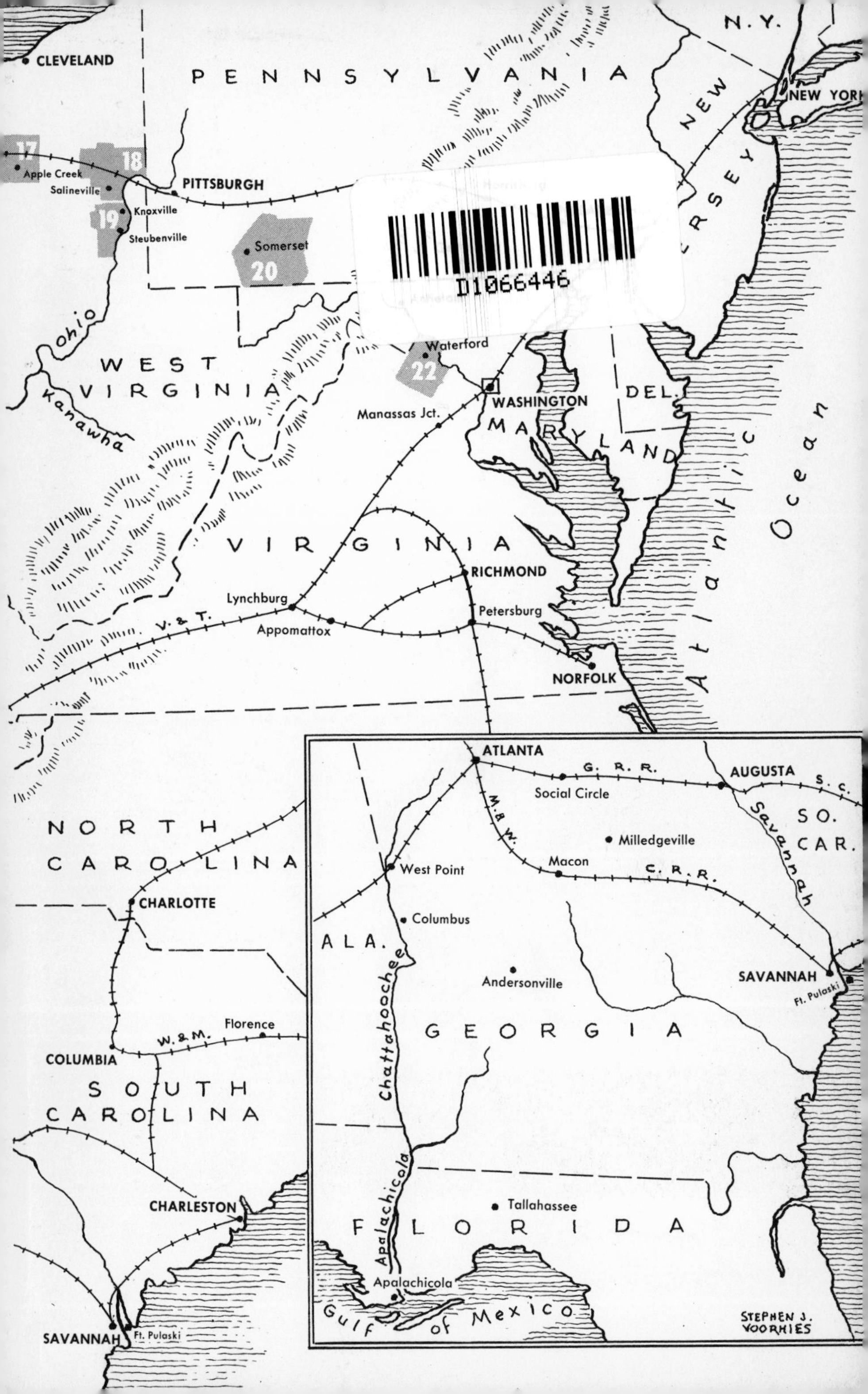
CLEVELAND
PENNSYLVANIA
N.Y.
NEW YORK
NEW JERSEY
17
18
19
20
22
Apple Creek
Salineville
Knoxville
Steubenville
PITTSBURGH
Somerset
Waterford
Ohio
Kanawha
WEST VIRGINIA
WASHINGTON
Manassas Jct.
DEL.
MARYLAND
Atlantic Ocean
VIRGINIA
RICHMOND
Petersburg
Lynchburg
Appomattox
V. & T.
NORFOLK
NORTH CAROLINA
CHARLOTTE
Florence
W. & M.
COLUMBIA
SOUTH CAROLINA
CHARLESTON
SAVANNAH
Ft. Pulaski
ATLANTA
G. R. R.
AUGUSTA
S. C.
Social Circle
M. & W.
Milledgeville
SO. CAR.
Savannah
Macon
C. R. R.
West Point
Columbus
ALA.
Andersonville
SAVANNAH
Ft. Pulaski
Chattahoochee
GEORGIA
Apalachicola
Tallahassee
FLORIDA
Apalachicola
Gulf of Mexico
STEPHEN J. VOORHIES

WILD TRAIN

The Story of the Andrews Raiders

"James J. Andrews"

Wild Train

THE STORY OF THE ANDREWS RAIDERS

BY CHARLES O'NEILL

NEW YORK RANDOM HOUSE

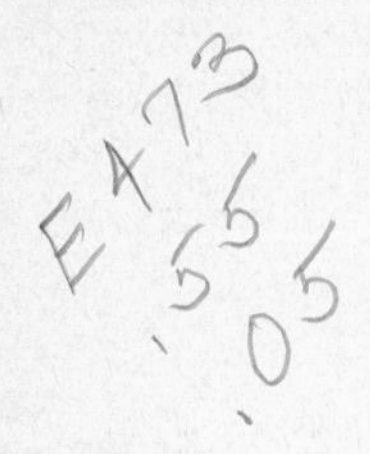

SECOND PRINTING

Published in New York by Random House, Inc., and simultaneously in Toronto, Canada, by Random House of Canada, Limited.
Library of Congress Catalog Card Number: 56-6347
Manufactured in the United States of America
by H. Wolff, New York

William H. Campbell — William H. Reddick — Martin Jones Hawkins

John M. Scott

Daniel Allen Dorsey

Wilson W. Brown

John Reed Porter

William Pittenger

Robert Buffum

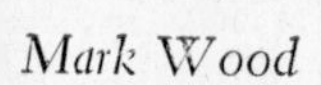

Mark Wood George D. Wilson Elizabeth J. Layton

Elihu H. Mason Jacob Parrott Samuel Slavens

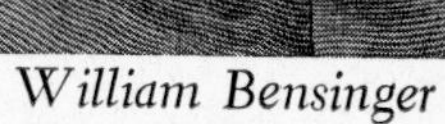

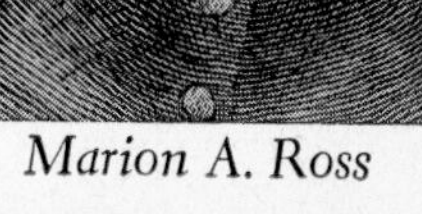

Philip G. Shadrach William Bensinger Marion A. Ross

This time, for Christy and Trev

Contents

Illustrations

Story of a Story 1

Less than eight hours of a wet April Saturday in 1862 along a stretch of Georgia railroad track have been widely acknowledged to contain the most melodramatic single sequence of events of the Civil War: the capture of a locomotive deep in the Confederacy by a party of twenty-two Union raiders and the ensuing eighty-six-mile chase led by a handful of determined and resourceful Georgia railroadmen.

Fact and myth concerning the day's action became almost immediately interwoven to form a durable legend. To its elements of pioneer war by rail, persistence against fantastic odds, and a secret service mission directed toward a crucial stake—in simplest explanation of the story's wide appeal—were added an agonizingly clear, followable course and matching sets of heroes to satisfy both South and North. Over the years it won telling and retelling in newspaper and magazine articles, pamphlets, lectures, books, film and radio reenactments, and even in narrative verse. As this note is written nearly a century later, facts and myths of that violent day march on, in current fiction, comic strip and motion picture treatment, to renewed and larger life.

The young Ohio soldiers who followed the man known as James J. Andrews have been honored in many ways. Holders of the first Congressional Medals of Honor to be awarded, many were given commissions and lifetime pensions as well. The graves of seven lie beneath a national memorial at Chattanooga. The final tribute most chroniclers have withheld is the attempt to make more than the barest try at finding out who these men of the Andrews raid were, how they came to be together on the train that made the breakfast stop that morning at Big Shanty, Georgia, and what actually happened to them then and afterward.

This book includes what should be as accurate and detailed an account of the chase itself as can be found in one place, thanks to the fact that it's told almost entirely in the sifted words of those on both sides who took part in it. In greater detail, it concerns itself with the men of the Andrews party—and a number of their opponents, fellow soldiers and families—in some of the meaningful days and years before and after the eight wild hours of April 12, 1862.

Although to most of its participants it was eventually to become the most important single action of their lives, the Andrews raid was no more than a minor incident of the Civil War. Surprisingly enough, however, the chief product of a closer look at the available writings and remembered talk of the raiders is a sharply increased understanding of the full war, the country it was fought in, and the day-to-day reality and life of the men and women caught up in it. Through the accident of their becoming the famous "engine thieves," six or eight of the surviving principals spent a good part of the following fifty years trying to remember exactly what had happened before, during and after the great day. Sharp-edged memories of all kinds of people, things and ways of life were pulled from the distant past, or put down close to the time of their observation, by men and women given reason to believe that what had happened to them would be important to others.

Actually, it was. What had happened to the raiders was life in America during a time of profound change and the unexpected first taste of total warfare. The American Civil War has the doubtful honor of being trail-breaker and killing kin of the savage, full-scale wars of the twentieth century, and within the American war, the two-day battle of Shiloh—with its twenty thousand killed and wounded, of some eighty thousand opposed—marked the shift from skirmish-style conflicts to the lethal entanglements where four, five or six of every ten men directly engaged might lie destroyed in a morning before the armies could be maneuvered apart again.

It was on the second night of Shiloh—a hundred-odd miles away, and before the deadly new price scales could be known—that the Andrews party started out south along the Wartrace road. Within ten weeks, all of them were to know that they had moved into a new kind of war. What happened to some of them was the first and most chilling proof that this contest was beyond the supposed limits of old-school chivalry and for keeps. As well, in their own tangled interrelationships, some were to foretaste the murderous cross-suspicions of twentieth-century men caught together in the mind-cracking pressures of imprisonment by the enemy.

As a layer of long-buried silt can preserve playthings and tools along with bones and weapons, the catch-all of the raiders' memories hung onto more than the sharp edges of the bad hours. Some of them may have noted the first military gains clearly chargeable to the Indian-borrowed Rebel yell. Through their help, we meet Union sympathizers in the South with a frequency that confirms the generally overlooked thousands that were actually to be found; we see and hear repeatedly of equally unstressed Northern-born officers and technicians serving the Confederacy. On the Chattahoochee, at Columbus, the hammers of workmen clang night and day to sheathe an ironclad that was to blow up before reaching the Gulf. In a mountain cabin, we learn that a bag of hot ashes applied to the abdomen by a dutiful wife might be the proper cure for a man's hard colic. Not far away, we find that the war never particularly cut into the drinking of jar-borne corn whiskey from mountain stills. The wedding night of a Southern girl and a Yankee soldier finds pistols under the pillow; awaiting death together, two near-strangers discover the bond of past hours in the Chillicothe singing school of a man improbably remembered as Newt Bookwalter.

In the introduction of one of the best accounts of the raid to be published—Frank M. Gregg's *Andrews Raiders,* Chattanooga, 1891, written after interviews with a number of men who took active parts in the chase and the events preceding and following the raid—Gregg wrote: "The writer of this doesn't apoligize for quoting narratives of the participants, since these are essential to fulfill the only reason this work has for existence: throwing additional light on this remarkable Andrews expedition into Georgia, which threatened to change a whole phase of the late Civil War."

Gregg's non-apology is echoed here, and more or less for the matching reason. *Wild Train* is made up almost entirely of the pieced-together first-hand testimony of those who took part in the events described. To this, where useful or otherwise unavoidable, explanatory notes by later writers—including Gregg—have on occasion been added. Where not self-explanatory, the assorted excerpts spliced in have been found in published and unpublished writings, in the case of raiders Alf Wilson, Dorsey, Knight, Pittenger and Porter; in letters, army reports, affidavits and speeches, as with O. P. Temple, W. A. Fuller, Anthony Murphy, John Woodruff, and raiders Parrott, Bensinger, Buffum and others; or, in a very few instances, are derived from remembered statements vouched for by surviving sons, daughters or other relatives of the witness used. Of these, the families of Knight, Alf Wilson, Murphy, Fuller and Peter Bracken have been particularly helpful. A full listing of such sources will be found in the general bibliography and credits section at the end of the book.

The escape report assigned Andrews is given as remembered by Sam Williams and others interviewed by Gregg. It shouldn't be taken as having anything like the word-for-word value of the two Andrews letters that have been found, the first of these the previously unpublished letter of December 6, 1862, reproduced here through the kindness of Mrs. Iolene Ashton Hawkins of Flemingsburg, Kentucky, to whose father it was originally addressed for handing on to the local ladies named. The Murphy account used is his long letter of 1891 to Dorsey; the Fuller passages come almost entirely from his Columbus speech of 1888, as reported by the *Dispatch*. Nearly all the Dorsey material drawn on, published and unpublished—and made available through the invaluable help of Mrs. Alene Lowe White—is to be found in the Western Reserve Historical Society's William P. Palmer Collection. George D. Wilson's few memorable words at Atlanta are given essentially as remembered by John Woodruff, who heard them spoken.

The Robert Selph Henry, Seymour Dunbar, and R. C. Black III extracts are from *The Story of the Confederacy*, *Travel in America* and *Railroads of the Confederacy*, respectively. The Whitelaw Reid passages are from his two-volume *Ohio in the War*, issued in 1868. Albert D. Richardson, the New York newspaperman who was himself to spend long months as a Confederate prisoner, is quoted from early pages of his *Field, Dungeon and Escape* of 1865. C. W. Evers, editor of the Wood County *Sentinel*, was a neighbor and friend of J. A. Wilson; Wallace P. Reed and F. J. Cook were Georgia newspapermen of the gneration after Bracken, Fuller and Murphy; Randell McBryde is quoted from his *The Historic "General"* of 1904; and the early passage assigned Oliver P. Temple, Knoxville attorney who took part himself in one painful aftermath of the raid, is from his *History of East Tennessee and the Civil War*. More complete identification is made in the closing section of the book.

In most cases, the material used is taken unchanged from the source shown except for standardizing of spelling and correction of clear error where the judgment or reportorial accuracy of the person quoted happens not to be in question. Cutting has been done freely, and—in the body of the book, at least—without the salting in of elision dots that might throw off the non-specialist reader for whom this book is primarily intended. In all cutting, responsibility has been taken by the writer of trying to make the reduced material not merely an actual slice of the original, but a representative one—even, in some cases, at the price of employing a few unbracketed connective words the better to let the excerpt convey the meaning or reproduce the original effect of the whole.

In Pittenger, the cutting has been frequent and deep. Pittenger in his various books could often load twice the words to a page that might be needed to carry his meaning, and he was fond of exclamation points and italics. A good part of the ornamentation has been dropped, and where the occasional insertion of a simple verb or neutral connective phrase can make possible the detouring of whole dispensable paragraphs, this has been done. In no instance has condensation or abridgment been used consciously to distort an original meaning, and in those places where Pittenger is later in any sense to be held to account for an opinion or manner of expression, the full original text has of course been kept verbatim.

With both Pittenger and Alf Wilson, substitutions have been made in a few cases of recurring word choice where later usage has substantially colored or altered meanings once intended. "Comrade" might have been an instance of this—given its present-day associations—but as neither "buddy," "pal" nor any later variation comes close to qualifying as a satisfactory replacement, the men of the G.A.R. have been left the term they favored for themselves. For an actual example, Pittenger had a fondness for the word "glide." Days glided into weeks; the watchful leader would glide from room to room; trains glide from stations. Almost invariably, this has been translated as "move." Wilson, as no dictionary would deny him the right to do, overly favored the word "secrete" for "hide." A canoe is secreted in the bushes, a man secretes himself in a pile of brush. Since current usage of "secretions" would seem to be crowding this one toward a special restricted meaning, in the pages of *Wild Train* Wilson's canoe is usually *hidden* in the bushes and a man *hides* as he can—except that in Alf Wilson's particular case, he was generally as ready to fight as to hide.

Reliable evidence about anything is rarer than most of us ordinarily take the time to remember. A street accident can be reported within minutes of its happening in half a dozen conflicting versions —some reflecting honest differences rising from varying qualifications or points of view of the observers, others influenced by the witnesses' opposing personal interests. Add tricks of memory over the passage of years, and the expected variations multiply. Not all the evidence presented in the course of this narrative can be taken as accurate or purely objective. Some was written or spoken years after the action described. A few witnesses were transparently trying some editing of earlier opinions or conduct to meet changed political realities. Some were magnifying their own parts in various situations at the expense of actual credit due others. All that can be promised the reader is that for each of the hundreds of pieces of interlinked action and conduct here examined, the attempt has consistently been made to hunt out the witness or witnesses best qualified to report on it. If several versions of a given incident exist, the one believed to be least distorted by personal interest or other factors has been picked.

Subject to these qualifications, *Wild Train* is a try for the most part at letting the Andrews raiders and those involved with them tell in their own words what they saw, heard, felt, tried to do, and did. After some years of looking into it, the writer might testify for himself that the actual story—as nearly as it now can be established—is an even more remarkable and absorbing one than all the myths, part-truths and cardboard heroics that have come close to obscuring it. Nearly all the Andrews raiders thoroughly deserved those first Congressional Medals of Honor they were given, and it's an honor fourscore and fourteen years later to be allowed to help tell how they earned them.

The hill country where the Andrews raiders were to meet the test of their lives was a land marked specially apart even in the years when most of them were just being born.

WILD TRAIN

The Story of the Andrews Raiders

ALF WILSON: *The trial of speed between these locomotives in Georgia was a race which for desperate, daredevil recklessness, velocity and the high stakes at issue was never equaled on land or water on the American continent. On what followed, I don't think I could withstand the same deprivations again, although a man doesn't know what he can endure until he tries it.*

The Hills of Home

EDITOR: April in northern Georgia can be a time and a place to remember. For centuries out of mind the red clay hills and sub-valleys of the long Appalachian Valley lying between present-day Chattanooga and Atlanta have borne a green, springing cover of gum, oak, shortleaf pine and hickory, and through it, bright scatterings of blossoming cherry, hawthorn, tulip-tree and dogwood. Up to something more than sixty Aprils after the American Revolution, the long valley was the home and heart of the Cherokee nation—most advanced of modern North American Indian civilizations—acknowledged by U. S. treaty to be a near-sovereign people.

Three facts were to operate against the Cherokees: The linked series of sub-valleys was a natural passageway between the level lands of Georgia and the western country beyond the Tennessee. The bottom lands and easy slopes of most of the area were fertile. Below the white sprays of hawthorn in Dahlonega was the yellow of proven veins of gold. Invoking not these considerations but the claims of a higher sovereignty, men of Georgia—and of Tennessee—levered the Cherokees from their lands, and in 1838 finished driving them by the stricken thousands into exile beyond the Mississippi over a sunset way the Indians were to call "the trail where they cried."

In the morning time of American railroading, Wilson Lumpkin—later elected governor of Georgia chiefly on the strength of this crusade—was the first powerful seer and advocate of a rail line striking up from central Georgia to connect the state's ports with the natural transportation gateway to and from the Ohio, the Mississippi and the West formed by the gap where the Tennessee River breaks through the mountain barrier of the Cumberlands. From 1826, when he completed a field survey of the Indian lands, Lumpkin kept calling with the untiring fervor of a prophet from the wilderness—and the matching skill of an interested land speculator—for the immediate development of that "excellent route over the rolling hills and through depressions in the mountain range for a railroad to Tennessee at the northwestern corner of Georgia."

In 1836—with the Federal legalities of purchase and "cession" of the Cherokee lands arranged, and the first evictions of the thousands of families concerned in prospect—the Georgia legislature authorized the construction of the Western & Atlantic Railroad, to be wholly owned by the state. In the spring of 1837, from the U. S. Army Engineer Corps, Governor William Schley borrowed a New Hampshireman to survey, lay out and begin building the new line. In the services at $5,000 a year of Lieutenant Colonel Stephen Harriman Long, a Dartmouth graduate of the class of 1809, Georgia found a bargain. It had hired a highly capable engineer, a noted Western explorer and a thorough original.

SEYMOUR DUNBAR: Major Long, who like his predecessors Captains Lewis and Clark was an army officer, had made [a notable trip of exploration] from Pittsburgh to the Rocky Mountains and return in the years 1819 and 1820. His expedition moved for some distance up the Missouri River by means of a little steamboat called the *Western Engineer*, which was built for the purpose at Pittsburgh, and was the first steam craft west of the Mississippi.

The boat was seventy-five feet long, thirteen feet wide, and drew nineteen inches of water. For the purpose of mystifying and impressing the native peoples along whom it might pass, the bow of Long's steamboat was fashioned in imitation of the neck and head of a serpent from whose mouth issued clouds of smoke. The propelling machinery was purposely hid from sight by a superstructure, as was the paddle wheel at the stern, which violently agitated the water like the tail of some strange aquatic monster. The speed of the boat was about three miles an hour. It is needless to say that the effect produced among the Indians by the apparition was extreme.

EDITOR: Resisting the temptation to devise steam-powered dragons to help him gouge his cuts, for three and a half years the sharp-faced, resourceful Long soberly chopped and twisted through and over the hills and numerous streams of the long, brokenly rising valley—improvising en route new techniques of bridge building, grading and curvature handling that were to be drawn on by railroad builders for decades after—until he had pushed his survey through to the town at the bend of the Tennessee, then called Rossville.

Actual construction was begun in March of 1838—and was to take thirteen years and something over four millions of dollars for full completion from Atlanta to Chattanooga—but in all except the eventual width of the road, the governing construction principles of the W. & A. from start to finish were those laid down by Engineer Long in his interim report of November 7, 1837.

STEPHEN HARRIMAN LONG: The gradations along the line of road should not exceed thirty feet per mile; its curvatures should be limited to a radius of one thousand feet; and the road surface should have a width of twenty-five feet.

EDITOR: The dragon-ship designer, never a man of undersized dreams, indicated as well the rank the completed road might one day expect to hold in the national transportation pattern.

LONG: The Western & Atlantic Railroad, when viewed in its relation to the natural and artificial channels of trade, is to be regarded as the main connecting link, in the chain or system of [American] internal improvements, more splendid and imposing than any other that has been devised in this or any other country.

EDITOR: It was Colonel Long's idea that the road should be graded for two tracks but rails laid for one, and later, when traffic conditions required, the second track could be built. In a few sections the extra width was constructed. On most stretches, for reasons of economy, no more than a single-track roadway was graded, and the W. & A., through the following years of tension and eventual war, was to remain a road on which passing had to be done at station sidings.

With the road surveyed and construction well started, Colonel Long returned to the U. S. Army late in 1840, and the line was carried to completion under successive chief engineers, James S. Williams, Charles F. M. Garnett and William L. Mitchell. Connecting with the Georgia and the Central of Georgia railroads, in what was originally almost blank wilderness, the railroad by its own coming into existence gave birth to the junction point first be to be called White Hall, then in turn Terminus, Marthasville, and—in 1847—Atlanta.

A great day for the line was the October one in 1849 when the

[*Editor*]
headings for the long tunnel through Chetoogeta Mountain were driven through and celebrated with band music and bottle after bottle of Madeira, port and Georgia scuppernong. A more serious —and perhaps prophetic—note was struck by the Reverend John Jones of Marietta, who presented to Chief Engineer Mitchell a small bottle of water brought from the River Jordan in the Holy Land. After being handed around for the inspection of the curious and the reverent, the Jordan water was poured out over the rail line.

In this same year—in illustration of Georgian concern over the wide-reaching, towering wooden bridges of the new line, and again, in possible foretaste of sharply increased attention to come—a Negro slave, Ransom Montgomery, was given his freedom in thanks for his alertness and prompt action in saving the Chattahoochee Bridge from destruction by fire.

In 1848, basic charter provisions of the road might have served to put possible future trespassers on fair warning:

". . . If any person shall intrude upon the said railroad without the permission or contrary to the will of the company . . . he, she or they may upon conviction be fined and imprisoned by the court of competent jurisdiction. Every obstruction to the safe and free passage of vehicles on said road shall be deemed a public nuisance, and may be abated as such by an officer agent, or servant of the company, and the person or persons causing such obstruction may be indicted and punished. . . ."

The completed railroad, from Atlanta to Chattanooga, was 138 miles in length. By 1858 its flourishing rolling stock inventory included 25 passenger and baggage cars, 606 freight cars and 52 locomotives—among these a powerful pair built by rival firms in Paterson, New Jersey: the *General* and the *Texas*.

The Mustering 1

ABRAHAM LINCOLN:

July 4, 1861

To the Congress:

At the beginning of the present presidential term, four months ago, all the functions of the Federal Government were found to be entirely suspended within the several states of South Carolina, Georgia, Alabama, Mississippi, Louisiana and Florida, excepting only those of the Post Office Department. . . .

By the affair at Fort Sumter . . . the assailants of government began the conflict of arms. In this act . . . they have forced upon the country the distinct issue: "Immediate dissolution, or blood."

This issue embraces more than the fate of these United States. It presents to the whole family of man, the question whether a democracy—a government of the people, by the same people—can, or can not, maintain its territorial integrity, against all its domestic foes. It presents the question whether discontented individuals, too few in numbers to control administration according to organic law, in any case can always upon the pretences made in this case, or on any other pretences, or arbitrarily without any pretence, break up their government, and thus practically put an end to free government upon the earth. It forces us to ask: "Is there, in all republics, this inherent and fatal weakness? Must a government, of necessity, be too strong for the liberties of its own people, or too weak to maintain its own existence?"

So viewing the issue, the administration had no choice left, but to call out the war-power of the government; and so to resist force employed for its destruction, by force for its preservation. . . .

I now ask that you give the legal means for making this contest a short and a decisive one—that you authorize to be applied to the work at least four hundred thousand men, and four hundred millions of dollars. . . .

This is essentially a people's contest. On the side of the Union, it is a struggle for maintaining in the world that form and substance of government whose leading object is to elevate the condition of men—to lift artificial weights from all shoulders . . . to afford all an unfettered start and a fair chance in the race of life. . . .

Our popular government has often been called an experiment. It is now for the people to demonstrate to the world that those who can fairly carry an election can also suppress a rebellion—that those who can not carry an election, can not destroy the government—that ballots are the rightful and peaceful successor of bullets; and that when ballots have fairly, and constitutionally, decided, there can be no successful appeal back to bullets. . . .

It was with the deepest regret that the executive found the duty of employing the war-power, in defence of the government, forced upon him. He could but perform this duty, or surrender the existence of the government. No compromise could, in his judgment, be a cure; but at best, only a little more lingering death to our popular institutions. . . .

In full view of his great responsibility, he has so far done what he has deemed his duty. You will now, according to your own judgments, perform yours. . . .

The Mustering 2

WILLIAM BENSINGER: I was born January 14, 1840, in Wayne County, Ohio, and was raised on a farm. At the age of eighteen I removed with my parents to Hancock County, Ohio, where my father purchased a piece of land all woods. For the next three years my daily occupation was in the use of the axe and maul. I had attended a district school in all about two years up to this time.

When Fort Sumter was fired on, I was one of the first in my neighborhood to enlist, but my parents pleaded so with me to remain with them—I being an only son—that I didn't go into the three months' service. When the three years' troops were called for, I enlisted, August 19, 1861, in Company G, 21st Ohio Volunteer Infantry and served with my regiment from then on.

EDITOR: William J. Knight—great-grandson of John Knight, a soldier of the American Revolution—was born at Apple Creek, in eastern Ohio's Wayne County, in 1837. Shortly after the early death of his mother, he and his brother James were left orphans at the ages of five and seven by the death of their father, Matthew Knight. Taken across the state by their grandfather, Jacob Knight, the boys were raised to manhood—in the company of a number of Jacob's remaining nine sons and a daughter—on the Knight farm in Farmer Center, near the border of Williams and Defiance counties. The aunt and numerous uncles, aided by the nearby family of Richard Knight—another son of the John Knight who'd taken up the Western lands his Revolutionary service had earned him—were soon linking the two boys by cousinship to the Sweets, Tomlinsons, Gardners, Hacketts, Wynns, Hemenways and other pioneering families of the area.

Quick of muscle and wit, and handy with tools, young Bill Knight became handier as he was allowed to help and learn the ways of turning wheels and gears at the sawmill Jacob Knight had assembled and built. Well started in mechanics at the sawmill, the growing young man took to the adventurous new craft of railroading and was a railroad shop hand within months of reaching voting age. In the maintenance shops at Logansport, Indiana, he learned how to take down and reassemble engines before being allowed to ride them as engineer in control on trains running between Logansport and Chicago. Knight's shop training seems to have been less than might have been required to qualify him as a fitter or master mechanic, enough to make him capable of handling all routine road repairs.

Promptly after President Lincoln's call for volunteers, both Knight brothers enlisted at Defiance and were mustered together into Company E of the 21st Regiment, Ohio Volunteer Infantry. (James Knight was never mustered out; although he, too, was eventually to reach Georgia. Taken prisoner in combat, he died August 4, 1864, and occupies Grave #4715, "Anasarca," in the cross-studded earth of a place once known as Andersonville prison.)

DANIEL ALLEN DORSEY: My parents were Virginians—of Waterford, Loudon County—who emigrated to Ohio a few years after their marriage. When I was about eight years old, they returned to Virginia, living there at this time about three years, during which time I learned much of the manners and acquired something of the dialect of the Southern people.

At twenty-one, I was teaching a country district school in Fairfield County, Ohio. I had closed my first term—and reached the age of twenty-two—when Fort Sumter was fired on. I had engaged to teach another term in the same county, but instead, I took leave of my mother and sisters and enlisted.

EDITOR: Ormsby MacKnight Mitchel—a distinguished and learned bantam-cock of fifty in the spring of 1861—took pride in an array of proven talents outstanding for variety even in an upswelling new country where some degree of versatility was expected of nearly everyone.

Born in Kentucky of Virginian stock and taken to Ohio at three after the death of his father, Mitchel was reading Virgil at nine, earning his own way from the age of twelve, and managed to win entrance to West Point before he was fifteen. In the Academy's memorable class of 1829, in which the twenty-two-year-old Robert E. Lee stood second, Mitchel—not quite nineteen—ranked fifteenth. Held at the Academy as an instructor of mathematics, Mitchel soon after courted and married Louisa Clark Trask, young widow of a fellow lieutenant. He left the army within four years, the better to support an increasing family and to find fuller outlet for his crowding energies and interests.

Basing himself at Cincinnati, Mitchel studied and briefly practiced law, served as surveyor and planning engineer of a proposed new railroad along the Little Miami River, and then turned again to education as professor of natural philosophy and astronomy at the new University of Cincinnati. Always a vigorous and interest-kindling teacher, Mitchel threw himself as violently into the practice of astronomy and became fired with the ambition to promote and build America's first major observatory. Lecturing widely to enlist support, boldly ordering in Munich a lens of a size and fineness then not equaled in the world, Mitchel pushed his project through to triumphant reality, and by 1845 had made his raw young Western town the leading astronomical center on the continent. To increase the scope and value of his observations, Mitchel proceeded to improve existing precision equipment and to invent recording devices incorporating early and imaginative use of principles a later generation was to call on in the field of feedback control and automation.

An inexhaustible Roman candle of varied enterprise, Mitchel in his spare time returned to railroading to survey and organize construction of the Ohio & Mississippi line. This time he turned financier as well, and on three trips to Europe marketed the road's bonds in such accomplished style as to invite later question in some quarters of the possibility that Professor Mitchel had been something less than as exact as a man of science might have been expected to be in distinguishing between the road's financial welfare and his own. He continued to make profitable lecture tours throughout the country; turned the collected lectures into successful books of popularized science; edited and published a magazine on astronomy; kept his military hand in by commanding and drilling a volunteer military company; and in the late 1850's accepted—while holding his Cincinnati post—the directorship of a new observatory at Albany, N. Y. None of these demands kept him from a keen and increasingly troubled interest in the course of national affairs.

On April 20, 1861, in New York City, eight days after the Confederate attack on Fort Sumter in Charleston Harbor, the one-time precocious West Pointer—now father of six grown and nearly grown sons and daughters—stood up at the great Union Square meeting organized to offset Mayor Fernando Wood's near-rebellious support of the Confederate position. Mitchel stirred the tens of thousands before him with the best-received speech of the day:

ORMSBY MACKNIGHT MITCHEL: . . . I've been announced to you as a citizen of Kentucky. I love my native state, and my adopted state of Ohio, but I owe my allegiance now to the United States of America. . . .

Listen to me. My father and mother were from Virginia, and I know these men of the South. I've been among them, I've been reared with them. They have courage, and don't pretend to think they haven't. It's no child's play we're entering on. They'll fight. Make up your mind to it. . . .

I for one say put me where I can do my duty. In the ranks or out of the ranks, I'm ready to fight. Having been educated at the Academy and in the army for seven years—serving as commander of a volunteer company for ten more—I feel I'm ready for something. I only ask to be permitted to act, and, in God's name, give me something to do.

EDITOR: Permission for the orator to act took nearly four months to process. On August 8, 1861, Mitchel was called to Washington and

[*Editor*]
commissioned a brigadier general of volunteers. The day after seeing her husband off—and with him, a son, F. A. Mitchel, who was to act as his father's aide—Louisa Clark Mitchel, who had had two strokes during the spring, suffered and died of the third.

WHITELAW REID: At the beginning of September, General Mitchel was assigned to command of the Department of Ohio, with headquarters at Cincinnati, and was entrusted with defense of the city against the early attack from Kentucky then expected to be made by the Confederate forces of General Zollicoffer. Despite the recent and sharply felt loss of his wife, Mitchel at once plunged into the work with his old zeal and energy. He placed the city in a posture of defense, supervised the erection of earthworks, took charge of the gathering troops, and strove to reduce them to discipline.

F. A. MITCHEL: These military departments, at the period of organization, tried severely every general who commanded one of them. Before the troops were organized into corps, divisions and brigades, every company captain, hospital steward or wagon-master felt at liberty to address the general direct for any required article, be it a hundred rounds of ammunition or a bottle of medicine. The throng of citizens requiring attention was countless.

My father, while often short with some, saw everyone who called at his office during certain hours of the day, and the rest of the time was free to visitors in his room at the Burnet House. Often on returning to his hotel he would find his apartment so full that, standing round against the wall, his visitors covered it completely. He would commence with the first of these, transact his business and dismiss him, and so on till the room was cleared. He frequently cleared one of these throngs in half an hour.

WILLIAM PITTENGER: I was born January 31, 1840, in Jefferson County, Ohio, not far from the panhandle section of what later became West Virginia. My father, Thomas Pittenger, rented a small farm near the village of Knoxville, and afterward bought a larger tract of land two miles north of the same town, to which he removed when I was twelve years of age.

I was the oldest of seven children. As a child, I was healthy and fond of all games, but badly near-sighted. When I began to read I could only see the letters at a distance of three inches, and the concave glasses which I long afterward procured for supplying the defect were of only two inches negative focus. I learned easily at the village common, and read all the books that could be borrowed for miles around.

When my father moved us to his own farm, my annual schooling was reduced to the three winter months. When I was sixteen it ceased altogether. I was then reading history with delight and hoping, like most boys, to share in great adventures. The work of education went on about as fast after school-days as before. Shorthand was mastered during the noon spells and rainy days of a busy harvest, and astronomy was studied with especial devotion. The constellations were learned, though I couldn't when I first began see a star of less than the third magnitude. At sixteen, I succeeded in getting a teacher's certificate. The teaching I found easy; but keeping order among sixty or eighty young people of all ages from twenty-one down to four or five was no light task.

Almost the first money so obtained went to securing a telescope. Not satisfied with a small one, I bought the mirror and eye-piece for a ten-foot reflector from Amasa Holcomb of Massachusetts, and made the rest of the instrument. A stepladder and a post on which the telescope was pivoted constituted the observatory. Here on a level spot above the farmhouse many happy nights were spent gazing on the wonders of the sky.

At eighteen, I left Jefferson County and taught a school of higher grade near Ravenna, Ohio. Later that year, I accepted an invitation by Alexander Clark, another Jefferson County teacher, to join him in editing and publishing the *School-day Visitor*, in Cleveland, Ohio. The next year, being nineteen, I taught school in southern Illinois, and during the winter indulged freely in the common pastime of debating. The question debated was nearly always some phase of the slavery controversy, and I soon became known as an abolitionist—far from a complimentary title in those days.

In the spring I returned to Ohio, and made some essays toward the business of photography. But I lacked capital, and in the fall of 1860, when twenty, I took a school for the winter in Beaver County, Penn. During the winter, while one after another of the Southern states were seceding, I wrote home stating that in the event of war, I had made up my mind to become a soldier.

At the close of the school term, I returned to Jefferson County and purchased a photographic establishment from Charles Williams. As well, for nearly a year I had been reading law in my leisure moments under the direction of Miller and Sherrard, of Steubenville. My first step, when the bombardment of Fort Sumter occurred, was to go to Attorneys Miller and Sherrard, and to Mr. Williams, and ask release from the engagements I had made.

That evening, a war mass meeting was held in the courthouse at Steubenville. I listened to the speaking, saw man after man go forward and put his name down, and heard the cheers that greeted each recruit. I was more and more inclined to go, but didn't want to decide finally under the excitement of a public meeting. I took a long walk alone, going beyond the outskirts of the city, then went back to the courtroom, went forward, and asked the privilege of saying a few words. The conclusion of the address—in which I expressed gratification that the long suspense of the winter, when traitors were destroying the government and no hand was raised for its defense, was now over—consisted of the adding of my name to the list of recruits.

C. W. EVERS: John A. Wilson was born July 25, 1832, near the town of Worthington, Franklin County, Ohio. When seventeen, he removed with his father, Ezekiel Wilson, to Wood County, the family locating not far from Haskins. (In the new northwestern country—by his own account—the boy explored the nearby Black Swamp; caught catfish in the Maumee River; and on occasion, dealt with the prairie rattlesnakes he called massasaugers.)

In stature, the grown Alf Wilson—as all his acquaintances call him—is medium, weighing perhaps one hundred and fifty pounds. He is of rather slender, but wiry build, of nervous temperament, light hair and bluish gray eyes. In manner he is deliberate, though quick of decision and action, and there is that in his appearance that denotes a fearless determination and tenacity of purpose. He is a man somewhat after the old John Brown make-up, at least in this one respect of tenacity of resolution, belief and purpose.

At the beginning of the Rebellion, in 1861, Mr. Wilson enlisted in Company C, 21st Ohio Volunteer Infantry.

PITTENGER: The company formed that April night in Steubenville was one of twenty forwarded to Washington, stopping at Harrisburg on the way, where we were organized into the 1st and 2nd Ohio Regiments. My one fear was that I might be rejected on the medical examination; but there was none worthy of the name. When we were mustered into service, the surgeon simply came into the room and looked around for a few moments, examined hastily any case that was reported to him by the officers, and all others were passed. I put my spectacles, which I always wore, in my pocket, and wasn't challenged.

We took our first lesson in the variety of a soldier's life by sleeping on the marble floors of the Pennsylvania State House. Anson G. McCook was elected captain of our company and we proceeded on our way. At every railroad station along the route we were greeted by enthusiastic crowds cheering, bringing coffee and other refreshments. In Baltimore we passed through rough and scowling crowds; but as our guns had been received we weren't molested.

When we arrived in Washington, daily drill, tent life, guard and picket duty began. Reviews were frequent; and on one occasion President Lincoln passed along the line, a tall, awkward, but noble man, who couldn't keep step with the little men who bobbed along on each side of him.

At length we entered Virginia, crossing Long Bridge by night. On the morning of July 21, 1861, we were roused at two o'clock, and made a long and tedious march upon the right wing of the enemy.

Bull Run was a defeat which came very near victory. The panic which closed the day was far more intense among the teamsters, sutlers and newspaper correspondents than the troops; and the dispersion of a large part of the army which hadn't been seriously engaged arose as much as anything from the fear of officers and men that they would be held for the defense of Washington beyond their three-month terms of enlistment, and thus miss the chances of promotion in new organizations. The 2nd Ohio was no better or no worse than others. It had seen no severe fighting, and could have gone back to Washington intact. Instead, in view of the feeling that they had already served beyond their time, the men straggled at their will, and when morning came the regiment had melted away.

When the day turned against us I decided to re-enlist, not wanting to quit defeated; and apparently the same feeling moved nearly every man of our regiment's three months' volunteers.

WHITELAW REID: The 2nd Ohio Volunteer Infantry Regiment was reorganized for the three years' service at Camp Dennison, near Cincinnati, in August and September, 1861. Before this period it had served in the three months' campaign, and participated in the first flurry of the war around Washington City.

In September, 1861, the regiment, with a full complement of officers and over nine hundred men, crossed the Ohio River, and by direction of General O. M. Mitchel, then in command at Cincinnati,

[*Whitelaw Reid*]
moved to Olympian Springs, in eastern Kentucky. As it was the first regiment of National soldiers seen in that section of the state, officers and men made a successful effort, by good conduct and courteous treatment, to show the citizens that the Yankees weren't so bad as they had been represented.

At Olympian Springs the 2nd was engaged in scouting and intercepting the numerous bands from central Kentucky on their way to join the Rebel army in the South.

DORSEY: Pittenger was rather tall, slightly stoop-shouldered, and quite talkative.

ALF WILSON: Mark Wood was an Englishman by birth. Before entering our 21st Ohio he lived at Portage, and was in the employ of an Austin Van Blarcum there. He was also for some time in the employ of William Wakefield, of Bowling Green. He was twenty-one years of age, a bright, free, thoughtless, rollicking Englishman; good-humored, impulsive, generous and brave, and had much of the spirit of adventure in his composition so characteristic of his countrymen.

PITTENGER: John Scott was well educated, and left brothers, sisters and a very plesasant home in Findlay, Ohio, to join the 21st Ohio. His father and mother had always been among the most respected of the citizens there. Scott married just three days before enlisting.

Private George D. Wilson of Company B [from Franklin, Warren County] 2nd Ohio was the most remarkable man of those who were to be thrown together on the special service with which this history is concerned. At thirty-two, well older than most of his fellow soldiers, Wilson had spent many years before the war going from place to place as a journeyman shoemaker. Not highly educated in the formal sense, he had traveled and observed much and forgotten nothing. In vigor and force of language I never knew a man who surpassed him. He delighted in argument on any topic—social, political or religious—and in the use of scathing language, in the power to bury an opponent under a flood of exhaustless abuse, he excelled. In coolness, bravery, natural shrewdness and quickness of intellect, this one-time leather worker was fully equal even to the unusual man who was to become our leader. The older of the two unrelated Wilsons who were to serve together, George Wilson was tall and spare, with high cheekbones, overhanging brows, thin brownish hair, long thin whiskers and sharp gray eyes.

As George Wilson excelled in intellectual powers, so did William Campbell in physical strength. A native of Salineville, Ohio, Campbell's muscular feats were astonishing. He weighed 220, was of fine build, and for all his size was as agile as a circus acrobat. Danger seemed to have an attraction for him, although he wasn't in the least quarrelsome, and often reproved wranglers. He had led an irregular life—including some hard drinking, it was said—and was staying in Louisville in the fall of 1861. Campbell hadn't enlisted as a soldier, but on occasion visited Shadrach of Company K or other friends of our regiment.

Perry G. Shadrach [christened Philip Gephart Shadrach, carried on the company rolls under a third variant: Charles P. Shadrach] was about twenty-one when he came from [Somerset] Pennsylvania to Knoxville, Ohio, and enlisted in the 2nd Ohio when it was being reorganized for the three years' service. Not tall, he was plump, solidly built, merry and reckless, with an inexhaustible store of good nature. His temper was quick, but he was as quick to forgive, and ready to sacrifice anything for a friend. His wit was frequently the life of any group in which he found himself, and his blue eyes sparkled with mischief on the slightest provocation.

EDITOR: Into the enlisted ranks of the 2nd, 21st and 33d Ohio Regiments at this time—along with hundreds of others—were going a number of men, the full facts of whose lives and histories were to remain known only to families, friends and fellow soldiers who in turn were to know this intra-American war chiefly as it shaped and was shaped by these young volunteers.

Of tall lean Martin Jones Hawkins, an experienced railroad engineer, we hear that he had spent much of several pre-war years in the South, and for one high-riding interval, was a professional circus performer. William H. Reddick's father had "abundant means"—at least, as financial worth was rated in the village of Locust Grove, Adams County—while Jacob Parrott, at eighteen, had neither father nor mother living to be concerned when he gave over plowing Hardin County earth to answer the President's call for enough men to keep the Union intact. Marion A. Ross, born October 9, 1832, had had two and a half years of schooling at Antioch. One of the sons of Levi and Mary Ross, of Adison, Champaign County, an experienced schoolteacher, Ross was serious, reliable, and a sharp enough soldier to become sergeant-major of the second Ohio volunteer regiment formed in 1861.

DORSEY: Robert Buffum had seen some rough life before the waı, being a resident of Kansas where he took a hand with John Brown and others in the struggles there that preceded the Rebellion.

EDITOR: Of Buffum, we know a little more than that. Small, black-haired and unpredictable—with bony, quick-moving arms that made him a spiky windmill in a fist-fight—a Massachusetts-born Free-Soiler slow to lose his nasal twang, given both to prayer and profanity, Buffum five years before had been one of the bristling young Yankees helped to emigrate to Kansas along with shipments of Beecher's Sharps-made "Bibles." Although not on the rolls of Brown's immediate company, the youth saw his share of the fighting and terror that served as sample of the full savage conflict to come. A crippled cousin, David C. Buffum—pulled from his fields while at work, shot and murdered in September of 1856 by a Missouri ranger later to be released unpunished—was one of the counterweights placed on the Free-Soil side of the bloody scales Osawatomie John Brown had set sagging with the hacked bodies of five pro-slavery settlers.

Robert Buffum, taking leave of his wife to go into Company H of the 21st Ohio in 1861, was getting back to unfinished business.

WHITELAW REID: The 21st Ohio was organized at Camp Taylor, near Cleveland, on the 27th of April, 1861. It moved on the 23d of May, passing through Columbus, where it received its arms, to Gallipolis. It was in camp here until the 3d of July, when it moved to Ravenswood, by order of General McClellan, to re-enforce the 17th Ohio, then expecting an attack from O. Jennings Wise, whose forces lay at a little town called Ripley, twelve or fifteen miles from the river.

The National force under Colonel Norton of the 21st Ohio made a forced march to Ripley, surprised the Rebels and drove them from the place. The expedition then returned by steamer to Gallipolis. A day or two after this, Colonel Norton made a reconnaissance up the Kanawha River, and captured forty prominent Rebel citizens as hostages for the good treatment and safe return of some loyal Virginians captured by the Rebel irregular, Jenkins. On the 11th of July, General Cox took command of the brigade in which the 21st was serving and marched to the Kanawha River. On the morning of the 17th, Companies D and K of the 21st were ordered to drive the enemy from his position. The fight opened at great disadvantage to the Nationals, from the fact that their old United States smooth-bore muskets didn't carry far enough to reach the enemy, who were stationed in the bed of the creek and protected by its high banks. Colonel Norton, seeing the disadvantage, determined to drive the enemy out of the creek with bayonets.

The charge was successfully made, the enemy lifted out of the creek, and the whole Rebel force driven back. Colonel Norton was severely wounded through the hips in this affair, but remained on the field. In the meantime the enemy received reinforcements; and discovering that the National force was not properly supported, again advanced their column, and in turn drove them, capturing Colonel Norton and other wounded. The loss in this engagement was nine killed and seventeen wounded.

The 21st Ohio remained in the field, under command of Lieutenant Colonel Neibling, until ordered home to be mustered out on the 12th of August, 1861, at Columbus, Ohio. It was again reorganized, on the 19th of September, 1861, for the three years' campaign and mustered into the service at Findlay, Ohio.

EDITOR: Wilson Brown of Dowling, Wood County, could run a locomotive. He'd learned his railroading—and something of the ways of the South—on the Mobile & Ohio which ran from Columbus, Ohio, the full way to the Gulf. John Wollam, as resourceful and unfazeable a young soldier as could be found in Company C of the 33d, was from Jackson in southern Ohio's Jackson County where he had grown up within easy visiting distance of Kentucky. John Reed Porter, of Wood County, a young recruit in Company G of the 21st, had a strong clear belief in God and a knack for finding and holding to a direction.

PITTENGER: Porter was the only one of our number in that first year of the war who had a clear religious faith and seemed to be happy in it. He told me he had got his faith by going to a Methodist "Mourners' bench" a year or so before the war, and seeking till he found it.

DORSEY: Samuel Slavens of Company E of our 33d was of stout build, full round figure, five feet eight inches in height, about twenty-five years old on enlistment, and weighed 180 pounds—a frank, open-faced jolly fellow. He and his wife Rachel had three young sons, all then below the age of five.

EDITOR: From Wakefield, in Pike County, Sam Slavens came down to Portsmouth, in Scioto County, to enlist. Dorsey, already serving, was five feet seven and slight of body. Like most of the young recruits, Dorsey was then unmarried, and the monthly $14 pay he drew was his own to keep, spend at the sutlers', send home to his mother, or risk at the chuckaluck games on spread-out rubber ponchos that were to be found during off-duty hours on almost every company street. Elihu Mason of Company K of the 21st, with a wife and child back in Pemberville, Wood County, in this first year of the war, had immediate use for all the pay he could send home, as had George Wilson, also married and a father.

DORSEY: As near as I can ascertain, the ages at enlistment of the men who were to make up our party were about as follows: Geo. D. Wilson, thirty-six; Buffum, Mason and Hawkins, thirty-one; Alf Wilson and Ross, twenty-eight; Knight and Slavens, twenty-five; Shadrach, Brown, Scott and Dorsey, twenty-two; Bensinger, Porter, Pittenger, Reddick, Wollam and Wood, twenty-one; Llewellyn, Smith and Robertson, nineteen; and Parrott, eighteen. James J. Andrews in 1861 might have been thirty-five, and William Campbell, twenty-three.

EDITOR: The 33d's Sammy Robertson of Company G was from Bourneville in Ross County. Like Knight, Bensinger and most of the forming soldiers he fell in with, the nineteen-year-older was of the first generation from the newly broken Ohio lands. Of pioneer fathers and mothers originally from Virginia, Pennsylvania, Kentucky, and New England, nearly all the Ohio-born sons had grown up to the common knowledge and use of ax, maul, knife and plow. None of them, in looks and ways, would have been alien to the man, born of their own moving frontier, who had called them—in sorrow, but in resolution—to the fields where the vintage of wrath was about to be trampled out.

WHITELAW REID: The 33d Ohio was organized at Camp Morrow, Portsmouth, Ohio, during the latter part of the summer of 1861. It entered the service with an aggregate of eight hundred and thirty-nine men. The Colonel (Joshua W. Sill) spared no pains to render the regiment perfect in drill and discipline. Upon entering the field it joined the forces of General William Nelson, at Maysville, Ky., and accompanied that command in its march to repel an invasion of the Bluegrass Region by the Rebel Colonel John S. Williams.

The Mustering 3

PITTENGER: Flemingsburg is a small rural county seat on the border of the Bluegrass Region of Kentucky. In the years before the Civil War, its population was about 1,200, and the town was somewhat isolated, being seventeen miles distant by turnpike from Maysville on the Ohio River, its nearest point of communication with the outside world.

In the spring of 1859, a traveler came either by stage or on foot into this secluded village. Of a group of idlers in front of the brick hotel opposite the courthouse, he made some inquiries, and in response to questions addressed to himself, said that he had just come up from Maysville, and had thought of seeking a position as schoolteacher. Noticing the name "Andrews" on a sign across the street, he asked if there were many of those people in town. Assured that they were among the leading citizens of the place, he said, "That's my own name, and I think I'll go no further, but make my home here for a while."

EDITOR: The Flemingsburg courthouse James Andrews saw—up to the 1950's Kentucky's oldest in continuous use—still stands, although most of the county's justice is now dispensed from a new building to which the courts have been moved. Present reckoning makes it eighteen miles to Maysville, although the population up to recent years has stayed within a few hundred of its 1859 level. A pleasant, hospitable town, Flemingsburg is still peopled by the immediate descendants of dozens of men and women who knew the striking stranger who introduced himself this first day as James J. Andrews.

PITTENGER: The stranger stated that he was a native of Hancock County back in Virginia, and that he had come down to Maysville on a raft. Though he had little apparent means, he was cordially received, and made to feel at home. No opportunity presenting for employment as teacher, the newcomer began work as a house and ornamental painter, and was quite skillful. He had an excellent singing voice, and taught several singing schools in the evenings, becoming a general favorite.

[*Pittenger*]

On arrival in Flemingsburg, James J. Andrews must have been just turned thirty years of age. Then, and later, he was a commanding figure—six feet in height, weighing approximately 185 pounds, inclined to hold himself something less than his full height except when excited. He had strong and regular features, a clear complexion, dark gray eyes, abundant black hair, and a short, curling beard—later to become luxuriantly full.

From the first, in Flemingsburg, Andrews' new neighbors sensed an air of reserve and mystery about him. His wide information and refinement of manner, his good looks and easy grace in any company gave him a marked ascendancy over his companions, even while he tried to be one of them. Very little was known of his former life; and while few cared to ask him directly on the subject, a story was generally circulated as originating with him to the effect that his father had entrusted him with $5,000, which he invested in a flouring mill with wool-carding attachment in Ohio. The mill—the story went on—had burned without insurance. He left home, resolving that his family shouldn't hear from him until he had more than made this amount good.

An elaboration of the same story was afterward told by him to Jacob Parrott and others of our party. Shortly before the burning of the mill—in this version—Andrews had been on very friendly terms with two young ladies, and eventually became engaged to one of them. When all his property was lost, this lady wrote him a chilling letter, asking release from the engagement. He at once went to the other lady, and finding the warmth of her sympathy a grateful contrast, he offered himself and was accepted. Within a month of the period fixed for marriage, the second lady—he never gave the names of either—suddenly died. The threefold disappointment drove him from home to make a new life amid new surroundings. His parents meanwhile had removed from West Virginia to southwestern Missouri.

No verification has been found by me for the story in either form, but the blankness of Andrews' record in the pre-Flemingsburg years, together with a kind of thoughtful melancholy which was manifest when he wasn't actively engaged, would seem to point to some decisive break in his history. Judge W. A. Cord later stated that Andrews told him on one occasion that he had come from Hollidays Cove, then a poor section of Hancock County in the panhandle area of western (later West) Virginia.

EDITOR: Another possible explanation of the mystery of James Andrews' early background is suggested in this book's second section.

PITTENGER: Most of the people of Flemingsburg were soon convinced that Mr. Andrews was anxious to make money, although he wasn't penurious, was strictly honest, and seemed to have done no more than maintain himself respectably.

Some months later, a gentleman named [William T.] Lindsay, who lived some seven or eight miles from Flemingsburg on the Maysville Turnpike, partially rebuilt his house and employed Mr. Andrews to do the necessary painting. Mr. and Mrs. Lindsay frequently jested with the newcomer about his growing to the ripe age of thirty without marrying. Andrews answered that he could find no lady willing to accept him who wouldn't be wasteful of the property that he wished to earn. Lindsay said he knew one who possessed every desirable quality, without being extravagant. Mr. Lindsay was a sympathizer with the South in the angry controversies that had already begun to presage war, while Andrews was as firm on the other side; but this didn't prevent a great esteem on the part of the older man for the younger.

Lindsay proceeded to introduce Andrews to a Miss Elizabeth J. Layton, a young woman who had been staying with the Lindsays for some time, helping in sewing and other ways.

EDITOR: James Layton, Elizabeth's father, died in 1849, leaving nine children, most of them under age.

PITTENGER: The lady was of medium height, graceful and well formed. She had dark eyes and hair and was of pleasing though not notably handsome countenance, and may have been a year or two older than Andrews. Her manners were quiet and grave, but she had a very decided character. She was a member of the "Christian church" (Campbellite) and her sympathies were entirely with the loyal side in the rising struggle. Andrews was busy most days on house painting and ornamental jobs throughout the village, and often had his singing classes at night, but many pleasant evenings were spent at the Lindsays', and it was in the large front room of their home that Andrews courted her.

"They were affectionate and happy together till the war came on," Mrs. Lindsay was to say. "Elizabeth wasn't rich, but she had a little property, and was economical and a good worker. In almost every way, she could have made Mr. Andrews a good wife."

EDITOR: For Flemingsburg at the time, and to a stranger of as little means as Andrews, Elizabeth's property and the advantages of a connection with her family might have seemed considerably more of a temptation than Mrs. Lindsay indicated. The Laytons had owned a great deal of good Mason and Fleming county acreage since 1812, and when Andrews first met her, existing court records show that Elizabeth Layton not only held land of her own, but was guardian and administrator of substantial property belonging to her younger sisters and a brother: Nancy, Malvina and Oliver Layton.

PITTENGER: Before the courtship had ripened into an engagement, the war came, and for a time the couple saw less of each other. Andrews took a firm stand for the Unionist position, and with his work in the Kentucky Home Guard, and afterwards in more important enterprises, his time was fully occupied.

When the war broke out in the spring of 1861, Kentucky occupied a peculiar position. The majority of the people had no wish to secede, but they wished as little to fight for upholding the Union. For a time the impossible task was essayed of remaining neutral. Troops were enrolled as a State Guard, not to be called into service unless the state was invaded, when they were to be used against the party making the invasion. Such a position of armed neutrality became increasingly untenable, since the border position of Kentucky made it sure that sooner or later the state would be forced to adhere to one or the other of the two great sections.

ALBERT D. RICHARDSON: Kentucky—in the summer of 1861—was disputed ground. Treason and loyalty jostled each other in strange proximity. At the breakfast table in Louisville, one looked up from his New York paper, forty-eight hours old, to see his nearest neighbor perusing *The Charleston Mercury*. He found *The Louisville Courier* urging the people to take up arms against the government. *The Journal*, published just across the street, advised Union men to arm themselves, and announced that any of them wanting first-class revolvers could learn something to their advantage by calling upon its editor. In the telegraph office, the loyal agent of the Associated Press, who made up dispatches for the North, chatted with the secessionist, who spiced his news for the Southern palate. On the street, one heard Union men advocate the hanging of Governor Magoffin. At the same moment, some inebriated "Cavalier" reeled by, shouting uproariously, "Huzza for Jeff Davis!"

Here, a group of pale, long-haired young men was pointed out as enlisted Rebel soldiers, just leaving for the South. There, a troop of the sinewy, long-limbed mountaineers of Kentucky and East Tennessee, marched toward the river, to join the loyal forces upon the Indiana shore. Two or three State Guards (Secession), with muskets on their shoulders, were closely followed by a trio of Home Guards (Union), also armed. It was wonderful that, with all these crowding combustibles, no explosion had yet occurred in the Kentucky powder-magazine.

PITTENGER: Andrews spoke decidedly in favor of maintaining the Union. He wasn't an abolitionist, but he held with the old flag and the nation undivided. He joined the volunteer organization of Fleming County, brought all his powers of persuasion to bear, and helped secure its unqualified adhesion to the Union cause.

The war excitement had brought all business to a standstill. There was little house-building or other improvements during the spring and early summer months of 1861, and consequently no demand for painting. Andrews was at this time boarding at the hotel of Mr. J. B. [Brack] Jackson, who, finding him out of employment, offered him the temporary position of clerk. This he held for several months.

At length Andrews made a journey to Louisville, and on his return announced that he had been appointed a deputy U. S. provost marshal, and that his jurisdiction in that capacity would be extended over Fleming and the adjoining counties. Despite the resentment of those whose sympathies were with the Confederacy, Andrews entered upon the duties of the office with much apparent zeal, purchasing a copy of *Conkling's Practice* to inform himself in regard to U.S. Federal court procedure. On the night of his return from Louisville, however, he informed his hotel-keeping friend Jackson that the provost office was only a blind. Andrews' real business was to be the secret collection of information for the Union army. From this time—by his admission to Jackson—he was to be a spy.

The account Andrews gave of his entrance upon this business was that he met a young lieutenant by chance, while on business in Cincinnati, who recommended it to him as an employment in which he could render great service to his country. Being at the time out of employment, Andrews went to Louisville, offered his services, and was immediately accepted.

EDITOR: Although no record of the connection has been found, the lines of authority for secret military service in the Ohio area prevailing in the spring and early summer of 1861 make it likely that

[*Editor*]
James Andrews was recruited and given his first training in undercover intelligence gathering either by Allan Pinkerton's deputy—George Bangs—by Pinkerton himself, or by a civilian or officer acting for one of these two.

On April 24, 1861, as one of his first acts on assuming command of the forming Ohio volunteer regiments, former railroad president George B. McClellan had sent for the Scottish-born detective he had first known in Chicago, and on Pinkerton's arrival, had placed him in charge of all secret procurement of military information. Pinkerton—or "Major E. J. Allen," as he chose to call himself on this and later wartime assignments—brought along George Bangs and the personable Kate Warne who had helped him smuggle President Lincoln through Baltimore in the touch-and-go days immediately before inauguration. With these and his favorite field agent Timothy Webster, McClellan's intelligence chief set up discreet recruiting, training and dispatching offices in Cincinnati and later at Louisville.

With McClellan's authority quickly expanded in May to cover the full department of the Ohio, Pinkerton within weeks found himself sending Webster, Price Lewis, Sam Bridgeman and other agents—and one occasion, going himself—out through Kentucky, western Virginia and adjoining Confederate-held states. Pinkerton and his men were much given to Vidocq-inspired lightning changes of hats, caps and hair-do to confuse possibly hostile observers—as they had even induced Lincoln to wear an embarrassingly out-of-character Scotch cap on the cloak-and-dagger trip through Baltimore—and similar headwear-juggling by Andrews was later to be noted and remembered by those traveling with him.

To Andrews, however, Pinkerton's most important legacy was probably the negative one of leaving the agent cut off from his normal channels of reporting and support when Pinkerton abruptly followed McClellan east at the end of July, 1861, to the latter's new command of the Army of the Potomac, taking Webster, Kate Warne and, later, George Bangs, and leaving most of the suddenly orphaned agents of his western network to make such new arrangements for themselves as might be improvised.

PITTENGER: [Brack] Jackson instantly opposed Andrews' entry into Federal secret service, not because of the nature of the employment, for Jackson was a strong Union man, but because of the danger involved. He told Andrews that if he didn't give it up, his being detected and hanged was only a question of time. Andrews didn't deny the probability, but said that he was doing no good now and that he was determined "to make a spoon or spoil a horn." Jackson understood him to mean that he would make a fortune in that business, or lose everything, life included.

In order that he not be compromised, Jackson suggested that his former room clerk find a new boarding place. Andrews agreed and at once removed to Mrs. Sarah Eckels' boardinghouse.

EDITOR: In September of 1861, General William Nelson—the big-bodied, headstrong, capable officer once of the U. S. Navy—established Camp Kenton, three miles from Maysville, as staging area and base camp for the forthcoming Union campaign in eastern Kentucky. The development placed an active divisional headquarters within a dozen odd miles of Flemingsburg and, for Andrews, probably marked the end of the getting-ready period and the beginning of active field assignments.

WHITELAW REID: The 21st Ohio was supplied with arms at Camp Dennison on the 2nd of October, and marched the same day for Nicholsville, Ky. From there, with the 33d Ohio, it was ordered to march to McCormick's Gap to join General William Nelson. During that campaign no engagement occurred, except that at Ivy Mountain, in which the Rebels attempted an ambush, but were whipped.

On the 22nd of October, 1861, the 2nd Ohio—after a night march of nearly thirty miles—surprised and defeated at West Liberty a band of Rebels under Jack May, inflicting some loss to the enemy and coming off scatheless. Subsequently joining the command of General Nelson, the regiment took part in a movement toward Prestonsburg, causing its evacuation by the enemy. The 2nd also assisted in the repulse of the Rebels at Ivy Mountain, quite a spirited affair, in which it suffered the loss of one man killed, and one officer (Captain Berryhill) and seven men wounded. The enemy was pursued to Pikeville.

PITTENGER: Andrews accompanied Major General William Nelson into the mountains of eastern Kentucky on the Pikeville expedition of November, 1861, in which my own 2nd Ohio, and the 21st and 33d Ohio Volunteer Regiments, took part along with other forces.

At the re-forming of the 2nd Ohio for the full three-year term, I had become a member of Company G of Captain James F. Sarratt. We were first ordered to Camp Dennison, and from there into Kentucky by way of Cincinnati. After camping for a time near Covington, we proceeded by rail to Paris, and thence on foot into mountainous eastern Kentucky. By a night march of thirty-seven miles we surprised and captured the village of West Liberty. At Prestonsburg, we met the 33d and 59th Ohio, which had passed through Maysville and nearby Flemingsburg. Here at Prestonsburg I myself first met the man I was to know as J. J. Andrews.

As our companies tramped through, Andrews was standing near the public square with a beautiful little repeating rifle—Winchester, I think—on his arm, which some of the soldiers were examining with much interest. He had a faraway look, and took little interest in the questions he answered about the gun. Some of us, noticing his striking appearance and the manner in which he watched the marching regiments, thought he might be a spy of the enemy.

Under the command of General William Nelson, the three Ohio regiments and one from Kentucky marched up the Big Sandy until we reached Ivy Mountain, where we suddenly found ourselves in an ambuscade with the 2nd in advance. We lost scarcely a man after we left the road, and soon dispersed the enemy.

DORSEY: J. J. Andrews was a large, well-proportioned gentleman with a long black silken beard, black hair, Roman features and an almost effeminate voice. I first met him to talk to up in eastern Kentucky during our campaign, under General William Nelson, against the Rebel general, Williams, in the fall of 1861.

Andrews was with the army there and had left an umbrella by the roadside. A member of my company found it. Seeing Andrews coming down the line and divining his intention of claiming it, the soldier handed it to me with the suggestion that I keep it. For some reason I was just contrary enough that day to refuse to give it up, and I did refuse, but I never forgot the gentlemanly manner of the claimant, the mild speech and pleasant smile with which he said it was all right, and left us, walking slowly back toward the head of the column as we stood halted in the road.

I didn't then know that this stranger was in any way connected with our army, but thought he was pretending to be a citizen of the country we were now in, and I didn't believe anyone of his ability, intelligence and apparent means could be found residing in all that vast region of mountainous and generally benighted country. For this reason I was disposed to doubt his ownership of the umbrella. I kept it for some time and later sold it to a citizen at Louisville for twenty-five cents, and gave the money to another citizen to fill my canteen with old Kentucky bourbon whiskey.

PITTENGER: Our force under General Nelson advanced but a short distance beyond Pikeville when we were recalled for the large-scale movement through central Kentucky. Steamboats were in waiting for us at Louisa, and we were conveyed down the Ohio to Louisville. Here we went into camp as part of the vast army assembling under General Buell.

WHITELAW REID: The eastern Kentucky campaign lasted about sixty days, in which time the Rebels were driven to Pikeville, and into Virginia. Taking transports at Louisa, on the Big Sandy River, the three Ohio regiments moved back to Louisville, the last of them—the 33d—being landed there December 1, 1861.

Dry Run 1

EDITOR: From the start of his active military service, General Mitchel—the one-time surveyor, promoter and builder of railroads—was sharply aware of the vital new role in warfare that the irregularly woven young railroad lines of the country might come to play. Up to this time, except for a brief, scarcely noticed experiment in the Crimea, the land forces of all countries had remained locked within rigid time-and-space limits set by the speed of marching men and the carrying power of mule-pack, horse teams and human backs. Ormsby MacKnight Mitchel, with the quick-leaping perception he had always shown, was one of the first to see how rail-carried steam power might shatter these ancient limits and enormously multiply the range and striking force of a given number of troops—and, for the other side of the coin, how the interruption of key enemy rail lines might at strategic moments equal in defensive value the employment otherwise of batteries of artillery and full divisions of infantry.

[*Editor*]

The project Mitchel here proposes had been more or less in the minds of McClellan and others since late spring, but once charged with his plan to fight for and by railroads, Mitchel was to be gripped by it for all his days of command.

O. M. MITCHEL:

September 30, 1861

Dear Governor [William] Dennison [of Ohio]:

I learn from reliable authority that from London, Ky., where we have an advance guard, it is but two days' march over fair roads to points beyond the Tennessee line in rear of Cumberland Gap, and from there only about thirty miles to the [East Tennessee & Virginia] Railroad. Were it possible to seize that road and hold it only long enough to burn two long bridges at and near Knoxville, it would be of vast importance.

[Senator Andrew] Johnson [of Tennessee] and others were with me last night. They all know the country in that region and assure me the people are with us almost unanimously, and that 10,000 troops entering Tennessee in rear of Cumberland Gap would electrify Tennessee and North Carolina.

Respectfully,
O. M. Mitchel

EDITOR: Mitchel actually won War Department approval on October 20, 1861, for the raid in the strength and manner here first proposed, but a tangle of the lines of army authority was to keep him from his first railroad bridge targets as effectively as though full Confederate divisions opposed him. Kentucky and Tennessee came within the Department of the Cumberland, commanded since October 7 by a touchy, red-haired brigadier named W. T. Sherman. Sherman promptly opposed the militarily unorthodox plan of having an independent command cross through his area of authority, and on October 26, Mitchel's expedition was called off, the regiments forming for it transferred to other assignments, and Mitchel himself ordered to return to "his proper command, the Department of the Ohio."

Mitchel promptly forwarded his resignation to Washington, but within a few days was persuaded—by the promise of an alternative field command—to withdraw the request that would have sent him back to civilian life. Relieved of departmental duties he was given command of a division—the 3d—in the army then organizing under

General Don Carlos Buell at Bacon Creek, Ky., between Louisville and Bowling Green. With this division promised for his own, Mitchel threw himself wholeheartedly into its training.

O. M. MITCHEL: The regiments going forward into Kentucky under me will go thoroughly equipped and prepared for the field as no regiments have yet been prepared elsewhere. Everything comes under my own eye, and a team of four horses, even to wagon and harness, I have tested by loading it fully with nearly double what is required to move, and then driving it down and up a steep rough hill.

EDITOR: However quickly—in the formation of this new division under Buell—Mitchel was able to forget his disappointment, there were others to whom the abrupt late October change of signals came as a more permanent letdown.

HOUSE REPORT 306, 56TH CONGRESS, 1ST SESSION: During the early part of the war of the rebellion President Lincoln earnestly sympathized with the Union men of East Tennessee, and tried to devise an effectual method of relieving them from the rigors of Confederate rule. The Confederate military authorities for their part were very bitter toward the East Tennessee Unionists, these Unionists being considered as rebels and traitors to the Confederate government, and many of them were arrested and imprisoned. To relieve these men, a plan was finally agreed on by President Lincoln and the military authorities of the United States.

Loyal refugees from East Tennessee, after conference with General George B. McClellan and General George H. Thomas, were authorized to return to East Tennessee and raise companies of loyal men to burn the great bridges along the line of the railroads between Stevenson, Ala., and Bristol, Tenn. The Federal army, then under General George H. Thomas in Kentucky, was on a given day to march into East Tennessee, and the companies of loyalists, that had been secretly organized for that purpose, were on a designated night to burn all of the bridges agreed upon.

EDITOR: As steadily reliable a general as either side produced in the war, George H. Thomas is in this report described as the invading commander expected by the East Tennessee bridge burners. He was one of two proposed at different times—Mitchel being the other—and the persisting confusion reflects the rival lines of authority between the Departments of the Ohio and the Cumberland at the time.

[*Editor*]

McClellan's consideration of the Tennessee bridge-burning proposal puts this first planning of the project in July or earlier. Andrew Johnson's part in rousing Mitchel's interest makes it likely that the new action was linked to the original plan.

HOUSE REPORT 306, 56TH CONGRESS, 1ST SESSION: The purpose of the bridge burning was to prevent the Confederate authorities from throwing reinforcements into East Tennessee, so that General Thomas would have no enemy to overcome other than the forces then garrisoning that section, for the Confederate authorities were at that time treating it as a hostile country.

Concerted action thus agreed on, a day was fixed for General Thomas to move his army toward Knoxville, Tenn., and a day fixed for the companies of loyal East Tennesseans to burn the great railroad bridges.

Unfortunately for all the loyal East Tennesseans, perhaps unfortunately for the general success of the Union cause, and certainly unfortunately for the bridge burners, the order for General Thomas to advance into East Tennessee was countermanded while he was actually on the march and the plan of immediate invasion abandoned without, however, notifying the prospective bridge burners.

There were nine bridges included in this plan of destruction. Two of these, the one over the Tennessee River at Loudon, Tenn., and the other over the same river at Bridgeport, Ala., were long and costly structures. The other seven were indispensable to railroad travel not only in East Tennessee, but through East Tennessee to Virginia on the east and to Alabama on the southwest.

On the night of November 8, 1861, the various companies of loyal East Tennesseans, wholly ignorant of any change of plans, and relying on the coming of a Union army under General Thomas, as had been agreed, collected and marched upon the Confederate soldiers guarding the various bridges.

The sanguinary battles fought in the darkness of that night between the various companies of loyal East Tennessee mountaineers and the Confederates guarding the bridges were as thrilling as they were tragic.

OLIVER P. TEMPLE: The news of the burning of the bridges in East Tennessee came upon the country on the morning of November 9, 1861, like the sound of a fire bell at night. The Confederacy was startled and stirred from end to end. Universal consternation prevailed in East Tennessee. Other and greater calamities were expected to follow, and the military authorities and railway officials were thrown into a wild panic. They hastened to and fro and stormed and issued orders as if they had just lost a decisive battle.

HOUSE REPORT 306, 56TH CONGRESS, 1ST SESSION: Had General Thomas then come into East Tennessee, as had been agreed upon, it is safe to say at least 20,000 loyal East Tennesseans would have joined his army, and by their aid that mountain land, in the heart of the Confederacy, could have proved a fortress of the Union cause.

But Union help never came, and the bridge burners were left to their fate. Some were shot down in their tracks, and others were captured, tried by drumhead court-martial, and hanged all on the same day, their bodies left swinging beside the ruins of the bridges they had burned. Hundreds were thrown into jails until they became so crowded that it was necessary to send many of these prisoners to the prisons of Georgia and Alabama.

DORSEY: Outstanding among the leaders of the loyal mountaineer men was a Captain David Fry of the 2nd East Tennessee Union Regiment, whose home was in Greenville, Tenn.

PITTENGER: Early in the fall of 1861, Captain David Fry of Greenville in eastern Tennessee had gathered a company of his Union neighbors, and under his guidance they had run the gauntlet of guarded roads and Rebel scouts, till they reached the Federal camp in Kentucky. He was here elected captain, duly commissioned, and served for some time at the head of Company F, 2nd Regiment, East Tennessee Volunteers. In October of the same year he was sent by General S. P. Carter back into East Tennessee, for the purpose of burning the bridges on the East Tennessee Railroad between Knoxville and Virginia, preparatory to a general Federal advance for the deliverance of that section of the country. The authorities at Washington had determined on such an advance through Cumberland Gap, by a special force under General O. M. Mitchel, who was then in command at Cincinnati.

Fry, with all assurances of support, was far on his way, and knew nothing of the cancellation of Mitchel's orders that followed. The great bridge at Strawberry Plains was burned with many others, and all Confederate reinforcements by rail were cut off. Fry held a considerable mountain district in Tennessee and North Carolina for

[*Pittenger*]
many weeks; but at length superior Rebel forces were accumulated, and he was forced to abandon much of the area taken.

During the whole winter Fry kept the field, on one occasion seriously threatening Knoxville. In March of 1862, with some six hundred men, he tried to fight his way through to the Federal forces. At the foot of Cumberland Mountains, about ten miles from Jonesboro, he was attacked by an overwhelming Rebel force, and defeated, his men scattered, and himself badly wounded. Soon after, he was captured and taken to Knoxville, where he would have been hanged had it not been for a vigorous letter with threats of retaliation from Union Generals Morgan and Carter. Captain Fry had thrown a citizen's coat over his uniform in his last effort to escape and this was held to constitute him as a spy as well as a bridge burner. At Knoxville, he was kept in the most rigorous confinement.

ALF WILSON: Captain David Fry first saw service in the Mexican War, and was a man of fine stature and great muscular power—brave as a lion, yet sympathetic as a child to those in need or distress. Had he been promptly helped when he went in to cut the mountain railroad line, he could have saved much of the suffering and persecution endured then and later by the people of Tennessee. As it was, he was left to his fate almost unaided.

EDITOR: Two of the nine bridges attacked on the night of November 8, 1861, were below Chattanooga on Georgia's Western & Atlantic line. For days—as a number of sharp eyes were to note—Chattanooga was cut off from Atlanta. Until Georgia's outraged Governor Joseph Emerson Brown could get the burned bridges replaced, neither troops nor supplies could move north of Dalton.

The Mustering 4

PITTENGER: James J. Andrews rendered considerable service as a scout or advance agent in the eastern Kentucky campaign of November,

1861, although not as much as he may have expected, for Confederate Colonel Williams' forces were driven out without large-scale conflict. What Andrews attempted, however, aroused the hostility of the enemy, and his escape from them was narrow in more than one instance. In reference to this he told another friend, Mr. J. H. Cooper, that as the Confederates were so bitter toward him, he had resolved to do them all the injury in his power.

It is doubtful whether Andrews up to this time can properly be called a spy, notwithstanding his use of the word to Jackson. He seems rather to have been a scout and agent for secret communication with the Union men of Kentucky. He was known in his own home, and generally in the towns through which he passed, as a Union man; and while he didn't wear a uniform, he seems to have been regarded as a Kentucky citizen rendering aid to the Federal army. This exposed him, when beyond the protection of our army, to the hostility of the Confederates.

EDITOR: It may have, and it may not. The 2nd and 21st Ohio Regiments returned to Louisville from the eastern Kentucky campaign in the last week of November, the 33d reached the brigade camp on December 1. Within a week of this return, James Andrews was placing himself so firmly and publicly on the Union side as to invite the suspicion—given the developments to follow—that the one-time house painter and hotel clerk was already becoming interested not so much in the good opinion of the ladies of Flemingsburg as in the creation of clear proof for Southern eyes that James Andrews was accepted by Union ladies and military men alike, whatever his actual business might be.

The evidence of this, which doubles the known existing letters of Andrews, is a message written and sent by him on December 6. Postmarked from Louisville by the Cincinnati mail line and addressed in care of Charlton H. Ashton of Flemingsburg, the letter was handed on to Mr. Ashton's sister Rebecca, then secretary of the Flemingsburg Ladies' Aid group. Kept in the family, the letter is here reprinted through the kindness of Mrs. Iolene Ashton Hawkins, of Flemingsburg, ninety-year-old niece of Rebecca Ashton Clark and daughter of Andrews' friend Charlton H. Ashton, through whom the message was first sent.

For clarity—and on one other ground that will be explained in the *Postscript* section of this book—a number of misspellings in the original letter have been corrected in the version printed below. Otherwise, it is given unchanged and in full.

JAMES J. ANDREWS:

Louisville, Ky
December 6, 1861

To the Officers and Members of the Ladies' Soldiers Aid Society of Flemingsburg

Dear Ladies:

If you will excuse the impertinence and intrusion, I propose to send you a few items that I picked up this morning that may be interesting and encouraging to you, in your noble effort of alleviating the suffering soldiers that have volunteered to drive the invaders from Kentucky soil, and protect your homes from the Southern vandals.

This morning as I was passing through the camps some five miles from the city I heard someone say, "Hello there, you from that town where the ladies are so clever."

On looking around I saw a countenance that had become familiar to me while on the march to Piketon, and which I recognized as belonging to one of the boys of the 33rd Ohio. As this was the first time I had met any of the 33rd since I left Piketon, nothing would do but I must go along to their quarters.

Arriving there, very few of them remembered my name, but they all recognized me as the "man from that town where the ladies were so kind." Be assured I felt proud of the compliment paid you and am very grateful to you for the kindness shown to me by the 33rd, which is all due to the fact of my hailing from "that town where the ladies are so kind." And when I told them that it was through your liberality and forethought that the wounded at Ivy Mountain had any hospital stores and that what you supplied was all there was with the army at the time, their praise seemed to know no bounds. Many of them related acts of kindness that they received from the ladies of Flemingsburgh as they passed through that they have not forgotten and they say they never will. Many of them described the generous donors so accurately that I could name them, but knowing their extreme modesty, I forbear. They all seemed anxious for an opportunity of becoming better acquainted with the ladies of Flemingsburgh and many of them declare that as soon as they could get ready to settle they would most assuredly give these noble hearted ladies a call before they made the final decision. So, young ladies, don't despair.

After spending an hour or more with the 33rd, I came on towards the city about three miles, where the 2nd Ohio Regt. is encamped.

I called to see them also, having become acquainted with them during the campaign up Sandy, especially with company A of Capt. [Alexander S.] Berryhill. The company had eight men wounded at Ivy Mountain, two of whom were thought at the time to have been mortally wounded. The captain had just received a mail for his company, among the letters two or three from his wounded men now in the hospital at Cincinnati, stating that the wounded were all doing well and those thought to have been mortally wounded are improving and will get well.

Our conversation naturally turned to the incidents of the fight and the sufferings and hardships of the men. When I told them that all all the hospital stores they had in that campaign were furnished by the ladies of Flemingsburg, and had it not been for your generosity they would have been without many of the delicacies they had, and the sufferings of the wounded would necessarily have been much greater, one of the party looked up with the tears glistening in his eyes and said, "God bless the ladies of Flemingsburg. I have never seen them, but were it possible I would suffer fifty times as much as I have to protect such disinterested kindness. The Southern marauder shall never disturb them, except they do it over my dead body," and many other such expressions.

You have no idea how much good it does men that are enduring the hardships and dangers of an active campaign to know that they are not forgotten by the noble mothers and daughters of America. You may think that those rough-looking soldiers (made rough by the hard service and thieving contractors) do not appreciate your kindness. Could you but see the heaving chest, the falling tear, and the fervent expression of thankfulness that I have, you would very soon conclude otherwise.

Need I say persevere in your noble work? I think not, for I am satisfied that the same patriotism that incited the first acts still burns in your hearts; all then that need be told you to stimulate you to further exertions is that Kentucky seems to be doomed to be the "Dark and Bloody Ground" again. It makes my heart bleed to see the mighty preparations that are being made by both parties to slay each other, and very soon the terrible work will begin in earnest. The mighty hosts that we are now hearing marshalled on Kentucky soil cannot remain idle much longer. The clashing of arms and the thunder of artillery will soon be heard from the Mississippi. Along the southern portions of the state clear to the mountains will be one vast field of carnage and death. Thousands of the noblest sons of America ere many weeks pass away will be made to bite the dust, awful thought, and many more will need the kind assistance of such societies as yours.

Persevere and may God bless you is the prayer of your humble servant,

J. J. Andrews

P.S. If your society has no correspondent in this part of the state and if you can put up with my blunders in spelling and composition, I will write you occasionally if you desire it. If so drop me a note to that effect. Direct to care of Louisville Hotel, Louisville, Ky.

PITTENGER: On return from the eastern Kentucky campaign, Andrews apparently resolved on a bolder course. The first step—as told by Mr. [C. H.] Ashton, later postmaster at Flemingsburg, who was an eyewitness—was striking.

Andrews had been absent for several days—at Louisville, it is presumed [presumed correctly, by the postmark of Andrews' letter of December 6]—and on his return was accosted in a friendly manner by Judge W. A. Cord, one of his intimate associates, and a leader among the Unionists. Andrews replied coldly and gruffly. As the other approached, and again spoke cordially, Andrews said: "I don't care to talk with you."

"What in the world's the matter?" Cord asked.

"I've been behind the scenes the last few days," Andrews answered. "I saw too much."

"Saw what?" asked the other, deeply puzzled by this extraordinary change of front.

"Why, I've seen how this war is carried on, and what it means," said Andrews. "It's all a great sell. Everybody's trying to make what he can out of it, and I'll have nothing more to do with it."

Mr. Ashton was astonished at such language from a man who had been virtually in the military service of the United States; but then he saw not far away, observing them, a certain William A. Berry—a bold, reckless man, the ringleader of the Rebel element in that entire district. Berry of course was greatly interested in this sudden conversion of Andrews.

About an hour afterwards, Ashton observed Berry and Andrews in close conversation at another part of the street. Andrews was telling of his changed views, and ended by asking Berry to get him admitted to the societies by which the friends of the South were bound together, as it was now his intention to serve the South with all his might. At this proposition, Berry, who had seemed pleased at first, broke out in a volley of oaths. "Andrews," he said, "do you take me for a baby or a fool? What you are is a blue-bellied spy!"

Andrews quietly said: "Berry, you're excited. You'll understand me better after a while," and strolled away from the raging Rebel leader.

From this time Andrews continued to avoid the Union men of Flemingsburg in public, but all his advances were coldly received by the opposite party. He had been too fully committed, and there was a time when he was in no small degree of personal danger.

At first the leaders of the Union party in Kentucky had held their partisans back from enlisting in the Federal army until the state's position had been fully determined, for the sake of their influence and vote in local matters. But soon the hot young men swarmed into the army in such numbers as in some places to reduce seriously the advocates of their cause at home. During this period, Andrews was more than ever threatened, but he was—as always—undismayed, and the Union sentiment soon became so firmly established and aggressive that Berry and his chief friends found it convenient to retire beyond the Rebel lines—the former engaging in business in Nashville.

In another conversation with his friend Jackson, Andrews declared his determination to follow this example, and also go to Nashville.

"Why, Andrews, what will you do about Berry?" Jackson asked. "He wanted to hang you even here, but if he finds you in Nashville where the Rebels have it all their own way, he'll surely do it."

"I can manage that," Andrew replied, and in due time made his way through the lines.

At Nashville he boldly went to the largest hotel and, registering as J. J. Andrews of Flemingsburg, Ky., went to bed. Before he was up in the morning he heard an impatient rap at his door, and a voice saying, "Let me in. I want to see you." He opened the door. The visitor entering announced himself as Judge Moore of Fleming County.

"What are you doing here?" Judge Moore asked. "I always heard that you were one of the head Yankees up there."

Andrews had seen Moore, though he had no personal acquaintance with him, and replied: "So I was, but the one difference between you and me is that you saw into these Yankees a little sooner than I did. When I turned over to the right side, it got too hot for me at Flemingsburg."

Moore grasped his hand, congratulated him on having come over, and welcomed him to Nashville. After breakfasting together, Moore took him up to military headquarters and introduced him to Beauregard, Hardee and other prominent officers, as "his friend Andrews from Flemingsburg." The latter told these officers that he proposed to run articles needed in the South through the Union lines—a profitable, though hazardous, business; and one that would be of great benefit to the Southern armies, which were in need of medical supplies, especially quinine. The stringent blockade had made all things not manufactured in the South excessively scarce and costly. The Confederate officers encouraged Andrews, giving passes and all necessary facilities.

Shortly after this, it may have been the next day, Andrews met Berry face to face on the street. The latter stopped as if thunderstruck, and exclaimed with a great oath, "Well, and what are you doing here, Andrews?"

Andrews greeted Berry cordially, told him that he had been intending to hunt him up as soon as he got settled, and added the same expression that he had used with Judge Moore, "The only difference between us, Berry, is that you saw how things were moving a little sooner than I did."

Just then one of the leading Rebel officers, passing by, greeted Andrews familiarly, and Berry could hold out no longer.

"Andrews," he said, "I was a little hard on you when I thought you wanted to play the spy on me, but I'm glad to find out that you're all right. If I can do you any favor here in Nashville, don't hesitate to call on me."

Andrews promised to bear that in mind, and as Berry had engaged in the saddler's business, he brought him through a cargo of buckles and other much needed articles on his first blockade-running trip. Afterward he had no better friend in the South than Berry.

Andrews now occupied a position, in this first winter of the war, where he could do the Union cause the most essential service. His business as blockade-runner gave him free access to the territory held by Rebel armies, and the purchase of new supplies furnished the opportunity and excuse for frequent visits to the Federal lines. The amount of trading that he thus did was duly reported, along with all other matters, to his employers.

At about this time, Andrews formed a business partnership with a Mr. Whiteman, a well-known merchant of Nashville, who supplied him with money needed for his purchases and aided him in the work of distribution. Andrews' own financial profits were considerable, and these he took pleasure in representing to his friends within the

Confederate lines as the motive which induced him to run such extraordinary hazards.

Late in January of 1862, before the general movement of the Union armies began, which resulted in breaking the enemy's lines, forcing him out of Kentucky, Andrews visited Fort Donelson, gaining admission probably as a bearer of medical supplies, and succeeded in getting a complete account of the Confederate forces there, together with a sketch of their works. In order that his information might be in time for the important movement under Grant which was then imminent, Andrews rode sixty miles in one night.

EDITOR: In the theatre, this might be called throwing a line away. If Andrews brought useful information from within Fort Donelson at the time named—when Grant's preparations for the attacks on Forts Henry and Donelson were being completed at Paducah—it could have been one of the most important reconnaissance feats of the war.

At Donelson, Grant with 15,000 men pinned down 18,000 Confederate troops. With gunboats brought up and a reinforcement of no more than 2,500, his men captured the fort and 14,000 of its defenders. In his *Memoirs,* Grant explains the apparent recklessness of his first investment as rising from a personal estimate that the overcaution of Gideon Pillow, one of the fort's three general officers, would prevail—"I had known General Pillow in Mexico, and judged that with any force, no matter how small, I could march up to within gunshot of any entrenchments he was given to hold. . . ." —and no mention is made of intelligence supplied by Andrews or anyone else.

Since Grant rarely mentions the contributions of scouts and spies even when these were known to be working effectively for him, lack of confirmation from him leaves the matter unproven one way or the other rather than throwing weight against the case for Andrews' participation in this campaign. The case stays a speculative one, but to it can be added the fact that General William Nelson's division, with which Andrews had served the previous fall, received orders from General Buell to join Grant for this attack. Andrews' services might have been offered as an advance part of this aid, which, in fact, didn't arrive until after the surrender. For another ounce or so of confirmation, the sixty-mile ride spoken of—allowing for some understandable twists and turns en route—wouldn't be too far out for a journey by horseback at the time from the Fort Donelson area to Paducah.

[*Editor*]

Whether Andrews can receive credit for helping prepare this victory has to remain in dispute pending the discovery and sifting of further evidence. On the value of the victory itself, two qualified authorities find themselves in no dispute whatsoever.

U. S. GRANT: My opinion was and still is that immediately after the fall of Fort Donelson the way was open to the National forces all over the southwest without much resistance. If one general who had taken the responsibility had been in command of all the troops west of the Alleghenies, he could have marched to Chattanooga, Corinth, Memphis and Vicksburg with the troops we then had . . . and there would soon have been forces enough at all those centers to operate offensively against any of the enemy that might be found near them.

ROBERT SELPH HENRY: Fort Donelson, in many ways, may be considered the critical event of the Civil War. Its direct military results were immense: the opening of much of Kentucky and half of Tennessee, including its capital, to the Union armies; the capture of nearly one-third of Johnston's effective force; the establishment of a firm base at Nashville, from which to push further conquests in the South. The moral and political effects were perhaps even greater. Deep discouragement in the South, in contrast with the undue elation after Manassas; a new start and a fresh grip on the war for the North, were some of the consequences.

To Make a Spoon 1

WHITELAW REID: In Louisville in December, 1861, the 2nd, 21st and 33d Ohio Regiments were brigaded with the 10th Wisconsin under Colonel Joshua W. Sill in Major General Don Carlos Buell's army. With General O. M. Mitchel as divisional commander, the regiments then marched to Bacon Creek, Kentucky, where they remained in winter quarters, perfecting themselves in drill and discipline. To the division at this time was attached Colonel Kennett's 4th Ohio Cavalry. While lying at Bacon Creek, the troops suffered severely from measles, smallpox and camp diarrhea.

On February 12 and 13, 1862, the division moved out in the advance of the Army of the Ohio, starting southward for Bowling Green, Kentucky.

PITTENGER: At some time near midwinter of 1861-1862, probably about the 1st of February, James Andrews visited Flemingsburg for the last time. He had returned once or twice previously and been kindly received, the good will inspired by former friendships having overcome the irritation occasioned by his professed change of views. There were only a few persons, however, with whom he held confidential communications. One was his friend Jackson, the hotel-keeper, who entreated him to leave a business so beset with danger. Andrews answered by telling Jackson how fully he was trusted by the Rebel authorities, and what an excellent chance he now had to make money. He assured his friend, however, that he wouldn't continue in the same line of service much longer.

Andrews didn't fail to visit Miss Elizabeth Layton during this final stay in Flemingsburg. Some time before this, he had proposed to her and had been accepted. He now tried to make her think there was no special risk in his present employment; but she wasn't easily deceived. Intensely patriotic, she was glad he was serving the Union cause; but there was so much mystery and danger in his form of service that she pleaded with him to give it up. Miss Layton's plea was no more successful than Jackson's. (Although presumably he told her as well that he hoped before too long to complete his special employment and change to other work or service. In confirmation of this intention, it was understood in Flemingsburg that Elizabeth Layton and James Andrews agreed during this visit—or had agreed prior to this—on a date in the forthcoming June for their wedding.)

EDITOR: During this Flemingsburg visit, Andrews made one other arrangement, almost surely not troubling Elizabeth Layton with a knowledge of it.

DAVID S. MCGAVIC: I knew James J. Andrews for more than a year prior to the 17th of February, 1862, when after several conversations, being intimate with him, he delivered me a check reading:

[*David S. McGavic*]

Flemingsburg, February 17, 1862

Cashier of the Branch Bank of Louisville, at Flemingsburg: Pay to David S. McGavic, or bearer, in coin twelve hundred dollars.

J. J. Andrews

Andrews was then in the secret military service of the government of the United States. On this occasion he told me he was engaged in rather a critical business—one from which he might not return. In this event, I was to carry out certain instructions.

"If I shouldn't get back," Andrews told me, "I want you to draw this twelve hundred dollars out of the bank and lend it out at interest, the proceeds to go to the poor of Fleming County perpetually."

After making these arrangements, Andrews left here for Louisville, and I didn't hear from him again.

PITTENGER: Another Flemingsburg man Andrews trusted was a Mr. J. H. Moore, then quite young. Andrews didn't talk to Moore of money as his motive in his hazardous career, but of the service he was rendering the country. He so enkindled Moore's imagination, that the young man wished to accompany him, and enter upon the same business. As he was intelligent and cool-headed, Andrews didn't at first try to hinder him, though he told him that it was a hard life, more dangerous than that of any soldier. Andrews consented to accompany Moore at least as far as Cincinnati, and the two left Flemingsburg in company. On the trip down the river Andrews was very sociable, and made no objections to Moore's expressed intention of going on with him to Nashville, so that the latter considered himself as fully embarked on the career of a spy. But when they were shown to their room at Cincinnati at night, and were alone, Andrews laid his hand on him and said: "Young man, you don't know what you've undertaken. I like your spirit, but you're ten years too young. I'm going to put the whole matter before you and then if you go on, it will be on your own responsibility."

Andrews then drew a picture so frightening that young Moore felt all his ardor ebbing away. The sober thought of the morning completed the work that Andrews' evening words had begun, and Moore informed the latter, apparently much to Andrews' satisfaction, that his mind was made up to return home and enter the army in the common way. Then Andrews made a simple request, which throws no small light on his character.

"Moore," said he, "Old Mrs. Bright asked me to send her back a dollar's worth of sugar from Maysville. I had so many things on my mind that I forgot all about it, and have her money yet. Will you get the sugar and take it home with you for her?"

At Louisville, Andrews purchased a lady's trunk, large and elegant, and left it empty in charge of the landlord at the Hotel Louisville, at which he was accustomed to lodge. The supposed blockade-runner then completed collecting his cargo of articles for sale in the South and returned to Nashville.

In February, when Buell's advance division under Mitchel reached Green River, opposite Bowling Green, and began throwing shells across, Andrews was in the town. It is even said that he rendered the Confederate commander a service by moving out from the station a train of cars which had been abandoned, just as it was ready to start, by engineer and train hands because of the severity of the Federal fire; and that he thereby won Confederate gratitude, and still more trust.

EDITOR: If Andrews won Confederate gratitude by helping move out a locomotive under Union artillery fire, in all probability he earned whatever credit he received. Corporal James Pike of the 4th Ohio Volunteer Cavalry and other Federal witnesses testify that the men of Captain Cyrus O. Loomis of Battery A, 1st Michigan, were zeroed in on the last rolling stock left unmoved.

JAMES PIKE: On February 12, 1862, our 4th Cavalry and the rest of the 3d Division left Bacon Creek and marched on Bowling Green, General Mitchel being, as was usual with him, in great haste to follow up the flying enemy. The obstructions in the roads, upon which the Rebels had wasted so much labor, scarcely blocked us at all. We had a regiment of pioneers from Michigan, who were the best working men I ever saw, and they cleared the way for the advance almost as fast as a man could find his way.

EDITOR: In his early twenties, in the winter of 1858-1859, James Pike—the restive, printshop-trained son of a belligerently Democratic Ohio newspaper editor—had thrown over his trade, made his way to Texas as a horse wrangler, and won recognition over the following two years as a venturesome and resourceful Indian fighter with the Texas Rangers. Holding with the Union, Pike had dropped out of the Rangers in July of 1861 and worked his way back to Ohio through Confederate-held territory. In September, 1861,

[*Editor*]
he was sworn in as a member of Captain O. P. Robie's company of Colonel John Kennett's 4th Ohio Volunteer Cavalry.

PIKE: At Russellville, Ky., scouting out alone ahead of our skirmishers one night, I succeeded in getting into the town, and rousing some of the inhabitants, represented myself as a Confederate quartermaster. I asked them to tell me where the Texas Rangers were—then on our front in this part of the country—and inquired about Colonel Wharton and other Rebel officers, with the air of an old acquaintance. The Russellville people told me that the regiment had left town about an hour before; but if I hustled on, I could overtake them at Whippoorwill Station, since they intended to burn the bridge at that place. I went to Grey's tavern and ordered breakfast for a hundred Texas Rangers, telling him to have it ready for us just at daylight.

The Russellville landlord took me at my word, and a troop of our 4th Ohio Cavalry had a first-class breakfast a few hours later, prepared for the Rangers, who turned out to be real blue-coated Yankees.

We arrived at Bowling Green just as Captain Loomis, of the Coldwater Battery from Michigan, was shelling the Johnnies out of the place. Captain Loomis knocked the stack off the locomotive just as a train loaded with Rebel soldiers was about to start out, and they barely had time to save themselves as we entered the town.

PITTENGER: Andrews remained in Bowling Green after capture of the town and was thus able to give precise information to the Federal commanders of the condition of the retreating Rebels. Then he passed on ahead of the Union columns and arrived at Nashville in time to witness the evacuation of that city by most of the Rebel forces on February 16; and to greet the Union armies on their belated entrance on February 23, upon which he reported directly to General Buell.

WHITELAW REID: Driving the enemy from Bowling Green, General Mitchel's division moved on to help take and occupy Nashville in the last week of February.

EDITOR: No reliable account of Andrews' movements at this period is on record. Nashville was in a lawless condition in the week between the departure of the Confederate army and the arrival of the first Union elements—a situation which could have offered rich picking for an agile between-the-sides dealer—but the check given David McGavic in Flemingsburg was dated February 17, which if dated on or near the day it was drawn makes it impossible that Andrews could have been in Nashville for all or much of the week from the 16th through the 23d.

PITTENGER: The Union capture of Nashville late in February made no change in the lucrative traffic carried on across the hostile lines by Andrews, except that he now took Nashville as his northern starting-point, staying at the City Hotel while there, and carried goods to Whiteman—who had removed to Chattanooga—and to other persons as far south as Atlanta. Andrews was several times seen in the latter city [at the reading room of the newspaper *The Southern Confederacy*, among other places] and still seemed to inspire the Confederate officers with full confidence. In possible confirmation of this, Andrews at about this time was said by Captain Sarratt to have brought a son of the resolute Rebel General B. F. Cheatham through the lines to leave in the care of connections at Nashville for education.

ALF WILSON: Andrews later confided to me, and perhaps to several of our comrades, something of his history. Before most of us first met him, he had been a Union spy, or secret service agent, and had made several trips into different parts of the Confederacy, obtaining much useful information, and invariably accomplishing whatever he was sent to do.

PITTENGER: While at Nashville, late in February, Andrews, already secretly in Buell's service, proposed to that general a daring plan. He offered to take a small party of men, disguise them as Southern citizens, and conduct them to Atlanta, where he would meet a friend of his who ran a locomotive on the Georgia State Western & Atlantic line connecting Chattanooga and Atlanta. Riding with his party as passengers to a favorable point, he proposed to capture the locomotive, cut the telegraph wires behind him, and run through Chattanooga and from this point westward, burning the bridges behind him, especially the great one over the Tennessee River at Bridgeport.

Carried out, the operation would have cut the main communication for some days or weeks between the eastern and western armies of the Confederate states at a most critical period. As General

[*Pittenger*]
Buell later confirmed, the bold plan originated with Andrews himself, who recognized the general's interest in destruction of the enemy's communications, and suggested the means for accomplishing that end. General Mitchel, whose division was nearest the scene of the proposed enterprise, was instructed to furnish volunteers for the purpose.

EDITOR: The commander of the Department of the Ohio wasn't nearly so convinced as were Pittenger and Wilson of the value of Andrews' undercover operations, and gaining his approval of the plans for the first railroad raid may have taken somewhat more sweating it out than Pittenger indicates. A quarter of a century later, looking back on the early movements of this violent spring, General Buell recorded himself as less than satisfied with his agent's services up to this time, at least as these were known to him.

DON CARLOS BUELL: Andrews was within the Confederate lines when I advanced upon Nashville. He reported to me there.

He had come into my employment in the capacity of a spy. Having traffic in quinine, etc., as an excuse for his movements, he had made one trip and returned without information of value. He started on a second at a critical period, full of important facts. While the crisis was pending, I expected him every day. He returned only after I entered Nashville, and then the current of events had told all he knew. . . . I had little confidence in Andrews' usefulness, apprehending that he thought more of his traffic than of the object for which he was engaged. When he proposed to attempt the destruction of bridges, I did not assent. . . . He, however, interested my chief of staff, and at the request of the latter, I consented to the arrangement that was completed between them.

EDITOR: The relationship between an able agent and the military commander he works with and for is a highly special one, easily wrecked by shaken confidence on either side. However caused, Buell's souring on the contraband runner in February—if sensed by Andrews—could understandably have helped deflect the agent toward Mitchel as a possibly more appreciative and cooperative military commander. As the movement of the armies stepped up, Mitchel's advancing division offered in any case a more accessible and effective operating base for swift trips across the lines than did army headquarters, and this in itself could have accounted for Buell's loss of first chance at the agent's information, and a resultant lack of awareness of such later contributions as Andrews may have been making.

On the full record, Buell's failure to make effective use of Andrews' services would seem at least as chargeable against the general as against the agent. Justly or unjustly arrived at, the departmental commander's low opinion in February of the agent's value could well have been an ingredient in Andrews' resolve that spring to prove himself before the army and the world to a spectacularly undeniable degree.

PITTENGER: The securing of volunteers for Andrews' audacious project was managed with the utmost secrecy. In addition to General Mitchel and General Joshua Sill—under whose brigade command our 2nd Ohio came—a few line officers of the 2nd Ohio were given a rough outline of what was wanted, and they induced men to meet Andrews. These volunteers, after consulting with him, entered upon their duties without giving a hint of the nature of these to their comrades.

Dry Run 2

EDITOR: As spring approached and his semi-independent division broke loose and moved southward, General Ormsby MacKnight Mitchel was relishing all the challenge, demands and privileges of his first undeniable wartime field command. A particular pleasure, for a man of Mitchel's unorthodox talents and temper, was the privilege of conducting his own secret service operations. For weeks—chiefly through projects involving heel-kicking Corporal James Pike of Kennett's 4th Cavalry unit—Mitchel had been having a fine time running a spare-time private duel with the cool and unpredictable Confederate irregular cavalry leader John Morgan.

PIKE: The celebrated John H. Morgan was then in our front. General Mitchel resolved to catch him, kill him or drive him out of the country. To enable me to find Morgan, the general gave orders that I should be fitted out to my own notion. Captain Prentice, the assistant adjutant general, furnished me with citizen's clothes and the general gave me his own saddle pony to ride, as it was the only unbranded horse in camp.

O. M. MITCHEL:

March 11, 1862

I have determined to take Captain John Morgan, the Dick Turpin of Tennessee, if at all possible, and last evening I started one of my rangers, Corporal Pike, to spy out Morgan's camp. The boys took the greatest interest in disguising him. One furnished a coat, another a pair of trousers, I the citizen's saddle and bridle, Captain Loomis the horse, Captain Prentice the money (Tennessee money, of course) and so we fitted out our spy and started him about eleven o'clock last night. In case he finds the camp, my scout Pike has orders to return to me like a streak of lightning.

March 14, 1862

. . . I can now give you the second chapter in our "Romance of the Civil War." The night before last, Pike returned and was brought to my tent, a prisoner of the guard, about midnight. He had penetrated Morgan's lines, passed all of his pickets, and actually been seven miles beyond Morgan's headquarters at Murfreesboro.

EDITOR: As a result of Pike's information, Mitchel on the following night—a forerunner of mechanized infantry planners to come—organized and started out a task force combining cavalry elements, light artillery and twelve hundred riflemen borne concealed within sixty teams and wagons.

Morgan, as uncooperative as ever, surprised Mitchel by appearing under a flag of truce almost at the moment of the expedition's start, his errand the return of a captured teamster. Mitchel—enormously exasperated, but bursting to have the results of his planning seen and appreciated by a qualified judge, even if at the cost of the original point of it—took Morgan along the road where the wagon-borne striking force was formed and showed him his formidable preparations. Gracefully—before taking his leave again—the Confederate irregular admitted himself thoroughly impressed, acknowledged his luck in escaping and granted this to be an "outstanding new feature in warfare."

The expedition of course had then to be abandoned, Mitchel reported regretfully, and "thus was a most capital adventure spoiled."

F. A. MITCHEL: When General Mitchel moved south from Nashville on March 18, a member of his staff had been left with an officer suffering from typhoid fever. The sick man a day or two later was sent back to Cincinnati. The staff officer then wanted to return to the division, which had meanwhile moved thirty-five miles further south. The trip through semi-hostile country alone seemed uninviting till the officer happened to meet—at General Buell's headquarters—Corporal Pike of the 4th Ohio Cavalry, who had been sent to get news of the man with typhoid fever.

Corporal Pike and the general's aide went through together, traveling by dark and with a thirty-mile ride to make before morning. After scouting Indian style through the night, they stopped at a farmhouse for breakfast.

At the table sat a tall man with a long brownish beard, eating in silence. No joke or banter could elicit either a smile or a word from this silent, strange-looking man who neither seemed to be a citizen of the country nor connected with the army.

After breakfasting, the aide and Pike mcunted their horses and proceeded to camp.

Upon riding up to General Mitchel's headquarters at Murfreesboro, who should be standing by the general's tent but the silent man with the long beard. He proved to be Mr. J. J. Andrews, then arranging with my father for his first attempt against the railroad in Georgia.

PITTENGER: To the soldiers of our 2nd Ohio not picked up for the first Andrews expedition, the whole affair was wrapped in mystery. Eight of our best men suddenly disappeared, and we didn't know what had become of them.

In March of 1862, my position in Company G was that of first corporal, and I was looking for promotion to sergeant. A sergeant had died at Nashville, and his place would naturally become mine unless Captain Sarratt carried someone over my head. One of the missing men—Alexander Surles—happened to be second corporal, a splendid soldier and a great friend of the captain. I had heard that he might be preferred to me, if for no other reason, because I was near-sighted. At the first opportunity I called Captain Sarratt aside and mentioned my fears. He assured me, somewhat impatiently, that my rights should be cared for, and added, "Pittenger, this is a very little matter of yours. I only wish the men were back in the camp again."

"But where are they?" I asked.

"I'm not permitted to tell anything," he answered.

Captain David Mitchel of Company K, 2nd Ohio, was a friend of mine, and a distant relative of our commander. His company had supplied one of the missing adventurers—my cousin, B. F. Mills—who had been my messmate during the three months' service terminating with the battle of Bull Run. I resolved to make an attempt on Captain Mitchel. The opportunity soon presented itself. I was war correspondent of the Steubenville *Herald* as well as soldier. It was time to write again. Taking pencil and notebook I walked off to the bank of the beautiful little Stone River. It was in the afternoon of a warm spring day, March 21, 1862. Three days before we had broken camp near Nashville and started for Murfreesboro, just reached the day before.

A short distance downstream a railroad bridge burned by the enemy a few days before was being repaired, under the vigorous direction of our General O. M. Mitchel. As large timbers were hewed, framed and slowly raised to their places, there was precision and speed such as I had never noticed before in similar work. The general himself, nervously eager, was encouraging the willing and rebuking the shirkers.

Just then, Captain Mitchel happened along. We talked for a time, and then I led the conversation to the destination of the men who had vanished, saying I was convinced they had gone south on a secret expedition. Startled at first by the accuracy of my guess, but then admitting his own uneasiness about the absent men, he gave the full information desired. Nothing I had ever heard so fired my imagination. The new bridge below, rapidly rising out of the ruins of the old, took on a fresh interest. The destruction the enemy had wrought was, perhaps, at that very moment, being repaid upon them with interest, far in their rear. The more I thought of it, the more attractive such service seemed. I was tired of the dull monotony of usual army life, and I was both ambitious and patriotic.

I went next morning to regimental headquarters, and told Colonel L. A. Harris, who then commanded the 2nd Ohio, that I knew the business on which some of his soldiers had been sent south, and desired, if at any other time there should be another such enterprise, that I might be chosen for it. Major Anson G. McCook, in whose company I had served during the first enlistment of three months, was also present, and at once objected. He had always been friendly; but now he thought my extremely defective eyes would unfit me for sudden emergencies in enterprises where each soldier is thrown on his own resources. I was greatly gratified to hear Colonel Harris say that he couldn't agree with McCook; wearing spectacles as I did, I looked so much like a school teacher and so little like a soldier that he felt the Southerners would never suspect me. The colonel then gave me his promise that if any other men were sent beyond the lines, I should be among the first called on.

A few days after, one of the absent men from Company C, 2nd Ohio Regiment, returned to the camp at Murfreesboro. He reported having gone as far as Chattanooga, where he was recognized by a Rebel acquaintance. For the sake of former friendship the Southerner hesitated to denounce him, but insisted that he should at once return northward, which he did.

D. C. BUELL:

Headquarters Army of the Ohio
Nashville, March 23, 1862

Maj. Gen. H. W. Halleck,
Commanding Department of the Mississippi:

General: If the enemy should contemplate an advance upon Nashville and our position in middle Tennessee under certain circumstances there are three routes by which it could be attempted: First, by the direct route across from Knoxville; second, by the Chattanooga Railroad; third, by the Decatur Railroad. . . .

I have intimations, not well defined yet, of the collection of a considerable force and a large amount of rolling stock about Atlanta. If they should be verified, it is a thing that must be watched. Floyd has gone to Knoxville, leaving Chattanooga with a guard of not more than a few companies. . . .

Respectfully,
D. C. Buell
Brigadier General, Commanding

PITTENGER: About a week afterward all returned. First was my cousin, Frank Mills; and on two consecutive days the remainder came. I learned the bizarre details of their journey from Frank Mills and later from Frank J. Hawkins, of Columbus, Ohio.

[*Pittenger*]

To go back before the start of this first expedition, James J. Andrews had become quite well acquainted with Captain Sarratt, and depended mainly upon the captain's company for volunteers for the venture. At first Sarratt regarded Andrews with some distrust; but his persuasive words overcame this feeling. Accordingly, when Andrews obtained the order from Buell for Mitchel to furnish him volunteers, he told the latter that he could easily find them in the 2nd Ohio. Sarratt agreed to furnish half of the eight men needed, and sent for Frank Hawkins, J. W. Holliday, Alexander Surles and B. F. Durbin. These were among his best men. Andrews told them that he wanted eight men to go south with him as far as Atlanta, from which he had just returned. He had made there the acquaintance of a railroad engineer who was also a good Union man. This engineer had agreed to run off with his train, if Andrews would furnish hands to act as brakemen, tear up track and burn bridges. When the four soldiers had heard his statement they all volunteered. Frank Mills of Captain Mitchel's company offered his service, as did a private named Horr from Company A. Two other volunteers—names not now procurable—made up the party.

The four from Sarratt's company made up one band who traveled by themselves. They were furnished with citizen's clothing in place of their uniforms, and forty dollars each in gold. The same evening they slept out at the reserve picket post, and started into the enemy's lines at four the next morning. They bent their steps first toward Tullahoma, forty miles distant, which was the furthest point northward to which the Rebels at that time ran their trains.

Twelve miles out they met three Rebel citizens in a spring wagon, who on inquiry were told that the four came from Nashville, and were on their road to Atlanta to enlist. The citizens stated their own business, which was to spy out the number of Yankees in Murfreesboro. Hawkins and his friends misled them as much as they could by stating that 25,000 troops had left Nashville.

By one o'clock of the next day the four had reached Tullahoma. From this point the adventurers proceeded by rail to Chattanooga. They spent the night at the Crutchfield House, the principal hotel, and at seven were off for Atlanta. At Big Shanty, they stopped for supper, and reached their destination at nine in the evening, finding lodging at the Trout House in Atlanta.

Andrews and others of the party arrived the next morning. He visited the four, and said that he hadn't yet found his engineer. He didn't succeed in finding him that afternoon. There were plenty of officers of the Confederate army at this hotel—General Johnston, among others—eating at the same table with them. Our men didn't go around the city much during the day, thinking it safer to keep close to their hotel; but at night they went to the courthouse, and heard a fiery secession speech from Robert Toombs. He said, among other things, that the Yankees were a distinct people from the Southerners—so distinct that he could tell one wherever he saw him. The four Yankees, looking right at him, cheered as heartily as the rest.

On this same evening Surles and Durbin had a very narrow escape. These two went out by Andrews' direction to cut the telegraph wire, in order that no word of their operations—if they should take the train next day—might be flashed ahead in time to hamper them. They found a solitary place, Surles climbed the pole, and with the tools brought for the purpose soon severed a wire. Durbin had just taken hold of it and was coiling it up for removal, when two Rebels belonging to an irregular cavalry company rode up. They carried shotguns.

"What are you at up there?" they demanded.

Surles was a man of great coolness. He answered by a burst of passionate imprecations on the Confederacy, declaring that it was high time the Yankees came in and took charge of the whole thing, if it couldn't be managed better.

"If I have to tend a key all day," Surles said, "and go around mending wires all night, I don't care how soon the whole thing goes to destruction."

The cavalrymen, convinced that they had to do only with an overworked operator, encouraged him to bear up under his trouble, and rode away. Surles and Durbin bore up long enough to finish the repair which consisted in getting down a large roll and throwing it into a neighboring cornfield. Andrews came to their room later and reported that he had finally heard of his engineer, but the news was no comfort. The man had been drafted off to the East Tennessee road to assist in the work of transporting troops toward Corinth, where the Rebel forces were concentrating in anticipation of the Pittsburg Landing battle.

Andrews asked each of his men whether he could run an engine. Not one of them could. Andrews himself knew nothing of a train except what he had learned by casual observation, and felt it would be too great a risk to attempt to force an unwilling engineer to do their work. It was to Andrews a most bitter disappointment, but he wasted no time in vain regrets. He told the men the fault was his

[*Pittenger*]

own in not having taken an engineer along, and now the only thing they could do was get back to the Union lines. The others started the same day; the four from Sarratt's company delayed till the next morning.

When they left Atlanta it was on a mixed freight and passenger train, which stopped for an hour at Big Shanty. It was then in the center of Camp McDonald, a Confederate camp of instruction. Having some time to spare, our soldiers went over to look with a veteran's interest upon the evolutions of the raw recruits. These were supplied only with pikes about four feet long, for arms were very scarce in the South at that period. After witnessing the recruits' performances for an hour, our men continued their own journey.

Durbin and Surles went into the forward end of the train while the others took seats in the rear car. Andrews was with them. A brakeman came into the car saying, in an excited tone, "We've got some Yankees out here." Their natural presumption was that their comrades had been arrested. Hawkins and Holliday stepped out to investigate, and found that the prisoners were a number of Union soldiers on another train they had just met. As they looked around, on return to their car, they could see nothing of their leader. But a man was there, with his face toward the window, whom they hadn't seen before. When he turned and asked them what prisoners it was they were talking about outside, they started, for it was Andrews. At the alarm of a few moments before, he had simply changed a hat for a cap which he carried, and thrown his hair in another way, so that it would have required a very close observer to identify him.

In the evening the train arrived at Chattanooga, where the four separated to cross the mountains back to the Union army.

O. M. MITCHEL:

Murfreesboro, Tenn.
April 2

Dear Mr. [George S.] Coe:

A week ago Friday a large force was put to work on three railroad bridges near this town. These must be rebuilt before we could advance, as without the railroad we could not feed the army. On Saturday morning I learned that we had framing tools for only two gangs of framers, when I wished to set twenty gangs to work. I at once mounted my horse, went to Nashville, purchased all I required, returned the same day, and on Sunday morning at daylight the wagon arrived with the tools. My journey was seventy-five miles.

Sunday everything was grooved up. Monday we framed and started raising butts.

This morning two bridges are finished, and the third one nearly ready for the iron. Thus in ten days a work has been accomplished which has no parallel in the histories of bridge building. But alas, it's of no avail. Some small bridges near Nashville, under repair for some six weeks, are unfinished, and thus my entire division is held back, after the most positive promise on the part of our general that these other bridges should occasion no delay.

Learning these facts, I sent one of my staff to Nashville to communicate by telegraph with General Buell, at Columbia, and I hope to be placed in command of the entire railroad to Chattanooga, and then my troubles will be over, for with a clear field and plenty of room in which to operate, and no one to depend on but myself, I ask no odds of anyone.

I hope one of these days to address you from Decatur, or, possibly, from Chattanooga.

Yours,
O. M. M.

PITTENGER: Two of the men returning from Andrews' first attempt at the W. & A. took the route toward Tracy City and Manchester. Holliday and Hawkins went by the train as far as Stevenson, to which point the road had been shortened since they had last passed over it. From this place they started on foot. A week later—after covering nearly a hundred miles, sleeping en route in fields, barns, Negro cabins and with farmers both Rebel and Union in sympathy—they found the Union pickets. Here they were promptly arrested, put under close guard, and conducted to Colonel Turchin's quarters. Some of their band had already returned. Colonel Turchin recognized this additional pair, treated them royally, and sent them to their regiments, where they were warmly welcomed.

Andrews himself returned a few days later. He reported only to Mitchel, and didn't seek the headquarters of General Buell, who was approaching Shiloh, nor, as far as can be ascertained, did Andrews make Buell any written or telegraphic report.

When Andrews and Mitchel settled on the plans which led to our raid, no witness was present. Andrews was undismayed by the failure of his friend, the Southern engineer, and proposed making another attempt with a larger force, carrying with him engineers and train hands from the Union army. Their interview was most probably held in Mitchel's tent, where there would be security from interruption and maps of the enemy's country spread out before them, and it took place the night of Sunday, April 6, or before daylight on Monday morning, April 7—on exactly the days the battle of Shiloh or Pittsburg Landing was being fought, a hundred and ten miles to the west.

General Mitchel was then in high spirits, for the obstacles which had so long delayed him at Murfreesboro had been overcome. He had built a bridge across Stone River at that point from his own resources with a speed unexampled in the army. General Buell, whose excessive caution was more dreaded by Mitchel than the forces of the enemy, had marched off days before to join Grant, leaving Mitchel buoyantly on his own. From nearly every aspect, the outlook of the Union armies at that time was more hopeful than we, with the memory of the years of bloody struggle that followed, can easily realize.

While Andrews and Mitchel considered the advisability of a second secret expedition, one fact was clear. The original instructions from Buell, given nearly a month before, no longer applied under the thoroughly changed circumstances. Any new enterprise must be directly on the authority of Mitchel.

DORSEY: One of the [first party of six later] declared that he wouldn't undertake it again for anything; said he felt all the time he was in the enemy's country as though he had a rope around his neck, and that if Andrews wanted any more bridge burners he might get them, but this man couldn't be one of the party. None of the original six would try it again. When they learned Andrews was going to try it again, one of them said he would fool with that scheme until he got hanged.

The Mustering 5

DORSEY: The 33d Ohio had been in quarters at Shelbyville, Tenn., about two days when after roll call on Sunday evening, April 6, 1862, a group of some half dozen of our Company H were standing about the campfire chatting about army matters, the fine climate and the budding springtime. We were joined by our company commander, Lieutenant A. L. Waddle, who entered into the conversation for a few moments, and then quietly informed us that one man was wanted from this company to go, in company with others from our brigade, on a secret expedition.

One or two newer recruits of the company at once offered their services. The rest of us, however, were disposed to inquire into the matter. We got a general idea of the expedition, and elicited the fact that the call came from high authority—the general in command. But we didn't learn where we were to go, nor the character of the work we were to do. Several of our best men signified their willingness to serve and finally—after still further questioning the officer until he declined to reveal anything more—I placed my services at his disposal. This, as I remember it now, seemed to satisfy the lieutenant, and he soon after turned the conversation again to casual matters.

One by one the boys dropped out of the circle and retired to their tents, until but three or four of us remained. Lieutenant Waddle excused himself and started for his quarters. When he had reached a secluded spot he halted, turned, and catching my eye, beckoned me to his side. Here he informed me that I was the man for this service. I told him that I was willing to go if he thought proper to send me, but insisted that better men had offered to go.

"No," said he, "you're the most suitable. You're cool and cautious, as you'll need to be, because you're to go disguised into the enemy's country, and we want to send men down there intelligent enough to know what they see and be able to tell it when they get back."

While I received this as quite a compliment, I believed then, and still believe, as I told him, that better men had offered their services. But he chose me, and that was his judgment—not mine. The additional information as to the destination of the expedition he gave me in confidence.

On retiring I found the comrades of my mess all awake in the quarters, and many were the jests gotten off, as it was understood that I was selected for the raid. "Dorsey, you're a goner!" "Good-bye, Dorsey!" "Say, Dorsey, they'll hang you as sure as—!" And from a comrade in a neighboring tent: "Leave us a lock of your hair, Dorsey!"

EDITOR: On Sunday, April 6, 1862, Private Sam Slavens of Company E, 33d Ohio Volunteer Infantry—father of three small sons aged five, three and one—wrote his wife Rachel from camp at Shelbyville,

[*Editor*]
Tenn. The Reuben of the letter is his brother, a volunteer in the same company.

SAMUEL SLAVENS:

Camp Harrison
near Shelbyville, Tenn.
April 6, 1862

Dear Wife Rachel:

Once more I have the pleasure of writing a few lines to inform you that I am well, and hope these few lines may find you and the children all enjoying good health.

We left Camp Van Buren the 4th, and marched twenty-six miles and came to Shelbyville. We came it in two days. The boys all came through that started with us. It wasn't hard marching. The first day we marched fifteen miles, and the second day we got here about eleven o'clock, although it rained both days. It is warm and nice, and we had a good turnpike, and had our knapsacks hauled.

We are forty miles from Alabama. Mitchel's division is all that is marching on this road. Nelson and McCook's divisions are to our right on another road, and Grant's is on the Tennessee River. We are going to march in behind them and try and surround them and see whether they will fight or run. If they run, I think they will have to break down through Alabama. If they run any other way like as not they will run against a "sawyer."

Well, enough of that, as I will write every three or four days when I have a chance, and let you know where I am and how I am getting along. I will tell you that Reuben was nearly well when we left Murfreesboro and Colonel Moore told him that he could stay there, as there had to be some left. He was all the one that was detailed out of our company. Colonel told him to stay at a man's house by the name of Murfree—it is about one mile from town—and to go to the hospital every day or two and see how the sick were getting along, and if any of them died to mark their graves so they could be found, and it may be some time before he comes up to the regiment. He may stay there as long as there is any of our regiment there sick.

Give my love to all, and reserve the largest portion for yourself and the children.

Good-bye.
Samuel Slavens

PITTENGER: On Monday morning, April 7, orders were sent in regular military channels to the colonels of the three Ohio regiments of Sill's brigade to have a man from each company selected for special and hazardous service. Each colonel called a meeting of captains, and gave them a general idea of the nature of the work required. (None of the members of Andrews' first expedition, all of the 2nd Ohio, had volunteered for a second attempt.) The officers were particularly instructed to search out men with railroad experience.

Two engineers, Wilson W. Brown and William J. Knight, were from the 21st Ohio. That whole regiment was called into line, and the statement publicly made that men who could run engines were wanted for detailed service; and any engineers or firemen having experience in that line were asked to step forward. Brown was one of the two men who did.

WILSON BROWN: The colonel then ordered me to report to his headquarters for instructions. When I did, he told me that there was a secret raid being organized to penetrate into the South to burn bridges, and that, to complete the work, a locomotive would have to be captured. He added that I had been selected to run this locomotive, though, to guard against all contingencies, two other engineers would be along to take my place if anything happened to me.

After giving me some advice the colonel ordered me to report to General Mitchel in person. I did so, and handed the general a note from the colonel, which he read. Then he said, "This is a dangerous mission you are going on, and the utmost caution will be necessary on the part of all of you." He next questioned me as to my competency to run an engine. This work Mitchel well understood, as his questions showed. I answered all he put to me, and he then asked if I had any papers to show. I drew from my pocket a paper signed by the master mechanic of the Mobile & Ohio Railroad, on which I had run in 1860, and other papers from other roads on which I had been employed.

The general carefully read them all and said they were sufficient on that point, adding, "On you rests a great responsibility. You're the first engineer selected, but there'll be two others from the other regiments."

"May I ask the object of this raid?" I inquired.

"To destroy the bridges over one of the main lines of the enemy's communications."

"What do you think of our chances of success?"

"If the enterprise can be carried out in the way and at the time planned by Mr. Andrews," he replied, "I think the chances very good."

"But if there's any delay?"

"As the armies draw nearer," he answered, "the roads will be more occupied with troops and stores moving back and forth, and these will be in your way. I don't deny your mission is hazardous. I do have great confidence in Mr. Andrews, however, and I'll trust that God will protect you all."

He grasped my hand and ended the interview. I never saw him again.

DORSEY: The next day I met Samuel Slavens of Company E. He was of stout build, full, round figure, five feet eight inches in height, possibly thirty-two years old, and weighed 180 pounds—a frank, open-faced, jolly fellow.

"Corporal," he said as we met alone on the parade ground, "I understand you're going south on this secret expedition. I'm going, too, and we'll go together."

The proposition was cheerfully accepted, and we became almost inseparable companions.

BENSINGER:

William Bensinger was duly sworn and examined:

Q. Your position in the service?

A. A private in Company G, 25th Ohio Infantry.

Q. In what part of the state did you enlist, and when, and for how long a time?

A. I enlisted in Hancock County, Ohio, on the 21st of August, 1861, for three years.

Q. Were you a member of this secret expedition sent out by General Mitchel?

A. Yes, sir.

Q. Where was General Mitchel's headquarters at the time this expedition set out?

A. It was close by the town of Shelbyville, Tenn., and just across the river—probably forty rods from the town.

Q. Under what circumstances did you become a member of it?

A. The day before we started, my captain called me to one side and told me that he wanted me to report to the colonel the next morning. I asked him if he knew what the colonel wanted with me. He said he supposed it was for a secret expedition, but he couldn't tell me what. I told him I would go, and reported to the colonel as ordered. The colonel gave me a pass and directed me to report to Mr. Andrews at Shelbyville, at a hotel there. The colonel told me I was to obey the orders of Mr. Andrews, and also told me to procure citizen's clothes, which I did. I went to Shelbyville and reported there.

DORSEY: The men designated by the respective company commanders were reported to the colonel of the regiment, and if he approved of the selection, they were by him introduced to the commander of the expedition, and if he approved, the soldier was elected. In our regiment—the 33d—the men first selected by their company commanders were all accepted save in the case of Wm. Hunter Myers of Company K. He was rejected for lack of sufficient physical ability to endure great hardships, and Jacob Parrott of the same company took his place.

JACOB PARROTT:
Jacob Parrott was duly sworn and examined:

Q. In the first week of April, 1862, what was your position in the military service?

A. I was a private in Company K, 33d Ohio Regiment.

Q. What was then your age?

A. Eighteen, sir.

Q. In what part of Ohio did you reside before entering the army?

A. I lived in Hardin County.

Q. Have you a father and mother living?

A. No, sir.

Q. You were a member of the expedition sent out by General Mitchel?

A. Yes, sir.

Q. Will you state the circumstances under which you joined the expedition?

A. My captain called me out of the tent and asked me to take a walk with him. We walked down towards the guard quarters, and he asked me if I would go on a secret expedition, and told me that, if I agreed to go, I should go up to his tent in about half an hour and report to him. I went up and told him I would go.

Q. Did he know the precise object of the expedition?

A. No, sir. He only knew that it was a secret one, and so told me.

WILLIAM J. KNIGHT: Captain Brewster reported my name to the Monday, April 7, meeting at the 21st headquarters as the man from his company for the expedition on foot. We were next called out as a regiment on parade shortly after dinner. While on the parade ground, the colonel made a call, that if there were any engineers in the regiment capable of running a locomotive, they should step two paces in advance. I stepped out thinking that I was going to get some soft snap, such as running a saw or grist mill; but it turned out not to be so very soft. He told me to report to headquarters immediately after being dismissed.

Captain Brewster offered to go along, and give me an introduction. On the way he told me the first I knew of the expedition, and that my name was already in as one of the men, but said I could use my own judgment about going. I said I would go and he introduced me as the man he had for that expedition, and also as having stepped out as an engineer.

I was presented to Andrews, who was there, and he asked me if I considered myself competent to take charge of an engine. I said that I was perfectly competent, and showed my papers.

Andrews had his maps of the country spread out on the colonel's table, and showed me on the map where I was at that time, and where he wanted me to go. It looked much better on paper than I afterwards found it on land. Andrews also told me that I would have to take off my uniform and put on citizen's clothes. He stated that if we were caught in the enemy's lines, and they knew us, we would be treated as spies. The colonel then gave me a pass to go down and procure clothing, saying to take nothing in my pockets that would give me away if captured; but if I should be captured, I was to get out by enlisting in the Southern army or any way I could, and it would be considered honorable when I got back.

DORSEY: During that day—Monday—the leader of the expedition appeared at regimental headquarters. Colonel Moore had a special guard put around his tent to keep off intruders. The tent was closed and the men designated for the raid were called in and introduced to a gentleman in citizen's dress, Mr. Andrews. His mild manner and gentlemanly appearance tended to make us feel free and unembarrassed in his presence.

When I was introduced to him he took me by the hand, and after looking me straight in the eyes for a moment, with a smile he said to the colonel, "He'll do." I thought as our eyes met that I had seen him before. (I had, although I didn't then at first remember where.

He was the civilian scout whose umbrella I had uncivilly taken in eastern Kentucky the fall before.)

With the information that the matter of the raid would be more fully explained by our leader after we had passed out of our lines, we were dismissed to make final preparations for the mission.

PITTENGER: William Campbell, irregularly of Louisville and still a civilian, was in the camp on a visit to Shadrach when the latter was selected for the Andrews expedition. Campbell requested permission to go along. Being well qualified for dangerous work by his great strength and adventurous disposition, his request was readily granted.

WILLIAM REDDICK:

William Reddick was duly sworn and examined:

Q. Your position in the military service?

A. A corporal in Company B, 33d Ohio Regiment.

Q. When and for how long did you enlist?

A. I enlisted on the 18th of August, 1861, for three years.

Q. Will you state the circumstances under which you were engaged in the secret expedition sent out by General Mitchel?

A. I was sitting by the campfire when the captain and second lieutenant called me up to them. The captain told me that there was a secret expedition on hand, and he wished I would go with it, stating that he had to furnish a man and that he preferred me for the service before any other of his company. He said we were to enter into the enemy's lines, capture a train and destroy the bridges on the road; that it would be very easily accomplished; that we had a good leader, a man who understood the business, and who had been employed in the service of the United States. He told me that he would give me three-quarters of an hour to study upon it, whether I would go or not.

I went to my tent, and after a time, I went up and reported that I would go. The captain took me to the colonel, and the colonel told me to get all the citizen's clothing that I could procure in camp. I only made out to get two checked shirts of one of our boys who had just returned to camp, and a pair of jeans pants from the cook in the hospital. We were then taken to Shelbyville, where we procured more clothes, and then we returned back to the camp for supper. After supper we were taken back to Shelbyville. We went out upon the railroad a mile and a half or two miles, and there we stopped and money was given to us. We were unacquainted, at that time, with each other.

MARK WOOD: On the 7th day of April, 1862, our company commander, Captain A. McMahan, came to Alfred Wilson and myself and informed us it was proposed by General Mitchel to organize a party of men who would volunteer to go on a secret service expedition to the state of Georgia, the purpose of which was to destroy railroad bridges and cut off the railroad communication between Georgia, Tennessee, Virginia and Mississippi. We volunteered to go, expecting not to return unless successful.

Our division was at this time encamped at Shelbyville, Tenn. As soon as we said we would go, we were ordered to report to J. J. Andrews, who was to be the leader of the party. Upon reporting we found there was to be a force of men from the various regiments of the division, and were also informed that we would be reimbursed for all money we might expend while on this service, if we returned, whether successful or not.

ROBERT BUFFUM:

Robert Buffum was duly sworn and examined:

Q. At the beginning of April, 1862, what was your position in the service?

A. I was a private in Company H, 21st Ohio Regiment.

Q. Were you a member of the expedition sent out by General Mitchel?

A. Yes, sir.

Q. Will you state the circumstances under which you joined it?

A. My captain came to me and called me from the tent, and asked me if I was willing to go on a secret expedition, and said that if I was I should report to him in twenty minutes, or as soon as I could. I asked him the nature of the business, and he said he couldn't tell me anything; but if I didn't wish to go, there would be nothing more said about it. I told him I would go. He then told me to report to the colonel, which I did, and he gave me a pass to Shelbyville, where I was to meet Mr. Andrews at a tavern. Shortly after I arrived there, Mr. Andrews appeared. There was a man with me by the name of Wilson, and another by the name of Wood, belonging to the 21st. Mr. Andrews gave me forty dollars to purchase citizen's clothes with. It being all in gold, I got our three suits for the forty dollars.

PITTENGER: Captain James F. Sarratt wasn't asked to select a man. To his surprise, he was simply required to "inform Corporal Pittenger, that he's selected as the man from your company."

Called to Captain Sarratt's tent, I was given a pass that I might go to Shelbyville, a mile distant, and purchase supplies needed for the expedition. The captain also told me that I would probably see Andrews there, and advised me that if he didn't perfectly satisfy me as to what he proposed, I was to return without hesitation to camp.

This Monday was very quiet, for Mitchel had allowed two days of rest and preparation before the effort of his next dash into Rebel territory. My comrades, as I walked down the street, were sitting around the openings of their tents, scouring arms and accoutrements, playing games, telling stories in little groups, or lazily sleeping either within the tents or in the shade just outside.

Out of the camp and arrived at the pleasant little town of Shelbyville, I began to inquire for clothing. Others were on the same quest. I didn't find a full suit to my taste, but knew that I could supply the deficiency in camp. Among those who were purchasing I noticed with pleasure Marion Ross, sergeant major of the 2nd Ohio. After a few cautious questions and answers, we both became convinced that we were on the same errand.

Our first business was to find Andrews. As both Ross and I had remembered him from the eastern Kentucky campaign, we recognized him at once as we saw him coming out of a store. Gaining his side, we reported to him.

At thirty-three, Andrews had now grown an imposingly full silken beard and was in manners and address the ideal Southern gentleman. He gave to everyone the impression of gentleness and strength. His voice was soft and musical, never strong, yet with a distinctness and firmness of tone which made it well suit the man.

Rather sharply on this occasion, he asked us what we were to report to him for. When satisfied that we were two of the men detached to his service, he told us he would be a mile or two out of Shelbyville on the Wartrace road shortly after dark, and if we met him there, he would give us full information. His manner was that of one who didn't care very much whether we came to the place or not.

There were some variations in the mode of selection. Porter went to the headquarters of the 21st and there found one or two others with Andrews. The latter entered with some detail upon the plan of his operations—showed a map of the country and pointed out the road over which they were to pass and the bridges between Atlanta and Chattanooga that were to be burned. Porter and the others were then shown what they were individually to do, and ordered, if willing to enter on the work, to report at the night rendezvous on the Wartrace road.

I was surprised to find Ross engaged in this expedition. He was fastidious, neat, fond of drill, parades, and generally of the pomp and glitter of war, and was often teased for these qualities. As we walked back to camp together, the sergeant major asked my frank opinion of Andrews. I answered with enthusiasm. The strong influence of this singular man was already at work—his thoughtful manner, his mild firm voice, his grace and dignity—and I was ready to trust him completely. Ross expressed a similar opinion, and yet along with it a fear that possibly Andrews had now undertaken more than he could carry through.

On nearing our tents we parted to make our separate arrangements. At the camp, indifference had given place to curiosity. Several soldiers, I was told, had arrayed themselves in citizen's dress and left the regiment. I went to the tent of one of the number who had been out with Andrews before, and from him borrowed the clothing needed to complete my outfit. Then I took off the army blue which I had worn so long, and getting all my arms and equipment in order, left them to be turned over to the proper authorities.

When I was clad only in plain garb, my changed appearance caused a sensation on the company street. Soon all that weren't on guard, or otherwise out of reach, came around me and began to shower questions faster than a dozen men could have answered.

"There's something up," was the commonest opinion expressed. I didn't care to contradict this, and answering all questions at random, I hurried across the line of tents to the adjoining company, and to the tent of my cousin, Frank Mills, who had been on the former expedition.

Mills was uneducated but very shrewd.

"So," he said in strong disapproval, "you're going with Andrews."

I assented, and then asked to borrow his revolver—he had a fine one. He freely gave the weapon, but added the opinion that if I knew when I was well off, I'd stay in camp.

When cartridges had been liberally supplied with the revolver, I had everything needed for starting. I resolved not to try to steal away as the first party had done, since by now their report to their comrades, and the excitement caused by seeing the adventurers arrayed in citizen's dress, rendered it impossible to conceal the fact that we were leaving the camp for some kind of perilous enterprise. First I went to headquarters to see Captain Sarratt, then I wrung the hands of all my old comrades as for the last time I walked down the company street.

DORSEY: It wasn't long that Monday evening until most of us were in citizen's dress, in whole or in part. I borrowed a coat, vest and cap of one of my messmates, Wm. Saint, and left my knapsack and suit of blue, except trousers, in his care. We also left with comrades all papers and other articles that might compromise our position to the enemy, for we knew now that we were to penetrate his country. I am free to say that if some one of the half-dozen others who had offered their services had been selected, I would have felt quite satisfied, and, no doubt, they breathed a little freer when they saw the duty fall upon other shoulders; for all recognized it as a sort of forlorn hope. I never forgot the last words spoken by Colonel Moore to me as we passed each other in crossing the parade ground before we left camp.

Said he, smiling, "Now, Corporal, don't let them get your napper down there"; to which I replied, "I'll try not to, Colonel."

The Mustering 6

KNIGHT: That Monday evening I went to Shelbyville, bought clothes, and got supper at the hotel.

PITTENGER: When the parting in camp was over, I looked up Sergeant Ross, and we returned to Shelbyville. It was still early. We made sure of the road to Wartrace, a small village east of the town, situated at a railroad junction where a branch for Shelbyville leaves the main Chattanooga & Nashville line. After an hour or so of lingering around the town, we started out toward Wartrace.

DORSEY: About dusk, as it was intended to conduct the matter with as much secrecy as possible, an ambulance wagon pulled up to Colonel Moore's tent and a minute later the eight from our regiment were seated inside. We were driven rapidly to Shelbyville, where we met several of those detailed from the 21st and 2nd Ohio Regiments, there being, however, but six from the latter regiment and nine from the 21st, eventually making twenty-four of us all told, including the leader.

Some of us hadn't completed our disguise before leaving camp, and further exchanges of the blue uniform for citizen's clothes—which were generally of cotton goods—were made here. I failed, however, to get a pair of trousers, and went out of our lines in my blue ones, hoping to be able to change them by a purchase at some country store before going far.

PITTENGER: Darkness was closing in on the Wartrace road, and we weren't sure whether our comrades were ahead of us or behind. At length two men came along whose watchful manner was so like our own that we joined them, and readily ascertained that they did belong to our band. Their directions were more explicit than ours, and they said that our only trouble arose from being too early.

KNIGHT: After supper at the hotel in town, I started out along the Wartrace road by myself, as Andrews had told me to do. Before I got outside the lines I fell in with two others.

DORSEY: We walked out from Shelbyville late in the evening. Some time after dark some of our party were at the outpost having trouble with the guards about letting them pass, when Andrews appeared on the scene, and with a word set all right, and we passed out. We followed the railroad track some two miles to a secluded spot at the roadside, where Andrews gathered us around him on a patch of underbrush, and laid out the whole plan, speaking in a low, confidential tone.

PITTENGER: More travelers overtook our party until we numbered nearly a score. Next Andrews himself came up. Proceeding a few hundred yards, we halted beside the road until another squad of our men arrived. We remained here a short time, talking but little, for our number wasn't quite full, and our leader had the air of a man not wishing to speak till all were gathered to hear.

After a time longer, when Andrews seemed satisfied that no more were coming, he arose and spoke in the low distinct tones that were to become so familiar to us: "Let's go a little way from the road, boys."

He led the way up a slight slope through stunted bushes to a level spot. We followed, and something more than twenty men gathered around him.

DORSEY: Twenty-three men met with Andrews at this night consultation on the Wartrace road. Their names are given by regiments and in grade and company order:

2nd Ohio Volunteer Infantry:

Sgt. Maj. Marion A. Ross
Cpl. William Pittenger *Company G*
Pvt. George D. Wilson *Company B*
Pvt. James Smith *Company I*
Pvt. Philip Gephart Shadrach *Company K*
(Also known as Perry G., or Charles P.)
William Campbell, of Salineville, O.
(Civilian who took place of a 2nd O.V.I. soldier)

21st O.V.I.:

Sgt. John M. Scott *Company F*
Sgt. Elihu H. Mason *Company K*
Pvt. Mark Wood *Company C*
Pvt. John Alfred Wilson *Company C*
Pvt. William J. Knight *Company E*
Pvt. Wilson W. Brown *Company F*
Pvt. William Bensinger *Company G*
Pvt. John Reed Porter *Company G*
Pvt. Robert Buffum *Company H*

33d O.V.I.:

Cpl. Martin Jones Hawkins *Company A*
Cpl. William H. Reddick *Company B*
Cpl. Daniel Allen Dorsey *Company H*
Cpl. Samuel Llewellyn *Company I*
Pvt. John Wollam *Company C*
Pvt. Samuel Slavens *Company E*
Pvt. Samuel Robertson *Company G*
Pvt. Jacob Parrott *Company K*

PITTENGER: A storm was rising, although the afternoon had been so bright. Andrews spoke quietly, stopping when the thunder rolled, resuming the moment it ceased.

[*Pittenger*]

To start with, we here were to learn enough of the plan and the risks involved to decide whether to go on with Andrews or to return to camp. In a sense this was a formality, since each of us had already made up his mind, but acceptance here did make all of us full volunteers. The more practical purpose of the conference was to receive instructions and such information as would enable us to cooperate intelligently with our leader.

The opening words of Andrews to the men packed around him were exceedingly informal, much more like conversation than a set speech. Though I listened with burning attention to every word, I cannot claim that the language used below is exact. There was explanation, repetition, and enlargement of parts not fully understood, with frequent questions and answers. In substance, he told us:

"You'll break up in small squads of two, three or four, and travel east into the Cumberland mountains, then south to the Tennessee River. You can cross the river and take passage on the cars at Shell-Mound or some station between that and Chattanooga on the Memphis & Charleston line. You must be at Chattanooga not later than Thursday afternoon, and reach Marietta the same evening, ready to take passage northward on the train the next morning. I'll be there with you, or before you, and will then tell you what to do.

"Your way is long and difficult," he went on, "and you'll have only three days and nights in which to reach Marietta. I'll give you plenty of money, and you may hire conveyances whenever safe and available. I'll ride along the same road that you are to travel—sometimes before, sometimes behind—and will give you any help in my power. If you should be arrested I may have influence enough to secure your release, but don't count on this in any way. Depend on yourselves and be watchful and prudent. Don't recognize me at any time unless sure we're alone."

Some of our party had traveled enough in the South to know that for inquisitiveness the people of that section aren't a whit behind the most curious of Yankees, and therefore inquired what account we should give if asked who we were, and why we were coming south.

"The most plausible thing," Andrews answered, "will be to tell them that you're Kentuckians escaping from Yankee rule, and that you expect to join some Southern regiment. Say just as little as will carry you through, and always have some reason for not joining just then. After you get into the mountains you'll be in the track of the Kentuckians who travel south, and will seem to be coming from there rather than from the Union army. But if you should be closely questioned, it'll be safe to say you're from Fleming County, in Kentucky, for I happen to know no Southern soldiers hail from that place, and you'll not be confronted by anyone who knows that you don't."

"But if we're completely cornered and they won't believe our stories," asked another of the soldiers. "What do we do then?"

"Enlist," said Andrews. "It'll be far better to serve awhile with the Rebels than to risk disclosing our plans by holding out. You can probably get away from them some dark night on picket."

"They'd let a man join their army, even if he couldn't give a satisfactory account of himself?"

"The hard thing's keeping *out* of the Southern army, not getting into it," Andrews replied. "They're picking men up everywhere and forcing them to enlist. Stick to whatever story you tell, and as long as they have no proof you're a Union soldier, they'll be glad to hustle you into the service even if they don't believe a word you say, as the best way of disposing of you."

I had no question on the first part of the expedition, for I could see how persons moving south would find it easy to allay suspicion, but there was a contingency far ahead which had a deep personal interest for me. I greatly disliked the thought of being left alone—probably because of defective vision. I asked Andrews whether after we had captured the train and used it in burning the bridges, we were to abandon it and try to steal north separately as we were now stealing south.

He answered explicitly, and in so doing revealed more of the general plan.

"No," he said. "General Mitchel starts south in the morning for a forced march, and he'll surprise and capture Huntsville on Friday, the day we're to capture the train. When we get back to that point we should find him ready to receive us. If we can't quite reach him, we'll leave the train close to our lines and dash through in a body."

This was glorious. The thought of such a coming into camp after piercing the heart of the Confederacy set every nerve on fire, and there were few questions afterwards. Andrews called on the men to form their squads according to their own preferences and then commenced distributing Confederate money among them, giving sufficient to one man of each group for all, although without constituting the man so favored the leader of his comrades.

The formation of these little traveling companies was a somewhat delicate matter, and wasn't always arranged to perfect satisfaction. I

[*Pittenger*]
wished the company of Ross, but he asked permission to go along with Andrews as far as he could accompany any of the party. One or two others making the same request, they were thrown together and I had to find other companions. I was fortunate, as Campbell, Shadrach, of Company K, and George D. Wilson, of Company B, fell to my portion. With the division completed, the hour for parting had arrived.

"Boys," said Andrews, "we're going into danger, but for results that can be tremendous. If we burn those bridges, General Mitchel can take and hold Chattanooga. But we'll have to be prompt. The last train for Marietta leaves Chattanooga at five in the afternoon. Be sure to catch it not later than Thursday, and I'll either be on it, or on an earlier one. Good-bye till then."

About this time the rain began to fall, and it soon come down in torrents. One group after another filed off, and Andrews shook hands with the members of each as they passed.

As our four picked our way along the railroad, stumbling over the ties, I looked back and saw Andrews, with none but the three members of the last group near him. He was looking after us, his head bent slightly forward in the pensive attitude habitual with him, and a broad stream of lightning made him at that moment stand out clearly. The next moment he disappeared in darkness, and the crash of thunder overhead drowned out every other sound. We hurried on our way and were soon far from the place of meeting.

Heading South 1

ALF WILSON: Having been supplied by Andrews with Confederate money to pay our expenses, we separated that Monday night into squads of four or five and directed our course toward Chattanooga, distant one hundred and three miles. We were soon clear of all our picket and vidette posts and in the enemy's country. Not until fairly away from sight of the old flag and our regiments could we begin to realize the great responsibility we had incurred. The military spy, in the ordinary line of his duty, isn't compelled to expose himself to detection. On the contrary, he conceals his identity in every possible way. This we could do only until in the heart of the enemy's country, the very place where we would be in most danger and where the blow would arouse against us all the hatred and most active energies of our enemies.

It commenced raining again the night of our departure, as it had done the week previous, and continued with but very little cessation during our entire trip.

BUFFUM: That night, the 7th of April, we commenced our march. About a mile from town Mr. Andrews gathered us together, as we came along in twos and threes, and told us that our object was to destroy the bridges, cut off communications, etc., and that he would meet us at Chattanooga. He gave me five men to take through.

REDDICK: We left camp on the 7th of April, divided into squads. John Wollam and myself went up the railroad about five miles that night. We stopped at a house where there was a light, and represented ourselves as strangers who desired to stop for the night. There was a lady there, a Southern woman, who told us we couldn't stay in the house, as her children were sick. She told us to go to the Negro quarters if we wished to get out of the rain.

We told the Negroes, when we went out to them, that we were trying to make our way to our command, which we represented to be at Round Gap. This the Negroes told to the lady of the house, who came down to see us, and desired us to go over to her uncle's, where we could get better accommodations. We didn't do so, but went to bed and slept until about four o'clock.

DORSEY: Slavens and myself started out together, but as it was now raining quite hard, we stopped under a woodshed by the side of the railroad on which we were traveling, and were soon joined by Mr. Andrews and some other member of the party, who were bringing up the rear. We lay there quite a while listening to the rain, the deep thunder, and the highly entertaining words of Mr. Andrews, as he still further explained to us the great importance of our mission and the grand results to follow.

But it was now after midnight, and it was important that we should get as far as possible from our lines before daylight; so we plodded

[*Dorsey*]
along the railroad through the rain and mud, the night being exceedingly dark, save when an occasional flash of lightning lighted the way. Slavens and myself struck out at a pretty lively gait, while Andrews and his companion moved more slowly, so that we might become more widely separated. Two together would attract less attention, if discovered by citizens, than four.

We tramped all night, or morning rather, except an hour or two, resting then in someone's barn loft.

PITTENGER: No start on a long journey could have been less promising than ours. The night was pitchy dark, the rain poured down, and the Tennessee mud was now almost unfathomable. While George Wilson, Shadrach, Campbell and I were able to walk the railroad track, the mud was avoided, but in the darkness the danger of tripping over cattle guards and other hindrances was greater. We had hoped to pass Wartrace—beyond the Federal pickets—before daylight, but an hour or two of toilsome trudging rendered the thought of rest almost irresistible. Unanimously, we resolved to find a house and make up for the delay by an early start on the morrow.

The country was thinly peopled; and a mist which began to creep along the ground prevented us from seeing a rod before us. We continued on the railroad until we felt sure there was no house that way before reaching Wartrace. Then, as we didn't wish to find lodging in the village itself, we turned out on the first road that crossed the railway.

A barn was our first discovery. Sweeping around in widening circles until the house was reached, we roused an old farmer, who on seeing us looked as if he would refuse us entrance if he dared. But the request of four able-bodied men, in such a storm and at such an hour, had a good deal of persuasive force.

The house, as we saw in the morning, was a rude log structure, consisting of two pens built ten or fifteen feet apart, and connected by a roof, thus making an open porch between them—a style of house very common in the South at that time. At our admission, fresh wood was thrown on the smoldering fire in the large open fireplace and there was soon abundant light and a most grateful heat. Then our host, who insisted on providing us something to eat, questioned us as to who we were, and how we came to be traveling so late on such a bad night.

It was a good opportunity to commence our drill in deception. We said we were Kentuckians from Fleming County, journeying by night to evade the Union pickets, and that we wouldn't have stopped till in safety if it hadn't been for the rain. Asked our reason for leaving home in these troubled times, we put it that we were disgusted with the tyranny of the Lincoln government, and meant to fight in the Southern army.

His reply gave us great—although unexpressed—pleasure: "You might's well save your trouble, for the whole South'll soon be as much under Lincoln as Kentucky is."

He advised us to go back home, for our errand was bootless and the rebellion would soon be put down as it deserved to be. We assured him we'd never submit, that we'd die first. He laughed and said time would show.

While we partook of a plain but good meal, and afterward for a short time around the fire preparatory to retiring, we continued to argue the great questions of the day. It was a novel experience, trying to maintain that the Rebels were right in seceding and our own people all wrong. I noticed that George D. Wilson, who spoke with great ease and force, seemed dissatisfied whenever Campbell and Shadrach took part in the conversation, as they did several times, expressing very radical Southern views with great emphasis of language. Repeatedly, Wilson would interrupt them and call on me for something in another direction.

When our host and his wife, who also had been aroused to minister to us, had retired, Shadrach asked the reason for the interruptions. Wilson replied that the two were making fools of themselves by being better Rebels than the Rebels themselves. He then complimented me for being moderate in statement and telling the necessary stories in a believable way. The truth was that the whole business of such false representations was distasteful, and I had used just as little of it as would suffice to make the stories plausible.

I supposed the frank words of Wilson would be resented. To my surprise, both Campbell and Shadrach admitted the justice of the criticism, and declared they would hereafter—in the presence of strangers—limit themselves to endorsing all that Wilson and I should say. This they faithfully did throughout the whole of the journey, always waiting for one of us to take the lead in conversation.

At length we lay down for rest, two in a bed. I think Wilson slept at once, but I lay awake for some time, watching the fitful light of the fire flicker over the bare rafters and rough side logs of the room. I thought of many things, but there was one line of thought which it may be as well to record with some care—even more than I gave it then.

[*Pittenger*]

The question was: how could we reconcile to our consciences the falsehoods involved in our expedition? The moral question involved is only a branch of the larger question as to the morality of war. In its nature, war is compounded of force and fraud in nearly equal quantities. If one of the necessary ingredients be wrong, the other can hardly be right. The most conscientious general thinks nothing of making movements with the sole purpose of deceiving his adversary, or of writing false dispatches for the same purpose. If it be right to kill our fellow beings, I suppose it's also right to deceive them in order to get a better chance to kill them. The golden rule has but little place between hostile armies or nations. To find where some unsuspecting persons are asleep, and steal upon them to shoot and stab before they can wake to defend themselves, would, in peace, be thought a crime of the most ferocious character. In war, it is only a surprise, and if successful, confers the greatest honor upon those who plan and execute it.

Some may wonder if constant resort to falsehood in a secret expedition isn't peculiarly dishonorable. Let's look this fairly in the face. All armies employ spies, and the old adage, "The receiver is as bad as the thief," is here applicable. A general who induces a man, by the hope of money or promotion, to go disguised into the enemy's lines—in part, for the general's advantage—is a full partner in the enterprise and cannot throw off his share of the guilt. It's true the laws of war throw all odium on the spy. But the generals, and not the spies, made the laws of war.

As to whether even these rules were to be taken as applying, let it not be forgotten that we didn't look on ourselves as upon the same plane with the enemy.

EDITOR: When did any soldier, whatever the circumstances, whatever the war?

PITTENGER: In our view our opponents were rebels, guilty of a crime justly punishable by death. We didn't think that men who had associated together against our government had acquired any more rights than a band of pirates or murderers. The manner in which the enemy carried on the war at the time intensified this feeling. Their soldiers were imperfectly uniformed at best. They had encouraged guerrilla warfare, and on more than one occasion, Federal uniform had been used to get within our own lines and work injury, as in the case of the capture of Gallatin by Morgan just a few weeks before this date.

Their citizens were often found living in apparent innocence within our lines, and yet sending complete information on all Union movements southward, and taking the oath of allegiance only to break it —often seizing their rifles and acting as soldiers against us without any organization. Our party, in disguise, went forth to play at the enemy's own game, knowing well its hazardous character, but feeling that the enemy should have no cause to complain.

Some Christian denominations consistently take the ground that war can never be lawful. With them I can have no controversy. It's enough for my purpose to show that deception is an element in all war. In our case, with the full sanction of our officers, we had entered upon an expedition which required disguise and deception. We had been expressly told that we weren't even to hesitate in joining the Rebel army if that step became necessary to avoid detection. In the whole of this expedition we were true to each other and to the mission upon which we had entered, but we didn't hesitate at any kind or degree of untruthfulness directed toward the enemy.

I confess that deception was very painful to me at first, and I used it as sparingly as possible, but practice made it less grating after a time, and eventually, there even came to be a certain pride of dexterity in doing it well. George Wilson stimulated this feeling by putting me forward on all possible occasions as spokesman, first of our own little squad, and, afterward, when we were united, of the whole party. On such occasions his praise for my being able to say plausibly and exactly what we had agreed upon beforehand was not altogether unrelished.

EDITOR: Wilson W. Brown and William J. Knight, two of the three engineers starting out with the party, met at the Monday night consultation and were together from that time for much of the expedition. On this first night, with two other men, Knight bucked the rain for a time, then found a barn and slept. At daybreak, after walking some five or six miles, they stopped for breakfast at the house of a strong Southern partisan. To this householder, Knight and his companions volunteered the information that they were en route to Chattanooga from Fleming County, Ky., with hopes of eventually finding and joining a Kentucky-raised Confederate regiment.

KNIGHT: Where we were getting breakfast, we asked the man for the names of some good men we could trust along the line of our journey, so that we could keep away from all Yankee sympathizers. These he gladly gave, and guided us past the last Federal outpost. Soon after he left us, we came to a Rebel picket post in the bend of the road, and were upon them before we saw them. They were armed with double-barreled shotguns and weren't slow in bringing them to bear on us, and in demanding that we give an account of ourselves or be blown through. The usual story proving satisfactory, they dropped the guns and presented a quart bottle, which, being less formidable, we didn't refuse.

DORSEY: Some of our party arrived at Wartrace early in the morning and took breakfast among Confederate soldiers—who still held the place at that hour—and then resumed the journey southward.

An hour or so later Slavens and I sat down to breakfast here, joined presently by Andrews and others, none of whom we presumed to recognize, although the place was now occupied by Federal cavalrymen, the Confederates having taken their departure.

On attempting to leave Wartrace, we found some difficulty in passing an outpost, but a word from Andrews with the officer aside left the coast clear, and we passed on. This was the last we saw of the boys in blue.

The mild-mannered Andrews soon convinced us that as a leader he knew his business, and could be an autocrat or desperado, if need be. One of our party had been reported to Andrews by another comrade for being too free with his tongue, and coming near revealing our true character to a Union lady, not through treachery or design, but through incautiousness, and overconfidence in the woman. Andrews dressed the man out the minute he came up with him. We weren't to trust anybody with the truth, he told us. Andrews used some pretty vigorous language on this occasion; threatened to shoot the offender on the spot, and promised death as the penalty for a repetition of the offense.

EDITOR: On the journey into Rebel territory—by at least two raiders' accounts—the horse Andrews rode in his role as shepherd of this straggling, hard-muscled flock, was one borrowed from his Southern business partner, Mr. Whiteman. From the merchant, by these reports, he had also received $10,000 for the purchase of quinine, needles and other articles of contraband which Andrews was to bring through to Chattanooga.

PARROTT: I didn't know Mr. Andrews before this expedition, but I had heard of him as a scout.

After the Monday night meeting on the Wartrace road I fell in with Samuel Robertson of Company G of the 33d, and we began the journey together. That night we stumbled ten miles in the darkness, knee-deep in mud and soaked to the skin. We slept in a shed, breakfasted at a farmhouse, and struck into the mountains Tuesday night.

KNIGHT: Tuesday we crossed the Cumberland Mountains and took dinner just beyond. An old lady and two daughters were the only persons in the house, and there was a small Union flag over the mantelpiece. We told them they were displaying the wrong kind of a banner, but they stood up for the old Stars and Stripes royally, and it went against the grain for us to have to disagree with them.

That night we lodged with a colonel who was a violent Rebel, and gave us a terrible downsetting on the sly. It mightn't have been safe for him to say what he did against Union soldiers if we'd been sailing under our own colors; but now he had the advantage and we took it meekly.

BENSINGER: That Monday night, Brown, Porter, Ross, Hawkins and myself composed one party. It rained incessantly for eighteen hours after we started. About four P.M., on Tuesday, the 8th, we arrived at a small town, Manchester, where we stopped for refreshments. The town seemed to be alive with secesh citizens inquisitive as to who we were and where we were "gwyn."

We told them we were citizens from Kentucky, and going to join the Rebel army, but while Hawkins and others were in a grocery store purchasing some corn juice for the party, I saw an old chap mounted on a horse, and who had the title of colonel, signal several others to follow him. He rode down an alley, and a half-dozen others followed him, when they held a short consultation. He then rode back to the grocery, and I followed, but wasn't noticed by him. He then told us that he lived four miles right on the road we wished to travel, and insisted we should go home and stay all night with him, which we agreed to do.

We took a square drink of corn juice, got two pints and started, but I had made up my mind that the colonel's roof shouldn't shelter me that night, and told Brown so on the road. I told all the boys just before reaching the house that we were suspected. By the time we reached the house the colonel was pretty well fired up, just what I had been working for.

[*Bensinger*]

When we entered the house, Brown remarked, "Your clock isn't running."

"No, she's broke down," said the old man.

"I can fix clocks," Brown said.

"Ah," said the old man, "you are a Yankee then."

Brown was equal to the occasion and said he had learned from a Yankee who had worked in Flemingsburg.

After supper we pulled out, even though the old man insisted we should stay. We afterward learned from others of the party who followed through the same town that a party had gone out that night from the town to question us more closely, but as we had impressed on the old man's mind that our reason for not staying over was fear of the Yankees, they concluded we were all right.

REDDICK: At four in the morning, when we got up at the Negro quarters where we were staying, our breakfast was sent over to us from the house, and we then started off. We went some seven miles, when we got a conveyance to Manchester, and from Manchester we footed it, procuring conveyance along the road as we could get it.

PITTENGER: We passed that night outside Wartrace in safety, and after breakfast went on our way. The sky soon clouded, and we were compelled to suffer the inevitable drenching which befell us every day on this weary journey. We reached Wartrace in the midst of a pelting storm. At first we intended to go around the town, as it was the last station on the Union picket line. But it was raining so hard that we thought we might manage to slip along the street unobserved. On making the attempt, however, we were promptly halted. For a time we tried to impersonate the innocent Southern citizen, but finally were compelled to admit our identity and wait under a sheltering porch until a messenger had ridden to brigade headquarters and brought an order for our release.

Then we traveled onward, through mud and swollen creeks. Early in the afternoon we reached Duck River at a point opposite Manchester, and as the river was at flood, we crossed by an unusual ferry—being taken up one at a time by a horseman, and thus carried through.

Here in Manchester we saw several others of our own party. There was no personal acquaintance between us previous to being detailed—I couldn't have given the name of a single member of the band apart from Andrews, Ross and my road companions—but there was something in the manner of each by which it was easy to recognize comrades. Reddick and Wollam had reached Manchester in advance of all the others. We greeted several of our squads here, but didn't remain long in company. Andrews also passed on horseback, but as all was well, we didn't speak to him.

DORSEY: This was our first day out, and the rain literally poured. The mud was terrible, streams swollen, and travel difficult.

Some half-dozen of us took dinner at a farmhouse. We hired our host to send us by wagon as far as a team could go and get back by night. A Negro boy of probably sixteen was detailed for the purpose, and we started out gay and happy, with a four-in-hand, that is, four small mules hitched to a wagon with a woodrack for a box or body, and we had to stand or sit on the boards constituting the bottom. The harness was of the old-fashioned kind. The collars, hames and traces, chains, back and belly bands constituted the "gears," save a light breaching on the rear or wheel mules, a head stall and bit for bridles, a light rope and jockey stick securing the off-lead mule to the near or lead mule, which latter was guided by a jerk line, a rope passing through the left hame ring to the bridle bit on the left side. This was the outfit, not a good article in it except the black-snake whip which was handed by the master to the slave, as he mounted the near mule, or "saddle hoss," as usually called, the saddle being a much worn old affair with no girth or cinch. The road in places was very rough, and at one place all our party except myself got off, fearing the thing would upset.

But the boy whipped right ahead as if he didn't care whether the wagon followed or not. In fact, we didn't more than get out of sight of our benefactor until we compelled the driver to put the mules on a full run where the roads would admit of it, for we were being delayed by bad weather, and we knew Andrews and most of the others were ahead of us.

We arrived at a ferry on a swollen stream just in time to cross with Andrews and his gray horse, which he had told us earlier he had left somewhere on the road, and which he said would help us to recognize him en route. It was nearly night when we reached the ferry. The Negro and the mules were pretty well fagged out when we turned them back.

Our Massachusetts Yankee comrade, Buffum, dropped into a store as we passed through Manchester, a small country village, and bought me a pair of yellow and white striped cotton pants. Buffum made the purchase because I still had on my army blue.

[*Dorsey*]

As we walked on briskly up the lane east of the village, we came straight onto four men on horseback, Rebel scouts. After some bad minutes, our railings at the Yankee high-handedness in Kentucky got us not only a friendly welcome, but a bid to join the local military company. We begged off, saying we had to keep on till we could enlist with a Kentucky company of friends down near Marietta.

Of our party there were present here Knight, Buffum, Slavens and myself. We felt a little anxious when one of the scouts thrust his hand in his coat pocket; but instead of drawing out a gun, he produced a bottle of whiskey, and proposed that before we separated we drink to Jeff Davis and the Confederacy.

Buffum first received the bottle, and holding it aloft gave the toast: "Here's to Jeff Davis."

We all drank, handed the bottle back, and the other fellows drank, and with a hearty good-bye, we parted as friends. This was our first full test in the art of deception, and our success was quite reassuring.

Soon after separating from the gentlemen, I left my blue pants under a pile of brush by the roadside and put on my nankeen striped ones, and felt more comfortable though a little cool.

ALF WILSON: During our first day's march we met, for a wonder, a true Southern Union man—as loyal a man as ever I met. He was an old man, who had remained true, although surrounded by disloyal neighbors. Though we professed to be Rebels on our way to enlist in the Rebel army, he boldly spoke his sentiments and did his best to persuade us to return and cast our lot with the Union army. After much urging he piloted us to the river, which was so swollen by rain that we couldn't ford it as we expected. The whole face of the country was a vast sheet of water, and we waded for miles through mud and water. The old man procured us a skiff, and we then, with a hearty shake of his loyal hand, bade him farewell.

In our instructions we were allowed just four days, not only to reach Chattanooga, but to accomplish the work. The continued rains and bad roads made this schedule a near-impossiblity.

During our journey to Chattanooga, Andrews, who was mounted, would ride ahead and make all necessary inquiries. Passing out of sight, he would allow us to go by, when he would mount and overtake us in some safe place where he would give us instructions, and then ride on, as though we were entire strangers to him. He would frequently pass us, simply bidding us the time of day in a careless way. Sometimes, when squads of Rebels were about, he would ask us where we were going.

"To Chattanooga, sir," we'd reply.

"Are you soldiers?"

"No, sir, but we expect to be as soon as we can get to one of the Kentucky regiments. We've got so disgusted with the cussed Yankees since they came into Kentucky that we can't stand it any longer."

"Glad to see you come out to fight for our country," Andrews would say. "If we don't drive out the Lincolnites, they'll take our slaves, and cut our throats in the bargain."

During these conversations the Rebel citizens would look on, and by their actions and words they seemed to think we were as good Confederates as ever lived.

PITTENGER: As we pressed on that Tuesday afternoon we realized fully that we were in the enemy's country.

It's difficult for people today to form an idea of the mysterious horror which clung about the South at the period of the opening of the war. Slavery had been separating the two sections more and more for a generation preceding that event. Terrible tales of outrage upon suspected abolitionists were told. If a Northern man traveled in the South—it was widely understood—he risked being dragged from his bed at night to be whipped, tarred or even hanged. These tales may have been exaggerated, but they were believed, and had some foundation.

That night we were still some miles from Hillsboro, having been greatly impeded by the muddy roads and swollen streams. The gentleman with whom we lodged this [Tuesday] evening was a slave-hunter, and tracked Negroes with bloodhounds for money, as we heard for the first time from the lips of one who practiced it. Our host said he had seen someone dodging around the back of his plantation just as it was getting dark, and that very early in the morning he would take his hounds and hunt him up; if it proved to be a Negro he would get the reward always allowed for a fugitive slave. He said he had caught a great number in that way, and that the business was profitable.

FRANK M. GREGG: The course generally followed by the raiders from Shelbyville southward was along the old Nashville and Chattanooga turnpike. From information picked up along the route, they were seen to pass at no great distance apart.

The party consisting of George D. Wilson, Perry G. Shadrach,

[*Frank M. Gregg*]
William Campbell and William Pittenger—the latter later traceable all along the route as the "spectacled Yankee"—crossed Duck River on the morning of Tuesday, April 8, and arrived at Manchester, county seat of Coffee County, in the afternoon of the same day. Continuing their journey along the road, they stayed Tuesday night a short distance out from Hillsboro, same county.

Heading South 2

EDITOR: In February, March and April of 1862, as General Mitchel's division drove south, Corporal James Pike and James J. Andrews—in dissimilar ways—were working two sides of the same secret service street.

Mitchel's drive for Huntsville, Ala., was his first chance at self-directed important action in the war. He understandably did all he could in advance to take out extra insurance against interference on his flanks. His chief irregular instruments in this were the men of the Andrews party, sent southeast on Monday night to work against counterattack by way of Chattanooga on the east, and Corporal Pike, sent southwest alone Tuesday morning to try for similar protection on the west by burning the M. & C. Bridge at Decatur.

In this and previous forays, Pike had the great advantage that Colonel Wharton's Texas Rangers were then detailed with the Confederate forces in the area. From his pre-war service, when he chose, Pike could draw out his vowels and reel off enough detailed information on the Rangers and their ways to satisfy the most suspicious of Rebel interrogators that this man could be no Yankee. To this accidental edge, Pike added his own boldness, a remarkable quickness with weapons, wide resourcefulness, and an unquenchable zest for operating against all normal odds and probabilities. On this trip, for an example of his increasing reliance on the value of crossing up all ordinary expectations, Pike held to his uniform and moved scores of miles into Confederate-held territory in full Union blue.

PIKE: On the 8th of April, I was sent by General Mitchel down to Decatur, to get information as to the state of the country, and to destroy the railroad bridge at that point, if possible. I set out for Shelbyville, mounted on old Punch, my pet horse, properly armed and fully equipped with turpentine and matches to do the required work.

Near to the town of Fayetteville, night overtook me, and I slept in the woods. This was on Tuesday night, and on Wednesday morning I rode into town. The citizens were astonished to see a single man dressed in full Yankee blue venture among them. Finding me cool, and of decent deportment, they at once took me for one of Morgan's own men in disguise.

EDITOR: The next day, cantering southwest in his dual capacity as scout and one-man task force—operating on targets of opportunity as these struck his fancy—Pike met and held up the wagon master and teamsters of a Confederate supply train. Disarming these, and compelling them to stand by in a corral improvised at a nearby fence corner, the ex-Ranger proceeded to set fire to the bacon-loaded wagons of the train.

PIKE: When the flames shot up, several citizens came to the scene of action, but I thrust them into the fence corner, along with the wagon master and teamster. As soon as the wagons were so far destroyed that I saw that it would be impossible to save anything of the wreck, I made the drivers mount the mules, and the wagon master his horse, and drove them off on the road to Fayetteville.

Wheeling my horse, I put out once more for Decatur. About ten miles farther down the road, I heard the deep tones of a preacher, belaboring a sinful congregation. Riding up to the door of the meeting house, I made my horse enter about halfway, so that I could see every man in the house. As his hoofs struck the floor of the church, the people were astonished to see a soldier under arms, riding boldly in among them.

Looking to the preacher, I inquired if there were any Southern soldiers in the house. I saw that there had been Rebel soldiers there, and that they had escaped in the direction of his glance. I rode on, after desiring the clergyman to pray for the President of the United States. The Rebel papers had an account of the affair, but they lied when they stated that I tried to make the preacher take a drink of whiskey; for I hadn't a drop to bless myself with.

[*Pike*]

Near sunset, I met with an old man, who had just crossed the Athens road, and he told me he had seen twelve of Young's Tennessee Cavalry and fifteen mounted citizens after a man, "who had been raising a disturbance up the country."

I saw that he was a Union man, so I asked him how I could give them less of a chance to bushwhack me. He told me of a good Union man, who lived down in the woods, and advised me to leave my horse there.

Leaving my horse, I took to the woods on foot, making direct for Decatur, taking the sun for my guide. The second night overtook me in the woods very near Madison Depot, on the railroad between Huntsville and Decatur. Being very tired, I slept soundly, with no cover but my rubber Talma.

Next morning, I was cold, wet, and hungry as a wolf. I made the railroad my guide, and passed through Madison just as the citizens were beginning to stir about, and I saw four or five Rebel soldiers starting at that early hour toward a saloon for their morning drinks. I followed the railroad till I reached a point near Mooresville, where I stopped at the house of a Union man for breakfast, or rather dinner, for it was about ten o'clock. He took me for a Rebel in disguise, sent there to try him and ascertain his sentiments. He gave his name as Porter Bibb, and I gave mine as Gabe Fitzhugh. I was trying to sound him and he was trying to sound me.

We spent about two hours in lying to each other, to discover each the other's opinions, but mutually failed. We were interrupted by the entrance of a quartermaster's sergeant, belonging to Young's 2nd Tennessee Cavalry, then guarding the identical bridge at Decatur I had been sent to inspect. I got into a conversation with them, and gave the 8th Texas—Wharton's Rangers—as my regiment.

They told me all about the bridge and its defenses, and how they were built of cotton bales.

"What's your regiment?" a new man asked.

"Wharton's Rangers."

"What is your captain's name?"

"Captain Cook," I told him.

"What part of Texas were you from?" he asked.

"From Waco," was my reply. "On the Brazos River."

"I've been in Waco," he said. "Do you know Dr. Tindsley there?"

"Yes, sir," I said, sure of my ground. "He's president of the vigilance committee of McClennan County."

EDITOR: After getting by the sergeant's cross-examination at Mooresville through his readiness with Texan information, Corporal "Gabe Fitzhugh" put away a full dinner with Porter Bibb and then walked it off along the railroad to Decatur until blocked by the camp of the 2nd Tennessee Cavalry unit guarding the first railroad bridge in the swamp, not far from the Y-switch in the road.

Pike was able to confirm the detailed information he had already gained as to the defenses of the main bridge, but found this too closely guarded to permit an effective attempt at firing it. Suspected and questioned again, he averted immediate arrest but was compelled shortly afterward to twist away on the run as squads of horsemen joined in search of him.

Late Thursday night, aided by an old Negro who prayed that the Lord might always keep this Union soldier "in His hand," Pike was guided across a three-mile swamp over an intricately disguised foot bridge of linked logs to a point safely beyond immediate pursuit. Friday morning he moved on, hunting Mitchel's advancing field headquarters.

PIKE: On Friday, I made my way across that immense body of timbered land which lies between Athens and Fayetteville, to a mill on the road to Huntsville and seventeen miles north of that town, and found that our army had encamped there on the previous night.

I was compelled to go on foot, till I reached Meridianville, where I met a Negro in a buggy, driving a fine horse. I stopped him, jumped into the buggy, and was off—not only with the horse, but with the Negro, baggage, and buggy, all of which were impressed into the service of the United States.

Heading South 3

DORSEY: On the way south, Sam Llewellyn and James Smith were stopped and questioned near Jasper, and then arrested on suspicion of not being what they claimed to be. Rather than be thrown in jail, they joined the Rebel army, enlisting in a light artillery battery on duty nearby.

PITTENGER: Wednesday morning, when we continued our journey, we found a man who agreed for an exorbitant price to give us a ride in his wagon for several miles. As it was now the 9th, and we were due in Marietta the 10th, this conveyance was a great aid. Room was made for several others whom we overtook, and we all were carried briskly and merrily along.

Soon we came in sight of the Cumberland Mountains, a mighty rampart of freshest green, although around their tops clung a mist. The mist quickly spread and thickened into clouds overhead, and again the interminable rain began to fall. The driver of our wagon, at about the same time, turned off and we were obliged again to plod along on foot.

At noon we stopped for dinner at a hut close to the road. The owner belonged to the class of "poor whites" whose condition in the old slavery days was little if any better than that of the slaves. Our entertainment was of the plainest, but we ate our corn bread and strong pork cheerfully, paid a round price, and passed on our way.

Soon after dinner we fell in with Mark Wood, who had possessed himself of too much apple brandy. He was talkative, and in no fit state for meeting strangers. We walked him along rapidly and gave no one a chance to say a word to him until the fumes had passed away; when he was so much frightened by his imprudence as to have no inclination to repeat the offense. This was the only instance of that kind during the whole trip; and there was but little even of moderate drinking in the company.

We had now reached the foot of the Cumberland Mountains. While going up the first long hill we overtook a Confederate soldier of the Eastern army home on a furlough. He had been in a number of battles, among them the first Bull Run, which he described minutely. Little did he think that I, too, had been there, as we laughed at the wild panic of the Yankees. He expressed great delight to see so many Kentuckians coming out on "the right side." When we parted, he said he hoped the time would soon come when we would be comrades, fighting side by side. I felt keenly the hypocrisy I was compelled to use, but having begun, there was no possibility of turning back.

On we clambered up the mountain, across the summit—a tolerably level tableland about six miles in breadth—then down again over cliffs, chasms and great gullies. This rough jaunt led us into Battle Creek Valley.

Just after sunset we found the house of a strong secessionist recommended to us by our soldier friend. The householder shared with us the best his place afforded, giving us his only bedroom and sleeping with his family in the living room or kitchen. This open-handed hospitality, given by those whose dearest hopes we were laboring to overthrow, was even more painful than the plentiful falsehoods to which we were compelled.

We here learned—from a group of our men who came along after supper—that Andrews had postponed the enterprise one day on account of unexpectedly bad weather, and the delay this might be expected to cause General Mitchel.

We spent the evening denouncing the abolitionists, which term was used indiscriminately, like that of "Yankees," to designate all Union men. Practice had rendered it nearly as easy for us to talk on this side of the question as on the other; and a little observation had shown us just how the Confederates liked to hear us talk.

One truth we told made more impression than all our falsehoods. In the character of Kentuckians we informed our host that we were forever exiled from our homes by the expatriation law recently passed by the Kentucky legislature. This act made the reasonable provision that any person going south to fight in the army of the Rebels should lose all rights of citizenship in the state which he thus forsook. The old man thought this unparalleled oppression; and in the morning asked that I write that law down that he might show his Union neighbors what the Yankees would do when they had the sway.

EDITOR: James Clepper of Battle Creek Cove, the Wednesday-night host of Pittenger's group, kept and showed to his neighbors the expatriation order written out by Pittenger and signed by the four. Later, despite the startling news that came, Gregg affirms that Clepper held stubbornly to his conviction that his lodgers had been, as they said, citizens of Kentucky and true to the Confederate cause.

F. M. GREGG: Early Wednesday morning, April 9, the party including George Wilson, Shadrach, Campbell and Pittenger struck the foothills of the Cumberland Mountains in Grundy County. Climbing to the broad plateau, they crossed it at Poplar Springs (now the watering place, Monteagle). Winding down the eastern slope of the Cumberlands, and into Battle Creek Cove, they stopped Wednesday night at James Clepper's, a staunch Southern man, living fourteen miles from Jasper and forty miles from Chattanooga.

From James Clepper's home, the writer has traced them by personal investigation, and the information is given as gleaned from the memories of parties directly concerned at the time.

DORSEY: I frankly confess that I felt ashamed to practice deception on the confiding people we met along the way southward. The only justification I can find for it is in the thought that if it is right to go to war under any circumstances and kill our fellow man, it is certainly right to deceive him, take advantage of him, and capture his strongholds, and thus avoid taking his life, and perhaps losing your own, thus choosing the lesser of the two evils. Success in our undertaking meant the saving of many lives on both sides, and therefore could be a mission of mercy, and we so regarded it at the time. We drew pictures in our minds of men on both sides of the conflict whose lives would be saved if we should succeed, and casually asked ourselves whether the lives thus saved would be worth the sacrifice, in the event of a successful termination of the expedition but the loss of the lives of the men engaged in it. Of course they would, but these thoughts naturally suggested themselves.

We found the people generally accommodating, confiding and easily deceived. My parents were Virginians, but had emigrated to Ohio a few years after their marriage, in Waterford, Loudon County, Va. When I was about eight years old they returned to Virginia, residing there about three years, during which time I learned much of the manners and acquired something of the dialect of the Southern people, which now came in good play, and I used it to advantage.

With most of us the idea of keeping mum and talking as little as possible prevailed. We made it a point to appear as insignificant or uneducated as we could. I know that I purposely mispronounced words; always said goin' or gwyin' instead of going; comin' instead of coming, etc.; called a horse, hoss; whip, whup; tobacco, tobacker; a Negro servant, boy; etc.

On the morning of the 9th we met a man whom we supposed to be a Southern spy. There were five of us together at this time—Slavens, Buffum, Wood, Alf Wilson and myself—and we debated the propriety of heading this man off and holding an impromptu court-martial over his case, but concluded if he could reach Chattanooga ahead of us, he was a good one, better than from appearances we took him to be; and thus the matter dropped. This was near the foot of the Cumberland Mountains. We five had taken breakfast at a farmhouse together that morning and here met the suspicious traveler. Slavens and I had traveled late and had slept in this farmer's barn. We saw the traveler several times during the day, always off the road, going across the fields.

PARROTT: On Wednesday a squad of Confederate soldiers halted us, but they believed our story as we were on the natural route south from Kentucky.

ALF WILSON: On Wednesday night, April 9, we arrived at the little village of Manchester. Near this village some of the party stopped for the night at the house of an old Rebel who bore the title of "colonel." It was our plan to avoid persons of his stamp, as we didn't care to undergo too close scrutiny. But night overtook a part of the squad there, and none who took shelter under the old colonel's roof had cause to feel sorry. He was a good entertainer, had plenty of the comforts of life about him and was an incessant talker, especially on the subject uppermost in his mind—the war. He was at first a little cautious and shy, but on being assured that his guests were Confederates of the best stripe, he relaxed and assured them he felt it a privilege to be able to serve such brave men—men patriotic enough to leave their homes in Old Kentucky and go voluntarily to the front in the great hour of danger. It didn't seem as though he could do enough for the boys; nothing he had was too good.

The colonel proved his good will to the boys the next morning, and his loyalty to the secession cause, by taking his team and wagon and hauling them as far as the mountains, to a little place called Pelham. In that part of Tennessee, the colonel's company was as good as a passport. Before leaving the men he took them to a tavern and treated them to whiskey, after which he bade them good speed and returned home.

For myself, I spent the same night with a farmer—a neighbor of the old colonel's—a mild, inoffensive old man. I was very hungry and tired and felt great gratification on seating myself at his table to see it bountifully supplied with substantial eatables. I ate heartily and said but a few words. There was a rather genteel, smooth-looking man at the table, whose presence and appearance I didn't exactly understand. I couldn't at first make out whether he belonged to the place or not, but soon discovered that he was a stranger.

[*Alf Wilson*]

I kept a discreet tongue and learned bye and bye that the stranger, too, was on his way to Chattanooga. He inquired particularly concerning the roads and very minutely in regard to the Yankees. The old man told him that he had never seen a Yankee nor heard of any being nearer than the coal banks at the mountains. The stranger seemed quite uneasy lest he should fall into Yankee hands.

Next morning, in good season, we were ready to continue our journey, and the stranger became one of our traveling companions. He didn't long continue with us, however, as we took a road that was supposed to come in close proximity to the Federal lines. He now took me to one side and proposed to give me forty dollars to pilot him over the mountains. He told me he was a spy, acting in the employ of the Confederate government.

My mind was thrown into a cloud of doubt and perplexity as to the proper thing to do. This man, in case he had seen reason to suspect us, could get to Chattanooga in advance of us and cause our arrest. At times I had a mind to accept his offer and go as a guide with him until I had a chance to lose him or get separated from him. At another time I had concluded to go with him until we could reach some secluded place and there treat him to the fate of a spy and enemy of my country—a fate he deserved, as I knew he was carrying important news to the Confederates. But on the other hand, if I did this, it might detain me so long that I would fail to be on time to discharge my part in the service for which I had been detailed. We finally let him go on his road and we went ours.

(When we arrived in Chattanooga, this stranger was the first man we met and he, supposing us to be friends, treated us with great cordiality and invited us to go with him and "have something." Since it was nearly train time, we politely declined, not caring to make his further acquaintance. This was the last we saw of the nice-appearing stranger and Confederate spy.)

EDITOR: The near-cutting of this adhesive wayfarer's throat has overtones of chilling irony. Timothy Webster, Allan Pinkerton's favorite agent, had traveled through Chattanooga ten weeks before, and other Union agents were frequently in the area. Had one of these fallen in with a squad of belligerent young Kentuckians proclaiming themselves hot supporters of Jefferson Davis, what cover could he have been expected to use but that of an equally strong Confederate partisan?

DORSEY: It rained almost incessantly on Wednesday. At a crossroads we came to was a cabin where whiskey was kept. As we approached we noticed a number of saddle horses hitched to the fence near the cabin, heads down, calmly taking the pouring rain. Entering the cabin we found a red-whiskered, sandy-haired citizen behind the counter, which was a puncheon laid on two whiskey barrels set on end, and the little room pretty well crowded with men, some of whom had evidently been drinking.

We ordered some whiskey, which was drawn in a stone pitcher and placed upon the counter, with a tin cup to drink out of. Buffum acted as master of ceremonies, and first passed the applejack around to the strangers; then we all took a drink, and again had the pitcher filled up, paid the bill, told the gentlemen to help themselves, and took our leave. We wanted to leave these fellows something to occupy their time so they would not interest themselves too zealously in our welfare. All we asked just then was to be let alone, as Jefferson Davis said in relation to their secession movement.

EDITOR: In most of the country, then and now, applejack is cider brandy and whiskey's base is fermented grain. This isn't to say Buffum's stone pitcher—given its effect on Mark Wood—couldn't have held a lethal mixture of both.

DORSEY: Wood drank too much, and we poured sweet milk into him later at a farmhouse where we got dinner, and churned it out of him. After dinner we divided up again, Slavens and myself going together. We had been changing partners frequently as we inadvertently came together, and thus became acquainted with each other, so that we might be able to recognize the members of our party in the event of any sudden emergency. While traveling together that afternoon Slavens paid me an unexpected compliment by saying he had walked with most of the party, and that I was the only one who could keep up with him. We had no time to waste on this trip, and kept up a brisk swinging walk, leaning right out from early morn until late at night.

Exchanging our warm army blue for much lighter clothing and then plunging out through mud and rain caused us to take cold, and I was threatened with an attack of neuralgia, but Buffum gave me a heavy dose of quinine which broke it up.

This was on April 9, and toward evening Andrews came riding by and quietly told us that owing to the swollen condition of the streams, Mitchel would be delayed in his movements, and we would take another day for it, and to be sure and reach Marietta on the night of the 11th. (One or two squads didn't get Andrews' orders to take another day for it and traveled all of one night in order to get there on time.)

That night we stayed with an old man at the head of Battle Creek Valley, Mr. Clepper. He was highly elated to see so many young men coming from Kentucky to join the Southern army, and boasted that he had been a secessionist for twelve years and now had twelve sons in the Confederate army. Pittenger gave him a glowing account of the uprising among the people of Kentucky, on account, as Pittenger alleged, of the passage by the Yankee legislature of that state of an expatriation law, by the terms of which all Kentuckians who took up arms for the Confederacy were to be forever disfranchised. It so aroused Mr. Clepper's ire that he wished Pittenger to write it up for him, which he did, and we all signed it.

I think there were eight of us with the old man that night. As change was a little scarce, Geo. D. Wilson paid the bills of all the next morning, handing our host a one-hundred-dollar bill. In making change the old gentleman by mistake gave Wilson a one-hundred-dollar instead of a ten-dollar bill, and Wilson called his attention to it, correcting the mistake. This confirmed our host in his confidence in our complete integrity.

It was now Thursday the 10th, and passing down the valley a few miles, we came to a mountain stream so swollen that we were unable to cross it. Fortunately a gentleman on a stout, well-saddled, light bay mule, arrived at the ford about the same time, going in the opposite direction. Seeing our dilemma he very politely offered us the use of the mule to cross the stream. The offer was of course accepted, and one would mount the mule, ride him across the stream, rein him up and send him back empty; another would take him, cross over, and so on, until the whole squad of eight was safely across. The animal was sent back with many thanks shouted across the roaring current to the gentleman for his kindness.

Soon again we broke up in pairs and scattered out so as not to attract attention. Near midday Slavens and I were sitting on a fence for a short rest when a couple of horsemen came riding by. As they approached we thought one was certainly a Confederate officer, and we felt a little anxiety about it, but as they passed we discovered to our amazement that the supposed officer was our own Buffum. He had bought a Confederate colonel's overcoat, and had hired a man to take him on horseback to Jasper, a few miles farther on.

At Jasper several of us went into a store and bought tobacco. I bought a five-cent plug, and handed the merchant a silver dime, which excited his curiosity.

"A silver dime!" he said. "That's good for sore eyes."

So saying, he handed me, as he supposed, a five-cent "shinplaster," but in fact it was a fifty-cent bill with the corner torn off so as to take the 0, leaving the figure 5, thus deceiving him. My first thought was to correct the error, but the thought that that would require conversation caused me to desist, so I wasn't as honest as Wilson had been with the one-hundred-dollar bill, and pocketed the change.

PITTENGER: Reddick and Wollam lodged on Wednesday night with an influential and hospitable Rebel. They overwon his confidence, for he became anxious that they should enlist in a cavalry company his son was raising for Confederate service. Fortunately they had told him a slight modification of the common Kentucky story—claiming that they were already enlisted in the regiment of a Colonel Williams from Kentucky and were now on their way to join him.

Their kindly host then told them it was two days' hard walk from where they were to Chattanooga, but he could suggest a better plan.

"My sons are ferrying bacon across the river for the army," he said. "It's supposed to be against the law for anyone else to cross, but you go down and tell them I said to put you over. It's only half a mile then to Shell-Mound Station, and you'll have time enough to catch the twelve o'clock train for Chattanooga."

He then gave Wollam and Reddick a guide to the ferry. The colonel's sons obediently set the two over and directed them to the station. Their train was several hours late. When it came they found a regiment of Rebel soldiers on board. These, sent on to Corinth to reinforce Beauregard, had been turned back for some reason that they didn't then understand. Reddick and Wollam were kindly received, but managed to say little till they reached Chattanooga. They were just in time for the down train to Marietta, but as they had learned that the attempt was to be laid over for another day, they preferred waiting till morning.

At the Crutchfield House to which they repaired, there was so great a crowd that the only bed they could get was in the same room with two sick Confederate soldiers. These had some kind of fever and kept calling for water continually. The bell-knob had a card on it, saying that twenty-five cents would be charged for every room call during the night. Our comrades, however, had money, and not only remained awake most of the night ministering to their foes, but invested a good many quarters on their behalf.

KNIGHT: The colonel we'd stopped with Tuesday night sent us for the next night's lodging along to a major, who was more quiet and seemed to be reading our thoughts in secret. He couldn't have succeeded very well, for he gave us a letter to a squire (*all* the people in the South had some kind of title) and directed us to reach his house for the following night's stop by a trail that led over the mountain spurs, through a most desolate part of the country.

It was rough traveling, and we didn't see a man or a house all day; but it brought us out all right in the evening, and only five or six miles from Chattanooga. The squire proved to be a good entertainer, which after our dinnerless jaunt was well appreciated. He seemed also well posted in army movements, telling us how the Yankees were moving on Huntsville, which was no news to us, though we hadn't before heard it intimated by any of the citizens. He said the Southern army was moving back only to get the Yanks in a trap, which they had already set. He told us that we might see the last one of them in irons in Chattanooga before many days. (We didn't believe him then, but we certainly did see some of them in that condition later.)

BENSINGER: We traveled all Thursday night without meeting anyone. The following day we met two Rebel scouting parties, but they gave us no trouble. Thursday we reached Pelham, where there was a squadron of Rebel cavalry and one brass gun. We were questioned closely by the commanding officer, a captain, who finally allowed us to pass, after taking our names, place of residence and destination. We flagged a train loaded with Rebel wounded, and soon landed at Chattanooga.

We had seen Andrews on the road, who was surprised at the rapid time we had made, and who told us we were thirty miles in advance of some of the parties, and that we couldn't get together to take the train until Saturday.

Being very tired when we finally got to Chattanooga, we registered at the Crutchfield House, and without waiting for supper, went to bed.

PITTENGER: Although by the original plan we should have been in Marietta that evening, Thursday morning found our quartet still more than a hard day's journey from Chattanooga. That noon we came to the town of Jasper, and walked quietly up the street to the principal grocery of the place, where we rested awhile and talked with the idlers gathered around. We told them Kentucky was ready to rise and shake off her Yankee chains. They gave us ready credence, and in turn communicated such news as they had.

Having been three days outside our own lines we were anxious for any kind of intelligence. Nothing could be heard in regard to Mitchel, which was a little disappointing, as we thought that his movement southward—if on schedule—would by this time have caused some excitement. We did hear the first indistinct rumor of the battle of Shiloh or Pittsburg Landing, believed to be a great Rebel victory. It was the impression that thousands of Yankees had been killed, and that the armies of Grant and Buell were totally destroyed. This didn't cause us great uneasiness, for we placed a low estimate on the accuracy of Southern news—being in this almost as extreme as some of the Negroes, who made it their rule to believe the exact opposite of whatever their masters asserted. One countryman gravely assured me that five hundred gunboats had been sunk. I told him I didn't think the Yankees had so many as that, but wasn't able to shake his faith.

F. M. GREGG: Thursday morning, April 10, the raiders left old man Clepper's house and traveled toward Jasper. About one mile out from that place, some of the party ate dinner with Amos Cox, a farmer. It was about noon when they commenced to pass through Jasper in groups of two or three, going through without stopping. A party of four, consisting of the "spectacled man; a big man with a full beard, wearing a pin with a woman's face in it; and two smaller men"—Pittenger, Campbell, Shadrach and Wilson—stopped at a grocery, now used as a bank, and bought tobacco from Billy Hatch. To use the expression of one of the witnesses, "they beat 'em all talking secesh." This, however, didn't convince the crowd of their true character, some of whom were doubtful whether the South produced such a "Yankee face as that man with the spectacles had." Another fact noticed was that one had on a pair of shoes with perforated tips, never seen before, and not made south of the Ohio River.

About this time Amos Cox, the man with whom they had eaten dinner, came in and whispered to a friend, "Them fellers are Yankees, they gave me a silver half-dollar for a dinner." Suspicion was thoroughly aroused by this time, and as the party started on, Major

[*F. M. Gregg*]
P. T. Rankin, a captain of a company, home on a furlough, stopped them and demanded some information of themselves. This was readily given. Being assured that they were going to join the Confederate army at Corinth, Major Rankin allowed them to continue on their way unhindered, in spite of the suspicions of the crowd.

Some of the party, on the same day, crossed the Sequatchie Valley near South Pittsburg, getting over the river at that point. Most of the party, however, followed the road to Chattanooga, crossing the Sequatchie River at Quarrel's Ferry, at a spot now spanned by an iron bridge. Twelve miles out from Jasper, on the bank of the Tennessee River, Widow Hall kept a hostelry for the convenience of travelers. In the spacious guest room at her house a number gathered on Thursday night and spent the evening in merrymaking.

PITTENGER: From Jasper we journeyed directly to the banks of the Tennessee River with the intention of crossing in the morning and taking passage on the Memphis & Charleston Railroad. We were recommended for the night to a kind of rude country hotel, well known in the neighborhood as "Widow Hall's." The entertainment here was excellent; and as we believed the harder part of our travel to be over, we were in high spirits. Andrews and several others joined us, and for the first time, as we spent a social evening together, we had a chance to become in some degree acquainted.

The large guest-chamber with its great roaring fire, and two beds in the corners opposite, was exceedingly comfortable; and after a smoking hot supper, we gathered around the open fire and began to talk. The family were with us, and we impersonated strangers who had met for the first time. Many stories were told of our home life in Kentucky, and the different parts of Fleming County from which we came. Andrews was, according to his wont, rather silent and reflective, but appeared greatly to enjoy the conversation of others. Especially did he show that he appreciated the wit of Shadrach—which seemed to pour forth in an unending stream—remarking: "That man never opens his mouth but he says something."

George Wilson, who had traveled so widely, dominated the conversation in all serious and political matters as much as Shadrach did in sport and humor. Dorsey, who like myself had been a schoolteacher, formed the idea that it might be better for him to appear to know but little, and carried out this notion during all the expedition as well as this evening. He was amused and felt complimented when told by a member of a squad who had followed him, that some of the citizens of Jasper had referred to his party as a "lot of country jakes, who hardly knew enough to come in when it rained."

DORSEY: We reached Widow Hall's, some miles east of Jasper, about dusk and put up. Soon after we arrived here, a stranger on a gray horse rode up and asked for lodging also. It was Andrews. There were by this time, I think, eight of us at this one house—Andrews, Geo. D. Wilson, Pittenger, Campbell, Shadrach, Buffum, Slavens and I—and a merry crowd we were. Of course, to all appearances we were strangers, but the fact was soon developed that we had all come from nearly the same place, and we were leaving there for the same reasons—to get rid of Yankee rule, and go south to join our friends, the Confederates.

After a bountiful supper, we were soon left mostly to ourselves around the log fire in the sitting room, and the jests we got off at each other's expense provoked at times roars of laughter, never to be forgotten by anyone present. Andrews seemed to enjoy the sport as much as any, though he had but little to say. Buffum, Shadrach, Geo. Wilson and Pittenger, who was always a good talker, were chiefs in the sport, while the rest of us occasionally threw in a droll remark for the sake of variety. At a rather late hour we retired to sleep.

I had always been disposed to talk in my sleep, and on this trip had no little concern lest I should in my dreams utter a word that would lead to detection. We were under a constant mental strain, sleeping or awake. What if this stranger, Andrews himself, whom we were trusting to lead us, should prove to be a Rebel spy and betray us into the enemy's hands? All these thoughts naturally suggested themselves to our minds; and so with Andrews. Here he had more than twenty men, any one of whom might prove false and betray him. We were all in a boat that might at any time spring a leak, and by now, it was well out in mid-ocean in some deep and strange waters.

All passed off well at the Widow Hall's, though, and all that happened for the rest of that night was some assorted hard sleeping.

PITTENGER: Just such another evening as the one at the Widow Hall's I have never spent. The absence of all restraint in speaking of our former life; the equal freedom as to our plans and hopes; the presence of some hearers who either believed all we said, or, thinking us only using a traveler's privilege, were too courteous to contradict us; and another portion of the audience who knew we were acting, and could appreciate and imitate from that standpoint—all com-

[*Pittenger*]
bined to make the whole like a stimulating and highly interesting game, and our gaieties were prolonged to a late hour.

Several of our number were in advance, and four spent the same evening south of the Tennessee—two who hadn't been notified of our plans even reaching Marietta. These latter were Porter and Hawkins; and as they found that the party were not on hand to start Friday morning, they remained in their hotel at Marietta awaiting us.

Heading South 4

D. C. BUELL

Headquarters Army of the Ohio
Camp near Columbia, Tenn.
March 27, 1862

Brig. Gen. O. M. Mitchel,
Commanding Third Division, Murfreesboro

General:

I have already informed you in conversation of certain dispositions which affect your part in the campaign just commencing.

It is not necessary to point out to you how [your] force can be concentrated either for an advance or defense, if necessary. It can by marches of from twenty-five to thirty-five miles over good turnpikes concentrate at Shelbyville or at Columbia or Pulaski; or still farther in advance, at Huntsville or Decatur. . . . Fayetteville is also important, as affording by the branch railroad from Dechard a good depot for operations against any position south of it.

I do not think it necessary to do more than suggest these general features to you. You will understand well how to take advantage of them or guard against them, according to circumstances.

Move one of your brigades, with a battery and the principal part of your cavalry, at once to Shelbyville. As soon as the bridges you are at work on are so far advanced that you can leave them, carry forward the principal part of your division to that point, and throw a brigade and strong force of cavalry forward to Fayetteville. Endeavor, in connection with these movements, to secure some of the rolling stock on the roads north of Dechard by a rapid movement of cavalry through Manchester to that point.

Inform yourself by all possible means of the position, movements and strength of the enemy.

D. C. Buell,
Major General, Commanding

PITTENGER: General Mitchel occupied Shelbyville on March 28, the day after his orders were sent. When he broke camp there on April 8—the Tuesday morning following the dispatch of the Andrews party on Monday night—his destination was a secret.

Two railroads slanted south from Nashville—the Tennessee & Alabama southwesterly, the Nashville & Chattanooga southeasterly—which, after running about a hundred and twenty miles each, struck the east-west Memphis & Charleston Railroad at Decatur and Stevenson, points about ninety-five miles apart. There is a great bridge over the Tennessee River at Decatur and another long double bridge, with an island in the center, near Stevenson at Bridgeport, both on the line of the Memphis & Charleston Railroad. Between these bridges, the Tennessee River arches south like a great bow, of which the railroad forms the cord. Huntsville was situated on this railroad, nearer Decatur than Bridgeport. The first part of Mitchel's plan was to move south quickly between the two railroads—the Wartrace-Stevenson line to his left, the Columbia-Decatur connection to the right—to Huntsville; and then, dividing his force, to occupy all the Memphis-Charleston line north of the Tennessee.

The force immediately under Mitchel's control consisted of the three brigades of his own division with infantry and cavalry, amounting in all to about 10,000 men. General Negley's brigade at Columbia, and additional scattered regiments guarding Nashville and lines of communication, numbering 7,000 or 8,000 more, were to be under Mitchel's command only in case of emergency.

On the Monday night our raiding group left, there was an almost tropical rainfall, which continued with but slight intermission the following day. This made the process of striking tents and preparing for marching Tuesday forenoon far from pleasant.

No soldier is likely to forget the discomfort of moving camp in the midst of a rainstorm. The tents are wet through as soon as struck, uniforms are soon in the same condition; the three days' rations carried in the haversacks tend to melt into a pastelike mass. The forty rounds of ammunition and the loaded musket must be kept dry at any cost. Then the slow plowing of the wagons through the mud, the sticking fast of cannon, the roads soon trodden into thick jelly—these are but ordinary discomforts. A forced march under such conditions doubles and triples the hardships, and is an achievement which only a general of great ascendancy over his men can exact.

On this night, cavalry was thrown far out ahead and on the flanks to bring in all travelers, and to guard against enemy reconnaissance, while picked companies of skirmishers in the woods kept even pace with their comrades on the roads. Fayetteville, a distance of twenty-seven miles, was reached in two days. Here one brigade was left behind as guard for that part of the baggage and wagons not immediately needed. The other two brigades rested till noon of Thursday, April 10, and then went swiftly forward. One brigade continued longer on the march than the other, pressing on till at dusk they turned into the fields for rest—pitching no tents, kindling no fires, and sleeping on their arms.

Now they were within ten miles of Huntsville. Pickets were thrown out in all directions, and every person stirring was arrested, both to gain information and to prevent any being carried to the enemy. The Huntsville mail coach was captured and brought into the circle of peopled fields.

From twilight until the moon went down at about two o'clock, all was quiet, and the soldiers not on outpost duty rested as best they could. The interval was one of intense anxiety for the commander, alert and at work all that night. He visited pickets and personally questioned local citizens willingly or unwillingly brought within the lines. At midnight a Negro just captured made the startling assertion, on the authority of his master, that 5,000 troops had arrived at Huntsville. [The story was in part true. Kirby Smith reports Brigadier General S. B. Maxey as passing through Huntsville on the 10th with three regiments and a battalion.]

By Mitchel's knowledge at the time, there was nothing improbable in such a body of the enemy being there, for Huntsville was important and in direct communication with the principal armies of the South. Mitchel didn't hesitate, however; orders were to hold unchanged. The cavalry was divided into three bands. The first and second, accompanied by two or three light guns, were to diverge in opposite directions from the main body and strike the railroad some distance on each side of town, to prevent the escape of any engines or cars and to cut the telegraph wires. The third detachment was to gallop directly into town for the telegraph office and depot, stopping for nothing else.

Before two in the morning, the men were aroused without sound of drum or bugle, and Mitchel—who was a ready and inspiring speaker—briefly addressed each regiment as it filed past into the road. Then they moved on like an army of shadows. Talking was curbed; horses were held carefully reined in; wagons were left behind; even the few cannon taken were moved so steadily and carefully over the muddy roads that, except on striking an occasional stone, or rumbling over a bridge, they gave no sound.

As the early morning hours wore on, the silent, yawningly wary columns reached and passed Meridianville—halfway point of the night's march—without alarming the sleeping residents of the village. At first morning light, the cavalry party assigned to the western rail attack galloped off.

Two miles from Huntsville, the Fayetteville road draws close to the rail line to the east. On order, the second cavalry force broke for the left across the level fields, while the infantry swung to the side of the road to allow the few pieces of artillery to roll rapidly through. From beyond the cavalry racing east, the smoke of a locomotive was seen as the morning's first regularly scheduled train for Chattanooga pulled away from the town.

The engineer of the oncoming train saw the oncoming troopers, checked for a moment, then pressed on under an open throttle. A cannon was thrown into position and fired. Unhurt, the locomotive roared off among the hills. Another train followed, its speed building in alarm, but a second Union gunner was ready with sharper aim. One long-range shot disabled the engine, killing the engineer. The cavalry closed in, and took over the track, blocking further escape to the east for the valuable engines caught in the town. The trap was equally tight on the west, as it proved, for the first party sent out had had complete and eventless success.

The troopers of the third cavalry detachment, accompanied by General Mitchel, galloped at breakneck speed for Huntsville, itself followed fast by the infantry.

O. M. MITCHEL:

Hq. Third Division
Huntsville, Ala.,
April 11, 1862

Capt. J. B. Fry,
Assistant Adjutant General,
Army of the Ohio

Sir:

After leaving Fayetteville yesterday at twelve noon, my advanced guard, consisting of Turchin's brigade, Kennett's cavalry and Simonson's battery, entered Huntsville this morning at six o'clock.

The city was taken completely by surprise, no one having considered the march practicable in the time. We have captured about 200 prisoners, fifteen locomotives, a large amount of passenger, box and platform cars, the telegraphic apparatus and offices, and two Southern mails. We have at length succeeded in cutting the great artery of railway intercommunication between the Southern states.

Respectfully,
O. M. Mitchel,
Brigadier General, Commanding

F. A. MITCHEL: The town—with its important machine shops of the Memphis & Charleston Railroad—had been captured without the use of a pound of powder, except to shoot engines. General Mitchel had marched his men fifty-seven miles in forty-eight hours, but by their rapid movements they had possessed themselves of a more comfortable means of transportation for future operations.

The railroad was in fine condition; the depots, water and wood stations, turn-tables, engine-houses, locomotives and cars all in prime order. The road didn't cease to be operated; it simply changed hands. The workmen employed by the Confederate government, who went home the night before from their labors in the machine shops, either came back to work for Uncle Sam in the morning or were replaced by Yankee mechanics.

EDITOR: A prize of potentially greater military value than even the M. & C. railway shops, rolling stock and trackage was taken by—or given to—Mitchel at Huntsville in the form of an intercepted telegraph message in cipher from General Beauregard to the Confederate authorities at Richmond. Mitchel, the jack of many professions, proved himself cryptographer enough promptly to break the apparent jumble of words found, starting with "Whiraly, Ndirt 9."

Actually—lacking nulls, fixed-number letter groups, and most safeguards now considered advisable for any cipher of more than schoolboy utility—the message might have seemed written almost in clear to a code specialist, or even a sharp schoolboy, since "Whiraly, Ndirt 9" at the top turned out to be "Corinth, April 9," and the rest of the message wasn't particularly more opaque. The facts given and the appeal encased, however, were of a seriousness considerably beyond schoolboy games. This was the situation report by the commander of the Confederate western army two days after the stand-off butchery of Shiloh.

P. G. T. BEAUREGARD:

Corinth
April 9, 1862

General S. Cooper, Richmond, Va.:

All present probabilities are that whenever the enemy moves on this position he will do so with an overwhelming force of not less than 85,000 men. We can now muster only about 35,000 effectives. Van Dorn may possibly join us in a few days with about 15,000 more. Can we not be reinforced from Pemberton's army? If defeated here, we lose the Mississippi Valley and probably our cause; whereas we could even afford to lose for a while Charleston and Savannah for the purpose of defeating Buell's army, which would not only insure us of the valley of the Mississippi but our independence.

P. G. T. Beauregard

PIKE: I drove into Huntsville just as General Mitchel's men were raising the headquarter tents. I reported the condition of the country, down below, on both sides of the river, as far as Tuscumbia, and that it was clear of Rebels with the exception of the 2nd Tennessee and 1st Louisiana, both cavalry regiments. It had been impossible for me to get close to the Decatur bridge, but I'd learned that the Rebels had it already tarred, and that pitch-pine was piled in it, ready to be fired at a moment's notice.

The occupation of Huntsville took place on the 11th day of April, 1862; and the amount of public stores which fell into General Mitchel's hands was immense. We likewise took about five hundred prisoners; and in the telegraph office was found a dispatch from General Beauregard, giving the strength and disposition of his force at Corinth; and adding that if that place fell into the hands of the enemy, the cause of the South was lost. This dispatch was given to me a few hours after I got to Huntsville, and I was ordered to take my own way to get the document to General Buell, at Corinth, but to get it there without delay.

I mounted my wild horse—the one General Mitchel had given me —and, as the general handed me the document, he told me that he had sent two other men with copies, and expressed the fear that they wouldn't get through, as they were inexperiencd in the country.

"Now," said he, "I depend on your getting through with it."

I turned my horse down toward the Fayetteville road, and put him out at a rapid gait. He made the trip to Fayetteville in three hours, a distance of thirty-six miles.

Mounting a commandeered horse at Fayetteville, I went by the way of Fishing Creek Ford, to Columbia, the county seat of Maury County, Tenn., which place was commanded by General Negley. (About four miles from Columbia, I had fallen from my horse from fatigue, and I presume I lay for at least an hour, entirely unconscious. On recovering, I found my horse tied to a bush near by, and in the vicinity a woman's track in the dust.)

I delivered the deciphered dispatch to General Negley at Columbia, with the request of General Mitchel that it might be sent immediately by telegraph to General Buell, at Pittsburg Landing. General Negley was in bed when I arrived at his quarters, but he rose and called on his adjutant general, Captain Hill, to take it to the telegraph office; while he directed me to the best hotel in the place, offering to pay my bill.

EDITOR: The Beauregard message deciphered by Mitchel at Huntsville—which Corporal Pike, among others, had ridden so hard to get back for Buell's attention—was to cause more anxiety among the Confederate military leaders in the following weeks than interest or action on the part of the Union commanders.

Released to the press in Nashville on April 15 by hands unknown, an eventual reprint of the message in the Richmond *Examiner* was put promptly before General Lee by Adjutant General Samuel Cooper.

SAMUEL COOPER:

April 25, 1862

General R. E. Lee, &c.:

General: In the *Examiner* of today is published an article from the New York *Herald*, giving verbatim the telegraphic dispatch of General Beauregard of the 9th instant to me, which was in cipher.

This information appears to have been communicated from Nashville under date of April 15. The only copy that was made from the original dispatch was sent to you, together with the telegraph, in cipher; the rough, from which the copy sent you was made, has never been out of my possession, and I am therefore led to the conclusion that the telegraph communicated from Nashville must have been obtained somewhere in that quarter. . . .

Respectfully,
S. Cooper
Adjutant and Inspector General

ROBERT E. LEE:

Headquarters, Richmond, Va.
April 25, 1862

General P. G. T. Beauregard,
Commanding, &c., Corinth, Miss.:

General: My attention has been called to an article published in the New York *Herald* of the 21st instant, which contains a copy of your telegraphic dispatch of the 9th instant to General Cooper, and which it is stated was intercepted at Huntsville. As the telegram received here was in cipher, I have deemed the matter of sufficient importance to bring it to your notice. It may be necessary to change your cipher or adopt a new one altogether.

I have just received the enclosed note from General Cooper, and enclose it, together with the article in question, for your perusal.

Respectfully,
R. E. Lee
General

EDITOR: General Beauregard's aides made "diligent inquiries" into the early April telegraph situation at Huntsville and came up with a strong guess which makes it possible now to speculate that

[*Editor*]
O. M. Mitchel in his occupation of northern Alabama may have arranged to have more advance agents than the Andrews party and Corporal Pike operating for him behind the enemy lines.

The Confederate investigators—in addition to questioning the "soundness" of a tinsmith named J. G. Heap, previously used on occasion as a spy or scout for the Southern forces, but now believed to have gone over to the Union invaders—decided that the interception of the message could most probably be charged to a northern-born couple, Mr. and Mrs. C. E. (or J.H.) Larcombe, both on duty as telegraph operators in Huntsville at the time of the attack. (The Larcombes—promptly rated as "Lincolnites and Yankees" by investigator L. F. Zantzinger—were thought even less sound at the end of April when Zantzinger heard by across-the-lines grapevine that Larcombe had been appointed railroad superintendent at Huntsville by General Mitchel.)

Interest in Mitchel's prized intercept didn't develop for some two weeks, and then came almost entirely from the Confederate side. At Buell's army headquarters on this weekend of April 12 and later, Beauregard's detailed admission of vulnerability at Corinth was being disbelieved or disregarded.

Heading South 5

BENSINGER: First thing Friday I saw the captain, who had questioned us the previous day, looking over the Crutchfield House register and eying us sharply, but he said not a word. About eight o'clock that morning we boarded the train, paying our fare to Marietta, where we arrived around four o'clock.

KNIGHT: On Friday morning, our host the squire was kind enough to give us a letter which he said would pass us over the river to Chattanooga and introduce us to a colonel there. We didn't need to use it for the first, as there were no guards set that day; and we had no inclination to use it for an introduction.

During the day we strolled around the streets of the village—for at that time Chattanooga was nothing more—and saw whatever we thought worth looking at.

PITTENGER: On Friday morning, as it was to prove, there were at least seven of our party south of the Tennessee, and it was necessary that we overtake them before they arrived at Marietta, or join them this evening at that point. Notwithstanding our protracted gaiety at the Widow Hall's, we were up by daybreak, and Andrews mounted and rode back into the country without waiting for breakfast.

It was but a few hundred yards to a place where an old flatboat was kept, by which we intended to cross the Tennessee. As the owner of the flatboat was bailing it out, a man rode up with a stringent order to permit no person to cross during the next three days. The only explanation given was the rumor that the Yankees were coming.

The best thing we could think of was to go up the west bank of the river and try to get over directly at Chattanooga. This involved a laborious half-day's journey mostly over mountain paths and rugged valleys. The river is very crooked, and as we journeyed, we were sometimes on its banks, and again, miles distant. At length we turned into a valley road leading directly to the river bank nearly opposite Chattanooga. Travelers were now more frequent and from them we learned many items of news. One from the East was interesting: it was that the Confederate ironclad *Merrimac* had steamed out, and after engaging the Federal *Monitor* for some time without decisive result, had thrown her grappling irons on the latter, and towed her ashore, where of course she fell an easy prey. Our informant claimed that now, as the Confederates had the two best gunboats in the world, they would soon be able to raise the blockade and burn the Northern cities. I needn't say that the histories of the war have all neglected to record this wonderful capture.

F. M. GREGG: There was a private ferry at Mrs. Hall's landing, by which the Union men hoped to get across the river, reach Whiteside Station, and take the train for Chattanooga. As they were preparing on Friday morning, April 11, to get into the boat, orders were given to the ferryman not to let anyone cross. It was fourteen miles across

[*F. M. Gregg*]
the mountains by a steep trail. Striking Walden's Ridge, they came into the regular Jasper and Chattanooga road below Williams' Island. Some of the party stopped at Captain Samuel Williams' residence for dinner. Andrews himself, stopping with his party, had a conversation with men at the gate.

PITTENGER: On reaching the river bank across from Chattanooga shortly after noon, we saw a large number of persons, several of them belonging to our own party. The ferryman was also here with his craft, a frail boat driven by horses, but such a windstorm was raging that he feared to attempt the passage. We waited as patiently as possible, although as others of our number came up, the danger of detection increased.

Our train on the other side—the last which would be of any service to us—was to start at five o'clock in the afternoon, and it was drawing uncomfortably near that time.

At length, when we couldn't persuade the ferryman, we tried another plan. Talking up the bravery of Kentuckians or even of Ohio Yankees, as against his cowardice, we soon goaded him into saying he'd put us across or drown in the attempt—and for his part, he didn't much care which. When all who were willing to risk the passage were on board, we took hold with pushing poles, and also pulling on overhanging limbs—for the river was flooded, swift and choppy—we succeeded in getting a good start up the river, and after some tossing, landed safely on the other side.

We looked with keenest interest across the turbid water toward the town. We had every reason to anticipate a strict guard on the Chattanooga shore, and supposed that at the Rebel headquarters they would be less easy to satisfy than the citizens in the mountains had been. We saw no sign of fortifications, and at this date there were none.

Many valleys converge at or near Chattanooga—the upper and lower Tennessee, North and South Lookout, Chickamauga and Sequatchie—and all the common roads and railroads of the area. The town, if adequately fortified and held by a moderate force, could serve to dominate all the surrounding country. If Mitchel were able to reach Chattanooga a day or two after we stood gazing at the town, and with the W. & A. bridges south of it burned, the one useful rail connection between Richmond and the west would be broken, Mitchel's own rail lines to Nashville and the North would be open, while on the south the enemy couldn't come nearer than fifty miles by rail. Let Mitchel's army be increased; and he'd be the great man of the day and, possibly, even the first Union commander in chief.

The immediate question for us that day was thought to be how to pass the guard on the further side of the river. On crossing, to our pleased surprise, we saw no guard whatever and were permitted to pass directly to the railroad station, where we had less than an hour to wait for the train. The panic produced in Chattanooga by Mitchel's occupation of Huntsville was intense, and the attention of the enemy seemed about equally divided between preparing to resist, and preparing to evacuate. The occupation of the M. & C. had cut Chattanooga off from direct communication with Beauregard at Corinth, leaving only the circuitous route through Atlanta.

At the station we found waiting several of our party who had come earlier. We also found a large number of passengers, many of them soldiers. Of the town itself, we saw almost nothing.

ALF WILSON: We reached the north bank of the Tennessee River, opposite Chattanooga, on Friday, the 11th, one day behind the time agreed upon with General Mitchel, and were compelled to wait for some time for the wind to subside so that the ferryboat—a little, crazy, frail affair—could carry us safely across. At length, however, we had the satisfaction of landing safe and sound in Chattanooga, where we found we had been preceded by most of the party. We went to the depot and purchased tickets for Marietta, Georgia. Some of the party bought several tickets, so that there would not be so many of us at the office at once. Everything thus far appeared to work finely.

At this time or somewhat later, Andrews told me that this expedition of ours was to be his last—that if he got out alive, he meant never to undertake another trip.

DORSEY: We reached the ferry at Chattanooga just in time to get across to the depot in time for the southbound train. Andrews had reached the ferry ahead of us, but as the wind was high and the river rough, few trips were made that day, and the boat was held until our group all came up.

All who had spent the night at the Widow Hall's were on this boat, but again we were total strangers. With great anxiety we looked upon the opposite shore as we approached it, a little doubtful if we would be able to deceive the Confederate soldiers whom we expected to find stationed there as guards, but there being no guards on duty at that point, we passed on up the main street, unmolested.

PITTENGER: On Friday, after their night at the Crutchfield House, Reddick and Wollam—as they were to tell us later—strolled for a time about Chattanooga, looking in on both the commissary and ordnance departments of the military establishment. They also witnessed the burial, with honors of war, of some officers who had been killed at Pittsburg Landing.

Happening on a photographic gallery, they were seized with the desire to have their pictures taken. The artist asked them to wait awhile, as he was engaged in whittling out a frame, with his penknife, from a cigar box, explaining that since he had been "cut off from Yankeedom," he had been compelled to make everything for himself. The pictures that were then taken for them were prized the more because of this homemade setting.

In the evening, Reddick and Wollam were at the depot when the remainder of the party came in. Andrews gave them a warm grasp of the hand, and assured them that all was right.

PARROTT: At the ferry below Chattanooga on Friday morning a rumor had it that the Yankees were coming, and as orders had been issued against anyone crossing, we trudged upstream to Chattanooga to take our chances at the ferry there.

It was on this walk that we fell in with members of our party who said that they had seen Andrews, and that he had given orders to assemble at Marietta on Saturday instead of Friday. On our way we met a man whom we had seen at the ferry.

"Hello, Yanks," he said.

Were we recognized? It was a lonely spot, so Robertson said to me, loud enough for the man to hear: "He's a Yankee spy. He takes us for Yankees."

We turned on the man with drawn revolvers, making him throw up his hands.

"We've come a long way to fight such fellows as you," Robertson said.

We searched the man, found by his papers he was from Chattanooga, and then let him come along with us.

At the river, more of our party were waiting to cross. The ferryman said the wind and waves were too high. It was nearly five o'clock, and we were getting desperate, when the man we had held up on the road, who knew the ferryman, spoke up for us.

"These fellows are all right," he told the ferryman. "Kentucky boys sick of the Yanks, who've got to get down by the cars tonight to join our army."

The ferryman believed him, and we started across. We stepped ashore unchallenged in Chattanooga. The train for Marietta hadn't left, and our Chattanooga friend even helped us to buy our tickets.

DORSEY: After crossing the river and getting into Chattanooga, we scattered out somewhat; but a group of three or four of us, going up the main business street toward the depot, attracted the attention of some men about a store. We were walking along in as aimless and ungainly a way as possible, when some fellow called out: "Hello, who's them fellows?"

To which another replied, "Oh, some country jakes, I reckon."

Andrews had instructed us to be on our guard, and avoid the soldier step, and also all such commands as, "Halt! Attention!" etc., as these might be used as a means of detection by any who might suspect us. We were now in the midst of our enemies, and an act or word might entrap the whole party. As for myself I never dared look a man square in the face when talking, for fear my eyes would give me away.

At the depot we found quite a rush for tickets going south. General Mitchel had already captured Huntsville and cut off communications with Corinth and the west. Soldiers en route to Corinth had been turned back and with many citizens were fleeing southward. Conversation among the people soon disclosed this unwelcome news to us—unwelcome, that is, as far as its being twenty-four hours too soon for best fitting in with the work we had ahead.

F. M. GREGG: It was about four o'clock on Friday when the largest group of Union travelers arrived at the lower ferry at Chattanooga, run by W. L. Dugger. It was a windy day, and the ferryman wasn't anxious to make the trip. He was persuaded by the party to make the attempt, and succeeded in landing them at the foot of Pine Street in Chattanooga. Here General William I. Standifer (of Marion County) met them as they got on the boat.

W. I. STANDIFER: They were a motley-looking set. If you had met one or two together, you would never have noticed them, but when seen together, there was an evident attempt to deceive in their appearance. Some wore long coats, one had one coat-tail gone, straw and felt hats of the oldest kind were worn. In fact, they would have aroused suspicion at once if they hadn't been so far inside the lines.

F. M. GREGG: The party came up Pine Street to the Union Depot, arriving in time to take the five o'clock train for Marietta. Here were

[*F. M. Gregg*]
first shown the difficulties they would have to contend with in their attempt to execute the work planned. Mitchel was at Huntsville; overcoming all obstacles, he had fulfilled his part of the expedition. As the outcome of his position at Huntsville, the road was crowded with extra trains removing provisions to more distant and safer quarters. Andrews was fully aware of the fact of the increased danger of the expedition, for he had said, "If Mitchel gets to Huntsville before we leave Marietta, the road will be crowded, so that our task will be much harder."

KNIGHT: Toward evening, we saw many of our party coming in. I didn't know them personally, as I hadn't yet had an opportunity of becoming acquainted, but I could have picked them out from the whole Southern army. We were at the depot in time to take the down evening train, with the others.

BENSINGER: Four of us arrived at Marietta about four o'clock in the afternoon on Friday, the 11th of April.

ALF WILSON: When we had all secured our tickets, we went aboard the train, and to our great relief, no one seemed to pay any attention to us. We took seats in the cars and were soon moving off into Dixie at a good rate of speed. I felt that this was a much easier and more expeditious way of getting on than the tedious marching of the previous four days.

Just before leaving, Andrews divided $700 in Confederate scrip among the eighteen of us who were there and told us that we were soon to enter upon our dangerous duty. He warned us, though, that the first man who got drunk, or flinched in the least, he himself would shoot dead on the spot.

After getting seated, and there being no further cause for concern for the time being, I began carefully to study over the situation with all the thought I could, and to calculate our chances of success or failure. The result of my deliberations was by no means encouraging. We were one day behind the time appointed. With General Mitchel in Huntsville, there would be little room to hope for our success. It would cause the road to be crowded with trains flying from danger, and it would be difficult for us to pass them all in safety. But it was too late now to change the program. We must make the effort, come what might.

I said nothing to anyone except Andrews; but on listening to my opinion on the situation he encouraged me by saying there was yet a good chance to succeed. Indeed, he expressed himself in so sanguine a manner that I made no further argument; although I still thought my course of reasoning correct, whether the result would accord with it or not.

PITTENGER: When we had purchased our tickets at Chattanooga, and had ceased to walk about the station for the purpose of looking for others of our party, we got on board. Many of the passengers were furloughed soldiers, who were going back by the southern route to join Beauregard. The conversation still turned to the mighty battle of Pittsburg Landing, which the soldiers regarded as a great triumph. We took part in the talk, expressing as much interest as any. There was no system of passports then in use on that line, or, indeed, in most others in the South, and travel—at least up to that time—was entirely unrestricted.

The sun was about an hour high as we moved from the depot, and it soon sank behind the hills of Georgia. On the northern end of the road, which frequently crosses the crooked Chickamauga Creek, there are many bridges. With one additional over the same stream on the East Tennessee road, there are eleven large ones within thirty miles; and as we ran southward over these, we couldn't help picturing our proposed return on the morrow, and the destruction we hoped to contrive.

Darkness closed in amid the laughter and oaths of the Rebel soldiers, many of whom were intoxicated. Drowsing on an improvised seat on the coalbox, I was aroused by the call of Dalton, the supper station. It was after dark, for the train had been making very slow time.

Whether it was behind schedule or not, I didn't know. The running on all Southern railroads during the war was but moderate, since the scarcity of iron and other material had caused them to fall into bad repair. The fastest train on this road at this time, I was informed later, rarely got beyond eighteen miles an hour. This factor wasn't in our favor, nor was the great traffic on the road, which had become one of the most important in the South. We saw many freight trains standing at the stations, and everything indicated that the capacity of this line was being pressed to the utmost, which would operate to make the running of an unscheduled train—if we should capture one—that much more difficult.

There was a great rush for places at supper. There was not even room for all at the second table, though the conductor was very patient.

DORSEY: Andrews and several others of the party got seats at table at the Dalton supper stop, thirty-eight miles south of Chattanooga, but some of us weren't so fortunate. I stood well back on the left-hand side of the dining hall, and as the meal progressed, I met the landlady, a portly, motherly-looking woman, assisting the servants in waiting on the tables. I asked her if she could spare me a piece of pie, as I wouldn't have time to get supper before the train left.

"Certainly, sir," she said.

With a pleasant smile, she handed me a piece of pie from the plate in her hand, receiving the ten-cent shinplaster I tendered in payment. How forcibly this incident reminded me of my mother and home!

Andrews was one of the most conspicuous personages in that dining room. I think he had the most commanding presence of anyone there, Confederate officers, citizens and all. But little Buffum made himself conspicuous by standing behind a Rebel captain at the table, urging him to hurry up. As the captain finally rose from the chair, Buffum literally slid right in under his arm and took the seat almost before the captain was off of it. This provoked from the officer the remark, "Well, if that isn't a Yankee trick!" The movement had been observed by many, and this sally of the captain's caused a roar of laughter. Buffum knew the ropes, and while at supper got someone to refill his bottle with whiskey, which, when we had resumed the journey south, was indulged in as we felt the need of it, that night and the next day.

We arrived at Marietta about midnight, and put up at the hotel near the depot. The hotel was so full that we could scarcely be accommodated. Slavens, Pittenger and I piled into one bed, and catnapped it until morning.

PITTENGER: Near midnight we were waked by the conductor calling, "Marietta." The goal was reached. We were now almost directly in the center of the Confederacy. Before we could return many miles toward our own lines, we were to strike a blow that would either make all Rebeldom vibrate to its center, or be ourselves at the mercy of the merciless. Nearly all of our group registered at the Tremont House, under all kinds of names. As the hotel was much crowded, we took a few rooms close together and packed into them to their utmost capacity.

F. M. GREGG: The southbound train the raiders took left Chattanooga at five P.M. At Dalton, supper was had, and about midnight of Friday, the 11th of April, it reached Marietta. The twenty-two Union men reunited there were 200 miles from their comrades, whom they had left less than five days before at Shelbyville.

DORSEY: Except for Llewellyn and Smith—who had been stopped en route near Jasper and were already "enlisted" in the Rebel army —all the men who had started from Shelbyville made it here to Marietta. There were now twenty-one of us in the party, with Andrews as the twenty-second.

PITTENGER: Andrews was with our larger party in the hotel near the railroad station, the Tremont House, while Porter and our three engineers—Hawkins, Knight and Brown—were in the other hotel at some distance. Our chief scarcely slept at all that night. He first went to the other hotel and saw that Knight and Brown had made arrangements for being called on time in the morning. Porter and Hawkins, who had come down the evening before and had gone to bed much earlier this night, weren't seen and it wasn't then known that they had overlooked paying a fee to a room waiter for rousing them the following morning.

We were sleeping three or four to a bed at the large hotel, but young soldiers aren't fastidious, and the greater number slept soundly.

ALF WILSON: We left Chattanooga a little while before sunset on Friday and arrived at Marietta soon after midnight. We at once repaired to the nearest hotel and registered, of course giving fictitious names. Before retiring, arrangements were made to have the hotel men awake us in time for the northbound train in the morning, which they promised to do without fail.

No man knows what a day may bring forth. The uncertainty of what the light of the next day's sun would bring in our particular cases was the reason some of us, myself at least of the number, didn't sleep very much. By the setting of another sun we might be hanging to the limbs of some of the trees along the railroad, with an enraged populace jeering and shouting epithets; or we might leave a trail of fire and destruction behind us and come triumphantly rolling into Chattanooga and Huntsville, within the Federal lines, to receive the welcome plaudits of comrades left behind, the thanks of our general and the praises of a grateful people. Such thoughts as these weren't calculated to make for sound sleep, and even this broken rest wasn't to continue long. In two or three hours we were to be called.

New Management on the M. & C.

PITTENGER: Back at Huntsville, the capture of the town and its railroad shops on Friday morning hadn't finished Mitchel's work. He promptly reorganized the railroad management, and spent the day in getting ready two other expeditions, this time by rail.

The first expedition planned consisted of a single regiment, the 24th Illinois, under the command of Colonel J. B. Turchin. Packed on a train, the force left Huntsville at six P.M., steaming warily westward in an attempt to capture the Decatur Bridge twenty-five miles away, and if possible to open communications with Buell. Arrived before Decatur the following morning, the rail-borne Union force drove a surprised guard detachment from its fortifications. The bridge was fired by its defenders as they fled, but Turchin's men moved in quickly enough to extinguish the flames and take over the bridge intact.

To the east there were greater obstacles. The distance to Stevenson was some seventy miles, and the morning train which had escaped had put the enemy on warning that some kind of a demonstration was being made at Huntsville, although they couldn't know whether it was only a quick-hitting raid, or an advance in force. Another factor might be either of the greatest help or a serious disappointment. Our party under Andrews would early on this Friday, if on time, be starting up from Georgia toward Chattanooga and Huntsville. Even if fully successful, we couldn't be expected to move out on the M. & C. line before late afternoon, but if we came then and had succeeded in burning the Chickamauga bridges, all Mitchel's next work and the grandest opportunity of the war would lie clear before him.

But on that Friday the 11th, when the whole M. & C. road from Chattanooga westward might have been open for us, we were only going toward our destination as ordinary passengers, with all our work still to do.

Colonel Joshua Sill's brigade—that from which our raiding party had been selected—was chosen for the eastern expedition. The troops, fully equipped, were loaded on boxcars and long flatcars with low sides. Two cannon mounted on a flatcar pointed diagonally ahead on each side of the locomotive and were formidable in appearance if not in fact.

No other such advance as the one planned over an enemy's railroad directly into an enemy's country had been made up to that time in any war. Preparations were completed at about midnight of the 11th, when some two thousand troops were aboard the train.

It was a perilous novelty, with progress necessarily slow. On a clear track, the seventy miles to Stevenson might have been made in two or three hours. This trip—moving warily against the possibility of ambush or collision with an armed train sent out by the Rebels to learn why no trains or telegrams had come from Huntsville—took nearer ten to cover the distance.

A. L. WADDLE: At Huntsville on Friday, April 11, the brigade of Colonel Sill [including the narrator, Lieutenant A. L. Waddle, Company H, 33d Ohio Volunteer Infantry] was ordered to Stevenson—junction of the Memphis & Charleston and the Nashville & Chattanooga—by way of the newly captured M. & C. Railroad line. The brigade was placed in the cars the same evening; the men were compelled to remain closely packed in these uncomfortable quarters the entire night in that disagreeable state of uncertainty which always exists when one is expecting to start at every moment, but never goes.

Soon after daylight on Saturday, however, we were off, and a novel train it was. Before the locomotive—in the cab of which General Mitchel was riding—a platform car was driven, on which was placed a piece of artillery, and on which Colonel Sill stood the greater part of the trip. Then followed a motley collection of passenger, freight and construction cars, all filled with armed men.

Cautiously, if such a thing as caution was possible under the circumstances, we moved forward, through cuts where whole troops of hostile soldiers might be hiding, over bridges and embankments where a misplaced rail might send us all to destruction. We steamed along until a run of seventy miles brought us to our destination.

[*A. L. Waddle*]

Our coming at Stevenson had been heralded by an engine which escaped from Huntsville the day before, and there was great excitement among such of the citizens as had remained to receive us. After stopping at the principal hotel for a dinner of fried pork, corn bread and rye coffee, we proceeded a few miles further on to a bridge over a small stream called Widden's Creek.

DORSEY: Although Huntsville had been captured on Friday, General Mitchel and his railroad force didn't get off by rail for Chattanooga until the next morning.

Mitchel came to within thirty miles of Chattanooga on the west, having run seventy miles through the enemy's country by rail, and stopped, burning a bridge in front of him. The enemy had but one regiment in Chattanooga at that time, the 43d Georgia, and it was poorly armed.

PITTENGER: As the troop-packed, gun-displaying train bearing Sill's brigade approached Stevenson, a startled enemy force there—reportedly 2,000 in number—cleared out without firing a gun. Mitchel remained a short time, securing the five additional locomotives found at Stevenson, and then, reboarding the train, steamed seven miles further to Widden's Creek and pulled up at the small bridge there, the extreme point of the advance.

Here with his vanguard, as the tense hours of that Saturday, April 12, 1862, wore on, General Mitchel waited.

Georgia, Georgia

JEFFERSON DAVIS:

Richmond, Va.
April 10, 1862

Governor Brown, Georgia:

General Beauregard must have reinforcements to meet the vast accumulation of the enemy before him. The necessity is imminent;

the case of vital importance. Send forward to Corinth all the armed men you can furnish.

Jefferson Davis

[Same to governors of Alabama, Louisiana, Mississippi and South Carolina.]

EDITOR: In the spring of 1862, the railroads of Georgia were still among the best in the South, and of the lines in the state, the state-owned Western & Atlantic continued to be Governor Joseph E. Brown's particular pride and concern. It had earned nearly two million in clear profit for the state treasury in the four years it had been under Brown's watchful eye, and with the testing of war it was proving itself as strategically valuable a line as the South had.

Despite the loss in 1861 of 180 cars taken for use elsewhere in the Confederacy—a drain the governor had ended by threatening Richmond with counter-seizures in reprisal—and the burning of two bridges below Chattanooga by the East Tennessee partisans the November before, the governor and general superintendent, John S. Rowland, could take satisfaction in their inventory of locomotives, rolling stock and maintenance supplies. Thoughtfully, the governor had picked up eleven hundred spare tons of bar iron the winter befor at $50 a ton—iron which now couldn't be found at $200 a ton—and with the spare parts, tools and reserve supplies forehandedly found, bought and laid in by the master mechanic, Flynn, and the motive power superintendent, Murphy, the state road was readier than most to meet maintenance demands for the hard year or two to come. Particularly, when the Atlanta rolling mill and Mark Cooper's iron works at Etowah offered the heaviest and most versatile iron-working facilities in the Confederacy after the Tredegar works in Richmond.

New Hampshire's Stephen Harriman Long had designed and built a first-class road for the times; Georgia's Governor Brown, ex-Superintendent J. W. Lewis and current Superintendent Rowland had seen to its defense and maintenance. The Georgian forests were supplying nearly limitless fuel at under $2 a cord; Negro track gangs were still hirable from owners along the right-of-way. The road's basic need continued to be trained manpower at the operating level: the engineers, firemen, conductors and shop mechanics required to keep the W. & A. up or near the standards set for it in the years immediately before the war. In these, the W. & A. had a strength to match its inventory of cached supplies.

[*Editor*]

The operating railroad men of the South in the 1850's and 1860's were as often Northern- or Irish-born as not. For an example, in the spring of 1861, twenty-nine-year-old Peter J. Bracken—engineer of the W. & A. locomotive *Texas*—was originally a Philadelphian, his mother of County Cork. Not too many months before, railroader Bracken had courted, won and married Louisa Sewell of Virginia, and the couple had set up housekeeping in the pleasantly named town of Social Circle, east of Atlanta. Qualified engineers, at the war's opening, were drawing a substantial $70 monthly—more or less on a wage par with conductors, something under the $90 or more that master machinists were beginning to command—and often greater rewards in the prestige accorded them by awed bystanders at the stations. Bracken had a married sister in Stonington, Connecticut, and a half-brother and sister in Philadelphia, but his immediate fidelity was to his engine and his W. & A. job, and it was to be said of him, then and later, that "no matter what happened, Pete Bracken would always bring his train in."

Since the W. & A. Railroad was state-owned, many Georgians, besides Governor Brown, were able to feel an almost matching proprietary interest in its operations. Men like N. White Smith and Captain W. J. Whitsitt of Ringgold could look on threats to its smooth running as they might look on interference with their own property or activities. With the coming of war they were seeing this smooth running increasingly dependent, in some respects, on younger hands: Henry Haney, Bracken's fireman, not yet sixteen; Ed Henderson, Dalton telegraph operator at seventeen. At every station along the line, in war as in peace, the road had attentive amateur inspectors of operations in the idlers and nearby tradesmen drawn to the tracks at the stopping of nearly every train. For most of these self-constituted local boards of review, the sources of freshest news and most authoritative channels for the transmission of complaints or inquiries were the conductors who commanded the comings and goings of each passenger train, mixed or straight.

William Allen Fuller, on April 12, 1862, was within three days of his twenty-sixth birthday. Born in Henry County, Ga., the grandson of a veteran of the American Revolution—his middle name a salute to an ancestor on his mother's side, Jesse Allen of the Green Mountain Allens—the young Georgian took advantage of such schooling as could be secured, and in 1855, at the age of eighteen, gave over chopping cotton on his father's farm to head for Atlanta and a job with the state-owned railroad.

For a youngster not mechanically bent or trained, but long of wind and quick of foot, the first chief assignment as a W. & A. train hand at the time was almost automatic: jogging for miles daily as advance flagman for wild freights or before scheduled trains on particularly twisting sections of the Atlanta-Chattanooga run. Proving himself ambitious, aggressive, and quick to learn, Fuller won promotion to the responsibilities of a train conductor by 1857 and for the several years to follow was kept busy balancing the daily accounts that included half-price commutation books, checking consignment deliveries and pick-ups on mixed freights, and—among numerous other duties—trying to keep order on Saturdays when countrymen delighted to come exuberantly to town.

A born partisan, of quick and stubborn convictions, Fuller at the approach of war had drilled with a militia company and considered going with it when the local military organizations of the state were called to active service at the outbreak of war. Governor Brown promptly made it clear that experienced railroad men could best serve Georgia in the emergency by helping to keep the supplies and men rolling over the state's own W. & A. line. The young conductor took the governor's word for it, and stayed where he was. A general Confederate conscription law was expected before this April of 1862 was out, but Georgians hadn't yet seen the law from Richmond that could make Governor Brown shift an inch from any policy he held to be in the interest of his belligerently sovereign state. Unmarried as yet, his home base an Atlanta hotel, Fuller handled his wartime assignment—the full Atlanta-Chattanooga runs—with pride, zeal, and growing self-assurance.

Conductors were responsible directly to Superintendent Rowland, but the quiet-spoken, capable man to whom Jeff Cain, Peter Bracken and all the engineers and mechanics of the line were immediately responsible was Anthony Murphy, foreman of motive power and machine shops of the Western & Atlantic.

WALLACE PUTNAM REED: Born to Thomas and Elizabeth (Keyes) Murphy in County Wicklow, Ireland, in 1829, and brought by his family to Schuylkill County, Pennsylvania, nine years later, young Anthony Murphy was educated in public schools until the age of eighteen. He went then to Trenton, New Jersey, where he was apprenticed to the machinist's trade. After serving there three years, he moved to Pierpont, N. Y., worked for a year in the Erie Railroad shops and then went to Pittsburgh for a further year in the Pennsylvania Railroad shops there. His father, meanwhile, had removed to Iowa.

In 1854, at the age of twenty-five Murphy came to Georgia, and after working four years as a W. & A. machinist, was assigned to the road for eighteen months as a locomotive engineer. Shortly after his arrival in the South, he married an outstanding Atlanta beauty, dark-haired Adelia McConnell.

EDITOR: The thirty-two-year-old Anthony Murphy—whatever his first views may have been—made the decision after Fort Sumter to stand by his wife's people and the friends with whom he had worked and lived for seven years. He was an immediately useful accession to the Confederacy. Within a few weeks of the outbreak of war, as a special agent of forehanded Governor Brown, Murphy completed a bold undercover mission to Pennsylvania, where he recruited—with the promise of high wages and rapid promotions—a number of skilled mechanics and returned with them to Atlanta. Shortly afterward he resumed his normal responsibilities.

In the spring of 1862, as the W. & A. Railroad shops and the Cooper furnaces at Etowah were helping make the Atlanta area the second most important weapons-producing center of the Confederacy, the company of skilled machine workers Anthony Murphy had pried loose and spirited south from Pennsylvania were proving themselves invaluable industrial reinforcements to the side where weapons and machines were always in shorter supply than zeal and valor.

W. P. REED: While his head is cool, his heart is warm, and a more evenly balanced mind is rarely found. Quiet, reticent and undemonstrative, Anthony Murphy is yet an almost invincible power when brought into action.

EDITOR: In the spring of 1862, the superintendent of motive power and machine shops still had dozens of locomotives to look after and call on. Two of the best of these—described by Murphy as equal in power and of the same class—were the *General* and Bracken's engine, the *Texas*, both of five-foot driving wheels. The two had been built in Paterson, New Jersey: the *Texas* by Danforth, Cooke, & Co.; the *General* by the rival firm of Rogers, Ketchum and Grosvenor, shortly to become the Rogers Works. The locomotives of both firms were rated highly throughout the country. It was a Rogers wood-burning engine much like the *General*, for an example, which did the pulling on the first train ride taken on the Illinois Central by a young former storekeeper named Abraham Lincoln, a passenger whose chalked top hat was later to indicate his status as part-time railroad attorney and annual-free-pass holder.

Louis L. Park, a later chief draftsman of the Rogers Works, put down a detailed description of the *General*, which can be taken in most respects as supplying, as well, the specifications of the *Texas*.

LOUIS L. PARK: Built by the Rogers Works for delivery in December, 1855, for the Western & Atlantic Railroad, the *General* is an eight-wheel, wood-burning locomotive of type 440-50, weighing 50,300 pounds; gauge five feet, cylinders 15x22 inches; piston rod, two and a quarter inches in diameter. It has four driving wheels, each sixty inches in diameter, made of cast iron, with journals six inches in diameter; driving wheel base, seven inches; total wheel base of engine, about twenty feet, six inches. The weight on drivers, 32,000 pounds; weight on truck, 18,000 pounds. Heating surface: flues, 748.38 square feet; fire box, 71.08 square feet; total heating surface, 819.44 square feet; grate area, 12.46 square feet.

The *General's* boiler is of the type known as Wagon Top, covered with felt and Russia iron; diameter inside first course, forty inches; working pressure, about 140 pounds; thickness of barrel of boiler, five-sixteenths of an inch; thickness of dome course, three-eighths of an inch. Fire box: thickness of shell, three-eighths and five-sixteenths of an inch; thickness of crown, three-eighths of an inch; thickness of flue sheet, one-half inch; thickness of sides and back, five-sixteenths of an inch; length of grate, forty-six inches; width, thirty-nine inches. Contains 130 flues, each eleven feet long by two inches in diameter. Steam pipes five inches in diameter. Engine truck, four-wheel, rigid center; tender trucks, four-wheel, inside bearing. Diameter of wheels, thirty inches. Has two escape valves and two pumps. The smokestack is of the old balloon type, and the cow-catcher is much longer and larger than those on modern engines.

EDITOR: Joseph Emerson Brown, the Union County mountain boy who had made his own way to and through Yale Law School, and in 1857 to the governorship of Georgia, was fiercely dedicated to the survival of his sovereign state. Whatever his frequent differences with Confederate President Jefferson Davis over the manner of their employment, Georgian troops and Georgian supplies were helping stand off Union forces on nearly every battlefield of the war. On this

[*Editor*]
Palm Sunday weekend of 1862—in addition to the apparently desperate position of the Confederacy's chief western army under Beauregard at Corinth—a pair of paralyzing home blows suddenly threatened Georgia itself with the most disastrous weekend since its founding.

On the heels of President Davis' appeal of the 10th, word came to Brown early on Friday, the 11th, that Mitchel's Federal force was at Huntsville, astride the M. & C., and threatening Chattanooga. The Tennessee railroad junction was Georgia's northern bastion. Once in Chattanooga, the enemy could be within minutes of ripping into unfortified northern Georgia. One almost unarmed Georgia regiment, the 43d, was holding the town. To the barehanded companies at Chattanooga that Friday, Governor Brown ordered pikes, knives and any weapons at hand.

The threat from the north, bad as it might be, was well less than another from the sea. On Thursday, the 10th, a Federal naval and army force had begun bombarding Fort Pulaski, chief defense of Georgia's vital port of Savannah. For the first time, from long range, rifled cannon were to prove that they could blast open fortifications previously thought invulnerable. Governor Brown wasn't to appreciate the demonstration of military progress. While Pulaski held, Savannah was a working port, sending out and receiving blockade runners. On Friday afternoon, Pulaski was pounded into surrender.

Union victories on all fronts had seemed so encouraging to the North that Abraham Lincoln had designated Palm Sunday of April 13 to be observed as the first day of national thanksgiving. On the morning of this Saturday the 12th, both Savannah and northern Georgia appeared to be under immediate threat of occupation. To Saturday's usual call for militia muster and drill, Governor Brown added the life-and-death urgency of a rally against invasion and possibly double-edged disaster.

Whatever new turns were to be met during its own up-coming hours, this April Saturday—first anniversary of the attack on Fort Sumter—was already certain of being no ordinary run-of-the-mill day for Georgia, nor for her native and adopted sons.

Frederick Hill Meserve

Ormsby MacKnight Mitchel

Library of Congress

Abraham Lincoln

TWO WHO CALLED THEM OUT

William Knight

John Alfred Wilson
(with Clara and Algeretta Hale Wilson)

TWO OF THOSE WHO WERE CALLED

FOUR MEN WHO HELPED PICK, TRAIN AND SEND THEM

Library of Congress

"Major E. J. Allen" (Allan Pinkerton)

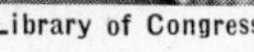

Library of Congress

William Nelson

Library of Congress

Don Carlos Buell

Library of Congress

Joshua W. Sill

TWO MEN WHO SHARED THE SPECIAL HAZARDS MET

David Fry

Carl L. Cannon and Princeton University Press

James Pike

National Archives

Heading South at Tunnel Hill, Georgia

Library of Congress

Heading North at Allatoona Pass

THE WESTERN & ATLANTIC LINE THEY WENT TO TAKE

John H. Morgan

Library of Congress

Joseph Emerson Brown

Library of Congress

Danville Leadbetter

Library of Congress

E. Kirby Smith

Library of Congress

William A. Fuller

Anthony Murphy

SOME OF THE MEN IN THEIR WAY

Heading North 1

ANTHONY MURPHY: On Saturday morning, April 12, 1862, at about four o'clock, I went aboard a W. & A. passenger train in Atlanta that started then for Chattanooga, Tenn. The train, known as a freight and passenger train, was in the immediate command of Engineer Jeff Cain and Conductor W. A. Fuller. As foreman of machine and motive power of the road, my business on that day was to examine an engine that furnished power to cut wood and pump water for the locomotives at Allatoona, a station forty miles from Atlanta.

PITTENGER: On the morning of April 12, we were all roused promptly at the railroad hotel, a little before daybreak. While we were dressing, Andrews, who had slept little if at all that night, moved quietly from room to room seeing every man. Each of us was asked his name, to close out the last possibility of mistake, and then told exactly the part he was expected to take in the enterprise of the day. There was suppressed fire in Andrews' low, whispered words, a calm confidence in his manner that was contagious. There seemed to be no doubt, hesitation or shrinking on his part, but on the contrary, almost an eagerness and joy that the test was so near at hand.

When we were ready, and finding it still lacked a little of train time, most of us gathered in Andrews' room for an informal council of war. Its windows overlooked the railroad, so that we were sure to see the train coming. Behind the locked door, some of us were seated on the bed, one or two on chairs, and the remainder stood around as best they could. We all kept our voices down. Andrews gave no exhortation, and stressed the need for caution, if anything, in preference to rash, overly hasty movements.

"Get seats near each other in the same car," he told us, "and of course say nothing of our business on the way up. When the train makes the Big Shanty breakfast stop, keep your places till I tell you to go. If anything unexpected happens, look to me for the lead. You and you"—designating Knight, Brown and J. A. Wilson—"will go with me on the engine. The rest will go on the left of the train, forward of where we'll uncouple it. Climb into the cars as quickly as you can when the order is given. If anyone interferes, shoot him, but don't fire unless you have to."

[*Pittenger*]

Andrews went on to lay out every action with the nicest accuracy. Our engineers, Knight and Brown, were told the signal on which to start. Wilson as fireman and others as brakemen were assigned their work. The rest of us were constituted a guard to shoot down anyone attempting to interfere with the work. All orders were to come from Andrews, and he was to do any part of the work not otherwise provided for. Any man not aboard when the signal to go was given was to be left, since a delay of thirty seconds after our designs became clearly known could result in the slaughter of the whole party.

At this point, Sergeant Major Marion Ross, the ranking soldier of the party, and as brave a man as we had, offered a respectful protest against going further. In substance, he said that circumstances had changed since we set out. It was a day later than planned. Many more Confederate troops were at Big Shanty than had been reported a few weeks before. We'd all seen the overloaded traffic of the road as we came down, and the full effects of Mitchel's attack would probably throw Western & Atlantic schedules into even worse confusion. On these counts, Ross thought it better to postpone the attempt or give it up altogether.

Andrews answered quietly. He admitted the facts as stated, but suggested that they operated in our favor, rather than against us. The military excitement, extra trains on the line and general commotion would make our irregular train the less likely to be suspected. As to the several thousand troops at Big Shanty's Camp McDonald, if we did our work promptly, they'd have no chance to interfere. Capturing the train at the moment it was surrounded by armed regiments might actually be easier than anywhere else, because no one would believe it possible and there'd therefore be no guard and little watchfulness.

Andrews could be plausible at any time, and with nearly any material, but on this morning, he hadn't yet completely convinced his hearers. Several others, among them J. A. Wilson, placed themselves frankly as sharing Ross's misgivings. I'd said nothing, for I felt at the time that we were under Andrews' leadership and should simply carry out orders, leaving the responsibility for them to rest on him.

In final answer to the doubts raised, Andrews first made plain that he wanted no man to come against his better judgment. Anyone in the room who thought the attempt too hazardous to try was still at liberty to switch to the down train for Atlanta and thereafter work his way back to the Union lines as best he could. For himself the decision was made.

"Boys," he said, "I tried this back in March and failed. Now I'll succeed or leave my bones in Dixie."

The words and manner won us all. He grasped our hands all around, and we hurried down to the platform, for the train was now almost due. By the time tickets had been procured, the train swept up to the platform. Hastily glancing at it in the early morning light, and seeing only that it was very long and apparently well filled, twenty of us—nineteen and Andrews, since Porter and Hawkins couldn't be seen—entered by different doors, but finally took places in one car.

KNIGHT: I sat up near the front of the car. Looking back I saw that most of our men were pale but steady.

DORSEY: It was just narrowly daylight on the morning of the 12th of April, when we boarded the northbound train at Marietta, twenty miles north of Atlanta, 118 miles south from Chattanooga, and more than 200 miles from General Mitchel at Huntsville, 100 miles west of Chattanooga. We took seats in the cars in a sleepy, drowsy manner, and to observers must have appeared indifferent to all surroundings. The conductor passed through the car, took up our fares apparently without noticing that we were strangers, and asked no questions. Some paid their fare to one point, some to another, so as not to attract attention, as all paying to one point might have done.

JOHN REED PORTER: Through some mistake or negligence of the hotel porter, Martin Hawkins and I weren't called in time for the train, as it left quite early, although we arrived at the depot in time to see the cars before they were out of sight. We gazed intently until the smoke of the locomotive disappeared in the morning twilight. I can't describe my feelings at that moment. I glanced at Hawkins, who appeared to be as much bewildered as myself. There we were in the heart of the Confederacy, knowing that if we were suspected of anything wrong we could expect death.

Trying not to make any move that would create suspicion, we started walking around the town, as if on no more business than a stroll.

WILLIAM A. FULLER: Early on the morning of April 12, 1862, a Saturday, I left Atlanta in charge of the passenger train, having three empty freight cars, next to the engine, which were intended to bring commissary stores from Chattanooga to Atlanta on the return trip.

[*William A. Fuller*]

When we reached Marietta, twenty miles from Atlanta, a considerable party of strangers, dressed in citizen's clothes, got aboard and paid their fare, some to one point and some to another. All that talked claimed to be refugees from within the Yankee lines, desirous of joining the Confederate army.

At that time, Big Shanty—the breakfast stop above Marietta—was the location of an army instruction center called Camp McDonald, and there were about 3,000 Confederate recruits there just then, being drilled ready to send to the front or into active service elsewhere. Deserters had been reported as slipping out from the camp, and the commanding officer had asked me and the other W. & A. conductors to be on the lookout and to arrest any soldier who got on the train without a pass. On men going to the camp, as anyone from below Big Shanty could be, we weren't keeping such a close watch.

MURPHY: The train arrived at Marietta, twenty miles from Atlanta, shortly after daylight. I stepped from the coach and noticed a number of men getting on the car forward of the one I rode. They were dressed like citizens from the country, and I supposed they were volunteers for the army, going to Big Shanty, later known as Kenesaw, a station about eight miles from Marietta, where troops were organized and forwarded to the Confederate army in Virginia and other points.

ALF WILSON: Hawkins and Porter being left that morning was a serious loss, for Hawkins was the most experienced engineer of the party, and the one originally selected to take first charge of the engine. It's not likely, though, that the result of the expedition would have been different, even with his practice and experience.

It can be seen by glancing at a map of Georgia that just to the north of Marietta, on the railroad, is the town of Kenesaw, or Big Shanty. It was the latter place, also called Camp McDonald, a place where Rebel recruits in great numbers were brought for organization and drill, that had been selected to strike the first blow by capturing the train, or such part of it as was wanted. Big Shanty is only eight or ten miles from Marietta, and there were two good reasons why we selected that particular station: there was no telegraph-sending officer there; and it was an eating station, where passengers were allowed twenty minutes for refreshments. This second point might save us the necessity of killing the engineer and fireman, who would, in all probability, leave the engine to go to the refreshment room. Aside from considerations of humanity, it was our wish to avoid any collision or delay, for there were thousands of Confederates camped within sight of the station.

The train we had taken passage on was the express, heavily loaded with passengers and drawn by a fine-looking locomotive. There was many an anxious gaze from one to another of our party after we had taken our seats in the cars that morning, as if to read the thoughts of each, as men will sometimes do drawn up in line just before a great battle when the skirmishers are slowly retreating before the advancing columns of the enemy. For my own part, I couldn't discover on a face in our party any sign of nervousness or fear. Each appeared cool, decided and resolute. Few words were spoken and we all seemed impatient for the decisive moment to arrive.

When the shrill whistle announced that we had arrived at the station, and the conductor sang out, "Big Shanty! Twenty minutes for breakfast!" and himself started for the restaurant, followed by the engineer and fireman, we felt a happy relief. The passengers were swarming into the eating house for breakfast pell-mell. Now was our time.

PITTENGER: The passengers, as we boarded at Marietta, had that listless and weary air generally prevailing on an early morning train. The conductor, whose name we afterwards learned to be William A. Fuller, entered and began to take tickets. He looked narrowly at us, for it was an uncommon thing for so many persons to enter in a body as did at Marietta. We also studied him carefully, for it was possible, if his suspicions were in the least aroused, that we'd have a fight in trying to take his train. Fuller was quite young for a conductor, being—as we afterward learned—only twenty-six, though he had been for seven years in that position. He had a frank, genial but resolute face, was of medium size, and looked active and strong. He accepted our tickets and moved on.

From Marietta to Big Shanty the railroad sweeps in a long bend of eight miles around the foot of Kenesaw Mountain, which lies directly between the two stations. The train ran slowly, stopping at several intervening points, and didn't reach Big Shanty until it was fully daylight. We had had little leisure for looking at the grand form of Kenesaw on our left; the question of deepest interest to us, and one which would be quickly solved, was how much of a fight we'd have at Big Shanty. If the train were left guarded during breakfast time, we would have to overcome the guards in a close-quarter fight. Every revolver had been carefully cleaned and loaded at Marietta before we slept, but the hope was that we wouldn't have to call on our weapons.

As we drew into the Big Shanty stop, we could see the white tents of the Rebel troops and even the guards slowly pacing their beats. When Andrews had been here on the previous expedition, few troops were seen, but the number was now greatly increased. It was difficult to establish even later how many were here on this day, because units and individuals were constantly coming and going, but there seem to have been three or four regiments, numbering not far from a thousand men each. They were encamped almost entirely on the west side of the road, but their camp guard included the railroad depot.

When the train stopped and the call came of, "Big Shanty! Twenty minutes for breakfast!" the conductor, engineer, fireman and most of the passengers covered quickly the forty feet over from the tracks to the long low eating shed, on the east side of the road. No guard whatever was left, yet for a moment we were compelled to keep our seats and await the appointed signal by our leader. It required a strong effort of will to keep from rushing forward. If anything could be gained by waiting five or ten of the twenty minutes scheduled for the stop, we knew that Andrews, with his marvelous coolness, would wait and expect us to do the same. It seemed already a considerable interval, for the last of the passengers who wanted and could pay for breakfast were leaving the car.

But Andrews meant no delay. Absent from the car for a time as we neared Big Shanty, he had only just returned and resumed his seat close to the door. Now he quietly rose, and without turning his head toward us, stepped toward the door with the passengers crowding out. Engineer Knight, whether from natural impulsiveness or at a signal from Andrews, rose also and went out with him. These two swung off on the side next to the military camp, and opposite the depot. They walked forward at an ordinary pace until abreast of the locomotive, which they saw to be vacant—engineer and fireman had gone to breakfast. [A brass plate bore the engine's name: *General*.]

Andrews walked a few steps farther forward, with Knight still at his side, until he could see ahead of the engine that the switches were open and the track clear as far as a curve a little way up the road, which blocked the view. Then they turned and walked back until just in advance of the first baggage car and behind the three empty freight cars, when Andrews said with a nod, "Uncouple here and wait for me." Complying, Knight drew out the pin and carefully laid it on the draw bar.

Back at the door of our car, Andrews opened it and spoke in his ordinary tone, not a whit louder or more hurried than usual.

"Come on, boys," he said. "It's time to go now."

Our hearts gave a great bound, but we rose quietly and followed him.

DORSEY: Since Andrews' last trip over this W. & A. line—and he had made two with the express object of surveying the line with a view to this expedition, actually walking many sections of the track between Big Shanty and Chattanooga for the purpose—a military camp of instruction had been established at Big Shanty. This camp was on the left or west side of the road, the guard line coming down to within perhaps fifty feet of the railroad track. The sentinels were pacing their beats, and we could hear the rattle of their tin cups and bayonets, as the soldiers getting breakfast in the camp pounded their rye coffee.

As the train came to a stand and trainmen and passengers rushed to the eating house, Andrews quietly stepped off on the opposite side, next to the camp, followed as quietly by Knight and Brown. On signal, some moments or minutes later, the rest of us in turn quietly stepped off on the same side, some of us at the front of the car where Andrews got off, some at the rear end of the car. There was no running, no excitement. Andrews walked rather briskly up to the head of the train, followed by the rest of us, all leisurely following with feigned indifference, but in reality with a resolution we had never felt before.

Although I had been in the army for about eight months, I had never been in a battle. I had enlisted under the impression that many young men had entertained on both sides, North and South, that if we put on a bold front, showed the opposite side that we meant to raise a large army and that the war would be a desperate one, the other side would give in rather than have a prolonged and desperate struggle. I say many of us enlisted under that impression, not that we weren't willing to fight if need be, but with a strong hope that it wouldn't be necessary to do much of it. Having lived a quiet, peaceful life up to the time of my enlistment, I had never before made up my mind that I could get the consent of my conscience to kill another unless in absolute self-defense, or in some equally justifiable cause.

But now I found myself placed in a position where, if need be, I

[*Dorsey*]
felt that I could have no regard for any man who might put himself in our way. We were there to get that engine and meant to have it. As I walked up along the side of that train with my hand on my revolver, for the first time in my life I felt that if a man opposed me, I could shoot him with perfect deliberation.

PITTENGER: Nothing that we had yet done was likely to attract the attention of the few passengers remaining in the cars, although this scarcely mattered any longer since the time for concealment was almost past. Outside, Andrews moved forward very swiftly and Knight, seeing him coming, ran on ahead and jumped on the engine. Seizing the throttle bar, Knight stood leaning forward, eyes on Andrews.

Andrews didn't follow immediately. He stood a step back from the locomotive, with one hand on the rail, watching the rest of us as we ran forward. Brown and Alf Wilson raced ahead and took their posts beside Knight on the engine. As soon as the rest of us reached the rear car of the three boxcars forward, we saw that its sliding door was wide open. Whether this was a happy accident, or whether, as is more likely, Andrews had gone forward at one of the earlier stops, with his usual audacity, and opened it himself, I don't know. But now as he motioned with his hand to us, calling, "Get in! Get in!" we needed no urging. The floor was breast-high, but the hindmost shoved and lifted the foremost and were themselves pulled up in turn. I helped throw Shadrach up and had my arm almost pulled off as I was dragged in by him a second after.

All this time a Rebel sentry was standing not a dozen feet from the locomotive, casually watching, as though this were the most ordinary proceeding, and a number of other soldiers were idling but a short distance away. They hadn't made up their minds what to say or do, and we were hidden by the train itself from the view of persons at the depot.

The scramble into the cars took seconds only, and as the last man was being yanked in, our chief swung up on the locomotive step and nodded to Knight, who hadn't taken his eyes from Andrews' face. Instantly the valve was thrown open, but for a terribly long moment, the locomotive seemed to stand still. Knight had thrown the full power on too suddenly, and the wheels slipped on the track, whirling with swift revolutions and the hiss of escaping steam, before the inertia of the ponderous machine could be overcome. But this was an instant only. None of the nearby soldiers had time to raise their muskets or give an alarm before the wheels "bit" and the train shot away.

ALF WILSON: Brown, Knight and myself, and then Andrews, sprang on the engine and we were off. The rest of the men had leaped into one of the boxcars. The Rebel guards on duty about the platform didn't at first seem to comprehend what was up, and when it was too late, looked after us in blank amazement.

We shot out lively for a short distance, perhaps nearly half a mile, as Knight had thrown the valve wide open, when we discovered that the engine had been damped and left with little steam or fire. We were compelled to come to a dead stop, and the way we put in wood and poured on oil wasn't slow by any means. We could see the surprised, dumfounded crowd—citizens, soldiers, officers and railroad men—gazing after us and running about in confusion. Several squads of soldiers, with their guns, started for us on the dead run, yelling like wild Comanches. Our fire was burning briskly by this time and we had no fear of them. We waited until they came within thirty or forty rods, then pulled the lever and rolled on slowly for some distance till we could gain a good head of steam. When the soldiers saw we had steam up, they came to a halt and opened a lively musketry fire on us. They did us no harm, and every revolution of the big wheels carried us farther beyond their reach.

FULLER: Seven miles from Marietta, at Big Shanty, the train made its breakfast stop. From before the war, Lacy's place there had been known for its first-rate food. Most of the passengers and train's crew went to the dining room of the hotel which was situated some forty feet from the track.

The passengers had taken seats at the table. I was on the opposite side of the table from the railroad, facing the train. Through the window, I saw some of the strangers who had got on at Marietta get up on the engine in an excited way and start off with it and three freight cars uncoupled from the passenger cars.

To my engineer, Jeff Cain, and to Anthony Murphy, then foreman of the Western & Atlantic Railroad shop, I said: "Someone who has no right to has gone off with our train."

All three of us got up and hurried out of the house just as the engine passed from sight.

MURPHY: At Big Shanty the train stopped for breakfast, and as the engineer, conductor, myself and passengers went to get our meals, no one was left in charge of the locomotive. The explanation of this apparent carelessness is found in the fact that Big Shanty was a recruiting station and a sentinel was stationed near the railroad track.

I had about finished breakfast when I heard a noise, as if steam were escaping, and looking through a window, I saw the cars move. Calling to our engineer and fireman at the table, I said to them, "Someone is moving your engine."

By this time, I was at the front door, and saw that the train was divided, the engine and three cars already passing out of sight. All at the table were at the door in a few seconds. What was the cause, and by whom was the engine moved? was asked by many voices. Cain, Fuller and myself consulted a moment. I asked Fuller about the great number of strangers who got on at Marietta.

"They had tickets to this point," Fuller said.

I was suspicious in a moment, and said, "They're the men who took the train!"

We, however, thought they were deserters, who would run the engine as long as the steam held out, the road being downgrade for many miles, and then abandon it. Fuller, Cain and myself concluded in a few minutes that our duty was to proceed after them.

DORSEY: The capture of the train—by the account of a Mr. Allen Price, a Confederate soldier at the time of the raid and in camp at Big Shanty—caused great excitement. The soldiers, disregarding discipline and guard-lines, ran pell-mell across lots in their wild effort to head off the captured *General*.

MURPHY: At Big Shanty Station itself, nothing could be done. There was no telegraph at this point. We started, and just at that time I saw Lon Kendrick come down the hill. He was connected with the road. I requested him to get a horse and go to Marietta, the nearest telegraph station, as fast as possible, and communicate with the superintendent at Atlanta, which he did.

In starting, various comments were made by those standing around as we put out on foot after a locomotive under steam. But knowing that we would reach a squad of track hands somewhere on the line, not far away, we jogged along and had some hopes.

Heading North 2

DORSEY: Away we sped. As we rolled out around a curve, far enough from the starting point to feel out of range of the enemy's guns, our spirits rose to a high pitch. The trees by the roadside seemed to wave us Godspeed, while the scream of our engine was like a shout for the Union. Andrews had told us, from the beginning, that to reach and take the train would be our hardest job. Once past that, success should be practically sure. We had taken our train, and we felt jubilant. I well remember that I jumped up and flourished my revolver over my head.

"Thank God, boys," I cried, "we're done playing Reb! We're blue-bellied Yankees again!"

George D. Wilson, older than most of us, wasn't as carried away.

"Don't be too fast, Dorsey," he cautioned me. "We're not out of the woods yet."

PITTENGER: And soon enough, it seemed as if we were to have serious trouble right at the start. The engine ran slower and slower, until it finally came to a full stop, not yet far from camp. There had been just one burst of speed, and then this alarming failure of power. We asked eagerly of those forward what it meant, and the answer was far from reassuring—"The steam has gone down."

DORSEY: Alf Wilson had taken station on the top of the cars as brakeman, which place he held throughout, except when serving as fireman, which he did for a good part of our run. Wilson, Andrews, Knight and Brown were all of the party readily visible to onlookers. The rest of us were in the boxcar, closed up from view except for occasional intervals between stations.

PITTENGER: At a second stop—beyond Moon's Station, something over two miles from Big Shanty—the telegraph wire was cut and we made our first attempts to obstruct the track. Cutting the wire was necessary, for though there was no telegraph office at Big Shanty, a portable battery might have been found, or a swift messenger sent back to Marietta to flash word ahead. No scheduled time was lost in this, for we'd started ahead of Fuller's usual time for leaving Big Shanty, and had some leeway.

Breaking a wire isn't as easy as it might seem; but we here adopted a plan which worked all day, and took up no time that wasn't utilized for other purposes. John Scott, who was as agile as a cat, scrambled up the twenty-foot pole, and knocking off the insulating box at the top, swung down on it. A small hacksaw found on the engine easily cut the tightly stretched wire close to the box. This didn't take more than one or two minutes.

At this first deliberate stop, Andrews came back and clasped our hands in triumph, showing more excitement than I had ever seen in him. We had the enemy now at such a disadvantage, he held, that they couldn't harm us or save the engine.

"When we've passed one more train," Andrews declared, "the coast will be all clear for burning the bridges and running on through to Chattanooga and around. For once, boys, we've got the upper hand of the Rebels."

By saying we had only one more train to pass before doing this, Andrews didn't mean that there was but one train coming toward us. Three scheduled southbound trains had already left Chattanooga; but only the first of these, a local freight which might be met at any point between this and Kingston, was a real obstacle. Andrews knew the time schedule of the other two, and could plan to meet them at any given station, even if we were far ahead of Fuller's time. Had there been none but these three trains, his first joy would have been well warranted.

The following—to the best of my knowledge—is the basis upon which Andrews made his calculations: he believed that no locomotive could be had nearer to Big Shanty than Kingston on the north, or Atlanta on the south, each about thirty miles distant. If the Rebels pursued toward Kingston, the best they could do was follow us on horses, and the time, allowing for delay in starting and the poor state of the roads, couldn't well be short of three or four hours, by which time we ought to be out of reach, with all our work done. If they rode or sent back to Marietta, which would seem to be their best plan, that would take at least an hour. A telegram then to Atlanta could very soon start a train after us, but by then it would be forty or fifty miles behind; and long before it could catch up, bridges would be burned, track and telegraph cut, and the road completely destroyed.

We expected to run on our train's regular time to Kingston, which would thus take about two hours, but to obstruct the track at several places on the way; then with the local freight safely passed, hurry on to the Oostanaula Bridge just before Resaca, twenty-four miles farther, in half an hour more. Burning that, we'd sweep on over the eleven bridges of the Chickamauga—also the one of the East Tennessee road, over the same stream—and leaving them in flames, bypass Chattanooga on the Y-switch running over to the Memphis & Charleston road, and press as rapidly as possible westward to Bridgeport, or wherever Mitchel might be.

It will be seen that leaving out of account any accident to our train, and any difficulty in passing the trains we were to meet, our calculations were reasonably sound. With two experienced engineers, and caution in running, accidents weren't likely to occur; and Andrews trusted to his own resourcefulness and commanding presence to disarm suspicion in any train crews met. On Friday, these calculations might have worked out with the precision of a machine. This day there were new elements that were to try our powers to the utmost.

All careful preparations were now made for a long run. A red flag placed on the last car showed that another train was behind, and served as a kind of unspoken excuse for being on the schedule of the morning mail. The engine was also closely inspected by Knight—whose mechanical knowledge was most useful throughout—and found to be in excellent working condition. After oiling it thoroughly, we moved leisurely onward until we came near Moon's Station, where some workmen were engaged on the track. The opportunity of getting necessary tools was too good to be lost. Brown sprang down and asked a man for a crowbar with which he was prying. The man gave it at once. Brown stepped back with his booty, a little disappointed, for one of the bent claw-footed bars, for pulling our spikes, would have been worth much more, but they had none.

As we went on, Andrews cautioned the engineers not to run too fast, which they were inclined to do. In this first part of the journey, it was important to hold to the train's usual time schedule.

DORSEY: Andrews wanted the road clear before beginning the work of destruction. We seemed to have things all our own way, calmly moving along as if we were to have no opposition, little dreaming of the awful storm that was gathering about us.

PITTENGER: Thus we passed through Acworth, and Allatoona, and then stopping again to cut the wire, also endeavored to lift a rail. While we were sure no train from Big Shanty could follow us, we wished also to block the way against one from Atlanta, if any should be sent from there. Of equal importance, we didn't wish the local freight to proceed southward after we met it, to avoid having it turned after us by pursuers.

A lifted rail is almost sure to derail an unsuspecting train. Yet the process of taking one up was far from easy without proper tools. A single pinchbar constructed for drawing out spikes would have enabled us to baffle all possible pursuit. But this we didn't have, and for each rail taken up, more than five minutes were consumed in battering out spikes with our crowbar, and afterwards prying others loose with handspikes, and with the rail itself. This delay wasn't immediately dangerous, for in this first stage of the run we had spare time if we were to hold to schedule. The rails when lifted were carried away with us, and the break thus left was for a time a barrier—to a train not supplied with track-laying tools—as absolute as a burnt bridge.

There was an exultant sense of superiority while running along in the midst of enemy country in this manner, such as a man in a balloon might feel while drifting over hostile camps or over the raging waves of the ocean. As long as all is well with his balloon, the man needn't care what takes place in the world below; and as long as our engine retained its power and the track was clear before us, we were in a similar state of security. But a knife-blade thrust in the silk globe overhead, or the slightest tear in the delicate fabric, will in a second take away the security of the man in the clouds. So the loosening of a bolt, or the breaking of a wheel, would have left us powerless among our enemies; and the chance of these hazards, always near, couldn't be forgotten for any part of our passage through the towns and fields and woods of the enemy's land.

At length we reached the Etowah River and there safely passed over the great bridge. No stop was made, though the first serious cause for anxiety was here visible. Up to this point everything had worked as calculated, and our confidence in our leader and in final success was correspondingly increased. Now, on a side track—which connected with a spur line that then ran up the river about five miles to the Etowah iron works and rolling mills—there stood a locomotive. It was but a short distance from us, and the smoke rising from the funnel showed only too plainly that it was ready for work, thus constituting an element, of the most dangerous character, which hadn't been included in our planning.

It was named the *Yonah*, an engine used by the owners of the iron works for their own purposes. Thoroughly as Andrews had explored the road, I believe he was unaware of its existence until the moment when he saw it standing on the side track not a dozen yards away, and looking as if it were ready to enter upon a race with our *General* on equal terms. It was still thirteen miles to Kingston, and the enemy, if there was any direct pursuit, would be able to get a locomotive there much sooner than we had supposed possible.

Several men were gathered around the *Yonah*, but not enough to seem formidable to our party. At the first sight of the standing engine, Knight spoke his mind directly to Andrews.

"We'd better destroy that," Knight said. "And this bridge with it."

Andrews shook his head.

"It won't make any difference," he said.

The morning was damp, and it had already begun to rain slightly.

FULLER: The enterprise, while daring, was both practicable and possible. Andrews had traveled over the Atlanta-Chattanooga route many times, and acquainted himself with its location and condition. He was familiar with the stations, passing points and the manner of running the trains. He knew the location of all the bridges on the line, and that they were wooden structures of the Howe truss pattern, weather-boarded, covered with shingles, and very combustible. He also knew that at the time they were guarded by but a single guard each.

Mr. Andrews' plan worked without a hitch, at least up to the time of the capture of my engine, the *General*, and the three freight cars attached between it and the passenger cars. When I discovered that someone had run away with the engine and a portion of my train, I at once sent out in pursuit on foot. This seemed to be funny to some of the crowd standing around by the hotel there, but it wasn't so to me.

I ran two and a half miles, and when I say run, I don't mean trot, gallop or pace. I mean run. At this point I came upon the section hands, who were in great surprise at the conduct of some strangers who had just left there. In a hurry, they told me that the captors of the train had stopped there and taken their tools from them, and that there were about twenty of them, all strangers, and working in

[*Fuller*]
great haste. Up to this time I'd supposed that the captors were Confederates, in camp at Big Shanty, who wanted to ride out of the camp lines and thus pass the guards so they could visit home, without a passport. But when I heard the story from the track hands I knew it must be a Yankee trick, and from there on I was twice as sure I'd have to get my train back.

I put the hand car (a pole car used for hauling crossties) on the track as quickly as possible and pushed back with all the strength in me to Jeff Cain and Anthony Murphy, who were coming along after me. When they were on the hand car, we turned north again in the pursuit. We pushed by turns, one riding at a time. I fully believed that by a desperate effort I could run to Etowah Station, distant twenty miles, before the *Yonah*, the engine of the Cooper iron works, left that station. And if I could possibly succeed in doing so, I'd take that engine in the pursuit. This plan I made known to Cain and Murphy, and we all bent ourselves to the work.

ALF WILSON: The men around the *Yonah* evidently regarded us with surprise or suspicion. The railroad men knew the locomotive we were on, but the hands were all strangers to them. Besides, we were a wild train ahead of the express, and unannounced. But we didn't parley or answer questions nor stop until we reached the tank, where we took on water and wood. Then we pulled out at rapid speed.

MURPHY: We did meet a car and hands near Moon's Station, about two miles from the "Shanty." We pressed into service their car and two hands to propel it. (Hand cars in those days were driven by poles, men standing on the car and pressing the poles against the ties, or ground, as I have seen boatmen do with their boats on canals. There were no crank cars in those days in our section.)

We had proceeded but a short distance with our pole car, when we reached a pile of crossties on the track, and found the telegraph wire cut. This changed our minds as to deserters, for if they were, they meant more than we first expected. Clearing off the ties we pressed on, until we reached Acworth Station, six miles from Big Shanty. At this point we learned that the engineer had examined the journals, carefully oiling all parts, and then had moved off at a lively speed.

This satisfied me that whoever they were, they understood their business, and meant something more than deserters would attempt. Then we thought for the first time of enemies from the Federal army. However, we moved on to Allatoona, the point for which I had first shipped. There I found that the station engine was not in such bad order as to require my immediate attention, under the circumstances, and I moved on.

At Allatoona we obtained two old shotguns, one for Fuller and one for myself. I really didn't know how long they had been loaded, nor do I yet, for we never fired them. These were the only arms in our engine during the chase. Two citizens went along from there, making about seven men on our little pole car, pretty well crowding it.

As we proceeded toward Etowah, we moved rapidly, this being downgrade. We were making good time as we neared the place where we intended to leave the pole car, when suddenly we beheld an open space in the track. A piece of rail had been taken out by the raiders. Having no brake, we couldn't hold our car in check, and it plunged into the gap, turning over with all hands except Fuller and myself. We jumped before the car left the track. Putting the car back on the rails, we left one of our polers here to run back and have the next section crew repair the track.

F. M. GREGG: At Acworth, George Martin and George Rainey joined the chase, and another man, White Smith, was sent to Allatoona by horse, hoping that the engine would be abandoned, and he would thus be able to head them off. Seeing no one, [Smith] rejoined the pursuit at Allatoona.

FULLER: At Acworth, seven miles north of Big Shanty, we armed ourselves with double-barreled shotguns. I didn't have time all day to examine mine to see whether or not she was loaded. On we pressed and pushed. When our strength was nearly gone, we hove in sight of Etowah, and to our great delight the engine was there.

Just at that moment, in a short curve, looking ahead, we saw, but too late to stop, that the track had again been taken up. Again, pell-mell, into the ditch we were thrown, but we were too much elated at the sight of the engine, not more than a mile distant, to be bothered by anything so insignificant. We carried the car across the break in the track and pushed on to Etowah. In five minutes we had the engine *Yonah* running at full speed toward Kingston, distant fourteen miles.

PORTER: That Saturday morning in Marietta the news soon reached the town that a train had been captured at Big Shanty, while the passengers and crew were at breakfast, and that it had been done so quickly and easily, no one could imagine who did the deed, or what it meant. Soon everything was wild with excitement, and the town was thronged with excited Rebels, waiting to hear further developments regarding the wild train, as it was termed.

Hawkins and I concluded to skip out, one at a time, though keeping sight of each other, and make our way to the country unmolested, if possible. In this we succeeded, and after reaching a piece of woods we came together, congratulated ourselves upon our success thus far, but what to do next we hardly knew. We felt certain that the chances of our getting away in the present state of excitement weren't the best, and after much hesitation and doubt we determined to go to Big Shanty, to Camp McDonald, as it was a Rebel camp of instruction, and join the Rebel army, and thus be enabled to make our escape, when sent to the front, by deserting a picket post or taking the first opportunity that might offer for escape in any manner.

We proceeded on our way, intending to reach Camp McDonald about sundown, thinking perhaps that by this time the excitement would somewhat subside.

PITTENGER: The *Yonah* and Etowah Bridge left behind, we rolled on through Cartersville, a town of considerable size, leaving many astonished and disappointed passengers on the platform, and continued without incident until we reached Cass Station. The town of Cassville is some distance from the railroad, but the station was important to us as the regular place for taking on wood and water. Here we stopped and began to wood up.

William Russel—as we later learned the tender's name to be—was naturally curious about the appearance of such a bobtailed train running on the time of the morning mail, with no passengers and none of the regular hands.

ALF WILSON: Andrews went into the office and procured the switch keys and a schedule, telling the office man that he was running an extra train through with powder and ammunition to General Beauregard, who was hard-pressed at Corinth by Grant and out of ammunition, and the greatest possible haste was necessary. The story, trumped up on the spur of the moment or not, had much semblance of truth, although we didn't know it.

Not a week had elapsed since the battle at Shiloh, and Generals Grant and Halleck were at that very time confronting an outnumbered Beauregard at Corinth. To give further plausibility to our story, there was in the express car a prodigious iron-bound safe, containing probably a wagonload of Confederate scrip, with which to pay off the Rebel soldiers under Beauregard. The account given was satisfactory to the man, who said he'd willingly take off his shirt and send it to Beauregard if it would do any good.

PITTENGER: Andrews' powder story—I became convinced later—was adroit and carefully planned, with enough of foundation to make it probable. His claim was that he had been sent by General Beauregard, who was in desperate straits for ammunition, to impress a train, have it loaded with gunpowder, and run it through at top speed. Had he been pressed more closely, Andrews could probably have produced contrived passes proving himself worthy of belief. But it wasn't necessary to go so far. The very appearance of Andrews—tall, commanding, and perfectly self-possessed, speaking like one long accustomed to authority—was so much like the ideal Southern officer that Russel's credence was won at once. The station-keeper knew very well that after such a battle as the one at Pittsburg Landing, it was natural that gunpowder should be scarce, and if it didn't come at once, what more natural than to send for it?

Seeing the impression that he had made, Andrews, who of course didn't work at throwing on wood, but left that to his companions, asked if he couldn't be supplied with a current timetable, as it might be useful. Russel, in his patriotic fervor, took down and handed out his own schedule, saying that he'd send his shirt to Beauregard if the latter wanted it.

WILLIAM RUSSEL: I'd as soon have suspected Mr. Jefferson Davis himself as a man who talked with the assurance Andrews did.

PITTENGER: We were now within seven miles of Kingston, re-supplied with wood and water, and with a full, up-to-date schedule of the trains on the road. But at Kingston we had more reason to apprehend danger than anywhere else along the route. A branch road from Rome—linking with boat traffic on the Coosa River—connected at Kingston with the main track, and the morning train from that town would be awaiting our arrival. This, with the local freight which we hoped to meet, and the complicated arrangement of the switches, would constitute no small obstacle. Andrews had

[*Pittenger*]
made himself familiar with the working of the road at this point, as also at Dalton and Chattanooga, and we'd soon be able to see how he'd overcome the hindrances in his way.

Heading North 3

PITTENGER: We reached Kingston a little ahead of time. The local freight hadn't yet arrived. Without the slightest hesitation, Andrews ran a few hundred yards past the station, and ordered the switch-tender to set the switch so as to throw us on the side track. We then backed out on it, stopping on the west side of the station, and almost directly alongside the Rome passenger train, then lying on its own track, which joined the main line a few yards further north. This train was expecting the coming of Fuller's mail, and, of course, the arrival of our three-car train in place of the one they were expecting made their eyes pop. Their engineer stepped over to the *General*.

"How's this?" he asked, with an oath. "What's up? Here's Cain's engine with none of their men aboard."

ALF WILSON: Finding a new and strange set of men aboard and no passenger cars, the railroad men at Kingston didn't know what to make of us. They knew the locomotive and asked us what we were doing on it. We told them the same ammunition-for-Beauregard story that Andrews had told, but still they seemed to think something wasn't right. When Andrews, however, who was clothed in somewhat of a military dress, stepped back and told them the same story in his serious and impressive way—that he had charge of the train by government authority, and that it was very important that there be no delay—and also assured them that Fuller's express train would be along soon, they seemed a little more reconciled.

PITTENGER: Andrews waved his hand toward the car in which we were shut up—representing the powder, if we'd known it—and they inquired no further in that direction, but simply asked when the passenger train would be along. Assuming indifference, Andrews answered that he couldn't tell exactly, but supposed it wouldn't be a great while, as another train was being fitted out when he left Atlanta. With this cold comfort, the inquiring railroaders were obliged to be contented.

Andrews, leaving the *General* in care of Knight, Wilson and Brown, went into the telegraph office, which was on the western side of the depot next us. What was the matter with the local freight—he asked inside—that it wasn't yet at Kingston? In reply, he was shown a telegraph dispatch for Fuller, ordering him to wait at this point for the freight's coming, an indication that it wasn't very far away.

Andrews returned to the *General*, and stood or walked about on the end of the platform nearby during the hard moments of waiting that followed. He didn't seek to enter into conversation with anyone, but quietly answered any questions asked. He appeared abstracted and a little anxious, as of course might have seemed natural for one running a special ammunition train, on which the safety of an army might depend. His real and assumed characters here may have reached a point of nearly complete agreement.

Brown, Knight and Wilson attended to their engine, seeing that all was in good order with a reasonable head of steam, and refrained, as far as they could, from any kind of conversation, answering all demands, after the first, in monosyllables. Their position during this enforced stop was embarrassing, but possibly less painful than ours in the boxcar. The rest of us could hear low murmurs outside; we knew we were at a station, and alongside another train, and could hear the tread of feet; but we couldn't learn why we didn't press on.

A thousand conjectures will spring up at such times. We had a tolerably high estimate of our fighting power, and didn't doubt that we could capture any ordinary train, or the usual crowd around a village station. But to be shut up in the dark, while for all we knew the enemy might be concentrating an overwhelming force against us, was exceedingly trying, and put the implicit confidence we had in our leader to a very severe test. There was one precaution Andrews had neglected—probably because he trusted so fully in his own powers. No lieutenant was appointed. One who could have taken charge of the men, leaving Andrews free to plan and give general directions, would have been a support to us now, and a help to all of us later. With George D. Wilson or some other of the soldiers as authorized second, the force would have been in better fighting trim, and what's of more importance, Andrews would have felt more free to order the capture of any pursuing train. But at present we had nothing to do but wait till the road was cleared for us.

Before suspense became intolerable, the whistle of an approaching train was heard, and the local freight rumbled up to the eastern side of the depot, and stopped before it on the main track. Andrews made haste to begin the inevitable conference. He went over and spoke to the conductor, telling him to pull his train—which was quite long—southward on down the road so that we might get out of the switch and proceed on our way. In explanation, the same powder story was given. This conductor saw that Andrews was treated with marked deference by the people about the station, and didn't hesitate to believe his story and obey the order.

Before the train could be started up, Andrews noticed a red flag on the hind car.

"What does that mean?" he demanded. "I'm ordered to get this powder through to Beauregard, and here you are signaling another train after you on the track."

No doubt Andrews felt all the vexation he expressed. The freight conductor said he was sorry, but it couldn't be helped. The reason he then supplied was a startling piece of intelligence. Mitchel had captured Huntsville and was said to be advancing eastward toward Chattanooga by forced marches. As the Confederate officials there had no force to resist him, they were running everything out of Chattanooga, and had put a long extra train on the track to get the rolling stock, as well as the supplies, out of the way. Andrews thanked him for the information and told him to move on well down the track so that his northbound extra would have room enough to get by.

"I must be off the first possible minute," Andrews added.

The conductor made no objection, but asked what Andrews expected to do about Mitchel at Huntsville.

"I don't believe he's there," Andrews said. "But if he is fool enough to be, Beauregard will soon sweep him out. Either way, I have my orders."

The freight was shifted down the road enough to leave the way clear for us, and the tedious process of waiting resumed.

MURPHY: On arriving at Etowah we had found the engine *Yonah*, owned by the Cooper Iron Company, and run on a branch road for their private use. We pressed this locomotive into our service and left the little car that had proved so useful to us.

Getting an open car and stocking it with some rails, spikes and tools, to repair the track if needed, we moved on with the *Yonah* to Cartersville. At this point we had intended to get horses to ride to Kingston if we had failed to find the *Yonah* at Etowah.

Passing on to Rogers Station, we learned that the raiders had stopped there, and received wood and water, telling the station master they were under military orders and that the engine crew proper were coming on behind. We pushed on, pressing the *Yonah* hard.

PITTENGER: On our side track to the left of Kingston Station, the wait for the extra freight was agonizingly long. When we almost despaired, it finally came. On it, however, to the shocked dismay of Andrews, and those on the engine, was still another red flag. Asked the meaning of another train following, the conductor of this extra freight explained that there had been too many cars and too great a load for one engine. Accordingly, a second section of the extra freight had been made up, and would be along shortly.

The delay for these two trains had already been almost an hour; and here was a third train still blocking the road before us. Had Andrews taken the risk of running out in the face of the first extra, we might already have made at least the first station above. Now, unable to chance greater risk through trying to halt the second section by telegraph, it would be insanely rash to try running out between the two sections of a belated train. It was better to wait, even if that entailed the risk of a fight. Andrews signaled to Knight, quietly gave his instructions.

Leaving Andrews, Knight sauntered carelessly along down the train, just as though he were tired to death with waiting and didn't know what to do with himself. Leaning against our closed boxcar, without turning his head or eyes toward us, he spoke in a low tone, clearly heard by those of us within.

"Boys," he told us, "we've got to wait a while more for one more train that's behind time, and the local folks around are getting edgy. If you're called, be ready to jump out and fight."

We could only look to the priming of our pistols, and to the handiness of our spare ammunition, while we kept on waiting.

F. M. GREGG: The pistols Ross and Wollam carried were of Colt's make, shooting ten times and having two hammers. That of Andrews was ivory-handled and a fine weapon.

PITTENGER: Outside, the crowd gathered around had grown, and there was increased grumbling and resentment of Andrews' high-handedness. The questions asked—particularly by the old switch-tender in charge—grew sharper by the minute, such as why Fuller and the regular train weren't yet along, and why the superintendent of the road at Atlanta hadn't sent notice of the special ammunition train.

Andrews dealt with each question raised, briefly and plausibly, although without appearing at all concerned over anyone's opinion. He even did some grumbling of his own about the bad management of a railroad that would allow its track to be blocked at such a time of urgency, and added accounts of himself at Beauregard's headquarters—all of it with an air so confident and truthful that no one ventured to challenge him.

Our three men who were outside declared later that they hadn't seen the slightest indication of fear, disappointment or impatience on the part of Andrews, save such impatience as he showed when telling how much Beauregard was in need of his ammunition, and what a shame it was that the road should be clogged by ordinary travel when the fate of the Confederacy's brave soldiers was in the balance. To the questioners, Andrews explained that it was because Beauregard couldn't get his orders filled in time through ordinary channels that he had sent Andrews to bring the powder through by force, if necessary. And if the officials at home didn't support the army in the field better, Andrews had gone on, his own opinion was that martial law would soon be proclaimed. Such indignation and threats were applauded by those bystanders who wished to be thought especially loyal to the Rebel cause, and, for at least the first half-hour, served to curb all distrust.

I think there was only one thing, apart from the dangerous delay itself, which Andrews really dreaded. He kept very near the telegraph office, and without seeming to do so, closely watched the operator within. An attempt by the operator to send any kind of a message about us would probably have brought on an immediate collision.

Brown tells of a curious incident as occurring here. From the engine, he noticed a man standing by who watched Andrews for a short time, and then, when no one else was near, stepped close to him and handed him a large and seemingly well-filled envelope. Andrews smiled, placed the envelope in his breast pocket. With no further exchange, the man stepped away. Brown intended to ask about the matter, but more pressing business put it out of his mind. Probably this was an incident of Andrews' contraband trade, and the package contained an order for goods with the money to pay for them. If Andrews was recognized during this day by any who knew him, as he seems to have been more than once, he wasn't at all compromised by such meeting at the time, as long as the train wasn't known to be taken by the Yankees. Whether successful or not, of course, this day's work must eventually have ended his double role and closed the South to him.

We had been at Kingston a full hour—to those of us shut up within the boxcar, it seemed nearer a harrowing half-day—when the enormously welcome whistle of the third train from the north was heard. This last extra pulled in at the platform as the others had done, and was at once ordered by Andrews to draw on down the road that we might have room to go out. The conductor obeyed without hesitation, and this obstruction was removed.

It only remained to reset the switch so that we might again get on the main track. This Andrews directed the switch-tender to do; but the grumpy old yardman had been getting in a worse and worse humor for the whole of the last hour. Hanging up his keys, he now defiantly declared he wouldn't take them down again till this fancy stranger showed him by what authority he was ordering everybody around as if he owned the whole state road. We who were shut up in the boxcar heard the loud and angry voice, and supposed that the time for us to act had come, but Andrews only laughed goodhumoredly, as though the anger of the old man amused him.

"I've no more time to waste with you," he said.

Ignoring the old man's hot calls for aid from the crowd around him, Andrews stepped into the station, found the keys where he had seen them put up, took them down, walked out quietly and swiftly and made the change himself. The tender stormed after him, swore, said he'd report the trespasser and have him arrested. Calmly, Andrews handed back the switch keys and signaled to Knight. As our *General* came promptly up, Andrews lifted his hand in half-salute to the crowd and swung aboard the moving locomotive. We rolled out on the main track and were off.

It had been a fearful but well-met ordeal. The hour and five minutes we were at Kingston, added to the two-hour run preceding, made us three hours and five minutes from Big Shanty as we left the junction and started around the sharp northward curve beyond.

Just four minutes later, at Kingston, Fuller and Murphy arrived.

Heading North 4

FULLER: We made the fourteen-mile run from Etowah to Kingston in fifteen minutes. When we arrived there, greatly to our annoyance we found many heavy freight trains, which, at the demand of the raiders, had been run past the station in order to let them out at the further, or north, end of the siding. This forced me to abandon the *Yonah*, as it would have been sure defeat if I'd delayed long enough at Kingston to have had all those trains pull by so as to have let me pass them.

By double-quicking more than two miles to the north end of the town, to a point where I knew the Rome engine, according to the schedule, was standing, I, with a few volunteers, took that engine [the *William R. Smith*] in the pursuit. I took my stand on the cowcatcher of the Rome engine and told the engineer to watch me and I would look out for obstructions ahead. At very short intervals after leaving Kingston, there were crossties thrown upon the track. This they could do, without stopping, from a hole punched in the rear of their last boxcar, but I was forced to slack speed to remove the ties.

MURPHY: On reaching Kingston we found they had left, after assuming control of passing trains and stating that they were carrying ammunition to General Beauregard on the line of the Memphis & Charleston Railroad. They also said that Fuller and Engineer Cain were behind on another train.

At this point we came near losing the advantage we had gained by starting on foot. We met several trains that delayed us, and also had delayed Andrews. I gave up the *Yonah* to the engineer to return to Etowah, and coupled the engine *New York* to the supply car we had for emergencies, and was ready to start. Fuller, in the meantime, went forward to the depot, giving the news, which caused great excitement. I sent him word to clear the track so we could get out. Kingston is where the Rome road connects with the Western & Atlantic, and the Rome engine and train were in our way. I learned that Fuller couldn't control the crowd on the other train, and they pulled out for the chase with the Rome engine and some cars attached, greatly to my disappointment. I had to abandon my outfit and run to get on their train.

We had no control over this crew. Everyone was wild, the engine was small, with very low driving wheels, and there were several cars loaded with people, so that we made slow time and I feared the day was lost.

PITTENGER: The ceaseless rain was now severe. As soon as we were well out of sight of Kingston Station, we stopped, and Scott, with a man at each foot to give him a boost, was in a moment at the top of the telegraph pole, the box was knocked off and the wire cut. While this was being done, others threw a few obstructions on the track.

Once more on board, we noticed an exhilarating quickening of speed. We had been running slowly since leaving Big Shanty—to hold to schedule—but now Andrews said to his crew, "Push her, boys, push her."

Wilson heaped in the wood, and the fire was soon roaring, with great clouds of smoke escaping. Our leader's intention was to reach Adairsville in a few minutes, in order to meet there two further trains which were now overdue. These were the regular through freight and southern-bound passenger trains, normally scheduled to wait at this station for the train we had taken over. Our terrible delay at Kingston had been unfortunate in all ways. If there had been no extra trains, we could by this time in all probability have been at Dalton, forty miles farther up the road, with the Oostanaula Bridge burned behind us, and, these two trains passed, with no further serious obstacle to contend with.

But while so anxious to reach Adairsville, the next station above, where there was a side track, we couldn't afford to leave the way open behind us from Kingston, as the distance is only ten miles, and if a pursuing train were started from there, it could be dangerous. So it seemed that we had scarcely got under full headway when the tender-brakes—all that we had on our train—were put sharply down. We piled out, and under the energetic leadership of Andrews, went hard to work at lifting the track. We again cut the wire, and also loaded on a large number of crossties and other kinds of wood to be used in bridge burning. We were the more anxious for a great deal of fuel, since the hard and continuing rain would render difficult in any case the kindling of quick-spreading fires.

Lifting a rail may sound easy enough, but it was far from easy in practice. The rail is long and heavy; it's securely bolted to other rails and fastened with great spikes driven into solid oak ties, which in turn are deeply imbedded in the ground. This was the first place we wished to take up a rail very quickly, and accordingly we were far more aware of the difficulty than when we had had more time. We weren't overly agitated, for we still believed ourselves an hour ahead of any probable pursuit; but we wanted very badly to pass the two trains still before us and hurry to our real work of bridge burning. Slowly we drew out spike after spike, battering at the great nails with our one iron bar. A large load of ties was on board before the stubborn rail was half worked loose.

The rail was giving at the southern end, and for perhaps two-thirds of its length of sixteen feet or so was cleared of spikes. Eight of us took hold of it to try to pull out the remainder by the rail itself. The spikes were too firmly fixed. We were about to give up the attempt and wait to batter out a few more, when away in the distance we heard, faintly but unmistakably, the whistle of a northbound locomotive. It could only be in pursuit of us, and no sound more unwelcome ever fell on human ears.

DORSEY: A little way out from Kingston, we halted, cut the wire, and were tearing up the track when Andrews discovered a train from the south curling its smoke up over the tree tops as it came screaming along after us.

Some half-dozen more of us sprang forward and grabbed the end of the rail that had been half loosened by the men drawing out the spikes. With one convulsive effort we broke it, leaving perhaps one-fourth of it still on the ties. This was in a cut, and when the rail broke we fell, the end of the rail catching in the bank and checking our fall.

Throwing the broken rail into our car, we again pushed on for Adairsville, now at the highest rate of speed possible.

FULLER: Six miles north of Kingston the raiders had taken up several rails of the track in their rear and carried them away. As well, they had cut the telegraph wire, as they invariably had done wherever they stopped.

When I came to this gap—having neither tools to work with nor time to delay, and knowing that according to regular schedule, a down freight was at that moment due at Adairsville, four miles north—I abandoned the Rome engine and called for volunteers to join me in another foot race. When I'd run half a mile or so, I looked back. Anthony Murphy was the only man following me.

MURPHY: Luck, however, hadn't left us. A few miles above Kingston we found a pile of crossties on the rails, and the telegraph wires cut. Clearing the track, we moved on a few miles farther, where we found another gap in the track. A rail had been taken out and carted away. To me this was a relief—to get rid of our small engine and a crowd so wild. I knew that we would soon meet the engine *Texas* with a freight train, and probably an extra mixed freight and passenger train that was out of time and which might cause our quarry some delay.

Fuller and myself left the Rome train at this point and pressed on again on foot, advising the crowd to return, which they did; but if they would follow, we told them how they could take up a rail from behind the train, place it in front and follow us.

We expected to get to Adairsville, about five miles from where the rail was taken up, before the *General* could leave. Rain had commenced just before, and as we proceeded on foot with our old rusty guns, the ground proved too soft for fast walking and it became apparent we couldn't reach Adairsville before the locomotive left.

PITTENGER: As we came in sight of Adairsville Station, there lay the freight train. Actually, it had long been waiting for us, as we were now a half-hour behind Fuller's normal time. It was holding up as well for the overdue morning passenger train from Chattanooga, which should have overtaken the freight at this point. The panic in Chattanooga, and resulting extra trains on the road, had disordered the whole schedule and enormously increased our difficulties.

As we neared the station, speed was slackened, and we stopped on the main track beside the through freight. Andrews at once answered the usual storm of questions and asked others in turn. He heard still more of Mitchel's operations; the telegrams were being interrupted nearer and nearer east from Huntsville along the Memphis & Charleston line, so that, from every indication, the Union forces were coming to Chattanooga.

However it might be with Mitchel, Andrews' chief immediate interest was in news of the down passenger train, now a good half-hour late. Lacking information on it, the freight conductor had determined to run on south on arrival of Fuller's train, in line with their railroading rule at the time, by which a following train was to be waited for only a certain length of time. Andrews approved, saying that Fuller with the regular train would probably wait for the freight at Kingston. Andrews might have held this train here by giving a message as from Fuller, but he preferred to get rid of it, so that if compelled soon after to back before the belated passenger, the freight might not be in the way; and if compelled to fight, the fewer of the enemy the better. Otherwise, its running down to the site of the broken rail was undesirable.

As he prepared to leave, the conductor looked at Andrews inquiringly.

"You'll of course remain here till my passenger train comes?" he asked. "And tell them they can overhaul me at Kingston?"

"No," said Andrews. "I'll have to go out at once. If the Yankees attack Beauregard, he hasn't powder enough for a three-hour fight."

Startled by this possibility, and forgetting about Mitchel being in the way—the other men on both sides had heard this exchange, but hadn't joined in—the patriotic conductor gave way promptly.

"Get through by all means," he said. "But you'll have to run very slow and put a flagman on every curve, or you'll have a collision."

"I'll attend to that," Andrews answered.

He stepped back quickly to our engine, motioning to Knight, who was still at the throttle. Knight, having heard the supposed promise about running slowly, put on steam in a gradual manner, and we moved off at a moderate rate of speed.

But this wasn't to last; neither was any flagman to be sent ahead. There had been delays enough. Beyond the first concealing curve, the time had come to take a great and deliberate risk. We didn't dare wait for the passenger train because of the pursuers whose whistle we had heard—who might join with the freight crew above the rail break—and we were compelled to reach the station above before it could start out.

From Adairsville to Calhoun, the next station that had a side track, is a little more than nine miles. Running directly north, the road is almost straight and quite level, making it the most favorable stretch of the whole line for fast running.

"Let's see how fast she can go," was Andrews' order to his three-man crew. "We'll want every second we can save from here to Calhoun."

These orders were given to men who'd been straining all morning to break loose. The *General* was in the finest running condition. Knight had oiled its parts carefully during the long wait at Kingston, and again to some extent at Adairsville, and a heavy head of steam had been built up during the stop at the latter station. Now the full force of the mighty power was turned on at once, while oil was poured on wood-chunks and these fed into the firebox.

The three cars and twenty men were no load for the powerful engine, and it sprang to its work with a shock that nearly took all of us in the boxcar from our feet. Our car was so close to the engine that it felt every impulse of power, and there wasn't the weight of following cars to steady it. The engine itself seemed to be not so much running as coursing with great lionlike bounds along the track.

MURPHY: We met the *Texas* about two miles below Adairsville Station. I had great admiration for the *Texas*, and based on it my hope of still winning the race if we reached Adairsville in a reasonable time after the raider's departure. The *Texas* had the same class of engine as the *General*, and was in fine order, having five-foot wheels and being recently out of the shop, where a thorough repair had been given it under my own supervision. Driving wheels, truck and tender wheels were in fine shape, and it was almost as safe to run it backward as forward, and backward we had to run it.

Meeting this train, we motioned the engineer—Peter Bracken—to stop, went aboard, turned him back to Adairsville, placed the cars on the side track and proceeded in haste. From Bracken and his conductor, we heard the same tale about the wild train with powder for General Beauregard.

FULLER: When we got within a mile of Adairsville, having run three miles on foot, Murphy and I met the down express freight train, twenty-one cars in length. Seeing me, the engineer at once reversed, as he had been feeling somewhat dissatisfied at the strange conduct of the raiders whom he had just met at Adairsville. I took a position on top of the rear car of the train, while Murphy, coming up in a few moments, got on the engine. Backing, we rushed north again for Adairsville.

Within two hundred yards of the switch at Adairsville, I jumped off the train, ran ahead and changed the switch so as to throw the cars on the side track. With the cars shunted off, I threw the switch back for the main track and jumped on the engine as it came by. We did this throwing-off so quickly that for many yards the cars and the engine were running along side by side.

I now had just the engine, the *Texas*, with the following for crew: Anthony Murphy; Peter Bracken, the engineer; Henry Haney, fireman; and Alonzo Martin, wood-passer. We resumed the chase, heading for Calhoun ten miles away.

DORSEY: Soon after we pulled out of Adairsville, it was established later, the southbound train was about to pull out, when another engine—the *Texas*—was heard in the distance screaming and roaring at a fearful rate. It soon dashed by, leaving the people wild with excitement. This engine was closely followed by another, with two passenger coaches loaded with armed men, and from one of these someone on the steps or platform, either from his misunderstanding of the situation or on mischief bent, set the people wild by exclaiming: "The country's alive with Yankees! The country's alive with Yankees!"

At least, this startling rumor of an invasion in progress got out somewhere, and presumably it was here.

PITTENGER: In the boxcar, as we fled away for Calhoun, we were jerked about and thrown from side to side, and time after time, we had the temporary conviction that we had leaped the track. We hardly knew what the breakneck speed meant. Although we pushed our door partly open, the risk of being thrown out prevented us from opening it wider, and the glimpses of flying rock, woods and fields we could catch gave us no clue in explanation of the frantic pace, for we could perceive no sign of pursuit. There was slight danger of our being seen in the open door; the sight of the wild, spark-showering engine would have taken all the attention any chance onlooker had to give.

Andrews, we were told later, scarcely looked ahead while making this run. Brown and Knight, however, did keep a sharp lookout, trying to be ready when we came near Calhoun—if we should make it—to shut off steam and begin pulling to a stop. They had no hope of stopping in time if the belated passenger train should be met. They might as easily have reversed a cannon ball in flight. If the passenger train started out from Calhoun before we came in sight, it was almost inevitable death for all our party; and the people on the other train wouldn't have fared much better.

The race against time which followed was grand and terrible.

MURPHY: The raiders hadn't been gone long when we left Adairsville on Bracken's fast engine, and as the train from Chattanooga was behind and ought to have been at Adairsville ahead of the train hauled by the *Texas*, we feared a collision. Andrews did also, I think, for we heard that he blew the whistle of the *General* almost continuously from that point to Calhoun, nine miles.

ALF WILSON: When we found that we were pursued, we knew that the destruction of a bridge was the only thing that would save us, and to do this we had to outrun them far enough to burn the bridge before they came up.

The resulting trial of speed between locomotives was a race which for desperate, daredevil recklessness, velocity and the high stakes at issue was never equaled on land or water on the American continent. This was our last shuffle of the cards and the game was a desperate one.

Our locomotive was under a full head of steam. The engineer stood with his hand on the lever and the valve wide open. It was frightful to see how the powerful iron monster under us would leap forward under the revolutions of her great wheels. Over and over, Brown would scream at me, "Give her more wood, Alf!" Which command was promptly obeyed. She rocked and reeled like a drunken man, while we tumbled from side to side like grains of popcorn in a hot frying pan.

It was bewildering to look at the ground, or objects on the roadside. A constant stream of fire ran from the rims of the great wheels, and to this day I shudder when I reflect on that, my first and last locomotive ride. We sped past houses and fields and out of sight, almost like a meteor, while the bystanders, who barely caught a glimpse of us as we passed, looked on as if in both fear and amazement. It has always been a wonder with me that our locomotive and cars kept the track at all. At times the iron horse seemed literally to fly over the course, the driving wheels of one side being lifted from the rails much of the distance over which we now sped at a fearful velocity. We took little thought of the matter then. Death in a railroad smash-up would have been preferred by us to capture.

PITTENGER: Andrews kept his watch in his hand, seeming to notice nothing else, and Knight, who looked on the same watch, always joined in declaring that the interval of nine miles between the two stations was run in seven and a half minutes. Seventy-two miles an hour! And this not on a well-kept road with heavy steel rails, but over a light and poorly maintained track.

It must be allowed that Andrews may have reckoned the interval from losing sight of Adairsville until coming in sight of Calhoun. Even so, the rate would have been just slightly over a mile a minute.

Our escape on this run was exceedingly narrow. The passenger train had actually moved out from Calhoun before we arrived; but it had only just got under way as our men saw it while we were slackening up for the station. A minute earlier in this passenger train's start could well have ended the raid. But seeing us coming, our whistle screaming, they backed before us up the track, and a station official obligingly opened the switch to let us on the side track. This was done as much in the interest of the passenger train, which couldn't proceed till we were out of the way, as in ours.

But the passenger train didn't go on for some time. The engineer in backing had gone not only far enough to let us get on the side track, but also, as their train was a long one, to block the far end of it completely, barring our return to the main track until they should pull ahead. Before doing this they wanted some explanation. The lateness of the regular train; our having Cain's engine without Fuller or any of his men; and our racing in on them without any warning signalman ahead at a time when railroad rules entitled them to the road—all this called for explanation.

Andrews calmly told his story, and Beauregard's need for ammunition was accepted as justifying most of our irregularities. We had good right to be uneasy here at Calhoun, hemmed in as we were, for in our urgency to reach the station we hadn't even delayed to cut the wire on our wild way from Adairsville. A question might come over the wires at any moment, which Andrews, with all his adroitness, wouldn't find it easy to answer.

Although accepting our powder story, the conductor of the passenger train didn't share our sense of urgency. Andrews tried mild and indirect means to convince him that it was safe for his train to run down and get to Adairsville before Fuller's train could reach there, but the conductor wasn't easily persuaded. The bare escape from collision with our train a few minutes before had shaken his nerves too much for him to wish at once to repeat the experience. Neither did he seem at all in a hurry to move his train ahead and let us out on the main track. As his train was the only obstacle, however, it wouldn't have been long—had he continued obstinate—until our reserve force would have been brought out and into action.

It may be said here that Andrews was perfectly sincere in assuring this conductor that there would be abundant time for him to reach Adairsville before Fuller with his train would be along. We didn't think Fuller would be along that day, and with his own train he wasn't.

EDITOR: Pittenger is quibbling on this one, and not persuasively. If Andrews and most of the raiders—including Pittenger—wouldn't have welcomed a collision behind them, or any accident that could promise blocking off pursuit, they weren't the men otherwise on record before, during and after this chase.

PITTENGER: But as matters stood, if the Calhoun man had allowed himself to be persuaded to start southward, a bad collision would almost certainly have ended all possibilities of pursuit, and left us free to burn bridges at our leisure.

After talking with the conductor and engineer of the down freight for some time and finding them still indisposed to proceed, Andrews finally spoke out flatly.

"I've got to go on with no more delay," he said. "Pull your engine ahead and let me out."

Given in this direct form, the order had to be obeyed or openly disputed. The conductor and engineer chose to comply, and proceeded to pull on.

MURPHY: The delayed passenger train was at Calhoun, and about to start, but heard Andrews' whistle and didn't leave. We on the *Texas* were close behind and also blew our whistle, still preventing the southbound train from leaving Calhoun. We made fast time to this point, probably fifty miles an hour.

A large number of people were on that train and at Calhoun Depot. (Andrews and his men had waved their hands to the crowd as they pressed on.) Slowing as we reached the station, we told the people there what had happened and kept on through.

RANDELL W. MCBRYDE: The train which both Andrews and Fuller passed at Calhoun had as a passenger Captain W. J. Whitsitt of Ringgold, an officer of the 1st Georgia Confederate Volunteers, who with ten armed soldiers was returning to his command at Mobile, in charge of a number of recruits from Ringgold and vicinity. Suspicion already being aroused by the passing of Andrews, a brief explanation from Fuller sufficed to give the alarm, and Captain Whitsitt with his ten regular soldiers boarded the tender of the passenger engine and followed the *Texas* closely in the race the remainder of the distance.

FULLER: We made the ten miles from Adairsville to Calhoun in twelve minutes. As we came near the station, I recognized the telegraph operator from Dalton—young Ed Henderson, who'd come down the line looking for the break in the wire that was disrupting messages from the south—and gave him a hand up on the engine as we moved through, not coming to a full stop.

EDITOR: Boarding the *Texas* as well at Calhoun was a useful reinforcement in the form of a restive passenger from the down train held up there. A husky engineer of the Memphis & Charleston line, Atlanta-bound on leave but caught up in the excitement of the day, Fleming Cox took over from the fifteen-year-old Henry Haney and fired the *Texas* from Calhoun to the finish, while the willing Haney —Bracken's regular fireman in the wartime absence of older hands— helped at the brakes and wood-passing as directed by Murphy, Bracken and Cox, the three veteran engineers then in the cab.

PITTENGER: At last—once out of Calhoun—we were on the main track with no train between us and Chattanooga; and, if the rumors were true, with no obstructions west of there to Huntsville, since all traffic that way was cut off by Mitchel. An open road lay ahead, and behind us scores of miles of obstructed track. For the whole morning we had been running with a train directly in front of us, or holding up for a belated one. We had passed five trains—the achievement the greater since all but one had been either extras or behind time—and the Y-switch at Chattanooga promised no greater difficulty than any of the many side tracks we had already successfully met. Some of the first exhilaration we'd felt after capturing the train at Big Shanty was again ours, as we whistled swiftly on for a mile or more, and then stopped to cut the wire, and to take up a rail—as we hoped—for the last time.

The Oostanaula Bridge was just ahead, and when that was burned, our program seemed pleasurably simple. With no more of the drudgery of track-breaking nor the even harder work of crouching in the darkness of our boxcar waiting for trains to arrive, we'd sail along from bridge to bridge, firing them as we passed. We had heard the whistle of a following train a dozen miles back; but that probably had to be one from Kingston, which if not wrecked by the broken rail, would almost surely have had to return there for tools to help get across the gap. We knew nothing then of Fuller's and Murphy's pursuit, and if we'd been told the full story, we would have thought it too wild and improbable to believe.

It would be useful, however, to take up one more rail before we finally changed our mode of operations. A broken section behind this passenger train would insure that it couldn't turn back on any sudden rush of late-grown suspicion and perhaps come on us while we were at the destruction of the Oostanaula Bridge at Resaca.

We worked gladly and cheerfully. Scott climbed the telegraph pole with even more than usual agility. Some worked at the taking in of all kinds of burning material, for we wished to be well supplied with this at the bridge. Every stick and piece of wood we could get hold of was soaking wet, but by breaking and whittling, they could be made to add to a flame, and from the engine, which was kept full of wood for the purpose, we could give a good start to a fire. We had only our one iron bar to force out spikes—a bent "crow's foot" would have been worth more than its weight in gold—but we hammered away with what we had, and spike after spike was drawn.

It was here I saw Andrews show real impatience for the first, or perhaps I may say the only, time during our run. He had altered his dress, throwing off the cape and high hat he had worn while at stations, and had a small cap on, which greatly changed his appearance. The nearing of the time when his plans would come to completion seemed to thrill and inspire him. He snatched the iron bar from the hands of the man using it, and—though we had strong and practiced workmen in our party—I hadn't before seen the blows rained down with such precision and force. Some say that he was swearing on this occasion, but although standing by, the only words I heard were directions about the work, given in his usual mild tones but with quite an emphatic ring of triumph in them. He wanted that rail up in the fewest number of seconds, and then—the bridge.

Heading North 5

PITTENGER: As we worked at our track-lifting at the stop above Calhoun and short of Resaca, there were several of us using a lever of green wood and trying to tear up the end of a rail from which the spikes hadn't yet been drawn. The sap-filled wood bent too much to have effect. A fence rail was added, and we lifted again. At that instant, loud and clear from the south, came the whistle of the engine in pursuit. By the sound, it was near and closing in fast. A thousand thunderclaps couldn't have startled us more.

At the end, where we'd been prying the rail, it was bent, but it was still too firmly fixed for us to hope to lift it, or break it like the last. We did the best in our power: bending the loose end up still further, and putting the fence rail carefully under it, with the hope either of throwing our pursuers from the track or forcing them to stop and adjust it. We then piled into the car and engine, and with one of its old bounds that jerked us from our feet—for Brown and Knight threw the valve wide open—the *General* bore us rapidly on.

MURPHY: About three miles above Calhoun, we came in sight for the first time of the captured engine and the freight cars. They had stopped to remove another rail and were in the act of trying to get it out of place when we hove in sight. This to them, no doubt, was a revelation. Andrews was guarding against what really took place—a pursuing party—but I learned later he didn't think it would be anyone from Big Shanty. He supposed we were a party on the engine he had just passed at Calhoun.

As we neared them they cut loose one car and started again.

PITTENGER: The coming of the *Texas*, before the track above Calhoun was torn up, was by far the most serious misfortune we had yet encountered. The plan which promptly presented itself to the undismayed Andrews was to use two of our cars as projectiles and hurl them back at the enemy. This was more in accordance with his temperament, which delighted in strategy, than the plain course of a straight out-and-out fight with the pursuing train. Accordingly, our engine was reversed—could we have selected a downgrade, the chance of success would have been better, but we were coming so near the bridge that we couldn't delay to choose—and when the speed in this way had been checked and the pursuing train was quite close and still going fast, we uncoupled, and bounded on again. But the skilled pursuers saw what we were about. Checking their headway, they also reversed, and coming up to the boxcar with moderate force, coupled on, which was easier because their tender was in front.

FULLER: As we ran from Calhoun to Dalton, I wrote a telegram to General Leadbetter, at Chattanooga, stating that my train had been captured, that I was in pursuit, that the captors were evidently Federals in disguise, and that no doubt the object was the destruction of the Chickamauga bridges.

Two and a half miles north of Calhoun I came in sight of the raiders for the first time. They were taking up the track. When they saw me they detached one of their cars and left it before me, and made haste to depart. To this I coupled and sped on in the pursuit.

PITTENGER: The Oostanaula Bridge was now just at hand. To leave it intact was to be thought of only in the direst necessity. We had carried the fuel gathered into our last car, and while it wasn't as good as we would have liked, yet in a little time we could make a fire. We now punched a hole in the back of our car—we had started making this opening in passing from one car to another previous to dropping the last one—and began to let ties fall out on the track while we ran. They followed us end over end, bounding into the air and showing at all times a most perverse disposition to get off the track, but a few remained. This moderated the speed of the pursuing engine, which was a help that we sorely needed, for it was now evident that they had a faster engine than ours, or better fuel, or both. Their fuel supply certainly was superior, for we had been using wood lavishly without any opportunity for a long time past to replenish it.

The first despondency of the whole route took possession of us as we approached this bridge at Resaca with our pursuer close behind. If we passed by without leaving it in ashes, we felt that one important part of our business would be undone even if we were completely successful afterwards in evading pursuit and destroying the Chickamauga bridges.

MURPHY: Moving on to the boxcar they had dropped, we coupled it before our engine. I said to our party: "If they drop a car on the trestle approaching the Oostanaula Bridge and throw it across the track, we'll be troubled to prevent them from destroying the rest of the bridges, or any other damage they wish to do."

PITTENGER: There was at this time a long and high wooden trestle by which the Oostanaula Bridge at Resaca is approached. As we came near, we slowed up, and in the middle of this trestle we dropped our second car. We saw no opportunity to turn and fight at this point. The town of Resaca was within a few hundred yards of the bridge, and any noise would have brought help from that quarter. Had the day been dry, we could have flung faggots from the engine upon the roof, but now a fire even on the inside of the large frame bridge would require careful nursing. With a station only a few hundred feet ahead, where the track might so easily be obstructed, and with the pursuers behind, we couldn't give time for this; so we slowly and reluctantly passed over the bridge, after dropping the car, and on through the village of Resaca.

FULLER: Two miles above the first boxcar we took up, I came to another car the raiders had left. I coupled onto this, as I had the other, and away we went after the raiders, arriving at Resaca just after their departure.

From the instant we got over the bridge at Resaca, the race became one for life or death between the two engines, one the Rogers and the other the Danforth & Cooke, both of five-feet ten-inch drivers, with 160 pounds of steam, and throttles wide open. No such race has ever been run, either before or since.

MURPHY: On reaching the bridge we found they had dropped a second car on the trestle, but hadn't thrown it off the rail, nor was the bridge fired. (In my view, Andrews at this point was more anxious to escape than to destroy bridges.)

We coupled this car also and left the two cars on the side track at Resaca, a short distance beyond the bridge. From Resaca to Tilton the road is very crooked, and we had to move with some caution. (Looking back at it now, our whole course seems reckless in the extreme. But we were young then, and youth takes chances that are appalling to old age.) The distance between was short. I feared ambushing by Andrews—or that the raiders might abandon their engine and reverse it, starting it back under an open throttle valve against us. The consequences of either move might have been very serious to us, being poorly armed and only seven in number. To prevent us closing in on them, they broke out the end of their remaining boxcar and from this opening threw crossties they had previously taken aboard onto the tracks to check our speed or derail us.

This work was hard on us, and exciting. It required coolness to avoid accident or destruction. I had a long bar fastened to the brake wheel of the tender so four men could use it to help check and stop the engine suddenly. There were no air brakes then. I also stood by the reverse lever to aid Bracken to reverse his engine and stop suddenly, which we had to do many times to avoid obstructions. Fuller sat on the back of the tender, watching the track and signaling us when danger threatened.

PITTENGER: After passing Resaca, we again forced our pursuers back by dropping ties on the track, and not knowing whether it was a telegraph station or not, we again cut the wires. No obstructions were placed on the track at this point, but it was on a curve, and taking a rail which had been bent in lifting it, I placed one end under the rail at one side and the other projecting diagonally toward the train on the other side. (The pursuers saw us start—I was later told—but seeing no obstructions they ran at a good rate of speed right over this rail. Persons on the tender were thrown into the air, and their escape was marvelous.)

But what conjectures did we form to account for the unexpected appearance of this pursuing train? The actuality was totally unknown to us then, and we were greatly perplexed. The matter had great practical importance. Was this engine started after us by an authority which had also alarmed the whole road ahead of us? If so, we'd do well to abandon our efforts for the destruction of bridges, and seek our own safety. Of one thing we felt sure: it must have been one of the trains that we had passed at Calhoun or Adairsville, that was following. But why? The first and least serious possibility was that the suspicious conductor at Calhoun, who had been so unwilling to let us pass, had determined that we were impostors, and at his own motion had set out to follow us. Or it might be that the freight had run to where we had broken up the track, had escaped being wrecked, and, turning back, had telegraphed ahead before we had cut the wire. In this case all the road ahead would be alarmed. Or, for a third possibility, a messenger might have been sent down to Marietta from Big Shanty, and a dispatch sent to Atlanta and around the whole circuit of the Confederacy back to Chattanooga, and, before the wires had been cut, to one of the trains we had passed, with orders to follow us closely and prevent us from damaging the road until a train could be sent out from Chattanooga to secure our capture. Should either of these latter guesses be true—and they were the most probable—our race was almost run. We would be obliged to leave the railroad, and try the far more difficult task of escaping on foot.

If Andrews thought them true, it would fully account for his reluctance in ordering the capture of a pursuing train; for such a capture could do no permanent good, while everyone of his party wounded in the fight would be disabled for the inevitable and hard land journey ahead. In view of the almost hopeless situation as it appeared to us then—far worse than the reality, for the road ahead hadn't been warned as yet—the heroic steadiness of Andrews, who continued to put forth every possible effort as coolly and quietly as if success were at hand, was remarkable. There were now three chasing trains: first, Fuller, Murphy, Bracken and their men on the locomotive *Texas* of the down freight; second, the Calhoun passenger, which had immediately followed him and wasn't far behind; and last, the soldier-carrying train started from Marietta.

For a time after leaving Resaca, we didn't run very fast. It was evident that we couldn't get away from the engine behind us by mere speed; the only hope was in some way to disable them, or to obstruct the track; and we were obliged to be saving of our fuel. But now we were approaching Green's, a wood station near Tilton, and we were determined to have a fresh supply at any cost. So the last wood in the box, with a little of our precious oil, was shoved into the furnace, and Brown, who had now taken the throttle, turned on a full head of steam, and we once more flew along the track. At the same time, we who were in the boxcar put a line of ties along its floor and kept them moving to the hole in the end, and let them drop on the track. This was rapidly exhausting our ammunition, but it was effectual in enforcing slowness and caution upon the pursuers.

Fuller couldn't run swiftly in the face of such a succession of obstacles. He did the best he could—as I learned later—giving the signal to reverse whenever he saw a tie on the track, jumping off and removing it, and on again, when the engineer would start with a full head of steam, and reduce speed when another tie was seen. It was extremely dangerous; and the only wonder is that they weren't wrecked long before the chase was done.

ALF WILSON: Those after us had one of the best locomotives on the road, and a fresh supply of wood and water, while we had but little of either, our supply having nearly run out. The road was very rough here; but, rough or smooth, our last thread of hope hung on the swiftness of our tired locomotive. We crammed the furnace with every combustible we could lay hands on. Again she plunged ahead, reeling and rocking on the rough track like a drunken man.

MURPHY: Passing through and beyond Tilton, we again came in sight of the party ahead. At this point the road has a straight stretch of over a mile. A short distance from Tilton and just as we rounded the curve, the *General,* with the raiders, was rounding another curve, leaving the straight line and giving us a fine view for some distance across the angle.

We could see the top of the smokestack. It looked as though the *General* were sailing as it rounded the curve majestically and as fast as possible, probably a mile a minute. The fastest run of the chase was made at this point.

This left an impression on my mind never to be erased—the two great locomotives, with their human freight, speeding on, one trying to escape, the other endeavoring to overtake. And though we strained every sinew to overhaul the fugitives, if we had actually caught up with them, none of our band might have been left to give the particulars of the chase. The chances of battle were certainly against us if Andrews had attempted to fight. He had better than twenty well-armed men, and we were just seven, with two rusty shotguns.

PITTENGER: When we reached Green's woodyard, there was no lingering in the work of loading up. The wood was piled in frantically by men working for their lives; but before we had half filled the tender, we again heard our relentless follower.

So eager were we to get the largest possible supply of fuel that we didn't take their first whistle as a sufficient warning to start. Then came blast after blast from them, obviously designed to alarm the keeper of the woodyard in the hope that he might hinder us from getting a full supply. This didn't scare us into bolting, for even when Andrews reluctantly gave the word to come on board, Alf Wilson—who as fireman had a keen sense of the need of fuel—lingered still to get a huge armload more. The enemy, seeing us standing, were actually obliged to begin braking to avoid the collision that seemed inevitable.

ALF WILSON: "Wood-and-watering" at Green's tank and woodpile, we'd secured only a partial supply when the chasing train came in sight, loaded with armed soldiers. Our pursuers were worked up to an infuriated pitch of excitement and rent the air with their screeches and yells as they came in sight of us, like dogs when the quarry is sprung. They opened on us at long range with musketry. (This is the first instance I ever heard of where troops were put into action on a moving railroad train, and if everybody takes my view of it, it's a kind of warfare that won't ever get too popular.) The bullets rattled around us, but fortunately none of our party was hit.

EDITOR: Not hit, Fuller and Murphy would say, because no actual shots were fired from the *Texas* here or elsewhere.

PITTENGER: The stop had given us a good head of steam, and with a bound, our engine sped on again. We'd been careful to so obstruct the track that the enemy was obliged to come to a full halt, and this gave us time once more to get out of sight.

We passed Tilton in safety, and the water station, which at that time was at a different place there from the woodyard, was soon reached. As our water supply was dangerously low, we stopped, adjusted the pipes, and told the powder story. From the battered appearance of our only car, with a hole knocked in each end, that explanation was no longer too plausible, but it answered for the moment, and we succeeded in getting all the water we needed. Had any objections been made, we would have taken it by force.

Before the tank was full, the pursuers came in sight, but seeing us, they slowed up warily, and as a party of our men had run back and put some obstructions on the track, out of gunshot, they were obliged to come to a full stop there, thus giving us the time needed. Then we mounted and sped on toward Dalton.

It was advisable at once to get decisively ahead of the pursuers before reaching this town, which might present serious difficulties. As there were no burnable bridges for a considerable distance, the only other thing was to try once more to tear up the track. The engine was again in good running condition, and we rushed rapidly forward, putting frequent obstructions on the track—mostly by dropping ties or sticks of firewood, but in one or two instances, by reversing the engine, jumping out and piling up obstructions. At a favorable place we stopped again for a more permanent break.

Long practice had made us more skillful in this matter, and the last two stops had shown us that the enemy couldn't run upon us without great care. So we divided at once into four parties. Scott and a companion cut the telegraph; Knight carefully inspected the engine; two or three ran back just out of gunshot, and heaped obstructions on the track; while the remainder worked with might and main in taking up a rail. Some of us in the boxcar had come to feel that there was no need of running so long before the pursuing train, which we could see to be a short one, with probably not much if any greater force than our own. Now while as many were at the rail as could find places to work—the process of lifting it with our imperfect tools was very slow, requiring more than five minutes—I stepped over to Andrews.

"We can capture that train," I said to him, "if you're willing."

"How?" he asked.

"Find a curve where there are plenty of bushes," I answered. "Block the track and most of us take cover nearby. One of our engineers runs our locomotive ahead. When the enemy stop to clear the track, we'll rush them. When we've captured them, our other engineer can reverse their engine and send it back down the track to clear the road of any more trains that may be following."

Andrews said, in his quiet way, "It's a good plan. It's worth trying," and looked around in a meditative manner as if weighing the chances. How close he came to accepting it, I wasn't to know. When the enemy's whistle sounded, we saw them rush up to the obstructions we had placed on the track, stop by reversing, and labor as frantically to clear the road as we were doing in trying to raise the rail.

We didn't get it up. The stubborn spikes still held, and as the *Texas* was almost ready to come on again, Andrews called out, "All aboard," and we dashed away. That wasn't the place to make a fight, as we all knew, for revolvers against shotguns and rifles would have had no chance at long range. From an ambush, though, we could have been climbing into their engine and cars before they could pick up their guns, and the conflict wouldn't have been many minutes doubtful.

This was the nearest we came to what one Southern account later was to call mutiny. Andrews was heartily obeyed during the whole of this day, and none of us said anything more about this plan at the time, partly because we felt that our leader was better able to judge what was to be done than we, and partly because we thought he was only waiting for the best place to turn on our pursuers, and that we would soon have all the fighting we wanted.

The full speed of our engine was again called on as we neared Dalton, and by the aid of a few ties dropped on the track, we were once more a respectable distance ahead. We needed this interval badly, for if anything delayed our immediate passage through this station, serious difficulty could arise. We might have a battle, for Dalton, where the state road we were on met the East Tennessee & Georgia line, was the largest town between Marietta and Chattanooga. The connecting road there ran to Cleveland in Tennessee, where it joined the main line from Richmond to Chattanooga, thus making a large triangle. At that time there were no telegraph wires on this crossroad. There were numerous side tracks at Dalton, and a probability that cars might be left standing on some of them. As we had more than made up our hour's delay at Kingston, and were now much ahead of time, there was no certainty of the switches being rightly adjusted for us. We therefore had to stop at the opening of the switch, fortunately a little way down from the large passenger depot through which we still had to pass.

Here the coolness and adroitness of Andrews shone out. It is likely that when we had spoken of fighting a little way back, his mind was occupied rather with the problem of passing Dalton, and of judging by what took place there whether the enemy was warned. As the train stopped, he ran forward, observed that the track was clear, spoke to one or two bystanders, and was back to his post in an exceedingly short time. To one or two who had come up even in these few seconds, he said, "I am running this train through to Corinth, and have no time to spare."

He nodded to Knight, who once more put on the full force of the engine—there was nothing to be gained by care in avoiding alarm any longer, for the distant whistle of the pursuer was heard—and we rushed at the depot, the roof of which then extended across the double track.

DORSEY: Knight was at the lever when we dashed through the covered depot at Dalton, where the road takes a sharp turn, and as he could see no track ahead of the depot, he thought we had unawares taken a side track and were plunging into a shed at the end of the track. Making the apparent discovery too late to stop, Knight thought it was the last of him and us, but kept a tight grip on the lever. He shut his eyes in anticipation of the fatal wreck at hand, and was almost jerked off his feet as the engine at the sharp curve made a lunge to the left, righted itself and dashed on.

Heading North 6

MURPHY: Reaching Dalton, we dropped Henderson, our young telegraph operator, so that he could send the message to General Leadbetter at Chattanooga, informing him as to how things stood. This was done as a matter of precaution, for we didn't know what might happen to us.

FULLER:

Dalton, Ga.
12 April, 1862

To Gen. Danville Leadbetter,
Commander at Chattanooga:

My train was captured this A.M. at Big Shanty, evidently by Federal soldiers in disguise. They are making rapidly for Chattanooga, possibly with the idea of burning the railroad bridges in their rear. If I do not capture them in the meantime, see that they do not pass Chattanooga.

William A. Fuller

ALF WILSON: Discovering the track all clear at Dalton, we went through at a high rate of speed. Here was the only instance, I think, where we failed to do all that could have been done. We ran about two minutes too long before we stopped to cut the wire. I tried, and even insisted, with Andrews, that we should stop the train sooner, but for some unknown reason he didn't.

It was owing to this that our pursuers succeeded in starting an alarm through about two minutes before we ripped down the wire. I've since learned that the message, not all the way completed, caused the wildest stampede in Chattanooga. Troops were called to arms, the railroad track torn up and cannon planted covering the track, while a double guard was kept on duty all night.

MURPHY: Fuller's message to Chattanooga was delivered, all but a few words that were cut off when Andrews destroyed the telegraph wires just beyond Dalton, where he stopped again and attempted to lift another rail.

We came on them there before they had time to take up the rail or harm the track. They moved on. Their supply of crossties was exhausted, so they had no way of blocking our pursuit.

PITTENGER: A mile above Dalton, which was about as soon as the headlong rush of the engine could be checked, we stopped again, just opposite the point where a regiment of conscripts—commanded, we learned later, by Colonel Jesse Glenn—was encamped in a field. Their position, which was within two or three hundred yards of us, was probably not seen by those on the engine until we were close to the soldiers, and it was probably better to take the risk of their interference than to lose time by seeking another place. Again the wire was cut, but it was a second too late; for a message had just been flashed through, no doubt even as Scott was bringing the wire down. The usual obstructions were here piled on the track, and we again essayed to take up a rail, for the Chickamauga bridges were just above, and we wanted time enough to get them on fire. No men ever worked with more desperate energy, but long before the rail was loose, the pursuers were again upon us.

F. M. GREGG: In connection with this stop above Dalton, it might be recorded that on the morning of the 12th, a John H. Flynn, foreman of the works at Graysville, Ga., found himself down near Dalton. He had been drinking considerably and was on his way home along the tracks. The raiders happening to stop near where he was, he hailed them and told them he wanted to ride with them to Graysville. They responded that it was a train of ammunition for Beauregard. Flynn waved his hand affably and said, "Hurry her up, boys."

PITTENGER: The race recommenced with all its speed and fury. The great tunnel was a short distance ahead—a favorable place for an ambush. If Andrews was disposed to fight, there would be the place of all others to do it. With the smoke of our train filling the space, with our party concealed along the sides in the darkness, success would be likely even if they had twice our number, for of course we couldn't tell how much of a reinforcement they might pick up at Dalton. But no orders were given to stop. We kept right on through the tunnel and the village of Tunnel Hill beyond, where we carefully crouched down to conceal our number from the curious eyes of any who might be about the station.

MURPHY: There is a tunnel before reaching Tunnel Hill, the next station, and as we approached it we could see the engine about a mile beyond us. I had thought, before reaching the tunnel, that the raiders were short of wood, because they hadn't been making as much speed since leaving Dalton. Finding the tunnel clear, I was satisfied their fuel was low, for, if their furnace had been full of fire, smoke would have remained in the tunnel for some time, and we couldn't have seen the engine through the hole.

We knew the raiders couldn't go very far without stopping to fight, or abandoning the *General*. The fight we weren't prepared for, and would have tried to avoid, although it might have been forced on us.

WHITE SMITH: Leaving Tunnel Hill, the parties on the engine ahead weren't running as fast as before, we on the *Texas* were gaining on them.

We got to Ringgold about one o'clock, and were just a short distance behind them. Our engine didn't stop here, as we knew they couldn't go much further. When we struck the heavy grade on the straight track, we commenced to crowd up on them. We could see the men on the boxcar which they were still hauling.

PITTENGER: We now did what had doubtless been in the mind of Andrews for some time past. He ordered us to fire our last car while we were running. The rain fell in torrents, and the wood was drenched in the tender. It was only by much effort and skillful firing that the the engine fire could be kept at the heat required for fast running. But we tore everything combustible loose from the car, and smashed it into kindling. Some blazing faggots were stolen from the engine and the fire made to burn. One man stayed to the last in the car to tend it, while the rest of us crowded on the tender and locomotive. The steam was now gradually shut off that we might come slowly upon the bridge and be able to leave the car just at the right place.

DORSEY: After gaining a little on the enemy, who were at times in plain view, we set fire in the last boxcar to the remaining ties, and to some rubbish thrown in for the purpose, and tried hard to get up a good blaze. The rains had so soaked everything that this seemed impossible, and our fire burned aggravatingly slow.

PITTENGER: We came to a full stop at this first Chickamauga bridge, a large one, well covered with timber. Inside, it was at least drier than on the outside, and with time the bridge timbers might be made to burn. We added almost the last of our oil and nearly the last stick of wood—knowing that if this bridge could be made to burn well, we could have all the time we wanted to replenish wood and everything else.

ALF WILSON: We dropped off this last car on the bridge when we reached it, and stopped to assist the fire all we could. But we weren't permitted to complete the task. We had no more than fairly got to work before we saw the black smoke of the pursuing locomotive and had to move on again.

PITTENGER: For a considerable time, as it seemed to us, though it must have been measured by seconds rather than minutes, we remained on the other side of the fire, watching. Then the inexorable smoke of the following engine was seen, the pin connecting the burning car with our engine was pulled out, and we slowly moved on. Our foes were now near at hand, and we could see their rifles and shotguns, with which they would be able to fight us one-sidedly at long range. The car which, if the day had been dry, would long before this have filled the bridge with a mass of flame, was burning faster than the bridge. To take it to another bridge was useless, for the drenching rain would have given it little chance to burn away from the shelter of the bridge. Very sadly we left the column of smoke behind.

DORSEY: The engine showed signs of failing power and began to lag. The water in the boiler was low, the fuel gone. The oil cans, tools and everything that would burn had been thrown into the furnace. Andrews even threw in his leather saddle bags, either for fuel or to get rid of them.

After passing Tunnel Hill and Ringgold, it was clear that the game was almost up. The slowly burning last boxcar was still attached to the engine—not dropped at the first Chickamauga bridge, as some have said—but the grand old iron steed was dying in his tracks. Another bridge couldn't be reached. Our fire was sufficient to smoke us out of the car onto the engine and now empty tender, but not sufficient for the now impractical task of firing a bridge even if we could reach it. Our intrepid and exultant foes were right on our heels, in plain view.

Heading North 7

ALF WILSON: Our most strenuous efforts to place distance between ourselves and our pursuers had been in vain. Their locomotive was equal to ours and they were running it with equal recklessness. We had nothing left on board to throw off and thus obstruct the track as we had previously done. It was becoming more evident every moment that our only and last hope lay in an abandonment of the locomotive and fleeing to the woods. Already our speed began to slacken—we had neither wood, water nor oil.

The locomotive shook and reeled as she sped on. I could liken her condition to nothing else than the last struggles of a faithful horse, whose heartless master has driven and lashed him until he is gasping for breath and literally dying in the harness. The powerful machine had carried us safely for almost a hundred miles, some of the time at a rate of speed appalling to contemplate, but she was becoming helpless and useless in our service. She was shaken loose in every joint, at least she seemed so; the brass on her journals and boxes was melted by the heat; her great steel tires were almost red-hot, while she smoked and sizzled at every joint. Our race was almost run.

F. M. GREGG: Wood was getting low, and it was evident that a crisis was near. At Ringgold the speed was perceptibly decreasing, and the *Texas*, with plenty of fuel to have gone to the end of the line, was about four hundred yards behind. The oil cans of the *General* were thrown into the furnace with the last sticks of wood.

There is a long curve at Ringgold, then a stretch of straight track, with a heavy up-grade. Down this straight track the old *General* was made to do her best, but, looking backward, the pursuing engine could be seen coming up the grade, gaining on them rapidly. Slower, slower, the drive wheels of the *General* turned. Backward came the hand on the steam gauge. It was a final effort; a little more steam and the top of the grade would be reached.

FULLER: In this terrible strain of speed and tension we sped on and on, both engines, until we had passed Ringgold three miles, when

[*Fuller*]
the fuel and water of the raiders gave out, and those brave men could have had no further hope of success. To save themselves was all that they could hope or try to do.

PITTENGER: We were now on what proved to be our last run. I have often been asked if this day wasn't one of great fear and terror for us. For my own part, I can't honestly claim greater fear than I had often felt in ordinary military service. No matter what happened, it was generally felt among the men that we still had one strong resource—the power to turn around and attack the pursuing enemy. We didn't have the boastful feeling that we were an overmatch for a large body of Southern soldiers, for we all knew how desperately they could and often did fight; but of the ordinary citizens, gathered up as we presumed our pursuers were, or even of conscripts, we had no great fear. That we hadn't our usual weapons was a serious disadvantage, but this could be remedied by getting into close quarters.

We again crouched down as well as we could in the tender while passing Ringgold, that the enemy might not see our number; and when beyond the town, we arose and looked about us. The country was mostly wooded and rough, being much cut up by the branches of the swollen Chickamauga Creek. We had no fuel. Every loose combustible scrap was carefully gathered up and thrown into the engine. Worst symptom of all, a large pair of saddle bags which we had never seen Andrews without from the time of the midnight conference, together with his cap and some other pieces of clothing that he didn't need for immediate use, were flung into the furnace. Various papers followed. Such preparations were ominous. But the next command—the last he ever gave to us as a party—was to me more dreadful still.

We were now beyond Ringgold, and within a mile or so of Graysville, or some nineteen miles by the longest railway course from Chattanooga. From that city westward to Bridgeport was twenty-eight miles farther. The nearest way to Bridgeport, however, was not through Chattanooga but further south, and by that route it was not distant more than thirty-five or forty miles. The direct course was at right angles with the numerous mountain ranges which here run almost north and south, a route difficult for cavalry and known to more than one of our party. Two comrades had pocket compasses to guide us day or night in any weather. Although it was now late to accomplish our original purpose, it wasn't too late to save our lives. My conviction then and now was that to have left our train in a body, without delaying to seek concealment, and together to have struck out westward as rapidly as we could go, would have been our most hopeful course.

The command which Andrews gave instead, as we huddled together in the wood-box of the tender, was to jump off one by one, scatter in the woods, and each man strive to work his own way back to the Union army. It may have been that what he felt confident of doing he assumed others could do; or if we should be captured, that he might thereby better be in a position to give us more efficient help. He may have thought as well that each man of the party would find the same relief that he did in being cast entirely on his own resources; but to me, it was a fatal order.

It must of course be remembered in explanation of this order that Andrews had slept little or none the night before, and that he had spent nearly two days and a night in the most exhausting labors, both mental and physical. As well, he had seen his cherished plans overthrown when on the brink of success. It had ever been his tantalizing lot almost but not quite to achieve; to succeed grandly up to a certain point, and then to fail through some cause too strong for human power, and too obscure for human foresight.

Perhaps under his calm appearance Andrews realized this, and felt the greatest favor he could render those he had led was to separate them at once from his own dark destiny. If so, that was the most tragic mistake of all.

ALF WILSON: A few minutes before we came to our final halt, Andrews, Brown, Knight and myself, who were on the engine and tender, having given up all hope of success, hastily discussed the best thing to be done, and it was concluded that the best course was to separate and scatter in all directions. In this way some of the party might possibly get away—and eventually, be able to help the others—while if we went in a body and continued together, with the great number of Rebel troops in our front and in the rear, and, in fact, on all sides of us, the capture of the entire party would be certain.

In accordance with this conclusion, Andrews now told us all that it was "every man for himself," that we must scatter and do the best we could to escape to the Federal lines.

PITTENGER: The *General* had served us well since the morning, and it was hard to abandon her now. She was substantially uninjured. The engineers, Brown and Knight, had taken good care of her, and, with wood and oil in abundance, there should have been no difficulty

[*Pittenger*]
on her part in completing the run to Huntsville. She was still jogging along at the rate of eight or ten miles an hour, and could maintain that pace a little longer. The pursuers had also diminished their speed, so as to keep us just in sight, having apparently no wish to press upon what may have seemed to them like a wounded and dying lion.

The command to "jump off and scatter" was repeated with the injunction to be quick about it, as the engineer wished to reverse the engine and drive it back upon the enemy.

Now one after another clambered down on the step and swung off. I was neither among the first nor the last; and jumping unskillfully out from the step, instead of forward, whirled over and over on hands and feet. Rising in a dazed condition, though unhurt with the exception of a few scratches from the briers with which the place abounded, I could see that the men who had jumped off were, according to instructions, flying in different directions. Others were just coming off the engine in almost the same way that I had done, while the engineers were attempting to carry out their scheme of reversing the engine.

DORSEY: We all left the engine at Andrews' order, except Knight and Brown, who stuck to her until the last of us jumped off; then, with a sudden jerk of the lever, they reversed it and jumped themselves, Knight right after Brown. Slowly, the engine moved back.

PITTENGER: The brakes of the tender were put on still more to diminish speed, and the reversal was made. The steam power was so low, that though the engine moved back, it was with moderate velocity, and I saw the pursuers reverse also, and coming to a full stop, whistle two or three times as it approached—a seeming whistle of alarm, though there was little now in the approach of our poor *General* to fear. Then they moved slowly before it for a short distance till the two were in contact, when the weaker stopped, and the steam was shut off. The great railroad chase was over.

Heading Nowhere 1

SMITH: Those of us on the *Texas* were in a small cut about two miles from Ringgold, just below the Fowlers' place, when I noticed the men ahead had commenced jumping off. Their engine was pulled up next, and the engineer reversed her without shutting off steam.

"She's coming back, Pete!" I yelled to Bracken.

Waiting just till we got across a small culvert, I jumped off.

MURPHY: Passing through the tunnel, we kept on, and beyond Ringgold about two miles the raiders left the *General* and made for the woods, some going on one side of the railroad and some the other side. We were in sight of them as they fled for safety, not knowing which way to go.

Nearing the *General*, we stopped. Fuller and others went after the raiders, but didn't reach them. I climbed on the abandoned engine to examine it, and found no wood in the furnace, but plenty of water in the boiler. The engine was all right, except for one truck brass that had become heated for want of oil. On the footboard we found the switch keys that Andrews had received from the agent at Kingston, where he took charge and changed the switch to run on the side track while the southbound train passed him.

In his endeavor to make steam, he had thrown all the oil cans and oil into the furnace. The last boxcar wasn't burned, as has been said, but splinters were prepared and placed in one end of the car where an effort had been made to burn it, which failed.

FULLER: The raiders abandoned their engine, and took to the forest.

SMITH: The *General* came back slowly, and Bracken, backing the *Texas*, eased her down without doing any damage. When the *General* was examined she seemed to be in good condition except that the forward engine truck brasses were heated.

"Those damned Yankees," one of the railroaders said. "They can run an engine as good as any of us."

MURPHY: A short time after we caught up with the *General*, the engine that was out of time—the one we passed at Calhoun—came up to where we were. Several men were aboard this engine and tender, and for the first time I knew that it had joined in the excitement of the chase and had been following us. I then instructed the engineer, Joe Renard, to return to Ringgold and give the news, which he did.

As we had passed Ringgold, I had seen many people there from the country. They generally came to town on Saturdays for the war news. The county was represented from nearly every district. So the news of the capture of the train went as fast as if there were a telegraph in every section, and in a short time the country was full of men and boys on horseback and afoot, making the escape of Andrews and his men almost impossible.

EDITOR: There's a variance of detail greater than usual in Fuller's and Murphy's accounts at this point, perhaps reflecting the intense excitement of the minutes immediately following recovery of the *General*. During this, it's easily understandable that two or more messages might have been rushed off calling for militia help from Ringgold.

FULLER: I ran upon their engine, the *General*, and coupled to her and hastened her back to Ringgold in the care of Peter Bracken, my engineer. I remembered that as I passed Ringgold I had seen a company of militia drilling. I sent a message to them by my engineer, informing them of the nature of our experience, and begging them to mount their horses and aid my party consisting of four men besides myself, in the capture of the raiders. They readily complied, and by this means the entire country was soon full of pursuers. My duty ended here.

PITTENGER: Campbell, the Hercules of the party, Slavens, also a man of massive proportions, and Shadrach were the first to leave the flagging *General*. It has been said that they jumped off under the command of Andrews before we reached Ringgold, and that as we came near the town the departure of the others was suspended for a little time, so that these were widely separated from the rest.

ALF WILSON: We put down the brakes, and as we sprang off and the *General* stopped, her motion was reversed with the hope that she would run back and either cause collision or delay to the onrushing train, with its frenzied passengers behind us, thereby giving us a little start. She wouldn't budge a wheel nor move an inch, just stood useless and sullen on the track—she was dead.

We didn't stop even to take a farewell look, but all struck for the woods, scattering in all directions. The locomotive after us came up to within two hundred yards of where we stopped, and we could hear them shout, "Halt! Halt!" and while some were leaping off the cars, others opened fire on us with their muskets. Between the shrill whistle and steam of their locomotive, their screeches and yells and the musketry fire, it seemed as if all bedlam had been turned loose. The musket balls began to fly uncomfortably thick.

As I jumped and ran from the train I heard my name called, and looking back, saw my comrade, Mark Wood, hastening after me. Halting for him, we continued our flight together.

BUFFUM: Mr. Andrews retained his presence of mind until the last moment. Finally our wood and water gave out, and he told us to shift for ourselves.

DORSEY: Leaving the *General*, I was with Bensinger, Buffum and George Wilson. We were near the last to cut out over the fields, running in a northeastern direction. As we ran, Buffum shed his Confederate overcoat by throwing his arms back and literally running out of it. Neither of us took time even to get the bottle which he had secured when we took supper at Dalton, and in which we both had felt quite an interest. Wilson was hurt and later had trouble walking, but in this first lighting out he was moving right along with us.

Some of our party were met in this flight through the woods by women who had taken alarm at the reports of the presence of the enemy and were trying to get themselves and children away in a panic. They told our boys to "run for God's sake; the country's alive with Yankees."

PARROTT: After we left the train, Sam Robertson and I took to the woods together.

KNIGHT: I will say I was first on the engine and last off. When the order was given by Andrews, "Every man for himself," the boys lit out like a flock of quail. I reversed the engine and started it back, but our steam being so low, it amounted to nothing. The pursuers were in plain sight. The boys had got a little the start of me, but I soon overhauled some of them.

[*Knight*]

There were five of us got together—Scott, Mason, Brown, Reddick and myself—and we ran as nearly as I thought by the compass, although we had none, in a southwest direction.

PITTENGER: When we left the train, I could see the soldiers pouring out from the pursuing trains—for a second one arrived almost immediately—and hear their loud shouts, and very soon the firing of guns. I didn't know where I was. I only knew that to go far enough north or northwest would bring me to our own lines; but the sun didn't shine, and I had no compass.

As I saw the fugitives a short distance ahead or to one side of me, I thought it would be a great advantage if I could reach those three who had been my companions day and night for a week, and from whom I had become separated in the confused tumbling from the cars. It was a pity that I thought of this, for in the attempt to find Wilson, Campbell and Shadrach, I lost the opportunity of finding some others whose companionship would have answered as well. My second thought was that getting away from the immediate scene of the abandoned train would be far better than to attempt concealment. Traveling never would be more easy or safe for us than that afternoon, if we but kept in advance of the enemy. By the next day it was sure that horsemen starting out from every telegraphic point would alarm the whole country.

If the description of the country given by different members of the party at starting differs somewhat, it's to be remembered that we had dropped off in scattered fashion along the road for the space of half a mile or more, which may have somewhat changed the surroundings. I climbed up the small bank which I found myself facing as soon as I recovered from the slight dizziness produced by tumbling off the train, and found a strip of woodland before me separated from the railroad by a fence. From the top of the fence I looked about, striving to get as good an idea of the situation as my bad eyes would permit. Our own train, which had gone ahead, was now halted or coming back, while the pursuing trains were very near.

They had stopped and men were getting off. Our boys were flying across the woods. Jumping down, I ran in the same direction. I crossed a little brook and came out into a large wheatfield that sloped up a moderate hill. There were three of our party a little ahead and it seemed as if I could overtake them. I put forth my best exertions, calling as I ran. They didn't hear me, and I couldn't overtake them. The wheatfield was very soft, and mud in great masses clung to my feet. Convinced that I couldn't overtake the men running uphill before me, I dropped into a walk, and plodding on, reached the other side of the field. As I left it, the first of the pursuers, Fuller at their head, mounted the fence and entered behind me.

In the woods beyond, I found with anguish that the last of my comrades had vanished, and I was alone. I continued on, keeping the noise of firing and shouting directly behind me as well as I could.

KNIGHT: Running hard, the five of us—Scott, Mason, Brown, Reddick and myself—soon came to the Chickamauga River. It had rained till the rivers and creeks were bank-full.

We jumped in, waded part of the way, and swam the balance, holding our revolvers over our heads to keep the powder dry. We got across, and hid in the brush on the far bank.

It happened that the day we captured our train, there was a general muster of the militia of the state of Georgia, and enrollment of the citizens. That brought everybody to the different towns along the road, and when they went home, the entire country knew of this railroad chase, and joined in the pursuit. They picketed the country and hunted for us as they would for wild animals.

We could lie where we were hid on the bank, and see more after us when they came up the river. At the same time we could see part of our party running still farther up the river on the other side. Our pursuers saw them about the same time and started for them. We lay where we first hid till dark.

F. M. GREGG: The race had gone on for about six hours, the captured train having arrived at Big Shanty at 6:45 A.M., and the *General* being abandoned about one P.M., in a small cut with a dense pine thicket on both sides of the road. When overtaken, the car that was still coupled to the engine was smoking from a fire built in one end of the car. The rain falling during the latter part of the race so wet the sides of the car that it didn't kindle well.

The engine pulling the passenger train which was passed at Calhoun came up just after the desertion of the *General*, having followed from that place with a carload of soldiers under Captain W. J. Whitsitt, who were passengers on that train. These started in pursuit and the engine was sent back to Ringgold to spread the alarm. This being muster day of state troops at Ringgold, it was soon known in all parts of the county, and pursuing parties were organized and scoured the country, arresting all strangers.

[*F. M. Gregg*]

When the raiders abandoned the engine they separated in all directions, some going east toward White Oak Mountains. The members of the expedition who went west ran through the woods, closely followed by Fuller and others, Murphy staying by his engine.

When the fugitives had gone about one-half mile through the woods, they came to the field of Judge T. M. Gordon, in which the Negroes were working at the time. While going through the field, attempts were made to get mules. This excited the hands, and they rushed to the house, crying, "The Yankees are coming, the Yankees are coming."

Beyond the field, there were woods bordering on Chickamauga Creek; through these they ran down to the creek to be confronted on the other side by a precipitous bank about ninety feet high and extending for about three-fourths of a mile up and down the creek. This bank was full of coverts and hiding places, offering them ample opportunities of secreting themselves. Captain Whitsitt, who was pursuing the raiders, was familiar with this place. Guessing that they would probably hide in it, he stationed a cordon of troops around this point. His hopes, however, were frustrated by the accidental discharge of a gun by one of his soldiers, which wounded a comrade. This attracted the attention of the rest of the party, who crowded around him, leaving the lower point unguarded, through which most of the raiders escaped.

When General Leadbetter, at Chattanooga, received by telegraph the startling information of the coming of the Andrews' party, he hastened a body of troops on flatcars out the Western & Atlantic road to meet them. Arriving at Chickamauga Station, they tore up the track. For one and a half miles on both sides of the road, a guard of soldiers was stationed, forming a trap in which it was hoped the quarry could be captured, but before the troops' arrival at that place, the engine had been abandoned ten miles below. Waiting until late that evening, the soldiers received word from their commanding officer, ordering them back to Chattanooga.

PORTER: Hawkins and I came in sight of Big Shanty late that Saturday. We marched into camp and reported at headquarters. Here we found several Rebel officers, one of whom, a colonel, turned his attention to us. After a short interview, which seemed plausible to him, he ordered us to report to the commanding officer of the 9th Georgia Battalion for enlistment. One of the companies, not being full, was called into line and took a vote whether or not we should be received into the company. The vote was unanimous in our favor, and we, after giving fictitious names, were assigned to a certain mess for our suppers. After supper we made the acquaintance of some of our new messmates, relating dismal stories of our treatment by the Yankee hirelings in Kentucky, which made a good impression on our comrades as to our loyalty to the Confederacy.

MURPHY: I took charge of the engine *General*, had it placed on a side track at Ringgold, and waited for the first train from Chattanooga to Atlanta. It reached Ringgold about dark. I went aboard, and reaching Dalton, the first telegraph station, I sent the news of the chase and recapture of the *General* to Atlanta that night. That ended my active participation in the memorable chase.

ALF WILSON: After running some distance, Wood and I came to a wide field, on the slope of a mountain. To cross this wide, open space would expose us too much. We could hear the enemy shouting, and the constant report of firearms. The woods were too open for a man to hide in, but as I glanced about, I saw where a tree had been cut down. The brush which had been trimmed off lay scattered around. Wood lay down, and I hastily laid a few leafy boughs over him. Mark was soon out of sight in a little flat pile that would scarcely be noticed among the other rubbish, and I slipped out of sight next to him, drawing my revolver and bidding him do likewise.

We were surrounded on every side. As I afterwards learned, within a few hundred yards from where we left our engine, two regiments of cavalry were encamped. It was muster day at Ringgold, two miles away, and hundreds of farmers armed and mounted were collected there. The day was dark, cloudy and rainy. Our boys were unacquainted with the country, and with the stars and sun hidden, most of them couldn't tell south from north. Within an hour or two the whole country was alive with scouts and hunters.

Several times parties after us passed so close to our hiding place that I could have reached out and touched their legs. The way our hearts thumped it seemed to me they could be heard twenty yards distant. But our pursuers made so much noise themselves that they could hear nothing else. They were all yelling, swearing and shooting, and on the style of dogs chasing a rabbit in tall weeds—all jumping and looking high, while the game was close to the ground.

F. M. GREGG: When Andrews jumped from the *General* he was joined by Ross and Wollam. Together they traveled westward, and were first seen at Daffron's Ford, about two miles south of Graysville. About dark they were seen again at Ellis' Spring, making their way toward Reed's Bridge road. From this time until the next day, Sunday, no trace could be had of them as they traveled through the woods.

That Saturday night at Graysville, John H. Flynn—the tipsy works foreman who'd thought in the morning only to catch an unexpected train lift that might get him home—was visited by a crowd. Taken from home, he was tied to a tree and unmercifully beaten as one of the sympathizers of the raiders.

A. L. WADDLE: We [of the advance Federal detachment on the railroad line beyond Stevenson] destroyed the bridge at Widden's Creek that Saturday afternoon, thus cutting off an attack by rail from the east, and returned to Stevenson, where Colonel Sill, with his command (General Mitchel having returned to Huntsville on the locomotive), remained several days, interviewing and being interviewed by the citizens.

Heading Nowhere 2

DORSEY: Run down near the railroad, Sammy Robertson and Jacob Parrott, two of our youngest men, must have been the first two captured. They denied all knowledge of the raid and their participation in it. Parrott was stripped, held down over a large rock by four men, and unmercifully whipped with a rawhide by a lieutenant, John Sauden, in an effort to extort a confession, but to no avail. Finally, it is said, Robertson sickened at the sight of his comrade's punishment, and seeing his back all gashed and bleeding, told his persecutors that they were United States soldiers, and that they were in the raid. This put a stop to the whipping. These were the only ones captured the day of the raid.

Parrott's back was fearfully cut up. When asked later if he intended to die there among strangers without letting them know who he was, Parrott said he intended just before he was actually killed—when he thought the end was near—to tell them his name and where he belonged and let them do their worst.

PARROTT:

Q. Will you state the circumstances of your capture and the treatment you received?

A. After a time, Robertson and I came down out of the woods. When we came out on the railroad, there were four citizens there, who saw us and took us. We were taken to Ringgold, where a company of Confederate soldiers were stationed.

When we got into the hands of an officer, one of them took me out and questioned me, but I wouldn't tell them anything. An officer and four soldiers took me out and stripped me, and bent me over a stone and whipped me. They stood by me with two pistols, and said if I resisted they would blow me through. I was whipped by a lieutenant, who was with the party, and who had on the Confederate uniform. He gave me over one hundred lashes with a strip of rawhide.

He stopped three different times during the whipping, let me up, and asked me if I would tell, and when I refused to do so, he would put me down and whip me again. He wanted me to tell who the engineer of the party was, and all about the expedition, but I wouldn't do it. I didn't tell him anything about it.

Q. Were other persons present when you were flogged?

A. Yes, sir; there was a crowd there. It was right by the side of the railroad, and the people there wanted to hang me. They got a rope and would have hung me, but for a colonel who came up.

Q. Did you have any trial of any sort?

A. No, sir.

Q. Your companion Robertson was with you at the time?

A. Yes, sir.

Q. Why wasn't he whipped?

A. I don't know. He told the regiment that he and I belonged to. I suppose, as I was the youngest, they thought that they could make me tell the most; but I wouldn't tell them anything, even the regiment I belonged to.

Q. Were you searched when you were taken?

[*Parrott*]

A. We were searched, and our money taken from us, before we were taken to Chattanooga.

DORSEY: George Wilson, Buffum, Bensinger and I traveled pretty rapidly until night came on. Then, owing to the cloudy weather—it was so dark we couldn't fix on a star—we simply wandered. Wilson thought he must have something to eat, and so we called at an isolated cabin, but as the gentleman of the house was prone on his back, his bare feet to the open fire, his abdomen covered with bags of hot ashes in the efforts of his faithful wife to relieve an attack of colic, we were neither fed nor admitted, and so wandered on.

PITTENGER: The certainty with which members of our party were identified when arrested arose from two causes. The first captures were so near the abandoned train that the men could be traced directly back to it. None of those first captured betrayed their comrades, and no one of them could have given names or descriptions of more than two or three of his associates, so little had we been thrown together. Not the slightest blame can be attached to these first captives, therefore, for revealing themselves; but, unfortunately, they first told the old Kentucky story which had already served us so well that we forgot that it might wear out. After that, whenever a man was found hailing from Kentucky's Fleming County, he was set down as one of us, and no denial would even be listened to.

Campbell, Slavens and Shadrach were the first to leave the *General*. Pursued by a large party with dogs, they were soon discovered and caught. Examined, they told at first the Kentucky story, and, afterwards, finding that circumstances had fixed their connection with the train, they gave their names and positions in the army—Campbell claiming, as it had been agreed, that he belonged to Company K, of the 2nd Ohio. They did this as they thought their fate as soldiers might possibly be better and couldn't be worse than that of citizens. They were loaded with heavy irons, conducted to Ringgold and afterwards to Dalton, in which place they remained for two or three days, when they were forwarded to what proved to be a general rendezvous —Chattanooga.

As to my own experience, for some time that Saturday afternoon, I kept on alone until I found myself in a bend of Chickamauga Creek. It was now swollen by the continuous rains into a formidable stream. Holding revolver and ammunition over my head, I succeeded in reaching the opposite shore, and climbing up an almost sheer cliff. At the top of the bank a sound reached my ears which set every nerve straining. It was the distant baying of a tracking dog. I ran in what I hoped was a westward direction until the noise of the dogs finally grew fainter.

On descending into an isolated valley, I saw a cabin and a man in the truck patch beside it. I approached him and asked the distance to Chattanooga. The answer was "eight miles." I must already have covered a long distance, as we were nineteen miles distant by rail when I started. I started along the road for Chattanooga, but as soon as the house was out of sight, turned off to my left for what I hoped was the direction of the Tennessee River.

I had walked fast for perhaps an hour, when to my great surprise I came to a road junction I had passed before, its appearance unmistakable. A short time later I struck either the Chickamauga, which I had crossed hours before, or one of its branches. I seemed to be in a labyrinth, where all my labor was worse than thrown away. In desperation I took the first road I came to and followed it, almost regardless of where it led or whom I should meet.

In the twilight, pressing on, I met a Negro driving a team. From him I learned that I was within four miles of Chattanooga. Vexation swept over me. Learning from the Negro the direction both of Ringgold and Chattanooga, that I might have two points by which to set my course, I once more set out for the Tennessee, not more than six or seven miles away. Although I didn't know it, the formidable Lookout Range was still before me, but I think I could have climbed anything if only sure I was going in the right direction.

Miles later, there did come a brief rift in the clouds, and by the stars, I was disheartened to find that I was again heading eastward—directly toward the railroad, which it seemed I had left an age ago. I had taken the highway to Ringgold. Wearily I retraced my steps. In less than half an hour, storm clouds again covered the stars. Rain fell in torrents, and a cold wind drove it against me till I shivered to the bone.

Knowing I must rest somewhere, I stumbled through some woods to a large log that lay only a few hundred yards from the edge of the road. I crawled partially under it, for shelter and concealment, and soon slept the dreamless sleep of exhaustion.

DORSEY: Before morning, George Wilson, Bensinger, Buffum and I tried again at a house for food, but failed to get admission, the people not wishing that night to open their doors to strangers. On the porch, however, we found a bucket of milk, which we were glad to drink. We pushed on again, and at daybreak, with no sun to guide us, we decided to hide till night.

We saw pursuers at a distance nearly all the morning, but weren't discovered. Then we saw three hounds coming right along our trail. There were four men following close and not allowing the dogs to get far ahead of them. We arose to meet them with the determination to fight these four if we couldn't deceive them, but one of them stopped and called lustily for help. He was answered with a whoop and yell from every quarter as we were advancing to meet the four. Evidently we were surrounded.

"Bagged, by—!" I said to my associates as we heard this response.

From every quarter came men, on foot and on horseback, whooping and yelling. We four were soon surrounded—this was on Sunday, April 13, about noon—by an excited crowd of perhaps fifty, Bensinger says eighty.

George Wilson had said that it might be well to drop the Kentucky story and try something new, but he didn't have time to get us drilled in anything. He talked up and pretended that we were from Loudon County, Va.—where I'd lived as a boy—and that we were down this way hunting Negroes. He made a pretty plausible story of it, but it wouldn't go down. Nine miles from Ringgold, and hiding in the woods as we were, it would have been hard to look innocent no matter what we did. We stood side by side, each with a hand on his pistol in his pocket, but if we'd started shooting, it would have been certain death on the spot, outnumbered by that crowd as we were. It was touch and go for a tight half-minute or so—I can remember a big, rawboned man with a double-barreled shotgun right in front of me; a man on horseback called "Major"; an old man nearby with a coil of rope, who looked as if he usually shaved once a week, on Sundays, but had been too busy on the man-hunt to get to it this day; and a yellow dog just to the left of the old man, sitting on his haunches, his head drooping, half asleep—and then we finally gave up our arms. Several of the crowd then wanted to shoot or hang us right off, but the major on horseback stopped them.

Bensinger had figured that naming ourselves as Union soldiers and claiming rights of war would give us our best chance, and he spoke up saying we were U.S. army, and asking that we be taken before regular military authorities. Whether from that, or from curiosity about our expedition, they tied our hands and took us to a house a mile away, where they even gave us a good dinner. Then we were marched to Ringgold and put into jail.

BUFFUM: I was captured with Mr. George Wilson, and Mr. Dorsey, and Mr. Bensinger. Money was taken from us by the officers—from some at the time we were taken, and from others when they were confined in prison. Mr. Wilson and I had $96 between us. They took away all our money, and our revolvers, pocketknives, and everything that could be of any use. We four were taken to Ringgold, and when we were taken into the jail we were stripped, our clothes turned inside out and everything examined.

Mr. Bensinger, who was with me when we were captured, was taken before a colonel, who took him into a room and questioned him. That night they took us to Marietta, where we were confined in a dungeon under ground. The rats were running over us in every direction. We could hardly get our breath. There were 150 guards around the jail to keep the mob from taking us out, as they would have done but for the guard. The next day we were taken to Chattanooga.

PITTENGER: How long I slept on the water-soaked leaves I have no idea—probably not a great while; but I seemed in an instant to be wide awake. Probably the nearest analogy to the state in which I found myself is that of the drunkard who experiences the horror of delirium tremens. The cause was no doubt purely natural, arising from fatigue, hunger, dampness and intense physical and mental exertion. But I will state exactly what occurred.

I seemed to hear someone whisper, as plainly as I ever heard human voice: "Shoot him! Shoot him! Let's shoot him before he wakes."

It flashed across my mind that a party of Rebels had discovered my hiding place and were about to murder me in my sleep. But immediately after this followed another thought only less appalling: "Was I insane?"

Slowly I opened my eyes. Directly before me stood a small tree. In a moment the tree seemed to break up into an innumerable multitude of the most beautiful forms—angels, ladies, flowers, children, nodding plumes, brilliant colors and all the pleasantest and most melodious objects and figures the mind could conceive. I got up, crawled back to the road and traveled on as if floating in a dream—but the dream was a reality, and mile after mile passed with an unrivaled ease and swiftness.

With the approach of morning, my visions began to fade. The

sense of weariness came back as I trudged on, and slowly my plan changed. Even before the day broke I resolved, if it still remained cloudy, not to try to avoid capture, but getting away as far from the scene of the raid as I could, to permit myself to be stopped and questioned with a view of enlisting.

Traveling on, I determined to keep a short distance from the road that I might not be discovered by those who were on it, many of them already going to church. At this time I was a believer in the Bible, but hadn't tried to make any practical use of it. I concentrated on devising the best methods of answering the questions that would follow arrest. A line of pretense as to my Southern sympathies and history from the time I left Kentucky to the present was outlined, and left to be filled up as occasion rendered expedient. In arranging such lines of defense, my partial legal education wasn't without value; but unfortunately the basis of the whole continued to be the same Fleming County story we had all told.

Noon brought me to the village of Lafayette, in Georgia—some twenty miles from Ringgold, the nearest railway station, and twenty-seven from Chattanooga. Several roads met here. I asked the way to Rome, and from there to Corinth in Mississippi. The direction was given and I continued on, but a mile or so from the village, I heard a loud voice behind calling: "Stop there! We want to speak with you."

Turning, I saw a party of more than twenty men, armed with various kinds of guns. Now was the time to try the plans I had been meditating all morning.

"What do you want, gentlemen?" I asked.

A little fellow called Major said that they wanted to talk with me. "There've been some strange happenings," he said, "and we're questioning every stranger."

I gave my name as John Thompson of Kentucky. I had left home because of the terrible oppressions of the Lincoln government, and meant, as soon as I had looked about me a little, to enlist in the Confederate army. He said they would have to search me. I felt safe enough on this score, as I had divested myself of all Federal marks. In fact, the South was so full of Northern manufactured products, that it would have been hard to name any article of general use that would have been compromising.

The major found a good revolver with plenty of ammunition, but that was in keeping for a Kentuckian. My money was all Confederate, and everything else right. I always wore my silver-framed spectacles, keeping them tied on my head for safety. Had they been taken, I would have been well-nigh helpless. But no reference was made to them either at this or any other time.

The major asked me where I came from the day before. I told him Chattanooga. Then he wished to know why I didn't enlist there. On the cars two days before, I had heard the soldiers boasting of the 1st Georgia, and now told the major that I wanted to go on to Corinth and try to get into the 1st Georgia. This flattered his state pride, and he seemed about to let me go when a dark-complexioned horseman, hat over his brows, spoke up.

"Well, ye-e-es," he drawled out. "Perhaps we'd as well take him back to town, though, and if all's right, maybe we can help him on to Corinth."

I pretended to be glad of the opportunity, and went promptly along. They took me down the single long muddy street of Lafayette, and brought me to the Goree House. People of the town gathered rapidly, and apparently many from the country also.

My reception was kind enough, but lawyers of the village came in and commenced asking all kinds of questions—many of them much harder than I had previously answered.

The situation was a terrible one. If I refused to answer at all, silence would be set down as a confession of guilt and myself as a stubborn and morose fellow. There might be no small danger of the lash and the halter. My only hope was dim and far off—that of being permitted to go on my way and meet similar perils; or of being enlisted in the Rebel army to face Union bullets, and possibly die in an attempt to desert. That was the future. In the present, a careless word or an outside incident might in a moment break up our truce and leave me at the mercy of a howling mob.

Lawyer-like, my inquisitors wanted to know about a host of minute matters. They asked me from what county in Kentucky I came. I said, "Fleming." They asked the county seat. I gave the name Flemingsburg without difficulty, then was asked to bound the county. I mentioned a few counties at random that I thought were in that part of the state. They procured a map, and said it looked rather suspicious to find a man who couldn't bound his own county. I offered to bet that none of their neighbors standing around the door could bound the county we were now in. They wouldn't make the bet, but tried the experiment. Not a man was able to do it entirely; and as they were comparing the map with the answers, I received a better idea of the geography of that part of the state than I had had before.

Then these inquisitive people wanted to know all about my journey from Kentucky down to that very day and with what people I had lodged. I think from some of their questions that they imagined me to be a Rebel deserter. All of them kept in a fairly good humor, and jests passed frequently.

For four hours the catechism went on, when a noise was heard outside, and a horseman dashed up to the door.

"They've caught the bridge burners," he shouted.

Question after question was hurled at him.

"They said at first they were citizens of Fleming County, Kentucky," the messenger answered. "Afterwards they owned they were United States soldiers sent south to burn the bridges on the state road."

Fierce eyes gleamed on me, and there were no more jests or questions. Some of the leading men went into another room, but came back in a few minutes, and one of them said to me simply: "We'll have to take you to jail."

Without a word, I rose from the chair by the window on which I had been sitting so long, and went with them.

DORSEY: I am not clear just where Slavens was captured. Campbell and Shadrach were taken together, as I was later to learn from a Mr. Richard L. Rhodes of Chattanooga.

Campbell and Shadrach at a rather late hour on the night of the raid, April 12, put up at the house of Mr. Rhodes' father, near Lafayette, and after a hearty supper, retired to bed. But their host suspected them as members of the raiding party and sent for help. Early next morning men came. Entering the room in which our comrades slept, these men picked up the revolvers, which lay on the pillows between the heads of the unconscious sleepers, and made them prisoners. So thoroughly exhausted had our comrades become from the week's toil and excitement—this was on Sunday morning, and we had been detailed for the expedition on Sunday evening, a week before—that Campbell and Shadrach had to be pulled and shaken before they could be roused from the heavy sleep into which they had fallen.

Mr. Rhodes also says Pittenger was captured near Lafayette about seven o'clock Sunday morning, and taken with the other two to Ringgold, and thence by rail to Chattanooga. This latter report is confirmed in part at least by others, although a medical man—name not available to me now—of Lafayette says he took Pittenger to Chattanooga in a buggy; and this confirms Pittenger in his account of his capture, except as to time. They all say he was captured early in the morning.

KNIGHT: We undertook to travel Saturday night, but made poor headway. When it came daylight Sunday, we kept slipping along through the woods till we saw the enemy scouring the country in all directions for us, then we hid ourselves again till dark.

PITTENGER: The little major who had acted as spokesman now escorted me to jail. I was taken up a narrow stairway, and entered a fair-sized room, with bars across the windows. The noticeable feature of the room was a large iron cage, nine by twelve feet, which stood in the middle. It had an iron door, which the jailer unlocked, and I was bidden enter. One man was in it—a Union man, as he said, though I was disposed to believe him a detective, put there for the purpose of finding out as much as he could from me.

My reflections couldn't have been more gloomy. I was locked up as a criminal, and too well did I realize the character of the Southern people to believe they would be fastidious about proof. A high value was never set on the life of a stranger, and now with the fierce war fever, and the madness caused by our raid, the situation was desperate. The thought of dying unknown—of simply dropping out of life without anyone ever being able to tell what had become of me—seemed terrible. That all my hopes should perish, as I then had every reason to believe, on a Southern scaffold, was almost unbearable. For a moment only did these thoughts sweep over me; the next they were rejected. At least here was rest and quiet. No more questions to answer, no straining to the last limits of physical endurance, but shelter, warmth and rest. To these was soon added another great comfort, for a fairly good supper was brought.

My cagemate wanted to ask me some questions; but I had been questioned sufficiently, and gave him very short answers. There were plenty of blankets, and wrapping myself in them, I soon fell into a deep sleep.

I didn't wake until next morning. At first I hadn't the slightest idea of where I was. Then when the terrible memories of the past two days came trooping back, despair didn't come with them. There might yet be the opportunity of escape, if a little time was given. I well knew that being inside the enemy's lines in citizen's dress gave them the right to put us to death by a sentence that would have at least the color of military law; but no military law required the exertion of that power. If they simply held us as hostages or exchanged us for men of theirs in similar condition—such as those of Morgan's men who were often taken even in Federal uniform—all military usages would be satisfied. While, then, the great probability was that the enemy in the heat of passion and vengeance would put me to death either by mob law or by a drumhead court-martial, yet if they could in any way be induced to let some little time pass, and cool reason to get the upper hand, there was a chance that I might either be able to break away or be saved by the power of threatened retaliation.

But that there might be the slightest chance for interference on our behalf, our character and position must be clearly known. Very quaintly did my prison companion put this thought. "If you're innocent of being one of the bridge burners," he said, "as they call you, they'll be sure to hang you. But if you *are* one, and should claim to be a soldier, your government won't let so many of you perish without making some effort to save you."

Slowly I came to the conviction that I *would* be better off in my own name and character. I had time enough for deliberation. Questions were asked—as visitors came in and passed around the cage and out again, a continual procession—but I didn't care to answer. I was too busy trying to arrange plans that might get me out of the position in which I was placed. I knew that there was no regularly constituted military authority at Lafayette, and that if I should be dealt with while there, it would only be the act of an irresponsible mob—in that lonely region a thing by no means unlikely. I now felt that Chattanooga, the headquarters of that district, was the best place to be. I thought that by working on the curiosity of my captors I might induce them to send me away.

Accordingly I told the guard, who carried word to the jailer, that I would like to see the vigilance committee. In a little time I was taken before them. They had their lawyers and clerk ready, but I cut the whole matter short.

"Gentlemen," I told them, "the statements I gave you yesterday were intended to deceive. I will now tell you the truth."

The clerk got his pen ready to take down the information.

"I'm ready to give you my true name, and to tell you why I came into your country."

"Just what we want to know, sir," said they. "Go on."

"But I'll make no statement till taken before the regular military authority of this department."

This took them by surprise, and they used every threat and argument in their power to make me change my resolution. But I told them that it was a purely military matter, and that if they were loyal to the Confederacy, they would send me as soon as possible to the commanding general.

They decided to send me that very day.

It was a journey of twenty-seven miles, and after dinner, a dozen men called and conducted me to the public square in front of the courthouse, where a carriage was in waiting in which I was placed; and then commenced a process of tying and chaining.

A great mob had gathered. They declared I could be hanged as easily there as at Chattanooga, and obviously didn't wish their village robbed of a tragedy or a sensation. They questioned me in loud and imperious tones, demanding why I came down there, what I meant to do with the train—for though I had not yet admitted being among its captors, they took that for granted—and added every possible word of insult.

My position was serious. The committee in whose hands I was had no more real authority than those who were hooting and howling around. I knew that the typical Southerner admires coolness and courage above everything else; so acting on Shakespeare's advice to "assume a virtue if you have it not," I selected some of those who seemed most prominent and addressed them. I spoke very quietly, and watching a chance to get in a joke about the manner in which I was being tied and affecting to treat the whole matter as hardly serious, I soon had some of the laughers on my side; and then I was less afraid, and could play my part still better. The insults and oaths decreased, and something of the qualified good feeling of the day before returned. During the whole time I was a prisoner I never had five minutes' conversation with any Southern man, or men, without all manifestation of angry feeling being suppressed.

I had now been secured in the carriage. One end of a heavy chain, eight or nine feet in length, was put around my neck and fastened with a padlock; the other end was carried back of and under the carriage seat on which I was sitting, and locked to one foot in the same manner. My hands were locked in handcuffs; my elbows were closely pinioned to my side by ropes. My conductor, the little major, took his seat at my side, and two men followed on horseback armed with shotguns. All preparations being completed, I took leave of the village.

As we journeyed, my companions were talkative, and though I couldn't quite forget that they were carrying me chained as a criminal, yet I knew it would be unavailing to indulge a surly disposition, and therefore talked as fast and as lively as they did. The guards them-

[*Pittenger*]
selves did not subject me to any insult. The most I had to complain of in their behavior was their conduct when we passed a house. They would call out: "Hallo! We've got a live Yankee here."

Men, women and children would rush to the door and stare.

"Whar did you ketch him?" they would call. "Goin' to hang him when you get him to Chattanooga?"

The perpetual recurrence of these questions grew wearisome, and wasn't without its effect in making me think that perhaps they still would hang me. In fact, my expectation of escaping wasn't very bright; but I considered it my duty, for the sake of others as well as of myself, to keep hope alive, that I might be ready to take advantage of any favoring circumstance. It wasn't so much death I dreaded—but to be hanged! Death in battle didn't seem half so terrible as the chill horror of the scaffold. These thoughts were almost too much for my fortitude but I knew no resource except patience and endurance.

F. M. GREGG: On Sunday, April 13, Fuller and Murphy arrived back in Atlanta from their chase after the raiders, and were seen by the editors of the *Southern Confederacy*, who then gave to the public the first real information of the "engine thieves," and their scheme. In general [in the main running narrative omitted here as a near-duplication of the Fuller and Murphy accounts] it was surprisingly accurate.

Southern Confederacy, ATLANTA, APRIL 15, 1862:

THE GREAT RAILROAD CHASE!

The Most Extraordinary and Astounding Adventure of the War; the Most Daring Undertaking that Yankees Ever Planned or Attempted to Execute.

Since our last issue we have obtained full particulars of the most thrilling railroad adventure that ever occurred on the American continent, as well as the mightiest and most important in its results, if successful, that has been conceived by the Lincoln government since the commencement of this war. Nothing on so grand a scale has been attempted, and nothing within the range of possibility could be conceived, that would fall with such crushing force upon us as the accomplishment of [these] plans [had they come to completion].

We will begin at the breakfast table, in the Big Shanty Hotel, at Camp McDonald, on the W. & A. Railroad, where several regiments of soldiers are now encamped. The morning mail and passenger train had left here at four A.M. on last Saturday morning as usual, and had stopped there for breakfast. The conductor, W. A. Fuller, the engineer, J. Cain—both of this city—and the passengers were at the table, when some eight men, having uncoupled the engine and three empty boxcars next to it from the passenger and baggage cars, mounted the engine, pulled upon the valve, put on all steam, and left conductor, engineer, passengers, spectators, and the soldiers in the camp hard by, all lost in amazement, and dumfounded.

This unheard-of act was doubtless undertaken at that place and time upon the presumption that pursuit could not be made by an engine short of Kingston, or from this place; and that, by cutting down the telegraph wires as they proceeded, the adventurers could calculate on at least three or four hours' start of any pursuit it was reasonable to expect. This was a legitimate conclusion, and but for the will, energy, and quick and good judgment of Mr. Fuller and Mr. Cain, and Mr. Anthony Murphy, the intelligent and practical foreman of the wood department of the state road shop, who accidentally went on the train from this place that morning, their calculations would have worked out as originally contemplated, and the results would have been obtained—the most terrible to us of any that we can conceive as possible.

These three determined men, without a moment's delay, put out after the flying train on foot, amidst shouts of laughter by the crowd, who, though lost in amazement at the unexpected and daring act, could not repress their risibility at seeing three men start after a train on foot. . . .

Through the great tunnel at Tunnel Hill, [the pursuers were] only five minutes behind. The fugitives, finding themselves closely pursued, uncoupled two of the boxcars from the engine to impede the progress of the pursuers. Fuller hastily coupled them to the front of his engine, and pushed them ahead of him to the first turnout or siding, where they were left, thus preventing the collision the adventurers intended. Thus the engine thieves passed Ringgold, where they began to fag. They were out of wood, water, and oil. Their rapid running and inattention to the engine had melted all the brass from the journals. They had no time to repair and refit, for an iron horse of more bottom was close behind.

Fuller and Murphy and their men soon came within four hundred yards of them, when the fugitives jumped from the engine and left it—three on the north side, and five on the south—all fleeing precipitately, and scattering through the thicket.

A large number of men were soon mounted, armed, and scouring the entire country in search of them. Fortunately, there was a militia muster at Ringgold. A great many countrymen were in town. Hearing of the chase, they put out on foot and on horseback in every direction in search of the daring but now thoroughly frightened and fugitive men. . . .

All of the eight men were captured, and are now safely lodged in jail. They confessed that they belonged to Lincoln's army, and had been sent down from Shelbyville to burn the bridges between here and Chattanooga, and that the whole party consisted of nineteen men, eleven of whom were dropped at several points on the road, as they came down to assist in the burning of the bridges as they went back.

One gentleman who went upon the train from Calhoun, who has furnished us with many of these particulars, and who is one of the most experienced railroad men in Georgia, says too much praise cannot be bestowed on Fuller and Murphy, who showed a cool judgment and forethought in this extraordinary affair, unsurpassed by anything he ever knew in a railroad emergency.

We do not know what Governor Brown will do in this case, but if such a thing is admissible, we insist on Fuller and Murphy being promoted to the highest honors on the road. Certainly their indomitable energy and quick, correct judgment and decision in the many difficult contingencies connected with this unheard-of emergency have saved all the railroad bridges above Ringgold from being burned. The most daring scheme that this revolution has developed has been thwarted, and the tremendous results which, if successful, can scarcely be imagined, have been averted. Had they succeeded in burning the bridges, the enemy at Huntsville would have occupied Chattanooga before Sunday night. Yesterday they would have been in Knoxville, and thus had possession of all East Tennessee. Our forces at Knoxville, Greenville, and Cumberland Gap would have been moved upon at once. This would have given them possession of the valley of Virginia, and Stonewall Jackson could have been attacked in the rear. They would have possession of the railroad leading to Charlottesville and Orange Court House, as well as the Southside Railroad leading to Petersburg and Richmond. They might have been able to unite with McClellan's forces, and attack Jo. Johnston's army, front and flank. It is not by any means improbable that our army in Virginia would have been defeated, captured, or driven out of the state this week.

The reinforcements from all the eastern and southeast portions of the country would have been cut off from Beauregard. The enemy have Huntsville now, and with all these designs accomplished, his army would have been effectually flanked. The mind and heart shrink back appalled at the consequences which would have followed the success of this one act. When Fuller, Murphy, and men started from Big Shanty on foot to catch that fugitive engine, they were laughed at by the crowd, but that foot-race saved us, and prevented the consummation of all these tremendous consequences.

One fact we must not omit to mention is the valuable assistance rendered by Peter Bracken, the engineer on the down freight train which Fuller and Murphy turned back. He ran his engine fifty and a half miles (two of them backing the whole freight train up to Adairsville), made twelve stops, coupled to the two cars which the fugitive had dropped, and switched them off on sidings; all this in one hour and five minutes.

We doubt if the victory of Manassas or Corinth were worth as much to us as the frustration of this grand coup d'etat. It is not by any means certain that the annihilation of Beauregard's whole army at Corinth would be so fatal a blow to us as would have been the burning of the bridges at that time by these men.

It was all the deepest laid scheme, and on the grandest scale that ever emanated from the brains of any number of Yankees combined. To think of a parcel of Federal soldiers, officers and privates, coming down into the heart of the Confederate States—for they were here in Atlanta and at Marietta (some of them got on the train at Marietta Saturday morning and others were at Big Shanty), of playing such a serious game on the state road, which is under the control of our prompt, energetic, and sagacious governor, to seize the passenger train on his road, right at Camp McDonald, where he had a number of Georgia regiments encamped, and run off with it; to burn the bridges on the same road, and go safely through to the Federal lines—all this would have been a feather in the cap of the man or men who executed it.

Let this be a warning to the railroad men and everybody else in the Confederate States. Let an engine never be left alone a moment. Let additional guards be placed at our bridges. This is a matter we specially urged on the Confederacy long ago; we hope it will now be heeded. Further, let a sufficient guard be placed to watch the government stores in this city. We know one solitary man who is guarding a house, of nights, in this city, which contains a lot of bacon. Two or three men could throttle and gag him and set fire to the house at any time; and worse, he conceives that there is no necessity for a guard, as he is sometimes seen off duty for a few moments, fully long enough for an incendiary to burn the house he watches. A well-armed guard should be placed around every house containing government stores. Let this be done without waiting for instructions from Richmond.

One other thought: the press is requested, by the government, to keep silent about the movements of the army, and a great many things of the greatest interest to our people. Now, we again ask, what's the use? The enemy get what information they want. They are with us and pass among us almost daily. It is nonsense, it is folly, to deprive our own people of knowledge they are entitled to for fear the enemy will find it out. We ought to have a regular system of passports over all our roads, and refuse to let any man pass who could not give a good account of himself, come well vouched for, and make it fully appear that he is not an enemy. This would keep information from the enemy far more effectually than any reticence of the press, which ought to lay before our people the full facts in everything of a public nature.

DORSEY: George Wilson, Buffum, Bensinger and I were taken from Ringgold by rail that Sunday night to Marietta and thrown in a stronger jail. A strong guard of cadets was thrown around the building to protect us from mob violence. The cadets were a jolly set of boys, and frequently came to our barred window to exchange greetings. They soon became so well acquainted with us that they could call each one by his proper name.

During the captures of members of our party that occurred during the next few days, word got out somehow that two of our number had been left off at Marietta, and suspicion at once rested on Hawkins and Porter—the two new recruits at Camp McDonald.

PORTER: Everything went all right with us in our 9th Georgia Battalion at Camp McDonald until in some manner it leaked out among the Rebels that the Yankee raiders, by mistake or accident, had left two of their party at Marietta. How this information got out I never learned, but it couldn't be otherwise than that someone of our party had indiscreetly told more than he ought to when captured; who the man was we never learned.

The excitement ran very high, and we discovered, when it was too late, that we had run into the jaws of danger, for immediately we fell under suspicion and were sent to headquarters and there ordered to give a truthful account of ourselves, under penalty of death if we lied. We were taken into a room, one at a time, and interviewed by a number of Rebel officers—Hawkins first and myself afterwards. When Hawkins came out I saw at a glance that something was wrong; but my turn had come and I took my seat in the room, confronted by six Confederate officers, when I put on the boldest front I could.

One of the officers, a colonel, took me in hand and began by first inquiring my name, which I didn't give in full, as I had used just the "John Reed" part of my name—John Reed Porter—when I enlisted with them. He proceeded in his order of examination as best suited him, and I tried to answer as best suited myself, just the reverse of what they desired. Finally, others of the party commenced asking questions and I found that John Reed was in a pretty tight place. On various occasions during nearly four years of army life I experienced some pretty close calls, but this was a little the closest corner I ever got into. They were very menacing and abusive, expecting, I suppose, to scare me into a confession.

The colonel finally said, "Mr. Reed, you stand there thrice damned. You may make your peace with your God, but you never can with Jefferson Davis, and we ought to hang you without any further ceremony."

I was permitted to return to the room with Hawkins, where we were closely guarded and weren't allowed to converse with each other. The word soon spread through the camp that we were Yankees and belonged to the railroad party. In a short time the building was surrounded with an excited mob that demanded our immediate execution—some threatening to shoot us and some to hang us before we should leave there. As they still gathered around, the excitement increased, until they placed a heavy guard around the building, and the crowd soon began to disperse, intent upon a fresh attack at night.

As soon as the first train came along going south, we were put aboard under guard and sent to Marietta, where we were handcuffed and chained together by the end of a trace chain being placed around the neck of each and locked with padlocks. Then, to make assurance doubly sure, we were placed in an inner cell of the jail for safekeeping during the night.

The news of our arrival soon spread through the town, and in a short time an infuriated mob gathered around the jail and demanded our release, that they might take out their vengeance upon us, otherwise they would burn the jail. As the night wore on, the crowd increased until they finally placed another heavy guard around the jail. That somewhat allayed our fears, although it seemed as though morning never would come. When it did, however, the jail was again surrounded by curiosity seekers and a mob-spirited crowd, to see the "wild Yankees," as they called us.

DORSEY: After a sojourn of about thirty-six hours at Marietta, the outside door was unlocked, followed soon after by a crashing noise made by the jailer throwing an armful of chains upon the floor. The jailer began to call the roll.

"Mr. Wilson."

The end of a bright new trace chain was passed around Wilson's neck, secured by a new padlock, and a pair of handcuffs was placed upon his wrists.

"Mr. Dorsey . . . Mr. Bensinger . . . Mr. Buffum."

I received the other end of Wilson's chain around my neck, secured by another padlock, and was handcuffed as well, Bensinger and Buffum being paired in the same style.

Stepping to the rear of the hall, the jailer opened the door to another cell and out stepped two others, full-jeweled like ourselves. We recognized Hawkins and Porter, but not knowing whether they had been identified as members of our party, we didn't speak to them, nor in anywise appear to recognize them. Taken out of our cell at Marietta, we were loaded into a boxcar, seated on cotton bales, and started northward.

PORTER: During the morning we were hurried to the depot under a strong guard to protect us from the mob, and were put aboard for Chattanooga.

DORSEY: A tall sergeant and squad of soldiers from a Georgia regiment constituted our escort. They were gentlemen, and treated us kindly; but were without means of feeding us or themselves. We reached Dalton about dark, and for some reason unknown to us, had to wait in the depot until another train arrived.

Quite a threatening mob gathered outside. Two ladies, a lad of twelve years and two colored servants came in and gave us all, guards and prisoners, an excellent supper. The ladies came and took seats facing us, inquired about our friends at home, asked if we had families and seemed to sympathize with us in our hopeless situation. I spoke feelingly of my mother and sisters, but not much more.

After returning to the opposite side of the room, the young lady sent her little brother to me with a red rose, with a single row of leaves around it, and with it her name. As the rose was placed in my hand, and the lady's name pronounced in my ear, I looked across the room in her direction, our eyes met, and for a moment we literally stared at each other. Of course, I accepted the proffered token of sympathy, respect or friendship, whatever it might mean, and returned my thanks, with my name, company and regiment. This display of friendship on the part of the ladies seemed to exasperate the crowd on the outside. They became quite demonstrative at one time, but the sergeant was cool and firm, and kept them off. At a late hour we boarded a passenger train and resumed the journey northward for Chattanooga.

Heading Nowhere 3

F. M. GREGG: Early Sunday morning, the 13th, Captain Hackett, a cavalry officer in the Confederate service, started out from Ringgold in pursuit of the three men who had been seen at Daffron's Ford, and later at Ellis' Spring, on the afternoon before. Hackett followed their supposed track across the valley but didn't succeed in overtaking them.

That afternoon, Hackett passed through Rossville Gap, Ga. On the western slope of Mission Ridge he rode up to a cabin on Thomas McFarland's place, and there saw Dr. [Thomas Y.] Park, a well-known physician who lived at the foot of Lookout Mountain, and who was on a professional visit at the time. Captain Hackett called the doctor out and told him of the pursuit and the character of the men sought, telling him at the same time that he was to organize a party and continue the pursuit. The doctor remonstrated, but to no purpose. The captain then rode off with his troopers.

As Hackett's party was returning that evening, they rode by a thicket where Andrews and companions were hidden, and the latter could hear the pursuers talk about "which way the rascals had gone." They had passed across Mission Ridge, at Rossville Gap, about dinner time. Andrews had a compass and by this means was making a straight line for Bridgeport, Ala., crossing Chattanooga Valley in a southwest direction. The three raiders stayed all night with a Union man named Merrick Earpes, at the foot of Lookout Mountain, about seven miles from Chattanooga, near Crutchfield's place.

DR. THOMAS Y. PARK: On Sunday afternoon, April 13, 1862, I was called over to McFarland's at foot of Mission Ridge, near Rossville

Gap, to see a patient. While at the house, Captain Hackett, of Ringgold, rode up with a troop. Seeing me, he called me out to the fence and said: "You're just the man I'm looking for." He then told me about the men running away with the engine from Big Shanty, and that some of the party had come through the Gap that day and were making their way across Chattanooga Valley to Bridgeport, Ala.

"I want you to follow them," he said.

I told him my practice wouldn't allow me to leave it and made other excuses, but he said: "You're the only man who knows all the paths through this section, and we've lost the trail. I order you to pursue these men and capture them. I shall hold you responsible if you don't."

It was nine o'clock Monday morning before I started with my party from McCullough's Mill, Tenn., at the foot of Lookout Mountain. There have been conflicting reports about dogs being used. There wasn't a dog in my party nor were there any in Captain Hackett's. The men we were after stayed all night at Merrick Earpes' and early next morning they started on their journey, Earpes piloting them around McCullough's Mill, which was the place of meeting for the pursuing party. On top of the mountain they took an old trail that goes near Lulu Lake.

Instead of walking in the path, the men we were after went along the side through the grass and weeds, enabling us to follow them readily. When my party came to the top of the mountain, it separated into two parts, one of ten men going down the Wauhatchie Trail. The other, consisting of Duncan Evans, Frank Harp, Isaac Wallen, James Wallen and myself, followed a blind trail that hadn't been used for years. We saw the signs along in the grass of persons having gone that way, but saw no one.

We followed across the top of Lookout Mountain, down the other side into the valley, crossing Lookout Creek. At a house where we stopped, a woman told us that three men had gone by there about a half-hour before. We then increased our speed, hoping to overtake them.

F. M. GREGG: When Andrews and his companions crossed the mountain they came down to Powell's Ford, on Lookout Creek. Here they met Sam Steadman in a canoe, who paddled them across the creek, passing Mrs. Powell's house. It was she that gave their course to Dr. Park's party.

Andrews, Ross and Wollam went down the road to the house of a man named Pierce Meadows. Here they ate dinner. Meadows had a cleared field south of his house, extending to the road, giving an open view on that side. When they had finished dinner they started down the road, and as they passed the field, entered into a white hawthorn thicket, wholly unconscious that as they were disappearing behind the screen of green leaves—which a minute later would have safely hid them from all pursuit—they were seen by Dr. Park's party.

DR. PARK: When we left the house where the woman told us of the three men ahead, we whipped our horses up until, going quite a distance, we began to think we were on the wrong trail. There was a cleared space ahead, and we came into this at a good pace. We could see no one about the house, but down the road a distance we saw three men go into a white hawthorn thicket. They didn't see us, but we whipped our horses to their utmost speed and raised the yell, and went into the thicket pell-mell.

Sure enough, about one hundred yards ahead of us, there were the three men running their best, but our horses were too swift for them. I had a double-barreled shotgun in my hand. One of the men we were chasing couldn't run as fast as the others; gaining on him, I ordered him to halt. He paid no attention to me, but coming to a thick part of the woods, jumped behind a post oak tree. When I came up to him he sprang from behind the tree with a cocked revolver nearly against me. Fortunately, Isaac Wallen was behind me with the handle of a large butcher knife sticking out of his coat pocket. He put his hand down to it, thus attracting the attention of the man. The latter lowered his revolver, saying that there was no use of having two dead men there in the woods. The whole party stopped and gathered around our prisoner. All we could get out of him was that he was from Kentucky and was going to join the Confederate army and that his name was Wollam.

In the meantime the other two men had disappeared over the hill. I then ordered Evans, James Wallen and Harp to follow them up. When they came to the top of the hill the two men could be seen quite a distance ahead. Duncan Evans was on a better horse than the other two, and he was soon well ahead in the chase. The taller of the runners was also well in the lead, and could no doubt have escaped, but returned to his exhausted companion. When Evans came up he covered the larger one—Andrews—with his rifle. The latter feigned to be surprised that Evans was after them, and said, "We are Confederate soldiers," then pulling out from his vest pocket, he showed him an old Confederate passport that he had used when he was a contraband merchant. He told Evans that they were going to the army, and that they had run from our party because they supposed us to be Yankee cavalrymen.

Evans believed this story and sent word back to me that he had two Confederate soldiers up there, and what should he do with them. I sent word back to hold them until I came. Going to them, I went straight up to the largest one—Andrews, as we found out afterwards.

"I know who you fellows are," I said. "You're some of the party that stole the engine at Big Shanty, ran it up as far as Ringgold and then left it. You're not looking for the Confederate army."

"Well, my friend," said Andrews, in a voice as cool and steady as if speaking to his best friend, "I'm surprised at your information, but you're right about it. I see there's no use trying to deceive you. Are you the leader of this party?"

I replied I wasn't elected leader, but I was at the head of it.

"Well," was the reply, "I surrender to you as prisoner of war, and expect to be treated as such."

He gave his name as Andrews and his companion's as Ross; we then walked down to where Wollam was. On the way down, Andrews put his hand in his overcoat pocket, and his pistol went off; he said that it was cocked in his pocket and he was trying to let it down, when the hammer slipped through his fingers. It was a fine ivory-handled weapon, which he handed over to me without further remarks.

When we came to where I had left the other party and my men had come together, Andrews said, "Where's the rest of them?"

"This is all," I told him.

"If we had known that," Andrews said, "you never would have taken us. We supposed the woods were full of you, from the noise you made, so we surrendered to your noise, and not to your numbers."

There's no doubt but that if Andrews and the others had made a fight at all, they would have succeeded in getting away, for our crowd had one shotgun, a rifle and a butcher knife. It wasn't because they were afraid that they didn't use their arms, but we made all the racket possible to deceive them, and they imagined that they were surrounded with superior force. All of them were grit to the backbone, but they supposed it was a hopeless fight.

We captured Andrews and his two comrades about twelve miles from Bridgeport, Ala., which point no doubt they would have reached the same evening, but for our discovery of them just as they went into the hawthorn thicket. It was about three-quarters of a mile above New England City, Ga., and about sixteen miles from Chattanooga, to which place we started with our prisoners riding behind us.

Ross rode behind me, Andrews back of Evans, and Wollam with Frank Harp. We had hardly mounted when Ross asked me if I was a Mason. I told him I wasn't, but would introduce him to a man who was when we met our other party; doing so shortly, I introduced him to Dr. Davis, and together they went to one side. I heard Dr. Davis say, "I recognize the link between us, but can do nothing for you under the present circumstances." Ross seemed somewhat disappointed at this, but said nothing further on the subject. His only response to my questions asked about the expedition was that they were enlisted men, and that Andrews was to have received $20,000 if he had succeeded.

PITTENGER: When Andrews, Ross and Wollam were finally surrounded, it was done so quickly at the last as to be something of a surprise, and Andrews was understood not to have completed the destruction of some papers which he had been unable to get out of the way. These, with the large amount of money he carried—more than two thousand dollars—at once marked him out as a person of consequence, and, in connection with his striking personal appearance, suggested the commanding stranger who had acted as conductor of the pretended powder train.

That same evening, Andrews and his two companions were heavily ironed and borne to Chattanooga.

F. M. GREGG: About ten miles out from Chattanooga, Dr. Park's party was met by a company of Ragsdale's cavalry under command of Lieutenant James Edwards, to whom the prisoners were turned over, together with their weapons. They were then conducted by that officer to General Leadbetter's headquarters at the old Crutchfield House. Andrews gave Lieutenant Edwards his compass as a gift; this, however, was turned over with other effects to General Leadbetter and not later returned.

DORSEY: Though we traveled some twenty hours after leaving the engine, we were captured about nine miles from where we had left it. In our wanderings we had unawares taken the back track.

We acknowledged, during the dinner hour, our participation in the raid as United States soldiers, and claimed the protection due us as such. There was loud talk of lynching, hence the claim of protection. En route to Ringgold, after dinner, the major asked who our leader was, and receiving no satisfactory answer, said: "It makes no difference, gentlemen; we know all about it; your leader's name is Andrews, and we've got him."

This was startling news, for we had fully expected that Andrews—separated from our party, and with the passes he had from Rebel officers—would soon be in General Mitchel's camp doing something to protect us.

F. M. GREGG: In Chattanooga, Andrews and his companions weren't taken at once to General Leadbetter's office, as the latter was busy trying to induce or scare information from another of their band who had been brought in before them.

PITTENGER: We reached Chattanooga before it was quite dark and at once drove to the Crutchfield House, the headquarters of General Leadbetter, then commanding. While the guards ascended to inform him of our arrival, I remained in the carriage.

I was the first of our party brought to Chattanooga; and the curiosity to see me was intense. In a few minutes the street in front of the hotel was completely blocked, the people jeering and hooting. My conductors were a good while gone, engaged, as I supposed, in letting General Leadbetter know the kind of a person I was, and how I came into their possession. No doubt they also told him what I had promised to reveal on my arrival. I hadn't forgotten this myself, and had gone very carefully over the ground and decided where the line must be drawn between truth and fiction—how little of the former would suffice to establish my standing as a Union soldier, and how much of the latter could be administered with probable profit. There was no qualm of conscience as to telling him—the enemy of my country, and in rebellion against lawful authority—anything that might injure him or his cause, or contribute to my own interest.

General Leadbetter was a hard drinker, and originally a Northern man; but as is not unfrequently the case, he was more extreme in his views than the natives with whom he had cast his lot. When I entered his room I saw that he had been drinking, though not so much as to render him incapable of business. He treated me with a kind of pretentious politeness, causing me to be seated in front of him, and then said that he had learned that I had a communication to make to him. Now I might tell him everything, and would find it to my advantage.

As he spoke I was carefully studying him, and trying to estimate the amount of deceit that might be profitably employed. I was encouraged; for he seemed like one who would deceive himself, and think all the while that he was showing wonderful penetration. I told him that I was a United States soldier, giving my name and regiment, declaring that I was detailed without my consent, that I was ignorant of where I was going, or the work I was to perform, which I only learned as fast as I was to execute it. He listened very attentively, and then asked who the engineer was who had run our train. I refused to tell. The Confederates were exceedingly anxious to find the name of this person, imagining that he was probably some high official of the Western & Atlantic Railroad. Any member of the expedition could at any time have purchased the promise of his own life by telling who our engineer was—that is, if he had been believed.

Then Leadbetter wanted to know the purpose of our expedition. I professed to be ignorant so far as any direct knowledge was concerned, but he still questioned and I gave him my conjectures as facts.

All that I told him was what any person of judgment would have supposed—the hopes of taking Chattanooga, cutting the Confederacy in halves and the rest of it. He acted as if receiving valuable information, but expressed doubt whether Mitchel could follow up such an enterprise; saying that by his information, Mitchel hadn't more than ten thousand men. I was determined to mislead him if I could, for his estimates were singularly correct. So I said that this must refer only to the first division of Mitchel's force, and didn't take into account the many thousands more that were ready to come to him by rail from Nashville.

Leadbetter seemed profoundly impressed. Then he wanted me to tell just how many men we had on the train, and to describe them. The latter I couldn't have done if it had been to save their lives and mine. The former I wouldn't do, as I could see a bearing it might have on the pursuit.

"General," I answered, "I have freely told you whatever concerns myself, for I want you to know that I'm a United States soldier, and under military protection; but I'm not yet base enough to describe my comrades, or help you in any way to capture them."

"Oh," answered he, as if the idea was amusing, "I didn't know that I ought to ask that."

"I think not, sir," I replied.

"Well," said he, "I know all about it. Your leader's name is Andrews. What kind of a man is he?"

I was thunderstruck. Perhaps Leadbetter was deeper than I

thought, and had been playing with me all this time. (For I have given a small part only of our conversation, but all the general drift of it.) But I had every confidence that Andrews would still get away and try some measures for our relief. So I answered boldly: "I can tell you only one thing about him. He's a man you'll never catch."

The smile on Leadbetter's face became broader.

"That will do for you," he said. And then, turning to a captain who stood by, "Take him to the hole."

The subordinate saluted, and took me from the room. At the door stood Andrews, heavily ironed, and Ross and Wollam with him. My heart sank, and I then knew why the general had smiled.

F. M. GREGG: While the examination of the man taken before them was going on, Andrews, Ross and Wollam had remained downstairs on the sidewalk, and by this time were surrounded by a crowd. The W. & A. train had just come in. Conductor Fuller, as he came out from the entrance of the depot, saw the people in front of the hotel. The crowd opened a way for him and for the first time pursuer and pursued in the famous railroad chase stood face to face. Fuller introduced himself and spoke in complimentary terms of their daring scheme. Andrews then congratulated Fuller on his successful chase, and for quite a while they talked and laughed over incidents of the race until the guards appeared to take him before Leadbetter.

Andrews and his companions hadn't been thoroughly searched until brought before General Leadbetter. Here the large amount of Confederate money found on Andrews and the spokesmanship he had assumed for the party during the locomotive run stamped him, in their minds, as the leader of the expedition. After vain attempts to get the three men to commit themselves they were consigned to the guards to be removed to prison. (While before General Leadbetter, Andrews asked the privilege of sending a flag of truce to the Union lines with news of the capture of the party. This request was denied.)

Followed by a large crowd, Andrews, Wollam and Ross were taken to a one-time slave jail on the corner of Fifth and Lookout streets, surrounded by a high fence. At the gate they were met by the keeper, an old man by the name of Swims, who stood dangling his keys as the prisoners filed by him into the building.

The following, from an eyewitness, describes the scene:

"Old man Swims had shut out most of the crowd from the jail so that there were very few persons except the guards who were in the upstairs room. Swims turned to the officer and said in his nasal tones,

'Where shall I put 'em?' 'In the hole,' was the response. The old fellow bent over, fumbling with his keys, then lifted up a trap door set in the floor, yelled, 'Look out below!' and slid a ladder into the space. The rising air was hot and burdened with an unpleasant odor. You could see the white, upturned faces of men moving around in the blackness. Andrews drew back, saying, 'That's no place to put a man. Let us stay up here where we can get some air.'

"It was to no purpose. Swims said, 'It's the best we can do now, but we'll do better after a while.'

"The guard closing up, Andrews—still protesting—was forced down the ladder into the thirteen by thirteen foot 'hole' below."

PITTENGER: Down in the darkness of Swims' fetid den—packed in with Union-sympathizing prisoners from various parts of East Tennessee—I heard the tramp of feet overhead, the clash of chains and felt the stream of comparatively cool air as the trap door was lifted and the ladder thrust down. A set of new victims clambered down slowly. I stationed myself at the foot of the ladder, and made to the newcomers some such safe remark as, "This is a hard place to come to."

In a moment I found my hand caught in a warm strong grasp, and "Pittenger," "Ross" were mutually whispered. It was Andrews, Wollam and Ross. I had last seen them chained in front of Leadbetter's room. Now they were here; and the sense of misfortune seemed lightened by half. To die in the company of friends was better than to die alone. I pitied them and wished them free; but it was far better to be confined together than for us to endure the same suffering in separation.

A whisper more to Ross brought me the information that they had given their names and character. The East Tennesseans kindly allowed us to take a corner close to one of the window holes, where we could more readily talk. Ross and Wollam agreed with me that our best course would be to claim to be detailed Union soldiers, not denying what we really did—only claiming that we weren't volunteers, but were ordered on this expedition, and simply obeyed orders. Andrews also approved, but said that his case was separate from ours, and much worse.

An hour or two passed in such conversation not altogether unpleasantly and it came time to sleep. One of the first things we had done was to disrobe as far as our irons would permit. Many of the East Tennesseans who weren't fettered were entirely naked because of the intense heat. The one advantage of the hole's close atmosphere was that the great heat and the slow carbonic acid poisoning from the impure air rendered slumber easy, and then and later we found little trouble in sleeping early and late. We adjusted ourselves in our corner, so that our chains might cramp us as little as possible, and ceasing to talk, were soon asleep.

DORSEY: We reached Chattanooga next morning a little after sunrise, and were led by the chains about our necks, under a strong guard, through a mob in the crowded streets, some of whom called out, "Will them houn's hunt?"

We were taken to the Crutchfield House where, by order of the proprietor, we were given a good breakfast. This was on the spot where Jeff Davis and William Crutchfield, brother of the proprietor of the hotel, had a little more than a year before made their impassioned speeches against and for the Union.

Before parting with us, our escort of Georgians took all our names in their little passbooks or diaries. The little books were placed between our ironed hands, and with pencils placed in hand by the same parties, we wrote our names. Another squad of Georgia soldiers now took charge of us and marched us to the corner of Lookout and Fifth streets, and into the odd-shaped oak-lined brick building we found to be Swims' jail.

We were pushed down into the hole, the ladder was taken out and the trap door fell with a dull thud. But in the darkness we felt the grasp of friendly hands and listened to words of friendly greeting. Among the first, we recognized the one man we'd been surest would escape—Andrews.

PITTENGER: Within a few days, as more of our party were put in the hole, I found that George Wilson and nearly all had done as I had in acknowledging themselves United States soldiers, influenced by the same reasons. We consulted about the matter, and concluded that the only hope we had was in adhering to the same story, and trying to make the Confederate authorities believe that we were actually detailed without our consent, and without a knowledge of what we had to do. We agreed to conceal the name of the engineer at all hazard, the fact of a previous expedition being sent down into Georgia, and that Campbell wasn't a soldier, also our previous acquaintance with Andrews, thus leaving him free to make his own defense. With the exception of these reserved facts, which were not even to be whispered among ourselves, we were to talk freely; to answer all questions and convey the impression that we had nothing to conceal. We carried out this idea, and, as more of our men came in, they agreed to it, and gave without reserve their true names, companies and regiments.

We afterward communicated our plan to Andrews, who cordially approved it—saying that if we adhered to it, there would be some chance for our lives. We did adhere to it, and no amount of persuasion, threatening or promises could induce any of the party to betray one of our reserved secrets. The Rebels were particularly anxious to discover who was the engineer, and would first ask the question in the most careless manner; then afterward would sternly demand to know. But all in vain.

Thus chained together, packed into a little cramped dungeon, deprived even of light, and almost of air, crawled over by all kinds of vermin, we presented a picture of nearly perfect misery.

DORSEY: Fifteen of our party were soon gathered at Chattanooga, crowded in a miserable dungeon but thirteen feet square and thirteen feet deep. All were in chains and irons except Pittenger. He wore handcuffs, but wasn't chained by the neck to another. Slavens, Campbell and Shadrach were linked together on one chain. The seven still missing were Alf Wilson, Wood, Scott, Mason, Knight, Brown and Reddick.

Heading Nowhere 4

KNIGHT: The five of us—Brown, Reddick, Scott, Mason and I—continued to hide by day and travel slowly by dark till the sixth night out. We had come down off a mountain, were crossing a valley and had just commenced to climb the opposite side of the slope and enter the woods again. Mason and Scott were a little ahead and a little off to the right of us, when suddenly a dog jumped up in front of them, and at the same time we heard: "Halt! Who comes there?"

[*Knight*]

Mason and Scott were so close to the enemy that they couldn't get away. Brown, Reddick and I dropped down in the bushes, crawled off to the left and around the pickets, and got clear.

Then in going up the mountain we came to where the rocks stood perpendicular. (The great rock parapet of Lookout Mountain.) We noticed a big hole in the top of this ledge, and we managed to clamber up and get into that. It was quite a natural cave, and as it was now getting daylight, we put in the day there. We could look clear over the tree tops, and see into a little town. I didn't know its name, but we could see a great commotion there. We knew from the activity that that's where they probably had Mason and Scott, but as we couldn't render them any assistance, we kept quiet till dark. We crawled out then and climbed till we reached the top of the mountain—it proved to be level on top—and started south.

After a fair night's travel, the three of us—at daybreak of the seventh morning—reached what must have been the lower end of Lookout Mountain, and were in sight of a little log cabin off to our left. Brown and Reddick wanted to go to this house for breakfast, but I tried to have them hold off till supper, by which time we'd have the night before us to escape in if we needed it. We took a vote, and as the two outvoted one, we went to breakfast.

We had made up a new little story of our own previous to this, that we were going to stick to in case of accident. When we got to the house, an old man there said we could get something to eat if we would wait for it to be cooked. You couldn't get a pick-up lunch in that country the same as we could in our own, as they only cooked each meal just what they ate; and I found out afterward that they cooked that pretty short.

I noticed also that the old man was very uneasy. He couldn't sit still, and finally went out and got a horse out. We all went out with the notion, if all didn't seem right, of stopping him till we got our breakfast. He said he was going to send his boy over to his neighbor to get his plow to plow his garden.

This was so innocent that we let him go, and got our breakfast. Then we asked the old man the road and distance to Bridgeport, but calculated not to go there. We started up a hill on the main road, but meant to hide in the woods till dark. Right off there was a party of cavalry coming up the other side and we met at the top. That was the kind of plowing that boy was after.

They halted us and started their questioning. We told them we were going to Chandler Springs, Ala., and had come from Fleming County, Ky. They accused us of being engine thieves and we said we didn't know what they were talking about. They asked us for passes, telling us that since martial law had been put into effect—it started that month—nobody was allowed to travel without a pass. We had none, so they said we'd have to come along with them to Bridgeport.

(By this time—we learned later—most of the rest of our party had been captured, and were in jail in Chattanooga. They had acknowledged themselves to be United States soldiers, and had given names, companies, regiments, etc., and claimed protection from our government. Someone had even acknowledged more than that, and had told how many there were in the party. It needed just five more to fill the quota, and we three looked pretty likely to cut that five to two.)

The road wound around the side of the mountain, and after a couple of miles, we came to what they called a mountain still. It was the first one I'd ever seen. It was a log cabin that sat in a ravine in the side of the mountain—a place where they extract juice out of corn and sell it for whiskey. I think there was a horse hitched to every tree around the building and three men were there for every horse. They were liberal fellows though. They were carrying whiskey around in gallon measures, with tin cups to drink out of. They hadn't told us that any of our party had been captured yet and I guess they thought they would fill us up with whiskey and we would give ourselves away. But the more we drank, the more independent we got.

They finally put us on horses and took us to Bridgeport, where we were taken before Colonel Claiborne, who had command of the troops there at that time. Claiborne was a Kentuckian, as we were supposed to be. We were first all questioned together, they accusing us of being engine thieves and we denying it just as hard. Finally they separated us and questioned us. They could get nothing out of us, nor find any papers that would convict us, so they brought us all together again. Then they called for rope. Quite a few of the Southern people were great for rope anyhow. Ropes were procured; they commenced fixing them up to some limbs, and it did begin to look bad for us. Then the colonel came to our relief, he said he respected brave men, and said he'd be d---d if he'd let them hang us. There was a train came along shortly for Chattanooga, and we were put aboard a car. They filled that car with guards just to take us three to Chattanooga.

[*Knight*]

At Chattanooga we were taken before old General Leadbetter. His headquarters were upstairs at the Crutchfield House. It so happened that I was the first one taken into the room. The general sat on a chair with one of those old-fashioned Dutch knit caps on. He looked more like a lager beer sign than a general.

The first question he asked was: "Where did you come from?"

I told him from Kentucky, and he gave a grunt.

"Well, where are you going?"

I said to Chandler Springs, Alabama.

"What is your captain's name?"

He kept questioning me in that manner for half or three-quarters of an hour. Finally he wanted to know what I was going to do at Chandler Springs. I had made up my mind that I was going to be just as independent as he was, and I told him I thought if I liked the place that I would buy it. He then wanted to see the toes of my boots. I stuck up my foot, and the soles of my boots at the toes were all worn off so that the upper leather had commenced to turn up. He said: "Those look like some other men's boots we have taken in off the mountains."

That was the first inkling I got at the time that maybe some of our men had been captured. The general then wanted to know if that was all I had to offer for myself. I told him it was, and he said I could go out.

When the door opened for me to go out, I found they'd brought Andrews up and stood him so that we'd come face to face. I suppose they put him there to see if we'd recognize each other. I stepped right by and took my place in the ranks. But I think if I'd been struck with seven kinds of lightning I wouldn't have felt any more streaked than I did just at that time.

They then took in Reddick. The old general went at Bill in a different way. He told Bill that they had the rest of our party in jail, and then bringing Andrews up, in part verified his statement. He said: "If you belong to that party, the only thing that will save your life will be to acknowledge it, and claim protection from our government, as the balance of them have done."

Bill being an easygoing kind of fellow, and one of the George Washington stripe that couldn't tell a lie, must have given it away. I noticed when he came out we were started off for jail without any examination of Brown. I suspected something wrong, and as soon as I got a chance to whisper to Bill, I asked him if he gave it away. He said he didn't. I told him something was wrong or they would have taken Brown in. He said he didn't care; he didn't tell anything. We were taken to jail just the same, or to the place better known in Chattanooga at that time as Swims' hole. We added a little to that after a while and named it hellhole.

EDITOR: Just two of the Marietta roster still were missing at Swims' lock-up: young English-born Mark Wood and Alf Wilson, the wiry, light-haired hundred-and-fifty pounder, boyish-looking even at two months short of thirty—"in manner deliberate, though quick of decision and action"—who had yanked brakes as needed and kept the *General's* firebox crackling through the racing hours of Saturday morning.

ALF WILSON: It was some time Saturday afternoon when Mark Wood and I took refuge in our brush-heap near the place where we'd left the engine, and in that spot we were compelled to remain that night, all of Sunday and far into Sunday night. With the almost incessant rain, much of the time the water was three or four inches deep where we lay.

On crawling out our limbs were so stiff that it was only by rubbing and working them vigorously that we could begin to use them. We decided to take an opposite course from that which our comrades had taken, thinking there might be less vigilance on the part of the hunters in that direction. We wanted also to get into the mountains. I suppose at this time we were less than twenty miles from Chattanooga. The rain still fell, but as we went on and our stiffened limbs got limbered up, we began to make good time.

About daybreak Monday, we found a barn, the mow of which was full of bundles of corn fodder. We made a hole down in the mow, covered ourselves out of sight and went to sleep.

About one o'clock, we were awakened by somebody in the mow and soon found out that two women were looking there for eggs. As bad luck would have it, one of them reached in looking for a hidden nest and touched one of my hands. She started back with a scream, which brought up the other woman and they threw off the bundles and there we were. They were both badly frightened and ran for the house with all their might.

Who has ever vainly appealed in a respectful manner for food, when hungry, to a woman? We went to the door, apologized for the scare we had caused them, gave a story of being in pursuit of the train robbers, and said that being wet, cold and sleepy we'd preferred to take shelter in the barn rather than disturb anyone. We then told them we were hungry and asked for something to eat. They gave us a pitcher of buttermilk and some corn bread, all they had unless we could wait for them to cook us something, which we didn't wish to do. This was the first food we had eaten since the morning we left Marietta. We paid them after eating, and left much refreshed and strengthened. That night we shaped our course as near as we could, without following any road, toward the Tennessee River, east of Chattanooga.

By Tuesday morning, we had just arrived at the foot of the mountains. We concealed ourselves in a comfortable place, fell asleep from weariness and didn't wake until nearly night. Again we had a toilsome night march, feeling our way over rocks, climbing cliffs and at other times descending the steep mountain side on the run, through bushes and among rocks.

Wednesday morning we found that we were still surrounded by mountains, with no signs of a habitation in sight. We had in all this time tasted food only once since the raid began and that was the scanty meal we made on buttermilk and corn bread Monday afternoon. We decided that there was no great risk in this lonely region if we traveled by day. Wednesday afternoon we came out by the foot of a mountain at a small log house. We ventured to apply there, saying we'd been lost in the mountains, and were given food by a friendly, young-looking woman. From her we learned that the next town—Cleveland, Tenn.—wasn't far and that there were no soldiers there. This was gratifying, but not near as much so as the savory ham, eggs, corn bread and rye coffee she prepared for us.

We felt very much the need of a map. After a careful survey of the little town of Cleveland, I left Wood in a secluded spot to wait while I walked boldly in and went to a book store and asked for a school atlas. I was soon in the woods again, when we tore out such portions of the atlas as we needed and hid the rest under a log, after which we took our course and pushed on, making good progress. Our plan was to reach the Tennessee River and secure a boat of some kind, after which we'd drift down the river to some point near the Federal lines.

Toward evening of this day we came down from a high mountain and found another cabin, where we concluded to apply for something more to eat. We'd been so hungry we hadn't dared eat all we wanted at the last place.

There was no man to be seen, but the woman, a dignified,

plainly dressed lady, told us to be seated. She was looking at us with that scrutinizing gaze of a woman in doubt. I knew enough about women to guess that whatever her first impressions were they'd be unchangeable, so I said, "We're in need of something to eat."

She said if we could put up with such fare as she had we were welcome. She proceeded about her work, and asked us where we were traveling. I said to Harrison, a small village a few miles from there. She still eyed us closely, and suddenly she turned and faced us.

"You're Union men," she said. "I can tell by a man's look every time. You don't have to be afraid to own it either. I'm Union, and I'm not afraid to own it to anybody. If you're trying to get to the Federal army, I'll do anything I can to help you."

She seemed to have made up her mind, so we let her have it her own way and we had ours. Soon after her husband came in—a frank, fine-looking fellow.

When supper was over we offered this loyal woman pay, but she refused to take our money. She said she just wished the Union army would come—she'd give them everything she had.

As we took our leave, she told her husband to make sure we knew our route.

"For," said she to him, "you know old Snow and his cavalry are around, and he's watching every road to keep Union men from getting away from the conscription."

We were sorry to part with these good people—even if we couldn't afford to show how much—for we seldom met with their like.

Wednesday night we passed in the woods, and continued our journey Thursday morning—as we thought, being careful. All of a sudden we heard a stern order.

"Halt there, you!"

Old Snow had us. This elderly captain of the cavalry squad that came up around us seemed to be by his own account a bloodthirsty warrior, for he said it wasn't his custom to take prisoners but to hang and shoot all who fell into his hands. He asked us a great many questions, including, of course, our place of residence and our names, all of which we answered very promptly. We told him we lived in Harrison, nearby, and gave him some names we had picked up, which must have struck him just right, for at once he inquired after our fathers, whom he said he knew. We told him they were in excellent health. He said he was glad to hear it, for he was well acquainted with both of them.

"But," he continued, looking at us very sternly, "boys, it's my impression that you're running away from the conscription and you deserve to be shot for wanting to join the damned Yankees."

We told him we hadn't the slightest intention of enlisting in the infernal Yankee army, which was fast ruining the South and its people. After a moment's silence, and looking at us steadily, he said: "For all I know you may belong to those spies and bridge burners, and if I didn't know your folks I'd send you to Chattanooga, under arrest. But I'll tell you what I'll do. If you'll take the oath and promise to go back home and stay until I call for you, I'll let you go."

We accepted the conditions right off. The old captain at once ordered us to follow him, leading us back to what proved to be the house of a rank old Rebel. Here he went through the ceremony of what he termed administering the oath, after which he, with the aid of the hot-tempered old woman of the house, gave us the most fiery lecture on the subject of Southern rights and Northern wrongs we had ever heard. After it, we told the captain we hoped it wouldn't be long until he would find it convenient to call upon us for our services in the cause. He seemed much pleased at the favorable effect of his harangue, and as we hastily shook hands with him preparatory to leaving, he handed us back our revolvers.

This we considered a lucky escape, and we started off in fine spirits. It wasn't long until we were again in the mountains, where we soon after found a place of safety, and rested and slept till near night.

After we awoke, Wood and I talked over the situation. We were somewhere northeast of Chattanooga, and what we desired was to get to the Tennessee River and find a boat. Our great trouble had been, in this mountainous region, to keep to a course. Even if we knew the direction we wanted to take, it was next to impossible to follow it at night, on account of the unevenness of the country. It was this that made us so anxious to reach the river, which should afford us a sure means of night travel, and eventually guide us to a point near the Federal army.

EDITOR: That Thursday night Alf Wilson and Mark Wood made a second trial of the hospitality of the young Unionist couple who had warned them against the Confederate irregular cavalry. Welcomed again and installed in a nearby hiding place, the two raiders were given food, shelter and a chance to recover their strength over the full week-end of Good Friday through Easter Sunday.

On Monday night they were guided to a creek (Wilson couldn't be sure later whether this was the Chickamauga, McLarimore's Creek, or a third stream) and shown an unguarded canoe. In this, on Monday and Tuesday nights, Wilson and Wood managed to reach the Tennessee and work their way past Chattanooga undetected. With the help of a local man hired at three dollars' Confederate for temporary pilot duty—and a great deal of luck and frantic paddling—the fugitives got through the racing waters of the Suck below the islands badly shaken but intact.

Late Wednesday night they drifted through the great piers of the railroad bridge at Bridgeport, not sure whether they had yet come within the area recently brought under Union control.

ALF WILSON: I may state just here a fact well known to all men who in time of war have tried to escape from prison. The most critical part of a journey is that which lies immediately between the two contending armies. At such places, between two hostile lines, patrols are constantly moving about. Outposts are established on all important roads, while vidette and picket posts, in command of the most active and vigilant officers, are constantly on the alert for spies, scouts or prowling bands of cavalrymen from the enemy's camp. Every stray man is picked up and sent to the officer of the guard; and perhaps ordered tried by a drumhead court-martial, charged with being a spy. It is the worst place in the world to be caught fooling around—this ground between two hostile armies.

About sunrise of Thursday, April 24, Mark and I pulled in below Bridgeport and hid our canoe. Feeling hungry and also anxious to learn something about the Federals, we concluded to skulk off a short distance and see what we could find. It wasn't long until we found a cabin, where we got breakfast and learned that the Yankees were at Stevenson, or a short distance the other side.

Soon after leaving this cabin we met a squad of Rebel soldiers in full retreat. They told us that we had better be lighting out; that the roads and woods were alive with Yankee cavalry.

"They're in Stevenson, and pushing on this way in heavy force," we were assured.

We went on a little further, when we met more Rebel militia, who told us the same story.

We went back to our canoe and paddled down the river again,

until we thought we were about opposite Stevenson, which is about four miles north from the river. Then we tied up the canoe and struck out through the woods for the town. Just before reaching the place, we had to cross a creek, after which we ascended a long, steep hill. When we reached the top of this hill, we were somewhat surprised to find ourselves right in the town, but not half so much astonished as we were to find no blue-coats there, and the streets swarming with Rebel soldiers. We had been woefully deceived by the stories of the frightened fugitives we had met in the forenoon, and had unwarily trapped ourselves.

We determined to put on a bold front and take our chances. Some of the officers noticed us carelessly, while others paid no attention to us as we passed them. We went into a store and bought some tobacco, and then started off as unconcernedly as if we were a couple of country fellows, accustomed to visiting the town. We had gone some little distance, when we were met by an officer, who stopped us and said that he would have to inquire our business there, and who we were. He appeared well satisfied with our answers and was about to dismiss us, when unfortunately for us another man, I think a citizen, came up, and, pointing at me, said: "That's one of the rascals that was here with the Federal cavalry last night. He rode through the town, cutting all the flourishes he knew how. I know him. He daren't deny it, either."

In explanation of this man's singular accusation, I later learned that a squad of troopers from the 4th Ohio Cavalry had, on the previous night, made a dash into the place. This explained the stories told us by the flying fugitives.

From the minute we had been detained, I had been destroying the map in my possession, by tearing it in pieces in my pocket, dropping portions of it whenever opportunity offered, and chewing up much of it, until I finally succeeded, without detection, in disposing of the whole of it.

This man's story, wrong as it was, ended all hope of our getting away, and we were prisoners a second time. In spite of our protestations of innocence, we were bundled off under guard, put on a hand car and run up to Bridgeport, where the commanding office was stationed.

We reached Bridgeport soon after dark. Boots, hats, coats, socks and every undergarment underwent the strictest scrutiny. They could find nothing, and were about at a stand-off, when a circumstance ended all hope in our favor. An excited fellow, who came and stuck his head in among the gaping crowd who were staring at us, declared, in a loud voice, that we belonged to Andrews' spies and train thieves.

All eyes were turned on him instantly, my own among them. I could have killed him without compunction if I had possessed the power, for in the next breath he said: "I know those fellows. I saw them on the train."

Or Spoil a Horn 1

PARROTT:

Q. Will you state how long you felt the effects of the flogging you received?

A. I was very sore for about two weeks afterwards.

Q. You and your fellow prisoners were chained in the jail at Chattanooga?

A. We were all handcuffed together. I and some others had trace chains around our necks, secured by padlocks. We were secured in that way, two by two.

Q. What food was furnished you?

A. At Chattanooga we got some wheat flour mixed up with a little water and baked, and some spoiled pickled beef. We had it only twice a day.

Q. What was your condition in other respects?

A. We had scarcely any light at all. The windows were small and the room so close, and we were so warm, that we had to take our clothes off entirely. The room was so small that we couldn't all lie down, and we had to rest ourselves by leaning against the walls. We weren't allowed to leave the room under any circumstances while we were confined in it.

PITTENGER: Within a day or two after Andrews' capture, a number of persons were found who had known him previously, and his identification was made complete. Too many persons were acquainted with him in the South for him to have long remained unknown in any event.

FULLER: A few days after he was caught, I visited Andrews in the jail at Chattanooga and had a long talk with him on the chase and object of their expedition. Andrews told me, in the presence of all the rest, that he had suggested to General Mitchel at Shelbyville that he could take a detachment of soldiers, descend as far south as Marietta, and on their return trip burn all the bridges on the W. & A. Railroad in their rear. General Mitchel told Andrews that if he could do this, he would give him $50,000 in gold. This was agreed to, and soldiers volunteered to go with him. It was afterward concluded that a larger force would be necessary, and $60,000 was asked for and agreed upon. The additional $10,000 was to be divided among the volunteers, seven in number.

F. M. GREGG: The jail in which the raiders were confined in Chattanooga occupied the northwest corner of Fifth and Lookout streets. It was a brick structure, built early in the fifties by the county, although the county seat was at Harrison, fifteen miles distant. The building was a queer freak of architecture. It was thirteen feet wide, about twenty-six feet long and nearly as high. The south end ran into a hill about eight feet in depth; the north end was on a level. This end was occupied by the jailer's family. The south end was used as a prison. The room upstairs was well lighted and aired, although made secure by heavy iron bars across the windows.

The room below was of an altogether different structure. On the inside the lower room had been lined with heavy oak timber, twelve by fourteen inches, standing on end. To give it further security, only two windows were in the thick walls—each about fifteen inches square. Both were banded with heavy iron bars that occupied nearly all the space, kept out all sunshine and nearly excluded all air. Its only means of entrance was through a trap door above and down a ladder. It was in this hole that the raiders were placed.

Swims, the jailer, had been promoted from his public dray to the office of jailer. He was an inoffensive old fellow, but blinded by a strong prejudice against his Yankee prisoners. Old age hadn't softened his nature, and he turned a deaf ear to all entreaties of the prisoners of the simplest nature; except that at times, under the influence of liquor, he would give them a good opportunity of getting a breath of fresh air by talking to them.

DORSEY: The chains and irons were new when first put on us, but soon became red with rust, so damp was the atmosphere, and our profuse sweat facilitated the rusting process.

Knight had held onto his jackknife by keeping it under his arm and switching it around when they first searched him, and later he was able to whittle out with it some keys from the bones in our food that freed some of us from time to time from our irons. In addition, he had managed to hide and hang onto some gold coins, which we used after the first few days to buy tobacco and extra provisions when old Swims was in good humor enough to make purchases for us. The tobacco was in large plugs of old navy. These were stuck up in the windows between the bars, and when a man wanted a chew, the plug was taken from the window, a chew bitten off and the plug passed around.

As well—and how he did it I don't know—Knight had kept a package of gunpowder with which he proposed to blow our way out of the jail. Some protested the risk, and nothing finally was done, mostly because there wasn't enough powder to make a good job of it.

At first we had no rule for dividing out the food. When it came down, we sat or stood around looking up to old Swims, like so many young birds in their nest. Every fellow for himself, and the devil take the hindmost. Sometimes one or two were left clear out—didn't get a morsel. This, of course, wouldn't do, and we organized a government, and elected Andrews president, with full power to appoint assistants, and run things right. After that everyone got his dues—all shared their proper proportion of the food.

If profanity could explode anything, that old dungeon would have blown into a million atoms within the first twenty-four hours after we got into it. I thought everybody swore, but found out, after getting out in the light where we could see around and know who was making the noise, that several of our comrades didn't use profane language. These were Ross, Slavens, Porter, Pittenger and Andrews. But that hole was enough to make a preacher swear. Knight generally tried to make light of our situation, and said once he had but one request to make of the enemy, and that was that they gave him one good square meal before hanging him, so that his body would be heavy enough to break his neck fast.

We were in the dungeon but a few days when Corporal Pike, of the 4th Ohio Cavalry, was put in the upper cell. He'd been scouting across the river from Chattanooga and got "taken in out of the dew," as Buffum said we had been. Pike's eulogy upon the Rebels and their claim to a chivalrous spirit, when the trap door opened and he got a look down into our den, was something to hear. We didn't know then what became of him, but if he didn't get away from them it was for the want of half a chance.

EDITOR: Corporal James Pike, pushing his luck once too often, was captured near Bridgeport, Tenn., on April 24, when he ran into nine enemy pickets while on one of his usual single-handed scouting patrols. Pike killed a sergeant, was taken by the rest. Brought to Chattanooga, Pike was placed for some days in the upper room at Swims'.

PIKE: In the dungeon were confined twenty-one men of the 2nd, 21st and 33d Ohio Infantry, charged with being spies. They were under command of a Captain Andrews. I once went into the dungeon where these men were, and found them handcuffed and chained in pairs by the neck with a heavy chain, which was locked around each man's neck with a padlock that would weigh two pounds. These padlocks were larger than a man's hand. We were fed twice a day on tolerably good bread, spoiled beef, and coffee made of cane seed.

From Chattanooga I was taken to Knoxville to another jail, and confined in an iron cage.

EDITOR: Pike didn't get the half a chance Dorsey wished him, or muffed it if it came. Transferred from prison to prison, the one-time Texas Ranger spent six highly resentful and non-jaunty months in confinement before being exchanged in October, in such poor shape as to require further weeks of enforced inactivity in a military hospital near Washington before return to duty.

DORSEY: On another occasion early in our stay at Swims', I broke the quietude by striking up an old familiar song I had learned in an Ohio singing school. After my singing a few notes, Andrews asked: "Who's that singing?"

I answered him, and the next question was: "Where'd you learn that?"

"Of Newt Bookwalter," I said, "a singing master in Ross County."

"Newt Bookwalter?" said Andrews. "Do you know Newt Bookwalter?"

I replied that I'd known him at home, and had attended his singing school. So had Andrews. He assured us that he and Bookwalter had spent many pleasant hours together. Both being good singers made them congenial companions. Many incidents of this kind occurred. A mere word served to recall to some mind an incident, or the name of some mutual friend, about whom pleasant talk followed, to the entertainment of all.

Other times, complete silence might last for many minutes, all wrapped in meditation. Did our captors under the rules of war have the right to treat us as spies? That was the great question.

Geo. D. Wilson took what I then thought the right view of the case: that the raid had been a military expedition, which was fully shown by what we did; and that as we had passed no line or outpost of the enemy, they couldn't sustain the charge of lurking in and about their camps, necessary to conviction on the charge of being a spy. But with the manifest feeling against us among the authorities, most of us could see there was little hope of a successful defense before a Rebel court-martial. Although we were in a bad boat, we determined to make the best of the situation. We made it a point whenever in the presence of the enemy to appear defiant, and when taunted about the fate that awaited us, we had a stereotyped reply: "Hang and be d---d. Our fellows will hang twenty of you for everyone you hang of this party."

That threat of retaliation on our part seemed to have its effect on the soldiers, and may have had something to do in shaping the course many of the guards took in opposition to treating us as spies.

F. A. MITCHEL: Soon after General Mitchel's occupation of Huntsville, the enemy sent him news of the expedition's disaster. They reported that Andrews and all his men had been executed at Chattanooga. This was doubtless to avoid the retaliation which Mitchel might threaten if he should know the truth.

PITTENGER: There were times during the Chattanooga confinement when our situation seemed overwhelming; but usually we kept our minds busy during waking hours in telling stories, speculating on the prospects of the war, or planning escape. It seems scarcely credible that, among us all, there were but two out-and-out abolitionists—Buffum and myself—although slavery couldn't long have been maintained had its existence depended on a vote taken in our prison.

[*Pittenger*]
Many a heated discussion all of us had on slavery and on the propriety of arming the Negroes. Andrews took no part in our discussions beyond saying that he was no abolitionist, but believed that Negroes should be better protected against cruelty.

Soon there came a diversion which enlivened our conversation by giving us new themes, and secured for some a brief relief from the "hole," but which brought the deepest fear with it. Andrews, our leader, was summoned for trial. He procured able lawyers, who interposed all possible objections, and succeeded in securing considerable delay. Indeed, in all the proceedings there was a slowness and apparent hesitation which bore striking testimony to the importance they attributed to him.

When all of our party had first been brought into the prison, we had carefully reviewed the situation and ascertained how much the enemy had learned in regard to us. Most had already given names and regiments, and had claimed to be American soldiers. Nothing could be gained, therefore, by denying what we had done, or our true character. The first could be proved by those who saw us on the train, by our captors, or by our own admissions; the latter was our only possible defense. To George D. Wilson and myself fell the main task of outlining our defense and drilling all the party in it.

There was no difference of opinion as to what was best. It was only important that we all tell consistent stories. We resolved to say, when examined, that we had been appointed by our officers to serve under a man whom we supposed to be an officer from some other regiment or brigade; that the nature of our service wasn't clearly made known to us further than that it was to destroy some line of communications in the enemy's country; that we were in citizen's clothing only that we might not alarm the citizens among whom we were to travel; that we didn't see any pickets of the enemy or pass them at any point; that we were in no camp; that we supposed ourselves within the rules of war and entitled to protection as prisoners of war; that we had obeyed Andrews as we considered ourselves bound in duty to do. We were to say nothing about Campbell being only a citizen; and were to refuse to tell who our engineer was. It's by no means certain the enemy would have dealt any more severely with the engineer than with the others, had they ascertained that he was merely a soldier. But we couldn't know this, and judged from the persistency with which they sought to discover him that his fate would be sealed as soon as he was known.

Admitting that we were under the orders of Andrews wouldn't in the least embarrass him, for this much could be proved from what he was actually seen to do on the train; and he had already declared as much when captured. But we never revealed anything that would throw light on his employment as a spy in our service. The story which we thus planned to tell was so closely adhered to that the enemy never learned that we were volunteers and intelligent participants in the enterprise.

All were examined at least once, either on being brought into prison or afterward. My own ordeal was more protracted, probably because I had been the first brought before the commanding general, and also because I had been very willing to communicate what I knew—up to a certain point.

WOOD: A court-martial was ordered for Andrews, and Pittenger was taken out as a witness. By alternate offers of pardon and persecution, the Confederate authorities endeavored to make Pittenger testify against Andrews, but Pittenger was true to his word and his companions, and the court could gain nothing from him.

PITTENGER: The effort to gain additional information was less simple and more protracted than indicated. I was called out, went through the street once more, still wearing my handcuffs on both hands, attended by eight guards, and was brought before an officer, I presumed either the judge advocate or the president of the court-martial. Here I was told that they wanted to learn several things, among others, the name of our engineer, who were engaged in this affair, and the relation that the man Andrews bore to us and to the army. The officer said that he thought I could tell if I wanted to; and that if I did, I need have no fear of any prosecution for myself. It would have been easy to refuse to say anything, but I thought it better to answer, "Everything that concerns me alone, I'll tell you freely, as I want you to know that I'm an American soldier, and that I've done my simple duty; but I won't tell you anything that might tend to injure my companions."

He answered that he could promise me nothing unless I would tell all I knew. I said that I asked no promise, believing that when they understood the case they would only hold us all as prisoners of war. He said that this was very probable, but that he would have me separated from my companions and see me again in a day or two.

Accordingly, when taken back I wasn't put in the jail but kept in the yard outside under the charge of six guards, who stood by me day and night in regular reliefs of two at a time, with orders not to let

[*Pittenger*]
me, on any account, speak with those inside. There was no need of any further communication. For days previously, Wilson and I had been drilling the others just in view of making our stories harmonize. One of the guards, however, with possibly a little humane feeling in his veins, did tell my comrades just what I had said to the officer, and thus relieved any uneasiness they may have had—though they had little.

When taken before the officers again, I told my story in just the lines we had laid down, which made us simply detailed soldiers acting under orders. They questioned and examined a good deal. I refused, directly, to name the engineer, and varied from the truth in other matters just as far as I judged it expedient. At length I overheard one of the officers say to another, in effect, "It's no use. He's either ignorant, or too sharp to tell us anything we want to know."

Then I was informed that if I didn't know anything more I would have to be put back with my companions. I said, "As you will"; and soon found myself in the "hole" again, where I received a warm welcome. I didn't like the place, but was glad of the company.

F. M. GREGG: Near the Swims' jail in Chattanooga was the residence of Judge Reese D. Brabson, who at this time was Confederate congressman from this district. Several members of the Brabson household had called at the jail and conversed with the raiders through curiosity.

PITTENGER: One lady from the large mansion on Brabson's Hill—being permitted to talk to Andrews—expressed great compassion for him and afterward sent several gifts.

F. M. GREGG: The communication thus begun ended in Judge Brabson's offer to defend Andrews at his trial. This was sustained by an order of the court, also appointing another attorney from Holly Springs, Miss., as assistant, and Colonel Joseph McCollum and Captain Leander V. Crook, both of the 39th Georgia, for the prosecution.

PITTENGER: Back in our regiments in camp—as we couldn't then know—deep anxiety was felt in our behalf. When we didn't return at the appointed time, all believed we had perished. Every prisoner was closely questioned, but no positive tidings could be gained. Even General Mitchel couldn't learn where we were confined, or whether we had been captured at all. He finally declared to his son, F. A. Mitchel, that all of us had been hanged. The enemy wished apparently to hide the knowledge of us, probably fearing retaliation on the part of our commander; and it's possible that this was the reason for our confinement in the tomblike Swims prison, from which no word could reach anyone.

DORSEY: The trial of James J. Andrews took place while we were in the Chattanooga jail, Pittenger being witness for the prosecution, with the idea of establishing that we were legally detailed U. S. soldiers on a military expedition to cut enemy communications. I regret that I didn't learn more at the time of Andrews' opinions about Pittenger's course. I think, however, that Andrews originally approved of Pittenger going on as a witness in his case. He seemed to think that while it wouldn't help him—for he had little hope of saving himself—yet it might possibly help us in some way, and he would have done anything to save his men, even though it might make it worse for himself.

Andrews was tried on the charge of being a spy, though I believe another charge was brought against him, because of his previous Southern connections—that of treason to the Confederate government.

PITTENGER: None of us knew just the line of defense taken by Andrews nor upon what he based the hopes he did, certainly, to some extent, entertain. While all his money had been taken from him, he was still believed to be able to command it from outside sources, or could make promises which were believed. He was charged with spying and treason. He seems to have sought to make the work that he did appear as small as possible, and his own motive to be only moneymaking, with resulting benefits to the South far greater than the loss. What follows is built upon scattered hints, and is therefore offered with diffidence, yet comprises the only theory that seems to meet the facts.

He was known to the Southerners as a blockade-runner. This trade, if he could only persuade the Federals to permit it, was of great advantage to the Confederates. He might afford to do a good deal for the Federals and the balance of advantage be still on the Confederate side. Now he claimed that he was offered by General Mitchel, who greatly wanted an engine, the privilege of trading south to the extent of five thousand dollars per month as long as the war lasted, on the simple condition that he would seize an engine and carry it through. Andrews did disclaim to the enemy that he intended to burn any bridges, or do any harm beyond the comparatively trifling one of carrying off this engine. In harmony with the same line of defense he tried to make himself appear very ignorant, and in letters intended for their eye, his spelling was fearfully bad—so bad that it looks as if he overdid his part. As a help to the men who were under him, Andrews declared his belief that they were all detailed without their previous consent, and that they knew nothing about what was to be done. He summoned his old partner, Mr. Whiteman, to prove that he was a blockade-runner, and that this was his real business. He was greatly dissatisfied with the conduct of Mr. Whiteman at the trial, thinking that he received far more injury than good from him.

The defense was feeble, though possibly as good as could have been made under the circumstances. The car left burning on the bridge, and the admissions of the men who were first captured as to their intentions of bridge burning, tended to discredit the idea that the running of the engine through was the only object. Neither would the Confederates easily believe that the Federals would send men to the heart of Georgia for an engine, when experience showed engines could be had by the score in Kentucky and Alabama. The facts were that Andrews had gained their confidence, and had been admitted as their trusted ally, when suddenly they found him at the head of the most daring enterprise the enemy had yet undertaken. Andrews had played back and forth once too often; and the Confederates' enmity now was in proportion to their former confidence.

But it's possible that Andrews didn't look for an acquittal, only delay in the hope of a Federal advance, or of finding an opportunity to escape.

We remained at Chattanooga almost three weeks, during which time Andrews received his trial. The evidence was strong against him. Mr. Whiteman, whom Andrews himself had directed to be summoned, testified that Andrews had been repeatedly in the South, that he had professed allegiance to the Southern Confederacy, and in all things represented himself to be a citizen of the same. In fact he had passes in his possession when he was captured that could hardly have been obtained without his taking the oath of allegiance. This did much to sustain the charge of treason against him, as he admitted being the leader of the expedition.

The other indictment, that of being a spy, wasn't supported by any evidence, so far as I could learn; but this was of no importance, as the punishment of the first charge was death. However, the sentence wasn't then given, and Andrews' lawyers gave him some reason to hope that there was an informality in the proceedings which would render the whole trial void.

F. M. GREGG: For three weeks the court considering Andrews' case convened, in the second story of a building (later police headquarters) at the corner of Fourth and Market streets. Andrews appeared in court, and his defense was so ably conducted by Judge Brabson, that that gentleman was notified he was taking too much interest in the man's case and it might be better for him not to be so much concerned. Considerable sympathy had been aroused in Chattanooga by the prisoner's general good appearance, and as the first wrath of the populace wore away, the hardihood and recklessness of the raiders won favor with the people. One instance of an attempt to interfere in their favor is given by Dr. Thomas Y. Park.

DR. PARK: Andrews was a man of prepossessing appearance. His cool and determined manner impressed me as he faced his accusers at this trial. My sympathy aroused—although I had helped in his capture—I determined to appeal on his behalf to Captain Crook, one of the prosecuting attorneys, who was a personal friend of mine.

Calling Captain Crook from the courtroom, I told him what Andrews had said when we captured him, that he was a soldier and claimed the treatment of a prisoner of war, and that the men were enlisted and in force and couldn't be treated as spies.

"Enlisted or not enlisted," Crook said, "they were down there where they ought not to have been and I'll hang everyone of them if I can."

This seemed to have been the general sentiment of the court. Although the sentence wasn't given out at the time, Andrews virtually was a doomed man when he returned to the prison.

Southern Confederacy, ATLANTA, APRIL 26, 1862:

We learn that the court-martial at Chattanooga have completed the trial of the ringleader of the bridge-burning party. Their decision in the case will not be made public, however, till their finding is approved by the Secretary of War. We learn that no more of them will be put on trial till this decision is passed upon.

The leader of the party is named Andrews, and is said to be a partner in a well-known firm in Nashville, and had not heretofore been suspected of hostility to the South. He was hired by the Lincoln authorities to burn the State bridges, and, if possible, to bring through to them an engine. Those accompanying him belonged to the army, and had been detailed to do the work.

We are informed that the one who turned State's evidence against them is a Kentuckian. He said he was one of the State Guard in the days when neutrality was in vogue; that he was entrapped into the service by belonging to this State Guard and accepting arms from the Yankee Government before the Yankees came into the State, and was unable afterwards to get out of the service; that he was always friendly to the South, and that it was always his determination to fight for the South if forced to take any side; but that neutrality and the State Guard had deceived him as it had thousands of others. Before he was fully aware of the fact, he was in the Lincoln army and could not escape from it.

PITTENGER: The closing paragraph of the report above is hard to understand, even allowing for the usual latitude of misinformation. No member of our party was from Kentucky except Campbell, who carefully concealed the fact. It may be simply a reminiscence of our Kentucky pretensions. Andrews himself had been a member of the Kentucky State Guard; but it isn't likely that he would give that as a reason for being in the Union service.

Whatever the misunderstandings at Atlanta, there was no mistaking General Mitchel's determination to secure his victory. On April 28, he began his movement toward Bridgeport to throw the enemy on the defensive, while securing his own lines of communication to Stevenson.

DORSEY: In Mitchel's demonstration against Bridgeport and Chattanooga late in April, some units of our own Sill's brigade had a brush with the Rebel battery Sam Llewellyn and James Smith—the original twenty-third and twenty-fourth men of our party—had gone into, claiming themselves as brothers. Making a run for it over the bridge from Bridgeport, Llewellyn escaped back to his and my own old regiment, the 33d.

Smith wasn't able to get away. As they had told the same story when first arrested which we had all told while going south—that we were citizens of Fleming County, Ky.—and now Llewellyn had deserted, Smith was arrested on suspicion of being of our party. Some days later, he was put in with us. But we didn't pretend to recognize him, and he was moved out again, and later was able to escape.

It was Corporal Llewellyn, on about May 1—although none of

us knew it then—who brought the first news back to our regiments that all the raiders had been captured and that one of them was testifying against the others.

EDITOR: Llewellyn's news had competition for attention at divisional headquarters. On May 2, one of General O. M. Mitchel's sons [the second on his staff, Captain E. M. Mitchel] was captured near Pulaski, Tennessee, by Morgan's men. Negotiations for the younger Mitchel's exchange were completed promptly, aided greatly by the matching Federal capture, during these weeks, of Confederate General John Morgan's brother.

E. KIRBY SMITH:

Headquarters Department of East Tenn.
Knoxville, April 28, 1862

General S. Cooper,
Adjutant and Inspector General,
Richmond, Va.

I have not more than 500 troops at Chattanooga, which is in great danger. The enemy are at Stevenson. Cannot reinforcements be sent there from Georgia or Alabama?

E. Kirby Smith,
Maj. General, Commanding

Knoxville, April 28, 1862

Brig. Gen. D. Leadbetter,
Commanding,
Chattanooga, Tenn.

General Smith directs that the spies be tried at once.

Respectfully,
J. F. Belton, Aide-de-Camp

DORSEY: In the early part of May we were suddenly notified to get ready for the morning train south. As we believed the cause of our removal to be the fear of an advance of the Union army on Chattanooga, Alf Wilson couldn't get his shoes on. Finally, for all our dragging and dawdling, we were ready; and a little after sunrise, we scrambled up the ladder, and under guard were marched to the depot.

[*Dorsey*]

We were too late; the train had gone and we had to be returned to the hole. Anxiously we waited for the expected storm of battle, but night came and no battle. The order to be ready for the train next morning was renewed, and this time we were called so early that we couldn't kill sufficient time to miss the train, and away we went again southward, over the line of our exciting raid.

The rebel *General*, captured and disabled by us on April 12, had recovered from his wounds, and returned to duty, and was now pulling the train that was carrying his former captors. In spite of the rather shabby, if not filthy, appearance we must have presented, we were visited at every station in our car as we moved southward—always under a strong guard—by many curious people, anxious to see the chained Yankees. Everywhere we heard the cry: "Hang 'em!"

Or Spoil a Horn 2

DORSEY: We arrived at Atlanta from Chattanooga sometime in the afternoon and had to remain in the car for several hours awaiting a train to take us somewhere where prison accommodations could be had. As we lay there in the depot, a mob such as we had met nowhere else gathered to take us, and at one time it looked as if they had us sure. They were strong in numbers, and their leaders were very determined. As they closed in on the car, a policeman hit one of them with his mace. The car windows were open. Reddick saw the officer strike the fellow and called out: "Give him h--l, Reb!"

This struck me as very inopportune, and I shouted to Reddick: "Shut your mouth!"

The words were probably scarcely out of Reddick's mouth until he, himself, saw that they were out of order. Not another word was spoken. Prisoners and guards all watched the steadily advancing mob, which filled the depot and extended back into the street beyond for a block or more.

To the credit of the police force of Atlanta, be it said, they were equal to the occasion, and beat the mob back, bleeding some of the leaders severely. I saw one big, burly fellow with the blood running to his shoe, from a gash in his head inflicted by a policeman's club.

Presently a locomotive backed part of another train up and hitched onto our car. At this juncture someone in the crowd slipped a newspaper through the window and whispered the one word: "A friend."

In a moment the wheels began to roll. We were soon out of harm's reach, and the paper handed us contained great news—the capture of New Orleans by General Butler's army and Farragut's fleet.

Southern Confederacy, ATLANTA, MAY 3, 1862

THE ENGINE THIEVES

These notorious individuals arrived here yesterday morning on the train from Chattanooga. The leader, Andrews, has often been in our reading-room during his peregrinations in the Confederate States since the fall of Nashville.

Before that time he was engaged in running the blockade, bringing articles of necessity for merchants, manufacturers, etc., from Cincinnati, Louisville, and other points in the enemy's domain. He made it a business, and was quite successful in it, and he retained the confidence of our people in Nashville, where he resided while so engaged.

The other prisoners, his compeers in the attempt to burn the bridges, are all sharp, intelligent-looking men, no hard-looking cases like Yankee prisoners and East Tennessee Tories usually are. We learn they will be sent to Milledgeville for confinement.

PITTENGER: Instead of to Milledgeville, we were taken to Madison. We passed the dilapidated cotton factory where six hundred Federal prisoners were kept, and on to the old county prison which was then unoccupied. It was a gloomy stone building with two rooms. The party was divided between the rooms. The captain of our guard showed us kindness, though he didn't dare to take off our irons.

DORSEY: Tempers were short in our situation, and as before, it frequently happened that two men chained together by their necks quarreled. Here at Madison, Porter jerked my neck by the chain for some fancied grievance, and I of course paid it back in kind with interest. And thus it went, jerk, jerk, jerk, back and forth, until each flew at the other, and grabbed his chain around the neck and tried to choke his chainmate. There we stood like great gawks, trying to fight, both chained together, and both handcuffed. The other boys set up such a laugh at our folly that we cooled down and became better friends than before.

We had visitors here at Madison as well as elsewhere, and among them on one occasion was a man in Rebel uniform whom Andrews recognized as a former acquaintance and Union secret agent, though he didn't let the fact be known except to us afterward. The agent—we heard from the guard captain that night—narrowly avoided being arrested at the station as he was about to leave. Being asked for a pass he began fumbling in his pockets as if he had one, until the train was under a good motion, and as the last car came by, he suddenly jumped aboard, leaving the guards with guns in hand, standing on the depot platform, minus a Yankee spy.

A widespread pass system had been put in operation as one result of our expedition, and hundreds of soldiers were put to guarding property, especially railroad bridges where no guard had been before; so that we had done some good after all. But it was a hard way to serve the Lord, or our country either, though there was a grain of comfort in the thought.

PITTENGER: The Confederates—after the commotion over the "Lincoln spy"—stopped all our visiting; but we felt sure that news of our situation would reach our own lines directly. (In this we were disappointed. We were unable to learn anything about this man thereafter. Whether he was captured somewhere else, or his information lost in the rush and hurry of other events, we never knew.)

Our stay in Madison was only three days, after which the Confederates, relieved of the fear of an immediate advance by Mitchel, ordered us back to Chattanooga. Again we were compelled to run the gauntlet of jeering mobs that marked our course on the southward journey. We traveled in boxcars. The journey was rendered easier by the fact that since leaving Chattanooga we had been in the hands of one set of guards commanded by a Captain Lawes, who talked freely with us, and did all that they safely could to render our condition more endurable.

DORSEY: On arriving at our old quarters at Chattanooga—through the kindness of Captain Lawes and Colonel H. L. Claiborne, the new provost marshal—we were allowed to stay in the upper room instead of being put in the dungeon. But the poor Tennessee loyalists—

those grand old men of East Tennessee—had to go down into the dungeon. The chains were taken off our necks, and they put us together in pairs by means of handcuffs embracing the right hand of one and the left hand of another.

When this shift was made, we changed partners, some of us at least. Bensinger and myself now became partners and remained together until the irons were entirely removed. I had learned to remove the cuff from my left hand. This was done by wetting the left hand with saliva from my mouth, then clenching the cuff in my right hand, putting it between my knees, clasping it tight, and forcing the cuff off by a sudden jerk of the hand upward. When the officer came to make the change, I took good care to make it most convenient for him to release my right hand.

With the new arrangements, some began to think the enemy was feeling better toward us, and regarded the change of treatment as an omen of better things than we had been expecting.

Reddick and Pittenger shared a pair of cuffs and by some means Pittenger got his off. I think Knight unlocked it for him, and this left the cuffs in Reddick's possession. They served him the purpose of knuckles on one occasion. He and Shadrach had a difficulty one day, and Reddick using the cuff as a knuckle, struck Shadrach with it. Tempers were very short, the boys were full of vim, and a little tilt was liable to occur on the slightest provocation. But these little unpleasantries were of short duration, and generally there was good feeling among us all round. We were a jolly crew in a bad boat, liable to sink at almost any time, and on short notice—and we couldn't hold any grudge against each other. There was a small rope or heavy cord left in this cell by someone, and some of the better educated among us taught the next how to tie a hangman's knot. I was one of the students and the subject was one I wasn't ever to forget.

On some days we held mock court. Campbell, being the largest man among us, was made judge. Pittenger and George D. Wilson acted as counsel, one for the state, and the other for the defendant. Wilson made a practice of scoring his opponent in the most scathing manner, but Pittenger didn't lag in the amount or character of the abuse employed in replying. It was refreshing to hear the testimony of some of the witnesses. According to the sworn evidence, they had spent the night previous in Cincinnati, or Columbus, Toledo, Chillicothe, Kingston, Hallsville, or perhaps on Wall Street dealing in stocks. Anywhere, of course, but in the old Swims jail, in Chattanooga.

[*Dorsey*]

We had some sport, too, at the expense of the guards, who were comparatively raw and drilled on the hill near the prison in plain view. We jeered at them, sometimes even venturing to give them a command.

One favor from the guards was an old pack of cards. Pittenger and some others were disposed to object to card playing, but they were given to understand that the rest of us had just as good a right in that jail as they had. That settled it. No one was disposed to claim a better right to be in jail than his neighbor.

PITTENGER: We were still guarded with elaborate care. Even when below, where a man unassisted could scarcely have got out if the locks had all been taken off, the jailer had never raised the trap door unprotected by a strong guard. Now that we were in the upper room, their vigilance increased—guards on hand with leveled bayonets when our door was unlocked, the stairway guarded below, and a strong guard detail always walking beats clear around the prison. As well, we were all this time closely chained.

These chains actually meant very little. Knight had concealed his pocketknife when first taken by putting it up his sleeve, and adroitly turning his arm as they felt for concealed articles. Now from some small bones in our meat he made keys which unlocked the handcuffs. With strings and hairs, the padlocks on the chains had been opened before. We were given a good deal of trouble, for these fastenings had to be put on again when the door was opened. The outside stairway was useful as a warning. As soon as a foot was heard on it, the signal would be given for rapid locking up.

DORSEY: Andrews and Ross were fine singers, while Porter, Wood and others were fair assistants in rendering a few favorite songs which were run through every evening to the delight of us all, including the citizens, mostly ladies and children, who, hearing the melodies, came by permission of the guards into the prison yard.

The evening song service was usually opened with "Do They Miss Me at Home?" Porter's favorite was "Nettie Moore," or "The Prairie Queen." Mark Wood was fond of "A Life on the Ocean Wave." Wood was an Englishman by birth and education, and hadn't long since crossed the Atlantic. I think he had been a seafaring man, and this song of the sea seemed to rouse his naturally jolly spirits to their highest pitch. Andrews enjoyed "Riding on the Rail," which he sang at times with evident glee. Ross loved "Kissing

Through the Bars"—a strange fancy, but he loved it, and sang it to perfection.

Mr. Andrews was to have been married June 17, 1862, to Miss Elizabeth J. Layton, of Kentucky. But now that he was in the power of the enemy, with little hope of ever again meeting his intended bride, he seemed to take special comfort in singing the appropriate song, "Carrier Dove." The sweet melody of Andrews' voice, with the pathos and tremor of tone in which he sang the following lines, wasn't easily forgotten:

Fly away to my native land, sweet dove,
Fly away to my native land,
And bear these lines to my lady love . . .
I can bear in a dungeon to waste away youth . . .
But I can't endure she should doubt my truth. . . .

But the song of songs was the old "Star-Spangled Banner." We took good care to make that ring in the ears of friends—and we had some friends, though they didn't dare let themselves be known—and foes, at least once nearly every day during our entire imprisonment. If we were all to be executed together, we intended to sing "The Star-Spangled Banner" on the scaffold, and sometimes practiced it with that object in view.

PITTENGER: Our days were much longer and more pleasant after they'd put us in the upper room, as we awoke earlier and sought out more employment than below. Mock trials gave us much amusement. We needed some kind of government, and had to try, and punish, offenders. Campbell was made judge, and had usually the sport of carrying out his own sentences—a task for which his immense strength well equipped him.

More enjoyment was found in singing. Our special time for singing was in the twilight. Someone would start a song quietly, others would join, and then for hours in the gathering darkness we would have song after song. The guards liked to hear us sing; and frequently citizens of the town would gather outside the jail fence to listen to the caged Yankees. These songs, and the favorable report of the guards who were brought into contact with us, caused a sentiment in our favor to spread through the town.

DORSEY: Colonel Claiborne now allowed us another privilege which was greatly appreciated. He permitted half our number to spend an hour in the yard in the afternoon of each day for recreation, and after the first half had had their outing the others were allowed a like treat. On these occasions an extra line of sentinels was posted, and generally some of the soldiers not on duty came in the yard and talked with us. Colonel Claiborne was there one day—with quite a group of us around him as he sat on a camp stool making out a list of our party, I think—and some of our boys thanked him for his kindness.

His reply came as calmly as you please. "While you're in my hands," he said, "I'll treat you as gentlemen. If I should ever meet you on the battlefield, I'll kill you if I can."

ALF WILSON: All were anxious for an early escape attempt at Chattanooga, if I remember rightly, except Marion Ross and George D. Wilson, who thought the proposed attempt premature. They relied on the talk of the officers in charge of us that we would be exchanged—a reliance based on a sandy foundation. But there were some flying reports and rumors current that did, for a little time, cause a rainbow of hope to appear in our cheerless, cloudy horizon. These and the opposition, more especially of George Wilson, who was a ready talker, well educated, full of experience, fertile and ingenious in resources, a close reasoner, and a man who had much influence with us, temporarily lulled the clamor for openly jumping the guards and trying to escape.

Although I was in the minority, I didn't feel that the escape attempt wasn't both justifiable and feasible. We were all trying to do for the best, though we differed in judgment. Yet I have learned by experience that when a fellow is in a tight place, especially where his life and liberty are at stake, prompt, decisive, fearless action wins oftener than any other. The very boldness of the act sometimes confuses and paralyzes the enemy beyond successful effort at resistance.

PITTENGER: The word had gone out that we were only detailed men —not volunteers. All of our number had told this story. Andrews had been careful to confirm all that we said, and it was accepted as truth.

Meanwhile, there was great talk of exchange. Mitchel had captured a younger brother of Colonel John Morgan, but his own son had been taken by that chief, and now they, with many more on each side, were to be exchanged. A lieutenant who had been paroled for the purpose of effecting the exchange, visited us, and the brightest hopes were raised that we might be included. It's possible that if our authorities had known of our condition and had made a peremptory demand, backed by the threat of retaliation, they might have accomplished this. But the Confederate officers told us that we must first have a trial to show that we were soldiers. Andrews had originally proposed to send a flag of truce through to get from our officers a statement of our true character; but the Confederate authorities had refused to permit this.

Despite our hopes and the rising tide of local sympathy, we didn't give over plans for escape. At Andrews' suggestion, we settled on one plan in which Wollam—while we were being brought in from our breathing time in the yard—was to hide himself under the bed in Swims' room, through which we always passed. Remaining there till late at night, he was to open the door from that side, and let us out.

DORSEY: Around then, some of the officers gave us assurances of a possible exchange of prisoners between General Mitchel and the Confederates, in which it was thought we would be included. In fact, a cartel for the exchange of prisoners between them had been arranged, and a boatload of prisoners who had been captured at the battle of Pittsburg Landing, or Shiloh, was landed on the north side of the Tennessee River below Shell-Mound, I believe, and received by General Mitchel, who returned a like number of Rebel prisoners, in exchange.

But when the next boatload steamed down to the place of landing —we heard later—a line of Union soldiers was drawn up on the north bank of the river, and their officers forbade the boat to land. For some reason, the exchange plans had broken down.

Some of our party had for a time great hopes of our release, among them George D. Wilson, but so far as I was concerned I had no faith in it at all, nor do I think Ross had, nor Slavens.

EDITOR: From March of this year until the signing, on July 22, of the first extensive exchange cartel between the Federal and Confederate governments, no dependable procedure for substantial exchanges of prisoners existed. Varying individual arrangements continued to be made by commanders in the field, but these were always subject to abrupt changes of signals from the respective war departments.

DORSEY: Conductor Fuller made us a call one day at Chattanooga while we were in the upper cell. He didn't come in among us, but stood in the door entering from the jailer's room, and after passing a few words with us in a rather friendly manner, got off a speech I shall never forget. Said he: "The trouble with you gentlemen was that you had the wrong man to follow you. I'm the man that followed you, and I'm not done yet. I'll follow you to the scaffold, and see you at the end of a rope."

I don't know whether Fuller was drunk that day or not. (I can't even say for a complete certainty the visitor was Fuller, but someone did address us this way, and after he had gone, Mr. Andrews said it was Fuller.)

PITTENGER: In the Swims prison a short time before we left it, we differed, as usual, about our prospects. Some maintained that there was hope even yet, while J. A. Wilson, Dorsey and Mason were rather disposed to regard hope as useless and deceptive. They thought that we would have to die at any rate, and the sooner we passed out of such misery the better.

DORSEY: Ordinarily I was reserved, and without much to say. I offered advice to our leader but once, and that was when, from movements among the Rebel officers, it was apparent to most of us that some change in our situation would soon be made. I felt sure we must act without delay or it would be too late, and I urged Andrews to lead, and we would assault the guards and escape, or be killed in the attempt. But George D. Wilson and Pittenger objected, and carried their point, Andrews deciding against the proposed attack.

Most of the others agreed with me. Brown especially joined me in urging Andrews to go, and when the latter decided against us, Brown asked me if I would lead. I was surprised at the suggestion, as I was one of the youngest and, as I felt, humblest members of the party; but after a moment's hesitation I answered in the affirmative. I was so impressed with the importance of immediate action that I was willing to lead if the party wanted me to try it, though I felt that it was putting the cart before the horse; for there were evidently several others much better qualified for the high office of commander in such a moment.

Having signified my willingness to lead the way out, I awaited the will of the rest. It required urging to induce me to assume command over our cool-headed leader, whose judgment was averse to the move, and as no one else urged the matter, the subject was dropped, and no attempt to escape was made at that time.

ALF WILSON: Finally, after days of vain hope to hear something favorable, we again came around to escape plans and set a night for a determined strike for liberty. But it so happened that on the very day of our proposed night escape, an order came for twelve of our number to be sent to Knoxville. The order didn't designate by name those who were to go. It merely said twelve of us.

The officer handed the order to George D. Wilson, who happened to be down in the yard, where he was allowed on account of his being sick that day with cholera morbus or some ailment of the kind, and asked him to fill in the names. Wilson selected all of his own regimental friends (the 2nd Ohio) first, and afterwards some of his favorite comrades from other regiments, as he still clung to the exchange delusion and supposed he was doing his friends thus selected a favor. I wasn't of the number sent away, but this order, taking away twelve of our party, upset our arrangements for an escape.

After shaking hands with our departing comrades, we were compelled to change our calculations, although we didn't abandon the fixed purpose of getting our liberty in some way.

DORSEY: When it was decided to remove part of our number to Knoxville, George Wilson was told by Captain Lawes that they wanted him and Pittenger to go, and that he, Wilson, might choose the other ten, as they had no choice after himself and Pittenger. The twelve taken to Knoxville were George D. Wilson, Pittenger, Mason, Shadrach, Ross, Campbell, Scott, Buffum, Brown, Knight, Slavens and Robertson.

The uncertainty of our ever meeting again caused a gloom to fall over us and the parting was especially painful on Andrews' account, as all felt his days were probably numbered, though he had had no notice of the fact as yet.

PITTENGER: The departure of the twelve of us for Knoxville—after our six weeks of imprisonment together—roused a great deal of excitement. With Andrews the parting was peculiarly affecting. He was specially marked for vengeance; officers who had encouraged us had uttered no word of hope for him. He bore this like the hero he was, and continued mild and cheerful as ever, kind to all of us, always ready to sink his own sorrow in comforting others. He seemed willing even to offer his life if the giving of this could have availed for our safety. At his trial he hadn't spoken a word which could shake credit in the detailed-men story upon which we had risked our hopes, though it provoked the question: "How could you be so cruel as to lead men into these perils without giving them fair warning?"

We had never heard Andrews utter a word of repining. He had played a fearful game and lost; he was ready if need be to pay the penalty. One evening after we had ceased to sing, and had been silent for a time, Andrews had said thoughtfully: "Boys, I have often thought I'd like to see what's on the other side of Jordan." We weren't anxious to cross that final river so soon, and the subject wasn't pursued. But now at this splitting of our group, he recurred to the same word again. When we had sung our songs together for the last time, the twelve of us leaving for Knoxville came to bid him farewell.

Andrews pressed our hands one by one. "Boys," he said, in a low clear voice, "if I never see you here again, try to meet me on the other side of Jordan."

To Make a Spoon 2

DORSEY: The twelve were started for Knoxville on the morning of Saturday, May 31.

PITTENGER: The twelve of us who had been separated from the others at Chattanooga were escorted by Colonel Claiborne to the cars, ironed as usual, and committed by him to the care of a band of Morgan's guerrillas, with the injunction: "These are men, like other men, and gentlemen, too, and I want them treated as such."

Morgan's men were well dressed in citizen's clothes (for they weren't always uniformed, even in the enemy's country) and treated us kindly on the nearly twenty-four-hour train trip. A little after noon the next day we arrived in Knoxville and were lodged in the old jail, a square and massive building, far stronger than any jail we had yet occupied.

F. M. GREGG: In the old courthouse at Knoxville a court-martial, with Colonel J. B. Bibb as executive officer, convened to try the raiders as spies for passing through the fortified camps at Chattanooga and Camp McDonald at Big Shanty.

PITTENGER: At Knoxville, we were soon visited by Captain Leander V. Crook, the judge advocate, and other members of the court-martial, and notified of the trial. Captain Crook told us we could employ counsel, if we could find anyone to serve. Judge Oliver P. Temple—reported to be a kindly and able man—was promptly sent for, and I think it was on his suggestion that we also sent for Colonel Jonathan Baxter. Both were of first-class ability, and we couldn't have done better had we been able to pay a magnificent fee.

When we learned that it was the intention of trying us one by one, we protested that this was useless, as our cases were precisely alike. If one was guilty, so were all; if one was a prisoner of war simply, the same was true of all the others. Our request was refused. We then asked that one be tried and the result in his case be accepted for all. We also offered to tell just what we did, thus saving them all trouble about proof, for we didn't wish to deny being on the train, or engaged in its capture. But they gave us a clear intimation that they knew their own business best, and we were obliged to take it in the manner of their choosing.

The nature of the charge against us gave some uneasiness. It was of being spies, and of lurking about Confederate camps as spies, and hinged only on our going south, without anything being said of the capture of the train, or our return. This was suspicious; but we were led by their explanations to think that possibly they only wanted to get the case into such a form that we could consistently say, "not guilty," without denying what we really did. Afterward we found the intent far more serious. The charge was of violating a certain section of their Articles and Rules of War; and the specifications were two: first, coming to Chattanooga, and lurking as a spy about the Confederate camp there; and second, going through Dalton and Camp McDonald to Marietta, and lurking as a spy in those places.

The Knoxville trials began. Each day began and finished the trial of a man. The charges and specifications of William Campbell were first handed in. He was a civilian, but claimed to be a soldier, and we

[*Pittenger*]
endorsed his position. There seemed to be no rule followed as to the order in which the cases came, and probably they were taken out just as they happened to come on the prison list. One of our number was taken out, the charges and specifications read, a few witnesses heard, and then in about an hour he was returned to us. The charge against all who were brought to trial was "lurking in and around Confederate camps as spies, for the purpose of obtaining information." Not a word was said of taking the cars, or of anything we really did do. The next day another comrade was treated in the same manner. In no case did the proceedings occupy any great period of time, and as each one was a mere repetition of those that went before, the members of the court soon became very inattentive. The table in the courtroom was covered with newspapers, bottles and novels.

Our plan of defense has been partly indicated. It was to tell just who we were, and what we had done, and to claim that we were United States soldiers, detailed on a military expedition without our consent, and therefore entitled to the protection accorded to regular prisoners of war. This was put into words, and read on the trial as the acknowledgment of the party while pleading "not guilty" to the charge. The only evidence they had was of the men who pursued us on the train, and also of those who afterward arrested us; but of course none of these knew anything of our lurking around the camps.

The request to hear pleading of counsel was made by us and denied. This was the more strange because Andrews had been allowed that privilege. After three or four of the trials had passed, Judge Baxter visited us in prison and read the able plea which Judge Temple and he read at each trial. The only real question was one of interpretation, as there was no dispute about facts.

Did the mere fact of our having come into the territory under Confederate authority, in ordinary dress, render us worthy of death? And if so, would it be to the interest of the Confederacy to inflict the supreme penalty, and in what time and manner? Judges Temple and Baxter contended that the whole case against us consisted in our being dressed in citizen's clothes instead of our regular uniform; that this was nothing more than what Confederates frequently did, sometimes from necessity and sometimes for their own advantage; that they had many regiments in service that weren't yet in uniform, and that they had expressly encouraged guerrilla bands to raid Federal communications. They cited the instance of General Morgan having dressed his men in Federal uniform and passed them off as part of the 8th Pennsylvania Cavalry, by which means he succeeded in reaching and damaging a railroad. Some of these men had been captured by the Federal government and treated as prisoners of war.

As stated, no prisoner was allowed to hear the pleading of counsel for or against him, and although each case was concluded the same day it was begun, the several decisions were reserved that all might be rendered and approved together.

A great part of the testimony in our favor depended upon our own admissions, but as this was adduced by the enemy and not contradicted, they couldn't know how much of it was overdrawn—especially in reference to our ignorance, and the involuntary character of our service. Judges Baxter and Temple were far abler men than any on the court, and therefore managed to arrange the testimony in the best possible manner. Our lawyers were delighted with the course we took, and said that the prosecution hadn't a particle of evidence against us. As the trial of different ones proceeded, we had still greater encouragement from the court itself. Members called on us, and told us to keep in good heart, as there was no evidence before them to convict anyone. It's no wonder we were confident and believed that protracted imprisonment was the worst we had to fear.

DORSEY: On the afternoon of the same day the twelve left for Knoxville—Saturday, May 31—while we ten remaining at Chattanooga were outside for our afternoon airing, Captain Lawes entered the yard and quietly approached Mr. Andrews as he and Hawkins, who shared Andrews' handcuffs, walked to and fro along the north end of the prison in the shade of the building. Captain Lawes handed him a large envelope. Andrews received it coolly, and placing it in his pocket, resumed his walking for a few minutes, and then he and Hawkins leisurely walked up the stairway to our cell.

I don't think Captain Lawes said a word when he handed the envelope to Mr. Andrews; in fact, I think he was too much affected. Shortly after Andrews and Hawkins had gone up, Captain Lawes told the rest of us, in a manner that showed that something of unusual weight was on his mind, that maybe it was time to close the prison.

On returning to the cell we found Andrews and Hawkins seated at the west side of the room reading a document. We didn't need to ask what it meant; Andrews' countenance told that. For once there was a deathlike pallor upon the face of the man who seemed to have no fear. Andrews voluntarily told us the nature of the document he had received, and as he did so he smiled, but it seemed the smile of a corpse. However, as he talked with us his face gradually resumed its accustomed color and composure.

ALF WILSON: Andrews passed the paper to us. He was perfectly calm, with no perceptible emotion, but as we read the words, "and then and there be hanged until he is dead," there was not a man of us who didn't show signs of anguish. There wasn't one who wouldn't have fought to the death for our leader. He had, by his manhood and kindness, endeared himself to all. His unselfish regard for everyone of the party, his cheerful, quiet, encouraging manner under the most trying ordeals had caused us to regard him with the greatest confidence and love.

The time fixed in the sentence for his execution—June 7, the following Saturday—gave Andrews just one week longer in which to live. But we had no idea of using all this time in preparing Andrews for death. We all realized the reality that stared at us. This didn't mean simply the execution of our chief. It was a forerunner of the fate that awaited every man of us.

F. M. GREGG: When the finding of Andrews' court-martial had been referred to Secretary of War Leroy P. Walker and President Jefferson Davis, and had received the latter's sanction, it was at once made known to Andrews. On Saturday he was notified that one week later, on the 7th, he would be executed. He was at once put back in "the hole" for security.

The men immediately began planning to help Andrews escape, applying all their fertile ingenuity. By some means they had found that there was an attic above their cell. If they could succeed in getting up in it, by tearing a hole in the outside wall they could drop down and escape. The ceiling was made of two-inch oak planking; their only tool a jackknife.

DORSEY: That Saturday after supper the trap door was opened, the ladder thrust down, and once more Andrews was told to go down into the hole.

But we hadn't been idle during our stay in the upper cell. With Knight's knife we had cut the planks in the ceiling so that with a little work we could soon make an opening into the loft above, where there would be but a brick wall to work through in order to get out. Andrews himself had done most of the work, standing on the shoulders of two others while doing so. Andrews was pretty heavy, even when his weight was divided between two of us. More or less time had been spent at this work early each morning for a week or more, and now that Andrews was in the hole again, we proceeded to cut the lock out of the trap door so as to get the condemned leader out of the dungeon, and then try to effect an escape all round up through the attic.

Knight had left his knife with us in anticipation of just some such need for it.

ALF WILSON: We now set to work with the quickened energies of desperate men. The building was of brick, lined with heavy plank. Three men stood on the floor together and the fourth, with Knight's case knife made into a saw, stood on their shoulders, and was thus enabled to reach the plank ceiling overhead into which by patience and perseverance we succeeded in sawing a square hole large enough to admit a man's body. We bent ourselves to the task before us, with a watchman at every window to guard against the discovery of our operations. The noise made by our case knife saw was effectually drowned by stamping, loud talking, yelling, singing, or anything to keep up a din, and our singers and noisemakers were about as weary with the monotony of their efforts as the saw-shovers.

When two of the planks were so nearly cut out that they could be speedily finished, we filled up the cut so that it couldn't be noticed easily, and then the fellows below in the hole, Andrews among them, in the same manner, sawed out notches in the plank which held the bolts of the trap door. This was discouragingly slow work. The knife blade would get hot and bend up, and the man who worked it would soon get a tired, blistered hand; but a relay was kept ready, and when the hand of one became too lame to run the saw, he would take his place among the choir of noise-makers, while a fresh man would take the knife.

F. M. GREGG: Saturday night found the work on the hardened timber overhead only partly done. On Sunday night the prisoners resumed the efforts by which they hoped before the morning to look out into the free air.

ANDREWS: Under sentence of death I was separated from my comrades, and placed in the hole on Saturday. That night something was up I knew, for our men were singing and shuffling around nearly all the time. The next day was Sunday, and without my knowledge they completed the plot by which they hoped to set me free. Soon after dark they tore their clothes in strips to make a rope, and the others cut away with a jackknife on the heavy oak timber overhead, completing a hole commenced some time before. Then I heard a raking noise on the trap door above. I was certain there was something in the wind.

They soon cut the lock out, and with the stealth of a cat the trap door was raised. You couldn't see anything, but the cool air coming down told of relief at hand. I heard my name, "Andrews," whispered; then, "Catch this."

I couldn't see what but I felt for it and caught a ragged rope, which they had made. Putting it under my arms, in an instant I was swung up to the floor and caught by hands from above. My shackles were unlocked with keys made of bone. Looking upward they whispered of the hole in the ceiling; it seemed as if I was going to have another chance for my life.

We took off our shoes. Climbing on the backs of our comrades below, we were able to reach the attic above. Each took a turn and scratched with an old knife on the outside brick wall. It was a hard task, and nearly morning before we got a brick out.

ALF WILSON: Old Swims, the jailer, afterwards said he might have known there was some devilment up, the way the damned Yankees were singing hymns. Singing, however, had remained a very common pastime with us in the evening, even though our best vocalists had gone to Knoxville.

While our cutting work was going on, others had twisted old blankets and pieces of carpet into ropes with which to get the men out of the "hole" and by which to descend on the outside.

When everything was in readiness, Andrews, who was to go first, went up in the loft. The work of making a hole out through the brick wall under the roof was a much more difficult job than we had expected, and proved to be slow work with our case knife. It had to be done, too, without noise. We at last succeeded in getting out brick enough to allow a man to pass out, just as dawn began to show. If I remember correctly, each man had his boots or shoes off, so that we could avoid making noise. We could see the dim gray form of the sentry, and hear his tread as he paced back and forth. It was an anxious moment of suspense, when at last, in a whisper, word was passed that all was ready.

ANDREWS: A few were up in the attic now. We carefully removed the last brick while those behind fastened the ragged rope. When the hole was large enough to let a man through, we pushed the rope out and everyone whispered, "Andrews first." It was no time for leave-taking, so with my boots held in my teeth by the straps, I pulled myself out through the opening. I was nearly out when one of the boots or a brick fell, and the guards started firing.

Dropping to the ground, I lost both boots and hat in the rush. I made for the south fence, got over all right and found myself in a road, Fifth Street they tell me it was.

ALF WILSON: Andrews crept out and swung down, but in some manner some loose mortar or a boot fell to the ground and attracted the notice of the sentry. Almost instantly we heard the report of a gun. John Wollam, who was next behind Andrews, paid no heed to the shot, but lunged out head over heels. Bang! Bang! went the muskets, and there was loud shouting: "Corporal of the guard! Post number—Captain—captain of the guard! Halt! Halt!"

Dorsey, following Wollam through the hole, halted between two opinions, whether he had better jump down while the Rebel sentry stood beneath holding a cocked gun with fixed bayonet on him, or crawl back into the old prison cock-loft and bear the ills he was certain of. He crawled back. We were crowded in the loft waiting for our turn to go out, and listening to the racket on the outside. Within a very few moments the yard was filled with troops, and by their loud, excited talk we learned, to our unspeakable joy, of the escape of Andrews and Wollam.

The Rebels, of course, didn't at that moment know who or how many of their prisoners were out, but we in the loft already knew that the excited sentries had fired wildly. At all events, neither Andrews nor Wollam were to be seen anywhere, either dead or alive. We took new hope. While we felt the keenest disappointment at our failure to get out, yet we would call ourselves a thousand times repaid for our effort if it proved that Andrews had actually escaped. We knew that Andrews would put forth superhuman efforts to gain the Federal lines, and, if he succeeded, we felt that Chattanooga would in all human probability get a visit very shortly from General Mitchel.

The musket-firing and the news of the jail break spread through camp and town like the wind, and soon the whole population was in a fever of excitement. All the available man-hunting force, dogs included, joined in the pursuit.

[*Alf Wilson*]

It is hardly necessary for me to say that those of us who failed to make good our escape were now put back down in the hole, loaded with heavy irons, and treated with the greatest severity. However, we cared nothing for these rigors in our great solicitude for the success of Andrews and Wollam. Hour after hour we passed sleeplessly, waiting to catch the first tidings from the returning pursuers.

ANDREWS: I was fired at by the guard as I scaled the prison yard fence. I ran away from the town and made for the river, wading in to prevent dogs from tracking me, then came out, going up the river bank about two miles. I minded not having my boots, as there were briers in the bushes along the bank through which I traveled. Since it was now getting light, I climbed up in a leafy tree and stayed all day. I could see off in the level men with guns, and two came near the tree, but never thought of looking up. I stayed there all day, Monday, and was very tired, but fixing a cushion of my coat in the forks, made myself comfortable.

PITTENGER: Andrews and John Wollam were separated from the moment they left the prison. Wollam broke through the guards, and ran the gauntlet of hasty shots without injury. Soon he reached the river bank and, not wishing to attempt the passage in the growing light, hit upon the happy expedient of making the enemy believe that he was across. To this end he threw off his coat and vest, dropping them on the river bank, and then waded a little way in the water to throw the hounds off the scent. Quietly slipping back, he hid himself in a dense thicket of canes and rushes.

The fugitive soon heard the hounds and men who were pursuing on the bank above and all about him. At length they found the clothing and concluded that he had taken to the river. They crossed over and searched unsuccessfully with their hounds along the water's edge on the other side for the place he had come out. Concluding that Wollam was drowned, the party pursuing him returned.

When Monday night came, Wollam cautiously left his hiding place and worked his way along the river till he came across a canoe, which he took and paddled downstream all night.

Register, KNOXVILLE, JUNE 4, 1862:

THE ESCAPED TRAIN-STEALERS

The despatch below was sent from this city yesterday to the provost-marshal at Chattanooga by Mr. William A. Fuller, authorizing him to offer a reward for the recapture of the train-stealer, Andrews. Mr. Fuller, the conductor of the stolen train, is in this city, attending as a witness the court-martial in session here on others of the party.

June 3d. Knoxville

Colonel Henry L. Claiborne

Is it possible that the infamous Andrews escaped? Is he pursued? If not, offer in my name $100 reward for his recapture and reincarceration.

Wm. A. Fuller

Andrews, we learn, is tall, about 180 pounds, and is supposed to be about thirty-five years old. He has short black hair, and a heavy black beard. His voice is fine, and his general address good. We trust that this description may lead to his recognition and arrest.

PITTENGER: At Knoxville, the time was passing not unpleasantly. Although newspapers were forbidden, good friends would often bring them to us, and we were kept fairly well informed. This place was a great improvement on any which we had endured, and we spent the days in comparative pleasure, and in a great degree of hope. (The chain of reasoning by which I had demonstrated that it would be unprofitable for the Rebels to hang us was very plain—possibly because I wished it to appear so.) We were visited by Confederate officers who took a great deal of pains to confirm these hopes. Whether this was because as they grew to know us they didn't wish us to die, or whether they wanted to keep us in good heart that we might not make desperate efforts to escape, I can't positively say.

We here received with great pleasure a paper containing an account of the escape of Andrews. I also met with a great piece of personal good fortune. Before leaving Chattanooga I had asked the captain of the guard if he couldn't borrow a law book from some lawyer for me that I might have it to read during the long days. Very much to my surprise, he brought me the book. When we were moved, it had to be returned, and I thought that my prison law studies were ended. But at Knoxville, Judge O. P. Temple was kind enough to lend me a copy of *Greenleaf on Evidence*. The opportunity for studying law was a grand one.

Or Spoil a Horn 3

ALF WILSON: Those of us still in the jail were overjoyed when we first heard that Andrews and Wollam had baffled the skill of both men and dogs. After two nights had passed, and still they hadn't been caught, we began to feel even more confident.

PITTENGER: At daybreak on Tuesday, John Wollam sunk the canoe he had found, and hid in the woods till night allowed him to recover the canoe and continue. This procedure he repeated daily on his way down the Tennessee River. Twice he could have been saved if he had known it. General Mitchel had constructed an extemporized gunboat with which to patrol sections of the Tennessee within the area he controlled, and twice Wollam passed within hail of it. But he had heard nothing of any such Union craft being on the river, and imagined it to be some Rebel boat, perhaps searching for him.

At last, far into what should have been Federal-occupied territory, Wollam paddled boldly on in the daytime. A band of Rebel cavalry, who were making a raid into Mitchel's territory, saw him, and procuring a boat with several pairs of oars, came out after him. There was a hot chase, and Wollam was retaken. A Lieutenant Edwards, who had been with the party who captured him the first time, identified him, and he was sent back to rejoin the rest of us.

ANDREWS: As Monday night came on, it commenced to cloud up and the wind began to blow. I came down the river, until I could get no further, a bluff cutting off further travel along the bank. It was raining hard and the river was very rough. I went back upstream a short way. Rolling up my pants in a bundle, I fastened them around my neck, and started in opposite a big hollow [foot of Georgia Avenue] to swim the river. I had no trouble until nearly across, when the river got so rough I could hardly get along. One wave washed over me, throwing me around and taking my pants with it. I was almost exhausted when I reached shore. I rested but a short time, as I wanted to get as far away from Chattanooga as possible before daylight. Traveling through the night, briers were bad, and my legs and feet were torn by them, giving me considerable pain.

ALF WILSON: Andrews—we learned from him later—continued his flight in an almost naked condition. He tore out the arms of his coat and with these encased his legs as much as he could, so as to afford them some protection against the brambles and rocks of that mountainous region. Early Tuesday morning, as he was going across an open field to another tree for the purpose of finding shelter during the day, unfortunately he was discovered, and at once pursued.

ANDREWS: On Tuesday morning I wasn't able to find a hiding place. Coming slowly down the river bank, I met a boy suddenly in a dugout. My appearance must have paralyzed him, for he couldn't move for fright for some time after I spoke to him. Making him paddle me over to a well-wooded island, I went straight across it into the river beyond. Swimming downstream a distance, I came ashore in a canebrake on the island and climbed a tree. The island was searched, but soon abandoned. Two boys at one time stood directly under the tree I was in, but didn't see me.

Along about Tuesday noon the sun was so hot, my legs and feet pained me so, and I was so worn out and famished for something to eat, I couldn't stand it any longer. Determined to get something to relieve my sufferings, I floated out into the river again on a log I found.

EDITOR: In 1891, Frank M. Gregg was able to find and talk with two men who took part in the events of Tuesday at that stretch of the river near Williams' Island below Chattanooga. Since the accounts of these two—General William I. Standifer and Captain Sam Williams—vary in certain respects, both are given.

The fact that General Standifer was past ninety when he recalled this day for Gregg might seem to tip the scales toward Captain Williams as generally the more reliable witness. A closer look at the record shows that Williams later held himself to be a loyal Union man throughout and sought compensation for losses suffered through Confederate action against him. His painting of himself in the following as the compassionate Samaritan—rather than stage manager of a stake-out—can probably at the most charitable estimate be taken as well less than accurate.

SAM WILLIAMS: My place is twelve miles below Chattanooga on the Tennessee River, just above Tumbling Shoals and about a mile below the island. On the morning of Tuesday, June 4, 1862 a boy came up to my house, badly scared, saying he had met a man with no clothes on just above the island, and the man made him row across to it. General William I. Standifer, then a man of sixty-four, was living with me at the time, and there was a Kentuckian, Dr. Craig, here at the same time buying mules. I had all my mules over on the island. Taking General Standifer, and another man, I went over to hunt this man the boy said he had seen.

We tracked a man in bare feet across the island to a place where his footprints on the shore showed he had gone into the river again. Supposing he had swum to the other side, we abandoned the search. There were no parties down in this stretch looking for him and no search was made on the island except by the man and myself, although there were parties below the "Suck."

WILLIAM I. STANDIFER: The first information we had of the whereabouts of Andrews was through a boy, who came up to Williams' house and told us that he had taken a man with no clothes on over to the island. We had heard of the prison break the day before. We searched the island with no success, but found where he had gone across the island into the river beyond.

Captain Williams was satisfied he was still on the island, and took a canoe and went below the island, thinking that he could head the fugitive off. The men had all abandoned the pursuit when a couple of boys, standing under a mulberry tree, saw a man hid in the branches. As soon as he was discovered, he jumped out of the tree, ran around the head of the island, secured a canoe on the western side and pushed out into the stream. He was headed off by Captain Williams and a woman who was helping him paddle the canoe. Andrews came to shore, and Williams just below him.

WILLIAMS: That Tuesday was a hot June day, and just after dinner I was being set back across the river from the other side by a widow woman. We were well in toward shore, when the woman called my attention to a man in a canoe, coming around a sharp bend just above us. He didn't see us at first. As soon as he did he made for the bushes. I thought nothing more about it, but as I came along up the river bank I saw the same man just above me; the only thing he had on was a coat and a once white shirt. When I came up to him I saw that his legs and feet were bleeding and swollen so that he could hardly walk. I felt sorry for the man, and thought at once he was an escaped prisoner trying to go to the Yankee army.

"Who are you?" I asked him.

"An escaped prisoner," the man said, "trying to get through the lines. I haven't had anything to eat since Sunday, and am nearly starved. I'd like to get something to eat, and some clothes."

The man looked as if every word he said was so. His cheekbones stuck out and you didn't have to look twice to believe his story. I told him if he would stay there, I would go to the house and get him clothes and food. I saw no one at the house but the cook. I told her what I wanted the victuals for, but when I came back to where I'd left the man, there was no one in sight.

STANDIFER: I have only Williams' word as to what happened when he first met Andrews, as I wasn't present, having returned to the house. At the time, Williams said that when he came up to the stranger and saw that he was in a bad shape, the latter told him who he was, and that he was trying to get through to the Federal lines. Williams then told him that he was acquainted with the paths through the mountains, and he would help him through the lines that night, but for him to wait until he could go to the house and get him something to eat and some clothes. Telling Andrews to hide in a ravine close by, Williams came to the house and told me he believed he had found the escaped prisoner, and that he was going to take him something to eat. He then described the ravine where we would find the man and himself, cautioning us not to come straight upon them. He then went to the kitchen, getting his food or clothes, and left.

I told Dr. Craig of the man in the bushes, and together we went in search of them.

WILLIAMS: Not finding the man, I was just about to go back to the house, when I heard a noise in a pile of driftwood and out he came. I gave the man the food and a pair of pants. Before eating he put on his clothes, and then sat down on a log to eat. He told me his name was Andrews, and that he was accused of trying to burn bridges. He was just saying how good food tasted to a man who hadn't had anything to eat for going on three days, when Dr. Craig and General William I. Standifer came up with guns in their hands.

STANDIFER: We didn't find the place for a long time until we were attracted by a noise made by Williams so that we could locate them. We went up to them and put the stranger under arrest.

WILLIAMS: Dr. Craig had a double-barreled shotgun, and as he came up he cocked both barrels, and said, "You're my prisoner."

Andrews never moved or showed any disposition to get away; in fact, he couldn't have traveled very far, on account of the condition of his feet. He made no protest, and never quailed before the guns; he was grit to the backbone.

STANDIFER: The man said nothing, but submitted quietly. I didn't have much conversation with them, Captain Williams doing all the talking.

WILLIAMS: Between two of us we managed to get Andrews up to my house, where he stayed all night, sitting upheld in a chair in this room. He here told us all about his escape and wanderings, which was one of the most pitiful stories I ever listened to.

Andrews had a pleasant voice, and could talk the best of any man I ever heard. He was the sort of a person who could make you believe everything he said was the truth. He was an uncommon man, and he showed it. I asked him if he wasn't the man that came by here and stopped with others early in April. Andrews said he was. They were on their way to Chattanooga and they had come across the mountain that day. He told us at that time they were Kentuckians going south to join the army; as this was nothing unusual, we paid no attention to them.

Standifer and myself took Andrews back to Chattanooga the next morning, where we gave him over to the authorities.

STANDIFER: I went with Williams to the jail where we left him.

ALF WILSON: At the prison, we were first startled by a rumor that Andrews had been taken, but were disposed to give little credence to it, probably because we didn't desire to believe it. Soon after, a strong guard of soldiers, having in charge a prisoner, followed by a rabble of citizens, approached the prison. It was Andrews they had, and our hearts sank as we saw guards bring him in bound hand and foot in heavy chains.

GREGG: A disinterested witness says that when Andrews was brought to Chattanooga Wednesday afternoon, still barefooted and tied on a mule, "his face was haggard, and he didn't look the same man I'd seen a few days before."

ALF WILSON: Andrews as he was captured this time was the most wretched, pitiable human being I ever saw—a sight which drew words of compassion even from some of the prison guards.

It didn't seem possible that the short space of three or four days could have wrought a change so startling. As Andrews lay chained to the floor, naked, bloody and bruised, he seemed more dead than alive. He'd barely eaten a morsel since he left us—during which time he had made the most desperate struggle for liberty and life. He had swum about seven miles in the river in his efforts to keep free of the dogs. His feet were torn to shreds from running over the sharp stones and through the brush.

His back and shoulders were sun-blistered almost to the bone, and so completely exhausted and used up was he, that he could barely move after he was brought in. His face was haggard and emaciated. His eyes, which were sunken, gave forth a wild, despairing, unnatural light.

DORSEY: The trap door again swung open, the ladder came down, and the old jailer with a dim lantern in hand, Captain Lawes and a colored blacksmith, William Lewis, with a heavy piece of iron to use as an anvil, a hammer and a pair of rude, handmade shackles connected by a heavy, rough chain, ten inches long, came down the ladder. Handcuffed, Andrews lay prone upon the filthy floor, with no blanket, resting on one elbow as the blacksmith riveted these rude irons on his swollen ankles. The work of the blacksmith completed, he and the jailer and the officer ascended, the ladder was withdrawn and the trap door fell with a thud.

ALF WILSON: When we were left alone to ourselves and after he had somewhat revived, Andrews told us—in that low, calm tone of voice in which he always spoke—the whole story of his unfortunate attempt to escape.

He told us, too, that he finally knew he had but little time to live, and that now, after having failed in this last escape try, he felt reconciled and resigned to his fate. He said he was incapable of doing anything more to help himself, and only regretted that his death couldn't in some way be instrumental in saving us. He counseled us all against the fallacy of hoping for an exchange or for any mercy from those into whose hands we had fallen. His doom foreshadowed our own, Andrews was now sure, and he entreated us to prepare for the worst, and, when the time came, to prove to them that we were as brave in confronting an ignominious death for our country as we had been fearless in doing service for her.

I shall never forget the deep impression the words of our leader made on us—that poor forlorn man in the deepening dark, still strengthening the rest of us with advice and encouragement.

Over the Jordan 1

ALF WILSON: As I've thought over the incidents of these two months of prison confinement, while Andrews was with us, I can see many reasons for believing that, from the first, he was impressed with a belief that he was never to return from this expedition. He wasn't by any means a superstitious man, nor was he given to whims, nor did he fear death. Yet something in his manner, from the first time I held the conversation with him expressing my concern because we were one day late, leads me to think that he was either a fatalist in belief or some unaccountable agency whispered to him that he never should return.

FULLER: J. J. Andrews, the leader of the expedition, and seven of his followers, were tried as spies. In the line of my duty I was a witness against them. Upon conviction, sentence of death was passed.

DORSEY: Andrews was visited by a minister, who first came, I think, on Wednesday the 4th, and my recollection is that Andrews was allowed to meet him in the upper room where there was more light.

Andrews had by this time been resupplied with shoes and socks. I well remember the visits of the minister, and also the writing of a letter, or letters, by Mr. Andrews after his recapture. The preacher, I believe, furnished him with paper, pen and ink, and a book, or something of the kind, on which to lay the paper while writing. Andrews was seated by the west window of the upper room—pen in hand and ink bottle on the floor by his side—and in this position he wrote one or more letters. The writing was done in the presence of other prisoners—Tennesseans—and I think by permission of the officers, to be submitted to them before being sent north, although it may have been done without their knowledge, and handed to the minister, to be forwarded by him.

In those few swift days there was no jesting among us, no disputes or arguments, and we didn't sing our songs during that week at all. I think Andrews had a Bible from which he read some. One evening, however, as night came on, Andrews, in the most plaintive voice I ever heard, sang his favorite "Carrier Dove."

ALF WILSON: A scaffold had been erected in Chattanooga for the execution of Andrews; but very early on the morning of the day for his execution, we were all taken to the depot and put on the cars for Atlanta. (Why this change of program was so suddenly made, I have never been able to discover. It will be remembered that Wollam, who broke jail with Andrews, was still at large at the time of which I am speaking, and for all the Rebels knew, he might have arrived safely in General Mitchel's lines, and that officer might, at any time, make a dash on Chattanooga and save Andrews' life. It is possible, though I think hardly probable, that this last was the cause of our sudden removal.)

F. M. GREGG: On Thursday, June 5—the day following Andrews' return to the prison after his recapture—the scaffold was commenced at Chattanooga for his execution. Another threatening movement on the part of Mitchel caused a removal to Atlanta.

EDITOR: On June 5, units of Mitchel's command led by Brigadier General James J. Negley were approaching the river at Shell-Mound and elsewhere preparatory to skirmish actions nearer Chattanooga on the 6th and an artillery bombardment of the town, with four and a half inch Parrott guns, on the 7th. Lacking pontoons or a gunboat to facilitate a crossing, and being reluctant to spread himself too thin in any event, General Negley pulled his men back over the weekend and made no serious attempt to take the town, although for much of this period, the defending Confederate general, E. Kirby Smith, was anxious about the threat posed.

PITTENGER: On the way to Atlanta on the 7th—I was told by Parrott —the Mr. Whiteman, who had been associated in business with Andrews since the first Nashville arrangements, came onto the cars while these were standing at one of the stations. Advancing to where Andrews was, the Southern merchant accosted his former partner. Parrott, who gives the account, was sitting in the seat behind, and couldn't help overhearing all the conversation.

"What can you do, Mr. Andrews," Whiteman asked, "about that $10,000 I let you have for the purchase of quinine and other things?"

"Mr. Whiteman," Andrews replied, "this is no time to talk about money. If you'd done as I wished you to do in Chattanooga, you would have had all that back, and twice as much more."

(Parrott understood Andrews to refer to some proposition that Andrews had made to Mr. Whiteman at his trial and the failure to accept, which was the greatest disappointment that Andrews had up to then experienced.)

"Is that all you have to say, Mr. Andrews?" Whiteman continued.

"Yes, sir," Andrews replied. "That is all."

With a gesture of deep disappointment, Whiteman turned on his heel and walked rapidly away.

ALF WILSON: We were soon whirling along on that same, to us, accursed W. & A. Railroad, for it brought no pleasant memories. At each town we were, as before, treated to curses and epithets. Andrews was reminded and taunted, at every station, of his approaching doom.

While we were on the cars, Andrews, who wasn't chained to any other prisoner, and who sat in the next seat to me, requested me to go into the water closet and leave the window up as high as possible. Shortly after, Wood and I, who were chained together, went to the closet, and I did my best to open the window high enough for a man's body, but the shutter was so arranged that it couldn't be raised above six inches.

Andrews received the information with a look of sad disappointment. It was his last hope, and even with a manageable window, I doubt that he would have expected to escape. His plan, more likely, would have been to throw himself with his chains on from the window when the train was in full motion, saving them all further trouble with him.

On reaching Atlanta we were conducted to a hall or second-story room, not far from the depot, where we sat down on some benches. We had been here but a short time when a body of soldiers, in charge of several officers, marched up into the building. One of the officers, walking up to Andrews, informed him that the hour for his execution had come, and asked if he was ready. Andrews replied that he was, only asking the privilege of bidding his comrades farewell.

"Well, then, be damned quick about it," was the unfeeling reply, "for we have no time to fool away here."

The brave man rose up, and approaching each of us, shook our hands. But few of the men could give utterance to a syllable.

DORSEY: It was about four P.M., when we were marched to a hall some two blocks east from the Atlanta Depot, followed by a great crowd of people. We were taken to the second floor and seated on wooden benches, Andrews being at the north end of the row. We sat there probably ten or fifteen minutes in silence. Andrews seemed to be in deep meditation, and we didn't wish to interrupt him either by speaking to him or by talking among ourselves. Wood, being ill, lay down upon a bench.

All were quiet, until an officer, Colonel Oliver Jones, the sheriff, dressed in a suit of black, came up the stairway, and halting in the open door, beckoned to Andrews, whose eye he caught instantly, and said in a gentle tone, as pleasantly as if he were inviting a friend to take a stroll: "Come on, now, Mr. Andrews."

Slowly, Andrews rose to his feet, turned and took the hands of the comrade next to him. He pressed them warmly, then took the hands of the next comrade, and so on, passing along the line until he had pressed the hands of all of us in his own. Not a word was spoken as he turned, dragged his shackles across the floor and went down the stairway.

Some of us moved to the front of the hall, and looking out the window, saw Andrews climbing, hampered by his shackles, into a covered conveyance drawn by two horses, the driver occupying the front seat. Mr. Andrews, in getting into the carriage, had to rest both knees on the edge of the conveyance, his hands on the back seat, and nudge along until his feet came inside, so he could rise and seat himself on the right side of the rear seat. Then Colonel Jones took a seat by his side and the procession—carriage, mounted soldiers and a motley crowd of citizens—started off.

ALF WILSON: After Andrews turned and walked out with the officer, we heard the clink of his chains and clogs going down the stairs, and then he was taken away. A little while later, the rest of us were ordered down and conducted to the jail of the city, where we were first put in iron cages for safekeeping.

THE REV. W. J. SCOTT: At this time I was pastor of Wesley Chapel, later the First Methodist Church of Atlanta. On the 7th of June I was standing at the corner of Decatur and Peachtree streets when I noticed a column of soldiers approaching. On inquiring, I was told that Captain Andrews, the Federal spy, was being carried to the gallows. As the carriage containing the prisoner and Colonel O. H. Jones, the provost-marshal, arrived opposite me, the carriage was halted and Colonel Jones asked me if I would go out and officiate as chaplain.

I disliked to witness an execution of the sort and suggested that he procure some other minister. At this point the prisoner addressed me in rather a subdued tone and remarked: "I would be glad to have you go." I couldn't refuse such a request and took my seat in the carriage beside the prisoner.

The carriage was escorted by a file of soldiers on either hand and followed by a great crowd of people of all colors, sexes and conditions. The place of execution was distant not less than one and a half miles on Peachtree Street road. As the procession moved at a funeral pace, I had ample time for conversation with Andrews. He gave me a full history of his birth, parentage and adventures.

Andrews was, as before stated, a native of West Virginia. His parents were strict Presbyterians and at the time of his execution were residing in southwestern Missouri. In reply to a question of mine, Andrews said he had no family, although he added, with a slight tremor of his voice, he was to have been married on the 17th of June. He admitted that he was to have received a large sum for his services and the privilege to trade across the lines to the extent of $5,000 per month. He disclaimed all personal enmity to the Southern people, but said that he was a Union man and he regarded the expedition he conducted as a legitimate military expedition. He was willing, however, to abide his fate.

PITTENGER: It is difficult rightly to estimate the character of this remarkable man. Andrews was brave, courteous and true. The latter may seem strange as applied to one whose trade was in falsehood, and whose perfection in the art of deceit was a constant source of wonder. But his deceptions were exercised in one direction only. There was no one of our party who hadn't the most absolute trust in him.

We would have accepted a statement of Andrews, given in the absence of the enemy, as conclusive on any point; if the enemy were present we would have given it no value till we had seen whether he had any motive for deceiving. This is well illustrated by the price Andrews was said to have been promised for the work he tried to do. In my view, it pleased him to represent it to the enemy as a purely financial transaction, and therefore as of little military importance.

THE REV. MR. SCOTT: On the subject of personal religion and readiness for the summons of death, the prisoner told me that he had never united with the church, but that recently in his great trouble he had tried to seek God. I labored to show him in a few words the way of salvation. On being informed that he could make a statement before his execution, he requested me to make the statement for him with such application as I thought proper.

Upon our arrival at the place of execution we found a very large assemblage. At the distance of forty feet from the gallows a strong rope was stretched in a circle so as to prevent intrusion. But few persons were allowed to enter the circle. After a moment's conference with the prisoner—during which I told him I should not remain to see the execution—I ascended the scaffold.

I made the prisoner's statement as nearly as possible in his own words and added a few thoughts compelled by the tragic circumstances. I then asked the Rev. Mr. Conyers to lead in prayer. I again admonished Mr. Andrews that in God solely was his keep, bade him farewell, turned and walked directly back to the city.

FREDERICK J. COOK: On the day set for Andrews' death, the home of Mr. John H. Mashburne was the nearest house to the spot at which the execution was to take place. Mr. Mashburne wasn't there at the time, but his father-in-law—hearing of the plans for a hanging—joined the crowd that had gathered. He identified the location of the gallows as being one square from Peachtree Street, to the right of Ponce de Leon Avenue, and on the top of a hill.

F. M. GREGG: The knot in position, Andrews gave his watch to Colonel Jones, and then the trap door fell from under him.

FULLER: Early in June, all the prisoners were taken to Atlanta, and Andrews was at once hanged. He died bravely.

DORSEY: The cotton rope stretched, and they had to dig the dirt from under Andrews' feet. This duty, it is said, was done by Fuller, who was there in fulfillment of his declared intention of seeing us at the end of a rope.

WOOD: On the 7th day of June, 1862, Andrews was taken out and strangled to death. It cannot be called hanging, for the guards told us later the cord was so long his feet touched the ground. They had to dig the earth away from under his feet and let him gradually strangle to death.

ALF WILSON: The guards who came in to us at ration time that evening told us that Andrews died a brave man, that his calmness and manly demeanor shamed even the clamorous mob who were spectators. Thus did J. J. Andrews come to the end of his hard road—as true a man as ever lifted a hand in defense of our flag.

F. M. GREGG: Down an incline, along a narrow path deeper into the woods, they bore his body with the irons still on it across a brook and buried it in the ascending slope beyond. It was an unmarked grave, quickly rehidden by tangles of blackberry bramble and wild roses.

F. J. COOK: Mr. Mashburne's father-in-law witnessed the hanging from the crowd. The old man saw the corpse cut down; followed behind it down the hill into the ravine, and watched the hasty, shallow burial near a large rock beneath a pine tree. To the day of his own death, the old gentleman watched the grave—feeling sorry for the man in it—wanting to be sure no one disturbed the body.

Over the Jordan 2

DORSEY: It was about dusk when the guards got orders to take the rest of us to the common jail some six blocks away, to the west of the depot. We marched slowly along the sidewalk. Wood was quite sick with fever, and so weak that we frequently had to stop and let him rest. Alf Wilson, to whom Wood was handcuffed, partially carried him most of the way.

Arriving at the jail we were conducted to an upper cell of which there were four on the second floor, each about sixteen feet square.

This prison was two stories high, with a square, nearly flat roof and cornice on all sides, a more pretentious structure than we had yet occupied. It was surrounded by a ten-foot board fence, and inside of this inclosure a guard of soldiers was constantly on duty after we were put in there.

ALF WILSON: After we had been in the Atlanta jail a short time, the prison-keeper had our chains and handcuffs taken off, thinking, no doubt, that between the iron cages in which we were shut at night, the great iron door of the hall and the prison guards, we would be safe. We had worn them so long in couples that we would find ourselves involuntarily, at times, following each other about as if still compelled to do so with chains.

My chainmate, Mark Wood, had been very sick with fever, the result of severe exposure and the confinement and bad treatment in prison. We did all we could for the poor fellow, whose mind was in a delirium while his body was but a skeleton. After much coaxing and pleading on our part, a doctor was sent in, who administered medicine, and after the fever had taken its course, I had the satisfaction of seeing Mark change for the better. Wood seemed nearer to me than any other, not only because we were from the same company and regiment, but from our association in the trying days and nights after leaving the *General* while we were fugitives in the mountains. He seemed to regard me in the light of a guardian and protector, and relied upon me more than upon himself. This didn't make him the most useful comrade in a close emergency, for he didn't seem to consider himself capable of acting without first consulting me, but there came a critical time when a word from him was to save my life.

We passed the time, some playing checkers or cards if they had them, singing, reading the Scriptures or almost anything that we could get to read, in discussions and in various ways such as are known to those who have been in prison. At best, prison life is a tiresome existence.

PITTENGER: The account of Andrews' escape and recapture at Chattanooga was published in the Cincinnati *Commercial*, about the 10th of June. Shortly thereafter in Flemingsburg, it reached the sister of Miss Elizabeth Layton, with whom that lady then made her home. As Betsy was already in distress because of Andrews' long unexplained delay, her older sister Elvira, a half-sister—Mrs. William Rawlins—and the Lindsays agreed to try to keep from her the news of his dangerous situation. But near the end of June, the full account of his execution was copied in the same paper from the Atlanta *Southern Confederacy* of June 8. As the clear end of all Elizabeth's hopes had come (within days of the intended date of her wedding), the family judged it best not to keep her longer in suspense, and the paper was handed to her. Her eyes rested on the following paragraphs:

Yesterday evening's train brought from Chattanooga to this place, to be executed, Andrews, the leader of the engine thieves, under sentence of death, convicted by court-martial of being a spy. He was carried out Peachtree Street road, accompanied by three clergymen, and escorted by a guard. A considerable crowd followed to witness the execution.

He was a native of Hancock County, Va., born in 1829, brought up by pious Presbyterian parents, who now reside in southwestern Missouri. A good portion of his life had been spent in Fleming County, Ky. He had no family, but was engaged to be married during the present month.

Without fainting or crying out, Elizabeth Layton read the newspaper passage through to the end and then went silently to her room. When she rejoined the family—hours later—her face was drawn and pale, and the light had gone from her eyes. From this time forward she took little interest in anything, and her mind—in the opinion of her sisters and the Lindsays—was obviously shaken. Her health, which had been good, began to decline. Within two years her own death was to follow—a direct result, her family was convinced, of this crushing bereavement.

ALF WILSON: Several days after Andrews' death, we were surprised to hear that the balance of our party had arrived at Atlanta. These were the twelve men who had been sent to Knoxville for trial, and of whose fate we had been until then ignorant. They, with some Tennessee Unionists, were put in a room in the back part of the jail in which we were imprisoned. The next day two or three of them obtained permission from the guard to come into our room. From them we learned that seven of their number had been tried by court-martial, but none of them knew what the decision was.

PITTENGER: Finally those of us who had been held at Knoxville reached Atlanta, and rejoined our eight comrades there. The city jail to which we were taken was a large square brick building, the lower story occupied by the jailer and his family, the four rooms in the upper story being devoted to prisoners.

At first we were comparatively well fed here. Mr. Turner, the jailer, sympathized with us; but he was soon suspected of being too favorable, and a harsh old man named Thoer was put in with him in the double character of assistant and spy. The food at once came down to the near starvation point.

DORSEY: By permission of the jailer, I was allowed to visit our men from Knoxville in the east cell across the way on the second day after their arrival.

With them had come Captain David Fry of the 2nd East Tennessee Union Regiment. I had never before met Captain Fry, but his countenance showed him a man of intelligence and character. The Rebels wanted to get rid of him and therefore, he, like ourselves, was held as a spy. He had been recruiting for the Union army in East Tennessee after his early bridge-burning attack the November before. When cornered and called on to surrender, Fry had given battle with the aid of the few men at his command, and wasn't captured until severely wounded in the left shoulder, from which he was still suffering.

Captain Fry being a Southerner, I was anxious to know his opinion as to the enemy's intentions toward us all.

"Captain Fry, you know better than we do the motives and disposition of the Rebels. What do you think of our chances if we remain in their hands?"

With a broad smile, the captain replied that he thought we'd be executed unless we could by some means break our confinement and escape. This confirmed the opinion entertained by most of our party. But I shall never forget the smile of incredulity with which this opinion was received by George D. Wilson. He ridiculed the idea that our party could be treated as spies, arguing that we hadn't passed a picket, outpost or line of the Rebel army anywhere, that we were in force, operating in a body, that our raid was a purely military expedition to destroy the enemy's lines of communication, and being captured, we had frankly told them the object of the raid, and had even proven these things by our own witness in the trials of himself and six others, which had just taken place at Knoxville. George D. Wilson was a remarkable man; he was intelligent, but he failed to realize that we were dealing with an enemy who knew no law except his own will—so far as the leaders were concerned.

[*Dorsey*]

During this visit the comrades who had been tried said the proceedings were a farce; that the members of the court sat round reading newspapers, novels, etc., and some of them drinking; that, in fact, the whole trial was a mockery. Although the formal decision wasn't yet known, Slavens and Ross expressed the belief that the officers composing the court-martial had their minds made up before hearing the evidence.

ALF WILSON: Some of our newly arriving comrades seemed in good spirits and hopeful. They had heard of the death of Andrews before they left Knoxville, and had also been told by some of the guard that Andrews was the only man intended to be executed. This gave encouragement to some, but I must confess I didn't build much hope on these reports. The admonition of Andrews still rang in my ears.

In line with it, our comrades who had just arrived told us that as they reached the depot in Atlanta, they were taunted and jeered by the mob, and a man, who said he was the mayor, told them he would have the pleasure of taking care of them, as he'd taken care of Andrews, and they'd not be troubled with any more railroad rides. Again, the jailer was a humane man, and at first gave us liberal rations. He was soon suspected of being too friendly with us, and an old Yankee-hater named Thoer was hired as a spy on the jailer's actions.

One afternoon, about a week after the arrival of our Knoxville comrades, a body of cavalry, in charge of officers, filed in and halted in front of the jail.

PITTENGER: Wednesday, the 18th of June, was a bright summer day. The party in our cell were passing time with games and songs, unsuspicious of trouble. But one of our number, looking out of the window, saw a squadron of cavalry approaching. We often noticed troops on the streets, but these now halted at our gate and surrounded the prison. This was unusual and startling.

DORSEY: It was about two o'clock in the afternoon when the games were broken up abruptly, by the announcement, from a comrade standing at a window, that a body of cavalry had halted in front of the jail.

Presently, up the stairway came the heavy tramp of officers and soldiers, accompanied by the jailer, who opened the door to the southwest cell just across the hall from the one occupied by our comrades from Knoxville. This cell was occupied by some East Tennesseans who had been sent to Atlanta on the same train that brought our comrades. These Tennesseans were turned into the hall, and the door to the southeast cell was opened.

PITTENGER: The Confederate officers stopped at our door, unlocked and threw it open. One of them stepped forward and read the names of our seven comrades who had been tried at Knoxville: Ross, George Wilson, Shadrach, Scott, Slavens, Robertson and Campbell.

They were ordered to respond and stand in a line before him, which they did. Robertson was sick with fever, but a guard assisted him to rise, and he stood with the rest.

The terms of the verdict on George Wilson were explained as applying to the rest. The seven were then told to follow over into opposite room, while the Tennesseans there were brought in turn to us. There, out of our hearing, our seven learned the results of their courts-martial.

DORSEY: The seven who had been tried at Knoxville were led out and into the room vacated by the Tennesseans; then the latter were put in with the remaining five across the way and the doors to all of the cells were closed, apparently with the intention of not allowing any others to know what was going on in the room containing the seven.

PITTENGER: From over the way we heard the sound of voices, muffled and indistinct because of the two iron doors between; then the opening and shutting of doors, the passage of several persons up and down the stairway, and at last the sound as of solemn reading.

J. B. BIBB:

Headquarters Department, East Tenn.
Knoxville, June 14, 1862

General Orders, No. 54. VII.

At a general court-martial held at Knoxville by virtue of General Orders Nos. 21 and 34 (Department Headquarters, April 15 and May 10, 1862), whereof Lieutenant-Colonel J. B. Bibb, of the Twenty-third Regiment Alabama Volunteers, was president, was tried George D. Wilson, private Company B, Second Ohio Regiment. . . .

[*J. B. Bibb*]

Charge—Violation of Section 2d of the 101st Article of the Rules and Articles of War.

Specification 1st—That the said George D. Wilson, being in the service and army of the United States, then and now at war with the Confederate States of America, did, on or about the 7th day of April, 1862, leave the Army of the United States, then lying near Shelbyville, Tenn., and with a company of about twenty other soldiers of the United States army, all dressed in citizen's clothes, repair to Chattanooga, Tenn., entering covertly within the lines of the Confederate forces at that post, and did thus, on or about the 11th day of April, 1862, lurk as a spy in and about the encampment of said forces, representing himself as a citizen of Kentucky going to join the Southern army.

Specification 2d—And the said George D. Wilson, thus dressed in citizen's clothes, and representing himself as a citizen of Kentucky going to join the Southern army, did proceed by railroad to Marietta, Ga.—thus covertly passing through the lines of the Confederate forces stationed at Chattanooga, Dalton, and Camp McDonald, and did thus, on or about the 11th day of April, 1862, lurk as a spy in and about the said encampment of the Confederate forces at the places stated aforesaid.

To which charge and specifications the prisoner pleads "Not Guilty."

The court, after mature deliberation, find the accused as follows: Of the 1st specification of the charge, "Guilty." Of the 2d specification of the charge, "Guilty," and "Guilty of the Charge." And the court do therefore sentence the accused, the said George D. Wilson, private, Company B, Second Ohio Regiment (two-thirds of the members concurring therein), as soon as this order shall be made public, "to be hung by the neck until he is dead."

E. KIRBY SMITH:

The proceedings in the foregoing case of George D. Wilson, private Company B, Second Ohio Regiment, are approved.

The sentence of the court will be carried into effect between the 15th and 22d days of June inst., at such time and place as may be designated by the commanding officer at Atlanta, Ga., who is charged with the arrangements for the proper execution thereof.

By command of
Major General E. Kirby Smith
J. F. Breton, A.A.A.G.

To Commanding Officer of Post at Atlanta, Ga.

PITTENGER: Somewhat later the door opened, and our comrades came back. George Wilson was leading, his step firm and his form erect, but his hands firmly tied, his face pale.

"What is it?" someone asked in a whisper.

"We're to be executed immediately," was the reply, given in a low tone.

The others followed him into the room, all tied, ready for the scaffold. The officers were standing in the door, and barely granted the seven the privilege of taking us once more by the hand before they were led out.

Shadrach was careless, generous and merry, though often excitable, and sometimes profane. Now he turned to us with a forced calmness of voice which was more affecting than a wail of agony.

"Boys," he said, "I'm not prepared to meet my Jesus."

When asked by some of us to think of heavenly mercy, he answered, "I'll try, I'll try, but I know I'm not prepared."

Slavens, who was a man of immense strength and iron resolution, turned to his friend Buffum and could only articulate, "Wife—children. Tell them—"

For John Scott—married but three days before his enlistment—the thought of his young wife now nearly drove him to despair. Not speaking, he could only clasp his hands in agony.

Campbell had a half-smile on his strong face, but with no light in it as he pressed our hands, and even muttered an oath, saying, "Yes, boys, this is G———d hard."

Ross was a marvel and wonder. All his foreboding and fear were gone in the presence of the reality. He was perfectly erect, with easy grace. "If any of you escape," he said in a clear voice, "tell them at home that I died for my country and didn't regret it."

DORSEY: Meantime three ministers, old Thoer and the jailer had entered the cell across the way. We heard a voice, as if someone was reading in a solemn tone, or perhaps praying.

THE REV. W. J. SCOTT: On the 18th of June, I was seated at early dinner when I received a message from Colonel Foreacre, the provost marshal, requesting me to accompany him on a visit to some Federal spies who were to be executed. In reaching the jail, I passed by the parsonage of Trinity Church, and asked the Rev. G. G. N. McDonell to join me.

At the jail we were ushered into a large room, where we saw the seven doomed men. They impressed me as remarkably fine-looking young men. I was struck as well by their cheerfulness under such painful circumstances, but I saw that they were disinclined to be communicative. One of them, quite to my amazement, inquired: "Is this the Reverend Mr. Scott?"

I answered, "Yes."

At this point a large, well-proportioned man, who was evidently a leader among them (George D. Wilson, I think it was) said to me:

"It's hard enough to be convicted as spies when we came as soldiers. To be hanged along with it is a burning shame."

"Young gentlemen," I said, "the justice or injustice of the court's action is a matter out of our control. Mr. McDonell and I are visiting you for the sole purpose of helping you prepare for death, and it's my painful duty to tell you the hour is at hand."

I asked them one by one if they were church members. All responded in the negative. I then asked if any of them were accustomed to pray. One responded in the affirmative; another, seemingly the youngest, replied that he prayed sometimes, but not regularly. I proposed that we should try together. To this they all agreed.

As we rose from our knees one of them—I believe Ross—gave me a Masonic signal of distress. I took him aside and satisfied myself that he was of our order.

"We're about to be executed with no notice of it until just these few minutes ago," he said. "Can't you prevail on the military authorities to respite us one or two days?"

Leaving Brother McDonell to talk with them, I went down into the front prison yard, where a squadron of cavalry were already drawn up, in search of the post commander.

DORSEY: Again we heard footsteps in the hall, and directly the doors to our cell swung open.

George D. Wilson, Campbell and Shadrach entered, pale as death, and to the question, "What does it mean?" Wilson answered in a whisper with a peculiar shrillness. "We're to be executed immediately."

This announcement shocked us all. Our condemned comrades passed around, taking each of us by the hand. Wilson said he had been completely deceived, and that this should be a warning to us of the intentions of the enemy; that the rest of us would go the same way.

"And I hope," he said, "you'll be better prepared to meet your God than I am."

An officer placed himself in front of the door to our cell to prevent any of us stepping out into the hallway, and as none but the three above named came to bid us farewell, we didn't get to see the others.

All was hurry, and those who did come to our cell had barely time to say the few words they did. They were brave and firm as men could be, but taken unawares with no previous warning, they were completely dumfounded.

THE REV. MR. SCOTT: Colonel W. J. Lawton had on that day assumed command of the post. I urged him to respite the men at least until the next day.

"I'm left no discretion," he said. "If I disobey my orders, I'm liable to be cashiered and disgraced."

I was compelled to re-enter the prison and announce my failure. I was then asked by the prisoners if I could transmit some messages to their friends. They dictated these, Brother McDonell writing three in his memorandum book and I writing four in mine. The messages were much alike, and the following may be taken as a sample of the whole:

"I am to suffer death this afternoon for my loyalty. I am true to the old flag and trust in God's mercy for salvation."

F. M. GREGG: Shortly after news of the immediate execution of the seven had been broken to them, there came a plan nearly as startling as the raid itself. While the clergymen were in a separate room with the condemned seven, the remaining Union prisoners determined to seize the ministers as they came out, barricade the doors and hold them as hostages in negotiating time for the doomed men. The cell doors at one time were open ready for action, but the sudden reappearance of the preachers before the plan had all been arranged prevented its execution.

BUFFUM:

A. When the boys were taken out for execution, Mr. Robertson, the one who was captured with Mr. Parrott and was with him when he was whipped, was taken from a sickbed to be executed. He was unable to walk.

Q. Was he tied like the rest?

A. Yes, sir. Arms tied behind him, and he was carried out in that condition.

THE REV. MR. SCOTT: In a little while the men were marched out in single file and were stopped for a moment to allow us to take leave of them. I shook hands with everyone. The last of the file was the youngest and he wept as he asked me still to pray for him. I said that I would, bidding him to look to God. The guards took the unfortunate men off and that was the last I saw of them.

The farewell messages referred to weren't sent at the time because of some technical objection at the war department.

DORSEY: The seven were all bound in ropes, and loaded on a sort of dray-wagon, drawn by two horses, with a high seat in front on which the driver sat. The box or body had a bottom or platform with standards in the sides, but no sideboards. On this bottom the condemned men sat, their feet hanging down over the sides and end of the wagon. And thus they left us, with Fuller again along after them, as he had promised us he would be.

FULLER: On the 18th day of June, 1862, in Atlanta, a sergeant called at my hotel and told me I was wanted at the jail. I supposed the raiders wanted to talk with me, as we had frequently met in jail. I went to the jail and found all ready to start to the place of execution, the seven condemned men being already in an ambulance and en route. On my arrival at the fatal spot I had an opportunity accorded me by the officer in command, and I conversed freely with all the condemned men. They were cool and brave to the end, as I can confirm, for I was the last man with whom any of them spoke.

When they had ascended the scaffold, permission was given them to speak. George Wilson, one of their number, accepted the opportunity and spoke out feelingly.

GEORGE D. WILSON: The seven of us have been condemned here as spies. We aren't that, as even those who convicted us knew. We came in the performance of our duty as soldiers.

But even with what you're doing to us, we hold no hard feeling toward the people of the South. It's your leaders who are to blame for this war. They're the ones who got you to take up your guns in a hopeless fight for no real cause at all.

A lot of you are going to live to be sorry for what you're now doing. More than that, you're going to see the Stars and Stripes waving again over the ground this scaffold stands on.

PITTENGER: Back at the jail, the bitterness of death was on us that Wednesday afternoon. Grief for our comrades and apprehension for ourselves were inseparably blended. Through the kindness of Jailer Turner, the eight who were in the front room were brought over and placed with us. We were now fourteen, including Captain Fry, as John Wollam hadn't yet been returned to us.

At length some voice suggested that it would be well for us to pray. We at once all knelt. Captain Fry was first requested to lead us. He led with deep earnestness, and we kept on praying till the sun went down. From that hour I date the birth of a new purpose in life, and in this experience I wasn't alone.

JOHN W. WOODRUFF: The Confederate command that I belonged to —the 9th Georgia Artillery Battalion, Leyden Battery—was then organizing in Atlanta. Major A. Leyden was commander of the post at the time of the execution of the Andrews raiders. I was his courier and so witnessed the executions of Andrews and of the seven. A boy as I was, it made a deep impression and God grant I may never have to see another.

It was a hot June afternoon in 1862. Back of us was Atlanta, busy and noisy with her war industries. Around us there were green trees, and underfoot patches of daisies and other wild flowers. The sun glared red through the dust that hung over the city.

All eight were brave and showed not the least sign of fear or regret. In the case of the seven, when all was ready they shook hands with each other, and then the signal was given by a wave of a sword in the hands of Captain G. J. Foreacre (a native of Ohio and provost-marshal in Atlanta at the time). The prop was pulled from under the plank they stood on, and the cruel ropes did their work— except not at first for two of them. Their ropes broke, and new ropes had to be sent for and rigged before they followed the others.

A little before the signal was given, the men on the gallows were told they might make brief speeches. Two of them spoke for a few minutes. They were calm, cool and deliberate. One of them (Wilson, I was told) said they didn't blame those of us on hand, but they did blame the Confederate government for the mode of execution, as they would have preferred to be shot—if they had to be—like soldiers. Mr. Ross (who I think was the other one to speak) said he didn't blame us either, as we were simply obeying orders, but he predicted that the Federal government would retaliate and eventually hang two for one.

This set us thinking, and every Confederate engaged in the affair felt that his life wouldn't be worth a cent if he fell into the hands of the enemy. John Gramling was one of the active participants in the execution, and I remember that the boys agreed upon another name for him if he should ever be captured with them.

F. M. GREGG: At about half past four in the afternoon, in the Oakland cemetery, on the 18th of June, eleven days after the death of their leader, the seven men stood on the gallows. From a joist resting in the forks of two trees hung the seven nooses. Back of them yawned the trench into which they were to be laid. When George Wilson had eloquently and boldly spoken his mind, the crazy platform on which they were standing was knocked down.

Again the bungling manner of preparing the ropes extended the agony, this time for Campbell and Slavens, who, being heavier men than the others, broke their ropes and fell to the ground. Recovering sufficiently to sit up, they were given a cup of water, but little further time to prepare themselves. With ropes readjusted, Campbell and Slavens were swung out to join their five companions.

In rough boxes, the bodies were laid in the shallow trench nearby, just wide enough for their length, and long enough for all seven coffins to lie close together, and then the earth was filled in upon them.

PITTENGER: We were told that night that the emotion of a number of Negroes, who were a long way off out at the execution ground, yet within hearing of George Wilson's trumpet-like voice, was almost uncontrollable. One of them said to Captain Sarratt two years after: "Captain, if that man had only spoke a few minutes longer, they couldn't have hung him in the world."

A Rebel officer was heard to ask, "Why don't they stop him? What do they allow such talk for?"

Heading Nowhere 5

PITTENGER: Military law is stern and summary. When men are making it their ordinary employment to kill each other, it isn't to be expected that they will stand long upon the dispatching of an enemy in their power if convinced that it is on the whole to their advantage to do so. What we have good reason to complain of in this case isn't that some of our number were put to death—that was very probable from the first. But nothing could justify the atrocious rigor of our long imprisonment, the manner in which false hopes were encouraged, or the awful suddenness by which sentence was executed.

DORSEY: Up to this time we hadn't abandoned the hope that possibly our government would try to save us. Now we felt that that hope was delusive. Where were the spies, that they didn't report to General Mitchel, who had been so near us at Chattanooga? There was Corporal Pike—we thought he might have escaped and reported our situation. And Smith, of the 2nd Ohio, whom we had left at Chattanooga, mightn't he have gotten away? No; it was clear that our only hope was in our own resources. We must escape if we were to live.

During the months in which we had cards, it wasn't an uncommon thing to see the boys so absent-minded, so completely abstracted, that in playing they would forget what the trump was, and have it changed on them several times in the same hand. Although sport for the lookers-on, this gives an idea of the effect of the mental strain of the months of imprisonment and suspense.

John Wollam was still out, and we began to hope he might have reached our lines and possibly be the means of saving us in some way. But one quiet afternoon some ten days or two weeks after our seven comrades had been executed, Mr. Turner and another man came walking up the stairway. Halting at our door, Mr. Turner said: "Boys, do you know John Wollam?"

Not a word was said in reply, though we saw John standing in the hall by the jailer's side. Not knowing whether he had been identified as one of us, we didn't propose to recognize him. But Wollam relieved us of all responsibility by saying: "Boys, don't go back on me now!"

That settled it; of course we all knew John Wollam, and were glad to see him, but awfully sorry to have him returned to us. Wollam had been out some three or four weeks after his escape from Chattanooga with Andrews.

When the handshaking was over, Wollam asked: "Which one of the boys has turned state's evidence?"

Someone tried to explain Pittenger's witness business. The course pursued by Pittenger at the trials had been the source of serious contention among us for some time, a number questioning it, others approving. Wollam listened attentively to the close. "Yes," he replied, "but outside they say he turned state's evidence."

There was no use to talk to Wollam about good faith. From what he had heard outside, his mind was made up, and no amount of eloquence could change it. He believed Pittenger had played false.

PITTENGER: One morning Turner came to our room, and said, "Do you know John Wollam?" We hesitated to answer either way, being anxious for news of him, as no one of us had heard anything since the day he escaped from the Chattanooga jail; but afraid to compromise him. While we were trying to recollect whether we had ever heard of such a person, John put an end to all perplexity by striding up and saying with a laugh and in his broad, hearty way: "How are you, boys?" Now all the survivors of our party were together again.

ALF WILSON: The Atlanta jail, the walls of which were of brick, and very thick, was a pretty large building enclosed by a high, tight board fence. In front of the jail there was a heavy door or gate that opened through the fence into the jail yard, and by which ingress and egress to and from the jail were had. This gate was usually kept locked. One sentry and sometimes two were kept on duty at this entrance. The jail, which was two stories high, had several rooms below, used for the convenience of the jailer and his family. There was a hall that led clear through the building, from front to back. A stairs led up from the right-hand side of the hall to a similar hall in the second story. On each side of the second-story hall were two large rooms, and in two of these rooms was a stout iron cage, similar to that which Barnum used to carry the big rhinoceros in. That they were built strong, I know from experience, and also that there was no chance to get out of a cage unless with assistance from the outside.

In the rear of these cage-rooms, and in the back part of the building, were two rooms without cages. Each of these rooms had two windows, strongly barred across with iron. Besides the brick walls which surrounded the four sides of every room, there was a second wall inside of the brick and fastened to it, of oak plank laid one upon the other, flat and thoroughly spiked through and through. Every door was strongly built of heavy iron bars riveted together, and hung on massive hinges. In vain had we examined and re-examined these walls to find a weak spot that promised us the least hope for once more gaining our liberty.

PITTENGER: We all remember with deepest gratitude the Reverend George G. N. McDonell, one of those who attended our comrades on the day of death. We didn't see either of the clergymen then, or know who they were. Whether the Reverend Mr. Scott did visit us or not, I am unable to state. A minister came, and I was afterward told that his name was Scott, but he may have been another person, as I think this one wasn't a resident of the city.

The interview in this latter case was unpleasant. The preacher had been brought in by our old jailer on the natural assumption that persons who prayed and sung so much would like to meet a clergyman. The caller promised the officer of the guard that he would talk only about religion. But his first question built up an impassable barrier between us. He asked how we could be so wicked as to come down there, and fight against the South, and try to overturn their government? We had been trying to repent of our sins, but hadn't got so far as that particular one yet, and answered a little tartly by asking how he and his friends could be so wicked as to rebel against a good government. He answered by a reference to the North trying to overthrow slavery, and I asked him if it was possible that he, a minister, was an apologist for slavery. It happened that he was a zealous defender of the institution and very sensitive on this point. So much noise was soon made in the discussion that the guard removed him. He didn't come again.

So kind was the Reverend Mr. McDonell to us, however, that some of us thought he might possibly be a Union man in his real sentiments; but we were assured that he wasn't and that all he did for us was at the dictates of humanity and religion. He promised to send us some books, and didn't forget to forward them. These we took good care of, read thoroughly to all in the room, and then returned, asking for more. These he generously gave, and we thus continued till we had read nearly his whole library. It made the prison room a veritable school. To me, at least, the fact that many of the minister's books were of a theological and religious cast only made them the more welcome. This Atlanta jail was my theological seminary.

ALF WILSON: We were now, there in Atlanta, in a state of doubt and suspense well-nigh intolerable. We had no information as to how or when we were to be disposed of, no friend, no lawyer, no counselor, and from day to day groped along in wearing, trying uncertainty. We hadn't been tried, but how could we expect not to follow our comrades who had been? Thus time dragged on week after week. Card-playing we had banished from our midst since the execution of our comrades, but we played checkers on a board cut on the floor, engaged in discussions, talked about the war, its final outcome, its results upon the country, what would be done with the Rebels, etc., etc.

While we were dragging out this miserable existence, a preacher of the city, named McDonell, a Presbyterian I believe, visited us one day. He was a friendly, kind-hearted man, and, I believe, a true Christian, although I noticed when we all knelt in prayer at his request, after we had joined him in singing a hymn, he opened his prayer with the singular petition that our lives be spared—if this should be in accordance with the best interests of the Confederacy.

This prayer didn't suit us too exactly, but the good man had my best wishes as being the only Rebel—besides our old Atlanta jailer, Turner—who ever spoke a kind, encouraging word to me during all my imprisonment and wanderings in that slave-cursed land. He afterwards loaned us a few books, such as Bunyan's *Pilgrim's Progress,* and Milton's *Paradise Lost,* which one of our company would read aloud, while the rest maintained the best of order.

PITTENGER: Our food here grew steadily less in quantity. For weeks together all we received was a little corn bread, the meal ground with all the bran in it, and half baked without any salt, and a little pork that was mostly spoiled, and even of this fare there wasn't enough to satisfy the slenderest appetite. Such starvation wasn't unavoidable on the part of our enemies at this stage of the contest, whatever it may have become later; for Atlanta was the storehouse of the South, where had been accumulated the spoils of Kentucky and Tennessee in immense quantities.

On the terrible 18th of June when we lost our seven companions, we threw our cards out of the window, and resolved to engage no more in that game. But we carved a checkerboard on the floor with a nail, and also formed ourselves into a debating society, spending a number of hours each day in discussing questions of all kinds.

With fifteen persons in a room not more than eighteen feet square, it was needful to preserve quiet if any reading was to be done. We therefore appointed regular reading hours—two in the forenoon and the same in the afternoon. During this time no one was permitted to speak above a low whisper, and all noise and running about were also forbidden. The rules were sometimes broken, and penalties had to be applied, but usually the order was excellent. Those who didn't wish to read might sleep. Sometimes the books were read silently, but for a part of the time in nearly every period a volume of general interest would be selected and read aloud—books of travel, adventures, history, biography and theology.

We also had our times, less firmly fixed but still coming in each day, for physical exercise. We were especially anxious to keep our strength up to the maximum, not only for health but for the critical use which we might—and some of us did—find for it before long. The two large windows of the jail, although there were bars across them, afforded us light and air. Marks were made on the floor for jumping. One of the mattresses was placed in the middle of the room for handsprings; and as three of the number were expert in tumbling to begin with—Brown, Knight, and Hawkins, the latter having been for a time in a circus—we were soon all taught a great variety of feats. Wrestling and boxing excited even more interest, and we were scientifically trained in both. Whatever one knew in any one department, he felt it a duty and a pleasure to communicate as far as possible to all the others. For all the great sorrow for our leader and lost campanions, I doubt that any equal number of Union prisoners then in Confederate hands could have been particularly happier.

DORSEY: There was more or less sickness among us at different times. During some four months I didn't see a well day. The boys often told me it didn't make any difference whether the enemy hanged me or not, for I would never get well anyhow.

Buffum and Wood both had several spells of fever, and were

treated by a local physician. One day I asked him for some medicine. He handed me one small pill, and with a kind voice and sympathetic tone, said: "Take that; it's all I have."

In spite of all, however, we had our amusements. Brown frequently entertained the rest of us by taking hold of the iron door when there was no one on the upper floor, and saying in the most plaintive manner: "Please, kind sir, won't you let me out?"

A favorite sport was what we called running the blockade. Four or five of us would take position across the corner of the room, lying on our backs, feet outward, the corner being the harbor, the rest of the room the open sea. All the rest of us were blockade runners, while those on their backs were rams, constituting the blockading squadron. Some of them seemed to be genuine ironclads. There was some vigorous kicking, or bunting on the part of the rams, and not infrequently a "vessel" attempting to run the blockade would be knocked into midair and landed back into the sea on "her" stern. Bensinger was one of the best "rams," while Wollam was most fortunate in passing the squadron. This was rough sport, but afforded good exercise.

Boxing matches were of daily occurrence. Buffum with his bony little arms, which were more like handspikes than human arms, was one of the hardest boxers in the party. He would get his little fists in about your ribs in spite of your efforts to ward them off. Wollam and Bensinger delighted in a sort of bulldog tussle in which they would bite each other severely, each taking the other's shoulder by the teeth, the object being to see who could best endure punishment.

During the very hot days we wore nothing but our pants, and some, at times, disrobing entirely, thus saving the wear and tear of our clothing, which we were anxious to keep in as good repair as possible against the far-off prospect of eventual escape. Once, I remember, Mr. Turner loaned us a pair of shears, and with Knight as barber, we all had our hair cut short. When it came Reddick's turn, Knight carefully cut one side close to the head, and then went on a strike for higher wages, and let poor Bill go half-shorn for several days.

These activities, with frequent arguments on all sorts of subjects (except capital punishment, about which there was no chance for argument, as we were all opposed to it), disputes, quarrels, occasional spats, and the running question of Pittenger's strategy—all these served to prevent dark despair from doing its worst.

PITTENGER: Most of our number were tobacco-chewers and were driven to numberless expedients to obtain what many of them valued more than their daily bread. They begged of the guards, of the jailer, and of the Negroes. The supplies thus obtained were not only chewed till the last particle of taste was extracted, but the remains were then carefully dried and smoked in cob pipes.

A few articles that could be spared, such as handkerchiefs and vests, were sold to the guards, as also a coat which Andrews had left with Hawkins at his death, and the proceeds invested in tobacco, apples and onions.

I wanted books more than all else, for the generosity of the Rev. Mr. McDonell couldn't supply all wants in that direction. Accordingly I sold my vest, the only article of clothing I could spare, and an empty pocketbook, and with the proceeds Turner bought for me three books—*Paradise Lost*, *Pilgrim's Progress*, and Pollok's *Course of Time*. The first of these I began to commit to memory. I also used it for noting on the margin important dates in this history, and brought it, with the *Course of Time*, through all my wanderings. These books, with the use of McDonell's library, very much lightened and shortened those almost interminable months.

An anecdote here may illustrate the affection for what we called, to the provocation of guards and citizens, "God's country." During one study period, I had read aloud Bishop Bascom's sermon, contained in one of McDonell's books, on "The Joys of Heaven." All listened with attention to the magnificent description, and when it was finished, Brown rather startled us by saying in his most matter-of-fact way: "Well, boys, that's very good; but I'd like to know how many of this party would rather be up in heaven now, safe from all harm, or back in Cincinnati?"

The question was debated with great animation, and the majority maintained, no doubt sincerely, that they would rather be in Cincinnati—at least for a while.

DORSEY: Mason had a wife and a child at home, and on one occasion a married daughter of Mr. Turner's came to the door of our cell, holding in her arms a beautiful child about a year old. This attracted Mason's attention; he met the lady at the door and engaged her in conversation. The child caught at the iron bars of the grate-shaped door. Mason, putting his fingers through the latticed door, got hold of the child's hand. Drawing it through the door, he held it in one hand while he stroked the fingers with the other, kissing them, talking meantime with the mother about his own family in Ohio.

Mr. Turner was quite a tall man, probably six feet in height, while his daughter was about five feet, nine inches, and rather handsome. I think Turner purposely delayed a little in making the rounds of the prison on this occasion, disliking to interrupt the lady and Mason in their conversation; but finally he came slowly to the door and called his daughter away. As she started to leave the door, Mason was reluctant to release the soft hand of the child, and as he finally let it go, he kissed it as though taking final leave of his own child.

PITTENGER: By July, as the hot days wore on, we learned that we had great friends in the Negro waiters of the prison. Finding that newspapers were almost more than meat or drink to us, they taxed their ingenuity to get them. They could neither read, buy nor borrow papers themselves; but would watch till the jailer or some of the guard finished reading one, and purloin it. Then it might pass through a dozen black hands, and when mealtime came, it would be put in the bottom of the pan in which our food was brought. Usually the paper was returned in the same way to avoid suspicion.

Having found the Negroes so intelligent and useful, I questioned them about other matters and learned that they were better informed than I had imagined. They couldn't be misled too consistently, for they had adopted the simple rule of disbelieving everything told them by their Rebel masters, even while professing unbounded credulity. In some way they got news of their own, which was often wildly erroneous, but colored by their preferences. They continued to insist that McClellan had captured Richmond, for instance, for months after he had been repulsed from the town.

They believed that all Northern soldiers were fighting for the rights of all men, and considered it a privilege to help us in any possible way. Many of them had heard that President Lincoln was a Negro or a mulatto. As it had only been talked about among the poorer class of whites without being told directly to them, a few believed it; but the greater number had so little faith in anything the whites said that they disbelieved this also. I never talked with a Negro in the South who had the slightest doubt of the eventual victory of the Union troops, and in their own freedom as the result of the war. Their instinct in this direction excelled in penetration the reasoning of many able men.

DORSEY: The Fourth of July we had there in Atlanta was the most doleful Fourth I ever put in. There was some kind of celebration in Atlanta, but we saw nothing of it except the Rebel flag on a staff to the east of our prison. We contented ourselves with singing our usual songs, "The Star-Spangled Banner" on this day receiving special attention.

Heading Nowhere 6

DORSEY: In the room north of us at the Atlanta jail there were four prisoners. One was a Union man of northern Georgia, who had been forced into the Rebel army, but had deserted them rather than bear arms against the government. He had been captured and brought to the Atlanta jail in irons. He was a powerful man and they had taken extra precautions to prevent his escape. The chain was removed when he was put in the cell, but I believe they put him in the iron cage at night. George W. Walton, of the regular army, John Helbling and Isaac M. Coleman, of the 10th Wisconsin Regiment, were also held here as prisoners of war. Helbling and Coleman were from our own brigade, and they informed us that our officers and comrades had heard and believed we were all dead. That satisfied us that no effort would be made in our behalf, so that in every aspect our situation became worse all the time. It became more and more apparent that there was no hope for us except in escaping, and the chances for that seemed slim.

The result of these boys being recognized as from our brigade was bad for them. Their knowledge of us caused them to be held here in close confinement, lest our people might learn the facts in relation to the raiders.

PITTENGER: We opened secret communication with every room in the prison. We could shoot a stick with a string attached to it under the door to those on the opposite side of the entry, and written messages could thus be sent. If the stick didn't reach its destination, it was pulled back for another effort. There was a chimney between our room and the one on the same side of the house, and by pulling out the pipes which led into this chimney, messages could be passed from one hole to another.

As each month dragged its length along, the long reprieve we were enjoying seemed to us increasingly incomprehensible. Why didn't they put us to death if they meant to do it? If not, why weren't we placed on the footing of other prisoners of war? There seemed no reason for any middle course. It's likely we were forgotten in the rush and hurry of great events, but at the time, we couldn't understand that.

EDITOR: Although Pittenger's guess that the surviving raiders were kept alive as much by oversight as design is as likely an explanation as any, the uncertainties of their situation reflected accurately the tangled cross-hauling that went on between Union and Confederate authorities over policies of prisoner treatment and exchange. The fourteen Ohio soldiers and several East Tennessee irregulars held with them at Atlanta were a handful of counters on a board much larger than they could have known—and in a game played by rules far from being yet worked out by the chief players.

In the first year of the war, holding more prisoners than the Union armies had taken, the Confederate government pressed steadily for a general exchange agreement. Washington, not wanting to recognize the Rebellion as a war, had persistently refused to consent to one. Formal negotiations started on February 13, 1862, were broken off soon after when the large batches of Southern prisoners taken at Forts Henry and Donelson shifted the rough balance of pressures and counter-pressures that had been reached. Realities of the situation forced a re-examination of the question that summer. Taking most of its features from the British-American cartel of the War of 1812, a reasonably flexible exchange plan was decided upon and signed on July 22, 1862—on behalf of the carefully undefined "authorities they respectively represent"—by Major Generals D. H. Hill and John A. Dix. Hill took pride in listing his rank as one in the C.S. Army. Dix, at the more awkward end of the stick in the matter of recognition, signed himself simply as a "major general," presumably in the service of an unidentified army.

Thousands of officers and enlisted men were exchanged under the provisions of this cartel in the following months, although official comment in the field continued to run chiefly to wrangling and name-calling. On July 31, President Jefferson Davis wrote to General R. E. Lee: "Scarcely had that cartel been signed when the military authorities of the United States commenced to practice changing the character of the war from such as becomes civilized nations into a campaign of indiscriminate robbery and murder." The Davis outburst was in response to stiff guerrilla-control measures announced in Virginia by Generals Pope and Steinwehr and to an order issued by Secretary of War E. M. Stanton, on July 22, authorizing Union commanders under certain circumstances to seize private property without promise of compensation. Slaves—in the official Confederate view—were private property, and this was getting close to the bone.

It was shortly afterward that the surviving raiders elected to make what now seems the mistake of formally petitioning the Southern authorities to be placed on normal prisoner-of-war footing, eligible for exchange. The mistake, if it was that, lay in the fact of calling attention to themselves at all. Collecting nothing more damaging than noncommittal or frankly buck-passing endorsements as it rose through channels, their petition of August 17 was forwarded by Secretary of War George W. Randolph to President Davis on September 11, with the recommendation that the "engine thieves" be respited until further orders, and detained meanwhile "as hostages for our own people in the hands of the enemy." Davis—apparently in no mellower a mood on receiving this than he had been on July 31—took a chillingly prompt stand against discrimination.

"Inquire," he instructed Randolph, "whether there is anything to justify a discrimination between these and others who were executed for the same offense."

Randolph, by way of a message to Major G. W. Lee, provost marshal at Atlanta, began inquiring.

PITTENGER: Although Atlanta was virtually the center of the Confederacy, and a journey of several hundred miles—since General Buell had been driven back in Tennessee—would be necessary before we could reach the shelter of the old flag, talking about escape was a constant pastime. As well, it was a chance to impart the knowledge of each to all. All our former attempts were discussed and the particular causes that led to the capture of each person

[*Pittenger*]
were carefully gone over. These discussions awakened confidence, and were in some measure a substitute for experience.

DORSEY: From time to time we had held what amounted to classes in escape tactics, discussing the proper course to pursue when, if ever, we should get into the woods again: how to throw the dogs off the track, how to approach a house in search of food, how to cross streams, what direction to take, the probable whereabouts of the Union forces. These last we hoped might be found in Tennessee, somewhere within reasonable reach. We eventually learned that our own command at this time, instead of being in the vicinity of Chattanooga, or perhaps approaching Atlanta, had gone clear back to the Ohio River, and was in the vicinity of Louisville, Ky. Actually, the Union lines were then nearly four hundred miles away, and perhaps it was as well we were ignorant of this.

PITTENGER: Back in August, a Major G. W. Lee had been named as provost marshal and placed in command of us at Atlanta. He seemed interested in us and sympathetic at that time, but in September, when he visited us in search of new information about our cases, his inquiries persuaded some of our party that we were again in danger and that it was time to bend all efforts toward an early escape. I was reluctant to agree, convinced that no mode of escape was feasible which didn't involve the nearly impossible task of conquering the guard.

ALF WILSON: We communicated with the prisoners in the room opposite to us through the stovepipe, which entered the same chimney from both rooms, the pipe holes being almost exactly opposite. We would take off the pipe elbow and speak through, tube fashion. It was by this means that we learned, from some new prisoners brought in, of the Emancipation Proclamation of President Lincoln. This caused great commotion among the Rebels, and brought down bitter maledictions upon the President's head. The Negroes, ignorant as they were, seemed to take a lively interest in the Proclamation, and were never so pleased as when they could speak to us on the sly about it.

EDITOR: President Lincoln's preliminary Emancipation Proclamation was announced on September 22, 1862, five days after the bloody stand-off of Antietam had forced Lee's return to Virginia. As commander-in-chief of the Union's armed forces, Lincoln declared that on the first day of the coming January all slaves within any state or district then still in rebellion against the United States would be "then, thenceforward and forever free."

In the violent Southern reaction against this move—which included President Davis' decree that Negro Union troops and their white officers, on capture, thereafter were to face state-imposed death penalties for slave insurrection and incitement to such insurrection; and was to bring about in December complete suspension of the exchange of officers—the raiders still alive were put in new jeopardy, as their ears, eyes and prison-sharpened sixth sense of danger quickly confirmed.

ALF WILSON: As we moved into October, the evidence was increasing daily that something was in the wind that boded no good to us. At about this time, a couple of regular army soldiers, confined in the next room, overheard Major Lee, the provost, telling the officer of the guard that he hourly expected an order for the execution of "those raiders."

DORSEY: A little while after Colonel Lee had looked in on us again, there came a call at the stovepipe hole. Knight was first over, and received the announcement from Ike Coleman, "A message, boys."

Presently the stick that had served the purpose for some time came through with a bit of paper tied on it. The message, written by Walton, conveyed the startling information that Colonel Lee had called Turner, our jailer, out and had had a confidential talk with him. When the colonel had gone, the jailer talked with the guards loud enough to be heard by Walton and the others in the north cell. Turner gave orders for a closer watch over us, saying: "Those Ohio men will all be executed in a short time," adding that he was sorry, for "there are some fine men in that room."

That settled it. Our time had come and everything went to prove it. There was no longer any doubt of the proper course to pursue.

ALF WILSON: After sifting and weighing closely all the information we had, it stood about in this way: a little formality—Confederate army red tape—was all that now stood between us and the scaffold. If we had any hope of getting beyond those prison walls, except on a death-cart to the gallows, the blow must be struck at once. I believe in the efficacy of earnest Christian prayer, but prayer in a Confederate prison seemed to have less effect than in any place I have ever before or since been. We resolved to make an attempt to regain our liberty and save our lives without further delay.

DORSEY: For the first time since our capture we were all of one mind about escaping. No question was raised as to the manner of our going. We must go, and there was but one way. There was no time for anything but an open, straight-out rush.

It was now October 15, and we must go that very night. If we delayed another day, the number of guards might be doubled. Captain Fry, in whom all had the utmost confidence, was placed in command.

PITTENGER: It was now mid-October and the weather was fine. In our room at the jail there were our fourteen of the Andrews party and Captain Fry, of whom two—Wood and Dorsey—had been sick so long that it didn't seem sure they could be efficient in a fight. There were four prisoners of war and a Rebel deserter in the front room, and some ten or twelve other prisoners in the remaining rooms. There were then usually seven armed guards on duty. The escape plan we eventually agreed on was simply to attack these in broad daylight, and get away before an alarm could bring the other soldiers in reserve nearby.

ALF WILSON: Our plan was quickly agreed upon. We had decided to seize the jailer, Mr. Turner, when he came to the door to put in our rations, take the keys from him, unlock the doors and let out the prisoners in the other rooms, then all descend the stairs and divide into two squads—one squad to go to the rear door and capture the guards there, while the other squad would capture and disarm the guards at the front door and in the yard. This was all to be done in a rush and as quietly as possible. Then, with the muskets so obtained, we might be able to march on the double-quick out of the city, at once scatter to the nearest woods, and make the best disposal of ourselves that circumstances would admit of.

When it is remembered that we were in the jail of a large city, not a street of which we knew, that soldiers, home guards and police could be rallied at a moment's warning, and that the whole population, dogs and all, would freely turn out to hunt for the train thieves, it will be seen that we had no small contract on our hands. But experience has taught me that man, in the fix we were, is the worst and most desperate creature on earth, and will do things that seem utter impossibilities before their accomplishment.

We at once set about preparing ourselves for a journey. We mended our old, worn-out clothes as well as we could, so that our appearance among strangers wouldn't betray us. We cut out old pieces of blankets and made socks to protect our feet from our old worn shoes and boots. We gathered up several hickory sticks that we had in prison—and also some old bottles and such other implements as we could lay hands on—to use as weapons in our assault on the guards. The time fixed for the assault was in the evening when our supper rations were brought in, which was some time before sunset, and when our movements outside, should we succeed, would soon be covered by darkness. The routes to be taken after we were out were discussed and it was agreed by all that we must avoid any of the principal roads or ferries of the surrounding country.

PITTENGER: We were to travel in pairs and in every direction. Captain Fry was to be my partner, and all the rest considered that I was fortunate, for he would be at home in the Cumberland Mountains toward which we were to journey. The intended course was marked out for each.

It was afternoon when we received the intelligence which determined our action. We patched our shoes as well as we could, and made cloth moccasins to protect our feet, for many shoes were worn out. We gave messages to each other beginning with the form, "If you get out and I don't—" for whether seven guards would allow their muskets to be taken seemed more than doubtful.

Captain Fry was to begin the movement. I was to stand by and help him with the jailer and the watchman, Thoer, if the latter was on hand as he usually was. Then Buffum, who was as agile as a cat, was to snatch the keys, and, waiting for nothing else, open all the doors above. All the others were arranged into two bands, with leaders, to slip down the stairway at the proper time and break out on the guards at the front and rear doors simultaneously.

DORSEY: Fry himself would take care of the jailer. Little Buffum was to get the keys from the jailer and release the prisoners in the cell just north of ours. The Georgian in that room was awaiting trial and probable shooting for desertion, and we had promised in return for the favors done us to release these comrades if we made the break.

KNIGHT: The main question was: Who'd take the guard at the front door?

All of us kept pretty still when this came up. With no one answering, I finally spoke up and said I'd take the man at the front door if someone would first get hold of and keep Turner out of it.

From a piece of two-by-four worked out of the wall, I was able to rig a club to have in hand when the break-out time came.

DORSEY: We were now about ready for the assault, with a faint hope of partial success. The task was a desperate one, and it was thought the hearts of some would fail them, since we knew that going out into the open country, we would be hotly pursued, and, if caught, were liable to be lynched on the spot.

Toward evening of the 15th it rained, and thinking the ground and the leaves in the woods would be wet, and thus enable the dogs to track us with greater certainty, we decided to postpone our move until the next evening. We decided to make the attack at supper time when the door was open to admit the Negroes who waited on us.

ALF WILSON: On the day following—October 16—the wife of a citizen prisoner came in to visit her husband, and she told him it was the general talk in the city that the Yankee raiders were to be executed within a day or two, and that everybody was going to turn out to see the execution. This man sent word to us as soon as he could, and further advised us to try to break jail. He didn't know that we had already decided to do so, for we kept our plans entirely secret.

DORSEY: As the guards were relieved each morning by a fresh detail, we had become accustomed to scan them closely, measuring and discussing among ourselves their physical powers and probable courage, predicting what each fellow would do if we should suddenly pounce upon them. On the next day, with sharp interest, we surveyed the detail for this, our last day among them, if our plans didn't miscarry.

To our delight, no extra guards had as yet been assigned. Still, there were seven of them, a sergeant and six men, all able-bodied fellows, and although we were double their number, we were unarmed and emaciated. We felt that some would surely be killed in the fight with the guards. Accordingly, we took leave of each other later by shaking hands and saying good-bye.

PITTENGER: Late the next afternoon, just before supper time, we all shook hands in final readiness. Captain Fry, who had two coats, loaned the extra one to me. Everything that we felt ought to be taken we secured about us.

ALF WILSON: Captain Fry engaged the party in prayer for our safe deliverance, and a few moments before ration time came, we all shook hands and bid each other good-bye, for we knew and felt that we should never all meet again in this world. It was decided not to make the attempt when the rations were passed in, but to wait until the door was opened the second time, after we had had time to eat, for the purpose of taking out the ration pan or bucket and giving us water. This would make the time so much nearer sundown or dark, which was important to us.

When the door was opened, we were in our usual places, and tried to look as composed as possible, as the Negroes came in and set down our food while the jailer held the door and looked in through the bars. The door was closed after the Negroes went out and into the other rooms. Most of the men, while pretending to eat all their rations, quietly hid away a morsel in their pockets for the morrow.

PITTENGER: At length the door was unlocked and our food was handed in by the colored women who generally brought it. The door was then relocked while they moved on to give rations to the other prisoners. With great satisfaction we noticed that the old watchman Thoer was absent. We ate a few bites of the food and secured the rest. Again we heard the shuffling feet in the hall as the women waiters returned. The men looked pale but set, leaning slightly forward in readiness. Captain Fry was perfectly calm and his face wore a pleasant smile.

ALF WILSON: Each man had his part assigned him. Captain Fry had the post of honor. To him by common consent, on account of his powerful build and great strength, was entrusted the ticklish job of seizing the jailer at the door. My own part of the work was with the squad that was to tackle the guards in the front yard.

We prolonged the supper ceremony as long as possible, in order to gain time. After some twenty minutes, perhaps, the jailer returned to the door, putting his bunch of keys down to the great lock. It loosened with a loud click and came out of the staple. The door swung open and Mr. Turner stood on the threshold.

DORSEY: As the Negro servants, Kate and John, passed in, Captain Fry—who with Brown, Knight and others had stood against the wall to the left of the door and out of sight of Mr. Turner—stepped quickly out, followed by others, in such a way that the door couldn't be closed.

We all had on our shoes and most of us had our hats or caps in our pockets so as not to lose them in the expected scuffle. As soon as enough were in the door to make sure it couldn't be closed on us, my spirits rose. In fact, I felt like a man for the first time since my capture. Up to now I had been powerless to help myself, pulled and hauled about at the back and nod of the enemy, but here there was a chance to do business again for ourselves. Even this slight prospect lifted us up.

Captain Fry stepped forward, the easy smile on his face, and said very quietly: "A pleasant evening, Mr. Turner."

Heading Home 1

ALF WILSON: We were all watching Captain Fry, for the noble man of prayers and tears was a cool-headed, brave soldier as well. As the jailer stepped in, the captain placed his hand on his shoulder as if to speak privately with him, and, with a smile as pleasant as a May morning, threw Mr. Turner entirely off his guard as he said: "A pleasant evening, Mr. Turner."

Reaching his arm around the jailer's neck, the captain continued, "We've concluded to take a walk."

At this instant Captain Fry clapped his hand over Turner's mouth, suppressing a half-started call for the guard, and held the surprised and struggling jailer as if in a vise. Robert Buffum, at the same time, sprang like a cat and wrenched the bunch of keys from the jailer's hand. Turner was a stout, wiry man, and struggled violently, but Fry held him with the embrace of a grizzly. While a steady hand over his mouth and neck kept Turner from making any alarm, Fry was at the same time cautioning him to keep quiet—that he wouldn't be hurt.

Buffum, in the meantime, keys in hand, was slinging the doors open right and left, and in a jiffy all the prisoners who wanted to go were marshaled in the hall and ready for a descent on the guards below. Luckily for old Thoer, he wasn't about; if he had been, he'd probably have got a bottle over the head.

DORSEY: Captain Fry had divided the party into two squads, one to attack the guards in front of the jail, the other to attack those in the back yard. Brown and Knight were to lead the front, and I believe Hawkins and Mason the rear attack. With the Rebel deserter there were five in the front room. If we could release them, there would be twenty of us, against seven guards. With my sickness, Fry must have thought me the weakest man of the party, for he named me last of all, assigning me to the task of bringing up the rear of the column to attack in the back yard.

Fry and Turner were both big men and a great struggle ensued, but Fry mastered his antagonist sufficiently to prevent his interference with the work of Buffum. I had passed Fry and Turner, and stood at the head of the stairs leading down to the hall below. Through an unlocked latticework door at the head of the steps I could see down through the front door into the yard, and from movements there I was afraid the guards would be alarmed or had already heard what was going on upstairs. These armed guards were our main foe.

Knight and Brown stood watching Fry and Turner—having faced about to observe the struggle between them.

I put my left hand on Knight's shoulder, and said: "We'll have to go. The guard'll be alarmed."

Knight slipped his hand past mine, and quietly opened the door. He and Brown, shoulder to shoulder, swung down the stairway with catlike silence, followed immediately by myself and others.

KNIGHT: I jumped from the head of the stairs, landed about halfway down, and kept going. The front guard was sitting down on a chair or a stool. He looked around and jumped up, jabbing at me with the bayonet on his gun. I grabbed at the bayonet with my left hand, and swung my club with the right. It caught him over the head and he went down, the gun coming loose out of his hands.

Keeping on out the front door, I found four of the other guards sitting around on the ground playing cards, their guns off leaning against the building. I got between them and the four guns and they scrambled away. The other prisoners piling out grabbed some of the guards' four guns and the other guards coming around broke and ran.

ALF WILSON: The guards were surprised and disarmed before they recovered their senses, except three who ran out of the gate shouting,

[*Alf Wilson*]
"Help! Corporal of the guard! Captain of the guard!" and other cries of alarm.

Still yelling, these guards took refuge behind the fence outside the gate and pointed their muskets inside. Several of the guards had been knocked down and roughly handled. One fellow, more of a scrapper than the others, brought his musket up and showed fight, but one of our party knocked him cold with a heavy jug. The ones at the gate had given the alarm, and spoiled our arrangements for getting away to the woods quietly, but I didn't realize this at the time, so intent was I in performing my part at the front gate.

I ran to a pile of loose brick, near the corner of the jail, and arming myself with these I ran for the fellows at the gate. They'd dodge back when I threw at them, but one of them I hit, and must have hurt.

DORSEY: As I went down the stairway, the thought struck me that instead of bringing up the rear of the back-door squad, I'd put myself in front of it, but this had hardly entered my mind when it was relieved by Bensinger, Porter, Hawkins and others bounding over the banister above me and taking the lead. It was all done in a twinkling. Knight, Brown and others leaped on the guards in front and disarmed them before they knew what was the matter. The Rebel deserter joined them and got a cut in the hand inflicted by a bayonet in the hands of one of the guards.

In the back yard Bensinger seized a guard by the throat and held him fast, while Porter grabbed the fellow's gun, taking it from him with such force that when the guard lost his hold upon it, Porter fell to the ground.

One of the guards wasn't disarmed and took position in a corner of the yard and drew a bead on Bensinger, threatening to shoot him and thus release his comrade. But Porter swung up the captured shotgun, glared him down and drove him off. Seeing that the front gate was still held by the guards, Wollam, Hawkins and myself piled our left arms full of bricks and stones that lay around in the yard, and were just in the act of charging on them when Knight came running through the hall to the back door.

"Boys," he said, "if we want to get away we've got to get out of this."

At this all hands flung away bricks and bottles. Bensinger threw his man against the fence with such force as to hurt him badly. All of us dropped our weapons of whatever kind (I had a long-necked bottle among mine) and lit out for the back fence.

KNIGHT: We started for the woods, about a mile off. We ran through gardens or anything else that came in the way, kicking the pickets off several garden fences as the easiest way to get over them.

ALF WILSON: Suddenly, while I was still out in front throwing bricks, I heard a familiar voice call my name.

"Alf! Come on, quick! The boys are getting over the fence at the back of the jail. Hurry up, for God's sake, for there's a company of guards coming."

This was my old comrade, Mark Wood, and his voice was the first warning I had of the danger that threatened.

"Then bounce that fence," I yelled to Mark.

Dropping my bricks, I also sprang for the back fence.

PITTENGER: Inside, where I still was, the Negro waiters had kept perfectly quiet, looking on the proceedings with the greatest interest, and only beginning to scream when the noise outside convinced them that they might as well contribute their share. Buffum had just succeeded in opening the last door of the other cells when the outcry from below warned him that his own departure must no longer be delayed. Fry and myself had been engaged in securing the jailer, who, though old, was powerful, and fought vigorously, but hadn't finished when we were warned by the uproar that all thought of a quiet departure was at an end, and that there was no longer a motive in holding on to Turner.

We all rushed down stairs as best we could, knowing that we would now be last in the flight. The Rebel deserter released by Buffum passed us all like a tiger on the leap—I never saw such speed in a narrow place—and getting to the back door found two guards awaiting him with bayonets. He seized one in each hand, cutting himself severely, but flinging them aside so forcibly that the men were very nearly overthrown, and then with the same swiftness continued over the fence, and on to the woods, soon being in advance of all the fugitives.

Buffum followed after him and got over the fence without difficulty, but though a brave man and a hard fighter, he was a poor runner. One Rebel who was quite swift-footed kept right after him.

Captain Fry and myself were close together in going down the stairs, he a little in advance. At a glance he saw there was no chance in the front yard—the way we had intended to take—and at once turned to the back door, which was left open by the passage of the Rebel deserter. He got over the wall with little effort, but finding himself chased as Buffum had been, he used a little strategy. A good many shots were being fired in all directions, and he suddenly threw up his hands and fell flat. Those who were following him passed on after unwounded game, and when the way was clear he arose and resumed his course. He was seen again and had a most desperate chase, but finally reached the shelter of the friendly woods.

At no point in all my Southern experience did I find defective vision to be such a misfortune as at this time. My eyes were easily dazzled by a sudden increase of light, and as I came out of the obscurity into the broad light, for some seconds I could scarcely see at all. In this interval I was parted from Fry by running to the front door according to our original plan. There were two frightened guards in the gate, tossing their guns about and seeming not to know what to do. These weren't dangerous-looking, but just as I was about to run out of the gate, I saw newly arriving guards outside. They called on me to surrender, but I hurried back into the yard. A sentinel tried to shoot me at point-blank range; fortunately, his gun failed to go off. I got back into the jail and started out the back way—the course I should have taken at first.

There were a number of guards in the back yard by this time, but in the confusion I got through them, and to the top of the fence. What was my dismay to see a considerable number of self-possessed soldiers outside waiting with lifted guns to shoot anyone whose head might appear above the fence. I jumped very quickly down on the inside with one hope left. I ran into the building and out at the front door, thinking that now the front gate might not be guarded. It was no use. A large number of soldiers were there.

ALF WILSON: Mark Wood and I both reached the top of the high back fence at the same instant, and not a second too soon. As I glanced over my shoulder from the fence-top, I saw the reserve guards pouring in at the gate, and before I could throw my leg over and spring off, a volley was fired, the balls rattling and whizzing all about us. One bullet struck the picket under my thigh, and so close that the splinters cut my flesh. As my feet struck the ground on the outside, I said to Mark, "I'm hit."

"Get up and run," said Mark.

I was on my feet in an instant, not knowing whether my thigh was shattered or not. As I ran I clapped my hand there. I had the satisfaction of finding that I had received only a slight flesh wound. Never did I make better use of my legs.

PITTENGER: Out by the front gate a second time, I saw that the first panic and all the advantages of surprise were over. I ran back into the jail to try the back door once more, but a sentinel was now standing at it and several soldiers followed me into the building. I didn't care whether they fired or not. I went up the stairway, the guards not molesting me, and looked out at the chase which was continuing over the adjacent hills.

It was a wild and exciting spectacle. Company after company of soldiers came up. The bells of the city were ringing, and shots were being fired rapidly, while loud commands and screams were mingled. I left the window and went to the front room where the prisoners of war were, and to my surprise found that they hadn't gone out of their room at all. They said that there was too much risk in it—that it wouldn't be possible for anyone to get off.

KNIGHT: We found the patch of woods to be narrow when we got to them, and we stopped there only long enough to catch our wind, and then pressed on again. Mason, Dorsey and Hawkins were now with us.

We'd hardly had time till then to figure out why there hadn't been any shooting, starting with the first guard at the door who'd jabbed at me with his bayonet instead of pulling the trigger. The reason was, all those guards' guns were empty all the time, although we hadn't known that before making the break.

When we got into the woods I broke the gun I'd got from the guard over a stump. I kept the gun barrel and bayonet, but the guns were heavy and no use to us without ammunition. We could hear a lot of hollering as we ran and then some shooting finally starting behind us, but none of it near enough to hurt.

DORSEY: Passing a little way into the woods, I found Brown and Knight leaning against a tree, gasping for breath. I leaned against the same tree. None of us could speak. As we recovered a little, one of the others gasped, "Guess we'd better go, boys."

On we went, but not so fast as before, for none of our pursuers was now in sight. We were soon joined by Hawkins, Mason and the escaped deserter, so that we were six in all.

PORTER: From the moment of the alarm in the jail yard, we found that we had to run for our lives and every fellow for himself. We made for the woods. In a very short time it seemed the whole city was alarmed and in hot pursuit. It was a close chase. We were fired upon by the pursuing Rebels, but none of us was hit. Everybody was wild with excitement, women screaming, men running, bells ringing, drums beating, dogs barking, in fact, a regular stampede.

As I approached the woods I found my strength failing, and I associated myself with John Wollam, according to previous arrangements. We soon arrived at a clump of bushes, and as both of us were nearly exhausted we concluded to stop, though fearing recapture, as it wasn't yet dark. We lay down, pulled some brush and leaves over us, and as everything was hurry and excitement, we weren't discovered, though they sometimes passed within twenty feet of us, but weren't expecting any of the party to stop so soon.

ALF WILSON: After having run a long distance in our flight, we passed Buffum, who had lost his hat in the attack. Now, bareheaded and with his eyes fairly starting out of his head with exertion, the poor fellow looked the very picture of a wild man. Wood had fallen behind me in the race, and I could hear Buffum cheering and urging him to "pull into it" for dear life.

"I can't run, but I can stop them!" Buffum called. "Run, Wood! Keep on running, and never let up!"

I was yards enough ahead so that I had time to select the most favorable course for us to take to save distance and find the shelter of woods or thickets.

PITTENGER: Parrott and Reddick were captured inside the prison yard and Buffum outside. Bensinger, who had been so gallant in the struggle in the jail yard, was discovered after the first race for the woods by some men with dogs. For some three hours they pressed him sorely. He could get out of sight of the men, but the hounds clung to his trail. When wearied almost to death, he found a stream of water, and by running for a long distance in that, was able at last to get away from them.

KNIGHT: We next entered a big field, in the middle of which was a deep ravine with brush grown up in it. Here we rested again briefly, took our bearings and then traveled on.

PORTER: We remained in our retreat until we heard the city clocks strike ten. By that time the first excitement had died away and we concluded to go. As the night was dark and we had no guide but the stars, we made slow progress. We agreed to travel only at night and lay up in the daytime.

DORSEY: The six of us—Hawkins, Knight, Brown, Mason, the Georgian deserter and myself—traveled a mile or so the first part of the night and then held up in an open field, judging we'd be safer there against surprise. We had changed our course after getting into the woods, and were going around Atlanta to the south, intending to go north as soon as we got clear of the town. Piled together like so many hogs, as a partial protection from the cold, all night we heard dogs and gunfire. The distance from which these sounds came indicated that the pursuers were beyond us, and that our best chance was in hiding where we lay and allowing them to pass still farther ahead.

The next day we changed position, but didn't travel far. We were discovered by some citizens with shotguns, but outran them and got away. As Mason was getting lame, and also became quite sick, Brown and Knight insisted on his going to a house. They went with him, leaving Hawkins, the deserter and myself together.

Striking out for the North Star, the three of us pulled through the healthiest patch of blackberry bushes I think I ever saw. They were way above our heads and thick, but we got down on our hands and knees and dug and scratched our way through. Next day our Georgia friend, the deserter, became a little too bold to suit us, and proposed to go to a house for food. We were very hungry, but wouldn't take any such chances, and parted company with the reckless Georgian. (I afterward heard that he reached Washington, D.C., safely, but subsequently returned to his home in northern Georgia to see his family and was captured and hanged by the Rebels.)

Bensinger—we were to find out later—being so hot when he took to the cold stream to shake off the dogs, where he fell several times and got thoroughly soaked, wound up with such bad chills and fever that he had to go to a house for help. The gentleman there said they'd do what they could, but Bensinger would have to be taken back to prison. The mistress dosed him with red-pepper tea, gave him some peppers to take with him, and he was carried back to Atlanta on horseback.

The account stood up to this point: five in custody, and eleven of us—including Captain Fry and the Georgian deserter in our party—still at large.

Heading Home 2

KNIGHT: Mason now began to get sick, but we worked him along till dark; then through the night we moved along slowly, hiding ourselves a good share of the time.

During the next day we hid, but some men searching around caused us to change our position once or twice to avoid them. The second night we also made but little progress on account of Mason's sickness, and after hiding all day again, we still found him no better. We held a consultation, Mason urging us to leave him to his fate and save ourselves. But we decided not to leave him in the woods, at any rate.

We picked a house at a little crossroad between two main roads about a mile apart, and with woods near. Brown and I went to the house and asked for lodging, telling the man that one of our number was sick. He didn't wish to keep us, but we told him that we were going to stay, as we could go no farther. As we insisted, he yielded and gave us our supper. Mason was put to bed, and we stayed up with him part of the night, and then left him the bayonet, went to bed ourselves and had a good sleep.

In the morning, we hadn't yet determined what to do, but we ate our breakfast in a back kitchen and then went into the large house to get our hats, which had been left there. Just then three men walked in. They talked a little time about the weather and the war, and we began to edge toward the door. They asked us if we hadn't broken jail in Atlanta. They being only three, we told them openly that we had. Then they advised us to surrender, saying that the ferries and roads were all guarded, and that part of our comrades had been shot down in the woods, and that they had come to take us.

"No, we won't surrender," Brown said. "Now you see if we do."

We jumped out the back door, and made for the neighboring wood, leaping the fence and running. The men ran out at the front door and around the house, calling, "Halt, halt," but we didn't. We had no choice but to abandon Mason, who was taken back to Atlanta the same day.

EDITOR: Still ailing, but on his way to recovery, Mason was returned to the Atlanta jail and again placed with Bensinger, Buffum,

Parrott, Pittenger and Reddick, under strengthened guard. Pittenger, in the following months, was given semi-"trusty" status at the prison and for a considerable period, aided the officers in charge on various clerical chores. The six were together in prison at Atlanta and Richmond until exchanged from Libby Prison, March 17, 1863.

KNIGHT: The old fellow with whom we had stayed when we had to leave Mason turned his hounds loose and put them on our trail. We put in our best licks, but could hear the hounds coming up. We prepared for battle by stopping in a stony place and getting a pile of rocks ready. We waited for them to come close up, took them at short range, and rolled them back down the hill. By this time, though, we could see our three callers coming around the road nearby, on horseback, to get ahead of us. We got to the woods, and changed our course so as to get away from the horsemen. They got part of their hounds rallied so that they would follow along and howl on our track, but they couldn't be made to close up on us any more.

About noon we came to a small stream of water. We kept in the bed of that stream for a couple of hours, and then the hounds lost track of us. Soon after we reached Stone Mountain, about eighteen miles east of Atlanta, and went on the north side of it and hid ourselves in the grass till dark, when we picked out the North Star and traveled by it.

DORSEY: Captain Fry made good his escape. Knowing the country well, he made his way to his home near Greenville, in East Tennessee. He remained there with his family a short time, but as the country was occupied by the enemy and they knew Fry had gotten away at Atlanta, a close watch was kept over his premises, and he had to keep concealed about his own house. For this purpose a trap door was arranged in the floor, and he lay much of the time under the floor, often listening to the conversation going on between his family and the Rebels who had come to inquire after the welfare of the captain. He subsequently rejoined his regiment. Captain David Fry was wounded several times during the war, but became a colonel and fought through to the end.

PORTER: After three nights Wollam and I were still in hearing of the city bells. The slow progress was chiefly due to our reduced condition and the difficulty of traveling at night over hills and valleys in a country we knew nothing about. Many difficulties had to be met, the worst being that of crossing turbulent streams at night. Generally we crossed on logs, if we couldn't ford the stream, in order to keep our clothes dry.

For three or four days before the break, we had been saving morsels from our scanty rations to have something for this emergency. We had scraped together less than enough for two meals, and it was all we had for the first twelve days. By this time we were ready to run some desperate chances for supplies.

Being in the mountainous districts of northern Georgia, where the country was only sparsely settled, we concluded to visit houses occasionally, one of us to be on the watch while the other asked for food. We were hardly ever turned down, owing to an impressive appeal we made on the ground of our service to the Confederate cause. We generally made these visits about dusk in order to have the advantage of darkness for escape if suspected. Often the one who called at the cabin home was generously asked to stay all night, but under the circumstances couldn't accept these hospitalities, although the inmates were usually harmless old men, women and children.

As the dawn approached, each morning we would hunt a place to stop for the day. After finding some dense thicket, or a cave in the mountains among the rocks, we would stop and listen for the barking of dogs or the crowing of roosters. If there were none in hearing, we considered our retreat safe. Otherwise we would continue our journey for a better hiding place. Several times we slipped into the fields where the Negroes were at work, and stole the provisions they had brought for their dinner. One night we traveled till we were chilled and weary, when fortunately we discovered a drove of hogs. Immediately we routed them up, and lying down in the warm retreat they had left, slept till morning.

All this time Wollam was longing for the Tennessee River. He would speak of the rapid and easy manner in which he had passed down the stream when he and Andrews escaped at Chattanooga, and he believed that if we could once reach it and get a skiff, a few nights' journeying would carry us out of the Rebel lines. Accordingly, we kept going northwest, through the mountains, hoping to reach the river well below Chattanooga.

KNIGHT: For twenty days we traveled at night and hid by day. Each day, for several days, we could see men after us, sometimes with dogs. For six days after we left Mason, we were without a bite to eat save what the woods furnished, such as nuts, bark, buds, and the like. On the seventh day we were going along a little stream that we wished to cross, as there were mountains on the other side, and we thought we could get on their slope and be traveling in the daytime. We had great luck here, for we found two ears of corn on the bank and a flock of geese in the creek, one of which we captured by means of the corn. Then, getting into the mountains, we went along eating our raw goose, taking first a bite of it, then of corn.

On the tenth day out we reached the Chattahoochee River. There was a rail fence alongside the woods, and we took two large rails, crossed them near one end, lashed them fast with bark, and putting our clothes on the highest end, we floated at the other till we got across. We took a good sleep in the thick canebrake on the other side.

Near there we found an orchard from which all the good apples had been picked; but we ate and carried away as many of the poor sour ones as we could. We also got some strippings of tobacco that had been left in a field alongside.

The same evening we came to a drove of small pigs and began to figure for one. Finally I stood behind a tree with a club. Brown bit off little pieces of apple and pitched them to the pigs. Soon one little fellow commenced to pick up the pieces; then Brown kept working backward till he passed the tree where I stood. When the pig followed up, I let him have it with my stick. Previous to this we had found an iron strap that had fastened a shovel to its handle, and one part of it had been worn thin. This we rubbed up a little on a stone and it made a very good butcher knife. We split the pig, and each with a half, ran up the side of the mountain, and waited till dark for a wonderful feast. We could see over the farm where there was a fire burning out in a back field, and we went there and roasted the pig most of the night.

That pig lasted us till we struck the Hiwassee River in the corner of North Carolina. Here we had thought we could run a boat down by night and hide in the daytime. But when we saw the river we changed our mind, for it was a swift stream, full of great rocks. The tug of war came when we were on the other side—after being soaked and knocked around against the rocks in getting over—for now we had to cross the mountains which we had been traveling lengthwise before. They were so high and rough that we were four days going eight miles.

One day in a deep mountain valley beside a river we met two men armed to the teeth. We all stopped but quickly moved on again.

We simply spoke when we met, and all seemed glad to get by without having anything more to do with each other.

The next morning we continued down the river, making good progress. Around a sharp bend, we came to quite a large house with two men sitting on the porch. We concluded to go up to them and ask how far it was to Cleveland, Tenn. When we hailed them and asked, one of the men came down to us and told us it was sixty miles. Then we asked for some dinner, telling him that we were sick soldiers. He said we could have some dinner, but for his part he was opposed to the war.

We got some water and some soap, which improved our appearance a good deal, and finally dinner was ready. There were two ladies, one old and the other young. The old lady was one of the kind that do a good deal of thinking and say just what they think. At the table, she said she wished the Yankees would get there, so that they could get some Lincoln coffee. I said that I wished so, too. Then she accused us directly of being Yankees ourselves, and as we concluded that those two men couldn't arrest us, anyway, we said that we were Union soldiers, and belonged to the party called "engine thieves." They had all heard of that raid, and now really made us welcome. They invited us to stay a week and rest up. We were willing, if we could be hidden somewhere. They told us that they could hide us where the first "Great Rebel" himself couldn't find us.

We had a good time, being kept in the back room during the afternoon. They put a large dog out on picket, and we told them army stories and sang songs till dark. Finally the dog's master came. He took us by the hands, and told us some hard tales about his being imprisoned because he was for the Union.

It was now settled that we should stay for a few days. A large basket of grub was prepared, and their boy, pretending to be going coon hunting, made ready a torch. We were to follow a short distance behind, with quilts and provisions. We first went down the river, and then turned up the mountain and went up. We turned into another ravine, and again went up, till we came to a solid wall across our ravine. It looked as if the top of the mountain had slid down and barred the passage. Our guide turned a little to the left, and among the bushes he got down and showed us a hole big enough to crawl in. He entered with his torch and we followed. There was a good-sized room in the cave, and he said we could have all the fire we wanted, and hallo as loud as we pleased without danger. Then he gave us countersigns and promised to come again, and left us. We began to eat the provisions brought along, and continued till they were nearly gone. We would eat and lie down, but get hungry again before going to sleep, and eat some more. Finally we quit lest our friend shouldn't come back in time; but he did, and brought plenty of food with him.

For five days we were fed and rested in this safe retreat; then our friend took us down again to the river and gave us a guide whom we followed over the mountains. After a long time I noticed a light in the woods and saw that he was making for it. There we found an old house standing alone. When we got to the door, my guide opened it, and to my surprise it was full of men. They told us to come in, for we were among friends. We had a good handshake all around, and then one old man asked us if we had any money. We told him we hadn't. He said that our looks showed that we had no clothes, and turning to the company, he said: "We must get them clothes and money, for men can't travel without them."

We were taken to a barn and kept till the next night, and were then given a suit of clothes and ten dollars each, and a guide who was to receive thirty dollars for taking us three nights' journey.

This placed us across the Tennessee River, when we were sent with instructions from one house to another. By comparatively easy traveling, we passed rapidly and safely on till we reached our own lines. We had spent forty-seven days and nights, passing over some of the roughest country that ever laid out of doors.

PORTER: After twenty-two days of hardship and danger, Wollam and I struck the Tennessee River about twenty-five or thirty miles below Bridgeport. Soon after we started down along the river bank, we saw a large canoe chained to a tree with a padlock. We twisted the chain off and sailed out. We ran our canoe at night and hid in the canebrakes during the day. This was very pleasant, but it didn't afford us the same opportunity of visiting houses as when we were traveling overland. During this time the cold caused as much suffering. After having been three nights on the river without anything to eat, we concluded to take some chances on the following day.

After our regular rest in the canebrakes, we started out early in the evening. We soon saw a house on the island. I ventured up and found the place vacated, but there still remained several stands of bees. We hunted around, found an old crock, and raised the top from one of the hives, filling our vessel with honey. We put the honey in the boat and pulled out, intent on having something more to eat. When it was nearly dark we observed a cabin near the bank of the river. We hid our boat, and both headed for the house. A dog gave the alarm, and a lady came to the door. We told her that we were Confederate soldiers, had been sick and were on our way home to recruit, and that if she would be so kind as to give us a lunch we would travel on. She was baking corn bread, which was nearly done, and also frying meat, which we very readily accepted. After reaching our boat we opened up our treasure, and had a feast of corn bread, meat and honey.

Much invigorated, we again launched out and made good time that night. The next morning we stopped in a canebrake, hid our boat, hunted a suitable spot and fixed our bed for the day. The bed consisted principally of dry leaves and such other stuff as we could gather up. When we awoke, we got up, washed ourselves and finished up our corn bread and meat left from the evening before, but had still a supply of honey. After lunch we took a stroll. It seemed very lonely, but we were free; we breathed the fresh air. After the sun had set, we again launched our gum-tree canoe and floated on down the silent river.

At that season of the year the river was very low, and when we arrived at the head of the Muscle Shoals, we had to abandon our canoe. We journeyed on foot again, but were comforted by the hope of securing another boat as soon as the river could be navigated. The country being rough, we kept near the river and concluded to travel in the daytime when we thought it safe to do so. We soon found that this added to our progress and comfort, and with precautions was almost as safe as traveling at night, besides giving us a better chance of foraging.

Once we were traveling along the bank of the river when we came upon a small canoe that contained fishing tackle, which we supposed would be used for spearing fish that night, as there was a torch in the boat ready to light. A little distance from the boat we observed a sack placed in a tree. Wollam stepped on the fence, took hold of the sack and pulled it down. It proved to be a sack within a sack. The outer one contained some corn and the inner one provisions, which we shouldered and carried to the woods, double-quick. We traveled until nearly dark, and then hiding ourselves in a canebrake, proceeded to investigate the contents of the sack. We found a large loaf of corn bread, four or five pounds of bacon, a tin of lard and two or three pounds of salt. We considered this a bonanza, as it lasted five days.

We were now near Florence, Ala., about forty miles from where we had left our canoe, and at the lower end of Muscle Shoals, so that the river might again be navigated if we could obtain a boat. Everything was quiet, and we hunted until we found a boat made fast to a post. We loosed it and again launched out. But it leaked, and as we had no way of bailing, we were compelled to abandon it soon after midnight. We hadn't traveled far on foot before we found a skiff which proved to be a good one. From then until nearly daylight we pulled hard and made good time.

We learned from a Negro the following evening that Corinth, Miss., was in possession of the Federal army, and we concluded to make our way there when we should leave the river. At Hamburg Landing, about eighteen miles from Corinth, we left our boat and started across country. It was now evening, and as rain clouds were gathering, we looked around till we found a house. An old man came to the door and asked who was there. We said, "Friends who desire shelter and a place of rest for the night." He asked if we were soldiers and we answered, "Yes." He then invited us in.

They had just finished supper, and there was a nice blazing fire. The old lady commenced preparing supper for us, during which time we were questioned by the old gentleman. We told him that we belonged to a Mississippi regiment and that we had been sick at Florence, and were on our way home to recruit, and get new clothing, which we badly needed. The old man's name was Washburn; he lived fourteen miles from Corinth and had a son in the Confederate army. As the Rebels had been meeting with some reverses, however, he had lost confidence in the cause, and thought unless a change came soon, the South would not gain independence. An ample supper being ready, we were invited to sit up and help ourselves. It was quite late that night before we retired, as we were anxious to learn all the particulars about the country. Saying that we wanted to avoid coming in contact with the Yankees, we were careful to learn the most direct route to Corinth.

After sleep in a real bed and a good breakfast, Wollam and I took our departure before daylight. The kind old couple asked us to stop again if we should ever travel that way, and let them know how we got around the Yankees at Corinth. We promised we would and started on our way.

At about eleven o'clock, as we emerged from a strip of woods four miles from Corinth, we discovered some soldiers and teams. The men—we were delighted to see—wore blue coats. We were soon in the midst of a squad of the 9th Iowa, but we still looked like dilapidated Rebels, and after relating our experience, and telling the officer where we belonged, he laughed and said that our story *might* be true, and that he would take charge of us meanwhile. The officer in charge at the post was still more skeptical in regard to our character. He charged us with being Rebel spies and said they had a place for us.

A lieutenant from the 20th Ohio was less skeptical, and a guard was ordered to escort us to the provost marshal's quarters in Corinth. Several officers were in the room when we arrived. I soon observed that we were to undergo a very strict examination. They commenced in an insulting and sarcastic manner. In turn we were very independent, feeling much elated over our success in reaching the Federal lines, and were as tantalizing as they, knowing that we could easily establish our claim and turn the tables on them. After becoming convinced that we weren't to be scared, we were next conducted to General Dodge's headquarters. After a short interview he recognized our true character and received a full detail of our adventures. He then ordered the quartermaster to furnish us with a full supply of clothing and blankets.

We went to the quartermaster's department, drew our clothing, had a general clean-up, robed ourselves in army blue, and felt that we were no longer fugitives and wanderers, but free men. Some of the boys soon learned where we had been, and the consequence was that we had to relate our experience wherever we went. After taking supper with the quartermaster, we again reported to General Dodge, who made us a present of five dollars each and gave us an order for transportation to our regiments.

It was now the 18th of November, 1862—a month and two days since leaving the prison—and we had been absent from our regiments for over six months.

We had to go by rail from Corinth to Columbus, Ky. In due time we arrived at Columbus, where we took a boat for Cairo, Ill. Upon arriving we reported to the provost marshal to learn the whereabouts of our regiments, but could hear nothing of them. We then got transportation to Louisville, Ky., and after a weary night's travel arrived and reported to the proper authorities, but still failed to get any tidings of our regiments. After a few hours' delay in the city, we concluded to push on to Nashville, and took the first train south. When we reached Nashville, we had the luck to find the old 21st doing provost duty there, and the 33d—Wollam's—Regiment in camp only eight miles away.

Library of Congress

George H. Thomas

Library of Congress

William Tecumseh Sherman

TWO WHO CAME LATER INSTEAD

Etowah Bridge: Spring, 1864

Library of Congress

Joseph Holt — Library of Congress

Edwin M. Stanton — Library of Congress

ON THE JUDGE ADVOCATE'S REPORT, THE SECRETARY OF WAR AWARDED . . .

THE FIRST CONGRESSIONAL MEDALS OF HONOR

William H. Knight

Knight *Bensinger* *Pittenger* *Dorsey* *Parrott* *Alf Wilson* *Porter*

THE THANKSGIVING REUNION: MCCOMB AND FINDLAY, OHIO, 1886

Dorsey Porter Parrott Knight Anthony Murphy Bensinger

LAST MUSTERING: CHATTANOOGA, 1906

I'll never forget the expression of Colonel J. M. Neibling, when he took me by the hand and welcomed me back. I was heartily congratulated by all the boys and there was general rejoicing. After a few days' rest I was again ready for duty.

Heading Home 3

DORSEY: The day after the escape, we'd come on some wild muscadine grapes, which we ate by the pound. Our mouths afterwards were very sore, and the grapes may have caused the trouble.

Martin Hawkins had some knowledge of astronomy, which enabled him to keep the course quite well. The North Star and the Pleiades were our chief dependence, as we had to travel by night almost entirely for many days. On the fourth day out we were on ground over which the enemy had evidently made a thorough search, as every brush pile and bush had been turned up. We were hidden under some of these bushes when two of those who'd been after us rode back discouraged within four rods of where we were.

On the eighth day out we came to the ferry of the Chattahoochee River, far to the northeast of Atlanta. We took rails from a fence, and had begun to build a raft, when we saw a lighted torch on the opposite side of the river. When the party carrying it came nearer we saw that it was two Negroes with four dogs.

Hawkins, who had spent some years in the South, and understood the disposition of the Negroes, felt disposed to trust them—especially as we'd been living on grapes, sassafras bark and a few stray heads of cabbage and ears of corn since leaving Atlanta. Accordingly, we asked them to ferry us over, which they readily did, we giving them a little tobacco we had, which we couldn't use because of our sore mouths. They said they were Unionists, and we told them that we were Union soldiers, but said nothing about the fact of belonging to the railroad raiders. One of the two went for provisions, while the other stayed with us, kindling a fire. They told us that we were about forty-eight miles northeast of Atlanta, in the region of deserted gold mines, and proposed to hide us in one of those mines, supply us with quilts and provisions until we were well rested, and then direct us northward. It would probably have been better to have accepted their kind offer, which Hawkins wanted to do, but I was afraid we might be detected, so we turned down the proposal.

The one who had gone for provisions returned with a supply of boiled pork and beans, mashed Irish potatoes, sweet potatoes and corn bread. It was the first worthwhile food we had eaten for six months. What was left we carried away with us. Our African friends gave us an old broken butcher knife, which afterwards was very useful. They also gave us directions, telling us where the Rebel troops were, the lay of the country before us, and where we could find a colored slave who would ferry us over the Hiwassee (which runs down from North Carolina into the Tennessee). We assured them that they would soon be free, and parted with a mutual "God bless you."

We pushed on, made a good night's journey, and then laid by until evening of the next day. Seeing a house, and watching it till sure only an old man and woman were there, we went up to it, asked for and got some supper.

Early that night we came to a small stream, and attempting to cross on a fallen tree, I fell into the water and got soaked. Some hours after we came to a barn, the mows of which were filled with cornblades. We were glad to bury ourselves out of sight in the fodder, where we grew warm and slept all day. It was comfortable, but we paid for it. Some cavalrymen came into the stable under the mows and took out their horses. We could hear their talk and the jingle of their spurs, and scarcely dared to breathe. But they left us in safety. We stayed a day longer, as the bed was the best we had found since our first capture. A Negro boy came up to hunt eggs, and found us. He was so scared that we couldn't pacify him, and we had to go on. Some Negroes were again met starting on a possum hunt. On application they gave us a magnificent treat—a hatful of apples, a half pone, and two or three pounds of boiled beef on a bone. This supply lasted for several days.

On the night journeys we were much bothered by dogs at the houses we passed. For a while, after I sprained an ankle by a wrong jump, I had to walk by leaning part of my weight on Hawkins. We came to a wide river we couldn't cross, and going back into the fields, lay on the damp ground till morning. If I ever tasted cold, it was then.

Hawkins became reckless and wanted to go to a house—said he was going to have something to eat if he hanged for it. We found a hut, and watching it for some time, saw no one but a black woman there. She gave us a hot breakfast, a fire to warm by and some parched corn to carry. She also directed us to a ford. Thanking her, we got over the river and met a man who told us of the defeat of Bragg's army in Kentucky, and how the Confederates were coming south through the Cumberland Mountains, and then turning to concentrate at Murfreesboro.

This was bad news—the Rebel army in front of us. At this point Hawkins and I came near separating. He wanted to go toward Murfreesboro; I protested that the enemy was there in force, while if we went on north we would only have to cross the roads on which they were traveling, and thus have contact with a smaller number of them at a time. Hawkins insisted we could steal around the enemy's camps and reach our own lines much nearer than by going north to Louisville. Notwithstanding my great lameness, I refused absolutely to go by the Murfreesboro route, and Hawkins reluctantly gave in.

That night late we came on a bivouac of whites and colored people. All were asleep except one of the latter. We approached and, in a whisper, asked him who they were. He told us that his master was one of a band of fugitives coming south with their slaves to avoid the Union army.

The colored man gave us the few facts he had as to the retreating army and its baggage trains and, even better, some baked sweet potatoes. We traveled on, and twenty-four hours after, reached the Hiwassee River, having the luck to meet exactly the slave our colored friends on the Chattahoochee had said would be willing to ferry us over.

With his advice, after telling him we were escaped prisoners, we resolved to go down the Hiwassee to its junction with the Tennessee. To do this, we'd have to pass around a Rebel camp at Charleston, a few miles farther down the river. This was Friday. By waiting until Saturday, the young man could get a pass good until Monday, and could pilot us around Charleston. We resolved to wait. The youngster's father and mother treated us royally, sharing their rations with us and putting us in the best bed—a feather one—overnight, and the old colored woman even doctored my lame ankle with vinegar and salt.

We hid in the woods next day. On starting, the family gave us a bottle of molasses and a slab of bacon.

EDITOR: Wilson Brown and Bill Knight, after their hard travel through the hills and mountains of northeastern Georgia, struck the upper reaches of the Hiwassee River in eastern Tennessee, too far up

[*Editor*]
in the mountains for navigation. Dorsey and Hawkins—taking the same general route, but keeping more to the west—reached the Hiwassee at a point a number of miles downstream, just above Charleston, where the river had begun to widen and deepen, permitting boat travel.

DORSEY: Our pilot took us around the enemy camps without any trouble, and down below we first found an old leaky canoe; then saw a better craft with good paddles tied up, and "traded" without difficulty.

At daybreak we hid the boat, pushed in under some dry leaves and slept by turns till afternoon. That night, trying for supper at a house where we saw only some women, we got a good square meal, but then found a lot of other women turning up, and soon after some men also at the place. It was a "quilting," and they were to dance that evening. But we told a new story. We had been working at a sawmill in the mountains, were now out of employment and were going to Chattanooga to look for a job. They warned us that we would be arrested at Chattanooga, and would have to go to jail or join the army. They seemed to care nothing for the war, and to have no disposition to molest us. Probably they were Unionists, but we dared not risk a discovery.

About midnight, farther down the river, we came to what seemed to be a ferry. Suddenly two shots were fired at us. We lay down in the bottom of the boat, and taking in our paddles, let her float downstream. I suppose it was a picket of the enemy, who, after firing once, concluded that our boat was only a floating log and took no further trouble. After getting out of danger, an hour of vigorous paddling brought us to the river's mouth, and out on the broader Tennessee.

We were reluctant to abandon the river navigation, but it was clearly dangerous to continue unless we were prepared to take the risk of running by Chattanooga. So we rowed to the north side of the Tennessee, and turned our craft adrift, while we started across the mountains.

The first road we crossed gave evidence of the passage of a large body of troops, and this warned us that we were probably in danger of becoming entangled in the scouts and detachments of Bragg's army, still on its drawn-out retreat from Kentucky. Two boys we found by a schoolhouse—they had been out 'coon hunting—confirmed this report. Soon we saw the campfires of the army, and ascending a mountain, where we supposed we would be safer than in the valleys, we waited for morning. When it came, an appalling sight met our view. A large division of Bragg's army, with its seemingly endless baggage trains, well guarded by cavalry, was spread out beneath us. All day long we watched their movements from our eyrie with anxiety. We resolved at night to turn to the northeast instead of keeping due north, as we had intended.

EDITOR: Braxton Bragg, invading Kentucky, barely missed capturing Louisville in September of 1862. He and Kirby Smith started falling back to middle Tennessee after the sharp battle at Perryville, Ky., on October 8, carrying with them great supplies of food and other stores taken in Kentucky. The slow return of the heavy wagon trains clogged the mountain roads of southeastern Kentucky and East Tennessee from the 10th through most of October. Two of the escape teams—Knight and Brown, and Dorsey and Hawkins—had to work through this strung-out movement of over thirty thousand troops.

DORSEY: Before we had gone far, Hawkins whispered, "Al, we mustn't crack any corn tonight."

We came to a picket, and were only saved from running right into it by the snuffling of a horse. Soon a squad of cavalry passed up the road, and we crossed it right behind them, anxious to get over while the sound of their hoofs drowned any noise we might make.

When the daylight came we couldn't see the enemy any more, but heard his wagons rumbling off in the distance. Our parched corn was almost exhausted; and we resolved to try moving forward in the afternoon. We found a Negro, who, for a wonder, couldn't or wouldn't give any provisions or information. Late in the night we rested, tying some bushes together to make a shelter.

Very impressive were some of the hours spent in the forests of the Cumberland Mountains—although generally we couldn't appreciate the wild scenery as much as we might have if we didn't have to keep getting through the long miles of it, hungry, thirsty and on foot. Once we had to force our way on hands and knees through a mass of briers a quarter of a mile wide. Several times we hunted persimmons by moonlight—Hawkins shaking them off while I crawled on hands and knees feeling for them. Near a ford of the Sequatchie River we found a quilted skirt hanging out, which we appropriated, tore in two and made undershirts out of. The ford was waded with our clothes taken off and tied on our heads.

For two days more we traveled in the mountains—hungry, cold

and wet with the rain that now began to fall. Several times I fell. Hawkins later told me he thought he'd have to leave me in the woods, dead. I thought the same of him. He could see my features, while I could see his, but neither could see himself, hence each thought the other was about to give up the ghost.

Near sundown of the second day we heard some woodchoppers far below us. In our extreme hunger, we resolved to try for food from them.

We were an odd pair. Hawkins, six feet one, had no coat, no suspenders, wore a black slouch hat and boots. I, half a foot shorter, with a light summer coat and a cap, wore my old army shoes, which were now almost gone. We told the mountain men—a father and son—that we were Confederate soldiers who had been left in a hospital from which we had run away, and that we were now trying to get back to our regiments. They refused to do anything for us, saying that soldiers had already eaten them nearly out. This reception encouraged us. To test them further we talked of our Rebel cause, its justice, etc. They didn't pretend to agree with us, and finally told us bluntly that we were in what had been called "Lincoln District," because only two votes were cast there for secession. The conversation led them to a flat avowal that they were Union men. We then revealed the fact that we were Federal soldiers. The father smiled, said he'd mistrusted as much, and held out his hand.

The name of these men was Moyer—Alec and his son Albert—and where they lived was called Winesap, Tenn. Confederate soldiers straggled by their house almost daily and we had to take great care to keep out of their way. We lay in front of the open fire at the Moyers' cabin that night, clubs in hand, not quite sure that we could trust our hosts, notwithstanding their hospitality. Next morning there was snow on the ground. I believe we would have perished if we had laid out that night without food or shelter.

The Moyers told us we'd had the luck to strike an operating "underground railroad" getting Union friends north. The next morning, after a good breakfast, Albert piloted us to another friend where we got an excellent dinner, making three straight hot meals in a row—the first real meals since the breakfast at the Crutchfield House in Chattanooga, more than seven months before.

After dinner at the next place we were invited to remain and attend a whipping that was to take place a few miles distant that night. The war having interrupted the due course of law, stealing was usually punished by a flogging. We passed up the invitation, and were conducted by a new guide to the home of a pilot, called "Red Fox," which we reached after night. "Red Fox's" true name was Richard L. Flynn, post office Lantana, Tenn.

Mr. "Fox" wasn't at home when we arrived, but came in during the night. His father-in-law, aged ninety, was an enthusiastic Union man, and declared his intention to use his old rifle if the Rebels ever bothered him. The old gentleman literally forced upon us a dollar—the last one he had.

Early next morning "Red Fox" took his rifle in hand, and went "hunting." Of course we followed. About noon we crossed a well-traveled road, and a few rods further on, "Red Fox," who was at the end of his beat, sketched out our path and divided his jerked venison with us. We were about to separate, when we were startled by the tread of soldiers and the rattle of their tin cups and pans, as a brigade of Confederate infantry passed along the road we had just crossed.

After they had got well by, our friend marked out our way to the next stop on the underground route and bade us good-bye. We could only pay him with thanks, with which he was fully satisfied. Few persons outside of these districts have any idea of the services that were rendered and the dangers encountered by those loyal mountaineers.

That night we lost our way and had to sleep out in the woods. The next day's travel resulted in but little progress, and late at night we came to a cabin—not the one we'd been recommended to —and sought shelter. After breakfast we asked what our bill was, and were answered, "One dollar." If we hadn't been able to pay this, suspicion could have started up, and stopped us right there, for there was a camp of Rebel irregulars not far away. The dollar bill donated by "Red Fox" Flynn's old father-in-law met the emergency.

In addition to two men lodging with our host, there was a young fellow probably about eighteen years old. When we departed, he offered to show us the main road to Jimtown—on the maps as Jamestown. A little way out of the woods the young man frankly told us he took us for Union men trying to get to the Federal lines. He also named himself a Unionist and put us on a path that led us to the place we had started for two days before—a house belonging to a Squire W. H. Shillings. The squire put us up, and passed us on to a good friend in Jimtown. There were a lot of fine apple orchards in this section and we were eating chestnuts and apples most of the way.

At Jimtown, we had a narrow squeeze with guerrillas. News of us got to a woman whose husband was imprisoned in the South as a Union man. Her anxiety to get some account of her husband led her to betray us without meaning to, and we had to light out in charge of a pilot to safer quarters, which were found before morning some distance away in dense woods. Poor woman, we knew nothing of her husband.

From here we traveled without a guide, going by the directions given from time to time by friends to whom we had been directed. Usually we traveled by paths, avoiding main roads.

Over the Kentucky line at Monticello we reached a planter who received us in with that whole-souled hospitality for which the Kentuckians are noted. Our host (who had two fine-looking grown daughters) was a well-to-do slave-holder. From him we learned some of the divisions and dissensions that had sprung up in the North in regard to the prosecution of the war and the slavery question. We figured if the people of the North knew the Rebellion as we did, there wouldn't be much division going. Our host wanted to have his Negro shoemaker mend our shoes, but with scouting parties of Confederates around, we didn't want to give up our shoes even long enough to have them mended.

As it was now reasonably sure we would reach the Union lines, Hawkins began to talk of what we would say to Colonel Moore when we got to camp. Hawkins thought we ought to be promoted, but I thought it more likely we'd be reduced to ranks (we were both corporals) for not having burned the bridges.

We here got to see a Northern newspaper for the first time in seven months. The headlines of one article conveyed sad and unexpected news for us. They announced the death, at New Bern, N.C., of General O. M. Mitchel, of yellow fever. All the way through we had had General Mitchel on our minds. If we could get through and see General Mitchel, we felt that we would have a warm and prominent friend. Now we'd have to ask others to help those of our men still held.

EDITOR: Ormsby MacKnight Mitchel had never recovered the momentum of the high first days of April that saw him driving into northern Alabama. Although commissioned a major general after his capture of Huntsville, granted the privilege of reporting directly to the War Department at Washington, and given the challenge of almost independent authority over most of two railroads and dozens of counties of Tennessee and Alabama, Mitchel stumbled over several hazards not set by the enemy. His frank awareness of his own unusual merits understandably didn't endear him to his superiors, and professional rivalry between Mitchel and Generals Buell and Halleck undoubtedly heated differences of temperament and method, which could have caused friction in any case.

For specific ropes with which to pull Mitchel short, Buell was quickly handed two in the form of looting charges against Colonel Turchin's command, and the suggestion that Mitchel himself had become overly interested in the affairs of cotton speculators, then busily and profitably buying and shipping hundreds of bales north over Mitchel's newly won railroads. Mitchel vigorously defended his actions and those of his subordinates, and it would be difficult now to establish exactly where unsympathetic eyes misread creditable conduct and where actual fault or mistakes began. On July 2, after trying vainly to get Buell's approval for an early, swift advance in force to the east and to the south, Mitchel asked to be transferred from his command.

Called to Washington, for some weeks Mitchel was considered favorably by President Lincoln and Secretaries Stanton and Chase for top command either of the army about to drive down the Mississippi or the Union army of Virginia. Major General J. W. Halleck vetoed both suggestions, and in September was able to shunt Mitchel off to command of the resoundingly named but militarily unimportant Department of the South, an isolated beachhead at Port Royal on the South Carolina coast, chiefly held as a convenient rendezvous point for the East Coast blockading squadron.

As F. M. Mitchel puts it, his restless, scarcely used father had finally been granted a fully independent command, but one "located in the midst of swamps, shut in by estuaries, and threatening a coast guarded by fever."

DORSEY: After another good night's rest at Monticello, Ky., a lavish breakfast and a morning dram—which nearly turned our heads, as it was the first we'd had since in jail at Marietta back in April—our friend piloted us through the little town. Although our host was a Union man, he put up officers or soldiers from either side who called on him and had a good name with both. He gave us a note to his son-in-law, a Dr. McKinsey, at Somerset, whose hospitable house we reached the same day. The doctor next day fixed passage for us on some wagons that were going to Lebanon for salt. Two teams covered the seventy miles from Somerset to Lebanon in two and three-quarters days.

[*Dorsey*]

Near Lebanon we began to see blue coats—teamsters hauling wood, forage, etc. Old Glory was a mighty special sight for Hawkins and myself as we first saw it again there at Lebanon that evening—the 18th of November, 1862.

It was soon after the battle of Crab Orchard, and at that time there was an army convalescent camp at Lebanon. We weren't very cordially received by the officers in charge, as we looked a lot like some of the paroled Confederates still around. When we told the Union officers who we were and where we'd been, they seemed to doubt us. We added that we'd spent six months in the prisons of the South, and could stand a little more of the same treatment if they saw fit to lock us up. They then sent us to the barracks and promised to forward us northward in a few days.

I here saw my face in a mirror for the first time in nearly seven months, and was almost knocked over. My features were thin, spare, and bore unmistakable marks of the long-continued mental strain through which I had passed. The eyes in particular had a wild look, like those of a deer—full, round, protruding, as if looking away off in a strained effort to get a fast, wide-ranging look at everything and anything around. Undoubtedly Hawkins' face looked the same, but as I'd been seeing his face every day, I'd got used to the wild look on him—but not on myself.

Here at Lebanon, we gave our true names for the first time. The fear that a large reward was out for us had heretofore kept both names and share in the railroad adventure a secret.

At the barracks, almost the first man we met was George James, of my own company. He looked intently at us for a moment, then threw up both hands. "My God," he said. "Here's Al Dorsey!"

James remembered Hawkins, and at once called a company mate, J. B. Jacobs, who also knew him. It was a happy meeting, but our sad news of the deaths of Andrews and seven comrades, and uncertainty as to the rest, marred the occasion. From these friends we learned all about our comrades-in-arms: who had fallen in battle, who had been wounded, who discharged, and something about the friends at home. We borrowed a little money from these comrades and spent it right off for food and drink.

I think that Hawkins and I were sent to Louisville the next day. This was a regular military post and contained quite a number of troops.

We went to the office of the *Journal* there, and arranged with the old editor—George D. Prentice—to have a simple notice in about our escape and safe arrival, as we'd promised our mountain friends to do, by way of a report that we'd got through.

As Colonel Moore of our regiment was at his home in Portsmouth, having been wounded at Perryville the month before, and as we were so broken down that we weren't yet fit for duty, we went up the river by steamboat to that place to report to him. This was living high. Steamboat fare, as everybody knows, is of the very best, and we did justice to every meal. On the boat upriver from Louisville, Hawkins and I met Major Ellis of our regiment, and also a Mr. Brotherlin of Columbus, Ohio, who took a deep interest in us and our story, and requested us to call on him at his home. I did so afterward and was introduced by him to Governor David Tod [of Ohio] who promised to remember me. He did so, later, in the shape of a commission as first lieutenant, which I turned down then with the recommendation that our second lieutenant—V. B. Morrison—be made first and myself second, which was done.

Colonel Moore sent us home to remain until he was able to return to the regiment, when, he said, we would all go together. I couldn't wait so long, and went to the front on my own motion, rejoining my regiment at Murfreesboro, only thirty miles north of the place where we left camp on the raid, nearly a year before.

My captain, T. A. Minshall, showed me a longstanding entry in the company books:

"D. A. Dorsey—Executed by Confederate authority, exact date of execution not known."

Acknowledging that this now seemed out of order, the captain himself took pleasure in correcting the entry.

Heading Home 4

ALF WILSON: It was about a mile, the evening we broke out, before we struck the cover of the woods, and then the trees were so scattered that they didn't give us much protection. Wood had come up with me, and we dodged from one thicket to another until it began to get dark.

About this time, we found out we were coming to a public road. The sound of galloping horsemen and the clanking of sabers could be heard nearby. Looking around, we discovered a scrub pine with some thick bushes around it. We both dove under it and lay flat. We were so near the road that we could see the Rebel cavalry, who were deploying something on the style of skirmishers.

Two minutes sooner we might have crossed the road without being seen. We'd become separated from the rest of the party, but we could hear gunfire, and knew the chase was still going on. I'd seen Captain Fry reeling and stumbling in a way that made me think he'd been shot.

Compelled to keep on lying low, we saw the cavalry relieved by infantry, as far as covering the road went, and then the horsemen started out to scour the woods. The place where we lay wasn't fifteen steps from where an infantry sentinel was stationed. We could hear every word he spoke to the man on the next post. In their opinion there was no devilment a Yank would balk at, from stealing a black or a railroad to breaking jail and in various other ways defying the regulations and rights of the Southern people. They allowed that if any of the thieving raiders were caught, there would be no more foolish delay about hanging them.

Sometime late in the evening, still lying under our pine, we became aware that someone was crawling along near us, as if making a try for getting across the road. In the dark we could recognize the dim outlines of two men, and felt certain that it was two of our own; but we didn't dare take the chance of whispering to them.

After waiting a little while to be sure those two others weren't stopped getting across, and hearing nothing, we began to crawl out ourselves, concluding that there was no chance of the road guard being taken off that night. The sentries were stationed about thirty paces apart. I picked a place and worked over on my belly to the other side of the road safely, and then lay still, while Mark wriggled over after me. Luckily, the guards had been on the watch so long that they'd probably become drowsy.

On the far side of the road, after carefully getting over a fence, we found ourselves in an open field. When we finally got far enough from the road to be out of hearing, we struck out on a full run. Coming to a small stream, we traveled in it a way to throw off pursuit by dogs. Soon after, we struck a big wooded hill and climbed it for quite a while till we finally had to drop to the ground, too tuckered to keep on. We'd been shut up so long, that we found we had but little strength.

Up to this time, I think, neither of us had spoken, any more than if we'd been dumb. Now, I could hardly keep from shouting out, "Glory be to God! Free again!"

For a long time before our breaking out, I'd studied over the subject of escape routes pretty carefully. I'd seen enough of night travel in the mountains around Chattanooga and along the Tennessee River, and well knew the chances of our being picked up if we went that way. I'd made up my mind that in case I had the good luck to get away, I'd hit out south for the Gulf, and try to reach some of the ships of the Federal blockading squadron. While this would be much the longest route, the distance as near as I could calculate being over three hundred miles, I thought there'd be less vigilance and chance of pursuit in that direction. The country was unknown to me, except a slight general idea I had of it from the school geographies. I only knew that the waters of the Chattahoochee River, which flowed by west of Atlanta, entered the Gulf.

While we rested on the hillside, I whispered to Mark how I saw it and he agreed he'd go any way I thought best. Accordingly, we got up, moved along to an open place where we could see the stars, and fixed on our course—west by southwest to start with—and then we set out as fast as we could travel.

We soon came to the railroad track leading from Atlanta to Columbus and knew from this that our course was about right. Our march took us through some rough country and we had to halt and rest pretty often, so that when morning time started to come we estimated we still weren't more than about eight miles from the prison. We hunted out a hiding place for the day, and after getting each of us a good club, we slept until late in the afternoon.

We woke up feeling a lot better, but were so lame and our feet were so sore that we could hardly take a step without excruciating pain. We were hungry and the bits of corn bread we'd brought from the prison were gone almost right away.

I now saw a difficulty we hadn't had in our first escape try from near Ringgold. Our clothes had become dirty and ragged, and we had such a jailbird look that it seemed we'd give ourselves away the minute anyone saw us. I thought of this as I looked at Wood, and I suppose my own looks were no better than his. The miserable garments he wore didn't cover his nakedness. His face was begrimed; he'd become emaciated with fever and had a constantly ravenous appetite; his eyes were sunken in his head and seemed to have the wild, unnatural glare of a madman. We were in a country where we couldn't expect to find a friend, unless maybe in the Negroes, and of them we knew very little. Accordingly, we agreed not to go near a house if we could help it, no matter how hungry we got.

That night we got a few ears of corn in a cornfield we came to, and chewed them as we went along. After a toilsome night's journey, guided by the stars and keeping off the roads, we again hid ourselves as morning came. When we awoke, late in the afternoon, we each crunched what we could from an ear of corn and hobbled off, making but slow time for the first mile or so. The October nights were pretty cool, and dressed as we were, we had to keep moving all the time to keep reasonably warm.

Next morning we still hadn't reached the river. Again we hid and slept through the day. When night came we found our feet so blistered, galled and swollen that it seemed as if they'd burst with pain at every step. It began to be a serious question whether we wouldn't have to give up traveling. I encouraged Mark, telling him we'd soon have to hit the river. I suppose we'd shaped our course a little too far south and thus made the distance longer than it had to be. We struggled on for some time, sometimes crawling where the ground was stony. Finally I thought I heard running water. We forgot our tortures for the time being and scrambled on, and soon after had the satisfaction of standing on the banks of the Chattahoochee.

De Soto couldn't have felt more joy when he first discovered the Mississippi. We were by running water that led to salt water, hundreds of miles away, where we might find friends. We made sure of the way the river current ran, and started southward.

Not long after, we came across a skiff moored to a tree. We loosened the lock with a stone, and in a few minutes after were sliding smoothly down the current, and I doubt if two more joyful mortals ever navigated. Our painful feet now had a rest, and yet we were on our journey. We kept our oars busy, and when daylight started to show, we worked our craft into a bayou and hid ourselves in a thicket for the day.

It had been four days and nights now since we'd eaten anything but the corn bread from the prison and the hard field corn. Taking this and the murky river water we were drinking, our stomachs were starting to be in sharp trouble. On top of this, between our sharp hunger and the swarms of mosquitoes we weren't able to do much sleeping.

At early twilight, we pulled out of the bayou, bound on a raid of some sort for food, peaceable if possible, forcible if it had to be.

On hiding our boat and going up to a house near the river bank, we saw quite a number of Negro cabins near it, making it likely that this was the place of an extensive planter. The only occupants of the house were an old man and woman. We apologized for disturbing them and told them we were hungry soldiers returning from furlough to our regiments at Atlanta. They evidently credited our story, for we were told we'd be made welcome to such food as they had.

They were a quite intelligent, but unsophisticated, old couple in comfortable circumstances, living as most Southerners did, away from any highway, and I believe we gained their confidence. I had been in Dixie so long that I had acquired, from the guards and citizens, their vernacular of speech; besides this, we had learned the names of officers in a number of different regiments, such as the 8th Georgia Cavalry, etc., and could tell quite a plausible story if not too closely questioned.

We asked the old man if there was any late news.

"Well, not too much," he said, "except that they say in Atlanta the Yankee train raiders knocked over their guards, and most of them got away."

The old gentleman held that such a dangerous lot of scoundrels should have been hanged long before this. He was beginning to have his doubts, too, about the South being able to beat back such reckless freebooters as were swarming down from the Yankee country. All the worst thieves and scum of the great cities of the North—he let us know—were being hired to come down and take part against the South. We assured him that one Southerner could still whip five Yanks any day, and that there needn't be any doubt of the final result. In the meantime, we'd devoured everything the good woman had set before us. We were ashamed to accept so much, but our hunger was so much stronger than our sense of shame that we couldn't leave off.

A short time afterward we were in our boat pulling downstream with new vigor. Suddenly I found myself flat on my back in the river. What on earth had happened I didn't know. Luckily, one of my feet caught on the side of the boat, and I was dragged along until Mark pulled me out. The cause of my mishap had been a ferryboat wire stretched across the river and just low enough to catch me fairly.

Mark couldn't manage the boat very well, but needing my turn at sleep, I gave it over into his hands. Sometime in the night Mark aroused me, and told me we could go no further. We had come "to the end of the river." I began to look around, to find out what Mark's "end of the river" meant. I soon discovered that he had run the boat away under an overhanging rock ledge.

We worked the boat back into the current, and shortly after, the river began to grow rough. In the rapids, we got into so much fast water over the rock ledges, that we came near being broken up several times during the night's journey. The following night we came to a mill dam. We discovered what appeared to be an apron, near the center, and decided to risk running it. Bending to our paddles we came down with the velocity of the old *General* himself. What we supposed an apron was nothing but a break in the dam, and over it we shot. Below, plying our paddles frantically, we rode it out safely, but swore off on running mill dams in the night.

As we continued, the river was still rough and growing worse. We were constantly among rocks, the current got to racing along, and mountains loomed up on either side. It went on from bad to worse, till we lost all control in a gorge and were almost battered to pieces before we knew it. We had to abandon our craft and start a toilsome three days' land journey over rocky hills and bluffs along the river.

All the way down the Chattahoochee, Mark's condition was poor, and during this overland stretch it got worse. He'd often stagger and reel as if stupefied with liquor, and at times seemed to be almost blind, so that I was constantly on the watch, and oftentimes had to lead him by the hand. Our progress through these mountains was slow and painful, probably not more than five miles a day, although at some isolated cabins we were able twice to beg a little food.

At last, on the fourth morning, we saw the spires and smoke of a town in the distance. We took this to be Columbus, Georgia—as it was—and had heard that below it, the river was navigable clear to the Gulf.

When night came, we made a long, careful detour around the town, and then worked back to the river bank. During all the time we were near the town, we kept hearing sounds of a great hammering on iron. When daylight came we found out that a large number of workmen were covering a vessel with sheet iron. On closer inspection the following night, I found the craft to be a large, powerfully built gunboat, which the Confederates must have wanted badly to see finished, as the hammers of the workmen never ceased on her, night or day.

The gunboat was the rebel ram *Chattahoochee,* a formidable iron monster, built as an engine of destruction for the blockading Union fleet in Apalachicola Bay at the mouth of the river. (The first knowledge the Navy Department was to have of her was through Wood and myself, although the ram, on her first downward trip, blew up near the mouth of Flint River and never reached the Gulf.)

Our great anxiety now was to secure a boat. Wood was so lame he couldn't walk, and I wasn't much better. This delayed us here two days and nights. In my reconnoitering about the gunboat, I had discovered an old skiff chained to a stump, quite near and in plain sight of the workmen. I secured a stout stick for a lever, and watching my chance, got a pry in such a manner as to break the lock on the chain. The great work lights shone so brightly that I was afraid the workmen would notice me. However, I eased the boat away carefully, and half an hour after, Mark and I were pulling rapidly downstream. Our prize proved to be a leaky old concern, and one that kept us busy bailing.

Down some miles, we spied three boats tied to the shore on the west side of the river, and as we'd been giving our attention entirely to the Georgians all along, we concluded to be fair and trade boats this time on the Alabama side. Just as we'd loosened the one we picked out, three men came down the hill toward us, and the owner began hallooing and calling us thieves and the like. We speedily shoved all the boats into the water, and took a course upriver, as though we were going toward Columbus. We took a wide circuit, then headed downward under cover of several small islands near the Georgia shore, and came out in the main stream again far below, where we had the satisfaction of seeing the lights of our pursuers disappearing up the river.

With a good boat and an open river we felt now that our chances of escape were exceedingly good, provided we could keep from starving. Between our oars and the stiff current, we might be good for fifty miles of progress a night.

Thus we traveled, paddling or drifting through the night, and laying by in the daytime. The lower Chattahoochee is a vast water path through dense forests of cypress and other water-liking timber. On either side were endless swamps and the river channel was barely observable. Great festoons of gray, somber moss hung from the trees. I remember it as a dismal journey, where at times we wouldn't see a sign of civilization for forty-eight hours at a stretch.

Besides the torments of hunger, our nights were made almost unendurable by clouds of bloodthirsty mosquitoes. I thought I'd learned considerable about mosquitoes in my boyhood days in the Black Swamp of northwestern Ohio, but for numbers, vocal powers and ferocity I'd put the Chattahoochee skeeters against any others going. Our ragged clothing didn't much more than half cover us. To protect ourselves, we thatched our bodies all over with great skeins of the tree moss, and thus rigged out, two more comical-looking beings would have been hard to find.

We had two other annoyances—water moccasins and alligators. The latter, with which the water swarmed as we went farther toward the Gulf, were a terror to me. We knew but little of their habits. The largest water inhabitant I had ever seen, was a Maumee River catfish, and the most dangerous, a Black Swamp massasauger. Night or day, these "gators," as the Southern Negroes call them, were always within sight and hearing. Sometimes, during the day, we would take shelter in a pile of driftwood. When we would wake up, after a short nap, every old log and hummock about us would be covered with "gators." On the least demonstration on our part, these creatures would scramble out of sight, but Mark grew almost superstitious about them. He had read that sharks would follow a ship from which a corpse was to be cast overboard, even before death had occurred or was even suspected. What if alligators had the same sense?

After enduring hunger as long as we could, we were finally forced again to leave the river in search of food. This, I think, was about five or ten miles above Chattahoochee Landing. We were successful, and came back much strengthened, when, to our great dismay, we found that our boat had been stolen. Under other circumstances, we might have seen that as boat stealers ourselves, we didn't have much grounds for complaint, but we didn't feel too reasonable about it at the time.

After a long weary night, eaten by mosquitoes, I descried something on the far side of the river that looked like a boat partly sunk in the water. As the river was about three-quarters of a mile wide here, we had to hunt out an old piece of plank, which we lashed on three flat rails with a grapevine. Taking a piece of narrow stave for a paddle and to fight off "gators," I twined my legs firmly around the center of the frail craft, while Mark pushed it off into the stream.

The raft sunk down until the water came about my waist, but I stuck to it, and after about an hour's hard work, I found myself rewarded in the possession of a much better boat than the one we had lost the night before. After bailing her out and going back over for Mark, we plied our paddles until we felt sure we had passed out of reach of the owners of the boat, when we put into the cane and hid ourselves until night. After this mishap, we resolved that we wouldn't both leave our boat again while our journey lasted, starve or no starve. During the following day, while we were laid up fighting mosquitoes, and waiting for night, I went skulking about to see what I could see, and in an old vacant cabin found some fish hooks and lines, a godsend to us.

The country, from the point where we then were nearly to the Gulf, seemed to be one endless expanse of swamp, with scarcely a human inhabitant—the most forsaken, desolate country of all we had seen. We must have had a touch of scurvy, for out teeth were loose, and would bleed constantly when we attempted to chew the supply of field corn we had dragging behind the boat. But now with the hooks and lines we were in for a feast on raw catfish, of which we caught a plentiful supply as we journeyed on in the night. I had with me an old one-bladed knife without any back, which was our only weapon, defensive or offensive. This old knife I had hidden when we were in the Atlanta prison, and had kept as a precious treasure during all our wanderings. With this knife we managed to skin and dress the fish, which we ate raw with our soaked corn. Lacking matches, we had no fire.

I could eat only a mouthful or two of the raw fish at a time, palatable and welcome as it was. Mark, poor hungry fellow, tore it from the bones in great mouthfuls, until I begged him to ease up, fearing the results. He would sit and crunch the bloody flesh, and look at me with a wild, strange stare, and never speak a word. His eyes were sunk in his head, almost out of sight, and as he would seize a fresh piece, the pupils of his eyes would dilate with the gloating, ferocious expression of a panther or other wild beast. I had heard of men going mad from the effects of protracted hunger, and I sometimes shuddered as I looked at poor Mark's wasted frame and the unnatural glare of his eyes. He would mutter and groan in his sleep, and sometimes scream out as if pierced by a knife, when he would suddenly start up and call my name. Still, after we began to eat the fish, he seemed much better, and I only feared the unnatural quantities of the raw flesh he ate would kill him.

[*Alf Wilson*]

We were now—nearly two weeks from the time we left the mountains above Columbus—nearing the bay, for on each succeeding morning the river had grown wider. Finally we neared a large town, which afterwards proved to be Apalachicola, and this made us anxious to learn something of the state of affairs below—whether there were Rebel picket boats, or obstructions such as torpedo boats and the like.

About this time we discovered a cabin some distance from the shore, and, to have a plausible excuse, I took an old pipe Mark had and filled it with a few crumbs of tobacco which I fished from my old coat linings, and then left Mark and walked over to the house to get a light for my pipe. The occupants of the cabin proved to be an old Scotchman and his wife. He was very inquisitive, but I managed to evade suspicion and at the same time gained considerable information. I learned that we were about five miles above Apalachicola, and that the Federal blockading squadron was stationed at the mouth of the bay, eighteen miles below the city.

I hurried back to the boat, and found Mark rejoicing over a little armful of sweet potatoes he had stolen from a Negro's canoe in my absence. With the fire I brought we were able to roast fish and potatoes and dine in royal style. When night came on, we pulled out and passed down on the opposite side of the bay from the city, slowly and cautiously.

As soon as we had gone well past the city and pulled on down the bay, we ran along in the midst of a large school of huge fish of some description, from which we apprehended danger every instant. These monsters would swim along on all sides of us, with great fins sticking more than a foot out of the water and extended like a great fan. They would frequently whisk their fish-shaped tails above the water, which seemed to be as much as three to four feet across from tip to tip. One of these fish could easily have wrecked our boat with its huge body. I have never been able to learn to what class these finny monsters belonged.

EDITOR: Among all the real dangers he faced, inland-raised Alf Wilson probably can't be blamed for seeing menace in a romping porpoise school.

ALF WILSON: We hoped to reach the blockading fleet before daylight, but the night grew cloudy and we were unable to tell what course we were running, as the bay grew wider as we went out. We decided the best thing we could do was to pull for land, which we reached after midnight, pretty well exhausted. We tied up, went to a thicket and slept soundly.

When we awoke in the morning we were cheered by the beautiful surroundings. We had slept in a wild orange grove. The shore was lined with lemon, orange and palm trees, besides many other varieties of which I knew nothing. We made a hasty breakfast on our fish and potatoes and started for our boat. I was startled to find it distant at least two hundred yards from the water. Mark, who had lived in the old country, explained to me that this was the effect of the ocean tide, which had gone out since we landed and would not come in again until that night. There was no safe course left us but to drag our boat to the water, which we did.

When we were again on the water we pulled for the open sea. A little fishing smack passed away to the leeward of us, coming out from the city, but she kept on and either didn't notice us or care to inquire who we were. We plied our oars until about the middle of the afternoon, and had been out of sight of land for some time when we spied an island away in the distance. As we neared it we saw away in the distance something that had the appearance of dead trees. In the same direction, and right in our course, was something that appeared like a bar or gravel bank. We supposed the old trees stood on another low island or bar beyond.

But as we neared this bar, that which at first seemed to be dead trees began to take the shape of ship masts, and we imagined that we could see something that looked like the dark outlines of black smokestacks in the blue, hazy distance. We rowed away with renewed vigor and strength. We were close upon the bar, and presently we discovered a shallow channel through it. As we were going through, Mark gathered in a lot of rough, muddy-looking lumps, which I supposed were boulders, and soon called for my old broken-backed knife, after which I saw him open one of the muddy chunks and eat something from it.

"Taste this," he said, as he opened another muddy chunk, and I lapped up from the dirty shell the sweetest oyster I had ever tasted.

We were in the midst of a great oyster bed, the like of which I had never before seen. I had never, in fact, seen an oyster in the shell before. Mark gathered up as many as he could as the boat passed along, and when we reached the still water, we made quite a feast on them as we paddled on. We were still very hungry, and the moist, rich, salty flavor of the oysters seemed to suit our weak, famished stomachs to a nicety.

[*Alf Wilson*]

We could now plainly see the yards, cross-trees and great smoke-stacks of vessels ahead. We made the little boat scud over the still water at a lively rate and soon we could see the dark, somber-looking hulls of the ships. Suddenly a little breeze sprang up, and I shall never forget my joy on seeing the old flag, the glorious old stars and stripes as they seemed to extend their protection over us, after nearly eight months of bondage.

We threw down our oars in the boat and stood up and yelled and screamed. After we recovered our senses a little, we picked up the oars and began rowing again, directing our course again toward the largest vessel of the three in sight.

We were pulling our insignificant-looking little boat under the bow of a smaller ship, when a gruff voice commanded us to "Come to, there!" At the same time we saw a grim-looking old sea dog in blue uniform, leaning over the rail, motioning us in. When we came within better speaking distance, he interrogated us, in stentorian voice, about as follows: "Who in h—l are you, and what are you doing under my guns?"

We were half terrified that we had fallen into the hands of a Rebel cruiser under false colors. I stood up in our boat, and answered that we were two men trying to get back to God's country, among friends. I shall never forget the commander's stern but puzzled look. We'd been so excited that we'd forgotten to pull the old streamers of moss from our backs, and we must have looked like scarecrows. In our boat were a few catfish partly skinned, some oysters in the shell, some ears of scorched corn, a lot of moss and our old boots, for our feet were still sore and we went barefooted when in the boat.

When the commander again demanded some account of our strange conduct and appearance, I told him we were enlisted Federal soldiers, and belonged to the command of General O. M. Mitchel, in Tennessee, to which he growled something about our being a "d—d long ways from camp." I then explained to him briefly that we were fugitives, and the causes that led to it.

He said he had heard of the raiding expedition we spoke of, and commanded us to row up to the ladder and come up the ship's side. We did so, and Wood went up the steps first, so weak that he could scarcely raise his feet from step to step. The commander leaned over the rail and, reaching out, took hold to assist us up. It was with much effort that I was able to choke down my feelings, so that I could answer the few questions asked of us. Pretty soon the old commander's anger got the better of him, and he raved and swore as he stamped the deck until the air seemed blue. I think if he could have gotten hold of old Jefferson Davis at about that time, he would have hung him, and then tried him afterwards.

The vessel we had boarded was the United States gunboat *Somerset* of the East Gulf blockading squadron, and the officer in command, who had taken us up, was Lieutenant Commander A. F. Crosman. Peace to his ashes. A nobler and more kindhearted man never wore the United States uniform. He ordered us each a new suit of clothes, conducted us to his cabin, dirty and ragged as we were, and gave us each a few swallows of brandy, after which he sent us aft with the sailors, to wash up. We then rigged ourselves out in sailor's clothes, after which we were invited back to the commander's cabin, where we took dinner with him.

Commander Crosman cordially invited us to stay with him until we had fed ourselves back nearer form, but we told him we wanted to get back as soon as we could to some part of the Federal lines, where we could report, and, if possible, save our comrades in the Atlanta prison, if the poor fellows weren't already executed. He told us he'd be pleased to have us stay, but that if we insisted on going on, he'd signal the cruiser then lying not far away. This vessel was just ready to set sail for Key West.

After dinner, he interviewed us further, and again fell into a swearing frenzy. I thought he was the maddest, most furious swearer I had ever heard or seen. He wrote and forwarded dispatches to the Navy, and, I think, to the War Department, for my understanding of the case at the time was, and is still, that Secretary Stanton at once took the matter in hand, and notified the Confederate authorities at Richmond that any further executions of the members of the Mitchel party would be met with prompt retaliation. The commander also gave us letters to the commandants at the naval station at Key West and other points in our route. He furnished us with everything he could think of, even to a supply of tobacco, and with a hearty farewell handshake, Commander Crosman sent us off in a boat to the cruiser, on whose great dark hull was lettered her name, *Stars and Stripes.*

Soon after we came on board, the *Stars and Stripes* took up her anchor and was under weigh for Key West. Not long after, we were out of sight of the land where so many sorrows had come upon us, and of which we had but few pleasant memories.

Heading Home 5

WOOD: The 16th day of October, 1862, when the eight of us broke jail at Atlanta, disarmed the guard and made our escape, we took different directions. Alf Wilson and I struck out east at first. After we had traveled a few miles we proceeded south and west in order to elude pursuit.

We at last took a southerly direction, and traveled twenty-two days through Georgia, Alabama and Florida, eating only five meals of victuals during the twenty-two days, aside from berries we gathered in the woods, hard corn picked up in the fields and some fish we caught toward the end. We had no money, and had to travel nights to keep from being retaken. We at last arrived at Apalachicola, Fla., on the Gulf Coast, where we found the blockading gunboat *Somerset* of the Federal navy. We were taken aboard, treated very kindly by Commander A. F. Crosman, and sent on to Key West.

ALF WILSON: The 69th New York Regiment was on garrison duty at Key West when we arrived there, and the men and officers of it treated us with the greatest kindness. Soon after, the regiment received orders to go to Port Royal, S.C. After I'd recovered from a near-fatal bout of yellow fever, we took passage to that place on the same boat. On our arrival at South Carolina, to our sorrow, we learned that only a short time before—on October 29, 1862—our old division commander, General Ormsby M. Mitchel, had breathed his last in Beaufort. He had been placed in command at the South Carolina post but a little while before the yellow fever seized upon him and carried him off.

WHITELAW REID: Two years before Sherman, Ormsby MacKnight Mitchel showed how armies might depend on single lines of railroad through great tracts of the enemy's country for supplies. As early as Butler he showed how rebels could be made to support the war. Eighteen months before Rosecrans, he fastened upon the strategic point of the whole central half of the Southern states. Almost three years before Sherman, he showed how the shell of the Confederacy might be pierced, and how little resistance was to be expected when once this shell was passed.

Mitchel was comparatively untried. A brief period of subordinate service; a four months' campaign with an army of less than fifteen thousand, brilliantly managed but inadequately opposed; and five weeks preparatory to a campaign: in these short phrases his career in the war of the rebellion is told. Amid the stumblings of those earlier years his was a brilliant promise. He never fought a battle, never confronted a respectable antagonist, and never commanded a considerable army. Yet what he did had so won the confidence of the troops and the admiration of the country, that his death was deplored as a public calamity, and he was mourned as a great general.

ALF WILSON: What a privilege it would have been to us to have reached Port Royal in time to see General Mitchel before his death. I recall his words on that evening, far away in Tennessee, when he shook hands with a party of us and said, "Boys, I fear I shall never see you again." Nor did he, and I believe he died in the thought that our lives had all been sacrificed. Peace to his spirit.

We found good quarters at Port Royal and were royally treated by the eastern soldiers who were stationed there, and who understood and had the conveniences for making themselves about as comfortable as soldiers could well be. We soon got a chance to ship by small steamer to Hilton Head, and soon after shipped from there to New York on a large government transport, *The Star of the South.* On board also was the coffin containing the last remains of General Mitchel, being sent to his family and friends in Ohio.

We didn't stay long in New York. Commander Crosman had advised us to go immediately to Washington and personally see the Secretary of War, and lay all our facts before him. So we secured transportation orders to Washington, and kept on.

When we arrived in Washington, Mark took up temporary quarters at the Soldiers' Home, while I started out to find the commissary general's office, to get transportation for us to our regiment, after which we proposed calling at the War Department. I thoughtlessly started out without a pass, and hadn't gone far before I was confronted by a squad of nicely dressed provost guards, with bright new muskets, who "took me in," and not long after I had the mortification to see a prison door again closed on my liberty.

I didn't know at first how to go about it to get released. There was so much red tape about Washington military affairs that I knew I was liable to spend days in prison, if I went through the regulation course.

But a happy thought struck me. I had heard that President Lincoln was a very patient, kind man, and would give a hearing to a private soldier almost as readily as to an officer. I called for the officer in charge of the prison. He was a starchy, important kind of a man, who had, judging from appearances, never smelt Rebel powder, unless it might, perhaps, have been on a woman's face, and was disposed to treat me as such officials were too much in the habit of treating private soldiers. He impatiently demanded to know what I wanted.

I said, "Will you oblige me by sending me pen, ink and paper?"

He looked at me for a moment, and then condescendingly consented to the request.

I hastily wrote a note, about as follows:

Mr. President:—I have just arrived in the city, fresh from a long imprisonment in Atlanta, Georgia, from which place of confinement I took "French leave." The provost guards have imprisoned me here, because I was found without a pass, in which, I suppose, they did their duty. I know of no officer or friend in the city to whom I can apply for help. Can you do anything for me? If you can, you will greatly oblige your friend.

John A. Wilson
Of the 21st Ohio Volunteer Infantry

The messenger who took the note, which was addressed on the envelope, "A. Lincoln, President," hadn't been gone more than half an hour, until the prison door opened and the starchy officer called my name. I came forward, and a pleasant, gentlemanly civilian took me by the hand, at the same time handing the officer a written order for my release. The gentleman, who, I believe, was the President's private secretary, told me that Mr. Lincoln had requested that I come and see him, and that he would be glad to show me the way.

When we arrived at the White House, my escort said, addressing Mr. Lincoln, "Mr. President, this is Mr. Wilson, one of the Mitchel railroad raiders, who has just escaped from prison."

The President came forward and took my hand, much in the manner of a father receiving a long-missing son.

"Mr. Wilson," he said, "it's a pleasure to take you by the hand, and I thank God your life has been spared."

He then led me to a table where several gentlemen sat, to whom he introduced me, after which he showed me a seat. I was somewhat embarrassed, but I remember that Secretaries Seward and Chase were of the number. Mr. Seward, I recollect, seemed to be a serious, thoughtful old man, who said but little but listened attentively to the others. Mr. Lincoln sat down near me and showed as much interest in me as if I'd been an old and valued acquaintance. He congratulated me and my comrades for the spirit and devotion we'd shown, and the good luck which had enabled us to escape. He seemed perfectly familiar with all the details of our expedition—the cause of its failure, and the good results that could have arisen from its success.

I told the President that my business in coming to Washington was to see him or the Secretary of War, and ask them to intercede for those of the expedition still in captivity. Mr. Lincoln told me that Commander Crosman's dispatches had arrived at the War Department, and that steps had already been taken in behalf of the captives by Secretary Stanton. He said that not another man of them should be harmed if the power of the government could prevent it.

"When you go back to your regiment," said the President, "tell your comrades, and tell them to send word to the friends of those men of the expedition now imprisoned, that Secretary Stanton, and through him the government, has done, and is doing, and will continue to do, all that can be done to have them treated as regular prisoners of war, even if measures of retaliation are necessary."

As he shook hands with me, when I took my leave, Mr. Lincoln said, "Each member of your expedition shall have a commission, and if the Governor of Ohio doesn't give you a commission, Mr. Wilson, I'll give you a lieutenant's commission in the regular army."

A man was sent with me to the commissary general's office, where I secured passes and transportation for Mark and myself to go to our regiment, or to stop in Ohio until we received orders, as we saw proper. We decided to go right through to the Army of the Cumberland, stopping in Ohio only long enough to shake hands with our friends and to let them know we were alive.

We reached our old 21st Ohio in January, a few days after the battle of Stone River—December 31, 1862, through January 2, 1863. The men were camped near Murfreesboro, and only about twenty miles from Shelbyville, where we had left them nine months before. Our old comrades welcomed us back almost as though from the dead.

They weren't more rejoiced than we were, for after so many ups and downs, we felt about as much gratitude at being with our friends again as two fellows could well live through in one day, although we missed many comrades who were in new-made graves—along with General Joshua Sill and many more—on the bloody field of Stone River.

[*Alf Wilson*]

One of the pleasantest surprises in store was a meeting soon after with Captain David Fry, whom I'd supposed certainly dead, after seeing him go down—possum style, as it turned out—during our break from jail at Atlanta. What a change had come over the captain since I saw him—barehanded, starved, ragged and bony—grab Turner, the jailer, at the prison door and hold him with the firm grip of a giant.

Now as I saw the captain, he was robust, well-fed and soldierly, but in heart and character, the same man who had been our faithful comrade in prison. He kept on through the war with his Tennessee regiment—and, I believe, was on his way to becoming its colonel when last I saw him—and I know of few men for whom I entertain greater respect than Captain David Fry.

PITTENGER: That winter the six of us left in the prison—Bensinger, Buffum, Mason, Parrott, Reddick and I—were transferred to Richmond. On March 17, 1863, we were exchanged from Castle Thunder Prison there.

On March 28, soon after our arrival in Washington, we were taken in for an interview with Secretary of War Stanton. Stanton had lived for many years in my county town of Steubenville, Ohio, and I had seen him, though I could then claim no personal acquaintance. We were seated, after he had shaken each one of us warmly by the hand. We talked for a considerable time upon general topics—such as our impressions of the South and the Union men in it—and I was especially struck by his asking us how we had liked General Mitchel as a commander. When we spoke of him with enthusiasm, the Secretary seemed greatly pleased and said, "That's the way all his men talk about him."

Secretary Stanton told us that he had been aware of our expedition at the time, but had no accurate information of the fate of the party. His impression was that all had perished at first. On learning of the escape of the eight in October, he had made official inquiries of the Confederate government about us, threatening retaliation in case any more were put to death, and had endeavored to effect our exchange. He was very glad that these efforts had succeeded, and surprised us by saying, "You'll find yourselves great heroes when you get home."

Stanton seemed especially pleased with Parrott. He was the youngest of our number and of very quiet and simple manners. The Secretary gave him the offer of a complete education if he would accept it

—I understood him to mean at West Point. [Up to this time at least, by the testimony of his companions, Parrott hadn't had enough schooling to enable him to read or write.] Parrott answered that while the war lasted he didn't wish to go to school, but would rather go back and fight the Rebels who had used him so badly.

At this, Stanton smiled as if he greatly approved his spirit, and said to him, "If you want a friend at any time be sure to apply to me." Then, going into another room, he brought out a medal and handed it to Parrott, saying, "Congress has by a recent law ordered medals to be prepared on this model, and your party shall have the first to be given to private soldiers in the war."

EDITOR: Or to anyone. The medals given on this day by Secretary Stanton to the six exchanged raiders were the first awards of what has since become the nation's highest recognition for military valor: the Congressional Medal of Honor. Similar medals were later given the other surviving members of the party, all of them already back on active service—unmedaled—at the time of this award.

PITTENGER: Secretary Stanton then gave us a present of $100 each from the Secret Service Fund, and ordered all the money and the value of arms and property taken from us by the rebels to be refunded. Finding that we were all resolved to return to active service, he offered us commissions as first lieutenants in the regular army. We expressed a preference for the volunteer service. He promised to request Governor Tod of Ohio to give us equivalent commissions in our own regiments.

We had been invited to call upon the President the same day, and General Hitchcock accompanied us on this pleasant mission. A still greater crowd than at the War Office was awaiting admission; but as we came by appointment, we were conducted immediately to the private office of the President.

The office was very plainly furnished. There was a long table and some chairs, but scarcely anything else. Lincoln met us at the door, greeted us warmly and told us how much he had been interested in hearing of our adventures, and how glad he was that we had at last escaped from the hands of the enemy. We answered as well as we could. I remember telling him that we were very glad to see him, though we had been hearing a great many things not complimentary about him for the past year. He smiled, saying, "There are a good many people up here that say things about as bad of me."

While talking, Mr. Lincoln didn't keep one position, but shifted

[*Pittenger*]
from place to place, going from one to another of us, as he addressed each one with great courtesy. We ourselves made the first motion to leave. The President took the hand of each in both his own, saying again how thankful he was that we had been spared, and that he hoped we would find all our relatives living and well when we reached home. We left Mr. Lincoln, exceedingly proud of the honor he had conferred upon us. A furlough for sixty days was granted to us and an order given for government transportation to our homes.

The father of William Reddick had heard of his being still alive and in Richmond, and possessing abundant means, had started for Washington at once with the intention of trying to get a pass to go south in search of his son. Mr. Reddick arrived the day before we were ready to start for Ohio, and was in our company in the journey over the Baltimore & Ohio Railroad as far as Wheeling. He insisted upon buying for the whole party everything we could possibly eat on the way, and in the delight he took in the presence of his son we could see reflected what was in store for the rest of us.

When Bellaire on the Ohio River had been reached, the others took the road which carried them into the interior of Ohio, while I had to go up the valley to Steubenville, and from there on home for a welcome beyond description.

WOOD:

Murfreesboro, Tenn.
April 3, 1863

Lt. Ara Spafford

Sir:

During the month of February, J. A. Wilson and I were put on active duty in Company C and have been doing duty since. [In reference to possible reimbursement for expenses while away] I, Mark Wood, expended for a suit of citizen's clothes, revolver and other expenses incurred while traveling on the Andrews expedition, $125.

J. Alfred Wilson expended $15, money otherwise being furnished him by J. J. Andrews. Wilson expects no remuneration further than the above $15.

We certify the above to be a true and correct statement.

Mark Wood
J. Alfred Wilson
Members of Company C, 21st Regt.,
Ohio Vols., U. S. Army

Murfreesboro, Tenn.
April 12, 1863

Lt. Col. J. R. Paul,
Commissary of Subsistence, 14th Army Corps:

I beg leave to tender to you the circumstances and facts concerning a detachment of men sent from Shelbyville, Tenn., one year ago this April, with a view to collect if possible their loss in money and rations while absent. . . .

A resolution formed . . . to break jail at Atlanta was carried into effect by the surviving members of the party the evening of the 16th day of October, 1862. After being subjected to the severest of hardships, the following named persons finally succeeded in arriving safely to their regiments and companies at various times, with the loss of the sums set opposite their names:

Pvt. William Knight, Company E, 21st Ohio Vol. Inf.	$60
Sgt. Wilson W. Brown, Co. F, 21st O.V.I.	$29
Sgt. John R. Porter, Co. G, 21st O.V.I.	$30
Cpl. Mark Wood, Co. C, 21st O.V.I.	$125
Pvt. J. Alfred Wilson, Co. C, 21st O.V.I.	$15

[Dorsey, Hawkins and Wollam were of the 33d O.V.I. and accordingly not the responsibility of Colonel Neibling and the officers of the 21st.]

Others who were not among those who escaped have since arrived safely via Washington, D.C., and have been compensated for all their loss by the Secretary of War and assigned as a mark of honor a brevet lieutenancy and furloughed home for thirty days, a notice which is no doubt justly their due.

Therefore we, the officers of the 21st O.V.I. request most respectfully in consideration of the losses of the above-named enlisted men and trials they have undergone that they be compensated for said loss of private moneys and equipment and for rations not drawn.

Respectfully,

J. M. Neibling
Colonel, Commanding 21st Ohio Volunteer Infantry

(FIRST INDORSEMENT)

Commissary Department, 14th Army Corps,
April 20, 1863

Lt. Col. Flynt,
Assistant Adjutant General, 14th Army Corps:

This letter and the accompanying accounts are respectfully referred to you. I am satisfied of the correctness of the accounts. The men were sent from the division of General O. M. Mitchel while I was connected with it. Most of their comrades suffered death on the scaffold. These escaped by most daring measures, and I think it just that they should be paid for the loss of private property and also commutation of rations during the time of their absence from their commands.

J. R. Paul
Lieutenant Colonel and Commissary of Subsistence, 14th Army Corps

(SECOND INDORSEMENT)

HQ 14th Army Corps
Murfreesboro, Tenn.
April 20, 1863

Respectfully referred to Colonel Neibling to know if the men herein mentioned are as worthy of the compliment as those already complimented by the Secretary of War.

By command of Major General Thomas:

J. P. Willard,
Captain and Aide-de-Camp

(THIRD INDORSEMENT)

HQ 21st Ohio Volunteers
Murfreesboro, Tenn.
April 27, 1863

The within-named soldiers are as worthy if not more so than those complimented by the Secretary of War. They made their escape and endured unaccountable hardships and privations for weeks while in the enemy's country before reaching the Federal lines. A number of them also participated in the battle of Stone's River and behaved with great gallantry.

Very respectfully, your obedient servant,

J. M. Neibling
Colonel, Commanding 21st O.V.I.

(FOURTH INDORSEMENT)

HQ 14th Army Corps
Murfreesboro, Tenn.
April 29, 1863

Respectfully forwarded.

The within-named soldiers of the 21st O.V.I. appear from the accompanying statement of Colonel Neibling to be as worthy of remuneration and honorable mention for their losses and daring conduct while on the expedition referred to as their comrades who have already been so deservedly rewarded by the Secretary of War.

Geo. H. Thomas
Major General, U.S. Volunteers, Commanding

(FIFTH INDORSEMENT)

HQ Dept. of the Cumberland
Murfreesboro, Tenn.
May 1, 1863

Respectfully forwarded to the Adjutant General of the Army.

The Secretary of War having made a special case of men engaged with these in their enterprise, the accompanying papers are respectfully transmitted for his action.

W. S. *Rosecrans*
Major General, Commanding

(SIXTH INDORSEMENT)

Adjutant General's Office
May 12, 1863

Respectfully submitted to the Secretary of War.

The action of the Department alleged in the latter part of this letter is not of record in this office.

E. D. Townsend
Asst. Adjutant General

EDITOR: It isn't clear from the assistant adjutant general's comment whether he was scolding Secretary Stanton for keeping his files in his hat, or merely striking a blow on general principles for the normal viscosity of channels. Luckily—whatever his own first inclination may have been—he bucked it along.

EDWIN M. STANTON:

(SEVENTH INDORSEMENT)

War Department
May 21, 1863

The men referred to in (Colonel Neibling's] application will be placed upon the same footing as the other members of their party.

By order of the Secretary of War:

E. R. S. Canby
Brigadier General

Heading South 6

ALF WILSON: After rejoining my regiment, Mark Wood and I were detailed for detached duty. I remained at Fort Rosecrans, Murfreesboro, during most of the remainder of my term of enlistment, at the expiration of which I was discharged at Atlanta in 1864.

PITTENGER: After the expiration of my furlough at home, though still in poor health, I returned to the 2nd Ohio, which was again encamped at Murfreesboro.

I took part in the march from Murfreesboro toward Chattanooga, but finding my health so impaired that I wasn't able to endure the hardships of the campaign, I accepted a discharge for disability on August 14, 1863. In March of 1864, I was admitted to the Ministry in the Pittsburg Conference of the Methodist-Episcopal church, at its session at Barnesville, Ohio.

EDITOR: Except for Pittenger, all the surviving Andrews raiders remained in service for most or all of the war, and nearly all of them not recaptured fought the full way to Atlanta with their regiments. Since the long shot of a quick and possibly bloodless method of taking Chattanooga had failed, this time the raiders headed south the hard way—in uniform and with an army along. The line of attack was the same. It was over the Tennessee and along Stephen Harriman Long's original route through the Cherokee country, on the twisted tracks of Georgia's W. & A. Railroad, that the men of Generals George H. Thomas and William T. Sherman crunched their way in the side-slipping battles that were to take George Wilson's flag back to Atlanta.

WHITELAW REID: In the reorganization at Louisville in the fall of 1862, the 2nd Ohio Regiment was assigned to Rousseau's division. It took part in the battle of Perryville or Chaplin Hills on the 8th of October, losing in the action nearly forty per cent of all engaged. Captains [Alexander S.] Berryhill and Herrel, and twenty-seven enlisted men, were killed, and ninety officers and men, wounded.

On the 31st of December, 1862, in the battle of Stone River, the 2nd Ohio was closely engaged and suffered serious loss. Its colonel, John Kell, was killed at the head of the regiment; Major Maxwell was slightly wounded; Captain Hazlett, Lieutenants Chambers and Van Horn, and seven enlisted men, were also killed, and a large number of men wounded.

The division to which the regiment was attached had in the meantime been assigned to the 14th Army Corps, General George H. Thomas, in which command it remained up to Atlanta.

EDITOR: In the 21st Regiment, in the months to follow, Robert Buffum, Wilson Brown, Bill Knight, Elihu Mason and John Porter fought through some of the sharpest actions of the war.

WHITELAW REID: On the 24th of June, 1863, the 21st Ohio moved with the army upon the enemy at Tullahoma. On the 16th of August, it crossed the Tennessee River near Stevenson, and dragging its artillery and trains over Lookout Mountain by hand, it found the enemy at Dug Gap, Georgia, on the 11th of September.

Heavy skirmishing continued until the 19th, when the enemy was found in force on the line of Chickamauga Creek. The regiment immediately deployed into line of battle, under command of Lieutenant Colonel D. M. Stoughton, and opened a brisk fire upon the Rebels, which continued until night. Early the next morning (Sunday, September 20th) the battle was resumed. At eleven o'clock the 21st was posted on Horseshoe Ridge. Immediately it became fully engaged, and a severe contest resulted in the repulse of the enemy, not, however, without severe loss to the 21st. Lieutenant Colonel Stoughton had an arm fractured and soon after died. The command now developed upon Major A. McMahan.

By three o'clock in the afternoon the Nationals were forced back on the right and left by the greatly superior numbers under command of General Bragg, but the 21st, being armed with Colt's revolving rifles, continued to hold its position. The Rebels charged upon the regiment in this position five times without success. An hour before sundown a full Confederate battery was brought to bear upon it, inflicting severe damage. Under cover of the fire of this battery the Rebels charged again, but were met with a volley and a counter-charge, and the 21st continued to hold its position.

The scene at this time was horrible. The battery had set fire to the leaves and dry brush, and the dead and wounded were consumed by the fire. To remedy this was out of the question. To detain the Rebels, if possible, was all that could be expected while the troops of McCook's corps, which had been so severely crushed, could effect a retreat. The ammunition was now nearly exhausted, and a further supply couldn't be found nearer than a day's march distant. The cartridge boxes of the dead were searched and also the field hospitals for any that might have been carried there in the cartridge boxes of the wounded. By economy the regiment continued to fire until dark, when its last shot was expended. At this time the enemy had appeared upon the right and rear, and the regiment, now greatly reduced in numbers, was formed for one more desperate effort to hold the ridge. A charge was ordered by Major McMahan, and, though entirely without ammunition, the bayonet was applied with entire success. The enemy was forced back, leaving nine prisoners with the 21st Ohio.

The helpless condition of the regiment was discovered by the enemy in its inability to return their fire. It was now after dark, and, in a second attempt to push back the enemy with the bayonet, the 21st Ohio was overwhelmed, and Major McMahan and one hundred and fifteen of the officers and men of the command were captured. The 21st Ohio expended, in this battle, 43,550 rounds of Colt's fixed ammunition, and sustained a loss of one officer and fifty men killed, three officers and ninety-eight men wounded, and twelve officers and one hundred and four men captured.

EDITOR: Returning south with the 33d Ohio were Martin Hawkins, William Reddick, Daniel Allen Dorsey, John Wollam and Jacob Parrott—in the first brigade, of the first division, of the center of the army.

WHITELAW REID: On the reorganization of the Army of the Ohio at the beginning of November, 1862, under General W. S. Rosecrans and its rechristening as the Army of the Cumberland, the 33d Ohio had been placed in 1st Brigade, 1st Division, of General George H. Thomas' command. On December 26, the regiment moved out of Nashville toward Murfreesboro. At the battle of Stone River, it supported Loomis' Michigan battery, and rendered efficient service in checking the Rebels after they had broken through the National right.

The National army lay at Murfreesboro until June 24, 1863, when it moved on Tullahoma, and made the difficult march to Chattanooga and vicinity. About the 1st of September, the Chickamauga campaign opened. The 33d Ohio crossed the Tennessee River just above Bridgeport, marched over Sand and Lookout Mountains, and took part in the battle of Chickamauga on the 19th and 20th of September. The regiment went into action with 343 men and lost—in killed, wounded and missing—168 men.

EDITOR: Matching the stubborn courage of the men of the 21st and 33d—and of many other of the 14th Corps regiments engaged—the 2nd Ohio at Chickamauga lost 183 officers and men in killed, wounded and missing. Although the stand of dozens of rifle companies and batteries—on the pattern of the 21st on Horseshoe Ridge

[*Editor*]
—prevented a Union setback from developing into a rout and deservedly won for George H. Thomas the title of "The Rock of Chickamauga," the full two-day fight in the woods above Chickamauga Creek was a victory for the Confederate Army of the Tennessee. For weeks after it, the army that was to be taken from Rosecrans and assigned to Thomas was pinned within Chattanooga.

Two relief expeditions lifted the siege: a group of divisions under Hooker which made troop-hauling history by the speed of its rail trip from Virginia to Tennessee by way of Ohio and Kentucky; and a large force under Sherman which marched east from Mississippi.

Helping to get Sherman into action promptly and well-posted enough to throw the Confederacy on the defensive for nearly all the balance of the war was another ex-guest of Chattanooga jail-keeper Swims. Back in uniform and open again for any deal, his usual horse swapped for a canoe, Corporal Pike found himself out on his hardest and most important assignment of the war.

WILLIAM T. SHERMAN: Corporal James Pike, Company A, 4th Ohio Cavalry, in October, 1863, carried a message from General Grant to me at Iuka, Miss. He got a canoe at Whitesbury opposite Huntsville and came down the Tennessee, over Muscle Shoals—all alone for one hundred miles of river, every mile of which was picketed by the enemy, and reached me safely, as stated, at Iuka.

It was that message which hastened my movement at Chattanooga. The whole affair [was] highly creditable to the skill, courage and zeal of Corporal Pike.

DORSEY: Notwithstanding that I was in poor health, I remained in service until August 24, 1864, when I resigned my commission on a surgeon's certificate of disability. Before that, however, I had had the honor to participate in the battles of Chickamauga, Lookout Mountain, Missionary Ridge, Resaca, and some smaller affairs. I was anxious to get to Atlanta again, but the region of Burnt Hickory, or New Hope Church, saw the last of my service except some six weeks in the hospital on Lookout Mountain, and a short season after that on light duty in Chattanooga.

At the battle of Chickamauga, September 19 and 20, on Sunday afternoon, September 20, I received a slight wound of the right ear at the hands of a Confederate sharpshooter. The concussion dazed me for the moment, but resulted in no serious injury.

Lieutenants Jake Parrott and Bill Reddick fought in and came out of this great battle unharmed. Martin Hawkins, wounded during its course when hit in the back of the head by a piece of shell, got off the field in time to avoid capture when our forces fell back on Sunday evening.

EDITOR: Bill Bensinger of Company G of the 21st Ohio, reluctant to take a first lieutenant's commission that would lift him over the senior noncoms and second lieutenant then serving, had accepted instead the offer of a captaincy in one of the new Negro regiments Ohio and other states were finally authorizing in the summer of 1863. The necessary enabling papers for Bensinger took long weeks to process, and it was September—with the regiment in the broken country near Chattanooga, and a battle threatening within hours—before the commission came through. Bensinger postponed acceptance of his commission, looked to his rifle and stayed for Chickamauga.

Getting through the two days' carnage unwounded, Bensinger left from Chattanooga to report for his new privileges and responsibilities. The big man found more of both than he had looked for, and in unexpectedly pleasant form. In spare hours that could be pried from strenuous weeks of drilling and training the eager volunteers of his new company, Bensinger met, courted and married an East Tennessee girl who had continued to hold for the Union even with two brothers serving on the Confederate side.

Much of East Tennessee remained a no-man's land to the end of the war, subject to guerrilla forays by either side, and the bride-to-be lived in an exposed area a dozen miles beyond the picket lines of Bensinger's camp. On the wedding night, by the groom's report, the same two pistols that had helped guard the couple through the hazards of their courting meetings were tucked, loaded, under the nuptial pillow.

DORSEY: W. W. Brown, J. R. Porter, E. H. Mason and John Wollam—back with their companies—were all captured again on the second day of Chickamauga. Brown was wounded in the knee before being captured, and was exchanged with other wounded a few days after the battle. He was suspicious the enemy might recognize him, and hold him to answer the old charge of spying, hence he was exchanged under an assumed name.

EDITOR: After Sherman's, Hooker's and Thomas' forces had joined at the bend of the Tennessee, the break-out battles from Chattanooga came on November 23, 24 and 25 at Orchard Knob, Lookout Mountain and Missionary Ridge.

WHITELAW REID: The survivors of the 21st Regiment took part in the battle of Missionary Ridge, and thereafter remained in Chattanooga until January 1, 1864, when the 21st reenlisted as a veteran organization. The 24th of November, the brigade to which the 2nd was attached was sent to the assistance of General Hooker on Lookout Mountain, in his celebrated battle above the clouds. In the battle of Missionary Ridge, which occurred on the succeeding day, the regiment made its way to the crest with slight loss, and captured the colors of the 38th Alabama Volunteers. The 2nd, with its brigade, pursued the enemy to Ringgold, Georgia, at which place a halt was made.

On November 24, the 33d Ohio participated in the battle of Lookout Mountain, in which it lost heavily. On the 25th it took part in carrying Missionary Ridge. It here lost thirty-one men out of 200 engaged. The regiment followed the enemy to Taylor's Ridge, and there on the 27th had another fight. The day previous, at Graysville, it aided in the capture of five pieces of artillery and several hundred prisoners.

DORSEY: Just after Bragg's army had been driven from Chattanooga, Lieutenant Jake Parrott and myself were up on Lookout Mountain and had our pictures taken there looking out over all the battlefields round about—Chickamauga, Wauhatchie, Lookout Mountain and Missionary Ridge.

It is said that in the various battles around Chattanooga some fifty thousand men were killed and wounded. All of these were for the undisputed possession of the place Andrews and our raiders—if successful—might have helped get in a day with little or no loss of life. And if Chattanooga had then been taken and held, it's been maintained by many that there might never have had to be an Atlanta campaign.

After his capture at Chickamauga, Elihu Mason was actually held for a while by the Rebels at Atlanta on the old spying and engine-stealing charge, but was later taken to Richmond and finally exchanged. All the comrades taken except Wollam had received their lieutenant's commissions and were serving in that capacity when captured. Brown and Porter were later commissioned captains. (Hawkins didn't take a commission then or later, but served on to the last day of the war, as did Reddick and Bensinger.)

John Wollam was also held by the Rebels in Atlanta, on the original charge. A fellow soldier there at the same time—W. O. Johnson of the 3d Ohio Cavalry—later wrote of him:

> I was confined in the same prison with John Wollam at Atlanta in the winter of 1863. Comrade Wollam was a man of few words, but a braver or more patriotic soldier never enlisted in the cause of humanity and country. A ball and chain was fastened to his ankles, which made it very difficult to move about. I remember asking him why he was subjected to this barbarous treatment.
>
> "Prejudice," was his answer.

Late in February, 1864, on the day before that set for his trial, Wollam worked off his irons, broke out of prison and made good his escape. He rejoined his regiment at Chattanooga in April.

EDITOR: As experienced students of prison breaking and escape trips—Wollam and Porter were to show—the one-time raiders kept getting harder to hold.

PORTER: Shortly after I rejoined my regiment late in the fall of 1862, we started on the Stone River campaign. After a few months we again marched for Chattanooga. At Cave Spring, Ala., I was commissioned and mustered as second lieutenant of Company G, 21st Regiment, Ohio Volunteer Infantry, August 29, 1863.

I was captured at the battle of Chickamauga, September 20, in company with many more of the 21st. It was after dark, and we had run out of ammunition and were surrounded. Fearing that I might be recognized by some that knew us during our first imprisonment, I unbuckled and dropped to the ground my sword and belt, and having no other marks of a commissioned officer, gave a fictitious name and passed as a private soldier.

We were marched some distance from the battlefield that night. The next morning, after finishing our supply of rations, we were marched to Dalton, and after nine days' ride by rail, brought up at Richmond, Virginia. Here we were put in what was called Pemberton Building, nearly opposite Libby. We remained in Richmond until November 15. From Richmond we were taken to Danville, Va., where we remained during the following winter. Here we made several efforts to escape. We tried tunneling several times, but never

[*Porter*]
succeeded. The prisoners in one of the other buildings succeeded in tunneling out, and quite a number made their escape, consequently the guards were always on the alert for such things and searched the buildings every few days. During our stay here the smallpox broke out among us, and owing to bad treatment, many died.

We took our departure for Andersonville, Ga., May 15, 1864. When at Black Stock Station, S.C., I succeeded in making my escape from a train of cars in company with T. W. Harrison, a member of the 10th Wisconsin. After being out three days and nights we were recaptured, taken back to the station from which we had made our escape, put aboard the train and sent to Columbia, S.C. During our stay here, we tried tunneling again, but without success.

On the morning of June 29 we were again started for Andersonville. We arrived at Augusta, Ga., in the evening, and changed cars for Millen. Soon after leaving Augusta it became dark, and as there was no light in the car, we proceeded to cut our way out by sawing a board off in the bottom of the car with a table knife with teeth filed in the back for a saw. We succeeded in getting a hole through the bottom of the car large enough to crawl out at by nine o'clock, and as soon as the train stopped, we rolled out.

This was the night of June 29, 1864. We concluded to travel in a northwestern direction and strike the Federal lines somewhere between Dalton and Marietta, as we knew that General Sherman had reached Marietta on his way south. When we escaped we had two days' rations, this being the only bread we had during the journey, which was twenty-six days and nights. We traveled altogether at night depending mostly on blackberries and Irish potatoes for food. We were provided with a blanket each, one gallon coffeepot, and plenty of salt and matches, so we could boil our potatoes. We once got a goose, and had a regular feast on goose and potatoes. Occasionally we would get some apples for dessert. Having a pretty good knowledge of the country, we made good time. During our journey we encountered but one person. We had many streams to cross, but they were low at that time of the year.

On the morning of the twenty-sixth day out, we hunted a resting place as usual, expecting to hide for the day. We had been in our retreat but a short time, when we were aroused by a train whistle, and learned we had brought up near the railroad. We gathered up our traps and were soon upon the railroad—the same W. & A. line we had tried to break up better than two years before.

As the train had passed a short time before, we started for a water station that was in sight, and boarded there the next train that came along. We rode it to Marietta, where we reported to the provost marshal, who ordered us to General Thomas at the front. It was now the 25th of July, and Sherman's army was in front of Atlanta. We took the first train that came south, and were soon at General Thomas' headquarters. After hearing a full detail of our capture, imprisonment and escape, he promised us each a furlough to go home. We then started for our regiments, and were soon with our old comrades after an absence of over ten months.

Following a leave of absence for thirty days, I again joined my regiment (after the capture of Atlanta), and took part in Sherman's campaign to the sea, having charge of a party of foragers on that march. I was mustered out of service at Goldsboro, N.C., March 31, 1865.

EDITOR: Of the two men who had done the most to recover the *General* on April 12, 1862, Anthony Murphy by 1863 was on new duties with the Montgomery & West Point Railroad in Alabama. His enforced stays in Alabama for varying periods helped make possible a revealing glimpse of the growing pressure on Confederate rolling stock, along with an incidental wartime style note, left by his wife Adelia—a young woman increasingly proud, as the war wore on, of her kinship with a cavalry general whom even Mrs. John Morgan could respect: South Carolina's Wade Hampton.

ADELIA MCCONNELL MURPHY: I made one trip over to Montgomery, Ala., during the war, and when I returned, I came home in a freight car that had been filled with lime. I was wearing a handsome black brilliantine coat, and the lime ruined it. A few days after my return home, one of my children was born. In Montgomery I had had the pleasure of meeting the wife of General J. H. Morgan of Kentucky. She wore the tallest hat I ever saw. In those days the ladies made the crowns on their hats as high as possible, and often heightened them by inserting pieces of pasteboard, which were covered by the trimming.

WHITELAW REID: In the reconnaissance southward to Buzzard's Roost, in February, 1864, the 2nd Ohio was in the advance, and developed the strength of the enemy's position before Dalton. In May the regiment formed a portion of Sherman's force for the Atlanta campaign, and on the 14th of that month, at Resaca, suffered heavily. The 2nd Ohio then moved with the division through Georgia to the Chattahoochee River, and took part in the battle at Peachtree Creek, July 21, where Lieutenant John W. Thomas was killed—the last man of the regiment to offer up his life for the cause.

The 21st Ohio moved forward, March 6, to Ringgold, Ga., from which point it moved, May 7, with Sherman's grand army upon the campaign to Atlanta.

In May, 1864, the 33d Ohio Regiment joined in the drive for Atlanta. During that campaign it participated in the battles of Rocky Face Ridge, Resaca, Pumpkin Vine Creek, Kenesaw Mountain, crossing of the Chattahoochee, Peachtree Creek, and in the battles around Atlanta and Jonesboro. The aggregate number of officers and men killed and wounded in this campaign was approximately 170.

EDITOR: As Jacob Parrott, Bill Knight, Martin Hawkins, Alf Wilson, Mark Wood and many thousands more of the Union Army of the Cumberland came trudging south, however slowed by the defiant stands skillfully set up by General Joseph E. Johnston, the women of Atlanta had little attention to spare for the wonders of peak-topped millinery. Like many young mothers, Adelia Murphy was cutting and sewing soldiers' uniforms, and applying herself to service with the Hospital Relief Society. And the chief freight hauled south by the W. & A. these days was no longer cotton, corn and Tennessee bacon.

ADELIA MURPHY: The women of Atlanta had hot soups and coffee always ready to meet the incoming trains that brought the sick and wounded to the hospitals. My distributing point was at a building at the corner of Alabama and Pryor streets. I've seen hundreds of half-starved, sick Confederate soldiers and Yankee prisoners brought there and our women were always ready to minister to them with nourishing hot drinks—Yankees as well as our own boys, as far as most of us could manage it.

EDITOR: While the men under General George Thomas fought their way to Atlanta—biting off their chew of the W. & A. line each day, as the process was to be described, till they had it all—William Allen Fuller was still throwing himself strenuously into the service of his railroad, governor and state. Commissioned a captain in the Georgia militia by Governor Brown, Fuller in the hard days of 1864 became one of the governor's chief reliances in preserving the road's diminishing rolling stock and the archives of Georgia itself.

LOUIS L. PARHAM: In 1864, when the Federals had gained nearly full control of the W. & A. Railroad, Captain Fuller by order of the governor organized the white railroad force into a company which took charge of the entire rolling stock and other property belonging to the road, and removed them to places of safety. The archives of the state were later entrusted to his company's care and protection, and for the remainder of the war these [in one famous instance, along with Mrs. Brown's milch cow and a hastily pulled crop of cabbages from the governor's garden patch] were removed from place to place under the direction of the governor, and thereby kept secure from capture by the Federals. When hostilities ceased, Fuller's command returned the archives intact to their former and proper place.

WHITELAW REID: The 2nd Ohio Regiment remained in front of Atlanta until August 1, 1864, when orders were received to march to Chattanooga, preparatory to mustering out. The regiment was honorably discharged in Columbus, Ohio, on October 10, 1864.

EDITOR: With the cutting at Jonesboro of the Georgia Central line to Macon, its last supply line, Atlanta became indefensible by the forces left to General Hood, and on the morning of September 2, 1864, Sherman's regiments entered the city. Among much other military property taken over, they found in the railroad yards, rammed into a string of still smoking ammunition cars, an only lightly damaged engine called the *General*.

ROBERT SELPH HENRY: The War between the States was the first railroad war. The South had no other communication of consequence, with harbors blockaded and inland rivers controlled and patrolled by Union gunboats, but it did have two "interior" lines of railroad connecting its east and its west. So long as those lines [and the line connecting them, Georgia's W. & A.] could be held and kept open, the South could mobilize its strength and supply its armies. The loss of Chattanooga cut off one, the line through the valley of upper East Tennessee and southwest Virginia to Lynchburg and Richmond. The capture of Atlanta cut the second, from Mobile to Montgomery, through Atlanta, to Charleston, Wilmington and Richmond.

The holding of the key positions on these two lines more effectively dismembered the Confederacy than even the loss of the Mississippi River. Between the two great sections of the South, there remained but one roundabout and feeble line of rail communication, a collection of end-to-end branch roads, which did not always fit. With

[*Robert Selph Henry*]
Chattanooga and then Atlanta gone, the power of resistance went out of the South; only the spirit and the will remained.

DORSEY: After our army had taken Atlanta, the remains of our seven comrades who had been hanged together—Campbell, Robertson, Ross, Scott, Shadrach, Slavens and George Wilson—were discovered by Reuben Slavens, brother of Samuel, and others of his company. Later, these were disinterred, taken to Chattanooga, and reburied in the national cemetery there, the seven [eight, when Andrews' bones were found and brought to join them twenty-five years later] placed lying together in a semicircle.

EDITOR: The fall of Atlanta, Sherman's start for the sea, and the increasing pressure on Richmond seemed undeniable evidence in the fall of 1864 that the armies of the Confederacy could no longer dangerously take the attack. Hood and the half-strength army extracted from Atlanta promptly and astonishingly struck north for middle Tennessee, Kentucky, and the Ohio. By mid-December, the Union divisions of General George H. Thomas defending Tennessee were under serious siege in Nashville.

As unruffled as ever, Thomas methodically prepared his counterattack. On December 15, helped by a needed thaw, the Union army moved out of Nashville and smashed Hood's divisions in the single battle of the war that resulted in the rout of a major Confederate army, although a heroic seventy-five-mile running fight by a five-thousand-man covering force under Nathan Bedford Forrest enabled the remnants of Hood's invaders to get back across the Tennessee—the rear guard "ragged, bloody, without food and without hope," as Thomas reported of them, "but undaunted, firm and doing their work to the last."

As Brown, Buffum, Hawkins, Knight, Parrott, Porter, Reddick and Wollam of the original Andrews party were nearing the Georgia coast at the mouth of the Ogeechee with Sherman, Bensinger and the new soldiers of his Negro company had held and taken vital ground during the two-day fight at Nashville in some of the most murderous action of a war that wasn't lacking in it at any time. During one thirty-minute attack alone, death or a disabling wound cut down every fourth man of Bensinger's black regiment.

WHITELAW REID: The 33d Ohio followed Hood as far as Villanow, Ga., in his last mad movement toward Nashville, after which the regiment accompanied General Sherman in its march to the sea, and in the campaign up through the Carolinas. At Bentonville, N.C., it suffered severely, rendering there its last payment of lives to the cause of the Union. It then made the triumphant march through the Rebel capital to Washington.

In March and April, 1865, the 21st Ohio fought north through the Carolinas. After the surrender of General Joseph E. Johnston's forces, the regiment returned to Washington by way of Richmond.

ALF WILSON: Each member of our party, by act of Congress, received a Congressional Medal of Honor. We were also given $100 extra pay.

My story has been a longer one than I intended, but it still hasn't told a millionth part of what this war cost our people. I was revengeful once, and have hunted those who wronged me, and murdered my comrades, with violent intent. I hope I'm not unforgiving today and I'll hope the deadly strife which ceased at Appomattox Court House will never appear again, under any other form.

WHITELAW REID: The 21st and 33d Ohio—before being mustered out of service—were among the veteran regiments that took part in the grand review of the Union armies at Washington, on May 26, 1865.

EDITOR: There was a new President in the reviewing stand on that May 26th: Andrew Johnson from David Fry's East Tennessee town of Greenville. The life of the man who had called the 2nd, the 21st, the 33d and the men of all the regiments to the Union's successful defense had been added to the price of victory six weeks before.

REDDICK: I would just say that I served through the war as second lieutenant of my old Company B, 33d Ohio Volunteer Infantry. I was discharged July 12, 1865, at Louisville, Ky.

I have since the war fished a little in all kinds of labor, from farming to chopping cordwood, making railroad ties, peddling notions, book agencies, and township clerk, and am now back to honest clodhopping, which latter I hope will furnish me my daily bread for the remainder of my life.

Over the Jordan 3

EDITOR: The man known as James J. Andrews was nearly thirty before presently available history places him as even being alive. Three years later, a Cotton Kingdom cotton rope ended both that life and the chance that he himself might leave a fuller record of it than we have. In the second section of this book, a try will be made at adding some further guesses to the sparse bundle of intertwined fable, speculation and shreds of fact that make up the existing biography of the man who led twenty men to the winning of twenty Congressional Medals of Honor. Here, we'll still hold to the available record as it stands.

During the four June days at Chattanooga while the Union agent was preparing to die, as Dorsey remembered, Andrews put in some of his time writing letters. At least one of these letters—to Andrews' old Flemingsburg friend, D. S. McGavic—got carried across the lines and was eventually delivered to its intended readers.

DORSEY: Some days or weeks after Andrews' execution—near Stevenson, Ala.—William Hunter Myers, a sergeant of Company K, 33d Ohio, says that a citizen who came through the lines to the Union camp handed him a package of letters quietly, with the request that they be handed to the officers. The man then disappeared without further explanation. Myers knew of and had an interest in the Andrews expedition, since he had been the man originally picked from Company K to go on it, although later replaced by Jacob Parrott when it proved Myers wasn't then in good enough physical shape to go.

PITTENGER: On inquiry by Myers, the man carrying the letters said he was a fireman on the Georgia state railroad, and that he had so been employed for several years. His native place was Hagerstown, Maryland, however, and he said he had stood the ways of the Rebels as long as he could, and was now anxious to get back home. Myers asked the railroad man how he came in possession of the papers, but the man declared he didn't want to say. He was sent under guard to Huntsville, from which place he was able to return eventually to Maryland.

One of the letters the stranger carried—the one to Mr. McGavic—was placed in the mails at Louisville, and reached Flemingsburg in August of 1862, two months after it was written.

EDITOR: It isn't known whether Andrews wrote and tried to send out from the Chattanooga prison a farewell letter to Elizabeth Layton. If written, this message was intercepted or lost en route, as no direct word to her was delivered.

The letter to D. S. McGavic, appearing below, was entered at probate and is still recorded in Fleming County records as a will. McGavic and another trustee, a court clerk, Dudley, were believed by most of their fellow townsmen to have done their best with the trust imposed—placing out as directed, to various needy families, the $1,200 that had been on deposit in the Flemingsburg branch of the Bank of Louisville at least since February 17, 1862—although Andrews' hard luck held, even in this attempt to leave a few continuing cups of kindness for those of his one-time neighbors who might strike times as thin as the lean stretches he had often known himself. The principal was scattered and lost beyond hope or recovery within a few years and resulted eventually in no more than a series of sterile law suits.

The "Mr. Hawkins" of the postscript is Martin Hawkins of the raiding party. With Porter or Parrott, he later hunted out the new black trunk at Louisville and delivered it as requested to Elizabeth Layton. Unaccompanied as it was by an explanation, the yawningly empty trunk formed a wry final comment on the relationship of James Andrews and his one-time fiancée.

"A most singular bequest from a lover," Elvira Layton—Elizabeth's sister—was to term it years later. "And in itself, nearly enough to kill her."

No information has yet been turned up on the degree or duration of the romantic interest Andrews may have taken—or aroused—in the Misses Kate Wallingford and Nannie Baxter, particularly named of "the young ladies of Flemingsburg" in his letter. What can be established—chiefly through the extensive and cheerfully undertaken research of Miss Mary Pickett DeBell of Flemingsburg and Mrs. L. B. Reed of Maysville—is that neither young belle proved inconsolable, possibly a reflection of the current supply of young soldiers who kept on finding all through the war that the ladies of Flemingsburg were as amiable and clever as Andrews had reported the army's opinion of them to be at its beginning. On February 5, 1864, Nancy Baxter married Julius Herrick, a transplanted Vermont schoolteacher. Kate Wallingford, daughter of the Hiram Wallingfords, was the chief trophy of war Union Colonel Ira Grover brought back—as Mrs. Grover—to his home in Indiana.

There seems no way of determining now at which points in his final letter Andrews may have been writing at double or triple layers of meaning. In irons and under sentence of death at the time of its composition, Andrews must have understood—as Dorsey suggests—that the words written would probably have to pass official inspection before being allowed to be sent from Chattanooga. Andrews seemed aware of these possible Confederate eyes over his shoulder, at least in the passage where he insists that his men were "detailed"—thereby confirming the defense tactic agreed on as most likely to help get the men off lightly—and he may have been mindful that some of the Christian resignation expressed wouldn't have operated against such late impulses to mercy as might have happened to move his custodians.

To McGavic—or to the Union officers through whose hands Andrews may have hoped the letter would pass—the request to do exactly in "other matters" as the agreed-on "instruction" called for, may as easily have been meant to be a signal touching off rescue efforts as an order to dispose of Andrews' bank deposit. For an example of hope of this kind, we know that Andrews made an unsuccessful attempt during imprisonment at Chattanooga to enlist some sort of help from the merchant, Whiteman, who had been his partner in the blockade-running transactions. If such a distress call were intended, however, the message got to no one who could usefully decipher it in the short time Andrews had left to live.

The contents of the letter as a whole make it more likely that the simplest explanation of most of its passages is the most believable one: that Andrews, tired and beaten, within two days of a clearly approaching death, was allowing himself the rare luxury of putting down much of the truth as he saw it. Much of the truth and, possibly, very little but the truth, although not yet quite all the truth.

One notable omission—among others less clearly provable, to be dealt with later in this book's *Postscript* section—can be found in this account of the events leading to the cul-de-sac of Swims' dungeon. Andrews speaks of the use of dogs—when the spelling is thinned out—as being responsible for his first capture. He leaves out what even the leader of his captors thought to be the chief and much more creditable reason for his being taken: loyalty to his own men. When Andrews and Marion Ross were being chased by Dr. Park's mounted posse, the doctor was convinced, and later was to say, that

Andrews was "well in the lead, and could no doubt have escaped, but returned to his exhausted companion."

Whatever Andrews failed to include in his letter—or succeeded in packing in—he seems to have arranged for its eventual transmission by a courier who may have been a friend of the Union-favoring W. & A. engineer with whom a connection had been attempted on the first eight-man raid in March. Andrews dated his message—here given in exactly its original spelling, although punctuation has been supplied—from Chattanooga on Thursday of his last week, two days before the final train ride to Atlanta and the further shore of his self-sought Jordan.

ANDREWS:

Chattanooga, Tenn.
June 5, 1862

D. S. McGavic, Esq., Flemingsburg, Ky.

Dear Sir:— You will doubtless be surprised to hear from me from this place & more surprised to hear that I am to be executed on the 7th inst. for attempting to capture and run a train of cars from the Western and Atlantic R.R. to Huntsville, Ala., for the youse of General Mitchel.

I had a party of twenty-one detailed men from the 2, 21 & 33 Ohio Regiments with me. We succeeded in getting possession of the train and traveled with it some eighty or eighty-five miles, when on account of one extra train's beeing on the road, we ware compelled to abandon the train. The party scattered and trying to mak our way back on foot. The whole party, however, ware captured.

I was taken on the 14th of April. I am satisfied that I could easily have got away had they not put a pack of dogges on my trail. It was impossible to elude them. I was tried by court-marshall and rec'd my sentence on the last day of May inst., one week before the time set for my execution.

On Monday morning, the 2nd, I made an attempt to escape. I succeeded in geting out of prison and ran by the guard, they shooting at me but not hiting me. The whole country was immediately swarmed with soldiers. I succeeded in eluding them until Tuesday, about two o'clock, when I was recaptured & will be executed on Saturday.

The sentence seames a hard one for the crime proven against me, but I suppose the court that tride me thought otherwise. I am now calmly submitted to my fate and have been earnestly engaged in preparing to meet my God in peace and I have found that piece of mind and tranquility of sole that even astonish myself. I never supposed it possible that a man could feel so entire a change under simelar circumstances.

How I would like to have one hour's chatt with you, but this I shall never have in this life, but hope and prey we may meet in Heaven where the troubles and trials of this life never enter. What the fate of the balance of the party will be, I am unable to say, but I hope they will not share the fate of their leader. If they ever return, some two or three of them will call on you and the rest of the friends, and I hope you will receive them kindly. They are noble fellows and will give you a full history of the affair.

Please acquaint my friend of my fate. I shall try to wright to some two or three more before my execution. Tell J. B. Jackson should there be any little claims that I neglected to settle, to pay them and keep the horse. I don't think there are any, but there may be. In regard to other matters, do exactly as instruction before I left.

I have rec'd no letters from Flemingsburg since I left. I wrote several, but never rec'd any answers.

Please read this letter to Mrs. Eckels and tell her that I have thought of her kindness many times and that I hope we may meet in Heaven, where we shall enjoy the presence of the Lord forever. Give my kindest regards to Mr. Eckels, also. According to the course of nature it will not be long until we shall meet in that happy country. Blessed thought.

Remember me also to the young ladies of Flemingsburg, especially to Miss Kate Wallingford & Miss Nannie Baxter.

Hoping we may meet in that better country, I bid you a long and last farewell.

J. J. Andrews

Chattanooga, Tenn.
June 5, 1862

D. S. McGavic, Esq., J. B. Jackson, Mrs. Sarah Eckels,
Flemingsburg, Fleming Co., Ky.

You will find one trunk and one black valice. The valice has my name in read letters on the end. The other had my name on a paper pasted on the end. These are at the City Hotel, Nashville, in care of the old porter on third floor. These, with contents, I present to you.

Mr. Hawkins, you will find at the Louisville Hotel a large ladies' trunk. No mark on it and [it] is entirely empty. Please take it to Mr. Lindsey's near Mill Creek church, on the Maysville & Flemingsburg pike and request him to present it to Miss Elizabeth J. Layton for me and much oblige,

J. J. Andrews

EDITOR: On the night of April 6, 1862, in Shelbyville, after learning that he was to go on the Andrews expedition, Sam Slavens, the father of the three sons aged five, three and one back in Ohio, had put a brief postscript to the letter written earlier that Sabbath day to his wife Rachel. It perhaps can stand as a final word from—and fair sample of the character of—the seven young Union men who answered Lincoln's call of 1861 and followed Andrews to death in 1862 by Confederate order.

SLAVENS:

Shelbyville, Tenn.
April 6, 1862

P.S.

Dear Wife Rachel:

Since I wrote this morning I received your kind letter dated Feb. 18th, and was sorry to hear that you weren't very well, and sorry to think that the children will have the measles when you are by yourself. If I was at home it would be all right, but as it is I cannot help you. You will have to do the best you can until I get home, which I hope will not be long.

I don't want you to give yourself any uneasiness, any more than you can help, about me; but if anything happens to me that we never meet again on earth, I hope we will meet in heaven. Life is uncertain in war. Train up our babies the way they should go. Give them all the education you can, but live as comfortably as you can under the present circumstances. I know that you will have your hands more than full if the boys get the measles.

I would like to be there to help you to take care of them the best in the world, but all I can do is to wish you well, and think of you, which is very often.

Good-bye.

Samuel Slavens

POSTSCRIPT

DANIEL ALLEN DORSEY: It's easy to look back and see our mistakes.

KARL VON CLAUSEWITZ: Three-fourths of the things on which action in war is based lie hidden in the fog of greater or less uncertainty. War is the province of chance. In no other sphere of human activity has such a margin to be left for this intruder, because none is in such constant contact with it on every side.

WILLIAM PITTENGER: It's easier to imagine what might have been done, than actually to do it, even if circumstances were repeated.

The Story of a Story 2

History, among other things, is a general record put together from selected accounts of assorted events of which any record at all happens to have been made to start with. The form and force of its initial report can affect widely the chances of a given event's inclusion in the lasting register. One summary and appraisal—the Atlanta *Southern Confederacy* news story of April 15, its second one on the chase—threw the Andrews story into history with a momentum it was never to lose.

For its chances of being marked and remembered, the Andrews raid had the great advantage of taking place on the Georgia-owned W. & A. railroad at the time it did. From the start of the war, Governor Brown had been squaring off with the Confederate authorities at Richmond over the control of his state-owned rolling stock. Cars and locomotives lent early in the war to help get military supplies to Virginia, the governor complained, had come back damaged if at all. In September of 1861, after refusal by Brown of a War Department request for six W. & A. engines and seventy boxcars, Confederate transportation chief W. S. Ashe suggested that seizure powers might have to be invoked. Blasting back to Richmond came an indignantly clear expression of the Confederacy's favorite doctrine of local supremacy:

"If you seize our cars or engines," Brown had wired Richmond, "I shall by military force, if necessary, make counter-seizures."

Georgian touchiness as to Confederate War Department designs on W. & A. property make it by no means improbable—despite lack of mention of the point in Atlanta accounts then or later—that until hitting the first track break that Saturday morning, the angry energies of Conductor Fuller and the others may have been directed not so much toward overtaking supposed Rebel deserters or Yankee raiders as catching up with fellow Confederates believed to be attempting an informal engine-requisitioning coup in the interests of Richmond.

Even after the fall of Fort Pulaski and the first news of Huntsville, Governor Brown himself—had he been at Big Shanty watching the vanishing *General*—might as easily have thought of a Richmond-inspired impressment as a Union raid. Barely two weeks before, a bill had been introduced in the Confederate Congress providing that all Southern rail lines be placed firmly under central military control and all railwaymen, including station agents and conductors, put in the Confederate army; and calling for the "interchange of cars under public control." Brown and Georgia's legislative spokesman Augustus Wright were hotly fighting the proposed controls as completely "subversive of" Georgia's sovereignty. A vote on the measure was coming up on the 17th, five days after the attempted cutting of the W. & A.

Patriotic as they were, the editors of the *Southern Confederacy*—George H. Adair and J. Henley Smith—at Atlanta couldn't have been unaware of the pending rail control threat at Richmond when they settled themselves for the second processing of the startling information given them by Murphy and Fuller on their return to Atlanta. As supporters of Governor Brown, it's more likely than not that the editors shared the governor's hostility to the general provisions of the proposed measure—as on the 17th it was to prove that most Confederate legislators did—although in the story of the raid it was made clear that the *Confederacy* would welcome restrictions of passenger movement even to adoption of a passport system.

The issue the paper could join the governor on wholeheartedly was that of rousing Georgia. While even the armies scarcely realized the full nature of the war until the implications of Shiloh became plain, the Southern people as a whole were still more given to the easy-going ways of peace than of war, as confirmed by the case of the raiders' penetration south. What too many Georgians weren't realizing—in the paper's view, as seen in its stated anxiety about bridges, an unguarded bacon warehouse and other points—was that there was a war on.

Had the editors played down the Union raid as a casually mounted threat of little importance, they might have left Governor Brown with the embarrassment of explaining at Richmond—in the week of the vote on the proposed taking over of the railroads by the army—not so much how the *General* had eventually been recaptured, as how Brown's civilian hands had been so careless as to let the locomotive be taken from them in the first place. In this case the irresponsibility of Georgian railroadmen, rather than the dangers of Yankee daring, might have drawn most attention. As well, if the raid were shrugged off as an interesting but foolish attempt by the Lincolnites, the paper would have little chance of jolting the carefree bacon warehouse guard mentioned—"sometimes seen off duty . . . fully long enough for an incendiary to burn the house he watches"—or anyone else, into realizing that this was a time for taking off coats and backing up the Georgian boys out with the armies.

Given the full situation—plus the paper's declared stand against a misguided "reticence of the press," since the enemy was "passing among us freely" and getting "all the news he needed" in any case—there were almost no persuasive reasons for the editors' holding back on the story. Among the half-dozen good ones for playing it up was the simple—and probably controlling—consideration that it was about as solidly exciting a local story as a working newspaperman could ever hope to have dropped in his lap. It had beginning, middle and end; shock, suspense and triumph; and the squeezed-out eleventh-hour triumph was of theirs and the readers' side.

Editors Adair and Smith of the *Confederacy* were excellent newspapermen of a day when understating a story would have been ranked nearly with pieing it in galleys. They sorted out what they had heard from Fuller, Murphy and such other sources as they had had time to find and listen to, dipped vigorous pens in ink, and wrote the story to the hilt:

Southern Confederacy, Atlanta, April 15, 1862:

THE GREAT RAILROAD CHASE—THE MOST EXTRAORDINARY AND ASTOUNDING ADVENTURE OF THE WAR—THE MOST DARING UNDERTAKING THAT YANKEES EVER PLANNED OR ATTEMPTED TO EXECUTE.

Since our last issue we have obtained full particulars of the most thrilling railroad adventure that ever occurred on the American continent, as well as the mightiest and most important in its results, if successful, that has been conceived by the Lincoln Government since the commencement of this war. Nothing on so grand a scale has been attempted, and nothing within the range of possibility could be conceived that would fall with such a tremendous crushing force upon us, as the accomplishment of the plans which were concocted and dependent on the execution of the one whose history we now proceed to narrate. . . .

To make the matter more complete and intelligible, we will take our readers over the same history of the case which we related in our last, the main features of which are correct, but are lacking in details, which have since come to hand. We will begin at the breakfast table of the Big Shanty Hotel, at Camp McDonald, on the W. & A. R.R., where several regiments of soldiers are now encamped. The morning mail and passenger train had left here at 4 A.M. on last Saturday morning as usual. . . .

EDITOR: The Atlanta *Confederacy* narrative appraisal was the forerunner and solid foundation of all the legend to follow. It's possible that the actual raiders, packed dejectedly in their cell at Chattanooga, first saw in its bold-colored sweep the outlines of a far more heroic role in the war than they had realized themselves to have played. Pittenger was allowed to see the story there while held out away from the others, and managed to pass a copy on in to them. For him, even more than for most of his companions, the larger-than-life mirror of the *Confederacy* columns must have had a profound effect. He was to keep a copy of it to the day of his exchange eleven months later.

Alf Wilson and Mark Wood gave the country its first direct word from the raiders on November 15, 1862, through the Key West *New Era* after their escape down the Chattahoochee and to the Federal squadron in the Gulf. Excerpts from this were reprinted in Ohio papers, and the short narrative comprised part of the pamphlet "Ohio Boys in Dixie" which was published in the following year. In November and December of 1862, newspaper accounts were printed of the successful escapes of the Dorsey-Hawkins team and of Wollam and Porter. Knight and Brown were back as well in November of that year, although for some months this news didn't seem to be generally available. Pittenger, writing the following summer, wasn't sure even then that Knight had survived, although he was eventually to find him —as Knight himself took pleasure in pointing out—the "livest dead man he ever saw."

It was the report on March 27, 1863, of Judge Advocate General Joseph Holt to Secretary of War Stanton after the exchange of Parrott, Buffum, Pittenger, Bensinger, Reddick and Mason that gave the raid story the second great lift toward its permanent status. This was based on the depositions of five of the exchanged prisoners but was largely the work of Pittenger, the others chiefly speaking in confirmation of his presentation of the story. Pittenger, the one-time Steubenville *Herald* correspondent, had recognized the Atlanta *Confederacy* treatment for the convenient masterpiece it was, and it was the citing of this Confederate authority, more than any other one factor, that made it easy for Holt to accept Pittenger's assessment of the importance of the expedition.

The audacious nature of the nearly successful Andrews exploit offered a long-needed psychological answer to such swashbuckling Southern feats as Stuart's cavalry ride around all of McClellan's army, and the *Confederacy*-attested form in which this report of it came made it doubly acceptable. That the soldiers being honored were from Ohio didn't hurt the case with Ohioan Secretary Stanton, but the Congressional Medals of Honor given were probably won at the moment Judge Holt completed his report.

As Adair and Smith had brandished the astonishing Andrews threat as a means of alarming and arousing Georgia, Holt saw the matching usefulness of the story as an inspiration for the North. The Kentucky-born attorney had caught the full *Confederacy* swing, and hedged no more than his Atlanta counterpart had.

JUDGE JOSEPH HOLT: The expedition itself, in the daring of its conception, had the wildness of a romance, while in the gigantic and overwhelming results which it sought, and was likely to accomplish, it was absolutely sublime. [As] the editor [of the *Southern Confederacy*] says: "The mind and heart sink back appalled. . . . It is not by any means certain that the annihilation of Beauregard's whole army at Corinth would have been so fatal a blow to us as would have been the burning of the bridges at that time by these men. . . ."

EDITOR: Five months later, after seeing the Holt report in the "Official Gazette" of July 21, General Don Carlos Buell wrote the War Department and noted sourly that he didn't consider the raid —in its objectives or results—quite as sublime as it had been painted, but the general was commenting on the first unsuccessful eight-man raid he had authorized, apparently unaware that a second mission had gone out, and by this time the raiders' story was under too great a head of steam to be stopped.

Pittenger, after leaving the army in August of 1863, published his 288-page story of the raid and its aftermath, *Daring and Suffering,* in October of that year. Included in it verbatim, in nineteen book-length pages, was the Atlanta *Confederacy* account, again the most persuasive exhibit in the book. In the pages of *Harper's* magazine and elsewhere, before the war's end, the date April 12, 1862, was gaining acceptance as a day marking more than the first anniversary of the war.

In the postwar years, after Alf Wilson had added his "Adventures" in 1880, and Knight, Porter and others had put out briefer accounts in newspapers, Pittenger expanded his story—adorning it with such touches as the burning boxcar being pushed from the nearly blazing covered bridge—and reissued it in 1881 as *Capturing a Locomotive*. Southern accounts began to appear—Fuller's story in *The Sunny South* in 1878 for one—and it began to be evident that an unusual pattern of narrative teamwork was developing. Unlike many North-South battles which invited conflicting claims of achievement, this story was one in which the praising of the efforts of either side could serve not to detract from the other, but only to add to its credit.

The legend of gallant, mutually respecting fellow soldiers and opponents—the public face of this at least—was building year by year. The great railroad chase, with its built-in testimonial of awed admiration from the enemy, was unmistakably on the national record for keeps.

Appointment in Atlanta

At the running out of the little luck he had, the double agent called James J. Andrews left many deeper mysteries than the empty black trunk Parrott and Hawkins found in Louisville for Elizabeth Layton. The most troublesome one was the question of his origin and actual identity. He appeared in Flemingsburg, Ky., in 1859—of "strange reserve," courtly in manner and speech, a man of such marked differences from those around him as to impress almost all observers as having a hidden "story." Early or late in Flemingsburg—despite his good standing with Brack Jackson, Dave McGavic, the Eckels, Lindsays, Ashtons and others, and even the curiously unblazing relationship with Elizabeth Layton—no one could be sure he knew the soft-spoken Andrews well and none called him Jim.

"My parents both knew Mr. Andrews," Iolene Ashton Hawkins wrote early in 1956, at the age of ninety, "and they said that from the time he first came [to Flemingsburg] there was a whispered belief that there was something mysterious about him, though he attracted and kept the people as friends."

To Alf Wilson, Pittenger, Dorsey and the other young Ohio country boys briefly under his orders, Andrews was a striking and distinctive figure unlike any man they had known, reserved, gentle, speaking in a mild, almost "effeminate" manner, which in the area at the time might have been one way of describing an overly careful one. To Corporal Pike, over a shared Tennessee farm breakfast in no-man's land, the agent was a serious, withdrawn man of almost unbreakable reserve. None of these soldier witnesses of record did more than touch his surface. On the downward trip to Marietta, Andrews on his gray horse traveled for the most part alone. During the one social occasion of the journey—the night at the Widow Hall's—he kept in the background and let Shadrach and others take center stage. At Marietta on the night of the 11th, it's not clear where he slept or whether he slept at all.

Of the raiders, Ross, Hawkins and Wollam seem to have been the closest to him, although none could have been called a confidant. Ross traveled part of the way south with Andrews; he and Wollam were with him in the first flight from the *General;* and Wollam was the man chosen to follow Andrews in the escape at Chattanooga. Hawkins was Andrews' chainmate at Chattanooga, was left his coat on the day of execution, and is the one raider named in Andrews' last letter to D. S. McGavic. Of these three, Ross was executed at Atlanta, and neither Hawkins nor Wollam—third and fourth of the war survivors to die—left useful records of their impressions of Andrews or any personal information given them by him.

Generals William Nelson and the well-traveled Mitchel might have been sophisticated enough, and Captain Alexander Berryhill of the 2nd Ohio might have known Andrews well enough, to supply more revealing judgments than we have. By bullet or fever, all three were dead within short months of the raid. The Rev. Mr. Scott of Atlanta, of strong pro-slavery bias and a stiff, unsympathetic manner, learned from Andrews on their last ride together only that he was from "West Virginia," and that his parents were strong Presbyterians "then residing in southwestern Missouri." This may have been the truth, or it may have been a last mechanical repetition of a long-used cover story, well suited for a rootless man operating between North and South, since it couldn't readily be checked by either side.

In Flemingsburg, Andrews had once named himself as from Holliday's Cove, now included in Weirton, West Virginia. No birth records for this area were kept prior to 1853. The evidence turned up following the lawsuit over Andrews' legacy to the poor tended to knock the props permanently from under this explanation of the stranger's origin. The various melodramatic half-told bits remembered by Parrott or heard of by Pittenger in Flemingsburg as to the cold-hearted love thrown off by the lost patrimony sound like the gossip-born guesses or exercises in romance-spinning that they probably were.

The fact is—as Ohioan James Thurber seems to have been one of the few observers perceptive enough to note—the J. J. Andrews presented in the usual versions of the story is hard to believe. The closer the examination of the available record, the harder the believing gets. For lack of certain basic information as to where Andrews came from, how he was educated and what he had been doing in some of the years before he took the name Andrews from a Flemingsburg lawyer's sign, most of the actual shreds of fact we do have about him seem hopelessly contradictory or at odds with reality.

My guess is that most of the trouble has risen from a misreading of one key fact plainly on the record from the beginning. The newly available Andrews letter of December 6, 1861—which appears here thanks to the care given it over the years by Mrs. Iolene Ashton Hawkins and others of the Ashton family, and through the generous help of Miss Mary Pickett DeBell of Flemingsburg—would seem to confirm the point indisputably, but it has been there to be seen in the farewell letter to D. S. McGavic and others, since these pages were put on record at the Flemingsburg courthouse.

Pittenger and others—and even Flemingsburg townspeople up to the present day—have always spoken of Andrews' poor spelling as almost surely deliberate, to make himself seem less important to his Confederate captors or for some other purpose now obscure. Andrews wasn't in Confederate custody when he wrote the letter of December 6 from Louisville, nor had he an assignable reason then for making himself seem less educated than he was, but the pattern of the mistakes in it matches those of the McGavic letter at every point, and Andrews self-consciously included an actual apology for them.

The letter is here repeated, this time exactly as written by Andrews from his Louisville hotel. As the one record straight from his hands that we have—without the chance of possible adjustments for Confederate censorship—it deserves a second reading on many counts. In it we hear an Andrews of the early army days still hopeful and resolute even while foreseeing the carnage to come. Despite the surface mistakes and some of the elaborately put sentiments, he could thank the women of Flemingsburg for their merciful and needed work in as sensitive, warm and deft a tribute as they were probably to have in the war.

This reprinting of the letter in its original form, let it quickly be said, is being offered not as a deepener of the prevailing mystery, but as a probable aid to the explanation of a great deal of it.

J. J. ANDREWS:

Louisville, Ky.
December 6, 1861

To the officers and members of
the Ladys Soldiers Aid Society of
Flemingsburgh

Dear Ladies:

If you will excuse the impertinance and intrusion, I propose to send you a few items that I picked up this morning that may be interesting, and encouraging to you, in your noble effort of aleviating the suffering Soldiers, that have volenteered to Drive the Invaders from Kentucky Soil, and protect your Homes from the Suthern vandals.

This morning as I was pasing throo the camps some five miles from the City I heard some one say "Hellow there you man from that town where the LADYS are so clever."

On loocking around I saw a countinance that had become familiar to me, while on the March to Piketon, and which I recognised as belonging to one of the Boys of the 33 Ohio, as this was the first time I had met any of the 33 sence I left Piketon. Nothing would do but I must gow along to their quarters.

Ariving there, very few of them remembered my name, But they all recognised me as the "Man from that town where the Ladys were so kind."

Be ashured I felt proud of the compliment paid you and am very gratefull to you for the kindnefs showen me by the 33 which is all due to the fact of my Haling from "that town where the Ladys are so kind." And when I told them that it was through your liberality and forethought that the wounded at Ivy Mountain had any Hospital

Stores and that what you suplied was all there was with the army at the time, there praise seamed to know no bounds. Many of them related acts of kindnefs that they received from the Ladys of Flemingsburgh as they past throo that they have not forgot and they say they never will. Many of them described the Generous Doners so accurately that I could name them but knowing there extreme modesty I forbair. They all seamed anxious for an oportunity of becoming beter acquainted with the Ladys of Flemingsburgh and many of them declare that as soon as they could get Ready to settle in life before they would most ashuredly give those noble hearted Ladys a call before they made the final decision. So young Ladys, Dont dispair.

After spending an hour or more with the 33, I came on towards the city about three miles where the 2nd Ohio Regt is encamped. I caled to see them also, having become acquainted with them during the canpaighn up Sandy, especialy with Company A Capt. Berryhill whoos company had 8 men wounded at Ivy Mountain Two of whom ware thought to have been mortaly wounded at the time. The Captain had just recd. a male for his company. Among the letters received was two or three from his wounded men now in Hospital at Cincinnati, stating that the wounded ware all dooing well and those thought to have been mortaly wounded are improving and will get well.

Our conversation naturily turned to the incidents of the Fight and the sufferings and hardships of the Men. When I told them that all the Hospital Stores they had in that campaign, ware furnished by the Ladys of Flemingsburgh and had it not been for your generosity they would have been without many of the delicacies they had, and the suffering of the wounded would necessarily have been much grater, one of the party loocked up with the teers glistening in his eyes and said "God Blefs the Ladys of Flemingsburgh. I have never seen them, but ware it posible I would suffer fifty times as much as I have to protect such disinterested kindnefs. The Sutheren merauders shall never disturb them except they do it over my dead body" and many other such expressions.

You have no idea how much good it does men that are enduring the hardships and dangers of an active canpaighn to know that they are not forgot by the noble Mothers and Daughters of America. You may think that those Rough Loocking soldiers (made rough by hard service and thieving contractors) do not appreciate your kindness. Could you but see the heaving chest, the faling teer and the fervent expression of thankfullnefs that I have, you would very soon conclude otherwise.

Nead I say persvere in your noble work? I think not, for I am satisfide that the same patriotism that incited the first acts still burns in your hearts. All then that nead be told you to stimulate you to Further Exertions is that Kentuck seames to be doomed to be the "Dark and Bloody Ground" again.

It makes my heart bleed to see the Mighty preperations that are beaing made by booth parties to slay each other, and very soon the terible work will begin in earnest. The Mighty Hosts that are now beaing marshald on Kentucky Soil can not remain idle much longer. The clashing of Arms and the thunder of Artilary will soon be heard from the Mississippi. Along the Southern portions of the State clear to the Mountains will be one vast Field of carnage and Death. Thousands of the noblest sons of America will be made to bite the dust ere many more weeks pass away, Awfull thought, and many more will need the kind assistance of such Societies as yours.

Persevere and may God blefs you is the prayer of your humble servent,

J. J. Andrews

P.S. If your Society has no correspondent in this part of the State and if you can put up with my blunders in spelling & compositions I will wright you occasionaly if you desire it. If so drop me a note to that effect. Direct to care Louisville Hotel, Louisville, Ky.

EDITOR: If taken up on his offer to serve as informal war correspondent for the delicacy-supplying ladies of Flemingsburg—as isn't of record—the lines runner must soon have found difficulty prying loose enough spare minutes to attend to the self-assumed chore. No other reports from the field have been handed down, although in the last letter to McGavic there is mild complaint of no replies received in answer to several letters sent.

It will be noted that twelve words Andrews couldn't spell in the above and in the McGavic letter were: seem, tears, dogs, were, their, looking, called, falling, need, being, both, and go. Twelve that he did throw in easily and correctly were: acquainted, liberality, mountain, forethought, vandals, delicacies, glistening, necessarily, daughters, incited, Mississippi and tranquility. Despite the spelling stumbles, he could construct and without apparent effort steer through such sentences as:

[*Editor*]
"When I told them that all the hospital stores they had in that campaign were furnished by the ladies of Flemingsburg and had it not been for your generosity they would have been without many of the delicacies they had, and the suffering of the wounded would necessarily have been much greater, one of the party looked up with tears glistening in his eyes and said, 'God bless the ladies of Flemingsburg.' "

What kind of a man could misspell "dog," "look," and "go," and sail errorlessly through "tranquility" and "necessarily"? One plain answer—as impatient hands must have been up pages ago to point out—would seem to be a reasonably well-educated man who hadn't been born to the booby-trapped linguistic riches of English. A native-born American of little education could be expected to cope with the easy words first and the hard ones later. Andrews reversed the process, as any born European not from Britain or Ireland might be expected to do. "Clever" in one of the sung-out comments quoted is probably used in the archaic sense of well-shaped or pleasing—by a remote cousinship, it develops, with "cleavage"—but if "Hellow there you man from that town where the ladys are so clever" isn't a half-translated European rendering of something else, the homespun 33d Ohio must have been recruited even further afield than some of the German-speaking regiments of record.

One of the war's most reliable reporters of men and events, Colonel John Beatty of the 3d Ohio, was in Mitchel's division and might have left us a useful impression of Andrews had any of the raiders happened to have been selected from his regiment. By chance, none was. Another of Mitchel's colonels, John B. Turchin—once Ivan Vasilevitch Turchininoff of the Czar's armies—may have been qualified to make an even better guess as to Andrews' origin, but if such a guess was made, Turchin kept it to himself.

In 1850 an unmarried Finnish-born ex-officer of the Russian army called Andreas Johan Kars, thirty years old, emigrated to the United States. To his family's understanding he lived in this country under the name of J. J. Andrews. Within recent years, members of his family since moved to Norway have attempted to confirm their belief that Andreas Johan Kars died on a Confederate scaffold in Atlanta on June 7, 1862—brought there for his part in leading what has been known as the Andrews raid.

Investigation is now on here and abroad to prove or disprove the connection. As *Wild Train* necessarily goes to press, running down of the relevant evidence hasn't yet been completed, although some interesting coincidences can be noted. For a deck-clearing negative minor one, despite the favorable national mention given Andrews during and after the war, the parents supposedly in Missouri never came forward or made inquiries of record of any kind.

As Finland had been politically controlled by Sweden—ninety miles across the Gulf of Bothnia from Vaasa, the seaport in which Andreas Johan Kars was born—for the five centuries preceding 1809, the Swedish language would still have been a strong influence in the education of any Finnish child in the years of Kars' boyhood. A man raised and schooled in Vaasa at the time given, if later attempting to master English in adulthood, might have been expected to make occasional mistakes characteristic of the speakers of either language. For an American, putting in two g's is misspelling "dog" the hard way. In Swedish, "dogg"—as Andrews had it—is the only way of writing it. If misspelling "were," a characteristic error for Finns or Swedes might be to replace the *e* by an *a*. Andrews' consistent spelling of this word was "ware." In Finnish, as in Spanish, vowel pronunciations are constant. For a Finn to indicate the sound of open *o* in "go" or "hello," instinct and training would incline him to add a *u* or *w*. On both "go" and "hello," the spelling error Andrews curiously and consistently fell into was "gow" and "hellow."

As the case stands, the jury is out. In no way has it been proved that J. J. Andrews was born Andreas Johan Kars in the west central seaport of Vaasa, Finland. In no way has it yet been clearly shown that he couldn't have been. (Evidence bearing either way, or indicating another origin for Andrews, will of course be welcome at any time and can be sent the writer in care of the present publishers.)

Tabling the sub-question of exactly what country the raid leader came from until surer evidence can be found and tested, it's my belief from the two letters and other facts that we now have that "J. J. Andrews"—chief tragic figure of the most spectacular exploit of our Civil War—was born and educated in Europe. It's my guess that his ancestry was Finnish, Esthonian or Swedish. Wherever his birth, it's my unchanged conviction that he died the authentic American hero he has always been taken to be.

Blue vs. Blue 1

In late November, 1886, a few months from the twenty-fifth anniversary of the raid, eight of the eleven members of the Andrews expedition then surviving met for a Thanksgiving reunion at McComb, Ohio.

Fourteen raiders had outlived the war. Within two years of its close, the fever-worn young Englishman Mark Wood was dead in Toledo of tuberculosis. Robert Buffum's mind, rather than his body or heart, proved to be the second delayed casualty of the war. Killing a man in Orange County, New York, in a blaze of irrational anger over what he believed to be disrespect for Lincoln's memory, the one-time follower of John Brown was sentenced to life imprisonment and transferred soon after to the hospital for the criminally insane at Auburn. There, on June 20, 1871, he ripped a knife across the thin, troubled throat that had escaped a Confederate rope, and cut the total of surviving raiders to twelve. Martin Hawkins moved to the Mississippi at Quincy, Illinois, married, worked at various engineering jobs until his death ten months before the reunion meeting at McComb.

The McComb-Findlay area in northwestern Ohio was well chosen for the regathering. The eleven veterans were pushing for middle age, most of them seasoned family men, and for seven of them a Hancock County meeting required little travel time taken from business or farming. Apart from Wollam, Reddick, Dorsey and Pittenger—then living respectively in Topeka, Kansas; Louisa County, Iowa; Kearney, Nebraska; and Haddonfield, New Jersey—all the surviving raiders lived less than fifty miles from McComb, most of them no more than ten or fifteen miles from the next man.

In Wood County, Alf Wilson's grocery store in Haskins wasn't far from the Maumee where he'd dueled with catfish as a boy; Bensinger was farming at Deweyville just over the line from McComb; Mason was a solid businessman at Pemberville; and Brown was an agent for various lines of merchandise at Dowling. In Williams County, after a number of years of engineering in Minnesota, Knight was chief engineer for a wood-processing plant at Stryker. Parrott was a prosperous contractor and gravel bank operator in Kenton,

Hardin County. McComb, where Porter was currently giving his father a hand with a flourishing general store, was in Hancock County, as was nearby Findlay where the brothers and sisters of John Scott still lived. At Christiansburg in Champaign County, Marion Ross's brother and others of the Ross family were near enough to meet from time to time with several of the hanged sergeant major's one-time fellow soldiers. In the counties west of and below Toledo, the Andrews raid was still more than a spectacular footnote in the annals of the great American war.

Wollam, Reddick and Mason—by geography, from conflicting interests, or by choice—weren't to be on hand at McComb. Of those coming from out of state in the fall of 1886, the Rev. William Pittenger of the New Jersey conference of the Methodist Episcopal Church was more nearly a personal stranger to the rest than any, although the most widely known through his writings. Pittenger's first church posts had been near his native Jefferson County in eastern Ohio, and from 1869 on he had been in a series of small New Jersey towns in the Philadelphia area. Since publication of his first book, *Daring and Suffering,* in 1863, Pittenger had written textbooks on public speaking and had begun lecturing at Philadelphia's National School of Elocution and Oratory. In 1881 he had put out a second and expanded book on the raid, *Capturing a Locomotive.* The lean, stoop-shouldered clergyman-author felt his health to be in precarious condition, and for several years had been on a Federal disability pension.

Pensions were increasingly in men's minds in the third decade after the war. Since the summer of 1884, all of the raiders—and Sam Slavens' widow Rachel down in Pike County near the Ohio—had been drawing a special monthly pension of $24 granted the members of the Andrews party chiefly through the Washington lobbying efforts of Dorsey in 1881 and 1882; the writings of Pittenger and Alf Wilson; and the readily offered help of Ohio's senior senator, John Sherman, brother of the man who had led the western armies through Georgia.

Actually, through the seventies and the first half of the following decade, with more than a million Union veterans well into or past their forties, service pensions had become increasingly easier to get as politicians had taken note of the dimensions of the soldier vote. Starting in 1884, however, there had been a major change in Washington. Under the unwinking eye of New York's one-time reform governor, Grover Cleveland, the first Democratic president since the war, the loose-seamed pension system was getting an unexpectedly abrupt tightening. At McComb and elsewhere, at this Thanksgiving season of 1886, the current re-examination of the national pension rolls was arousing much pained and angry talk in an Ohio finding it hard enough in any case—after sending three of its Civil War generals in a row to the White House—to realize that the presidency was no longer a near-monopoly of the Republican party of Ohio.

Of those gathering at Porter's house in McComb, nearly all were in some way on the record. Balancing the newspaper accounts beginning to appear on the Southern side, with Conductor Fuller as chief source, Knight had given occasional lectures, and he, Porter, Dorsey and Alf Wilson had allowed Pittenger to use reports of their escape trips in his books. Daniel Allen Dorsey—in time taken first from farming and then from an undemanding frontier law practice at Kearney chiefly concerned with land sales—had written some newspaper articles, and in 1881 had come near enough writing a play on the expedition to copyright the title: "Andrews the Spy . . . A Drama Descriptive of . . . All Appertaining to That Secret Expedition." As well, by mail and in person, Dorsey had been pulling at and turning over various strands of the story and had had letters over the years on it from Fuller, Judge O. P. Temple, Secretary of War Robert Lincoln, and others. These he had been mulling over in company with an ex-soldier and fellow attorney at Kearney, a Judge James E. Gillespie who had spent hard months of his own at Andersonville. Alf Wilson's "Adventures," collected in book form in 1880 after appearing in weekly installments in the Wood County *Sentinel*, had carried as disarming a foreword as any raider was to employ.

ALF WILSON: This is the story of a private soldier who aspires to no literary honors, who claims no credit for martyrdom, whose deeds didn't change the tide of a single battle. . . . All I can claim for myself in [the Andrews] expedition is that I did all in my power to carry out the orders of my general, tried to serve my country faithfully, and believe I cheated the Rebels out of the pleasure of hanging me.

EDITOR: On this Thanksgiving weekend of 1886, thanks in great part to Pittenger's persistent and skillful presentations of the unique and heroic aspects of the raid, the eight ex-soldiers assembled were already minor celebrities in Ohio and elsewhere. All had Congressional Medals of Honor—most, in the later design that became the medal's permanent form; Knight characteristically had managed to wind up with both original and replacement, on promise never to wear the two together. Their story had been told and retold, and observers North and South were increasingly in agreement that April 12, 1862, had been one of the high days of the war. Stephen B. Porter of the Columbus *Dispatch*, Nelson Purdum of the Chillicothe *Leader*, C. W. Evarts of the Wood County *Sentinel*, and F. J. Oblinger of the Toledo *Bee* were just four of the many Ohio editors always glad to carry additional lore on the raid at times named for the general who had authorized it, at other times for the bearded, courteously spoken leader who had once sung with Newt Bookwalter —or Buchwalder—in Chillicothe.

As news of the forthcoming reunion had spread, through October and November, enough general interest had been shown in McComb and nearby Findlay to warrant tentative plans for the appearance of the full group at one or more paid public meetings.

The suggestion as to hiring a hall may well have come from Pittenger, although this isn't of record. The industrious minister himself had traveled the farthest, and most interestingly, of those turning up at McComb. From New Jersey, starting at the beginning of the month, he had come by way of Atlanta and Flemingsburg on a journey combining field research and sentimental pilgrimage. Pittenger's first stop on the roundabout research trip to McComb had been at Washington.

PITTENGER: To go freely amid scenes of peace, over the ground associated only in my mind with war, prisons and chains, was a pleasant experience which only limited means and the duties of an exacting profession long prevented me from enjoying. At length, in 1886, the wished-for opportunity came. Six years earlier, just before writing *Capturing a Locomotive*, I had made a hasty and partial visit to the South, and the information then received made me anxious to fully explore this field. . . .

On November 2, 1886, I arrived at Washington accompanied by Mrs. Pittenger. Mr. F. G. Carpenter introduced me to Mr. Spofford, Librarian of Congress, Colonel [Robert N.] Scott, Editor of the Official War Records, and Mr. Hodgeson, of the Records Department of the War Office, and I was soon hard at work. My only grievance was the shortness of working hours—from nine to four. Mr. Spofford, whose memory of books seems infinite, produced for me everything having any bearing on my subject, and also the files of Rebel newspapers for 1862-1863. From the books I secured no new facts, but several valuable illustrative items. The newspapers also were somewhat disappointing, for they were meager in historical material as compared with Northern papers. . . .

But a far deeper interest was evoked in Colonel Scott's office. The Government is there selecting from the official reports and correspondence of the war, those papers which possess permanent interest, for the purpose of publication. Already some twenty-five great volumes are in print, and the work is scarcely one-third done. No history of any part of the Civil War will have any standard value in the future which does not rest on these reports. [The full series, "*War of the Rebellion, Records of the Union and Confederate Armies*," and the corresponding naval records, on completion a number of years after Pittenger's visit, became and remain the basic documentation of the war.] Of that not yet printed, much has been classified by months and subjects, becoming thus easily accessible.

I was kindly supplied with a writing table, and all the bundles of MSS. I called for were furnished, with only the reasonable condition that I should rearrange each as I found it. Never have I had a more fascinating employment, though it sometimes became positively painful. To be thus groping among the very papers and orders which once had the power of life and death to thousands, to see the secret springs of events with which I was familiar on the outside and often wholly misunderstood, to feel that at any moment I might come across a great historical prize, to see the very hearts of men laid bare, often with startling revelations of greatness and meanness —all written in dim and almost faded characters which were never intended for the public eye—this caused the hours to pass by almost like minutes. . . .

But I was not satisfied with examining those documents which had been selected for publication. There might be others among the great mass in the war archives of even higher interest. Of one document published in the official reports, Vol. X [Parts I and II of Series I, Vol. X—published by the Government Printing Office in 1884] I wished to see the original, and secure a photographic copy for lithographing. This was the petition of our party which reached Jefferson Davis and received his endorsement upon it. . . .

The war records are guarded very carefully, as is right. The Government does not allow its own archives to be used as a basis for sustaining claims against itself. And there is always the possibility that some valuable but compromising paper might be abstracted. A letter to the Secretary of War, however, removed all obstacles in my own case. I not only found the document wanted, but another letter of even greater interest, written by myself to Jefferson Davis on a terrible day. I think I was able to get hold of everything in the department which could throw any light on the raid. Then a swift journey over the Piedmont Air Line carried us to Atlanta. . . .

EDITOR: Pittenger saw both William Fuller and Anthony Murphy at Atlanta, retraveled the old Marietta-Ringgold route accompanied by Fuller, and put in a day at Flemingsburg, Ky., hunting—without too much success—for substantial new information on James J. Andrews' prewar life. The Flemingsburg side trip ended in the last week of November at Maysville where Pittenger took a river steamer for Cincinnati.

PITTENGER: I was soon on my way to Cincinnati. This assured me of being able to reach the place appointed for the reunion of the survivors of our prison party at McComb, Hancock County, Ohio, the next day.

While waiting at Deshler, Ohio (the junction with the branch road leading to McComb), I saw a fine-looking man who had a familiar and preacher-like look, and who seemed to be watching me. I thought he was probably one of the members of the East Ohio Conference, of which I had been a member before being transferred to the N. J. Conference. At length he came up to me and said, "Is not your name Pittenger?" I assented, and learned that he was J. A. Wilson, my old prison comrade—the first time I had seen him since we had shaken hands, not without moist eyes, just before we attacked the jailer and the guard at Atlanta twenty-four years earlier. We were both boys then, and in the wonderful rush of memory and emotion which swept over me I began to realize for the first time all that this reunion—the first that our party had ever held—was likely to prove.

We talked rapidly, the minutes fled like magic, and it seemed almost too soon that we were at McComb. I learned that Dorsey had arrived from Nebraska, that Knight also had come, and that more were expected. This was the home of two others—Porter and Bensinger—and we were sure of a great gathering. Though already late, we had very much to talk over before we could sleep.

The next morning the lake winds blew cold, and the falling snow was quite a contrast to the warm days I had left behind in the South. But this did not diminish our enjoyment; perhaps, as the next day was Thanksgiving and we were to feast together at the house of Comrade Porter, the cold imparted additional zest. Of the whole number the only one I could have recognized—excepting Dorsey, who had visited me in New Jersey—was Bensinger. The grave, bearded men I saw were not much like the boys who had played games and sung in sight of the scaffold! But the very first tones of the voice of each one had a familiar thrill that flashed like lightning backward over all the intervening years. The citizens of McComb felt great interest in our meeting. The Methodist Church was crowded in the evening to hear the telling of experiences by the different members of the party. This entertainment was repeated the next evening and also for one evening at Findlay, an admission fee being charged, which went far toward defraying the whole expenses of the reunion.

The Thanksgiving dinner provided by the hospitality of Porter was excellent, and the contrast between that, and our boarding in Chattanooga and Atlanta, was duly dwelt upon. In the revival of old incidents I was much amused in noticing what all persons who have had much to do with sifting testimony have been forced to recognize —the uncertainty, in minute points, of the best witnesses. None of us had any motive to recall any other than the exact facts; but we differed in a thousand little matters, though none of the discrepancies were of practical importance. With this narrative in view, I questioned the others carefully about those things which I had not jotted down at the time, or which took place beyond the bounds of my own experience. Substantial agreement, with numberless minute divergencies, was the outcome. For example (and this was the more striking from its nonessential character) we began to talk of the number of windows in the upper cell of Swims' jail in Chattanooga. Some said there were three windows in the upper room, and others that there were but two. After the dispute had lasted for some time, another came in and was at once appealed to as a fresh witness, and unhesitatingly declared that there was but one. . . .

A more serious difficulty arose in apportioning the comparative labors of Brown and Knight. When the boxcar contingent, with which I was, broke out the end of their car and crawled on the engine and tender, Brown was acting as engineer. This mainly had led me to write and others to speak of him as "the engineer," sometimes without mention of Knight at all. But it appeared that while Brown was examined as to his qualifications as engineer by Mitchel himself, and approved; yet Knight had been spoken to by Andrews and the colonel of the 21st Ohio, and was also well qualified, had gotten ahead of Brown at the start and had taken the first turn at the throttle. Knight was also a mechanician, and probably better able than any man of the party to have repaired damages to the engine. These little discussions did not impair, but rather added spice to, an occasion which on the whole was such a time of tender, sad and triumphant memories as seldom comes in this world.

The photographs of the party were taken as a group in Findlay. Brown was not then with us, but he was seen afterward. Then, with tender and hearty farewells, we scattered on our several ways in life.

EDITOR: Differences among the raiders were brought into the open for the first time during the "magic" minutes of the McComb meeting, as Pittenger duly reported, but it's doubtful if the writer was as amused as he stated himself to be in the above passage from *Daring and Suffering* of 1887. The little discussions which "didn't impair, but rather added spice" to the whole occasion covered several points of considerably sharper interest than the number of windows in Swims' upper cell. Among these—raised bluntly by Dorsey—was the question of whether Pittenger had knowingly betrayed his comrades at Chattanooga and gained his own safety directly or indirectly at the cost of the lives of the eight men hanged at Atlanta.

The most probable explanation of the absence of John Wollam and Elihu Mason from the Hancock County reunion was their conviction that Pittenger had not only been weak enough to turn traitor under the pressures of Lafayette and Chattanooga, but hypocritical enough later to conceal his role and actually paint himself as one of the raiders ranking highest in fidelity, military judgment, and resourceful enterprise against the enemy.

DORSEY: For a quarter of a century, I had debated in my mind Pittenger's conduct and had never been able to satisfy myself fully about the matter. I had heard Mason and others condemn him, but it seemed so unnatural that a comrade should prove false, that I was reluctant to believe it.

EDITOR: Reluctant or not, most of Dorsey's digging and letter writing over the years—and possibly even his visits to Pittenger in New Jersey in 1881 and 1882, as Pittenger was to charge—had been directed toward finding clear proof or disproof of the black suspicions smoldering in the background since the day when John Wollam, on return to prison at Atlanta, had charged Pittenger as the man who had turned state's evidence to save his own neck. Soon after the war, Fuller had written to the family of Marion Ross placing the responsibility for the executions largely on the shoulders of Pittenger:

"Fuller said he learned," M. R. Ross, brother of Marion, had in

[*Editor*]
turn told Dorsey, "that Pittenger had gone north and published a book trying to acquit himself of all blame, and asked that his [Fuller's] letter be published, so that the people north might know the facts."

Pittenger was aware of the developing crossfire. When he wrote his second book, *Capturing a Locomotive*, published in 1881, he moved adroitly or charitably to disarm his Southern critic by an expanded and sweeping salute.

PITTENGER: As Conductor Fuller disappears from our story, where he has been so conspicuous, and where his energies, skill and daring shine in such brilliant colors, a few words may be appropriately devoted to his work. . . . All the evidence goes to show that the Confederacy had no other available man who could have saved the bridges on the Western & Atlantic Railroad that day.

EDITOR: In a letter to Dorsey, written October 31, 1884, after reading the above and the rest of *Capturing a Locomotive*, Fuller showed himself considerably mollified.

FULLER: Mr. Pittenger has seemed in his [most recent] work to give reasonable credit to me for my part in the chase. . . .

The impression upon my mind at the time was that the witness was in the interest of the prosecution, and indeed was; but from his [present] statement, it was by agreement . . . by all the prisoners as the theory less dangerous. Of course, the statement of the author is known to the survivors to be true or not, I cannot say which.

The author of *Capturing a Locomotive* was one of the only two witnesses in the several trials and I was the other. The author swore to who the prisoners were . . . while I swore to what they did, and when, how and where they did it. . . . Taking my testimony and Pittenger's together, the court found the prisoners, as they were tried, guilty.

Now I take the position that if [none] of the Federal party had testified, the Confederate government could never on my testimony [alone have] made out a case of spying. When I say that Wm. Pittenger's testimony was in the interest of the prosecution, I mean only to say that such was my opinion at the time, and [it] seemed to be the general opinion. [If] his testimony was that which was agreed upon by himself and all his fellow prisoners, of course no improper motive could be imputed to him.

EDITOR: In a footnote in his first *Daring and Suffering* of 1863, Pittenger had written:

PITTENGER: I do not pretend to justify the falsehoods recorded in this book, but it is better to give a true narrative, and bear the censure awarded by the reader, than to increase the guilt by omitting or misrepresenting facts.

EDITOR: Dorsey and others at McComb felt that Pittenger was a number of years overdue in acting on this excellent table rule for chroniclers themselves participants in events under description. The omitted facts they most missed in Pittenger's published writings were those concerned with the trials of the eight men executed. Nowhere in the first *Daring and Suffering* or in *Capturing a Locomotive* could the closest reader have learned that Pittenger had appeared as one of the two important witnesses against his companions. The omission was one of several Pittenger was asked to correct in his forthcoming expanded and revised version of *Daring and Suffering.*

There is no clear evidence that Dorsey in 1886 had yet become willing to charge Pittenger flatly with deliberate treachery. The points at issue were still mostly instances of evasion and omission in the books which kept Pittenger from even the appearance of weakness or double dealing. As well, for nearly five years—as Pittenger had good reason to know—Dorsey had had an endorsement of Pittenger of the most persuasive kind. Judge O. P. Temple and Jonathan Baxter were the Knoxville attorneys who had handled the defense of the seven raiders eventually executed. On January 14, 1882, referring to Fuller's identification in the Ross correspondence of Pittenger as the key witness against the men convicted, Dorsey had written to Judge Temple for further information on the trials, and for the attorney's opinion of Pittenger's conduct during them. The old Unionist answered without reservation.

O. P. TEMPLE:

Knoxville, Tenn.
January 21, 1882

Mr. D. A. Dorsey, Washington, D.C.

Dear Sir:

I have just seen Judge Baxter and we agree on the following facts: Mr. Pittenger did testify in the case, but under compulsion. In other words, he did not "turn state's evidence" but was put on the stand by the prosecuting attorney, with no promise of pardon to him, and when on the stand he testified to such a state of facts as we desired, and which we thought sufficient to acquit you all. He stated most clearly that it was a military expedition undertaken by the authority and command of General Mitchel, and that you were not spies.

At the time, those who were tried and who heard him testify did not complain of his conduct so far as I ever heard. If they had thought he was betraying them, I am sure Judge Baxter and I would have heard of it, for we saw and consulted with them every day, and you too would have heard of it.

No, I think Fuller was smarting under the exposure made by Pittenger in his book, and wished to break the force of it by making this charge, without giving all the facts. Both Judge Baxter and I thought, and still think, Mr. Pittenger acted with fidelity to his comrades.

Very respectfully yours,
O. P. Temple

DORSEY: When I received Judge Temple's letter I sent a copy of it to the friends of the deceased members of the expedition, and tried to persuade them that, maybe, after all, Pittenger acted in good faith, but some of them refused to be comforted even then.

EDITOR: At the McComb meeting—however the information was to be interpreted later—host Porter and guest Dorsey discovered for the first time that each had overheard the same possibly revealing exchange between Ross and Andrews at Chattanooga during the days of the leader's trial. As well, whether brought out by Pittenger or Porter, it was the agreement of the group that Pittenger's course at the trials had had at least initial approval by Andrews.

DORSEY: The trial of James J. Andrews took place while we were in the dungeon at Chattanooga, Pittenger being a witness for the prosecution. I think that Andrews approved of Pittenger's going on as a witness in his case. He seemed to think that while it wouldn't help him—for he had little hope of saving himself—yet it might possibly help us in some way; and he would have done anything to save his men, even though it might make it worse for himself.

The only intimation I had of Andrews' opinion of Pittenger was conveyed in a remark made by him one evening just after stepping off the foot of the ladder on his return to the hole at the close of a day's proceedings in his case. Ross said, "Well, Andrews, how did the trial go today?"

To which Andrews replied in sweet, plaintive tones, "Well, I hardly know, but I'm afraid that fellow has swatted me."

Porter and myself were at that time chainmates. We two sat near Andrews and Ross when the above dialogue took place, and although never mentioned between us until we met at McComb, Ohio, in 1886, both of us remembered it well, as did Knight also.

EDITOR: McComb was the first occasion for frankness on many subjects, large and small. Money was one that might have come under either heading. In *Capturing a Locomotive,* Pittenger had used extensive excerpts from the chase and escape accounts of Porter, Dorsey, Alf Wilson and Knight. The Pittenger books had always sold well, as a number of the raiders who had acted as salesmen for them on occasion could confirm. Sharing to some extent in the profits of the raid's history, as they had shared in its dangers, seemed to several no less than fair.

The clergyman-author pointed out that substantial expenses and outlays of time were on the other side of the profits coin. Were his old comrades offering to compensate him for his time, for the costs of cuts and plates, before calculating the theoretical gains available for whacking up? At the moment, the old comrades weren't. Remembering the sixteen to twenty months Pittenger had gained by leaving the army in August of 1863—rather than in 1864 or 1865 as most of the others had done—some weren't sure the principle of compensation for invested time didn't operate as much against Pittenger as for him, but no one of the group was qualified enough on the business side of publishing to propose an immediately acceptable, specific plan for dealing equitably with future returns from the books.

All had contributed in varying measure, however, Pittenger was prompt to concede, and it was the understanding of at least Knight and Dorsey at this time that a generous formula would be worked out at an early date allowing some cash dividends to accrue to Pittenger's military and literary companions in arms.

Pittenger was already the author of textbooks on extemporaneous debate, and awkward as were some of the magic moments at McComb, it's in no way certain that he left the area with fewer supporters than he had on arrival. He pointed out the practical difficulties of clearing himself of the implied charges of disloyalty. A great part of those Confederate records that hadn't been damaged or lost in the years of fighting and defeat had been deliberately destroyed to avoid just such postwar liability of various officers for possible crimes as might be involved in the raiders' trial records. Pittenger had hunted intensively at the Library of Congress and in Georgia and Tennessee for relevant documents and had found almost none. The attorneys of the executed seven had vouched for Pittenger's fidelity; he was sure Fuller and Murphy were now ready to confirm it as well; and he was persuaded that all the group, on more careful thought, would acknowledge the unfairness of blaming one man for a result that several of his hearers themselves had held in the prison to be inevitable from the beginning.

Equally to the point, could the airing of these unfounded and late-growing suspicions now serve a useful purpose for any of the party, living or dead? Putting aside unfairness to any one man, would such pointless bickering increase or decrease the audiences waiting to hear more of what was becoming a nationally accepted epic of boldness and endurance? Did the raiders—Pittenger was asking in effect—want to tip the boat that was carrying them all to permanent glory?

At least one published passage in *Capturing a Locomotive*—quoted from Porter's account of his and Hawkins' arrest after enlistment in the Confederate army—made it difficult for Dorsey to accept the suggestion that he pipe down and sit still in the boat.

PORTER: Everything went right with us [at Camp McDonald] until in some manner it leaked out among the Rebels that the Yankee raiders, by mistake or accident, had left two of their party at Marietta. How this information got out I never learned, but it could not be otherwise than that some of our party had indiscreetly told more than he ought when captured. Who the man was we never learned.

EDITOR: Suspicions of one kind or another, in Dorsey's view, were already abroad and Pittenger's books had helped give them circulation. While the clergyman evaded a full admission of his own wartime role, all survivors could find themselves undeservedly under a growing cloud. Before the reunion's end, several of these joined in a flat warning.

DORSEY: We survivors told Pittenger at McComb that we weren't satisfied with his explanations in *Capturing a Locomotive*, and that unless he told the whole truth in his forthcoming revised version of

Daring and Suffering, we'd tell it for him. Pittenger promised to make everything right.

EDITOR: It was only after the issuance and receipt of this plain ultimatum that the old wartime comrades—"with tender and hearty farewells"—scattered from Findlay on their several ways.

Blue vs. Gray and Blue

The differences at McComb had been private ones, kept among the raiders themselves. Two years later, the dissension broke into the open.

In the greatly revised 471-page *Daring and Suffering*, published in 1887, all but a few pages of Pittenger's narrative took its permanent form. More ample information was given on the trials and events following the chase, many minor errors had been corrected, and the book contained numerous passages of increased praise for nearly all concerned on either side. Despite the changes, the most careful reader would still have had difficulty learning that Pittenger had appeared as a witness against eight of his fellow raiders, and Pittenger's role as a leader in plans for resistance and eventual escape had been magnified rather than decreased. If open acknowledgment of fault in his prison conduct had been expected of Pittenger by Dorsey and others, the expectation hadn't been realized.

Dorsey stepped up his probing for information by mail. Colonel H. L. Claiborne, the one-time provost marshal at Chattanooga, was happy to be remembered as a straightforward, considerate man, but could remember no added information of value. Captain Fuller, responding to new inquiries, wrote on May 3, 1888, to Dorsey that he still felt Pittenger's evidence had been "fatal to the case of all those who were tried," and that he had "never been able to see why the counsel you had could consent to the line of evidence as given in by

Wm. Pittenger." Whatever the old fault or error had been, however, the Atlanta merchant—as the one-time conductor had become—suggested that all hands let it lie.

"Pittenger," he reminded Dorsey, "has made heroes of us all, and we ought to be satisfied."

Dorsey wasn't, even though great plans on foot in 1888 for new public honors to the raiders might have made restraint seem advisable. A good part of the nearly half-million members of the G.A.R. were heading for Columbus, Ohio, in September for their annual national grand encampment. Chiefly through the efforts of *Dispatch* editor Captain Stephen B. Porter, wartime sergeant in the 2nd O.V.I., the old locomotive *General* had been moved north for the occasion, and Captain Fuller had come with it to attend a special reunion campfire of the surviving raiders. Mrs. Slavens, other relatives, and all surviving raiders but Porter were on hand.

However Fuller's tact was to be appraised in the days and years to follow, there seems to have been no question as to his effectiveness in dealing with what could have been one of the most painful moments of the Columbus reunion. A reception had been arranged by Captain and Mrs. S. B. Porter on the first day of the encampment to allow Fuller on arrival to meet the surviving raiders and some of the relatives of the deceased members of the party.

DORSEY: Some of the survivors [at the reception] weren't at first disposed to treat Fuller kindly. Wollam, for instance, wouldn't shake hands with him. Before the time came for parting, though, even Wollam fell in with the others and took the hand of our old enemy in friendship. Pittenger, too, was treated kindly, though Wollam hadn't changed his mind about him; and Knight declared he thought more of Fuller than he did of Pittenger.

The meeting on this occasion of Captain Fuller with Mrs. Slavens, widow of Samuel Slavens, was especially pathetic, and was later described by Captain Porter in the *Dispatch*.

S. B. PORTER: [Mrs. Slavens] was about in the middle of the circle. As we approached her, I saw that her face was flushed. No one can ever tell the thoughts of this woman as she took the hand of the man who was responsible for her husband's death. Captain Fuller spoke so gently, however, and so kindly, that the lady was deeply touched. They sat down beside each other and conversed in undertones. What they said they alone know, though the house was silent, and we were all in the room.

Mrs. Slavens was a changed woman after their talk, for she said she felt all right now toward the men who captured, tried and hanged her husband.

EDITOR: At the raiders' ceremonial campfire before the State House the following night, the public reconciliation of old enemies reached its high point. An audience of five to six thousand veterans listened and watched in absorption as Pittenger, Fuller, Dorsey, Parrott, Knight, Brown, Mason, Bensinger, Wollam and Reddick spoke or stood in acknowledgment of the introductions made.

Fuller, introduced by Pittenger—and declaring it one of the great pleasures of his life to be "following" the preceding speaker once more—gave a detailed, swift-moving narrative account of the train-taking and chase, testified to the great potential military value of the attack had it succeeded, and closed with a strong tribute to the raiders, living and dead. In his mention of George Wilson, however, Fuller left the impression of a scaffold admission that the Confederacy had had legal justification for the verdict reached in the trials.

Dorsey, the following speaker, wasn't the man to let the reference pass, as Captain Porter was to report in the *Dispatch*.

S. B. PORTER: Captain Fuller's description of the last trying hours of these [seven] men, and the courage with which they proudly died for their country, was listened to with a silence almost oppressive, and right here came the event of the evening.

Captain Fuller stated that George D. Wilson made a "confession," or "confessed," and his comrades on the scaffold acquiesced. An inference was that Wilson admitted something which he had previously denied, which by the rules of war justified the findings of the court-martial.

Captain Daniel A. Dorsey, of Kearney, Nebr., the next speaker, immediately said that from the moment the capture was effected, the raiders held that they were detailed as soldiers who volunteered to perform extra-hazardous service, and that up to the time when George D. Wilson and his comrades were taken without a moment's warning to be executed, Wilson had always insisted that the party was entitled to the usage of captured soldiers. Captain Dorsey said he was not there to contradict Captain Fuller, but to do justice to the memory of Wilson, as information direct from other witnesses of the tragedy was to the effect that none of these men admitted that they were spies, but insisted they were soldiers sent out to do a perilous duty.

EDITOR: At the Columbus meeting, Dorsey's tact or sense of the most immediately useful course of action fell considerably short of Fuller's. A bill had already been proposed for action by the Ohio legislature to honor the raiders through a memorial at the Chattanooga National Cemetery, where the rediscovered remains of Andrews had been placed with those of his seven followers the year before. However uncharacteristic the words might have seemed from him in June of 1862, in September, 1888, Fuller pointedly and effectively approved the memorial plans—and threw in a bid for possible state pensions, if the state happened to be so minded.

FULLER: I say to the people of Ohio that though you have an abundance of wealth, you cannot do too much for the surviving members of this expedition, nor can you do too much in memory of the dead.

EDITOR: The speeches of Fuller and others at Columbus, and the national interest there shown in this spectacular near-coup by the men of an Ohio command, made certain the favorable action of the Ohio legislature that came in the following spring when $5,000 was appropriated for a suitable memorial at Chattanooga. Publicly, the raiders were becoming men of recognized note and group honors were being accorded them in increasing measure.

Privately, the discords first clearly acknowledged at McComb were becoming harder to muffle. The partial amends Pittenger had included in his *Daring and Suffering* of 1887 hadn't satisfied his critics. Although rooms had been arranged at Columbus for the raiders by Governor J. B. Foraker, the feeling against the writer-minister had become so intense—as Knight was to remember—that "Pittenger went to a hotel and slept away from the rest."

Immediately after the break-up of the encampment at Columbus, Dorsey followed the *General* south in first-hand search of more information than he had yet been able to collect. He found few actual new shreds of fact, but in a personal meeting with Judge O. P. Temple at Knoxville he heard an important qualification of the clean bill Judges Temple and Baxter had granted Pittenger in 1882.

DORSEY: Judge Temple still believed Pittenger hadn't betrayed us, but while he couldn't know whether there had been an agreement with the enemy that Pittenger should not be prosecuted, yet he said that, "as all lawyers know, there is an implied agreement or understanding, where one of a number accused of a crime testifies for the prosecution, such a one shall not be put on trial." Under this rule,

Judge Temple understood at the time of the trials that Pittenger would not be prosecuted.

That settled it in my mind. Pittenger had been accused while we were in prison of knowing he was safe from prosecution but had always denied it and said he would have to stand trial just the same as the rest of us when his time came. Now I was finally sure he had been playing us false all the way through. If any confession of ours was handed in under the table at Knoxville—and Judge Temple said none was read in court to his knowledge—I believe it was forged at Chattanooga by Mr. Pittenger, signatures and all.

Blue vs. Blue 2

A bitterly fought presidential election was on in the fall of 1888, incumbent Grover Cleveland against Benjamin Harrison, Ohio-born Republican. One of the campaign's heated minor issues, before its close, was the openly posed question of whether William Pittenger, while a Confederate prisoner, had been hero or traitor.

As Union army veterans and natives of the Republican stronghold of Ohio, a majority of the surviving raiders were natural opponents of the Democratic ticket, as Pittenger himself had been since reaching voting age as far as was known. In mid-campaign, the author of *Daring and Suffering* publicly took a stand for Cleveland. The repercussions of the move were being felt in the press of all parts of the country for weeks to follow.

Bridgeport, Conn., *Evening Farmer:*

Pittsburgh, October 24 [1888]

The Rev. William Pittenger, author of *Daring and Suffering,* and a life-long Republican, says:

"I have not been 'converted' and have not 'gone back on my record.' I hold just the same views regarding slavery, disunion, etc., that I held during the war, and if the issues between the parties were the same today as then, I would be on the same side still. But I never believed in high tariffs—in taxing the whole community for the benefit of a few. Every cent raised by the Government more than is needed by the Government, I believe to be a wrong done to the taxpayer.

"The President's message and the Mills bill meet my cordial approval, and I do not regard the taunt of 'free trade' any more than I used to regard the taunt of 'Abolitionist.' Therefore I expect to vote for the President's re-election."

EDITOR: It would be hard today to take issue with the stated reasons for Pittenger's decision. Harrison was far from a poor candidate, but in vetoing a come-one-come-all general pensions bill the year before, Grover Cleveland had taken one of the most courageous stands in American political history. The long-needed tariff revisions of the Mills bill and the recovery of millions of acres of public land illegally acquired by agile and well-connected individuals had added powerful strength to the opposition working strenuously for the defeat Cleveland was to meet. Had Pittenger been the most popular of the raiders, he could still have expected some hard words over this change of camp. With his position already as precarious as it was, the almost immediate result of his appearance as a political figure was a direct attack by the man who had stalked him over the years to the judgment reportedly reached at Knoxville.

Dorsey learned of Pittenger's political stand through a clipping sent him in October from Nelson Purdum of the Chillicothe *Leader*. [The excerpt below bearing on the sequence of events of October, 1888, is from a *Leader* article of the following February.]

Chillicothe, O., *Leader*, February 9, 1889:

One of the important elements of success in the campaign of last fall was the practical unanimity with which the old soldier vote stood up to the Republican ticket. . . . Of course there were some exceptions to the rule; and among those exceptions which attracted some attention was the case of Rev. Wm. Pittenger, a Methodist minister, of Hightstown, N.J., who suddenly declared his allegiance to the Democratic cause.

Pittenger had been a member of that gallant band of heroes who had been participants in one of the most daring and romantic episodes of the war—the famous Andrews Raid. His book, *Daring and Suffering*, was in half the old soldier households in the country. He had hitherto professed to be a Republican. . . .

So Rev. Wm. Pittenger was interviewed by the Democratic press; his connection with the famous Andrews Raid was retold; his book was extensively advertised; his face, his house and his town were photographed and made to furnish illustrations for the interview and the tale of his conversion to the Democratic faith.

This matter got into the "boiler-shops" of the cities, and done up in "plates," found place in the columns of every Democratic country weekly in the land. That is the way it happened to get into the columns of the Chillicothe *Advertiser*, and that is the way Treasurer Nelson Purdum came to see it. . . .

Now Mr. Purdum had been a member of the 33d Ohio, and he personally knew some of those who had gone out of his regiment on this dangerous expedition. So he clipped out the *Advertiser's* reference to Pittenger, and mailing it to Captain D. A. Dorsey, Kearney, Nebr., asked him what he knew about Pittenger.

Captain Dorsey's reply was published in the *Leader* of October 13, [1888] and when Rev. Pittenger of Hightstown, N.J., read it, it must have made his brain reel. . . . Captain Dorsey's letter more than intimated that Pittenger had turned traitor when the hour of danger came, and connived with the Rebels to furnish the evidence which would send all his gallant comrades to the scaffold, if but his own neck might be saved.

The charge was a terrible one; too terrible almost for belief. . . . Pittenger replied to Dorsey's letter, and the *Leader* published the reply; but it was weak, evasive and unsatisfactory. . . .

DORSEY: The whole tone of Pittenger's writings, on the subject of the trials, is calculated to deceive. There is a strained effort throughout to disguise the part he played. . . .

EDITOR: In effect, quoting the reports brought back through the lines by Samuel Llewellyn of the 33d Ohio and the several accounts printed in Confederate papers in 1862, which told of one of the raiders turning state's evidence, Dorsey charged that Pittenger had cracked at or almost immediately after his capture, and made himself a willing and fatally effective instrument of the Confederate authorities in return for promised immunity for himself and possible later release in "some distant part of the Confederacy." In all his writings since the war, Dorsey further charged, Pittenger had multiplied his guilt by consistently covering up or distorting the facts bearing on his own part in the trials.

Whether Pittenger's answers, in the Chillicothe *Leader* and the

Columbus *Dispatch*—to the columns of which the controversy quickly spread—were entirely "weak, evasive and unsatisfactory" depended to a considerable extent upon the varying political views and passions of the readers at the time. Pittenger had been a resourceful and quick-striking debater for nearly all the years of his life, and the stakes had rarely been as important to him.

Pittenger dismissed the Llewellyn story of his turning state's evidence as no more than unfounded rumor from the Rebel camp.

PITTENGER: A soldier who had started with us, but who had failed to get through the lines, and to save himself had joined the Rebel army, deserted from them and returned to our lines. He brought the news that the raiders were all captured and that one of the number—myself—was giving information against the others. Doubtless he gave the facts as they appeared to the Rebel soldiers with whom he was, for they could not know that all I did was as the spokeman for our whole party and for the purpose of showing that we were not spies, but soldiers regularly sent to perform a military service. His story caused no small controversy in our regiment—2nd Ohio—those who knew me well feeling certain that I could never be guilty of treachery, but having nothing but faith in my character to oppose to the man's positive statement.

EDITOR: In the heat of the 1888 election campaign, Pittenger wasn't counting on faith in his character on the part of probable political opponents in Ohio. Instead, he offered Judge O. P. Temple's statement of confidence in his fidelity as written to Dorsey in 1882, and added Dorsey's affidavit that the extract given was an accurate one.

PITTENGER: This very Dorsey, when he wrote his insinuations, had in his possession the following letter addressed to himself, proving their falsity. He had probably forgotten that he had given me a certified copy.

EDITOR: Pittenger proceeded to quote Judge Temple's clearly worded expression of confidence in his fidelity [the letter of January 21, 1882, already given] and added Dorsey's undeniable certification of the extract's accuracy: "I certify [on February 8, 1882] that the above is a true extract from a letter written to me by O. P. Temple who with Judge Baxter defended as counsel Marion A. Ross et al

. . . and that this extract covers all that relates to the matter therein contained."

The strongest answer for Pittenger came from a one-time opponent. As late as that spring, William A. Fuller had been writing to Dorsey with continuing reservations as to the wisdom or rightness of Pittenger's course during the trials. But Fuller was the man, among his several strong loyalties, who held himself to have been fired from the W. & A. service in the winter of 1869-1870 for no greater crime than "being a Democrat." If Republican partisan zeal could heat the words of those attacking Pittenger, Fuller may well have felt the need of some balancing warmth in favor of the new convert to the old party from which the Georgian had never wavered. On November 15 —late for the narrowly lost election, but not too late for the developing free-for-all—the "one man in the Confederacy who could have saved the W. & A. bridges that day" firmly chose his side.

FULLER:

Atlanta, Ga.
November 15, 1888

To the Editor of the [Columbus, O.] *Dispatch:*

I have your valuable paper of the 10th containing an article from the pen of Rev. Wm. Pittenger, a distinguished member of the deservedly notorious Andrews raiding party. I use the expression "distinguished member," because he has taken the pains, with great labor and tedious expensive research, to get together and publish all of the most important facts bearing upon one of the most daring, dangerous and thrilling expeditions of the late war. His book, *Daring and Suffering,* stands for itself, and the truths it contains will not be successfully contradicted. Looking at it from the standpoint of one who so hotly and vigorously contended against his party, I must say that on some points he makes, I think he draws strongly upon his imagination, as against the pursuing party, and then after the capture, as against the court trying the prisoners, and in favor, of course, always of his side. But this is so natural, that I hope I am charitable enough to excuse him for so doing. On the whole his story, as told in *Daring and Suffering,* in so far as I know, is true.

The article referred to in your paper of the 10th, by Mr. Pittenger, seems to have been made necessary in order to defend himself against what occurs to me to be an unwarrantable intimation or insinuation from the pen of Captain D. A. Dorsey, one of Dr. Pittenger's long-suffering companions. This insinuation, in effect, indirectly

[*Fuller*]
charges Dr. Pittenger with disloyalty and infidelity to his comrades when on trial in Chattanooga and Knoxville in May, 1862, while he, Dr. Pittenger, was attending court as a witness. . . .

As stated in my speech in Columbus in September last: When I had recaptured my train and the famous engine *General* and returned them to their legitimate service, and had personally or by other successful expedient captured the raiders, and they had been placed in prison, my duty as a public servant was at an end. But the cold iron hand of war's grip held the reins of government. The offended laws of cruel war had to be avenged. A court-martial was organized and the trial of the raiders had at once. The blood of the Southerner ran hot, and something must be done speedily as a preventive against a repetition of so daring an undertaking, the success of which was only thwarted by almost superhuman effort and peril.

A *subpoena ad testificandum* was served upon me and of course I served. The prisoners were brought into court, one at a time, as is usual in such cases, beginning with Andrews, the leader. The charges against each were similar, and they were that of spying, with the usual number of specifications. In each case tried, I testified. Dr. Pittenger was also a witness in each case. One of the specifications alleged that the prisoners lurked in and about the camps of the Confederates. Dr. Pittenger testified as to the route the raiders had taken from Shelbyville to Marietta on their downward trip. In each case tried, he gave the correct name of the prisoner, the letter of his company, the number of his regiment, and the state from which he came. My testimony was mainly as to the raiders boarding my train at Marietta on my upward trip, then in regard to its capture by the raiders at Big Shanty, then as to the effort made to destroy the road, the bridges and the telegraph, giving in detail, in each case tried, an account of the pursuit and the recapture of my train.

Now, it is due to candor and truth, that I should here state that when I heard Dr. Pittenger testifying, believing as I then believed, and as I now know, his testimony taken in connection with mine would prove fatal, I could but suppose that the witness had in view somewhat of an immunity from personal harm. But at the same time, I could scarcely believe it from the fact that his testimony seemed to be in accordance with the expectations of the prisoner in each case on trial, as well as their distinguished counsel, Judges Temple and Baxter. Not only so, but Dr. Pittenger seemed all the time to be on the best of terms with all the prisoners day by day as the trial of the several cases progressed.

In that cloud of mystery and uncertainty in reference to Pittenger's testimony my mind rested until the matter was made plain to me by not only Dr. Pittenger but others of the survivors.

As to the truth of Dr. Pittenger's statement, in substance, that the line of defense was agreed upon among the prisoners in jail, by and with the knowledge, consent and advice of their counsel, I now have not the slightest doubt.

Before this was made clear to my mind, in answer to some questions propounded to me by letters from Captain Dorsey, I may have written something that left doubt on his mind. If so, I sincerely hope that this impartial statement will at once dispel it. My mind is now clear, and I am firmly of the belief that Dr. Pittenger was at all times and under all circumstances true to his comrades and loyal to his cause.

I am, most respectfully,

Wm. A. Fuller

EDITOR: Two raiders joined publicly in Pittenger's defense.

WM. REDDICK: By this unwarranted attack Dorsey has done Pittenger great injustice. I never saw where Pittenger received any favor from the Rebels. If Pittenger has made any money by his books, he is entitled to it. He offered to share with the party if they would pay him for his labor.

J. R. PORTER: I cannot see how any member of the party can bear Dorsey out. He talked quite differently two years ago. I would like to know what members of the party, if any, will be influenced by a man who will falsify and vilify men who have been his best friends.

EDITOR: At Chillicothe, where the first open charges had exploded, Engineer Bill Knight in February, 1889, gave a partial answer to Porter's question.

Chillicothe, O., *Leader*, February 9, 1889:

On Friday and Saturday of last week, William J. Knight, another member of the famous band, and the man who took the throttle when the boys stole the Rebel train at Big Shanty, was a visitor to Chillicothe. . . . While he was here, he dropped into the *Leader* office to see the [issues] containing the Dorsey letter and the Pittenger reply.

The *Leader* [editor] watched Knight's face as he read. Under the overarching eyebrows he could see the stern eye flash, and under the bushy sandy beard, the square jaw working nervously, as the stories of each brought back to his mind the most eventful portion of his life.

The *Leader* knew that he was interested and he hoped that he might induce him to talk. . . .

"What do you think of Dorsey's accusations?" the *Leader* asked the engineer in an indifferent sort of a way.

"What do I think of them?" and the old soldier hastily arose to his feet and nervously paced the floor, "why, I——— but you will excuse me; this is a question that I have never discussed, save with my old comrades; and it is a subject that I do not care to talk about now."

"But, Mr. Knight, the issue had been made by Mr. Dorsey's letter. If his theory is correct he should be sustained by his old comrades; if Pittenger is wronged, he is terribly wronged, and those companions who believe that he has been wronged should say so."

"Well, sir," said the engineer, "as I have said, I do not care to discuss this subject; but I think as Dorsey does, and never have thought any other way. Why, sir, I had made up my mind immediately after I escaped from prison that if I ever met Pittenger, I would kill him; so strongly was his treachery impressed upon my mind. I never had any confidence in him from the first day I saw him. . . .

"I never ceased to mistrust him, and I haven't ceased yet," the old soldier continued. "I obtained and brought home with me the charges and specifications against George D. Wilson, one of our boys, upon which he was tried and hung. These charges and specifications bore the signatures of William Pittenger, and of Wm. A. Fuller, the conductor of the Rebel train that we stole.

"When we escaped from jail at Atlanta, Pittenger was there with us, and was as free to escape as any of us, but he preferred to remain."

"How many were there in the raid, Mr. Knight?" the *Leader* asked.

"Twenty-two."

"How many are there left?"

"But eleven. . . ."

"Can you tell the names of those who are yet living: where they live, and what business they are engaged in?"

"I think so. Well, to begin with, there is John Wollam. He was a 33d boy; is a bridge builder now, and lives at Topeka, Kansas. . . ."

"Who of all those living have confidence in Pittenger, and believe that he acted in good faith and did for the best?"

"But one that I know of—Wm. Bensinger. I think he feels that we have misjudged Pittenger."

"And the rest?"

[Knight's answer to this question was given without his knowing that Porter and Reddick had spoken or were about to speak out for Pittenger. Knight probably was as mistaken at the time on Brown, but no evidence of a greater error has yet been turned up.]

"All feel about him about as Dorsey and I do."

How Dorsey felt, by this time, was reasonably unmistakable.

DORSEY: "It was all the deepest laid scheme, and on the grandest scale," the Atlanta *Confederacy* had said, "that ever emanated from the brains of any number of conspirators combined." After years of mature deliberation and deep research, I take just that view of the case.

Chattanooga 1891

S. B. PORTER:

Columbus, Ohio
April 15, 1891

To the Posts of the Department of Ohio,
Grand Army of the Republic:

Comrades: Please ask the editor of your local paper to print the paragraph next following as news. It concerns the people. They pay for the monument:

(For the Press)

Ohio's tribute to the Andrews Raiders, provided for by Sixty-eighth General Assembly, is to be unveiled at the National Cemetery at Chattanooga, Saturday, May 30, 1891. The public are invited. The surviving raiders and the

[*S. B. Porter*]

widows, sisters, sons and daugthers of the men who were executed are to be the guests of the G.A.R. of that city. (Insert your post)

Post, No. has received an invitation to attend. The railroads have made a rate, and ex-Governor J. B. Foraker is to deliver the principal address.

The old soldiers and citizens of Chattanooga guarantee us a memorable visit.

Thaddeus Minshall, late Capt. 33rd O.V.I. President
Earl W. Merry, late Sgt. Major 21st O.V.I.
Stephen B. Porter, late Sgt., Co. G, 2nd O.V.I. Secy.
Andrews Raiders Commission (By authority
P. H. Dowling, Department Commander)

DORSEY: There was no use to talk to John Wollam about good faith. He lived and died—September 25, 1890—believing Pittenger had played false.

S. B. PORTER:

Columbus, Ohio
May 3, 1891

W. J. Knight, Esq.
Stryker, Ohio

Dear Sir:

Mr. Pittenger says: "If I should not get to the meeting [at Chattanooga] will you please say to the boys that I will now—if they still wish it—give them the history of our raid on very favorable terms. I will throw in the copyright and all plates and cuts which cost $1,600 for $1,000, or a 1/10 interest to any one of them for $100. This is much less than I offered it before because I have had 2½ years' sale of the book [*Daring and Suffering* of 1887] and have paid off, by means of it, obligations that then were resting on me." Pittenger, I am confident, will not be able to get to Chattanooga, but I look for all of the others with confidence.

You will apply for information concerning your transportation to the Big 4 agent at Findlay. . . .

I think Mrs. J. M. Powell, 131 Centre St., Findlay, a sister of John Scott, keeps a boarding house. If I were you I would go there when you get to Findlay. Scott's other relatives there are: Mrs. John W.

Exline, 509 Centre St.; Mrs. Geo. L. Arnold, Lincoln St.; Mrs. Chas. A. Ebling, 600 Main St.; Albert W. Scott, 214 Clinton St.

Very respectfully,

S. B. Porter

EDITOR: The raiders passed up the bargain-rate chance to become Pittenger's publishing partners, and *Dispatch* editor Stephen B. Porter guessed wrong about the clergyman-author's willingness to face hostile ex-companions. Brown, Knight, Reddick and Parrott didn't make it to the Memorial Day ceremonies at Chattanooga, but Pittenger did, along with John Porter, Bensinger, Alf Wilson, Dorsey and Mason. Sisters of Marion A. Ross and a nephew named for him, the sisters and brothers of John Scott, a sister of Sam Slavens, and a brother of Sammy Robertson were among the relatives attending. Rachel Slavens had come from Wakefield, in Pike County, with her sons now grown beyond the age Sam had been when he started out from Shelbyville. This time, too, Anthony Murphy and White Smith stood with Conductor Fuller as representatives of the pursuing party of 1862.

On the day of the memorial's dedication, floral pieces ordered from all parts of the country, including a pair from President and Mrs. Harrison, banked the marble block topped by a bronze replica of the *General*. At least one unguarded reference by Fuller—or the chance of an even greater audience—tempted Dorsey to take public exception again as he had done at Columbus, but his fellow raiders prevailed on the easily triggered Nebraskan to hold his fire, feeling that ex-Governor Foraker that day had stated the rights and wrongs of the case as plainly as the executed men themselves could have asked.

J. B. FORAKER: They [the seven men executed with Andrews] were typical Ohio boys, hardly out of their teens, without name, family, influence, or station, to cause them to be remembered and honored, as they are remembered and honored today. Why is it, then, that we are here? What purposes are we seeking to promote?

The answer is plain and simple. In the first place there is no bitterness, vainglory or unworthy spirit of any kind involved—although in no instance during the whole war, from its beginning to its ending, was any Confederate soldier, similarly captured, treated otherwise than as a prisoner of war. It is but stating the exact truth to repeat as fairly applicable to the whole of that great army who wore the blue, the dying words of Wilson, "that he had no hard feelings toward the

South or her people. That he loved the Union and the flag, and was fighting to uphold them, and not to do unnecessary injury to anyone."

Even in the midst of that great struggle [these eight men] did not want to kill anybody, except only as it became necessary to kill somebody to kill secession. They believed in the union of these States. They believed the highest interests of the South, as well as the North, required its preservation, and believing slavery to be the disturbing cause of all our differences, they gladly struck it down. But with it all there was no malice.

And as it was then, so is it now. The one great thought, that lies at the bottom of every such demonstration as this, is that of profound gratitude to the men who saved us, and supreme thankfulness to Almighty God for the great blessings that have come to our whole country through the victory of the Union armies. . . .

We erect and dedicate this monument in an impressive presence. Every spot on which the eye rests is hallowed ground. Visions long gone come back. A torn, dismembered and bleeding country rises before us. Grief and mourning are in every household. Countrymen are striving against countrymen. Two flags are in the sky. Two governments are struggling for the mastery. Hooker is again battling in the clouds, and once more Thomas is storming Mission Ridge. Again we see the moving roar and tumult of battle—the rattle of musketry, the shriek of shells, the shouts of the victors, and the groans of the dying. . . .

Break away from that nightmare. The armies have vanished. One flag floats for all. . . . [But the man] who would degrade the war to a mere trial of strength or display of valor is guilty of a crime second only to the rebellion itself. Valor there was on both sides, and that, too, of the highest quality, but the sublimity of the struggle was in the principles at stake. They related to our moral as well as our political welfare. Human rights and personal liberty, as well as American nationality, were bound up in the issue. Free, popular government was on trial. Success was our triumphant salvation—failure would have been our unspeakable ruin.

Who is so blind as not to see? Who so insensible as not to be proud of the United States of America? Soon the last of the war generation will be gone. . . . The prejudices that have drawn sectional lines will be swallowed up in a generous rivalry that knows not either North, South, East or West, but only a common pride in every portion of our common country. That glad day is swiftly coming. Let us run to meet it.

Showdown 1

JOHN T. RAPER:

The Ohio Soldier
Published Bi-Weekly: John T. Raper, Editor
Offices of publication: Cincinnati, O.
Editorial office: Chillicothe, O.
Saturday, January 28, 1893

THE MITCHEL RAID

We are enabled to announce this week that we have completed arrangements with Lieutenant D. A. Dorsey for his history of the famous raid organized under General Mitchel's orders—detailed from the ranks of the 2nd, 21st and 33d Ohio. . . . But one account of this, the most romantic incident in the history of warfare, has been published, and that has been pronounced by all participants as most unsatisfactory. It is therefore with peculiar pleasure that we announce this history of the raid by Lieutenant Dorsey. He is a comrade of intelligence, was a good soldier in every position in which he was placed, and enjoyed the confidence of the comrades who were with him in the famous raid, as well as his comrades in his regiment.

EDITOR: With the publication of Dorsey's own book-length account of the raid and its following events in the columns of *The Ohio Soldier* in 1893—the year of the Chicago World's Fair and of Grover Cleveland's return to the White House—the intermittently banked warfare between Dorsey and Pittenger broke into full flame.

The *Soldier* was taken or seen by most Ohio veterans, and the outspoken charges carried assured even wider circulation during the ten months the installments ran. In the spring of the year, with an eye to the sales possibilities at Chicago where the *General* was to be on exhibit with Knight and others lecturing, Pittenger brought out an essentially unchanged version of his *Daring and Suffering* of 1887, under the new and livelier title of *The Great Locomotive Chase*. The book was eventually to run gainfully through nearly a dozen editions, but for sharp reader interest in 1893—including that of the ten surviving raiders—the *Chase* ran well second to the fireworks touched off semimonthly in the *Soldier*.

Dorsey's opening profession was as rolling and decorous a one as even his opponent might have penned, although the health reference can be taken as possibly less than a literal report. In the pension-conscious postwar years, the actual physical condition of any G.A.R. man—Pittenger and others along with Dorsey—could be taken as somewhat harder to establish exactly than even the detailed truth of a wartime trial thirty years past.

DORSEY: Nothing but death will erase from my mind the incidents of the history I shall try to write. It is my desire to put things in their true light, and if the facts seem to reflect on anyone, it must be borne in mind that while I have no disposition to mar the happiness of any, yet the truth of history should be written.

I must ask charitable consideration of the fact that for many years after the events I describe, no survivor of the expedition was able to sit down and pore over the subject long enough to record the events except the Rev. William Pittenger, who accordingly has been permitted to be practically the sole historian of the "Mitchel Raid." Grateful for a restoration to health of what was once an almost wrecked constitution, I now venture upon the performance of a duty that has long pressed itself upon me, a duty which I feel is due not only the living, but the martyred dead, to whose memory these pages are most respectfully dedicated.

EDITOR: In his narrative account of the raid's preparation, the penetration trip south, the train capture and chase, and following escape attempts—from which a number of excerpts have already been taken for this book—Dorsey made a substantial addition to the factual record. It was with his handling of the trials and the part played by Pittenger then and later that the history-writing began to become hard to distinguish from a wide-ranging indictment.

DORSEY: Pittenger publishes to the world the report that one of our number was said to have turned "state's evidence," and says it is "hard to understand." He knew just what it meant but didn't dare to tell. He prefers to leave the reading public to suspect whom they will. He has been told that if he didn't tell the whole truth, we would tell it. He has failed to do so, and I shall try to fulfill our promise.

EDITOR: As late as the *Daring and Suffering* of 1887, and in *The Great Locomotive Chase*, published while Dorsey's series was running, Pittenger had spoken of the *Daring and Suffering* of 1863 as written in a manner "preserving the facts [of the raid] in their freshness, and attested in its recital of incidents by all the survivors of the expedition."

The important facts of the trials that led to the execution of eight men, in Dorsey's view, hadn't been given at all.

DORSEY: The depositions of March 25, 1863, by Bensinger, Buffum, Parrott, Pittenger and Reddick, on which Judge Holt's report of the Andrews expedition is based are recorded in the Army and Navy Official Gazette, of July 31, 1863. Not a word was said in these depositions (nor in Pittenger's books) about the witnesses against those who were tried by the Rebel court-martial—who they were, or what was their testimony. None of those who deposed knew of his own knowledge about these matters except Pittenger, who was the first and most extensively examined. His statement was quite full, and the others simply corroborated what he said, some adding their own testimony more fully about matters that had come under their personal observation, and were not personally known to Pittenger.

We cannot blame those who had no personal knowledge of the fact that Pittenger was a witness for the prosecution, and only knew of it by hearsay, for not mentioning it. But Pittenger knew all about it, and was sworn to tell the truth, the whole truth, and nothing but the truth. Since the war he has said to friends that the reason he said nothing concerning the fact that he testified for the prosecution was that part of his said testimony was "rank perjury." Is it not perjury to withhold part of the truth when sworn to tell the whole truth? Or was an oath administered by a Rebel court-martial more binding on his conscience than an oath administered by the judge advocate general of the United States? Or did he not consider the witness matter a material fact?

My judgment is that it was a very material fact, and if Pittenger had been as conscientious as he would have us believe him to be, he would have made a clean breast of the matter, and told all about it. But he was a lawyer and he knew Judge Holt was a lawyer. He knew as a lawyer that while he had made his uninformed comrades believe that he stood in the same light before the enemy in which they stood, he could not make Judge Holt believe it. Hence he said nothing about it.

After our capture, Pittenger had a plan of his own, to defeat, as he claimed we could do, the enemy in their attempt to prove that we were spies. His plan was to induce the enemy to put himself—Pittenger—on the witness stand as their witness, on the supposition, on their part, that he had turned state's evidence, when as a matter of fact, he was not to turn state's evidence, but to testify that we were regularly detailed soldiers, on a purely military expedition, and thus, as he claimed, disprove or contradict the assertion that we were spies.

Pittenger was a law student, in fact, quite a lawyer, and had a knowledge of law, both civil and military, and with his smooth tongue exerted quite an influence with the members of his own regiment and some others, who fell in with his proposition.

Pittenger knew that where one of a number of persons accused of a crime gives testimony for the prosecution, there is an implied agreement or understanding that such one will not be put on trial, and therein, I opine, was the "milk in the cocoanut" in this case.

This plan of Pittenger's was bitterly opposed by some. Others, like myself, paid no particular attention to it, except to maintain our position that there was no hope for us except in escaping. Those who indorsed Pittenger's plan to play the part of witness for the prosecution, in order to arrange an interview with the officers, set up a howl to the officer who always came with a squad of soldiers with the jailer when he opened the prison to "Take this man out! He is awful sick!"—which he feigned for the purpose—"For God's sake, don't let this man die in this hole!"

It worked, and Pittenger went creeping up the ladder, so faint and weak it seemed he would fall off before reaching the top. George D. Wilson, one of the oldest and most intelligent among us, strange to say, indorsed Pittenger's plan, and with others in the scheme gave muttered expressions of approval at their success in getting Pittenger out, while in other quarters of the "hole," there were deep-toned expressions of disapproval, mingled with curses upon "the fool scheme," with predictions of disaster.

Of his first interview with General Leadbetter, Pittenger says: "He began to question me, and without any regard to truth, I gave him the story that I supposed would be best for my own interest. I told him I was a United States soldier, giving my name, company and regiment correctly; but told him I was sent on this expedition without my previous consent, and was ignorant of where I was going or what I was to do, which I only learned as fast as it was to be executed."

Telling them we were United States soldiers, ignorant of what we were to do, is just what we all did, and how George D. Wilson could be brought to the plan of allowing Pittenger to go on the stand and testify that we knew from the beginning that we were to destroy some line of communication in the enemy's country, is more than I can understand. But Wilson is dead. The plan was arranged between Pittenger and Wilson almost exclusively, and whether "the lines laid down" were followed or not, I don't know. I wasn't a party to the plan and never consented to it.

Southern Confederacy, a newspaper published at Atlanta under date of April 24, 1862, says:

"One of them proposed to turn state's evidence against the balance if he could thereby save his own neck."

But Alf Wilson [and Mark Wood] in a letter published in the Key West, Florida, *New Era,* November 15, 1862, said, as Pittenger gives it:

"A court-martial was ordered for Andrews, and Pittenger of the 2nd Ohio was taken out as a witness; and by alternate offers of pardon and persecution they endeavored to make him testify against him, but he was true to his word and his companions, and the court could gain nothing from him."

Pittenger quotes the above, *Daring and Suffering* page 230, for the purpose, no doubt, of showing that he did not accept proffered immunity. Wilson [and Wood] knew no more about it at the time than I did, and I had no means of knowing whether they got anything out of Pittenger or not, nor could we ever have known if Pittenger had preserved silence on the subject. But Pittenger's writings are quite an eye opener. Reading Pittenger is like picking a millstone; the more you pick, the deeper you can see into the stone. Let us quote him again. Speaking of the examinations he says:

PITTENGER: "My own ordeal was more protracted, probably because I had been the first brought before the commanding general, and also because I had been very willing to communicate what I knew—up to a certain point. . . . I went through the street once more, still wearing my handcuffs *on both hands,* attended by eight guards, and was brought before an officer, I presumed either the judge advocate or the president of the court-martial. Here I was told that they wanted to learn several things, among others the name of our engineer, who was engaged in this affair, and the relation that the man Andrews bore to us and to the army. The officer said that he thought I could tell if I wanted to, and that if I did, I need have no fear of any prosecution

[*Pittenger*]
for myself. It would have been easy to have refused to say anything, but I thought it better to answer:

"'Everything that concerns me alone I will tell you freely, as I want you to know that I am an American soldier, and that I have done my simple duty; but I will not tell you anything that might tend to injure my companions.'

"He answered that he could promise me nothing unless I would tell all I knew. I said that I asked no promise, believing that when they understood the case they would only hold us all as prisoners of war. He said that this was very probable, but that he would have me separated from my companions and see me again in a day or two."

DORSEY: Let us look at this a little: Pittenger italicizes the fact that he had his handcuffs "on both hands," as if that were important. How else would a man wear handcuffs? Would anybody be foolish enough to put them on one hand, expecting them to restrain a prisoner? It seems to me he put that in to show that they regarded him as a bad man, from whom there had been no previous intimation that he might do to trust. It seems to me that the words that needed italicizing were "that if I did, I need have no fear of any prosecution for myself." Put that in italics as you go along and keep your eye on the indicator.

I believe he was not in irons at all [on the streets of Chattanooga] and that the officer alone guarded him or rather escorted him. When Pittenger is telling a falsehood he has a way of telling you how he knows it to be true. He says he was captured about noon. Knows it was near noon, for he saw people going to church. The fact is he was captured at seven o'clock in the morning, but puts his capture off until near noon so as to leave the impression that those captured earlier had told the story of the raid, which in fact he had done himself. He virtually says, "Of course I am a liar, boys. You know I am a liar, but *this* is true and I'll tell you how I know it is true," then relates the incident calculated to demonstrate its truth.

What "promise" was he seeking that prompted the officer to tell him he could promise him nothing unless he told all he knew?

I firmly believe he told the whole story including "the relation this man Andrews bore to the army."

Page 180 (*Capturing a Locomotive*), speaking of the questioning by General Leadbetter, he says: "For two or three days I was even separated from my comrades and daily questioned. . . . I could easily have secured my own safety by dishonor; but although I talked freely, I did not go a single word beyond the line which Wilson and myself, with the approval of all the others, had marked out."

Separated from his companions two or three days? At least ten days or two weeks. The line marked out by himself and Wilson was approved by all the others, was it? Not by any means, and he knew it when he wrote that. I for one wasn't a party to the plan and never consented to it. He manufactured that out of whole cloth. And then at last he "heard the acute lawyer who acted as examiner on these occasions say to General Leadbetter:

"'It is no use! He is either ignorant or too sharp to tell anything.'

"I felt greatly complimented, and was then taken back to the horrors of the old dungeon. . . ."

I think that "it is no use" is something else he manufactured himself. At the end of these interviews he was accepted as a witness for the enemy's side of a controversy that involved the lives of his comrades. Back to the "horrors of the old dungeon"? Back to the pleasures of the prison yard—quite a difference.

Again (in *Daring and Suffering*, page 232) he says, "None of us knew just the line of defense taken by Andrews, or upon what he based the hopes he did, certainly, to some extent, entertain." Now, what is the use of talking that way? Wasn't the whole matter talked over in the dungeon before Pittenger "was called out"? Pittenger was present at the trial and certainly knew "the line of defense taken by Andrews."

It will be observed that the charges and specifications [at Knoxville] make no mention of what we did or tried to do—burn bridges or steal or capture cars, etc.—but they charged spying, which there was no adequate evidence to support. Pittenger says (*Capturing a Locomotive*, page 211): "As to evidence against us, we knew that our recorded confessions, made when we were first brought to Chattanooga, could be used, and possibly the evidence of those who first captured us." What recorded confessions? Who made a confession, except to say he was a soldier, and entitled to treatment as a prisoner of war? They had no other confession from me.

Continuing, he says: "To make the greatest impression of candor, our story was sketched in brief, with the approval of the whole number, and, at a subsequent visit of the judge advocate, handed to him. He took our signatures to it, and it was read on the trials as our confession. It saved our enemies some trouble in the matter of witnesses, and put our case in what we judged the most favorable light." This so-called confession which he says was read before the court is not mentioned in his *Daring and Suffering*, and the survivors who were at Knoxville say no such paper was signed by them. Judge Temple also told me, in a brief interview I had with him in 1888, that no such paper was read before the court that he knew of. Can it be possible that Pittenger did this in some underhanded way, unknown to counsel and defendants alike?

I believed, and still believe, that the plan was to try the eleven, and execute them; then take the remaining nine to Knoxville, try and execute them. And then—what would they have done with Pittenger? Would he have been "turned loose in some remote part of the Confederacy," as he said in 1888 was one of the inducements they offered him?

(But keep your eye on the indicator. I wish I could wink at you, and by the way, if I were in the type-making business I would make such a type—a human eye with a wink on it. I would like to use it occasionally in writing this scrap of history. You see, we boys were in the soup, and in it bad, and I sometimes wish I could get out and write about something else.)

Or would they have made Pittenger a major in the Confederate army? I heard once, while we were prisoners, that some such proposition was made to some member of our party for some favor they thought he could do them. Perhaps, though, that was in their almost mad attempt to find out who our engineer was. They did pull every conceivable string to learn that, but all to no purpose. So far as we know they never did learn who our engineer was until after the war closed.

From what Pittenger has said I believe their anxiety to learn who ran the engine was because they had an idea that it was one of their own citizens, and from the fact that the efforts to learn who our engineer was practically ceased after it was arranged for Pittenger to go on the witness stand as their witness, I infer that Pittenger told them that it was not one of their citizens but some of our party, but of course would not tell who it was, and as we had repeatedly told them we were all in the same boat, all equally guilty or innocent, they could have no particular grudge against the engineer, nor would they care which one it was, for they meant to hang all except their friend Pittenger, and thus would be sure to get the engineer anyhow. I think that is the true solution of the engineer matter. . . .

According to Fuller, Pittenger gave the name of every man in the party, his company, regiment and corps. How dared he go in there and name any man who did not personally consent to it? What right had he to name me, or any of the nine who had been left at Chattanooga? I can only speak positively for myself, and if he named me before the court-martial he did that which he had no authority to do.

There had been some talk of the enemy sending a flag of truce to General Mitchel's camp to have our statements as to our character as soldiers verified, at least Pittenger says so, and on page 197 (*Capturing a Locomotive*) adds: "Our plans were carried out to the letter. Not one of our 'reserved facts' was ever known to the enemy until we were all beyond his power. . . . To this plan, conceived in the dungeon and consistently carried out, I attribute more than to anything else, the escape of any part of our number."

I think that to this plan, conceived in sin and born in iniquity, is due the fact that our leader and seven comrades were hanged, certainly the seven, and that if carried out to completion, it would have hanged every man in the party except Mr. Pittenger. There is no telling, from what he says, where it was conceived; for all we know, it may have been conceived in Lafayette, and there are some things that lead me to believe it was.

Pittenger quotes from the Atlanta *Southern Confederacy* a notice of the conclusion of Andrews' trial, the closing paragraph of which, on page 234, *Daring and Suffering,* is as follows: "We are informed that the one who turned state's evidence against them is a Kentuckian. He said he was one of the state guard in the days when neutrality was in vogue; that before he was fully aware of the fact, he was in the Lincoln army and could not escape from it."

Commenting upon this, same page, he says: "The report is hard to understand, even allowing for the usual latitude of misinformation. No member of our party was from Kentucky except Campbell, who carefully concealed the fact. It may be simply a reminiscence of our Kentucky pretensions. Andrews himself had been a member of the Kentucky state guard; but it is not likely that he would give that as a reason for being in the Union service."

Well! Why, Pittenger knew when he wrote that, that he was the very fellow referred to. What did the man mean in trying to cover his tracks when he knew there were so many living witnesses to the truth? It is unaccountable.

EDITOR: Apart from his record straightening and pointed speculations on the trials, Dorsey took the chance—while he had his audience

[*Editor*]
—to have his say on dozens of points in connection with the men and events of the raid, including an unusually frank report of his own mental condition as remembered from prison days.

An assorted sampling:

DORSEY: Our seven men were hurried off to their deaths without an hour's warning. Had the Confederates pounced upon us in the heat of passion at first capture and killed us all, there might have been some excuse for it. [Going through with the executions ten weeks later] was more barbarous than any of us believed [men] could possibly be.

Those who have read *Tom Sawyer* and *Huckleberry Finn* will recognize the striking characters in our party. Pittenger was Tom Sawyer, while all the rest of us were "Hucks." For instance, the case of Mason: bitterly opposed to the letter of August 17 addressed to Confederate authorities, knew it was wrong, yet when "Tom" wrote it, Mason marched up and signed it.

Quite a number of letters have been exchanged between Captain Fuller and surviving raiders since the war and in one of these the captain says, speaking of the raid: "But two things operated to prevent your success: first, unforeseen detention; second, but really the greatest of the two, you had the wrong man behind you in the race. Am I immodest in saying so?"

Answering his question, I will say it is simply a matter of taste.

I cannot describe the mental anguish I felt [in the prison at Chattanooga], but there was a deep regret at the thought that we had failed in our undertaking, and had literally thrown our lives away; then the thought of home, and friends and mother, whom I had no hope of ever seeing again, but instead must die among strangers on the scaffold; and that, too, for no crime, but for daring to do right. The thought was excruciating, and caused the heart and brain apparently to swell under the mental strain—the indisposition to yield—until it seemed both would burst and cause instant death. But just when it seemed death must ensue, a reaction would set in, and I gradually sank back into a sort of stupor, or sleep, which alone would give relief to an aching heart and a bursting brain. Following this feeling there was one of resignation, which, however, did not last long, until the same old feeling came over me again, only to be followed by the same stupor and resignation; and this was repeated over and again during my entire imprisonment, at greater or less intervals, and to this day I am not entirely free from these feelings if excited, or overworked mentally, and as of yore, sleep alone brings relief.

During my imprisonment, I often sincerely wished, when finding myself about to be lost in slumber, that God in His mercy might make it my last sleep; for in sleep there was rest, and I honestly wished death might claim me ere I awoke to another day of suffering. But, mind you, I felt quite sure that a more horrible death than dying in one's sleep was near at hand; otherwise I might have felt different about it.

Fuller's message from Knoxville after Andrews' temporary escape—"Colonel Henry L. Claiborne: Is it possible that the infamous Andrews escaped? Is he pursued? If not, offer in my name $100 reward for his recapture and reincarceration. Wm. A. Fuller"—confirms what I have said about his pursuing us to our death after we were in the hands of the military authorities. He has said since the war that he was at Knoxville in answer to a subpoena. Then why was not Anthony Murphy there also? He had seen as much of us on the day of the raid as Fuller had. It is clear to my mind that Fuller was there on his own motion, to urge on the prosecution, and that Murphy remained away because he did not wish to see us put to death. The two were at swords' points on that question and always have been, as I understand it.

I want to say here for Captain Fuller that he didn't attempt to deceive us. We knew just where to find him all the way through. He meant to hang us, and told us so from the beginning. Just what right he, a citizen, had to take a hand in prosecuting United States soldiers is another question, a question for our government and not us to answer.

[At one point in Atlanta] Pittenger tried to console us. As time rolled on and none of the rest of us were put on trial, it occurred to him that our leader and one-third of his men having been executed, the enemy probably intended to stop at that and allow the rest of us to live. To fortify us in this belief he argued very frequently, in the case of mutineers at sea, pirates, highwaymen, etc., the authorities would put the leaders and one-third of the men to death and spare the others.

He proceeded to cite instances of the rule which he claimed to have seen in the course of his studies as a law student. But [in my own law studies] I have never seen anything that leads me to believe there was such a custom, nor do I think Pittenger ever had.

Of course there could have been no compulsion on him if Pittenger had had any nerve, which "is doubted some on this side of the house" as the boys used to say in prison. In *Capturing a Locomotive*, pages 192-193, he says: "With many others I was convinced that we ought to make a bold push for liberty" and "Finally the majority decided in favor of an attempt to escape. Two plans were proposed—the first by the writer." The fact is Pittenger always opposed attempting to escape, giving as a reason that, being near-sighted, he couldn't make his way through the wood, especially at night.

EDITOR: Dorsey's *Ohio Soldier* account incorporated much more of Knight's first-hand reporting than had before been generally available, including one passage that might have been ground for lessening the pressure of accusations against Pittenger, had Dorsey felt himself less the prosecuting attorney with a jury-ready case.

KNIGHT: They then took in [before General Leadbetter, on first arrival of the captured men at Chattanooga] another one of our party, William Reddick, or as we always called him, Bill. The old general went at Bill in a different way. He told Bill that they had the rest of our party in jail, and then bringing Andrews up, in part verified his statement.

He said: "If you belong to that party the only thing that will save your life will be to acknowledge it, and claim protection from our government, as the balance of them have done."

William, being an easygoing kind of fellow and one of the George Washington stripe that couldn't tell a lie, gave it away. I noticed when he came out we were started off for jail without any examination of Brown. I suspected something wrong, and as soon as I got a chance to whisper to Bill, I asked him if he gave it away. He said he did not. I told him something was wrong or they would have taken Brown in. He said he didn't care; he didn't tell anything.

EDITOR: Dorsey may have shared Knight's original doubts about Reddick from the moment of hearing of them—or his willingness to throw a barb at the Iowan may have dated from Reddick's support of Pittenger in the election campaign clash of 1888—but Reddick had served creditably to the last day of the war, and had written no books.

The target remained Pittenger, although increasingly, Dorsey's exasperation was being directed even more at the later evasions and literary sleight-of-hand than at the original faults charged.

DORSEY: This man's efforts to cover up his tracks are remarkable. . . . In *Great Locomotive Chase,* page 102, he says: "They [the Confederate recruits at Camp McDonald] were encamped almost entirely on the west side of the road, but their camp guard included the railroad depot." He is determined to make it appear that we were inside the guard lines at Big Shanty, and thus as far as possible justify the enemy in treating us as spies.

The fact is, there was no depot at Big Shanty at that time, and all the troops were west of the track. No military man would lay out a camp of the kind so as to include a railroad station. In *Capturing a Locomotive,* page 211, he had put it: "But no one could say anything about our lurking around Confederate camps. We had been within the guard lines at Big Shanty, but we were no more lurking there than a body of cavalry who might charge into a camp." We didn't lurk in or about any camp; nor were we inside the guard lines at Big Shanty. That statement is false, and if Mr. Pittenger testified to it, he lied.

[On the selection of the twelve men to go to Knoxville] Pittenger says (*Capturing a Locomotive,* page 195): "Wilson asked who the twelve were to be, and wished he might be one. The captain told him that this was easily arranged, as the order called merely for twelve, without giving names. He further offered Wilson the privilege of naming eleven others besides himself to go. . . . Poor Wilson was completely misled. He told me that he considered those going to Knoxville would probably be exchanged first, if any difference was made. So he put down his own name first and mine next."

When it's remembered that Pittenger was a witness for the prosecution, the reader will clearly see that he wouldn't be left behind, but must be one of the twelve. And thus it was ordered, and thus reported to us by Wilson himself. The officer named Wilson and Pittenger, and told Wilson to name the other ten.

The misleading goes on and on. *Daring and Suffering,* page 269: "One of our number was taken out, the charges and specifications read, a few witnesses heard, and then he was returned to us." "Returned to us!" This conveys the impression that while the comrade on trial was out, Pittenger was in the iron cage—as of course he wasn't.

In his books, the mention of "we are informed that the one who turned state's evidence is a Kentuckian, etc.," together with the picture used in illustration further on of the court-martial at Knoxville with [a man resembling] William Campbell on the witness stand, are significant items tending to show a design on Pittenger's part to make it appear that Campbell, and not himself, was the one who turned state's evidence. Nowhere in his books does Pittenger ever name the two witnesses who appeared against our comrades.

Because he took no real part in it, Pittenger persistently tries to make little of the Atlanta escape effort that almost surely saved the lives of those raiders then surviving—both those who broke out and those who remained. In *Daring and Suffering*, page 368:

PITTENGER: It may be interesting to inquire whether the alarm under which we were led to break out of the jail was well grounded, or a mere scare. At the time we had no doubt. . . . Since examining so many of the records I am disposed to doubt whether anything had been discovered that would have led to a new trial. It was weeks after the escape before any court met, and then no one of our party was summoned before it. . . . The regular soldiers in the front room, from whom came the most alarming reports, were very anxious that we should attempt to escape and succeed, though they had determined beforehand, as we learned afterward, not to go with us; but they were anxious to be separated from us, believing that they would then be exchanged. But the strongest evidence is the simple fact we were not tried. There had not been time for any representations from our government to be made.

DORSEY: Pittenger had nothing to fear from the enemy; his danger was from his comrades. When it was seen that his "plan" had miscarried, and had resulted in hanging eight of our number, he became quite nervous, appeared to be agitated, and made a show of great fear that we would all, including himself, of course, be put to death soon. He began to gather up the cards and pitch them out the window, so as to put a stop to all gaming, and prepare for the end. I believe he felt some fear of violence at the hands of those who had not believed in his plan, but on the contrary had openly accused him of being false.

I have said before, and here repeat, that I think the "plan" was to execute the eleven comrades taken with Mr. Pittenger to Knoxville, and then take the rest of us to Knoxville and try us, and after putting us to death, release Mr. Pittenger. But the movements of our troops interfered with the workings of the "plan," and put Mr. Pittenger in a different situation from the one he expected to occupy. That is what set his head on fire: not the loss he had sustained, but the loss he feared he would sustain before the rising of the morrow's sun—his own precious life.

I believe that "confession" at Chattanooga was a forgery. I believe those men who were tried were inveigled into a trap and betrayed. In trusting Pittenger, George D. Wilson hugged a viper to his bosom and the viper stung him to his death.

Showdown 2

Pittenger's vigorous and extended reply to Dorsey began as *The Ohio Soldier* series was reaching midpoint.

The Ohio Soldier, August 26, 1893:

Colton, Cal.
August 3, 1893

To the Editor:

The July numbers of your paper have been sent me and I find in them a bitterly abusive attack upon me by Comrade D. A. Dorsey. That he is unjustifiably wrong in impeaching my good faith in connection with the Andrews raid will appear from the following four considerations:

1. The counsel for the Andrews raiders knew all the facts and heard all the evidence. They contradict Mr. Dorsey flatly. In their letter of January, 1882, to him they say: "Both Judge Baxter and I thought, and still think, that Mr. Pittenger acted with fidelity to his comrades."

2. Mr. Dorsey has searched long and in vain for any evidence from the records to show that I was promised or granted any immunity. In all orders, lists of prisoners and Confederate documents of every kind bearing on the subject my name occurs just as the others do. . . .

3. As I shared in danger and suffering, so I have shared fully in all rewards and public honors. Medal, pension, commission, name on monument were all accorded me. Would this have been possible if I had been a traitor? The whole story was investigated by Secretary Stanton on sworn testimony, and the raid had been written about and discussed for thirty years. There has not yet been produced one scrap of evidence to show bad faith on my part.

4. Until 1888 Comrade Dorsey was especially friendly to me. He came from a distant state to make long visits in my family. He repeatedly called me "Brother Pittenger" in public meetings. In two large group photographs of our party he is placed next me—in one seated by my side, in the other he stands with his hand affectionately on my shoulder. These are dated 1886 and 1888.

But something did happen in 1888 to change all this loving comradeship. A personal difference arose, part financial and part political. Had I agreed to share the anticipated profits of the new edition of my book with Mr. Dorsey and agreed with him politically, his tirades would never have been written. Since then he has been an unscrupulous enemy and does not hesitate to make utterly baseless assertions. . . .

Let any candid person read [me] and also Mr. Dorsey's philippics, and judge for yourself.

Sincerely yours,
W. *Pittenger*

The Ohio Soldier, September 23, 1893:

Colton, Cal.
September 7, 1893

To the Editor:

Your issue of August 26th presents a picture of myself so contradictory, grotesque and absurd that I cannot refrain from calling attention to the impotent malice it displays.

Let the reader note that Dorsey paints me as a traitor, cheerful in prison till my falsehood is detected, and then in mortal fear of being killed by my betrayed comrades. I am helpless in their hands for four months, fearing each night that I will be strangled before the next morning. The question might arise why I did not ask the Confederates whom I had served to take me out of such a fearful position. Instead, I make the raiders throw their cards out of the window, graciously permit them to play checkers, make them pray daily, compel them to keep perfectly still four hours a day that I may read undisturbed, make them take wholesale doses of the Bible, Milton, Bunyan, etc., and then sign just such papers addressed to the Rebel authorities as I please!

Can anybody outside of a lunatic asylum reconcile such things? . . .

But look upon the true picture in contrast. I will be a little more boastful on the strength of Dorsey's statements of August 26 than I have ever been before, for he certainly does not wish to flatter me! Yet he shows that I did invaluable service to the raiders during those four months. Remember that I had told the story on the trials upon which our able lawyers relied for saving the lives of the whole party. That failed and the seven brave men died. But I still gave every particle of head and heart I possessed to saving the party as I had from the first. I was by far the best-read of the party, in history, science and literature, and all that I knew was used without stint for the common good. What was it worth to this band in their terrible imprisonment to have the essence of good books given to them hour after hour, and the whole day to be filled with employment? Not one died from the imprisonment in the whole eleven months. Not one lost his reason from brooding over his troubles—unless Dorsey be an exception!

Dorsey believed in brooding over trouble. I have seen men die in a week from that cause alone; and, in other instances, become driveling idiots. Dorsey, at the window at midnight, his "heart bursting with grief," was in a dangerous way. But how all this was broken up like a breath of spring by the employments which Dorsey credits to me. In the morning we rose, sang, read some chapters from the Bible, and asked God's blessing on the day. After our meager breakfast some good book which I had provided was read aloud from day to day until completed. If no book was on hand I gave a sketch of one I had formerly read. Then came games, debates, physical exercises, and the day was filled, closing again with the Bible, song and prayer. Often an hour was allowed for telling some weird story or romantic history after dark, when we were lying on the floor, and poor Dorsey was kept so busy that he could only get a chance to do his brooding and fretting by waking in the middle of the night!

But Dorsey quotes the two letters written to Jefferson Davis and General Bragg by the raiders without seeing that they overthrow his whole case. Both sum up our story just as I gave it to the court-martial; both refer to the evidence on the court-martial for details; Dorsey endorses both; signing in one case next my name. By this signature he gives his adhesion to the "fool plan" of defense, and confesses his present opposition to it to be an afterthought and a fraud. . . .

Dorsey knows that I never turned state's evidence, and has said so over his own signature. He also knows that I never pretended to the enemy to do so, but was always on trial as the spokesman of the party.

Wm. Pittenger

The Ohio Soldier, September 23, 1893:

NOTE

I notice the letter of Mr. Pittenger in the last issue of *The Ohio Soldier*. I "have the floor," and propose to hold it until I have told the story of the Mitchel raiders fully, fairly and truthfully. Mr. Pittenger has held the floor nearly thirty years, and it is now my turn. Many of the points he attempts to make have already been answered as I have told my story from time to time, and others will be as the story progresses.

D. A. Dorsey

The Ohio Soldier, December 16 and 30, 1893:

Fallbrook, Cal.
November 30, 1893

To the Editor:

In this sunset land in the sunset of life, it is saddening to be drawn into a bitter controversy by a former comrade and long professed friend. . . . I have always welcomed every account of the "Andrews Raid" . . . by participants on either side. But in Dorsey's account "the true things are not new and the new things are not true." . . .

The editor of *The Ohio Soldier*, in introducing this serial, declared that my books, while popular and interesting, have never been satisfactory to the raiders. This is too broad. He might correctly have said that some things in my books were unsatisfactory to a few of the raiders. Then there was a question about participation in profits which made a little friction. But most of the raiders have contributed to my books, praised them and sold them. Dorsey also says . . . that the raiders were too sick to write till recently and thus left the field of narration to me. This is incorrect. Many accounts have been published by them. Wilson's book, written more than a dozen years ago, is in every way superior to Dorsey's. The fact is, that I had put time, money and research into the study of the great raid to such an extent that all other accounts were necessarily either personal recollections or a mere rehash of my work. Wilson's is the former, Dorsey's is the latter.

In this review I am driven to make perpetual comparison between Dorsey and myself. This is ungracious, but I have no alternative. But why should Dorsey thus attack me after the lapse of thirty years? He has found no new facts, but we did come to differ financially and politically. He made demands to which I would not accede and he became thus my foe and has written this account for the purpose of "getting even."

In the great outlines of the story by Dorsey, I find little to criticize, for the very good reason that it is taken substantially from me. In the escape, journey, and in his first prison experiences, Dorsey deals with his own feelings and there becomes interesting, displaying in several paragraphs no small degree of descriptive power. He always fails, however, when an incident of any complication is to be told or opposing accounts to be reconciled. . . .

[Dorsey says that at the] Chattanooga jail I proposed to "turn state's evidence" to mislead the Rebels. . . . This is a myth which has grown in Mr. Dorsey's own mind in the years of brooding over the raid.

The raiders were captured in the enemy's country without uniform, and in hostility to the enemy. The first question naturally asked was, "Are these men guerrillas and marauders, or U. S. soldiers?" They claimed the latter. This Dorsey declares as fully as I do. . . . How could we prove that we were such? . . . One thing [the enemy] did offer—to put one of our number on the stand. . . . The proposal was accepted, and I was the man named—Brown says by a direct vote. I do not remember the vote and rather thought it was by general consent.

A letter now before me from one of the party says that a Rebel officer addressing Wilson said that one of the party only could be used as witness, but we might select that one, and that several voices called out "Pittenger." The manner of the selection is not important. It is enough to know that we discussed the matter in advance, and that a witness was taken by arrangement with the Confederates to establish our character as soldiers. . . .

But was the witness thus taken for the defense or the prosecution? . . . The witness was simply brought out in irons and put on the stand for both sides to get as much out of him as they could. . . .

"The fool plan," to use Dorsey's phrase, was not what he supposes, but something much simpler and wiser. It was simply to establish our character as soldiers and put our story in the best possible light in the only way open to us. But this is too simple for Dorsey. Once he said to me in great glee, after he had received the letter from the lawyers proving my loyalty to my comrades: "Now I understand it all, and it was the shrewdest thing in the whole raid. To get one of our men to pretend to 'turn state's evidence' and fool them with their own witness! It was a regular Yankee trick, for sure! Put that in your book and we will all stand by you, and praise you to the skies!"

"But, Dorsey," I said, "I can't do that, for it is not true."

[The court-martial proceedings] were held in secret. The guards who saw one man taken out as a witness, and the newspapers, could only guess what was going on inside, and when someone had guessed that one of the men was telling on the rest, it was natural for them to take it up. But such outside rumors are worthless in establishing history. . . . This explains all the newspaper scraps and Rebel rumors which have so long disturbed Dorsey. . . .

The only thing that has ever given a moment's plausibility to Dorsey's assault is that I have spoken in my books and speeches with great reserve of my personal share in the trials. I had a very serious scruple which made the whole subject exquisitely painful to me, and for more than a score of years the whole party respected, if they did not share, my feeling. The story told the court was not "the whole truth and nothing but the truth," and while the tribunal was, in the eyes of the law, illegal, yet I suffered intensely from what seemed like trifling with judicial forms. Others of the raiders laughed at such scruples and recalled our instructions which advised us to enlist in the Rebel army if necessary, thus taking the oath of allegiance to the Confederacy. But I would rather have lost a right arm than to thus give testimony only partially true. So, in writing the account, I have always passed lightly over this whole affair, giving the facts, but with as little detail as possible.

With great delicacy, the members of the party all followed that course in all published accounts, until Dorsey arose, more than a quarter of a century after, who put the matter in the rudest and coarsest form, insinuating that my reason for reserve was that still darker treason was behind. This is brutal. The truth simply is, that I told on the witness stand the story of the party as we had prepared it, and the enemy could get nothing from me that we did not desire told for our own good. . . . This main fiction of Dorsey's being disposed of, his whole fabric based upon it falls. . . .

In the escape at Atlanta he gives me no credit for stifling the cry of the jailer, and getting my finger bitten by him. Parrott writes, "As for having your finger bit (in the struggle with the jailer), that is a fact. I remember the circumstances very well!" Bensinger bears the same testimony. . . .

In the fall of 1881 and the winter of 1882 [Dorsey] spent many weeks as a guest at my house in New Jersey, and then went to Washington where he was mainly supported by the sale of my new book, a part of which was a donation, the remainder sold on credit but never paid for, though I finally made him a Christmas present of them also. He turned over many papers with me, occupying my study alone for hours together at other times. . . . Was he doing detective work, seeking for something to blast my [name?] I know that he was then prying everywhere to find something against me. . . . He wrote to our lawyers in East Tennessee and got a letter [the O. P. Temple letter of Jan. 21, 1882, already given] which is now the most crushing answer to all Dorsey's slanders. He received it in my presence and after a little pressing he let me see it.

I said, "Oh Dorsey! How could you write in such a way?"

He was a little confused, but recovered and claimed that he was only getting evidence for the sake of others, who, as he pretended, had questioned him on this point. . . . Something impressed me with the necessity of having a copy of the letter, which I took, and made him certify to the correctness of it. . . . When he attacked me publicly in 1888, I had the copy and published it, completely breaking the force of his accusation. . . .

It is safe to say that none of the raiders ever in their heart thought I was guilty of treason to the party. But some may have supposed the plan of defense, though endorsed by Andrews and Wilson and our able attorneys, was a mistake. . . . If true, this would only show that a mistake was made where mistake was easy, and not criminal. . . .

I do not think that Conductor Fuller indulged in threats and profanity when he visited us in prison. I remember his speaking quite proudly of his exploits in pursuit, and that I was much interested in what he told us, but I think this story of his profanity and bloody threats is another hatching from Dorsey's Nebraska brooding. . . .

The [raider] from whom I have quoted says that in writing this account Dorsey has damaged the whole party in the estimation of the public beyond recovery, for they will think we are all liars, and the whole story a lie. No fear of that. People can read between Dorsey's lines and see . . . the essential truth of all I have written.

I quote here a letter from Captain W. W. Brown. . . . The

affidavits referred to are not needed, for the whole matter of Dorsey's accusation vanishes into thin air when tested.

BROWN:

... *Dowling, Ohio*
August 15, 1893

Dear Comrade Pittenger:

Please send me the papers that contain the Dorsey letters. I am informed that they are making charges against you of disloyalty to the party. I can see no foundation whatever for such a charge. When you went out to testify before the court-martial at Knoxville, you did so by the consent of the entire party present, and I have always been satisfied that you acted in good faith.

I can't see what object Comrade Dorsey has in bringing such charges before the public. You are at liberty to make this statement public if you desire to do so. . . . If you need more than this . . . I will make out an affidavit and will also get the affidavit of Comrade Alf Wilson and other members of the party. To make an assertion is one thing, to prove it is another.

Yours in F., C. & L.,
W. W. *Brown*
Eng'r on Mitchel Raid

EDITOR: To Brown's letter of August 15 that year, Pittenger added supporting extracts from the letters of Reddick and Porter written during the 1888-1889 exchange, and requoted Conductor Fuller's flat public statement of November 15 that fall:

"I am now firmly of the belief that Dr. Pittenger was at all times and under all circumstances true to his comrades and loyal to his cause."

PITTENGER: [From *The Ohio Soldier*, December 16 and 30, 1893, continued.] But it is surely useless to quote more in refutation of the slanders Dorsey has hatched. . . . It took him twenty-five years—he tells us—of hard labor, with the assistance finally of an "able lawyer," to arrive at the conclusion that he was a fool. The reader of these pages will not dispute that conclusion, at least!

When Dorsey and myself squarely differ, which shall be believed? He gives many reasons why the reader should rely on me rather than on himself. . . . I wrote while events were still fresh and had my notes to go by, and used all material from others while it was undimmed by time. Dorsey was so despondent that he did not charge his memory with what happened. . . .

Dorsey also impeaches my courage, but gives the strangest reasons man ever dreamed of. I was cool and collected, could read books, secure papers, make notes under all circumstances, talk to anybody, and avow myself an abolitionist openly in the South in war times! . . .

In closing this already too long review . . . I will make free to contrast the services to the raid of Dorsey and myself. I make no charge against Dorsey's conduct during the raid. I have no reason to doubt that he would have executed any reasonable order given him. But he originated nothing. . . . From the first I thought busily and suggested many things. There was no time that I was not felt as a force among the raiders. Several of the efforts on the chase were of my devising. . . . I stilled the cry of the jailer at the critical moment in the most desperate attempt to escape. Before that I kept the party employed in the most mentally healthful way, and secured for them a whole library of books, and gave them the substance of a still larger library out of my own head.

The contrast of service is still greater a little later. Dorsey and seven companions, all good men, escaped, and for five months were at liberty. No sensation was created, no medals or commissions were given them. The raid seemed to sink out of sight. When I was exchanged —the spokesman of the party, to use again a term that enrages Dorsey —I told the story to the Secretary of War, and to the people of the whole United States with the same clearness of explanation and heart-moving power as to the Confederates. Then Dorsey was hunted out and given his medal and commission, as were all. [Colonel J. M. Neibling and the officers of the 21st O.V.I., who had to initiate the fairly tart paperwork which secured several of the remaining medals, might have questioned this description of the process as a case of their men being "hunted out."]

That I have since told the story with a fullness of detail and an accuracy that few war stories have obtained; that the story is known throughout the civilized world and that the name of every raider is honored as the bravest of the brave is largely my work—a slandered man may speak frankly. If this is boasting, make the most of it. For all this I have been vilified and abused by a—Dorsey! "Little Dorsey," as we used to call him in the prison.

I recapitulate by quoting part of [the letter which we all signed and sent to Jefferson Davis from Atlanta in June] by which is summed up the story that I as spokesman told at the court-martial. The whole party in these letters—there was a second two months

[*Pittenger*]
later—take the story upon themselves, and share with me whatever of guilt there was in deceiving the Rebel generals in those few vital points where we deviated from the exact truth. The evidence on the court-martial went up to Davis just in advance of this letter, and in vain will any signer attempt to evade full responsibility for it:

Atlanta, Ga.
June 18, 1862

To His Excellency, Jefferson Davis
President of the Confederate States of America

Sir:

We are the survivors of the party that took the engine at Big Shanty, on the 12th of April last. Our commander, Andrews, and seven of our comrades have been executed. We all (with the exception of Andrews) were regularly detailed from our regiments in perfect ignorance of where we were going and what we were to do. We were ordered to obey Andrews, and everything we did was done by his orders, he only telling his plans when he wished us to execute them. . . . For fuller details we refer to the evidence in the cases that have been tried. No real harm was done, and as far as thought and intention is concerned we are perfectly innocent.

O! it is hard to die a disgraceful and ignominious death; to leave our wives, our children, our brothers and sisters and parents, without any consolation. Give this matter your most kind and merciful consideration. . . .

Wilson W. Brown, Co. F, 21st O.V.I.
William Bensinger, Co. G, 21st O.V.I.
Elihu H. Mason, Co. K, 21st O.V.I.
John A. Wilson, Co. C, 21st O.V.I.
John R. Porter, Co. G, 21st O.V.I.
Mark Wood, Co. C, 21st O.V.I.
Robert Buffum, Co. H, 21st O.V.I.
Wm. Knight, Co. E, 21st O.V.I.
Wm. Pittenger, Co. G, 2nd O.V.I.
Daniel A. Dorsey, Co. A, 33d O.V.I.
Jacob Parrott, Co. K, 33d O.V.I.
Wm. Reddick, Co. B, 33d O.V.I.
M. J. Hawkins, Co. A, 33d O.V.I.

. . . In gathering up every rumor, suspicion and possible blame against me and spreading them with such gusto before the public, I now think Dorsey has done me a real service. . . . It is said in old times the Roman Catholics had a custom, when a person was proposed for a certain high dignity, to appoint an officer called the "devil's advocate," whose business it was to hunt up and urge all that could possibly be found out about against the man before he could receive the high honor. What a splendid "devil's advocate" Dorsey would have made. His very initials fit. Behold! "D. A. D." "Devil's Advocate Dorsey!"

If Comrade Dorsey still feels that I am wearing laurels to which he or anyone else is better entitled, why not bring the matter to private trial? . . . I append the following direct challenge:

Comrade Dorsey:

I challenge you to formulate your charges with specifications as definite as you can make them and submit them with all the evidence you can produce to three impartial arbitrators who will decide whether I was guilty of bad faith or disloyalty on the raid. If they decide against me I promise to resign my medal and pension, and you must pledge yourself, if the decision is against you, to retract all your charges as publicly as you have made them and to make no more for the future. . . . I propose to choose one of the arbitrators, you another, and they two will choose a third. Let them all be Ohio soldiers of good repute and intelligence.

I also propose, in order to save time and to reach the exact issue, that the controversy be limited to the question of my loyalty and good faith during the raid. Mere vague suspicions or complaints about any of my actions or writings since will not affect the real issue.

I will even put before you, now, my whole line of defense. I deny that I ever pretended to the enemy to turn state's evidence for the purpose of deceiving them; but will claim that if I had done so with the previous knowledge of some, at least, of the party, that would have been no treason, but would have been in the line of our first instructions which contemplated deceiving the enemy whenever it was to our advantage. . . .

The distance between an unwise plan and treason is immeasurable. But I will claim that [having one of our number testify] enabled the Andrews' raiders to make the best defense on the court-martial that they could possibly make in any manner whatever. . . .

I will ask that your charges and specifications be at once formulated

[*Pittenger*]

and published in *The Ohio Soldier*. . . . Say exactly what you mean and bring on your proofs; then the arbitrators can soon declare whether in their judgment I am a traitor or you a spiteful and malicious slanderer.

Wm. Pittenger

The Ohio Soldier, January 27, 1894:

Kearney, Nebr.
January 6, 1894

To the Editor:

A lawyer in court with a bad case tackles the lawyer on the other side instead of the case. Pittenger tells you what a bad man "little Dorsey" is, instead of discussing the cold and awful facts.

In his letter of December 16, he says: "Mr. Dorsey has searched in vain for evidence that I was promised immunity." I find in the record made by himself that he was told he "need have no fear of any prosecution for himself" if he would tell certain things, "among others, who were concerned in this affair." . . . Pittenger, in order to save his own neck, [did] give the names of all who were concerned in the raid, those who opposed his "plan" as well as those who favored it.

In his second letter he says: "Dorsey believed in brooding over trouble, but that way lies insanity and death." He knows that is all moonshine, [but] if he could break the force of my plain statements by putting me in a madhouse he would do so, I believe, without hesitation. . . .

He likes Wilson's writings better than mine because Wilson ignored the witness matter. . . . When Wilson wrote, we were not in possession of Pittenger's last books and did not have the disclosures therein made for guidance.

By his own version of the case, he was to testify that we were soldiers regularly detailed to obey Andrews' orders—that we did not know where we were to go nor what we were to do, until the same was made known to us from time to time. . . . In his books he unwittingly reveals the fact that he, as spokesman, told more than that. The records made by Pittenger himself show that "we"—which stands for Pittenger—made admissions far more damaging than those made in the letters to Rebel officers which we all signed. . . .

He has stood aloof from us, has written book after book, hogged the profits and left the witness question to vex and annoy his comrades. We did propose to all join him in publishing the history, not share the profits, but to publish and all share the profit or loss. Knowing in that event all would be told, he "had made other arrangements." He feared the result of a history by the survivors. . . . It would not make him the hero he would have you to believe he is.

Pittenger knows that in 1884 I was writing a book. . . . From the Columbus, Ohio, *Dispatch* of November 5, 1888, I extract the following: "The letter was called out by the fact that Mr. Pittenger is supporting Mr. Cleveland, though the writer of the letter [Dorsey] is known to have entertained, for a long time, the opinion expressed in the letter with reference to Mr. Pittenger in connection with the raid."

The above shows that there was not a sudden change of my mind on account of politics or business. . . .

Captain [Stephen B.] Porter, the editor of the *Dispatch*, told me at the national encampment in 1888 that Pittenger denied that he named any to the court except the "man in the box." But Captain Fuller says in his letter that he gave the names of all the party, in each case, and this Pittenger has never denied in any of his published statements. Though Pittenger says, "But I would rather have lost a right arm than to thus give testimony only partially true," in the early part of his captivity he says he lied without stint, and would then have added the solemnity of an oath with equal recklessness. But at the trials (before a Rebel court) he disliked to "trifle with legal forms?" Nonsense! . . .

Why was Mr. Pittenger suspicious that I was playing detective when at his house? . . . I came to his house from Washington, and had told him of certain papers being there on file. He literally stared at me when I told him this, and gave a wild and suspicious look I never forgot. . . . Did he suspect that I was looking for lost papers? . . . As he has gone into personal matters I will mention another. On my first visit to Pittenger I found him in apparently good health, but he soon got sick—so much so, that on the Sunday I was with him he was unable to walk to church without leaning on my arm, and had to preach sitting in a chair, being unable to stand and preach. He called a physician, and I thought he would live but a few months, at best. I wrote the same day to Hon. E. K. Valentine, member of Congress from Nebraska, asking him to have Pittenger's claim for pension made special, telling him of the condition of his health. The case was soon after disposed of, and some $2,000 arrearages allowed him. He did not die as I expected he would, but is today, I believe, the healthiest man in the party. . . .

I did spend several months in Washington in the interest of the party trying to secure employment or pensions suited to their injuries, and Pittenger contributed twelve books for me to sell and apply to my support. Other comrades contributed money. I couldn't live on wind, and the comrades, Senator Sherman and others insisted that I remain. As to the "Christmas present," I quote his own letter of December 28, 1883: "Please consider that account [the twelve books] settled. Put it down, if you will, to copyright for manuscript you furnished which helped make the book more interesting than it would otherwise have been." . . .

I received Judge Temple's letter of January 21, 1882, at Washington. I voluntarily sent Pittenger and others a copy of it. He came to Washington afterward, copied part of the letter, and wrote a certificate to it, that it was a "true copy of an extract" from the letter. . . . This I signed (on February 9, 1882) at his request, not wishing to arouse any suspicion in his mind that I doubted his fidelity. . . .

Brown thinks Pittenger acted in good faith. . . . The trouble with Brown and some other comrades is that they haven't carefully read Pittenger's writings; they haven't studied the case.

Pittenger's gush over what he did when released [is] in contrast to what we, who escaped, did on our arrival in the Union lines. By escaping we saved the lives of those who were recaptured. This does not include Mr. Pittenger, for, as Hawkins always answered when asked why Pittenger did not escape, "Oh, he didn't have to run away. He was all right." Our escape was the crowning event of the raid—the only victory we gained. . . .

He proposes to arbitrate. . . . If there was anything to arbitrate, [one easy] decision might be that he was loyal and myself a truthful recorder of events as seen and understood by me. But as he has addressed himself to me, let me reciprocate. If there are any matters between us that demand a settlement we can settle them among the members of our party—the raiders. . . .

You say now that you deny you "ever pretended to the enemy to turn state's evidence for the purpose of deceiving them." Well, then, for what purpose did you pretend to turn state's evidence? Do you mean to admit that you intended to deceive your comrades? . . . You were pretending to serve two masters. Which one did you really serve? . . .

Did you not have in view your own personal safety above all things else? I have repeatedly asserted that you were safe from prosecution as a result of your services as a witness. You have never answered that. What do you say, safe or not? . . .

You think I do an injustice to the memory of our deceased comrades, who trusted in you to the last. . . . In all that I have written, I have had the memory of our departed comrades in mind. . . . I have felt that they were whispering in my ears: "Dorsey, pursue it; hunt up all the facts." I have studied the case, and have noted your efforts to disguise the part you played, and heard Fuller at Columbus, Ohio, try to make it appear that they confessed on the scaffold, and as I said then, it seemed to me their blood cried out from the ground, and said: "Speak!"

In their memory and, I believe, with their hearty approbation, I have spoken.

D. A. Dorsey

The Ohio Soldier, February 24, 1894:

Fallbrook, Cal.
February 3, 1894

To the Editor:

Mr. Dorsey in your issue of January 27 declines arbitration as I had anticipated he would. . . . In a way that is characteristically indirect he confesses that he has no valid case against me, and exposes the real motives which induced his attack. For he says that if I had written about the raid [with full frankness as to the trials] and had shared the profits, instead of having "hogged" them, all would have been well. This is a decisive confession that not what I did on the raid, but my manner of writing, and those terrible "profits" of publication, constitute Dorsey's grievance. . . .

Dorsey asks me to say if I was safe during the raid. I can gratify him by answering explicitly, "No." My testimony was in writing, like the admissions of all, and I could have been tried on that as readily as any other member of the party.

I have no wish to see Dorsey in a madhouse, [although the] whispers of the dead that he hears through all these years would be regarded by a physician as a very grave symptom. His friends ought, if possible, to get him into some new and healthful employment. . . . As he is now going on, the gates of bedlam loom not dimly nor distantly before him. When I think of the years and the money he has wasted on this bad business, I feel more of pity and sorrow than anger toward him.

Wm. Pittenger

The Ohio Soldier, April 16, 1894:

Kearney, Nebr.
March 14, 1894

To the Editor:

In his last article Mr. Pittenger lies down very nicely, just as I expected he would do, after a certain amount of bluster, fuss and feathers. He has nothing to arbitrate when it is to be left to surviving raiders. . . .

I have shown that after the offer of immunity, he was not taken "back to the horrors of the old dungeon," as he says, but was kept in the jail yard and used as a witness for the prosecution in the trial of Andrews. And yet he brazenly repeats that the offer of immunity was rejected. . . . He says he was not safe from prosecution. . . . I have asserted that he was lawyer enough to know that there is a well-established rule that one who "turns state's evidence" will not be put on trial, and this I repeat. . . .

In writing of matters that so deeply concerned [the executed men], I have tried to be governed by what I believe would have been their wishes, if they could have been given time to reflect. Thus influenced, the dead, figuratively speaking, whisper in our ears. It is plain and simple enough. . . . Eight noble souls [were] sent to an untimely and brutally tragic death. Others rescued themselves from a like fate by escaping from the enemy after six months of agonizing torture, in which we were held in part by the wiles . . . of the only black sheep in the flock.

Yours, etc.,
D. A. Dorsey

Showdown 3

At the close of *The Ohio Soldier* collision, Pittenger plainly offered to submit the wide differences between his and Dorsey's versions of the facts to a three-man arbitration panel. Not quite so plainly, Dorsey refused this solution and suggested instead an appeal to the raiders themselves. Both history and the most convincing presentation of his case might better have been served if Dorsey had accepted Pittenger's challenge at the time and in the form it was made. Since he didn't, and since Pittenger showed no apparent eagerness to take up Dorsey's counter-proposal, anyone in search of some form of a verdict is forced to depend in part on a belated tally of those close enough to the case to have had some grounds for a reasoned judgment on it.

Of those directly concerned, although not raiders themselves, Pittenger eventually made a sweep of the four men on record. Defense Attorneys Jonathan Baxter and Oliver P. Temple of Knoxville stated their confidence in 1882 that he had acted in good faith at the trials. Conductor Fuller, after condemning Pittenger in the immediate postwar years, declared himself in 1888 to be firmly persuaded of Pittenger's fidelity. Anthony Murphy made it clear that no condemnation of Pittenger could be expected from him: "Now as to parties turning state's evidence," Murphy wrote in an otherwise cordial letter to Dorsey of July 8, 1903, "I don't think any of your men ever did that. I am most certain Pittenger did not. I met Judge O. P. Temple at Tate Springs near Knoxville, Tenn., a few years ago, who was one of the attorneys who defended some of your party on trial at Knoxville. We talked that trial and its results, but he never intimated anything of that nature was mentioned during the trial."

Apart from Dorsey and Pittenger, twelve raiders survived the war. Had all of them lived long enough to hear and weigh the charges, and to sift such evidence as was offered, their verdict—clearly rendered—would have been at least the most interesting one any twelve jurors could have reached. Wood and Buffum, however, died too soon to leave votes that can be usefully counted, although Wood had joined with Alf Wilson in November, 1862—in the first relief at their escape—in the stated belief that the Confederate authorities had been able to get no damaging testimony from Pittenger, a view apparently shared at the time even by Dorsey.

Of the ten-man jury left, Pittenger in 1893 and 1888 won the public support of Brown, Reddick and Porter. Bensinger—by elimination quite probably the unnamed raider mentioned by Pittenger in 1893 as then gloomily certain that the public would come to think of the whole party as liars—can be counted as well for Pittenger on the strength of Knight's Chillicothe *Leader* interview of 1889.

No other raider can be firmly scored on Pittenger's side. Evidence from several sources, direct and indirect, puts Wollam, Hawkins and Mason among those earliest and most strongly against Pittenger, and the first indication of Mason's strong feelings may have been shown in his failure—reportedly, because of "sickness"—to confirm Pittenger's statements before the War Department notary on March 25, 1863. Knight—by the agreement in 1956 of his surviving sons—was bitter toward Pittenger to the day of his death.

With an even division of these eight votes, the opinions of Parrott and Alf Wilson could deadlock the poll or tip it either way. Neither opinion is easy to establish unmistakably.

Dorsey calls Parrott on his side, leaving a note in his papers that Parrott had told him Pittenger "coaxed the others, in their weakened condition" to say nothing about the witness matter at the time of the Washington affidavits. This alone couldn't be given much weight, and Parrott—unable to read and write in 1863—was never enough of a writer to get more on the public record than a few bits of his story, told to a magazine writer many years later. What may deserve weight is the fact that Pittenger's need of support at the time was far greater than Dorsey's. At the worst, during this controversy, Dorsey was being charged with envy, greed, lying, spite and near-lunacy—no roll of commendation, but crimes or failings well short of hypocrisy, cowardice and treason. If a man of courage had been even honestly undecided, given the circumstances, he might well have spoken up for Pittenger as the man more in need of aid. Parrott's courage was unquestioned, but he volunteered no statement and no affidavit was secured from him, although in Hardin County he was always within a short train ride of Brown.

Alf Wilson at Perrysburg was even closer to Brown at Dowling. Not ten miles separated them. Brown's offer to try for an affidavit from Alf Wilson was made to Pittenger on August 15, 1893. Pittenger's statement in December that such added support wouldn't be needed doesn't establish that he wouldn't have welcomed it, nor that Brown hadn't meanwhile made a try for it. Wilson's courage, like Parrott's, was well beyond dispute. In view of this—and of the showdown seriousness of the charges against Pittenger—Wilson's public silence ranged him nearer Dorsey's camp than Pittenger's. The 1897 National Tribune reissue of his *Adventures* still carried the statement that "not a man of that faithful band was base enough to betray his comrades," but three bits of evidence in the new edition indicated that Alf Wilson was giving Dorsey the edge on the close ones.

In the several accounts of the Andrews-Wollam escape from Chattanooga, the third man scheduled to go through the hole had always had the mixed honor of being described as deciding that the existing alarm made it too dangerous to try following Wollam. In all editions of Pittenger and in Wilson's first as quoted by Pittenger, the man was Dorsey—as he was frankly in his own account. In Wilson's 1897 version (page 122), the possibly unheroic hesitation is halfway ascribed to a once troubled soul a full quarter of a century beyond the danger of further misunderstandings. The third man now becomes: "The man (Robert Buffum I think) who was following Wollam through the hole. . . ."

In maintaining that he had contributed importantly to the success of the Atlanta escape, Pittenger had always insisted that he had been the man who clapped his hand over Jailer Turner's mouth at the crucial moment and that he had later made strenuous if misdirected attempts to leave the prison. On page 161, Wilson reports that it was Captain Fry himself who clapped his hand over the jailer's mouth, and that "in less time than I am telling it, all the prisoners who wanted to *go* were marshaled in the hall and ready for a descent on the guards below." The italicizing of "go" was Wilson's.

Reckoning Baxter, Temple, Murphy and Fuller with the raiders, Pittenger could be credited with more supporters than doubters. Holding it to the ten other raiders alive when the controversy broke into the open—if grays have to be scored either as white or black—the count would seem to be four certain for Pittenger's side of it, four certain and two probable for Dorsey.

Track's End

Dorsey couldn't let the bad business lie. Although he once almost wistfully confessed that there were times when he wished he "could be writing about something else," the aside itself came in the course of further footnotes to the King Charles' head of his endlessly running indictment. Bensinger, Knight, Alf Wilson, Fuller and the other survivors of the violent day were living their variously full lives and looking more to the promise of raising dozens of sons, daughters and grandchildren than to the closed ledgers of the past. The quiet man, Anthony Murphy—for one—was the father of seven, and in addition to lending a useful hand in the rebuilding or creation of Atlanta's school system, fire-fighting services and central water supply, he had managed through lumbering, industrial and transportation enterprises to reach a net worth of some half a million turn-of-the-century dollars. Such living-on with the present wasn't for Dorsey. While his marriage foundered and he drifted from his half-practiced law to a series of stop-gap occupations, he kept reckoning and rereckoning the old, old accounts.

No trial more conclusive than itself or its incomplete tally of raiders' opinion followed the spilling out of the bitter brew tapped by *The Ohio Soldier*. Dorsey had side-stepped the arbitration then proposed, but with the passage of time, the thought of a full-fledged trial became more tempting to him. As the century ended, much of the world was watching the second judging of a case once thought closed in France. To Dorsey, it was a renewed clang of the old fire-bell and a triumph of vicarious vindication.

"In the famous case of Captain Dreyfus of the French Army," he noted in an 1899 reworking of his *Ohio Soldier* series, "it now appears that his conviction was secured upon secret documentary evidence. So in our case, and part of the secret evidence in both was absolutely false."

Much of this secret evidence, Dorsey was now willing to charge openly—had he ever been able to find a publisher—might well have been removed by stealth from the official war records during the Library of Congress and War Department visits where Pittenger had had the private handling for hours at a time of sheaves of Confederate archives not yet fully catalogued. Dorsey had no proof whatsoever that this had been done, but he pointed to line after line in the *Locomotive Chase* report of this research to show that a realization of the possibilities of tampering with these records had clearly been in Pittenger's mind at the time of the Washington visits.

As the years wore on, no chance of a strike was too remote to try:

Columbus, Ohio
February 19, 1898

Hon. R. A. Alger
Secretary of War
Washington, D.C.

Dear Sir:

I write to ask if Confederate records show the name of William Pittenger as an officer or soldier in the Confederate army, and if so the rank and date of muster or enlistment of such officer or soldier. . . .

If Wm. Pittenger enlisted in the Confederate army it [might have been] as of October, '62. . . .

Very respectfully,
D. A. Dorsey

Record and Pension Office, War Department
Washington, February 23, 1898

Mr. Daniel A. Dorsey
Columbus, Ohio

Nothing has been found of record in this office to show that William Pittenger served either as an officer or enlisted man in the Confederate States Army.

F. C. Ainsworth
Colonel U. S. Army, Chief of Office

Or no showdown too formal—or improbable—to invoke:

Enid, Oklahoma
August 28, 1905

To the Honorable,
The Secretary of War, U. S. Army
Washington, D.C.

Dear Sir:

As one of the survivors of an expedition known in history as Andrews' Raid, I very respectfully represent that I have twice personally requested a court of inquiry into the hanging at Atlanta, Georgia, on or about June 18, 1862, of Samuel Slavens and Samuel Robertson of the 33d Ohio Voluntary Infantry, John M. Scott of the 21st Regt. OVI, George D. Wilson, Marion A. Ross and Perry G. Shadrach of the 2nd OVI.

The reason for my requesting such court of inquiry is the report that one of said party of raiders while in the hands of the enemy and at the time some of said raiders were on trial before a Confederate court-martial, at Knoxville, Tenn., turned state's evidence against them and that such report does not say which one of said raiders did so turn state's evidence, thus leaving all of said party open to suspicion.

I believe the facts to be * * *

All surviving raiders are to be at the great reunion to be held at Chattanooga, Tenn., September 17 to 20 [1906] and as the witnesses from both sides will then be on the ground where the raid was made, I beg leave to suggest Thursday September 21 as a suitable time and Chattanooga a proper place for holding the court of inquiry.

Very respectfully,
Daniel A. Dorsey
Late 2nd Lieut. Co H,
33d Ohio Voluntary Infantry
Enid, Oklahoma

War Department
Washington, September 9, 1905

Mr. Daniel A. Dorsey
Enid, Oklahoma

Sir:

. . . It is essential to the appointment of a court [of inquiry] that the applicant for the inquiry, and parties to the transaction which is to be inquired into, should be in the military service. In the case in reference [you and the parties concerned] belonged to the volunteer armies which were raised between 1861 and 1865, but have long since disbanded, and the officers and men who composed them have been separated from the military service by individual discharges, or by the muster out and general disbandment of the commands to which they belonged.

In view of the foregoing it will be observed the Department is without authority to grant your request.

For the Secretary of War
Very respectfully . . .

Subpoenas prepared for a trial during the 1906 reunion at Chattanooga, however misconceived and out of order on other grounds, couldn't have recalled the principals if service had been tried. In Atlanta, on December 28, 1905, a pursuer even more inescapable than he himself had once seemed on a long-gone April Saturday had caught up with William A. Fuller. And out in California, the Reverend William Pittenger—untagged turncoat, cruelly wronged patriot, or a driven man of the mixed strengths and weaknesses of most of us—

nger had been the traitor. On the question of escape, Pittenger
indisputably shown as being at nearly all times more for sticking
e he was than risking a break. Whether this reflected cowardice,
nderstandable caution imposed by poor eyesight, or misguided
idence either in the defense plans or expected Confederate
y, was guesswork before the presentation of Dorsey's indictment,
ined guesswork after it.
oof of extensive perjury at Washington would have required clear
nce that Pittenger had actually betrayed the others at Chatta-
a and Knoxville. This Dorsey didn't have. Pittenger's sworn state-
t there, however, was one stated to include all the material facts.
careful editing out of his own key role against the others, by a
ess of Pittenger's training and intelligence, clearly qualified as
swearing.
advertent disclosures by one or more raiders in the first excite-
t or panic of capture, followed by bad judgment in the choice of
and method on which to rest the defense, could have led as
y to the known results as the supposed treachery charged by
ey. In the case as proposed, Dorsey failed to recognize this alter-
e—or chose to overlook it—and accordingly offered an opening
which Pittenger struck promptly and brilliantly. If Pittenger faced
charge of treason, among lesser indictments, he had every justifi-
n to ask that the matter be resolved on the main indictment.
ad been so charged, and he so asked.
also propose, in order to save time and to reach the exact issue,"
nger wrote in his two-part answer in *The Ohio Soldier* of Decem-
16 and December 30, 1893, "that the [arbitration of the] con-
rsy be limited to the question of my loyalty and good faith dur-
he raid. Mere vague suspicions or complaints about any of my
ns or writings since will not affect the real issue."
e author of *Extempore Speech* and *The Debaters' Treasury* had
r been quicker on his feet. By this limitation, if Dorsey had ac-
ed the arbitration suggested, re-examination of the case would
been confined to an area in which Pittenger was practically in-
erable. No written transcripts of the trial had survived; General
ville Leadbetter and Colonel A. W. Reynolds and other officers
e court-martial had left no known word either way as to Pitten-
part; Defense Attorneys Baxter and Temple—and co-witness
r—were already on record as having faith in Pittenger's fidelity
s side. Ruled out—supposedly only "in order to save time and to
the exact issue"—was an impartial examination of the actually
aging tangible evidence against Pittenger: his actions and writings

had been, since April 24 of the year before, safely beyond the reach
of human justice, malice or misunderstanding.

Moot Court

Daniel Allen Dorsey brought two indictments: a minor and incidental one against William Allen Fuller, a major one against William Pittenger. In each instance, he much more suggested a case than proved it.

I

Dorsey raised no question of Fuller's tenacity, courage or loyalty to the Confederacy. Essentially, his charge was that the W. & A. conductor was overly vindictive during the war, unduly boastful after it, and untruthful or mistaken in his report and interpretation of George D. Wilson's last words on the scaffold.

From an examination of Fuller's Columbus speech of September, 1888, Dorsey would seem to have assigned it implications not necessarily intended. There's no clear evidence here or elsewhere that Fuller told more or less than the truth as it appeared to him, and there's a great deal of evidence that the conductor, on nearly all occasions, was a man unafraid to call the shots as he saw them. That Fuller wanted the raiders hanged and took something close to satisfaction in riding the full way to the scaffold with the eight so executed would seem borne out not only by the reported impressions of some of the raiders, but from the tone of a number of his own later statements. At no time was he reluctant to recall that he had followed the eight as closely and as unshakably in June as in April:

337 *Washington St.*
Atlanta, Ga.
November 15, 1895

Mrs. Harriet A. Scott
Auburn, Maine

My dear Madam:

. . . Yes, [the Rev. W. J. Scott] officiated in the case of J. J. Andrews, when he was hung in June, '62, as also when the other seven were executed a few days later, in Atlanta. He and Andrews rode in the same carriage with me from the city to the place of execution just outside. In the case of the seven others, Dr. Scott and myself rode in a carriage along with the commandant of the post, Col. I. G. Foreacre, just behind the ambulance in which the prisoners rode.

I am the man who was running the train as conductor when the Andrews raiders captured the engine *General*. It was I who pursued them under so many difficulties & finally captured them and recaptured my engine. . . . One of the parties I captured, Rev. W. Pittenger, has written a very interesting history of the incident in a book he calls * * *

I am very truly, etc.
W. A. *Fuller*

This letter of November, 1895, is a fair example of Fuller's increasing tendency—third point in Dorsey's bill—to look back on the Southern half of the chase as a one-man show. The names of Murphy, Bracken and others still warranted generous mention by him at Columbus in 1888; in the years to follow, as W. C. Dodson, W. P. Reed and other fellow townsmen of Atlanta were to note, the captain fell deeper into the habit of considering himself the single-handed hero of the old great day. Undeniably, Fuller had put in a strenuous and remarkable day's work on April 12, 1862. As undeniably, with no complications of diffidence or false modesty, he took pride for the rest of his life in admitting it.

On Fuller's side of the scales there should be added one instance of unexpectedly delicate tact. At the Columbus meeting with Rachel Slavens, he was able to find and speak the quiet words of comfort that helped dissolve the old anger of years' standing. Dorsey, on longer thought, might have remembered his own words—"When Fuller was seeking our lives it wasn't the individual he was after, but the

Yankee soldier"—and let it stand that this tough a
man was one better to have for a friend than an enemy

II

With Pittenger, for all concerned, it would have b
more helpful if Dorsey had condensed and organized
specific bill of particulars the clergyman-writer once
prepare. In substance, through the years, Dorsey cha
with:

(a) disclosure of damaging information at capture;
(b) treachery in varying degrees to his fellow raiders
ing the trials;
(c) persistent opposition, in prison, to escape plans;
(d) perjury at Washington in the sworn report of M
on the trials and associated events;
(e) evasions, falsehoods and assorted sins of omissio
and hypocrisy in his published writings directed
over Pittenger's actually discreditable part in
scribed.

Pittenger had studied some law, not practiced it. D
ticed it, but apparently without much study. On th
as it was made, the minister was a more skillful and p
than the attorney.

Dorsey's sprawling case in the columns of *The O*
more convincing in its entirety than any sample or co
might indicate. Its chief strength was the cumulative,
of scores of offered instances of Pittenger's bending
relevant facts, or insertion of extraneous material appa
a reader's attention from such awkward bits of straigh
be included. Its indefensible weakness was Dorsey's
scrupulous habit of treating possibilities as probabilit
in speculation and hearsay almost as willingly as reliab

The likelihood that one or more of the men capture
talked too much was established as a probability; tha
the one most at fault in this wasn't clearly confirmed.
out that deliberate betrayal could easily have taken
in some respects a more believable explanation of c
encies than other possible causes. He didn't establi
sonable doubt that such betrayal had occurred, or,

afterward. When Dorsey side-stepped the apparent put-up-or-shut-up offer, evidently more by instinct or luck than through a recognition of the mousetrap plan proposed, Pittenger was left as nearly a winner as that part of the controversy was to have.

Dorsey made wilder charges than his available evidence could bear out. In failing to make them all stick, it could have seemed to some readers of *The Ohio Soldier* that he hadn't had justification for bringing up any. Pittenger didn't make this mistake. The assorted charges of Dorsey's articles offered ample grounds for a libel suit had the injured man chosen to bring one. That Pittenger didn't may as easily have been due to Christian charity, or a natural reluctance to make a bad business worse, as to fear. The effect of Pittenger's restraint, whatever its cause, was to end the public aspects of the fight. My own guess—and most of such verdict as I can offer from here has to be made up of guesswork—is that William Pittenger would have suffered an even greater amount of public humiliation than he did rather than invite a close, widely followed assessment of all his "actions and writings" following the raid. In one, had it been made, I believe Pittenger would have been found to be nearly as vulnerable as he felt himself with reason to be unassailable on the straight treason charge.

Short of the discovery of presently unfound frank records left by General Leadbetter, Colonel Reynolds or other examining officers, there seems little chance now of establishing exactly what did happen at Lafayette and Chattanooga in the first few days after Pittenger was captured or gave himself up. From Pittenger's writings and the other evidence available, the probability would seem to be that Pittenger and perhaps several others talked too much almost immediately. It's doubtful, for instance, that the Fleming County cover story ever served as the dominating entrapment factor Pittenger names it to be in his writings. Alf Wilson and Wood didn't use it, George Wilson and Dorsey's party didn't, and it's not sure several others did, yet all were taken and almost immediately identified. Word of the Fleming parallel would have taken days to establish and circulate if deduced by the Confederate authorities themselves, and it quite surely wouldn't have been enough to generate the prompt order to pull two Confederate recruits from the ranks at Camp McDonald nearly a hundred miles away, as Hawkins and Porter were to be pulled. Porter—even though he was eventually to come to Pittenger's support—always believed someone had named two of the party as left behind at Marietta. When Alf Wilson was taken, the authorities already had his name. If some or all of this information came from Pittenger, the fact would still not necessarily have proved deliberate betrayal. The disclosures could have followed from temporary panic at capture or from a mistaken confidence in his ability to outsmart a battery of courthouse veterans twice his age.

Pittenger's next move of record—offering himself as witness in the trials—could have come whether or not he gave damaging information beforehand, and it could have had exactly the innocent explanation he gave it: that naming themselves U. S. soldiers seemed to most to offer the best chance of safety, and that Pittenger could have seemed as effective a spokesman as any in claiming such status. The death of eight of the raiders would seem at least as chargeable to Mitchel's negligence in initiating prompt and strong threats of retaliation as to anything Pittenger may or may not have done, and confirmation of the death sentences was clearly a Richmond decision—taken during the same weeks in which Timothy Webster was being tried, convicted and executed there—to move even deeper into total war than men like Colonel Claiborne wanted or had expected to go. The central decision, as a defiant assertion of sovereignty, might have produced the same results had any raider co-operated or not. Defense Attorneys Baxter and Temple, men of Union sympathies, found no fault with Pittenger's conduct during the trials.

What Baxter and Temple couldn't have known then or later, and what we can't know, is how honest Pittenger was with himself in identifying the course best for him as the one best for the party. He may have believed, or rationalized himself into thinking, that the course taken was the best for all hands, or he may deliberately have increased their danger to decrease his own. Essentially, Pittenger's strongest defense was the repeated evidence that Baxter and Temple had thought him a loyal Union man. This drew Murphy's later endorsement, by way of Judge Temple's persuasion. Dorsey's counterpoint was that the full truth hadn't then been known to any of the men later appearing as character witnesses—or, that getting away with a wrongdoing at the time of its commission needn't necessarily be taken as a complete defense later.

One point is clear. Testifying as he did—in the opinion of both Fuller and Temple—gave Pittenger a better chance of surviving than the others had, short of escape. It's hard to believe he was unaware of this at the time. Whether he had rationalized the situation to blur the best interests of the party with his own, or was deliberately looking out for himself first, it wouldn't have been expected that Pittenger would do anything but try his hardest to seem to the defense attorneys a man loyal to his companions. Had any under-the-table arrangement been made, it's equally unlikely that Union-sympathizing Baxter and Temple would have been told of it. In Pittenger's favor, it should be pointed out that nearly all the factors making it possible for him to have concealed acts of treason make it as difficult to prove innocence. From Korea and elsewhere, we've learned what a jungle of suspicion can grow in the steamy darkness of wartime prisons, and how difficult the later process may be of establishing the truth of any situation.

At Chattanooga and Atlanta, locked together as the men were, many personal traits of Pittenger grated increasingly on Dorsey and the others. If anything, these weigh for Pittenger as offering a simpler explanation of the frictions eventually to lead to the charges of treason. Nothing in the record—including Pittenger's reluctance to escape, and his later admitted status as a semi-trusty under Major Wells—confirms Pittenger as a deliberate turncoat.

Much in the record indicates that Pittenger made an inglorious try at carrying water on both shoulders—that whether from weakness or self-delusion, he played a part while in Southern custody that he himself later came to consider as discreditable, and on much stronger grounds than the professed reluctance to report "perjury" committed before the Rebel court. Pittenger, a man wanting very much to be a hero or have the respect given a hero—as can be seen in his speech at enlistment, his cover-breaking march of triumph along the company street at the start from camp, and elsewhere—made a poor fist of it when it came to the test. At the least, he made mistakes in judgment which facilitated the condemnation and execution of eight men. Had he acknowledged this, no one with justification could ever have made the attacks that eventually were to be made. Instead, in three published versions of the raid—by the weaving of an intricate fabric of half-truths, evasions and diversionary material—Pittenger undertook to cover all facts to his disadvantage and claim a number of virtues he didn't have in the measure suggested.

These notes are already much longer than they were intended to be. Pittenger clearly rates blame—in my opinion at least—not for anything he may or may not have done during the raid, trials and period of imprisonment, but for the nearly thirty years of hypocrisy and distorted reporting that followed.

I don't know that Pittenger took up the Christian ministry as a possible form of personal sanctuary ready to hand, any more than I can know that he left the army as quickly as he decently could to avoid the danger of a court of inquiry—or to avoid a part in the announced advance that led within a few days to the shambles of

Chickamauga—or than I can know that he changed his political party not so much from conviction as with the thought that the shift might offer a convenient explanation of the attack he had reason to expect from Dorsey at any time from the McComb meeting on. We can know that these several moves would have been shrewd ones had Pittinger been, or looked on himself as, a man once guilty of cowardice, fatally poor judgment or treachery.

It would be clearly unfair to Pittenger to suggest the preceding possibilities as having anything like the strength of probabilities. The possibilities are mentioned here because Pittenger's extreme carefulness in omitting or camouflaging in the record even the smallest facts unfavorable to him invites the guess that he looked on himself for nearly all his life as a man with a great deal to hide, and these could have been among the steps he took to make his concealment more secure.

Along with the three conflicting stories offered to account for the almost certain fact that Pittenger was in such standing at Chattanooga as to be allowed free access to newspapers, and such other minor clear twistings of the record as the attempted concealment of the fact that his presence at Knoxville was by his own choice and not George Wilson's, Pittenger gives even more grounds for distrust than Dorsey happened to find and name in *The Ohio Soldier* series. A clinching one, for me, became evident only after repeated examination of certain passages, and a recheck of Ohio geography. Hypocrisy is a strong word, but it seems impossible to avoid after considering the expressed sentiments of the published writings, and Pittenger's conduct toward the families of the executed raiders from April of 1863 on.

Pittenger became a probationary minister in the Methodist church on leaving the army, and served from his acceptance into the ministry until 1869 in several eastern Ohio churches. Perry—or Philip G.—Shadrach, as Pittenger mentioned very glancingly at one point, and one point only, in his last book, was from Knoxville, Pittenger's own village. Campbell's town of Salineville, otherwise located only as in "Ohio," is just over the county line from Jefferson County, within ten miles of Pittenger's home town. Pittenger speaks of Shadrach as having come at some time from Pennsylvania, and suggests Campbell as dissolute and brawling around Louisville when the armies came through. However recently Shadrach had come from Pennsylvania, and however Campbell might have been on the town at Louisville, it would be reasonable to believe that some members of the respective families would have been within a few miles of Pittenger during the years of his ministry.

A natural function of a clergyman is the giving of comfort and consolation where he can. A returned soldier, knowing the last days of a fellow soldier who didn't get back, might be expected to look up the man's next of kin, however painful the chore. At no time of record, to comfort them or to secure the personal information he hunted so diligently elsewhere, did Pittenger look up any member of the nearby Campbell or Shadrach families.

George Wilson left a wife and at least one child at Cincinnati or in nearby Warren County. Pittenger never looked them up. The family of Marion Ross were in Champaign County, Ohio, across the state but very much interested in news of their executed son, sergeant major in Pittenger's regiment. Pittenger kept completely away from the Ross family. At Findlay, although there during the reunion of 1886, he made no recorded attempt to see the brothers and sisters of John Scott. Bourneville in Ross County—where Sammy Robertson's people lived—would have been an easy trip for Pittenger at almost any time. The trip wasn't made. Portsmouth, where Sam Slavens enlisted, is on the Ohio River, up and down which Pittenger traveled several times in 1863 and later. Mrs. Slavens and her three young sons were there or at Wakefield in nearby Pike County through the years of the war and on. The Reverend William Pittenger apparently never found time to call.

Many elements of the story of Andrews and his raiders would never have come down to us if William Pittenger hadn't applied himself to its recording. Any latecomer dealing with it—this writer for one—is in his debt. Much of the honor accorded the raiders followed on his pointing out measures of honor due. That the honor we do them is deserved, however, was made clear by the courage and dedication of the raiders themselves, not to Pittenger's, this, or any other account of them. Of that company—by the kindest judgment the full record would seem to allow—Pittenger belongs after, and not before the rest.

A fictional treatment new in 1956 ends with Pittenger, rather than Parrott, getting the first Congressional Medal of Honor:

Pittenger came to attention, and Mr. Stanton pinned the medal to his chest. Pittenger knew he had to speak, but something choked him.

"I don't know what—" Pittenger said. "We don't deserve any medals, sir. We're just ordinary soldiers."

"That's all our country needs, Corporal," President Lincoln said.

Pittenger's eyes blurred behind his glasses, thinking of Andrew and the seven others, and he couldn't see Secretary Stanton or President Lincoln as the President said, "Just ordinary men, like you."

It's no pleasure to differ with even an invented statement of Abraham Lincoln, but I'll have to ride with Dorsey, Knight, Wollam and others, and call William Pittenger—by any standard—one of the least ordinary men in American history.

Story of a Story 3

Winston Churchill—an excellent if cheerfully high-handed historian—has written to the effect that if a certain heroic action belongs in history it will find its way there, and with his blessing, whether or not it happens to occur beforehand in the exact form described. By the rule, the burning boxcar on the Western & Atlantic's burning bridge must have been intended for the ages.

In the *Southern Confederacy* account, on the streets within three days of the chase, no burning of anything takes place: "The fugitives thus finding themselves closely pursued [beyond Tunnel Hill] uncoupled two of the boxcars from the engine, to impede the progress of the pursuers. Fuller hastily coupled them to the front of his engine, and pushed them ahead of him to the first turn-out or siding, where they were left. . . ." The third boxcar, unmentioned further, remained by implication firmly attached to the eventually stopped *General*.

Alf Wilson and Mark Wood, in their first report of the raid published in the Key West *New Era* in November, 1862—reprinted the following year bound together with the March 27 affidavits of the exchanged prisoners as "Ohio Boys in Dixie"—let some of the heat of their recent yellow fever bouts get back into a boxcar: "We came to a bridge, and here we set fire to one of our cars, piled on wood, and left it on the bridge, designing to set it on fire also. . . . Soon [the following engine] came to the bridge with the burning car, which had not yet caught the bridge. . . . [They] succeeded in turning the burning car off the bridge; they then started [again after] us. . . .

In Pittenger's first account, the *Daring and Suffering* of 1863, on pages 68-69, some smoke is rising, but not in spectacular fashion: "But before yielding, we decided to try one more expedient. For this purpose, we broke open the forward end of the only boxcar we had left, and with the fragments endeavored to kindle a fire in it. Had we succeeded, we would have detached it, left it burning on a bridge, and run on with the locomotive alone. But the fuel on the latter was too nearly gone to afford us kindling wood, and the draught through the car, caused by our rapid motion, blew our matches out. At length we succeeded in kindling a small fire; but the drizzling rain, which had been falling all morning, blew in on it, and prevented it from burning rapidly enough to be of any service. Thus our last hope expired. . . ."

Had they succeeded, Pittenger here notes wistfully, the car would have been detached and left burning on a bridge. They hadn't succeeded, and it wasn't.

Alf Wilson, or the newspaper editors for whom his articles were first written, kept working at the fire. On page 36 of Wilson's *Adventures*, published in 1880, the blaze was beginning to take hold: "We therefore determined to make another effort to burn a bridge. . . . We kindled a fire in the rear car and put the locomotive again at full speed, so as to have all the time possible for the bridge to get well to burning before the pursuing train came up. We dropped off this burning car on the bridge when we reached it, and stopped to assist the fire in the work of destruction all we could. . . . We no more than fairly got to work before we saw the black smoke of the pursuing locomotive rolling above the trees as she came thundering down. . . . They seemed to know our design on the bridge and were straining every nerve to foil the attempt. . . ."

Wilson lets it go at that—leaving the nerve-straining pursuers to get the boxcar off the bridge as they can—and passes on to the last stages of the race. The following year, in his *Capturing a Locomotive*, Pittenger saw Wilson and raised him a little. The hope of 1863, with the passage of eighteen years, was remembered as solid, crackling fact.

"We now resolved to play," Pittenger wrote, "what had been reserved as our last card . . . [lighting] a fire in our only remaining car. It was already open at both ends, and now as much of the sides and top as could possibly be obtained was also torn off and prepared for fuel." The speed of the flight still blew Pittenger's matches out, but this time—with Wilson's account to spur him on—a sterner try was to be made. "Fire was then brought back from the engine, but this seemed to smolder rather than burn, for the rain, which fell in torrents, blew through the unprotected car, and all the boards were soaking wet. Never did kindling a fire seem so difficult. When at length it fairly caught, and began to burn briskly, our dampened hopes began to brighten in sympathy with it. . . . Just then a long covered bridge was approached, which it was desirable on every account to burn. All of our party, whom the heat had not already driven forward, were ordered into the nearby empty tender, and the car was uncoupled in the middle of the bridge. We did not leave it hastily, but stopped near the farther end of the bridge to watch the result in breathless anxiety."

In his *How to Become a Public Speaker* of 1887, Pittenger was to write: "Nothing adds more to the brilliancy and effectiveness of oratory than the royal faculty of imagination. This weird and glorious power deals with the truth as well as fiction and gives to its fortunate possessor the creative, life-breathing spirit of poetry."

Oratory, Pittenger might have added, and competitive history. "We had scarcely halted," he continued in *Capturing a Locomotive*, "when the black smoke of the nearest pursuer was seen. . . . We could see that the flame was rising higher, but could also see that the enemy's train had a large number of men on board, some of whom had firearms. . . . We lingered, until we saw the enemy pushing our blazing car before them over the bridge; then . . . we again sought safety in flight. They pushed the blazing car before them to the first sidetrack, which happened not to be far away, and then left it to burn at its leisure. Thus our forlorn hope expired."

Full-muscled history had just two unkindled observers left to sidestep.

The first was William A. Fuller. In October 31, 1884, after seeing Pittenger's *Capturing a Locomotive*, Fuller was writing Dorsey: "I must spoil the romance. . . . The Federals took with them at the start only three boxcars at Big Shanty. Two miles north of Calhoun, where they were first discovered by me, they left one car. About one mile further north, and nearer Resaca, they left another. The last, and only remaining, car was captured by me, attached to the abandoned engine, two miles north of Ringgold. It had been set on fire, and was burning slowly, but was put out."

It hadn't been. In 1887, in his revised *Daring and Suffering* of that year, Pittenger showed that he, history and the fire weren't to be checked by a few buckets of cold water from Fuller. On its smoking bridge, the boxcar still blazed away. In 1891, in his letter to Dorsey, Anthony Murphy showed himself equally lacking in enough of the weird and glorious power to get with it.

"There were no bridges burned," Murphy wrote, "nor did Andrews attempt it. Nor were there any cars burned. An attempt was made to burn the last car just before they abandoned it, but that failed."

Murphy as an extinguisher was the one who failed. Pittenger hadn't started it, but if history demanded a blaze, history was going to get one. In the pages of *The Great Locomotive Chase* of 1893, without the change of a splinter from 1887, Pittenger reassembles his kindling:

"Desperate fingers tore everything combustible loose from the car, and smashed it into kindling. Some blazing fagots were stolen from the engine and the fire made to burn. The rapid motion with driving rain was an obstacle at first, but as we fed up the blaze and sheltered it as well as possible, it grew rapidly till soon but one could stay in the car and watch it, and all the others crowded on the tender and locomotive. The steam was now gradually shut off that we might come slowly upon the bridge and be able to leave the burning car just at the right place. We came to a full stop at this first Chickamauga bridge, a large one, and well covered. Inside it was at least dryer than on the outside, and we doubted not that with time it would burn well. The only question was, 'Will that time be given?' . . ."

In *How to Become a Public Speaker,* published in this same year, Pittenger stressed the value of what he described as the "thrilling pause." "It also requires a good degree of confidence," he noted in the handbook, "to firmly begin a sentence, even when the general idea is plain, without knowing just how it will end. . . . Yet a bold and confident speaker need feel no uneasiness." Nor a writer, when well squared away. The covered bridge fire buffs this time, after the thrilling pause, were getting the full treatment.

"We added almost the last of our oil and nearly the last stick of wood—knowing that . . . if this bridge could be made to burn well, we could have all the time we wanted to get wood and everything else. In fact we put life itself on this last throw, and left ourselves, in case of failure, hopelessly bankrupt. For a considerable time, as it seemed to us, though it must have been measured by seconds rather than minutes, we remained on the other side of the fire, watching. Then the inexorable smoke of the foe was seen; the pin connecting the burning car with our engine was pulled out and we slowly moved on. . . . The car which, if the day had been dry, would long before this have filled the bridge with a mass of roaring flame, was burning faster than the bridge. . . . Very sadly we left the tall column of smoke behind. The pursuers saw the car, and realizing how serious their loss would be if it was permitted to consume the bridge, they pushed right into the smoke and shoved the burning car on to Ringgold but a short distance ahead, where it was left to smoke and sputter in the rain on the sidetrack. We were now on what proved to be our last run."

The flaming boxcar wasn't. It was just working up momentum. By 1956, it was to be permanently out of control, and in Technicolor.

The Mustering Out

Knight, Porter, Bensinger, Dorsey, Brown, Parrott and Anthony Murphy met for the last time as a group at Chattanooga in 1906. In 1909, Murphy and Peter Bracken died. Within eleven further years, the last of the raiders followed—Knight and Dorsey living into, and Bensinger two years beyond, the first of the twentieth-century "total" wars, of which their own had been the unexpected and shattering example.

April 12, 1862, remains a day nearer our own than it might at first seem. Sons and daughters of the raiders and pursuers still flourish nearly a century after the raid, in Illinois, Georgia, Indiana, Michigan, California and elsewhere. The brass and iron of the locomotives the principals rode can be seen and touched in Chattanooga and Atlanta. With the intertangled written record and the product of the turned-out memories of the men and women who knew them still being put together, few final judgments on the assorted facets of the men and what happened to them can yet be made. For this writer, to offer one example, some four years of looking into the story have produced nearly as many new questions that need answers as old ones that have found them.

As a secret military mission of the kind World War II intelligence usage would have called special operations, the raid remains an impressive one in concept and execution. The objective would have been worth the risk of regiments, and the agent called Andrews and his hastily picked party of twenty-one came astonishingly close to achieving it on their own. It's late in this book to find space for second guessing as to how chances of the raiders' success might have been improved, but in general it would seem the young Ohio soldiers were more let down by others than by themselves.

For all the weeks preceding their mission, the chief daily business of Mitchel's division had been the repair of obstructed railroad track and wrecked bridges left by Johnston's army as it retreated from Kentucky. The Michigan engineering companies under Mitchel had "some of the best workmen" Corporal Pike was to see in his years of the war. An hour or two of instruction from these men for all the party in track blocking or bridge demolition could later have gained equal hours on the W. & A. run when unpressured minutes might have saved the day. Two or three of these experienced pioneer hands added to Andrews' party, as resourceful in demolition as in repair—as Sherman's task force of soldiers and pioneers was to demonstrate at Bear Creek, Ala., on the day after the Big Shanty raid—might have gone much of the way to offset the practical advantage Murphy's technical resourcefulness and Fuller's knowledge of the line gave the pursuers. Such trained equipment-foragers might have been used as well to make sure, even if they had to peel off at Calhoun, Kingston or elsewhere on the way down, that track-lifting tools, axes and kegs of Georgia turpentine were waiting to be picked up on the flying return trip of the main party.

Mitchel, who had been given to checking every detail months before—"Everything comes under my own eye, and a team of four horses, even to wagon and harness, I have tested by loading it fully with nearly double what it is required to move, and then driving it down and up a steep hill"—apparently didn't take time from his own main plans for the taking of Huntsville to work out the critical points of demolition equipment and techniques with Andrews. The leader, knowing railroading only by "casual observation," accordingly had to start his practical demolition studies on April 12, some days late for useful first classes.

Mitchel, the one-time railroad surveyor and construction engineer, missed an even simpler piece of insurance. A manual intended for the building of railroad bridges might serve as easily as a key to their efficient destruction. One available text that Mitchel himself must have known and used—although unfortunately he didn't now think to arm Andrews with it—was *"The Description of Colonel Long's Bridges, with Directions to Build,"* by Stephen Harriman Long, the man who had laid out the exact line under attack and from the actual bridges of which he had drawn many of his illustrations. The old New Hampshireman himself, had Mitchel thought to wire him for what could have been some interesting pointers, was in Washington on War Department duty while Mitchel and Andrews were settling on the details of the raid.

During the raid, on the evidence we have, there's no certainty that Andrews didn't let the raiders down in part, not by failing to take a possible measure for their safety, but perhaps by giving his and their safety more thought than they might have asked, considering the great risks already run. Whether fully aware of it at the time, most of the raiders came later to believe with other observers that the hope of seriously damaging the W. & A. by the burning of bridges was the overriding strategic justification for the chances taken. Murphy believed, as seen, that Andrews attempted no real attack on the bridges. If Andrews lost the edge of his nerve after the racking wait at Kingston, as Murphy implied, and strained for the balance of the race simply to escape—giving bridge burning only incidental thought as one of several ways, not of damaging the W. & A., but blocking his immediate pursuers—he could have done the raiders the greatest disservice then still possible: cutting the size of the stakes while the game was still on. If their goal in mid-run became merely the Confederacy's loss of an engine and some face, and not its loss for vital weeks of a railroad, the raiders were badly short-changed, since the basic bet of their lives remained on the board.

After their capture, it's possible that they were again let down by Ormsby MacKnight Mitchel, as he himself had been let down so often by those over him. The undeniably gifted general—rarely forgetful of the point himself: at a strawberry supper in Huntsville on May 17, by report of the generally sympathetic John Beatty, he monopolized the conversation with a determination "to make all understand that he was the greatest of living soldiers"—didn't see, or use if he saw, the one means of backing up that might still have saved the lives of the men he had sent out.

In no case during the war where matching sets of prisoners were named and specific threats of retaliation clearly made were executions attempted by either side. In mid-April, along with his new major-generalship, Mitchel had been given the right of reporting directly by telegraph to Washington. No report of the difficulties of the Andrews party was sent even after Private Sam Llewellyn had recrossed to the Union lines on April 29 with word that the raiders were alive and on trial, although a vigorous retaliation threat, as the events proved, might still have been effective at any time in May or early June. One tragic by-product of Mitchel's vanity may have been this failure to report to Washington the size, composition and plight of the party while this still might have helped, not by neglect or oversight, but in order not to let even the failure of a side mission tarnish the central triumph at Huntsville.

The heart of the Andrews raid story has never seemed to me a question of comparative locomotive speeds or even the workings of intricate and terrifying patterns of chance. It's not just the practical rarity of dependable evidence on anything, nor the mystery of the trials, and surely not the tragic cross-suspicions and sorry haggling over glory that followed for some, nor such unresolved minor points as whether the shine of a promised $50,000 in gold helped pull Andrews and some of the seven to the ends they met. These ingredients are all in the story, and important to it—as are the determination and resourcefulness of the defending Georgians whose own hardest days of trial were still to come—but its basic interest lies in the character and war-forced growth of the tested men themselves, the raiders whose lives were most immediately on the block before, during and after the chase. It was what these men were and did—then and in the full war—that would seem to warrant our remembering and knowing them as we can, in and out of the narrower story that threw them into history by some linked accidents of time, setting and form of first report.

The mention of possible degrees of letdown by others wasn't made before to give the impression that a few different acts by anyone might have made a major difference to the raiders. Had they not gone on the expedition, as many of them might still have died sooner or later in the war—as Bill Knight's brother Jim, Captain Alexander Berryhill of the 2nd Ohio, General Joshua Sill, Ormsby MacKnight Mitchel himself, and so many other hundreds of thousands did—but without the final mercy of being remembered by face and name. War is made up of thousands of assorted one-hour, one-day or one-week jobs of fighting and work done by thousands of teams of men. In these, as in life as a whole, each man's or woman's great test can come with unexpected speed and in an unexpected form, often without being recognized for the searching and final test it is until the score has already been irrevocably racked up. The men of the Andrews raid—including the lonely, mild-spoken leader who died without reproach and almost wistfully for a country not fully till then his own—met their testing over more days than the wild hours of April 12, 1862.

In sorrow and resolution, in his July Fourth message of 1861, Abraham Lincoln had called the people to the defense of the American union.

"In full view of his great responsibility," he had told them, "[the executive] has so far done what he deemed his duty. You will now, according to your own judgments, perform yours."

Along with enough hundreds of thousands more to give pledge that some of the hard, dark roads could lead back toward renewed morning, the men of the Andrews party—by their judgments—performed theirs.

Story of a Story 4

Participants' accounts of or comment on the raid and related events drawn on for quotation:

Andrews, J. J.: letters: to Soldiers' Aid Society of Flemingsburg, Dec. 6, 1861, and to D. S. McGavic, June 5, 1862; from words of, as remembered by Williams and Standifer in F. M. Gregg's *Andrews Raiders;* from accounts of Knight, Dorsey, Pittenger, Porter, et. al.

Bensinger, Wm.: from affidavit of March 25, 1863, included in report of Judge Advocate General Joseph Holt of March 27, 1863, also in House Executive Document #74, 40th Congress, 2nd Session, Dec. 18, 1867. (Hereafter cited as Holt Report.)

Brown, Joseph E.: A *Sketch of the Life and Times and Speeches of*—, by Herbert Fielder. Springfield Printing Co., Springfield, Mass., 1883.

Buell, Don Carlos: from "Notes on the Locomotive Chase" by James B. Fry, *Battles and Leaders of the Civil War*, Vol. 11, Century, 1887; and "Operations in North Alabama" from *Battles and Leaders;* dispatches and letters of, from *War of the Rebellion: Official Records of the Union and Confederate Armies.* (Cited hereafter as OWR.)

Buffum, Robert: from Holt Report.

Dorsey, Daniel A.: "The Mitchel Raiders," *Ohio Soldier*, Feb. 25, 1893, to Nov. 18, 1893; letters, in Columbus *Dispatch;* Chillicothe *Leader*, and other Ohio papers in 1888 and in *Ohio Soldier*, Jan. 6, 1894, through June 9, 1894; letters to and from Secretary of War Alger, Wm. A. Fuller, Anthony Murphy, John A. Woodruff and others; miscellaneous papers, Wm. P. Palmer Collection, Western Reserve Historical Society.

Fuller, William A.: "Muscles vs. Steam," in *Sunny South*, Feb. 16, 1878, as told to Dr. R. J. Massey; speech before GAR encampment, Columbus, Ohio, Sept., 1886, reported in Columbus *Dispatch*. (And see

"Epitome of the Andrews Raid," *Times-Union*, Jacksonville, Fla., March 8, 1904; "Battle of the Locomotives," Atlanta *Journal* magazine, March 16, 1930; letters to Dorsey, and others.)

Knight, William J.: "An Engineer's Story," Chillicothe *Leader*, Feb. 9, 1889; "How I Ran 'The General,'" article in *The Railroad Man's Magazine*, March, 1911, F. A. Munsey Co., N.Y.; letters and unpublished lectures; newspaper accounts quoted in Dorsey, Pittenger and J. A. Wilson.

Lincoln, Abraham: July 4, 1862, address as in *The Lincoln Papers*, Vol. I, edited by David C. Mearns, Doubleday, 1944.

Mitchel, Ormsby MacKnight: dispatches and letters from OWR; speech at Union Square, New York, in J. T. Headley's *The Great Rebellion*; *Ormsby MacKnight Mitchel, Astronomer and General*, by F. A. Mitchel, Houghton Mifflin, Cambridge, Mass., 1887.

Murphy, Anthony: "Pursuit of the Andrews Raiders," in letter to Dorsey, 1891; published in *Ohio Soldier*, 1893, reprinted in Atlanta *Journal* magazine, Nov. 8, 1931.

Park, Dr. Thomas Y.: own account, from F. M. Gregg's *Andrews Raiders*.

Parrott, Jacob: Holt Report and *McClure's Magazine*, Sept., 1903.

Pike, James: *Scout and Ranger: Personal Adventures of Cpl.* [*James*] *Pike of the 4th Ohio Cavalry*, J. B. Hawley & Co., Cincinnati and N. Y., 1865. (Reprinted in part with introduction and notes by Carl L. Cannon, Princeton, 1932.)

Pittenger, William: from Holt Report, 1863; *Daring and Suffering: A History of the Great Railroad Adventure*, J. W. Daughaday, Phila., 1863; *Capturing a Locomotive*, J. B. Lippincott, Phila., 1881; "The Locomotive Chase in Georgia," in *Battles and Leaders of the Civil War*, 1887; *Daring and Suffering, A History of the Andrews Railroad Raid into Georgia in 1862*, War Publishing Co., N.Y., 1887; letters, Ohio newspapers, 1888, 1893, 1894; "Chattanooga Railroad Expedition" in *Famous Adventures and Prison Escapes of the Civil War*, 1893; *The Great Locomotive Chase*, Penn. Pub. Co., 1893 (*Daring and Suffering* of 1887, with 19 pages added, ran through several reprints to 1929); *Capturing a Locomotive*, 1905 (re-issue), The National Tribune, Washington; *The Great Locomotive Chase in Georgia*, included in *The Blue and the Gray*, 2 vols., Commager, Bobbs-Merrill, N.Y., 1950.

Porter, John Reed: own accounts included in J. A. Wilson, Pittenger, Dorsey.

Reddick, William: from Holt Report, 1863.

Scott, W. J.: "An Episode of the War," in his *From Lincoln to Cleveland*, J. P. Harrison, Atlanta, 1886.

Smith, White: from Gregg's *Andrews Raiders.*
Standifer, William I.: from Gregg's *Andrews Raiders.*
Williams, Sam: from Gregg's *Andrews Raiders.*
Wilson, J. A.: report of Nov. 12, 1862, OWR and *New Era,* Key West, Fla.; *Ohio Boys in Dixie,* Miller and Matthews, N.Y., 1863; articles, Wood County *Sentinel,* Bowling Green, Ohio, and Toledo *Bee; Adventures of Alf Wilson, Blade,* Toledo, 1880; *Adventures of Alf Wilson,* slightly revised re-issue by The National Tribune, Washington, 1897.
Wood, Mark: reports from *New Era,* Key West, Fla.; OWR.
Woodruff, John: letter to Dorsey; Atlanta *Constitution,* July 28, 1902.

Non-participants' accounts of or comment on the raid and related events drawn on for quotation:

Dunbar, Seymour: *A History of Travel in America,* Bobbs-Merrill, N.Y., 1915; Tudor, N.Y., 1937.
Foraker, Joseph Benson: *Notes of a Busy Life,* 2 vols., Stewart & Kidd, Cincinnati, 1916.
Grant, U. S.: *Personal Memoirs,* Charles L. Webster & Co., N. Y., 1885; (Available in re-issue of 1952, World Publishing Co., N.Y., with introduction and notes by E. B. Long.)
Gregg, Frank Moody: *Andrews Raiders,* Republican Job Print, Chattanooga, 1891.
Henry, Robert Selph: *The Story of the Confederacy,* Bobbs-Merrill, N. Y., 1931.
McBryde, Randell: *The Historic "General,"* McGowan & Cook, Chattanooga, 1904.
Murphy, Adelia McConnell: from "Mrs. Anthony Murphy," by Lollie Belle Wylie, *Georgian,* Feb. 5, 1907.
Parham, Louis G.: *Pioneer Citizens' History of Atlanta,* Byrd Printing Co., Atlanta, 1902.
Porter, Stephen B.: editorials and articles, Columbus *Dispatch;* letters to Wm. Knight and others.
Richardson, Albert D.: *The Field, Dungeon and Escape,* American Publishing Co., 1865. (Re-issued by The National Tribune, Washington, 1897.)
Sherman, W. T.: letter quoted taken from *Adventures of Corporal Pike,* edited by Carl Cannon, 1932.
Waddle, A. C.: *Three Years with the Armies of the Ohio and Cumberland.*

Accounts of the raid, or of those concerned in it, general:

Abbott, J. S. C.: "A Railroad Adventure," in "Heroic Deeds" Series, *Harper's* magazine, July, 1865.

Adair, George H., and Smith, J. Henley: "The Great Railroad Chase," in *Southern Confederacy*, Atlanta, April 15, 1862; report of Andrews' death, June 8, and others.

Beatty, John: *The Citizen Soldier*, Wilstach, Baldwin & Co., Cincinnati, 1879.

Buchan, John: "The Railway Raid in Georgia," from *A Book of Escapes and Hurried Journeys*, Houghton Mifflin, Boston, 1922-23.

Canfield, S. S.: *History of the 21st Regiment O.V.I.*, Vrooman, Anderson & Bateman, Toledo, 1893.

Clark, Alexander: "Homeward from Dixie," Methodist *Recorder*, Aug. 8, 1874.

Cook, Fred J.: Articles for American Press Association, Atlanta, 1886-87.

Crosman, Commander A. F.: report reference, Wilson and Wood, Naval OWR.

Dodson, W. C.: "Story of the Andrews Raid," Jan. 18 and 25 and Feb. 1, 1903, in *The Age-Herald*, Birmingham, Ala.

Fry, Col. J. B.: "Review of Pittenger's *Capturing a Locomotive*," Journal, Military Service Institute, March, 1882.

Hanford, M. E.: *The General, Friendship Train*, 1952, unpublished manuscript.

Hearings, raiders' pension bill, Senate Report 361, 48th Congress, 1st Session.

Hubbard, Freeman, "The Other Side of Jordan," Railroad [Man's] Magazine, Jan., 1932, and in *Railroad Avenue*, Whittlesey House, N. Y., 1945.

James, Marquis: "The Stolen Train," *American Legion Magazine*, and included in *They Had Their Hour*, Bobbs-Merrill, N.Y., 1926.

MacKenzie, Robert: "The Andrews Raid; War by Rail," San Francisco Quarterly, Pre-Summer, 1948; reprinted in *Catholic Digest*, Aug., 1948.

N. C. & St. L. Railway: "Battlefields in Dixie," pamphlet, Nashville, 1928.

Reed, Wallace Putnam: "Hero of the Famous Engine Chase," Atlanta *Constitution*, July 15, 1899.

Reid, Whitelaw: wartime articles by "Agate," Cincinnati *Gazette*, 1861-65; *Ohio in the War*, Moore-Wilstach & Baldwin, Cincinnati, 1868.

The Story of the General, N. C. & St. L. pamphlet, Nashville, 1906.

Thurber, James: *Daguerreotype of a Spy*, Country Press, Inc., 1938, included in *Mixture for Men*, edited by Fred Feldkamp, Doubleday, 1946.

The New York Times: "Andrews' Daring Raid," April 17-18, 1892.

TVA: *Scenic Resources of the Tennessee Valley*, U. S. Government Printing Office, Washington, 1938.

Walker, Hugh: "The Great Train Chase," The Nashville *Tennessean* Magazine, Feb. 12, 1956.

Washington Chronicle: issues of March, April, 1863.

Some treatments of the raid in fiction, verse, radio and films:

Ashley, R. P.: *The Stolen Train*, John C. Winston Co., Phila., 1953.

Blair, J. F.: *The Andrews Raiders*, verse, 1898.

Houghton, Morris: *Adventure in Silk Hat*, radio play, Cavalcade of America, 1944.

Keaton, Buster: *The General*, motion picture, 1927.

Lancaster, Bruce: *No Bugles Tonight*, Little-Brown, 1948.

Lavender, David: *Mike Maroney, Raider*, Westminster Press, 1945.

The Railroad Raid, motion picture, 1912.

Roberts, MacLennan: *The Great Locomotive Chase*, with postscript by Wilbur G. Kurtz, Dell Publ. Co., 1956.

Robins, Edward: *Chasing an Iron Horse*, G. W. Jacobs & Co., Phila., 1902.

Watkin, L. E.; Disney, Walt; Kurtz, W. G.; and Lyon, F. D.: *The Great Locomotive Chase*, motion picture, 1956.

Zara, Louis: *Rebel Run*, Crown Publishers, N. Y., 1951.

With Thanks

The generous help of many more people than can be named here has been indispensable in the gathering and processing of the material from which this book has been made. Of the immediate families of the raiders, and those directly concerned with them, particular thanks are due three sons and a granddaughter of William J. Knight: James Knight of Cassopolis, Michigan, Jesse J. Knight of Goshen, Indiana, William H. H. Knight of Chicago, and Margaret Knight Hollenbeck of Menasha, Wisc.; the daughter and a granddaughter of J. Alf Wilson: Esther Mae Wilson and Gladys Hamilton Arneal of Los Angeles; Ella Mae Pennington of Macon, Ga., granddaughter of Peter Bracken; Wilbur G. Kurtz of Atlanta, son-in-law of William A. Fuller; Kate Murphy Sciple and Mary Louise Glenn of Atlanta, daughter and great-granddaughter of Anthony Murphy; Iolene Ashton Hawkins and Mrs. J. K. Grannis of Flemingsburg, Ky., daughter and granddaughter of Flemingsburg newspaper editor H. C. Ashton; Oliver R. Bright of Flemingsburg, grandson of James and Sarah Eckels; and a granddaughter and great-grand-niece of the William T. Lindsays, who once had their house painted by a man calling himself James J. Andrews: Frances Reed Kehoe of Flemingsburg and Lula Reed Boss of Maysville, Ky.

Unrelated to the raiders, but related essentially and invaluably to this book from start to finish have been Cornelia Rockwell O'Neill, my long-suffering, resilient and trouble-shooting wife; Mary Pickett DeBell of Flemingsburg, Ky.; Albert Hirsch of Chicago; Hiram Haydn and Bertha Krantz of Random House; and Alene Lowe White of Cleveland's Western Reserve Historical Society, who dug out and made available the published and unpublished wealth of previously overlooked Dorsey material in the Society's William P. Palmer Collection.

Help in the finding and reprinting of photographs used in *Wild Train* has placed me well in debt to the families of William Knight and J. A. Wilson, to Milton Kaplan of the Library of Congress, Frederick Hill Meserve of New York, and Mary Perry and Sam P. Senior, Jr., of Bridgeport, Conn. As well, in fairness, thanks more than to any other single individual should go to William Pittenger for preserving as many of the photographs and sketched likenesses of the raiders and principal participants as he did. Welcome aid on papers examined in microfilm form has come from the American Microfilm Service Co. of New Haven, Conn., Micro-Photo, Inc. of Cleveland, and National Microfilm Service, Inc. of Bridgeport, Conn.

Without the cheerfully shared resources of a number of libraries, this and most histories would still be unwritten. Thanks this time are owed the public libraries of Atlanta, Bridgeport, Chillicothe, Chattanooga, New York and Westport, Conn.; Baker Library at Hanover, N.H.; the Library of Congress; Georgia State Library; Hamilton County Medical Society Library of Chattanooga; the Ohio Historical Society Library at Columbus; the Pequot Library, Southport, Conn.; the Carlson Library of the University of Bridgeport; and the Yale University Library.

Needed help and encouragement on the book took many forms. An incomplete list of those rendering either or both in great measure would include Ruth Adams, Josephine Clifford, Rosalie Larthe, Archie Robertson and Eleanor Street of Westport, Conn.; Henry B. Bass, Enid, Okla.; Dellie Bochinski, Fairfield, Conn.; James G. Bogle, Mozelle Colquitt, Isabel Erlich, Edgar Kimsey, Walter R. McDonald, Jane Oliver and A. O. Randall of Atlanta; Norman Bradley and Frances Freedman of Chattanooga; Josephine Cobb of National Archives, C. J. Corliss of the Association of American Railroads, and Ann Costakis of the Library of Congress, Washington; Grace A. Donaldson and Margaret C. Farquhar of Southport, Conn.; Jean Ennis, Raymond Freiman, Robert Haas, Harry E. Maule and Fred Rosenau of Random House; Buford Gordon and W. S. Hackworth, Nashville; Frank Lozier Gregg, Coral Gables, Florida; Richard Holbrook, Bedford Village, N.Y.; Charles Grover Jones, Flemingsburg; Stanley T. Eddison, Jay Kelly and Frederick H. Wood of Bridgeport; George Kirk, Columbus, Ohio; Mildred M. Laning and Seville Young, Norwalk, Ohio; John T. Lindsay, Easton, Conn.; Olive, Karen, Meredith and Lewis Meyers, Laguna Beach, Calif.; and Harriette J. Nelson and Judge Harvey M. Wilson of Kearney, Nebr.

Thanks, finally, are due writers and editors of books useful in the preparation of *Wild Train*, or of value in increasing our understanding of the men, women and events dealt with in these pages. Some of these are:

Alldredge, J. A., et.al.: *Navigation on the Tennessee River System*, Govt. Printing Office, Washington, 1937.

Andrews, J. C.: *The North Reports the Civil War*, U. of Pittsburgh, 1955.

Baker, L. C.: *Secret Service*, John L. Potter & Co., 1894.

Black, R. C., III: *The Railroads of the Confederacy*, U. of N. Carolina, 1952.

Bruce, R. V.: *Lincoln and the Tools of War*, Bobbs-Merrill, N. Y., 1956.

Bryan, T. C.: *Confederate Georgia*, U. of Georgia.

Candler, A. D.: *Confederate Records of Georgia*, "State Papers, J. E. Brown, 1860-65"; "Official Correspondence, 1860-65," C. P. Byrd, Atlanta, 1909-11.

Cist, H. M.: *The Army of the Cumberland*, Scribners, N. Y., 1882.

Clausewitz, Karl von: *On War* (available in Modern Library, Random House, 1943).

Commager, H. S.: *The Blue and the Gray* (2 vols.), Bobbs-Merrill, N. Y., 1950.

Coulter, E. M.: *Georgia, A Short History*, Bobbs-Merrill, N. Y., 1933.

Crozier, Emmet: *Yankee Reporters*, Oxford Press, N. Y., 1956.

Donald, David; Milhollen, Hirst; Kaplan, Milton; Stuart, Helen: *Divided We Fought*, Macmillan, N. Y., 1953.

Duffus, R. L. and Krutch, Charles: *The Valley and Its People, A Portrait of TVA*, Knopf, N. Y., 1946.

Ellis, Daniel: *Thrilling Adventures of —*, Harper Bros., N. Y., 1867.

Farrington, S. K.: *Railroads at War*, Coward-McCann, N. Y., 1952.

Fish, C. R.: *The American Civil War*, Longman's, Green, N. Y., 1937 (edited by Wm. E. Smith from manuscript by Fish).

Fitch, John: *Chickamauga, The Price of Chattanooga*, J. B. Lippincott, Phila., 1864.

Ford, H. J.: *The Cleveland Era*, New Haven, 1920.

Ford, H. S.: *Memoirs of a Volunteer*, Norton & Co., N. Y., 1946 (reissue, with useful notes and introduction by Lloyd Lewis, of John Beatty's *The Citizen Soldier*).

Garrett, F. M.: *Atlanta and Environs* (3 vols.), Atlanta, 1954.

Gihon, J. H.: *Geary in Kansas*, C. C. Rhodes, Phila., 1857.

Govan, G. E., and Livingood, J. W.: *The Chattanooga Country*, E. P. Dutton, N. Y., 1952.

Hazelton, J. P.: *Scouts, Spies and Detectives of the Civil War*, McElroy, Shoppell & Andrews, Wash., 1899.

Headley, J. T.: *The Great Rebellion* (2 vols.), American Pub. Co., Hartford, Conn., 1867.

Headley, Phineas C.: *The Patriot Boy; or the Life & Career of Major-Gen. Ormsby M. Mitchel,* W. H. Appleton, N. Y., 1865.

Heartsill, W. W.: *1491 Days in the Confederate Army,* 1876. (Republished 1955 by Kingsport Press. Edited by B. I. Wiley.)

Henry, Robert Selph: *As They Saw Forrest,* McCowart-Mercier, Jackson, Tenn., 1956.

Hinshaw, David: *Heroic Finland,* G. P. Putnam, N. Y., 1952.

Horan, J. D., and Swiggett, Howard: *The Pinkerton Story,* G. P. Putnam, N. Y., 1951.

Huff, Sarah: *My Eighty Years in Atlanta,* 1937.

Humes, T. W.: *Report to the East Tennessee Relief Assoc.,* Knoxville, 1865.

Johnson, Gerald: *The Secession of the Southern States,* G. P. Putnam, N. Y., 1933.

Johnson, R. V., and Bull, C. C.: *Battles and Leaders of the Civil War,* The Century Co., N. Y., 1887.

Johnston, J. H.: *Western and Atlantic Railroad of the State of Georgia,* Georgia Public Service Comm., Atlanta, 1932.

Lewis, Lloyd: *Sherman, Fighting Prophet,* Harcourt-Brace, N. Y., 1932.

Long, S. H.: *Description of Col. Long's Bridges, Together with Directions to Bridge Builders,* J. F. Brown, Concord, N. H., 1836.

Lossing, J. J.: *Pictorial History of the Civil War,* G. W. Childs, Phila., 1866.

Malin, J. C.: *John Brown and the Legend of 1856,* American Philosophical Soc., Phila., 1942.

McLendon, S. G.: *History of the Public Domain of Georgia,* Atlanta, 1924.

Miller, F. T.: *The Photographic History of the Civil War* (10 vols.), Review of Reviews, N. Y., 1911.

Mitchell, J. B.: *Decisive Battles of the Civil War,* G. P. Putnam, N. Y., 1955.

Monaghan, Jay: *Civil War on the Western Border, 1854-65,* Little-Brown, Boston, 1955.

Morison, S. E., and Commager, H. S.: *Growth of the American Republic* (2 vols.), Oxford Press, N. Y., 1942.

National Cyclopaedia of American Biography (Vols. 9, 11), J. T. White & Co., N. Y., 1950.

Nevins, Allan: *Ordeal of the Union* (2 vols.), Scribner's, N. Y., 1947; *Grover Cleveland,* Dodd-Mead, N. Y., 1932.

Nichols, Alice: *Bleeding Kansas,* Oxford Press, N. Y., 1954.

Official Records of the Union and Confederate Navies in the War of the Rebellion.
Olmstead, F. L.: *The Cotton Kingdom,* 1861 (republished in 1953 by Alfred A. Knopf, N. Y., edited by Arthur Schlesinger).
O'Neill, E. J.: *Journals and Bearings,* Jellison Press, 1931.
Paris, Comte de: *Civil War in America,* Vol. II., Porter & Coates, Phila., 1875.
Parks, J. H.: *General Edmond Kirby Smith, CSA,* Baton Rouge, 1954.
Phillips, Ulrich B.: A *History of Transportation in the Eastern Belt,* Columbia Univ. Press, N. Y., 1908.
Pinkerton, Allen: *The Spy of the Rebellion,* Rose Publishing Co., Toronto, 1894.
Pratt, E. A.: *The Rise of Railpower in War and Conquest,* J. B. Lippincott, Phila., 1916.
Robertson, Archie: *Slow Train to Yesterday,* Houghton Mifflin, Boston, 1945.
Sanborn, F. B.: *Life and Letters of John Brown,* Roberts Bros., Boston, 1891.
Sandburg, Carl: *Abraham Lincoln* (6 vols.), Harcourt-Brace, N. Y., 1926, 1939.
Speed, Thomas: *The Union Cause in Kentucky, 1860-65,* G. P. Putnam, N. Y., 1907.
Starr, J. W.: *Lincoln and the Railroads,* Dodd-Mead, N. Y., 1927.
Starr, L. M.: *Bohemian Brigade,* Knopf, N. Y., 1955.
State Guides, WPA Series, Kentucky, Tennessee, Georgia, Ohio, Alabama, West Virginia, Florida.
Thomas, Benjamin: *Abraham Lincoln,* Alfred A. Knopf, N. Y., 1952.
Walker, R. S.: *This Is Chattanooga.*
War Department—Medal of Honor of the U. S. Army.
The War of the Rebellion: The Official Records of the Union and Confederate Armies.
Weisberger, B. A.: *Reporters for the Union.* Little-Brown, Boston, 1953.
Wigmore, J. H.: A *Pocket Guide of the Rules of Evidence in Trials at Law,* Little-Brown, Boston, 1910.
Wiley, B. I.: *Life of Billy Yank; Life of Johnny Reb.*
Williams, T. H.: *Napoleon in Gray, the Life of P. G. T. Beauregard,* Louisiana State Univ., 1955.

ABOUT THE AUTHOR

CHARLES O'NEILL was born in [illegible] in Bridgeport, Connecticut, and graduated from Dartmouth College in [illegible]. For the next ten years he did newspaper work in New Hampshire and Connecticut, traveled in Europe and Central America, wrote magazine stories and articles, radio and film scripts and plays.

During World War II he served in Latin America with Nelson Rockefeller's Office of Inter-American Affairs and then in North Africa, Italy, France and Germany with the U.S. Air Army. Married in Paris in [illegible], he and his wife now have four sons.

From [illegible] until recently he worked in documentary films and television. His historical novel *Morning Time*—which the late Carl Van Doren found "truthful and exciting," and *The New York Times* called "a rare triumph"—was published in [illegible]. He is a member of the Society of American Historians.

Mr. O'Neill reports that his father and one grandfather qualified as railroad mechanics, but makes no claim on his own part that he could deal, run or repair a locomotive, even after some four years of research and writing for WILD TRAIN.

ABOUT THE AUTHOR

CHARLES O'NEILL was born in 1909 in Bridgeport, Connecticut, and graduated from Dartmouth College in 1931. For the next ten years he did newspaper work in New Hampshire and Connecticut; traveled in Europe and Central America; wrote magazine stories and articles, radio and film scripts, and plays.

During World War II he served in Latin America with Nelson Rockefeller's Office of Inter-American Affairs and then in North Africa, Italy, France and Germany with the U.S. 7th Army. Married in Paris in 1945, he and his wife now have four sons.

From 1946 until recently he worked in documentary films, radio and television. His historical novel *Morning Time*—which the late Carl Van Doren found "truthful and exciting," and *The New York Times* called "a rare triumph"—was published in 1949. He is a member of the Society of American Historians.

Mr. O'Neill reports that his father and one grandfather qualified as railroad mechanics, but makes no claim on his own part that he could steal, run or repair a locomotive, even after some four years of research and writing on WILD TRAIN.

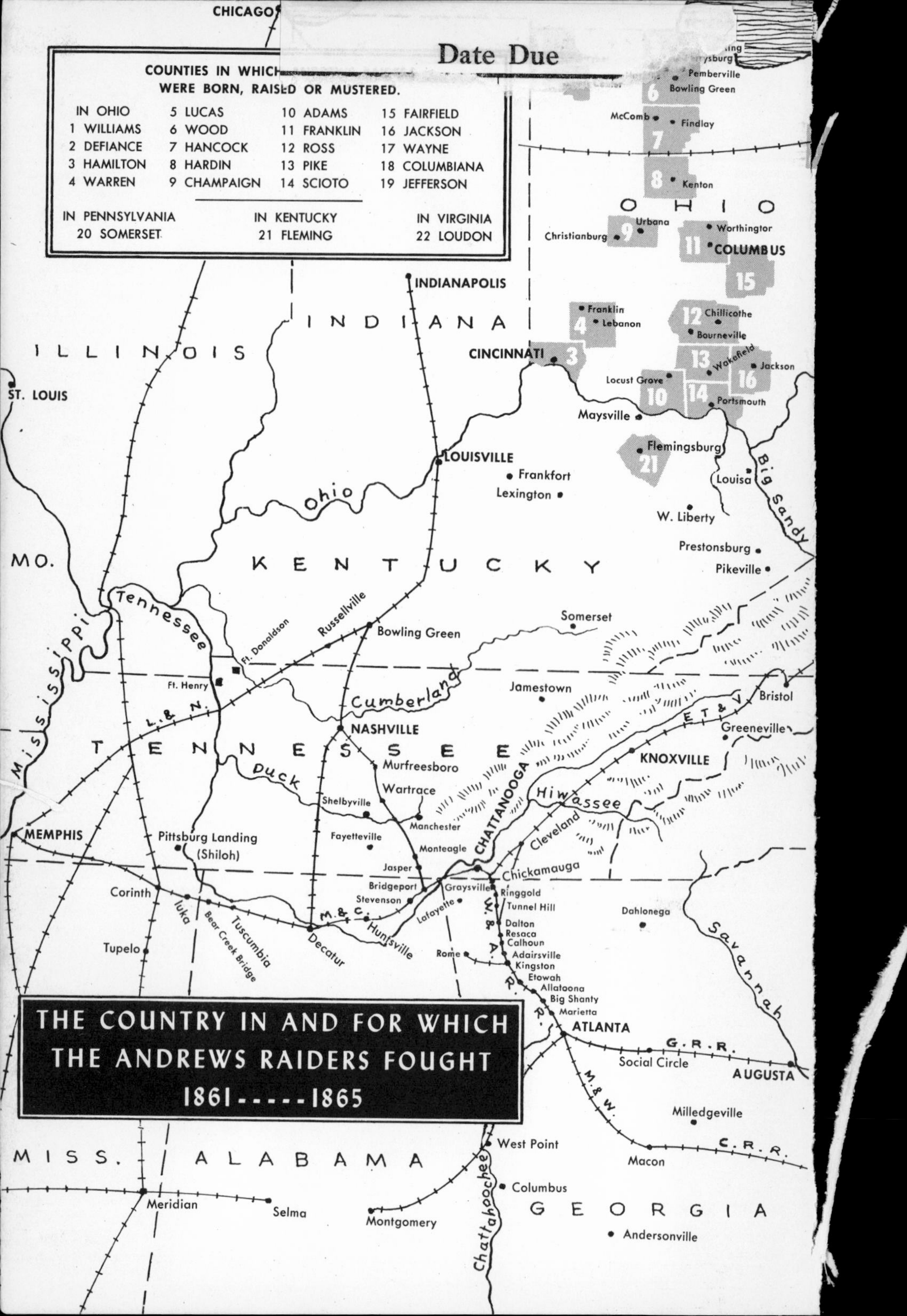

Date Due
COUNTIES IN WHICH
WERE BORN, RAISED OR MUSTERED.
IN OHIO
1 WILLIAMS
2 DEFIANCE
3 HAMILTON
4 WARREN
5 LUCAS
6 WOOD
7 HANCOCK
8 HARDIN
9 CHAMPAIGN
10 ADAMS
11 FRANKLIN
12 ROSS
13 PIKE
14 SCIOTO
15 FAIRFIELD
16 JACKSON
17 WAYNE
18 COLUMBIANA
19 JEFFERSON
IN PENNSYLVANIA
20 SOMERSET
IN KENTUCKY
21 FLEMING
IN VIRGINIA
22 LOUDON
THE COUNTRY IN AND FOR WHICH
THE ANDREWS RAIDERS FOUGHT
1861-----1865
CHICAGO
Pemberville
Bowling Green
McComb
Findlay
Kenton
OHIO
Urbana
Christianburg
Worthingtor
COLUMBUS
INDIANAPOLIS
INDIANA
ILLINOIS
ST. LOUIS
Franklin
Lebanon
Chillicothe
Bourneville
CINCINNATI
Wakefield
Jackson
Locust Grove
Portsmouth
Maysville
Flemingsburg
LOUISVILLE
Frankfort
Lexington
Louisa
Big Sandy
Ohio
W. Liberty
Prestonsburg
Pikeville
MO.
KENTUCKY
Somerset
Tennessee
Russellville
Bowling Green
Ft. Donaldson
Mississippi
Ft. Henry
Jamestown
Cumberland
Bristol
L. & N.
NASHVILLE
E T & V
Greeneville
TENNESSEE
KNOXVILLE
Murfreesboro
Duck
Wartrace
Hiwassee
Shelbyville
Manchester
CHATTANOOGA
Cleveland
MEMPHIS
Pittsburg Landing
(Shiloh)
Fayetteville
Monteagle
Jasper
Chickamauga
Bridgeport
Graysville
Ringgold
Corinth
Stevenson
Tunnel Hill
Dahlonega
Iuka
Bear Creek Bridge
Tuscumbia
M. & C.
Lafayette
Dalton
Resaca
Calhoun
Savannah
Tupelo
Decatur
Huntsville
Rome
Adairsville
Kingston
Etowah
Allatoona
Big Shanty
Marietta
W. & A. R. R.
ATLANTA
G. R. R.
Social Circle
AUGUSTA
M. & W.
Milledgeville
West Point
C. R. R.
MISS.
ALABAMA
Macon
Chattahoochee
Columbus
Meridian
Selma
Montgomery
GEORGIA
Andersonville